PRINCIPLES OF
MACROECONOMICS

THIRD CANADIAN EDITION

N. GREGORY MANKIW
HARVARD UNIVERSITY

RONALD D. KNEEBONE
UNIVERSITY OF CALGARY

KENNETH J. McKENZIE
UNIVERSITY OF CALGARY

NICHOLAS ROWE
CARLETON UNIVERSITY

THOMSON

NELSON

Australia   Canada   Mexico   Singapore   Spain   United Kingdom   United States

THOMSON

NELSON

Principles of Macroeconomics
Third Canadian Edition

by N. Gregory Mankiw, Ronald D. Kneebone, Kenneth J. McKenzie, and Nicholas Rowe

Associate Vice-President, Editorial Director:
Evelyn Veitch

Senior Acquisitions Editor:
Anthony Rezek

Executive Marketing Manager:
Don Thompson

Senior Developmental Editor:
Katherine Goodes

Photo Researcher:
Cindy Howard

Permissions Coordinator:
Cindy Howard

Senior Production Editor:
Natalia Denesiuk

Copy Editor:
June Trusty

Proofreader:
Gail Marsden

Indexer:
Jin Tan

Senior Production Coordinator:
Kathrine Pummell

Creative Director:
Angela Cluer

Interior Design:
Mike Stratton

Cover Design:
Peter Papayanakis

Cover Images:
People: www.firstlight.ca
City: Peter Gridley/Taxi/Getty Images

Compositor:
Nelson Gonzalez

Printer:
Quebecor World

Library and Archives Canada Cataloguing in Publication

Principles of macroeconomics / N. Gregory Mankiw ... [et al.]. — 3rd Canadian ed.

Includes bibliographical references and index.
ISBN-13: 978-0-17-641604-1
ISBN-10: 0-17-641604-8

1. Macroeconomics—Textbooks.
I. Mankiw, N. Gregory

HB172.5.P744 2006   339
C2004-906193-3

To Catherine, Nicholas, and Peter,
my other contributions to the next generation

To our parents
and
Cindy,
Kathleen and Janetta,
Muriel and Julia
Thanks for your support and patience

PREFACE

During my 20-year career as a student, the course that excited me most was the two-semester sequence on the principles of economics that I took during freshman year in college. It is no exaggeration to say that it changed my life.

I had grown up in a family that often discussed politics over the dinner table. The pros and cons of various solutions to society's problems generated fervent debate. But in school, I had been drawn to the sciences. Whereas politics seemed vague, rambling, and subjective, science was analytic, systematic, and objective. While political debate continued without end, science made progress.

My freshman course on the principles of economics opened my eyes to a new way of thinking. Economics combines the virtues of politics and science. It is, truly, a social science. Its subject matter is society—how people choose to lead their lives and how they interact with one another. But it approaches the subject with the dispassion of a science. By bringing the methods of science to the questions of politics, economics tries to make progress on the challenges that all societies face.

I was drawn to write this book in the hope that I could convey some of the excitement of economics that I felt as a student in my first economics course. Economics is a subject in which a little knowledge goes a long way. (The same cannot be said, for instance, of the study of physics or the Japanese language.) Economists have a unique way of viewing the world, much of which can be taught in one or two semesters. My goal in this book is to transmit this way of thinking to the widest possible audience and to convince readers that it illuminates much about the world around them.

I believe that everyone should study the fundamental ideas that economics has to offer. One purpose of general education is to inform people about the world and thereby make them better citizens. The study of economics, as much as any discipline, serves this goal. Writing an economics textbook is, therefore, a great honour and a great responsibility. It is one way that economists can help promote better government and a more prosperous future. As the great economist Paul Samuelson put it, " I don't care who writes a nation's laws, or crafts its advanced treaties, if I can write its economics textbooks."

It is tempting for a professional economist writing a textbook to take the economist's point of view and to emphasize those topics that fascinate him and other economists. I have done my best to avoid that temptation. I have tried to put myself in the position of someone seeing economics for the first time. My goal is to emphasize the material that *students* should and do find interesting about the study of the economy.

One result is that this book is briefer than many books used to introduce students to economics. As a student, I was (and unfortunately still am) a slow reader. I groaned whenever a professor gave the class a 1000-page tome to read. Of course, my reaction was not unique. The Greek poet Callimachus put it succinctly: "Big book, big bore." Callimachus made that observation in 250 B.C., so he was probably not referring to an economics textbook, but today his sentiment is echoed around the world every semester when students first see their economics assignments. My goal in this book is to avoid that reaction by skipping the bells, whistles, and extraneous details that distract students from the key lessons.

Another result of this student orientation is that more of this book is devoted to applications and policy—and less to formal economic theory—than is the case with many other books written for the principles course. Throughout this book I have tried to return to applications and policy questions as often as possible. Most chapters include case studies illustrating how the principles of economics are applied. In addition, "In the News" features (most of which are new to this edition) offer excerpts from newspaper articles showing how economic ideas shed light on current issues facing society. After students finish their first course in economics, they should think about news stories from a new perspective and with greater insight.

I am delighted that versions of this book are (or will soon be) available in many of the world's languages. Currently scheduled translations include Chinese (in both standard and simple characters), Czech, French, Georgian, German, Greek, Indonesian, Italian, Japanese, Korean, Portuguese, Romanian, Russian and Spanish. In addition, adaptations of this book for Canadian and Australian students are also available. Instructors who would like more information about these books should contact Thomson Nelson.

Special thanks go to Karen Dynan, Douglas Elmendorf, and Dean Croushore, who drafted many of the problems and applications presented at the end of each chapter. Yvonne Zinfon, my assistant at Harvard, as usual went beyond the call of duty as this edition was being prepared. I am also grateful to Fuad Faridi, a Harvard undergraduate, for assisting me in the final stages of this project.

The team of editors who worked on this book improved it tremendously. Jane Tufts, developmental editor, provided truly spectacular editing—as she always does. Peter Adams, senior economics acquisitions editor, did a splendid job of overseeing the many people involved in such a large project. Sarah Dorger, developmental editor, assembled an excellent team to write the supplements while managing thousands of related details. Dan Plofchan, production editor, along with the staff at Thistle Hill Publishing Services and GAC Indianapolis, had the patience and dedication necessary to turn my manuscript into this book. Off-Center Concept House professionally executed the production of the print supplements. Mike Stratton, senior designer, gave this book its clean, friendly look. Michele Gitlin, copy-editor, refined my prose, and Alexandra Nickerson, indexer, prepared a careful and thorough index. Janet Hennies, senior marketing manager, worked long hours getting the word out to potential users of this book, even as she gave birth to a future reader of it. Tom Gay, formerly of Harcourt, was instrumental in early stages of planning. Jeff Gilbreath worked as developmental editor until his untimely death; we will miss him. The rest of the South-Western team was also consistently professional, enthusiastic, and dedicated: Jon Schneider, Jenny Fruechtenicht, Terron Sanders, Carrie Hochstrasser, Vicky True, Peggy Buskey, Pam Wallace, and Sandee Milewski.

I must also thank my "inhouse" editor—Deborah Mankiw. As the first reader of almost everything I write, she continued to offer just the right mix of criticism and encouragement.

Finally, I am grateful to my children, Catherine, Nicholas, and Peter. Their unpredictable visits to my study offer welcome relief from long spans of writing and rewriting. Although now they are only ten, eight, and four years old, someday they will grow up and study the principles of economics. I hope this book provides its readers some of the education and enlightenment that I wish for my own children.

N. Gregory Mankiw
October 2002

PREFACE TO THE THIRD CANADIAN EDITION

As soon as we got our hands on the first U.S. edition of *Principles of Macroeconomics*, it was clear to us that "this one is different." If other first-year economics textbooks are encyclopedias, Gregory Mankiw's was, and still is, a handbook.

Between the three of us, we have many years of experience teaching first-year economics. Like many instructors, we found it harder and harder to teach with each new edition of the thick, standard texts. It was simply impossible to cover all of the material. Of course, we could have skipped sections, features, or whole chapters, but then, apart from the sheer hassle of telling students which bits to read and not to read, and worries about the consistencies and completeness of the remaining material, we ran the risk of leaving students with the philosophy that what matters is only what's on the exam.

We do not believe that the writers of these other books set out with the intention of cramming so much material into them. It is a difficult task to put together the perfect textbook—one that all instructors would approve of and that all students would enjoy using. Therefore, to please all potential users, most of the books end up covering a wide range of topics. And so the books grow and grow.

Professor Mankiw made a fresh start in the first U.S. edition. He included all the important topics and presented them in order of importance. And in the third U.S. edition, he has resisted the temptation to add more and more material. We have, in adapting the text for Canadian students, taken a minimalist approach: "If it isn't broken, don't fix it!" While the book is easily recognizable as Mankiw's, we have made changes that increase its relevance to Canadian students. Some of these changes reflect important differences between the Canadian and U.S. economies. For example, the Canadian economy is much smaller and more open than the U.S. economy, and this fact is explicitly recognized in this edition. Other changes reflect important institutional differences between the two countries, including the structure of the tax system and the nature of competition policy. Finally, the Canadian edition focuses on issues and includes examples that are more familiar and relevant to a Canadian audience.

We would not have agreed to participate in the Canadian edition if we were not extremely impressed with the U.S. edition. Professor Mankiw has done an outstanding job of identifying the key concepts and principles that every first-year student should learn.

It was truly a pleasure to work with such a well-thought-out and well-written book. We have enjoyed teaching from the first and second Canadian editions and we look forward to using the third Canadian edition. We hope you do, too.

HOW THE BOOK IS ORGANIZED

To write a brief and student-friendly book, Mankiw considered new ways to organize familiar material. What follows is a whirlwind tour of this text. This tour, we hope, will give you a sense of how the pieces fit together.

Introductory Material

Chapter 1, "Ten Principles of Economics," introduces students to the economist's view of the world. It previews some of the big ideas that recur throughout economics, such as opportunity costs, marginal decision making, the role of incentives, the gain from trade, and the efficiency of market allocations. The ten principles of economics are referred to throughout the book and an icon in the margin calls attention to these key, interconnected principles.

Chapter 2, "Thinking Like an Economist," examines how economists approach their field of study, discussing the role of assumptions in developing a theory and introducing the concepts of an economic model. It also discusses the role of economists in making policy. The appendix to this chapter offers a brief refresher course on how graphs are used and how they can be abused.

Chapter 3, "Interdependence and the Gains from Trade," presents the theory of comparative advantage. This theory explains why individuals trade with their neighbours, as well as why nations trade with other nations. Much of economics is about how market forces coordinate many individual production and consumption decisions. As a starting point for this analysis, students see in this chapter why specialization, interdependence, and trade can benefit everyone.

The Fundamental Tools of Supply and Demand

The next chapter introduces the basic tools of supply and demand. Chapter 4, "The Market Forces of Supply and Demand," develops the supply curve, the demand curve, and the notion of market equilibrium.

Macroeconomics

Our overall approach to teaching macroeconomics is to examine the economy in the long run (when prices are flexible) before examining the economy in the short run (when prices are sticky). We believe that this organization simplifies learning macroeconomics for several reasons. First, the classical assumption of price flexibility is more closely linked to the basic lessons of supply and demand, which students have already mastered. Second, the classical dichotomy allows the study of the long run to be broken up into several, more easily digested pieces. Third, because the business cycle represents a transitory deviation from the economy's long-run growth path, studying the transitory deviations is more natural after the long-run equilibrium is understood. Fourth, the macroeconomic theory of the short run is more controversial among economists than the macroeconomics theory of the long run. For these reasons, most upper-level courses in macroeconomics now follow this long-run-before-short-run approach; our goal is to offer introductory students the same advantage.

Returning to the detailed organization, we start the coverage of macroeconomics with issues of measurement. Chapter 5, "Measuring a Nation's Income," discusses the meaning of gross domestic product and related statistics from the national income accounts. Chapter 6, "Measuring the Cost of Living," discusses the measurement and use of the consumer price index.

The next four chapters describe the behaviour of the real economy in the long run. Chapter 7, "Production and Growth," examines the determinants of the large variation in living standards over time and across countries. Chapter 8, "Saving, Investment, and the Financial System," discusses the types of financial institutions in our economy and examines their role in allocating resources. Chapter 9,

"The Basic Tools of Finance," is new to this edition. It introduces essential tools—present value, risk management, and asset valuation—for students to understand the decisions people make as they participate in financial markets. Chapter 10, "Unemployment and Its Natural Rate," considers the long-run determinants of the unemployment rate, including job search, minimum-wage laws, the market power of unions, and efficiency wages.

Having described the long-run behaviour of the real economy, the book then turns to the long-run behaviour of money and prices. Chapter 11, "The Monetary System," introduces the economist's concept of money and the role of the central bank in controlling the quantity of money. Chapter 12, "Money Growth and Inflation," develops the classical theory of inflation and discusses the costs that inflation imposes on a society.

The next two chapters present the macroeconomics of open economies, maintaining the long-run assumptions of price flexibility and full employment. Chapter 13, "Open-Economy Macroeconomics: Basic Concepts," explains the relationship among saving, investment, and the trade balance; the distinction between the nominal and real exchange rate; and the theory of purchasing-power parity. Chapter 14, "A Macroeconomic Theory of the Open Economy," presents a classical model of the international flow of goods and capital. The model sheds light on various issues, including the link between budget deficits and trade deficits and the macroeconomic effects of trade policies. Because instructors differ their emphasis on this material, these chapters are written so that they can be used in different ways. Some may choose to cover Chapter 13 but not Chapter 14, others may skip both chapters, and still others may choose to defer the analysis of open-economy macroeconomics until the end of their courses.

After fully developing the long-run theory of the economy in Chapters 5 through 14, the book turns to explaining short-run fluctuations around the long-run trend. This organization simplifies teaching the theory of short-run fluctuations because, at this point in the course, students have a good grounding in many basic macroeconomic concepts. Chapter 15, "Aggregate Demand and Aggregate Supply," begins with some facts about the business cycle and then introduces the model of aggregate demand and aggregate supply. Chapter 16, "The Influence of Monetary and Fiscal Policy on Aggregate Demand," explains how policymakers can use the tools at their disposal to shift the aggregate-demand curve. Chapter 17, "The Short-Run Tradeoff between Inflation and Unemployment," explains why policymakers who control aggregate demand face a tradeoff between inflation and unemployment. It examines why this tradeoff exists in the short run, why it shifts over time, and why it does not exist in the long run.

The book concludes with Chapter 18, "Five Debates over Macroeconomic Policy." This capstone chapter considers controversial issues facing policymakers: the proper degree of policy activism in response to the business cycle, the choice between rules and discretion in the conduct of monetary policy, the desirability of reaching zero inflation, the importance of reducing the government's debt, and the need for tax reform to encourage saving. For each issue, the chapter presents both sides of the debate and encourages students to make their own judgments.

WALK-THROUGH

The purpose of this text is to help students learn the fundamental lessons of economics and to show how such lessons can be applied to the world in which they live. Toward that end, various learning tools recur throughout the book.

Chapter Openers Well-designed chapter openers act as previews that summarize the major concepts to be learned in each chapter.

Case Studies Economic theory is useful and interesting only if it can be applied to understanding actual events and policies. Updated or replaced with more current Canadian examples, this book therefore contains numerous case studies that apply the theory that has just been developed.

Figures and Tables Colourful and eye-catching visuals are used to make important economic points and to clarify Canadian and other key economic concepts. These have also proved to be valuable and memorable teaching aids.

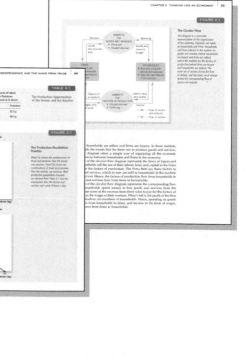

Updated Canadian "In the News" Features

One benefit that students gain from studying economics is a new perspective and greater understanding about news from Canada and around the world. To highlight this benefit, there are excerpts from many Canadian news articles, some of which are opinion columns written by prominent economists. These articles show how basic economic theory can be applied.

"FYI" Features

These features provide additional material "for your information." Some of them offer a glimpse into the history of economic thought. Others clarify technical issues. Still others discuss supplementary topics that instructors might choose either to discuss or skip in their lectures.

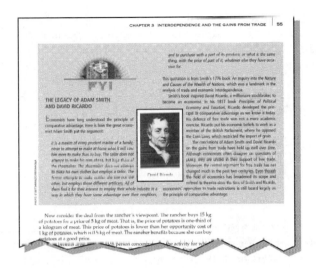

Key Concept Definitions

When key concepts are introduced in the chapter, they are presented in **bold** typeface. In addition, their definitions are placed in the margin. This treatment should aid students in learning and reviewing the material.

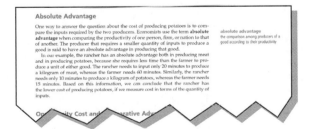

Interconnectedness of the Ten Principles of Economics

Whenever any of the ten principles of economics are discussed in the text, an icon appears in the margin. This draws the student's attention to an important discussion of one of the ten principles.

Quick Quizzes   After each major section, students are offered a "quick quiz" to check their comprehension of what they have just learned. If students cannot readily answer these quizzes, they should stop and reread the material before continuing.

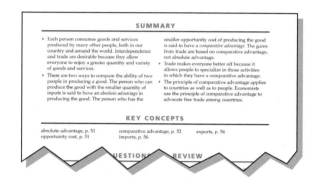

Chapter Summaries   Each chapter ends with a brief summary that reminds students of the most important lessons that they have just learned. Later in their study, it offers an efficient way to review for exams.

List of Key Concepts   A list of key concepts at the end of each chapter offers students a way to test their understanding of the new terms that have been introduced. Page references are included so that students can review the terms they do not understand.

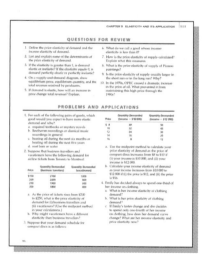

Questions for Review   At the end of each chapter are questions for review that cover the chapter's primary lessons. Students can use these questions to check their comprehension and to prepare for exams.

Problems and Applications   Each chapter also contains a variety of problems and applications that ask students to apply the material they have learned. Some instructors may use these questions for homework assignments. Others may use them as a starting point for classroom discussion.

Internet Resources   To end each chapter, some Internet resources are listed for students who like to search the Internet for further information on the chapter's topics.

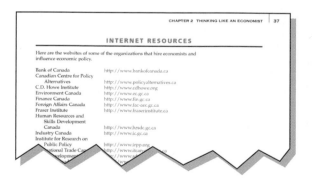

NEW IN THIS THIRD CANADIAN EDITION

New Chapter   Chapter 9, "The Basic Tools of Finance," introduces essential tools—present value, risk management, and asset valuation—to help students understand the decisions people make as they participate in financial markets.

Chapter 7   This chapter, "Production and Growth," offers a significantly revised section on population growth, incorporating a section on Malthus and new material on Kremer's study of population growth and technological progress.

Chapter 12   An improved and more detailed discussion of the Fisher effect, which clearly draws the distinction between expected and unanticipated inflation, is provided in this chapter, "Money Growth and Inflation."

Revised Content   The term "net foreign investment" has been replaced with "net capital outflow" in Chapters 13 and 14 to make this concept more intuitive for students.

Clear Explanations   In Chapter 15, the organization of the short-run aggregate supply theories has changed and now begins with the sticky-wage theory. Reviewers have indicated that this organization makes it much easier to present this material because it starts with the simplest theory for students to understand.

Internet Resources   The Internet is a vital study tool for students, so Internet resources have been added to the end-of-chapter material. Students will be able to delve deeper into a topic and gain a more thorough understanding of the intricacies of economics.

Current Canadian Information   Tables, charts, graphs, and figures have been updated to reflect the most current information available at the time of publication. Several "In the News" and "Case Study" features have been Canadianized, updated, or replaced with more current examples.

SUPPLEMENTS

For the Instructor

Instructor's Manual with Solutions and Classroom Activities for Microeconomics and Macroeconomics   For lecture preparation, the Instructor's Manual offers a detailed outline for each chapter of the text that provides learning objectives, identifies stumbling blocks that students may face, offers helpful teaching tips, and provides suggested in-classroom activities for a more cooperative learning experience. The Instructor's Manual also includes solutions to the Quick Quizzes, Questions for Review, and Problems and Applications found in the text.

Instructor's Resource CD-ROM for Microeconomics and Macroeconomics   Included on the CD-ROM are the key supplements designed to aid instructors: Instructor's Manual with Solutions and Classroom Activities, PowerPoint Lecture slides, PowerPoint slides of exhibits only, Computerized Test Bank, and a printable Test Bank for ease of use.

Test Bank   This updated and revised Test Bank consists of more than 200 questions per chapter. Every question has been checked to ensure the accuracy and clarity of the answers and painstakingly revised to address the text's revisions. Included are multiple-choice, true/false, and short-answer questions that assess students' critical thinking skills. Easy, medium, and difficult questions outline the process that students must use to arrive at their answers: recall, application, and integration. Questions are organized by text section to help instructors pick and choose their selections.

Computerized Test Bank   The ExamView Computerized Testing Software contains all of the questions in the printable Test Bank. This program is an easy-to-use test-creation software application that is compatible with Microsoft Windows. Instructors can add or edit questions, instructions, and answers, and can select questions by previewing them on the screen, selecting them randomly, or selecting them by number. Instructors can also create and administer quizzes online, whether over the Internet, a local area network (LAN), or a wide area network (WAN).

Microsoft® PowerPoint® Lecture and Exhibit Slides   Available on the CD and downloadable from the Mankiw website (http://www.mankiw3e. nelson.com) are two versions of the PowerPoint presentation. Instructors can save valuable time as they prepare for class using this comprehensive lecture presentation. This supplement covers all the essential topics presented in each chapter of the book. Graphs, tables, lists, and concepts are developed sequentially, much as one might develop them on a chalkboard. Additional examples and applications are used to reinforce major lessons. A separate exhibit presentation provides instructors with all of the tables and graphs from the main text.

The "Ten Principles" Video Set   This video series illustrates the ten principles of economics as introduced in Chapter 1. Instructors can show these videos as an interesting and visually appealing introduction to topics discussed through the textbook.

CBC Videos   Instructors can bring the real world into the classroom by using the CBC videotape for Mankiw, *Principles of Macroeconomics*, Third Canadian Edition. This video contains one video segment for each of the eight parts of the text, and provides current stories of economic interest.

Favourite Ways to Learn Economics   U.S. authors David Anderson, Centre College, and Jim Chasey, Homewood Flossmoor High School, use experiments to bring economic education to life. This is a U.S.-based lab manual for the classroom and for individual study that contains experiments and problem sets that reinforce key economic concepts (for both students and instuctors).

Economic Viewpoints   The shape, pace, and spirit of the global economy has been greatly impacted by the events that occurred on September 11, 2001. A new collection of essays is offered that provides a variety of perspectives on the economic effects of these events. Each essay in this U.S. supplement is written by a U.S. economics textbook author, all of whom are highly regarded for both their academic and professional achievements. This unique collaboration results in one of the most cutting-edge resources available to help facilitate discussion of the impact of September 11 in the context of economic courses.

For the Student

Study Guide   This study guide was prepared to enhance student success. Each chapter of the study guide includes learning objectives, a description of the chapter's context and purpose, a chapter review, key terms and definitions, advanced critical thinking questions, and helpful hints for understanding difficult concepts. Students can develop their understanding by doing the practice problems and short-answer questions, and then assess theory mastery of the key concepts with the self-test, which includes true/false and multiple-choice questions. Solutions to all problems are included in the study guide.

Microsoft® PowerPoint® Lecture Notes   A printable booklet available as a download from the Mankiw website (http://www.mankiw3.nelson.com), this supplement contains the lecture presentation in the PowerPoint slides, with space next to each slide for taking notes during class. This supplement allows students to focus on classroom activities by providing them with the confident knowledge that they have an excellent set of chapter notes for future reference.

Mankiw Website   Valuable resources for students can be found on the Internet at the Mankiw textbook support site: http://www.mankiw3e.nelson. com. Students will find more true/false, multiple-choice, and short-answer questions; links to economics-related Internet sites; PowerPoint slides for their review; and much more.

ABOUT THE AUTHORS

JORDI CABRÉ

N. Gregory Mankiw is Professor of Economics at Harvard University. As a student, he studied economics at Princeton University and MIT. As a teacher, he has taught macroeconomics, microeconomics, statistics, and principles of economics. He even spent one summer long ago as a sailing instructor on Long Beach Island.

Professor Mankiw is a prolific writer and a regular participant in academic and policy debates. His work has been published in scholarly journals such as the *American Economic Review, Journal of Political Economy*, and *Quarterly Journal of Economics*, and in more popular forums such as *The New York Times, The Financial Times, The Wall Street Journal,* and *Fortune.* He is also author of the best-selling intermediate-level textbook *Macroeconomics* (Worth Publishing). In addition to his teaching, research, and writing, Professor Mankiw is a research associate of the National Bureau of Economic Research, an adviser to the Federal Reserve Bank of Boston and the Congressional Budget Office, and a member of the Educational Testing Service (ETS) test development committee for the advanced placement exam in economics.

Ronald D. Kneebone is Professor of Economics at the University of Calgary. He received his Ph.D. from McMaster University. Professor Kneebone has taught courses in public finance and in macroeconomics from principles through to the Ph.D. level, and he is a two-time winner of the Faculty of Social Sciences Distinguished Teacher Award at the University of Calgary. His research interests are primarily in the areas of public sector finances and fiscal federalism. He shares with Ken McKenzie the Douglas Purvis Memorial Prize for the best published work in Canadian public policy in 1999.

Kenneth J. McKenzie is Professor of Economics at the University of Calgary. He received his Ph.D. from Queen's University. Specializing in public economics with an emphasis on taxation and political economy, Professor McKenzie has published extensively in these areas. He is the winner of the 1996 Harry Johnson Prize (with University of Calgary colleague Herb Emery) for the best article in the *Canadian Journal of Economics*, the 1999 Douglas Purvis Memorial Prize (with Ron Kneebone) for a published work relating to Canadian public policy, and the 2000 Faculty of Social Sciences Distinguished Researcher Award at the University of Calgary. Professor McKenzie has taught microeconomics and public economics from the principles to the graduate level, and has received several departmental teaching awards.

Nicholas Rowe is Associate Professor of Economics and Associate Dean of the Faculty of Public Affairs and Management at Carleton University. He received his Ph.D. from the University of Western Ontario. Professor Rowe has 25 years' experience in teaching economics at various levels, in Canada, Cuba, and Australia. His research interests are in the area of monetary policy, more specifically, inflation targeting by central banks. He is a member of C.D. Howe Institute's Monetary Policy Council, a panel of 12 top Canadian monetary economists that provides an independent recommendation for the Bank of Canada's monetary policy.

ACKNOWLEDGMENTS

In revising this third Canadian edition, we had the benefit of input from many talented people and wish to thank the following economics professors who read and commented on portions of the manuscript:

Aurelia Best, *Centennial College*
Bogdan Buduru, *Concordia University*
Byron Eastman, *Laurentian University*
Peter McCabe, *McMaster University*
Ugurhan G. Berkok, *Queen's University*

David Gray, *University of Ottawa*
Ather H. Akbari, *St. Mary's University*
Ibrahim Hayani, *Seneca College*
Michael Hare, *University of Toronto*

The success of the first two Canadian editions of this textbook was due, in part, to the many reviewers who helped us shape the manuscripts. We continue to be grateful for their comments:

Maurice Tugwell, *Acadia University*
Kevin Clinton, *Bank of Canada*
Keith Baxter, *Bishop's University*
Herb Emery, *University of Calgary*
Nancy Churchman, *Carleton University*
Stephen Rakocsy, *Humber College*
Chris McDonnell, *Malaspina University-College*
Costas Nicolau, *University of Manitoba*

Martin Dooley, *McMaster University*
Ernie Jacobson, *Northern Alberta Institute of Technology*
Robin Neill, *University of Prince Edward Island* and *Carleton University*
Pierre Fortin, *University of Quebec at Montreal*
Gregor Smith, *Queen's University*

Special thanks go to Bill Scarth of McMaster University, who offered invaluable advice regarding the structure and emphasis of the Canadian editions. Dr. Scarth is an award-winning teacher and author, and to ignore his advice would have been perilous indeed. His extensive comments were instrumental in helping us formulate our approach to the Canadian editions.

We would also like to thank our colleagues at the University of Calgary and Carleton University who provided invaluable informal input and useful examples and applications. We, of course, bear full responsibility for any misinterpretations and errors.

Canadianizing this book has been a team effort from the very start. We would like to acknowledge the editorial, production, and marketing teams at Thomson Nelson for their professionalism, advice, and encouragement throughout the process. Deserving special attention are senior acquisitions editor Anthony Rezek and senior developmental editor Katherine Goodes for helping to ensure the timely completion of our work.

Finally, we are grateful to our families for their indulgence and encouragement throughout the research and writing process. Their patience and understanding are greatly appreciated.

Ronald D. Kneebone
Kenneth J. McKenzie
Nicholas Rowe
November 2004

BRIEF CONTENTS

TABLE OF CONTENTS

© PHOTODISC

PART 1
INTRODUCTION   1

PART 2
SUPPLY AND DEMAND:
HOW MARKETS WORK 63

PART 3
THE DATA OF MACROECONOMICS 91

PART 4
THE REAL ECONOMY
IN THE LONG RUN 127

© GARY RHIJNSBURGER/MASTERFILE

PART 5
MONEY AND PRICES
IN THE LONG RUN   223

© JOSON/ZEFA

PART 6
THE MACROECONOMICS
OF OPEN ECONOMIES 275

© IMAGES CO./CORBIS/MAGMA

PART 7
SHORT-RUN ECONOMIC FLUCTUATIONS 331

CHAPTER 15
AGGREGATE DEMAND AND AGGREGATE SUPPLY 333

CHAPTER 16
THE INFLUENCE OF MONETARY AND FISCAL POLICY ON AGGREGATE DEMAND 367

1

INTRODUCTION

© PHOTODISC

TEN PRINCIPLES OF ECONOMICS

Learning Objectives

In this chapter, you will ...

- Learn that economics is about the allocation of scarce resources
- Examine some of the tradeoffs that people face
- Learn the meaning of *opportunity cost*
- See how to use marginal reasoning when making decisions
- Discuss how incentives affect people's behaviour
- Consider why trade among people or nations can be good for everyone
- Discuss why markets are a good, but not perfect, way to allocate resources
- Learn what determines some trends in the overall economy

The word *economy* comes from the Greek word for "one who manages a household." At first, this origin might seem peculiar. But, in fact, households and economies have much in common.

A household faces many decisions. It must decide which members of the household do which tasks and what each member gets in return: Who cooks dinner? Who does the laundry? Who gets the extra dessert at dinner? Who gets to choose what TV show to watch? In short, the household must allocate its scarce resources among its various members, taking into account each member's abilities, efforts, and desires.

Like a household, a society faces many decisions. A society must decide what jobs will be done and who will do them. It needs some people to grow food, other people to make clothing, and still others to design computer software. Once society has allocated people (as well as land, buildings, and machines) to various jobs, it must also allocate the output of goods and services that they produce. It must decide who will eat caviar and who will eat potatoes. It must decide who will drive a Ferrari and who will take the bus.

scarcity
the limited nature
of society's resources

economics
the study of how society
manages its scarce resources

The management of society's resources (e.g., people, land, buildings, machinery) is important because resources are scarce. **Scarcity** means that society has limited resources and therefore cannot produce all the goods and services people wish to have. Just as a household cannot give every member everything he or she wants, a society cannot give every individual the highest standard of living to which he or she might aspire.

Economics is the study of how society manages its scarce resources. In most societies, resources are allocated not by a single central planner but through the combined actions of millions of households and firms. Economists therefore study how people make decisions: how much they work, what they buy, how much they save, and how they invest their savings. Economists also study how people interact with one another. For instance, they examine how the multitude of buyers and sellers of a good together determine the price at which the good is sold and the quantity that is sold. Finally, economists analyze forces and trends that affect the economy as a whole, including the growth in average income, the fraction of the population that cannot find work, and the rate at which prices are rising.

Although the study of economics has many facets, the field is unified by several central ideas. In the rest of this chapter, we look at ten principles of economics. Don't worry if you don't understand them all at first, or if you don't find them completely convincing. In the coming chapters we will explore these ideas more fully. The ten principles are introduced here just to give you an overview of what economics is all about. You can think of this chapter as a "preview of coming attractions."

HOW PEOPLE MAKE DECISIONS

There is no mystery to what an "economy" is. Whether we are talking about the economy of Vancouver, of Canada, or of the whole world, an economy is just a group of people interacting with one another as they go about their lives. Because the behaviour of an economy reflects the behaviour of the individuals who make up the economy, we start our study of economics with four principles of individual decision making.

Principle #1: People Face Tradeoffs

The first lesson about making decisions is summarized in the adage "There is no such thing as a free lunch." To get one thing that we like, we usually have to give up another thing that we like. Making decisions requires trading off one goal against another.

Consider a student who must decide how to allocate her most valuable resource—her time. She can spend all of her time studying economics; she can spend all of her time studying psychology; or she can divide her time between the two fields. For every hour she studies one subject, she gives up an hour she could have used studying the other. And for every hour she spends studying, she gives up an hour that she could have spent napping, bike riding, watching TV, or working at her part-time job for some extra spending money.

Or consider parents deciding how to spend their family income. They can buy food, clothing, or a family vacation. Or they can save some of the family income for retirement or the children's college or university education. When they choose to spend an extra dollar on one of these goods, they have one less dollar to spend on some other good.

When people are grouped into societies, they face different kinds of tradeoffs. The classic tradeoff is between "guns and butter." The more we spend on national defence (guns) to protect our shores from foreign aggressors, the less we can spend on consumer goods (butter) to raise our standard of living at home. Also important in modern society is the tradeoff between a clean environment and a high level of income. Laws that require firms to reduce pollution raise the cost of producing goods and services. Because of the higher costs, these firms end up earning smaller profits, paying lower wages, charging higher prices, or some combination of these three. Thus, while pollution regulations give us the benefit of a cleaner environment and the improved health that comes with it, they have the cost of reducing the incomes of the firms' owners, workers, and customers.

Another tradeoff society faces is between efficiency and equity. **Efficiency** means that society is getting the most it can from its scarce resources. **Equity** means that the benefits of those resources are distributed fairly among society's members. In other words, efficiency refers to the size of the economic pie, and equity refers to how the pie is divided. Often, when government policies are being designed, these two goals conflict.

Consider, for instance, policies aimed at achieving a more equal distribution of economic well-being. Some of these policies, such as the welfare system or employment insurance, try to help those members of society who are most in need. Others, such as the individual income tax, ask the financially successful to contribute more than others to support the government. Although these policies have the benefit of achieving greater equity, they have a cost in terms of reduced efficiency. When the government redistributes income from the rich to the poor, it reduces the reward for working hard; as a result, people work less and produce fewer goods and services. In other words, when the government tries to cut the economic pie into more equal slices, the pie gets smaller.

Recognizing that people face tradeoffs does not by itself tell us what decisions they will or should make. A student should not abandon the study of psychology just because doing so would increase the time available for the study of economics. Society should not stop protecting the environment just because environmental regulations reduce our material standard of living. The poor should not be ignored just because helping them distorts work incentives. Nonetheless, acknowledging life's tradeoffs is important because people are likely to make good decisions only if they understand the options that they have available.

efficiency
the property of society getting the most it can from its scarce resources

equity
the property of distributing economic prosperity fairly among the members of society

Principle #2: The Cost of Something Is What You Give Up to Get It

Because people face tradeoffs, making decisions requires comparing the costs and benefits of alternative courses of action. In many cases, however, the cost of some action is not as obvious as it might first appear.

Consider, for example, the decision whether to go to college or university. The benefit is intellectual enrichment and a lifetime of better job opportunities. But what is the cost? To answer this question, you might be tempted to add up the money you spend on tuition, books, room, and board. Yet this total does not truly represent what you give up to spend a year in college or university.

The first problem with this answer is that it includes some things that are not really costs of going to college or university. Even if you quit school, you would need a place to sleep and food to eat. Room and board are costs of going to college or university only to the extent that they are more expensive there than elsewhere. Indeed, the cost of room and board at your school might be less than the rent and food expenses that you would pay living on your own. In this case, the savings on room and board are a benefit of going to college or university.

The second problem with this calculation of costs is that it ignores the largest cost of going to college or university—your time. When you spend a year listening to lectures, reading textbooks, and writing papers, you cannot spend that time working at a job. For most students, the wages given up to attend school are the largest single cost of their education.

opportunity cost
whatever must be given up to obtain some item

The **opportunity cost** of an item is what you give up to get that item. When making any decision, such as whether to attend college or university, decision makers should be aware of the opportunity costs that accompany each possible action. In fact, they usually are. College- or university-age athletes who can earn millions if they drop out of school and play professional sports are well aware that their opportunity cost of a postsecondary education is very high. It is not surprising that they often decide that the benefit is not worth the cost.

Principle #3: Rational People Think at the Margin

Decisions in life are rarely black and white but usually involve shades of gray. At dinnertime, the decision you face is not between fasting or eating like a pig, but whether to take that extra spoonful of mashed potatoes. When exams roll around, your decision is not between blowing them off or studying 24 hours a day, but whether to spend an extra hour reviewing your notes instead of watching TV. Economists use the term **marginal changes** to describe small incremental adjustments to an existing plan of action. Keep in mind that "margin" means "edge," so marginal changes are adjustments around the edges of what you are doing.

marginal changes
small incremental adjustments to a plan of action

In many situations, people make the best decisions by thinking at the margin. Suppose, for instance, that you asked a friend for advice about how many years to stay in school. If he were to compare for you the lifestyle of a person with a Ph.D. to that of an elementary-school dropout, you might complain that this comparison is not helpful in making your decision. You have some education already and most likely are deciding whether to spend an extra year or two in school. To make this decision, you need to know the additional benefits that an extra year in school would offer (higher wages throughout life and the sheer joy of learning) and the additional costs that you would incur (tuition and the forgone wages while you're in school). By comparing these *marginal benefits* and *marginal costs*, you can evaluate whether the extra year is worthwhile.

As another example, consider an airline deciding how much to charge passengers who fly standby. Suppose that flying a 200-seat plane across the country costs the airline $100 000. In this case, the average cost of each seat is $100 000/200, which is $500. One might be tempted to conclude that the airline should never sell a ticket for less than $500. In fact, however, the airline can raise its profits by thinking at the margin. Imagine that a plane is about to take off with ten empty seats, and a standby passenger is waiting at the gate willing to pay $300 for a seat. Should the airline sell it to him? Of course it should. If the plane has empty seats, the cost of adding one more passenger is minuscule. Although the *average* cost of flying a passenger is $500, the *marginal* cost is merely the cost of the bag of peanuts and can of soda that the extra passenger will consume. As long as the standby passenger pays more than the marginal cost, selling him a ticket is profitable.

As these examples show, individuals and firms can make better decisions by thinking at the margin. A rational decision maker takes an action if and only if the marginal benefit of the action exceeds the marginal cost.

Principle #4: People Respond to Incentives

Because people make decisions by comparing costs and benefits, their behaviour may change when the costs or benefits change. That is, people respond to incentives. When the price of an apple rises, for instance, people decide to eat more pears and fewer apples, because the cost of buying an apple is higher. At the same time, apple orchards decide to hire more workers and harvest more apples, because the benefit of selling an apple is also higher. As we will see, the effect of price on the behaviour of buyers and sellers in a market—in this case, the market for apples—is crucial for understanding how the economy works.

Public policymakers should never forget about incentives, because many policies change the costs or benefits that people face and, therefore, alter behaviour. A tax on gasoline, for instance, encourages people to drive smaller, more fuel-efficient cars. It also encourages people to take public transportation rather than drive, and to live closer to where they work. If the tax were large enough, people would start driving electric cars.

When policymakers fail to consider how their policies affect incentives, they often end up with results they did not intend. For example, consider public policy regarding auto safety. Today all cars have seat belts, but that was not true 50 years ago. In the 1960s, Ralph Nader's book *Unsafe at Any Speed* generated much public concern over auto safety. Parliament responded with laws requiring seat belts as standard equipment on new cars.

How does a seat belt law affect auto safety? The direct effect is obvious: When a person wears a seat belt, the probability of surviving a major auto accident rises. But that's not the end of the story, because the law also affects behaviour by altering incentives. The relevant behavior here is the speed and care with which drivers operate their cars. Driving slowly and carefully is costly because it uses the driver's time and energy. When deciding how safely to drive, rational people compare the marginal benefit from safer driving to the marginal cost. They drive more slowly and carefully when the benefit of increased safety is high. It is no surprise, for instance, that people drive more slowly and carefully when roads are icy than when roads are clear.

Consider how a seat belt law alters a driver's cost–benefit calculation. Seat belts make accidents less costly because they reduce the likelihood of injury or death. In other words, seat belts reduce the benefits to slow and careful driving. People respond to seat belts as they would to an improvement in road conditions—by faster and less careful driving. The end result of a seat belt law, therefore, is a larger number of accidents. The decline in safe driving has a clear, adverse impact on pedestrians, who are more likely to find themselves in an accident but (unlike the drivers) don't have the benefit of added protection.

Mick Jagger understood opportunity cost and incentives. In 1961, he became a scholarship student at the London School of Economics. In 1963, he abandoned a promising career as an economist, worked full-time on his music, and eventually earned millions of dollars with the Rolling Stones.

At first, this discussion of incentives and seat belts might seem like idle speculation. Yet, in a 1975 study, economist Sam Peltzman showed that the auto-safety laws have had many of these effects. According to Peltzman's evidence, these laws produce both fewer deaths per accident and more accidents. The net result is little change in the number of driver deaths and an increase in the number of pedestrian deaths.

Peltzman's analysis of auto safety is an example of the general principle that people respond to incentives. Many incentives that economists study are more straightforward than those of the auto-safety laws. No one is surprised that people drive smaller cars in Europe, where gasoline taxes are high, than in the United States, where gasoline taxes are low. Yet, as the seat belt example shows, policies can have effects that are not obvious in advance. When analyzing any policy, we must consider not only the direct effects but also the indirect effects that work through incentives. If the policy changes incentives, it will cause people to alter their behaviour.

QuickQuiz   List and briefly explain the four principles of individual decision making.

HOW PEOPLE INTERACT

The first four principles discussed how individuals make decisions. As we go about our lives, many of our decisions affect not only ourselves but other people as well. The next three principles concern how people interact with one another.

Principle #5: Trade Can Make Everyone Better Off

You have probably heard on the news that the Americans are our competitors in the world economy. In some ways this is true, for Canadian and U.S. firms do produce many of the same goods. Nortel and Lucent compete for the same customers in the market for telecommunications. Inniskillin and Gallo compete for the same customers in the market for wine.

Yet it is easy to be misled when thinking about competition among countries. Trade between Canada and the United States is not like a sports contest, where one side wins and the other side loses. In fact, the opposite is true: Trade between two countries can make each country better off.

To see why, consider how trade affects your family. When a member of your family looks for a job, he or she competes against members of other families who are looking for jobs. Families also compete against one another when they go shopping, because each family wants to buy the best goods at the lowest prices. So, in a sense, each family in the economy is competing with all other families.

Despite this competition, your family would not be better off isolating itself from all other families. If it did, your family would need to grow its own food, make its own clothes, and build its own home. Clearly, your family gains much from its ability to trade with others. Trade allows each person to specialize in the activities he or she does best, whether it is farming, sewing, or home building. By trading with others, people can buy a greater variety of goods and services at lower cost.

Countries as well as families benefit from the ability to trade with one another. Trade allows countries to specialize in what they do best and to enjoy a greater variety of goods and services. The Americans, as well as the French and the Egyptians and the Brazilians, are as much our partners in the world economy as they are our competitors.

Principle #6: Markets Are Usually a Good Way to Organize Economic Activity

The collapse of communism in the Soviet Union and Eastern Europe in the 1980s may be the most important change in the world during the past half-century. Communist countries worked on the premise that central planners in the government were in the best position to guide economic activity. These planners decided what goods and services were produced, how much was produced, and who produced and consumed these goods and services. The theory behind central planning was that only the government could organize economic activity in a way that promoted economic well-being for the country as a whole.

Today, most countries that once had centrally planned economies have abandoned this system and are trying to develop market economies. In a **market economy,** the decisions of a central planner are replaced by the decisions of millions of firms and households. Firms decide whom to hire and what to make. Households decide which firms to work for and what to buy with their incomes. These firms and households interact in the marketplace, where prices and self-interest guide their decisions.

market economy
an economy that allocates resources through the decentralized decisions of many firms and households as they interact in markets for goods and services

At first glance, the success of market economies is puzzling. After all, in a market economy, no one is looking out for the economic well-being of society as a whole. Free markets contain many buyers and sellers of numerous goods and services, and all of them are interested primarily in their own well-being. Yet, despite decentralized decision making and self-interested decision makers, market economies have proven remarkably successful in organizing economic activity in a way that promotes overall economic well-being.

In his 1776 book *An Inquiry into the Nature and Causes of the Wealth of Nations,* economist Adam Smith made the most famous observation in all of economics: Households and firms interacting in markets act as if they are guided by an "invisible hand" that leads them to desirable market outcomes. One of our goals in this book is to understand how this invisible hand works its magic. As you study economics, you will learn that prices are the instrument with which the invisible hand directs economic activity. Prices reflect both the value of a good to society and the cost to society of making the good. Because households and firms look at prices when deciding what to buy and sell, they unknowingly take into account the social benefits and costs of their actions. As a result, prices guide these individual decision makers to reach outcomes that, in many cases, maximize the welfare of society as a whole.

There is an important corollary to the skill of the invisible hand in guiding economic activity: When the government prevents prices from adjusting naturally to supply and demand, it impedes the invisible hand's ability to coordinate the millions of households and firms that make up the economy. This corollary explains why taxes adversely affect the allocation of resources: Taxes distort prices and thus the decisions of households and firms. It also explains the even greater harm caused by policies that directly control prices, such as rent control. And it explains the failure of communism. In communist countries, prices were not determined in the marketplace but were dictated by central planners. These planners lacked the information that is reflected in prices when prices are free to respond to market forces. Central planners failed because they tried to run the economy with one hand tied behind their backs—the invisible hand of the marketplace.

IN THE NEWS

PRICES CONVEY INFORMATION

In most markets, people buy and sell goods like eggs, oil, or computers. The following newspaper article describes markets in some very peculiar goods. The goods being bought and sold in these markets are futures contracts. A futures contract in the weather, for example, might be a promise to pay $100 if there is a frost in Niagara in May. (Niagara fruit growers might be very interested in buying that futures contract for insurance.) If the market price of that futures contract is $20, it suggests that traders believe there is a 20 percent chance of frost in Niagara in May.

Why Markets Come Up with the Right Answers

By Jason Chow

Washington balked this week in its controversial plan to offer traders a chance to buy futures contracts on, among other things, the odds of an overthrow of the King of Jordan. But while the Pentagon's futures market failed for political reasons, the rationale behind using market efficiency to predict events in public affairs has been proven to be successful. Investors can already bet on the outcome of the chase for Al Qaeda leader Osama bin Laden and bid on the winner of the 2004 U.S. presidential elections.

Earlier this week, it was revealed the Pentagon was designing a market that would have allowed traders to place bets on terrorist attacks and political events in the Middle East. The Pentagon was hoping its Policy Analysis Market (PAM)—the name of the ill-fated idea that was canned on Tuesday, only a day after the project was leaked to the public by two Democratic senators—would help the U.S. government intelligence agency predict events in the troubled region.

Though it was a public relations nightmare, fraught with objections of using public money to fund such an exchange and fears that terrorists might take large positions on the outcome of an attack and carry them out themselves, economists say, the idea in itself was a gem—both in its predictive abilities and in its broad appeal.

"It's bad publicity," said economist Robert Shiller at Yale University in New Haven, CT, and author of *Irrational Exuberance.* "But this idea could have worked, and it likely would have revealed information, just the same way as if you put up a US$15-million bounty for the heads of Uday and Qusai Hussein [sons of Iraqi leader Saddam Hussein]."

Alternative markets have been sprouting for some time to receptive audiences with strong reputations for being accurate.

The pioneering alternative futures exchange was the Iowa Electronic Markets, started in 1988, which allowed individuals to bet on the outcome of U.S. presidential elections. Research has shown that the IEM, even with its relatively small population of traders, has been a more effective forecaster than general opinion polls.

There are other similar exchanges. Dublin-based TradeSports.com has been the most active leader in the trading of futures contracts on political and cultural events. There, you can buy and sell contracts based on when you think Saddam Hussein will be captured and on whether you think basketball star Kobe Bryant will be found guilty on sexual charges. TradeSports attracted attention earlier this year when its futures contract on the date of the invasion into Iraq was on target.

The Athletic Stock Exchange allows individuals to ride the fortunes of sports stars while Hollywood Stock Exchange allows online traders to bet on the box-office success of upcoming releases. For example, the release of *S.W.A.T.*, starring Colin Farrell, is being primed as a bust, trading down US$5.67.

Why are markets so effective at predicting the future? Simply, markets can act as essentially virtual meeting places, where people get together to pay and profit for their opinions, economists argue, and the distilled collective thinking of several trumps the forecasting abilities of the individual.

Take the jar of jellybeans experiment: Ask a hundred people how many beans they think are in the jar. It's highly unlikely any one of the responses would have the exact number, but if you take the mean of all their answers you'll probably be close to the mark.

Markets are the same, economists say. Several participants are forced to answer an identical question i.e., Will current U.S. president George Bush win a re-election in 2004?—and have to pay for that privilege.

Stanford University professors Eric Zitzewitz and Justin Wolfers, who have been researching TradeSports and the Saddam futures, says the markets reflect more wisdom than any single individual can possibly have, and therefore are more effective at assessing probabilities.

"The market is one of the best aggregators of information," said John Delaney, chief executive of TradeSports.com. "In essence, I'm asking people for their opinions, but asking them to back it up with real money. They have to put their money where their mouths are."

There's also a psychological element, says Mr. Shiller at Yale, who also runs a private research firm that is currently looking into the creation of markets for house prices and other macroeconomic indicators. The market appeals to those who like to gamble, he says, while at the same time, forces people to think harder about their opinions.

"There's a gambling instinct and it's human nature," he said. "When people are asked their opinions for a survey, they'll say whatever first comes to mind. But if they have money on the line, they'll likely think twice. It's more honest. They'll say what they really believe in."

Of course, not all market predictions are on the money, even those made on alternative markets. Earlier this week TradeSports offered a futures contract on whether John Poindexter, head of the Pentagon's Defence Advanced Research Projects Agency and leader of the PAM initiative, would be able to keep his job after all the controversy surrounding the proposed market.

Traders on TradeSports were pricing in a 65% chance of him still being on the Pentagon payroll at the end of August. Mr. Poindexter was fired on Thursday.

Source: *National Post*, August 2, 2003. Material reprinted with the express permission of "The National Post Company," a CanWest Partnership.

Principle #7: Governments Can Sometimes Improve Market Outcomes

If the invisible hand of the market is so great, why do we need government? One answer is that the invisible hand needs government to protect it. Markets work only if property rights are enforced. A farmer won't grow food if he expects his crop to be stolen, and a restaurant won't serve meals unless it is assured that customers will pay before they leave. We all rely on government-provided police and courts to enforce our rights over the things we produce.

Yet there is another answer to why we need government: Although markets are usually a good way to organize economic activity, this rule has some important exceptions. There are two broad reasons for a government to intervene in the economy—to promote efficiency and to promote equity. That is, most policies aim either to enlarge the economic pie or to change how the pie is divided.

FYI

ADAM SMITH AND THE INVISIBLE HAND

It may be only a coincidence that Adam Smith's great book *The Wealth of Nations* was published in 1776, the exact year American revolutionaries signed the Declaration of Independence. But the two documents do share a point of view that was prevalent at the time—that individuals are usually best left to their own devices, without the heavy hand of government guiding their actions. This political philosophy provides the intellectual basis for the market economy, and for free society more generally.

Why do decentralized market economies work so well? Is it because people can be counted on to treat one another with love and kindness? Not at all. Here is Adam Smith's description of how people interact in a market economy:

Adam Smith

Man has almost constant occasion for the help of his brethren, and it is vain for him to expect it from their benevolence only. He will be more likely to prevail if he can interest their self-love in his favor, and show them that it is for their own advantage to do for him what he requires of them. . . . It is not from the benevolence of the butcher, the brewer, or the baker that we expect our dinner, but from their regard to their own interest. . . .

Every individual . . . neither intends to promote the public interest, nor knows how much he is promoting it. . . . He intends only his own gain, and he is in this, as in many other cases, led by an invisible hand to promote an end which was no part of his intention. Nor is it always the worse for the society that it was no part of it. By pursuing his own interest he frequently promotes that of the society more effectually than when he really intends to promote it.

Smith is saying that participants in the economy are motivated by self-interest and that the "invisible hand" of the marketplace guides this self-interest into promoting general economic well-being.

Many of Smith's insights remain at the centre of modern economics. Our analysis in the coming chapters will allow us to express Smith's conclusions more precisely and to analyze fully the strengths and weaknesses of the market's invisible hand.

---

market failure
a situation in which a market left on its own fails to allocate resources efficiently

externality
the impact of one person's actions on the well-being of a bystander

market power
the ability of a single economic actor (or small group of actors) to have a substantial influence on market prices

Although the invisible hand usually leads markets to allocate resources efficiently, that is not always the case. Economists use the term **market failure** to refer to a situation in which the market on its own fails to produce an efficient allocation of resources. One possible cause of market failure is an **externality,** which is the impact of one person's actions on the well-being of a bystander. For instance, the classic example of an external cost is pollution. Another possible cause of market failure is **market power,** which refers to the ability of a single person (or small group) to unduly influence market prices. For example, if everyone in town needs water but there is only one well, the owner of the well is not subject to the rigorous competition with which the invisible hand normally keeps self-interest in check. In the presence of externalities or market power, well-designed public policy can enhance economic efficiency.

The invisible hand may also fail to ensure that economic prosperity is distributed equitably. A market economy rewards people according to their ability to produce things that other people are willing to pay for. The world's best basketball player earns more than the world's best chess player simply because people are willing to pay more to watch basketball than chess. The invisible hand does not ensure that everyone has sufficient food, decent clothing, and adequate health care. Many public policies, such as the income tax and welfare systems, aim to achieve a more equitable distribution of economic well-being.

To say that the government *can* improve on market outcomes at times does not mean that it always *will*. Public policy is made not by angels but by a political process that is far from perfect. Sometimes policies are designed simply to reward the politically powerful. Sometimes they are made by well-intentioned leaders who are not fully informed. One goal of the study of economics is to help you judge when a government policy is justifiable to promote efficiency or equity, and when it is not.

QuickQuiz   List and briefly explain the three principles concerning economic interactions.

HOW THE ECONOMY AS A WHOLE WORKS

We started by discussing how individuals make decisions and then looked at how people interact with one another. All these decisions and interactions together make up "the economy." The last three principles concern the workings of the economy as a whole.

Principle #8: A Country's Standard of Living Depends on Its Ability to Produce Goods and Services

The differences in living standards around the world are staggering. In 2001 the average Canadian had an income of about $40 700. In the same year, the average Mexican earned $12 550, and the average Nigerian earned $1300. Not surprisingly, this large variation in average income is reflected in various measures of the quality of life. Citizens of high-income countries have more TV sets, more cars, better nutrition, better health care, and longer life expectancy than citizens of low-income countries.

Changes in living standards over time are also large. In Canada, incomes have historically grown about 2 percent per year (after adjusting for changes in the cost of living). At this rate, average income doubles every 35 years. Over the past century, average income has risen about eightfold.

What explains these large differences in living standards among countries and over time? The answer is surprisingly simple. Almost all variation in living standards is attributable to differences in countries' **productivity**—that is, the amount of goods and services produced from each hour of a worker's time. In nations where workers can produce a large quantity of goods and services per unit of time, most people enjoy a high standard of living; in nations where workers are less productive, most people must endure a more meagre existence. Similarly, the growth rate of a nation's productivity determines the growth rate of its average income.

productivity
the quantity of goods and services produced from each hour of a worker's time

The fundamental relationship between productivity and living standards is simple, but its implications are far-reaching. If productivity is the primary determinant of living standards, other explanations must be of secondary importance. For example, it might be tempting to credit labour unions or minimum-wage laws for the rise in living standards of Canadian workers over the past century. Yet the real hero of Canadian workers is their rising productivity. As another example, some commentators have claimed that increased competition from Japan and other countries explained the slow growth in Canadian incomes during the 1970s and 1980s. Yet the real villain was not competition from abroad but flagging productivity growth in Canada.

The relationship between productivity and living standards also has profound implications for public policy. When thinking about how any policy will affect living standards, the key question is how it will affect our ability to produce goods and services. To boost living standards, policymakers need to raise productivity by ensuring that workers are well educated, have the tools needed to produce goods and services, and have access to the best available technology.

Principle #9: Prices Rise When the Government Prints Too Much Money

inflation
an increase in the overall level of prices in the economy

In Germany in January 1921, a daily newspaper cost 0.30 marks. Less than two years later, in November 1922, the same newspaper cost 70 000 000 marks. All other prices in the economy rose by similar amounts. This episode is one of history's most spectacular examples of **inflation,** an increase in the overall level of prices in the economy.

Although Canada has never experienced inflation even close to that in Germany in the 1920s, inflation has at times been an economic problem. During the 1970s, for instance, average inflation was 8 percent per year and the overall level of prices more than doubled. By contrast, inflation in the 1990s was about 2 percent per year; at this rate it would take 35 years for prices to double. Because high inflation imposes various costs on society, keeping inflation at a low level is a goal of economic policymakers around the world.

What causes inflation? In almost all cases of large or persistent inflation, the culprit turns out to be the same—growth in the quantity of money. When a government creates large quantities of the nation's money, the value of the money falls. In Germany in the early 1920s, when prices were on average tripling every month, the quantity of money was also tripling every month. Although less dramatic, the economic history of Canada points to a similar conclusion: The high inflation of the 1970s was associated with rapid growth in the quantity of money, and the low inflation of the 1990s was associated with slow growth in the quantity of money.

Principle #10: Society Faces a Short-Run Tradeoff between Inflation and Unemployment

When the government increases the amount of money in the economy, one result is inflation. Another result, at least in the short run, is a lower level of unemployment. The curve that illustrates this short-run tradeoff between inflation and unemployment is called the **Phillips curve,** after the economist who first examined this relationship.

Phillips curve
a curve that shows the short-run tradeoff between inflation and unemployment

The Phillips curve remains a controversial topic among economists, but most economists today accept the idea that society faces a short-run tradeoff between inflation and unemployment. This simply means that, over a period of a year or two, many economic policies push inflation and unemployment in opposite directions. Policymakers face this tradeoff regardless of whether inflation and unemployment both start out at high levels (as they were in the early 1980s), at low levels (as they were in the late 1990s), or someplace in between.

The tradeoff between inflation and unemployment is only temporary, but it can last for several years. The Phillips curve is, therefore, crucial for understanding many developments in the economy. In particular, it is important for understanding the **business cycle**—the irregular and largely unpredictable fluctuations in economic activity, as measured by the number of people employed or the production of goods and services.

business cycle
fluctuations in economic activity, such as employment and production

Policymakers can exploit the short-run tradeoff between inflation and unemployment using various policy instruments. By changing the amount that the government spends, the amount it taxes, and the amount of money it prints, policymakers can influence the combination of inflation and unemployment that the economy experiences. Because these instruments of monetary and fiscal policy are potentially so powerful, how policymakers should use these instruments to control the economy, if at all, is a subject of continuing debate.

QuickQuiz   List and briefly explain the three principles that describe how the economy as a whole works.

FYI

HOW TO READ THIS BOOK

Economics is fun, but it can also be hard to learn. Our aim in writing this text is to make it as fun and easy as possible. But you, the student, also have a role to play. Experience shows that if you are actively involved as you study this book, you will enjoy a better outcome, both on your exams and in the years that follow. Here are a few tips about how best to read this book.

1. *Summarize, don't highlight.* Running a yellow marker over the text is too passive an activity to keep your mind engaged. Instead, when you come to the end of a section, take a minute and summarize what you just learned in your own words, writing your summary in the wide margins we've provided. When you've finished the chapter, compare your summary with the one at the end of the chapter. Did you pick up the main points?

2. *Test yourself.* Throughout the book, Quick Quizzes offer instant feedback to find out if you've learned what you are supposed to. Take the opportunity. Write your answer in the book's margin. The quizzes are meant to test your basic comprehension. If you aren't sure your answer is right, you probably need to review the section.

3. *Practise, practise, practise.* At the end of each chapter, Questions for Review test your understanding, and Problems and Applications ask you to apply and extend the material. Perhaps your instructor will assign some of these exercises as homework. If so, do them. If not, do them anyway. The more you use your new knowledge, the more solid it becomes.

4. *Study in groups.* After you've read the book and worked the problems on your own, get together with classmates to discuss the material. You will learn from each other—an example of the gains from trade.

5. *Don't forget the real world.* In the midst of all the numbers, graphs, and strange new words, it is easy to lose sight of what economics is all about. The Case Studies and In the News boxes sprinkled throughout this book should help remind you. Don't skip them. They show how the theory is tied to events happening in all of our lives. If your study is successful, you won't be able to read a newspaper again without thinking about supply, demand, and the wonderful world of economics.

TABLE 1.1		
Ten Principles of Economics	**How People Make Decisions**	#1: People face tradeoffs
		#2: The cost of something is what you give up to get it
		#3: Rational people think at the margin
		#4: People respond to incentives
	How People Interact	#5: Trade can make everyone better off
		#6: Markets are usually a good way to organize economic activity
		#7: Governments can sometimes improve market outcomes
	How the Economy as a Whole Works	#8: A country's standard of living depends on its ability to produce goods and services
		#9: Prices rise when the government prints too much money
		#10: Society faces a short-run tradeoff between inflation and unemployment

CONCLUSION

You now have a taste of what economics is all about. In the coming chapters we will develop many specific insights about people, markets, and economies. Mastering these insights will take some effort, but it is not an overwhelming task. The field of economics is based on a few basic ideas that can be applied in many different situations.

Throughout this book we will refer back to the ten principles of economics highlighted in this chapter and summarized in Table 1.1. Whenever we do so, an icon will be displayed in the margin, as it is now. But even when that icon is absent, you should keep these principles in mind. Even the most sophisticated economic analysis is built using the ten principles introduced here.

SUMMARY

- The fundamental lessons about individual decision making are that people face tradeoffs among alternative goals, that the cost of any action is measured in terms of forgone opportunities, that rational people make decisions by comparing marginal costs and marginal benefits, and that people change their behaviour in response to the incentives they face.

- The fundamental lessons about interactions among people are that trade can be mutually beneficial, that markets are usually a good way

of coordinating trade among people, and that the government can potentially improve market outcomes if there is some market failure or if the market outcome is inequitable.

- The fundamental lessons about the economy as a whole are that productivity is the ultimate source of living standards, that money growth is the ultimate source of inflation, and that society faces a short-run tradeoff between inflation and unemployment.

KEY CONCEPTS

scarcity, p. 4
economics, p. 4
efficiency, p. 5
equity, p. 5
opportunity cost, p. 6

marginal changes, p. 6
market economy, p. 9
market failure, p. 12
externality, p. 12
market power, p. 12

productivity, p. 13
inflation, p. 14
Phillips curve, p. 14
business cycle, p. 15

QUESTIONS FOR REVIEW

1. Give three examples of important tradeoffs that you face in your life.

2. What is the opportunity cost of seeing a movie?

3. Water is necessary for life. Is the marginal benefit of a glass of water large or small?

4. Why should policymakers think about incentives?

5. Why isn't trade among countries like a game, with some winners and some losers?

6. What does the "invisible hand" of the marketplace do?

7. Explain the two main causes of market failure and give an example of each.

8. Why is productivity important?

9. What is inflation, and what causes it?

10. How are inflation and unemployment related in the short run?

PROBLEMS AND APPLICATIONS

1. Describe some of the tradeoffs faced by each of the following.
   a. a family deciding whether to buy a new car
   b. a member of Parliament deciding how much to spend on national parks
   c. a company president deciding whether to open a new factory
   d. a professor deciding how much to prepare for class

2. You are trying to decide whether to take a vacation. Most of the costs of the vacation (airfare, hotel, forgone wages) are measured in dollars, but the benefits of the vacation are psychological. How can you compare the benefits to the costs?

3. You were planning to spend Saturday working at your part-time job, but a friend asks you to go skiing. What is the true cost of going skiing? Now suppose that you had been planning to spend the day studying at the library. What is the cost of going skiing in this case? Explain.

4. You win $100 in a hockey pool. You have a choice between spending the money now or putting it away for a year in a bank account that pays 5 percent interest. What is the opportunity cost of spending the $100 now?

5. The company that you manage has invested $5 million in developing a new product, but the development is not quite finished. At a recent meeting, your salespeople report that the introduction of competing products has reduced the expected sales of your new product to $3 million. If it would cost $1 million to finish development and make the product, should you go ahead and do so? What is the most that you should pay to complete development?

6. Three managers of the Magic Potion Company are discussing a possible increase in production. Each suggests a way to make this decision.

HARRY: We should examine whether our company's productivity—litres of potion per worker—would rise or fall.

RON: We should examine whether our average cost—cost per worker—would rise or fall.

HERMIONE: We should examine whether the extra revenue from selling the additional potion would be greater or smaller than the extra costs.

Who do you think is right? Why?

7. The welfare system provides income for people who are very poor, with low incomes and few assets. If a recipient of welfare payments decides to work and earn some money, the amount he or she receives in welfare payments is reduced.
   a. How does the existence of the welfare system affect people's incentive to save money for the future?
   b. How does the reduction in welfare payments associated with higher earnings affect welfare recipients' incentive to work?

8. In 1997 the Government of Ontario reformed the welfare system. The reform reduced the amount of welfare payments to a person with no income, but also allowed welfare recipients to keep a larger part of their welfare payments if they did earn some income.
   a. How does this reform affect the incentive to work?
   b. How might this reform represent a tradeoff between equity and efficiency?

9. Your roommate is a better cook than you are, but you can clean more quickly than your roommate can. If your roommate did all of the cooking and you did all of the cleaning, would your chores take you more or less time than if you divided each task evenly? Give a similar example of how specialization and trade can make two countries both better off.

10. Suppose Canada adopted central planning for its economy, and you became the chief planner. Among the millions of decisions that you need to make for next year are how many compact discs to produce, what artists to record, and who should receive the discs.
   a. To make these decisions intelligently, what information would you need about the compact disc industry? What information would you need about each of the people in Canada?
   b. How would your decisions about CDs affect some of your other decisions, such as how many CD players to make or cassette tapes to produce? How might some of your other decisions about the economy change your views about CDs?

11. Explain whether each of the following government activities is motivated by a concern about equity or a concern about efficiency. In the case of efficiency, discuss the type of market failure involved.
   a. regulating cable TV prices
   b. providing some poor people with free prescription drugs
   c. prohibiting smoking in public places
   d. preventing mergers between major banks
   e. imposing higher personal income tax rates on people with higher incomes
   f. instituting laws against driving while intoxicated

12. Discuss each of the following statements from the standpoints of equity and efficiency.
   a. "Everyone in society should be guaranteed the best health care possible."
   b. "When workers are laid off, they should be able to collect unemployment benefits until they find a new job."

13. In what ways is your standard of living different from that of your parents or grandparents when they were your age? Why have these changes occurred?

14. Suppose Canadians decide to save more of their incomes. If banks lend this extra saving to businesses, which use the funds to build new factories, how might this lead to faster growth in productivity? Who do you suppose benefits from the higher productivity? Is society getting a free lunch?

15. Imagine that you are a policymaker trying to decide whether to reduce the rate of inflation.

To make an intelligent decision, what would you need to know about inflation, unemployment, and the tradeoff between them?

16. Look at a newspaper or at the website http://www.economist.com to find three stories about the economy that have been in the news lately. For each story, identify one (or more) of the ten principles of economics discussed in this chapter that is relevant, and explain how it is relevant. Also, for each story, look through this book's table of contents and try to find a chapter that might shed light on the news event.

INTERNET RESOURCES

- Canadian economic and financial statistics can be found online through the University of British Columbia Library at http://data.library.ubc.ca/datalib/gen/analysis.html.

- Study original research and analysis of changes to the Canadian economy at the Industry Canada website: http://strategis.ic.gc.ca/sc_ecnmy/engdoc/homepage.html?categories=c_eco.

- The *Occupational Outlook Handbook* at http://www.bls.gov/oco describes the role of an economist, the future outlook of the position, and the training required. Although this is a U.S. site, much information relevant to Canadian economists is provided.

 For more study tools, please visit http://www.mankiw3e.nelson.com.

© PHOTODISC

2

THINKING LIKE AN ECONOMIST

Learning Objectives

In this chapter, you will …

- See how economists apply the methods of science
- Consider how assumptions and models can shed light on the world
- Learn two simple models—the circular flow and the production possibilities frontier
- Distinguish between microeconomics and macroeconomics
- Learn the difference between positive and normative statements
- Examine the role of economists in making policy
- Consider why economists sometimes disagree with one another

Every field of study has its own language and its own way of thinking. Mathematicians talk about axioms, integrals, and vector spaces. Psychologists talk about ego, id, and cognitive dissonance. Lawyers talk about venue, torts, and promissory estoppel.

Economics is no different. Supply, demand, elasticity, comparative advantage, consumer surplus, deadweight loss—these terms are part of the economist's language. In the coming chapters, you will encounter many new terms and some familiar words that economists use in specialized ways. At first, this new language may seem needlessly arcane. But, as you will see, its value lies in its ability to provide you with a new and useful way of thinking about the world in which you live.

The single most important purpose of this book is to help you learn the economist's way of thinking. Of course, just as you cannot become a mathematician, psychologist, or lawyer overnight, learning to think like an economist will take some time. Yet with a combination of theory, case studies, and examples of economics in the news, this book will give you ample opportunity to develop and practise this skill.

Before delving into the substance and details of economics, it is helpful to have an overview of how economists approach the world. This chapter, therefore, discusses the field's methodology. What is distinctive about how economists confront a question? What does it mean to think like an economist?

THE ECONOMIST AS SCIENTIST

Economists try to address their subject with a scientist's objectivity. They approach the study of the economy in much the same way as a physicist approaches the study of matter and a biologist approaches the study of life: They devise theories, collect data, and then analyze these data in an attempt to verify or refute their theories.

To beginners, it can seem odd to claim that economics is a science. After all, economists do not work with test tubes or telescopes. The essence of science, however, is the *scientific method*—the dispassionate development and testing of theories about how the world works. This method of inquiry is as applicable to studying a nation's economy as it is to studying the earth's gravity or a species' evolution. As Albert Einstein once put it, "The whole of science is nothing more than the refinement of everyday thinking."

Although Einstein's comment is as true for social sciences such as economics as it is for natural sciences such as physics, most people are not accustomed to looking at society through the eyes of a scientist. Let's therefore discuss some of the ways in which economists apply the logic of science to examine how an economy works.

The Scientific Method: Observation, Theory, and More Observation

Isaac Newton, the famous seventeenth-century scientist and mathematician, allegedly became intrigued one day when he saw an apple fall from an apple tree. This observation motivated Newton to develop a theory of gravity that applies not only to an apple falling to the earth but to any two objects in the universe. Subsequent testing of Newton's theory has shown that it works well in many circumstances (although, as Einstein would later emphasize, not in all circumstances). Because Newton's theory has been so successful at explaining observation, it is still taught today in undergraduate physics courses around the world.

This interplay between theory and observation also occurs in the field of economics. An economist might live in a country experiencing rapid increases in prices and be moved by this observation to develop a theory of inflation. The theory might assert that high inflation arises when the government prints too much money. (As you may recall, this was one of the ten principles of economics in Chapter 1.) To test this theory, the economist could collect and analyze data on prices and money from many different countries. If growth in the quantity of money were not at all related to the rate at which prices are rising, the economist would start to doubt the validity of his theory of inflation. If money growth and inflation were strongly correlated in international data, as in fact they are, the economist would become more confident in his theory.

Although economists use theory and observation like other scientists, they do face an obstacle that makes their task especially challenging: Experiments are often difficult in economics. Physicists studying gravity can drop many objects in their laboratories to generate data to test their theories. By contrast, economists studying inflation are not allowed to manipulate a nation's monetary policy simply to generate useful data. Economists, like astronomers and evolutionary biologists, usually have to make do with whatever data the world happens to give them.

To find a substitute for laboratory experiments, economists pay close attention to the natural experiments offered by history. When a war in the Middle East interrupts the flow of crude oil, for instance, oil prices skyrocket around the world. For consumers of oil and oil products, such an event depresses living standards. For economic policymakers, it poses a difficult choice about how best to respond. But for economic scientists, it provides an opportunity to study the effects of a key natural resource on the world's economies, and this opportunity persists long after the wartime increase in oil prices is over. Throughout this book, therefore, we consider many historical episodes. These episodes are valuable to study because they give us insight into the economy of the past and, more important, because they allow us to illustrate and evaluate economic theories of the present.

The Role of Assumptions

If you ask a physicist how long it would take for a marble to fall from the top of a ten-storey building, she will answer the question by assuming that the marble falls in a vacuum. Of course, this assumption is false. In fact, the building is surrounded by air, which exerts friction on the falling marble and slows it down. Yet the physicist will correctly point out that friction on the marble is so small that its effect is negligible. Assuming that the marble falls in a vacuum greatly simplifies the problem without substantially affecting the answer.

Economists make assumptions for the same reason: Assumptions can simplify the complex world and make it easier to understand. To study the effects of international trade, for example, we may assume that the world consists of only two countries and that each country produces only two goods. Of course, the real world consists of dozens of countries, each of which produces thousands of different types of goods. But by assuming two countries and two goods, we can focus our thinking. Once we understand international trade in an imaginary world with two countries and two goods, we are in a better position to understand international trade in the more complex world in which we live.

The art in scientific thinking—whether in physics, biology, or economics—is deciding which assumptions to make. Suppose, for instance, that we were dropping a beach ball rather than a marble from the top of the building. Our physicist would realize that the assumption of no friction is far less accurate in this case: Friction exerts a greater force on a beach ball than on a marble because a beach ball is much larger. The assumption that gravity works in a vacuum is reasonable for studying a falling marble but not for studying a falling beach ball.

Similarly, economists use different assumptions to answer different questions. Suppose that we want to study what happens to the economy when the government changes the number of dollars in circulation. An important piece of this analysis, it turns out, is how prices respond. Many prices in the economy change infrequently; the newsstand prices of magazines, for instance, are changed only every few years. Knowing this fact may lead us to make different assumptions when studying the effects of the policy change over different time horizons. For studying the short-run effects of the policy, we may assume that prices do not change much. We may even make the extreme and artificial assumption that all prices are completely fixed. For studying the long-run effects of the policy, however, we may assume that all prices are completely flexible. Just as a physicist uses different assumptions when studying falling marbles and falling beach balls, economists use different assumptions when studying the short-run and long-run effects of a change in the quantity of money.

Economic Models

High-school biology teachers teach basic anatomy with plastic replicas of the human body. These models have all the major organs—the heart, the liver, the kidneys, and so on. The models allow teachers to show their students in a simple way how the important parts of the body fit together. Of course, these plastic models are not actual human bodies, and no one would mistake the model for a real person. These models are stylized, and they omit many details. Yet despite this lack of realism—indeed, because of this lack of realism—studying these models is useful for learning how the human body works.

Economists also use models to learn about the world, but instead of being made of plastic, they are most often composed of diagrams and equations. Like a biology teacher's plastic model, economic models omit many details to allow us to see what is truly important. Just as the biology teacher's model does not include all of the body's muscles and capillaries, an economist's model does not include every feature of the economy.

As we use models to examine various economic issues throughout this book, you will see that all the models are built with assumptions. Just as a physicist begins the analysis of a falling marble by assuming away the existence of friction, economists assume away many of the details of the economy that are irrelevant for studying the question at hand. All models—in physics, biology, or economics—simplify reality in order to improve our understanding of it.

Our First Model: The Circular-Flow Diagram

The economy consists of millions of people engaged in many activities—buying, selling, working, hiring, manufacturing, and so on. To understand how the economy works, we must find some way to simplify our thinking about all these activities. In other words, we need a model that explains, in general terms, how the economy is organized and how participants in the economy interact with one another.

circular-flow diagram
a visual model of the economy that shows how dollars flow through markets among households and firms

Figure 2.1 presents a visual model of the economy, called a **circular-flow diagram.** In this model, the economy is simplified to include only two types of decision makers—households and firms. Firms produce goods and services using inputs, such as labour, land (natural resources), and capital (buildings and machines). These inputs are called the *factors of production*. Households own the factors of production and consume all the goods and services that the firms produce.

Households and firms interact in two types of markets. In the *markets for goods and services*, households are buyers and firms are sellers. In particular, households buy the output of goods and services that firms produce. In the *markets for the*

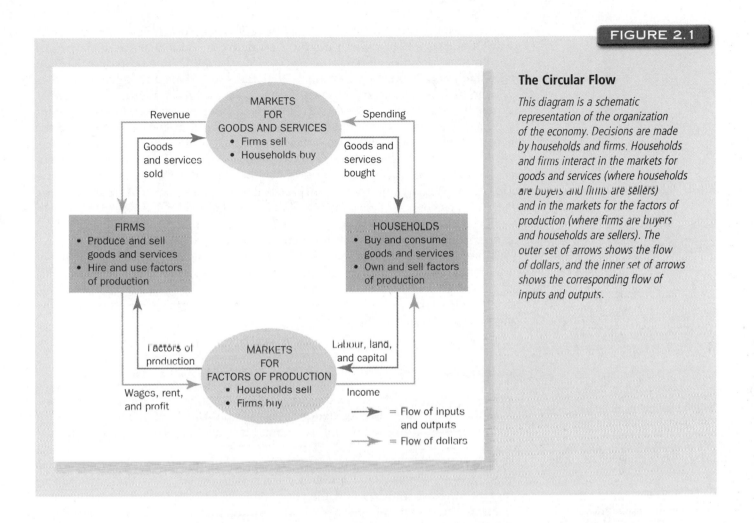

FIGURE 2.1

The Circular Flow

This diagram is a schematic representation of the organization of the economy. Decisions are made by households and firms. Households and firms interact in the markets for goods and services (where households are buyers and firms are sellers) and in the markets for the factors of production (where firms are buyers and households are sellers). The outer set of arrows shows the flow of dollars, and the inner set of arrows shows the corresponding flow of inputs and outputs.

factors of production, households are sellers and firms are buyers. In these markets, households provide the inputs that the firms use to produce goods and services. The circular-flow diagram offers a simple way of organizing all the economic transactions that occur between households and firms in the economy.

The inner loop of the circular-flow diagram represents the flows of inputs and outputs. The households sell the use of their labour, land, and capital to the firms in the markets for the factors of production. The firms then use these factors to produce goods and services, which in turn are sold to households in the markets for goods and services. Hence, the factors of production flow from households to firms, and goods and services flow from firms to households.

The outer loop of the circular-flow diagram represents the corresponding flow of dollars. The households spend money to buy goods and services from the firms. The firms use some of the revenue from these sales to pay for the factors of production, such as the wages of their workers. What's left is the profit of the firm owners, who themselves are members of households. Hence, spending on goods and services flows from households to firms, and income in the form of wages, rent, and profit flows from firms to households.

Let's take a tour of the circular flow by following a dollar coin as it makes its way from person to person through the economy. Imagine that the dollar begins at a household, sitting in, say, your pocket. If you want to buy a cup of coffee, you take the dollar to one of the economy's markets for goods and services, such as your local Tim Hortons coffee shop. There you spend it on your favourite drink. When the dollar moves into the Tim Hortons cash register, it becomes revenue for the firm. The dollar doesn't stay at Tim Hortons for long, however, because the firm uses it to buy inputs in the markets for the factors of production. For instance, Tim Hortons might use the dollar to pay rent to its landlord for the space it occupies or to pay the wages of its workers. In either case, the dollar enters the income of some household and, once again, is back in someone's pocket. At that point, the story of the economy's circular flow starts once again.

The circular-flow diagram in Figure 2.1 is one simple model of the economy. It dispenses with details that, for some purposes, are significant. A more complex and realistic circular-flow model would include, for instance, the roles of government and international trade. Yet these details are not crucial for a basic understanding of how the economy is organized. Because of its simplicity, this circular-flow diagram is useful to keep in mind when thinking about how the pieces of the economy fit together.

Our Second Model: The Production Possibilities Frontier

Most economic models, unlike the circular-flow diagram, are built using the tools of mathematics. Here we consider one of the simplest such models, called the production possibilities frontier, and see how this model illustrates some basic economic ideas.

Although real economies produce thousands of goods and services, let's imagine an economy that produces only two goods—cars and computers. Together the car industry and the computer industry use all of the economy's resources, or factors of production. The **production possibilities frontier** is a graph that shows the various combinations of output—in this case, cars and computers—that the economy can possibly produce given the available factors of production and the available production technology that firms can use to turn these factors into output.

Figure 2.2 is an example of a production possibilities frontier. In this economy, if all resources were used in the car industry, the economy would produce 1000 cars per year and no computers. If all resources were used in the computer industry, the economy would produce 3000 computers per year and no cars. The two end points of the production possibilities frontier represent these extreme possibilities. If the economy were to divide its resources between the two industries, it could produce 700 cars and 2000 computers, shown in the figure by point A. By contrast, the outcome at point D is not possible because resources are scarce: The economy does not have enough of the factors of production to support that level of output. In other words, the economy can produce at any point on or inside the production possibilities frontier, but it cannot produce at points outside the frontier.

An outcome is said to be *efficient* if the economy is getting all it can from the scarce resources it has available. Points on (rather than inside) the production possibilities frontier represent efficient levels of production. When the economy is producing at such a point, say point A, there is no way to produce more of one

production possibilities frontier
a graph that shows the combinations of output that the economy can possibly produce given the available factors of production and the available production technology

FIGURE 2.2

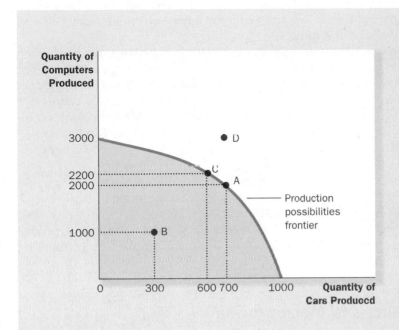

**The Production
Possibilities Frontier**

*The production possibilities frontier shows the
combinations of output—in this case, cars and
computers—that the economy can possibly produce. The
economy can produce any combination on or inside the
frontier. Points outside the frontier are not feasible given
the economy's resources.*

good without producing less of the other. Point B represents an *inefficient* outcome.
For some reason, perhaps widespread unemployment, the economy is producing
less than it could from the resources it has available: It is producing only 300 cars
and 1000 computers. If the source of the inefficiency were eliminated, the
economy could move from point B to point A, increasing production of both cars
(to 700) and computers (to 2000).

One of the ten principles of economics discussed in Chapter 1 is that people
face tradeoffs. The production possibilities frontier shows one tradeoff that society
faces. Once we have reached the efficient points on the frontier, the only way of
getting more of one good is to get less of the other. When the economy moves from
point A to point C, for instance, society produces more computers, but at the
expense of producing fewer cars.

Another of the ten principles of economics is that the cost of something is what
you give up to get it. This is called the *opportunity cost*. The production possibilities frontier shows the opportunity cost of one good as measured in terms of the
other good. When society reallocates some of the factors of production from the
car industry to the computer industry, moving the economy from point A to point
C, it gives up 100 cars to get 200 additional computers. In other words, when the
economy is at point A, the opportunity cost of 200 computers is 100 cars.

Notice that the production possibilities frontier in Figure 2.2 is bowed outward.
This means that the opportunity cost of cars in terms of computers depends on
how much of each good the economy is producing. When the economy is using
most of its resources to make cars, the production possibilities frontier is quite
steep. Because even workers and machines best suited to making computers are
being used to make cars, the economy gets a substantial increase in the number of
computers for each car it gives up. By contrast, when the economy is using most
of its resources to make computers, the production possibilities frontier is quite

flat. In this case, the resources best suited to making computers are already in the computer industry, and each car the economy gives up yields only a small increase in the number of computers.

The production possibilities frontier shows the tradeoff between the production of different goods at a given time, but the tradeoff can change over time. For example, if a technological advance in the computer industry raises the number of computers that a worker can produce per week, the economy can make more computers for any given number of cars. As a result, the production possibilities frontier shifts outward, as in Figure 2.3. Because of this economic growth, society might move production from point A to point E, enjoying more computers and more cars.

The production possibilities frontier simplifies a complex economy to highlight and clarify some basic ideas. We have used it to illustrate some of the concepts mentioned briefly in Chapter 1: scarcity, efficiency, tradeoffs, opportunity cost, and economic growth. As you study economics, these ideas will recur in various forms. The production possibilities frontier offers one simple way of thinking about them.

Microeconomics and Macroeconomics

Many subjects are studied on various levels. Consider biology, for example. Molecular biologists study the chemical compounds that make up living things. Cellular biologists study cells, which are made up of many chemical compounds and, at the same time, are themselves the building blocks of living organisms. Evolutionary biologists study the many varieties of animals and plants and how species change gradually over the centuries.

Economics is also studied on various levels. We can study the decisions of individual households and firms. Or we can study the interaction of households and firms in markets for specific goods and services. Or we can study the operation of the economy as a whole, which is just the sum of the activities of all these decision makers in all these markets.

microeconomics
the study of how households and firms make decisions and how they interact in markets

macroeconomics
the study of economy-wide phenomena, including inflation, unemployment, and economic growth

The field of economics is traditionally divided into two broad subfields. **Microeconomics** is the study of how households and firms make decisions and how they interact in specific markets. **Macroeconomics** is the study of economy-wide phenomena. A microeconomist might study the effects of rent control on housing in Toronto, the impact of foreign competition on the Canadian auto industry, or the effects of compulsory school attendance on workers' earnings. A macroeconomist might study the effects of borrowing by the federal government, the changes over time in the economy's rate of unemployment, or alternative policies to raise growth in national living standards.

Microeconomics and macroeconomics are closely intertwined. Because changes in the overall economy arise from the decisions of millions of individuals, it is impossible to understand macroeconomic developments without considering the associated microeconomic decisions. For example, a macroeconomist might study the effect of a cut in the federal income tax on the overall production of goods and services. To analyze this issue, he or she must consider how the tax cut affects the decisions of households about how much to spend on goods and services.

Despite the inherent link between microeconomics and macroeconomics, the two fields are distinct. In economics, as in biology, it may seem natural to begin

FIGURE 2.3

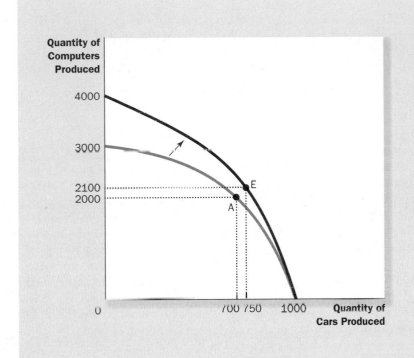

A Shift in the Production Possibilities Frontier

An economic advance in the computer industry shifts the production possibilities frontier outward, increasing the number of cars and computers the economy can produce.

with the smallest unit and build up. Yet doing so is neither necessary nor always the best way to proceed. Evolutionary biology is, in a sense, built upon molecular biology, since species are made up of molecules. Yet molecular biology and evolutionary biology are separate fields, each with its own questions and its own methods. Similarly, because microeconomics and macroeconomics address different questions, they sometimes take quite different approaches and are often taught in separate courses.

QuickQuiz   In what sense is economics like a science? • Draw a production possibilities frontier for a society that produces food and clothing. Show an efficient point, an inefficient point, and an infeasible point. Show the effects of a drought. • Define *microeconomics* and *macroeconomics.*

THE ECONOMIST AS POLICY ADVISER

Often economists are asked to explain the causes of economic events. Why, for example, is unemployment higher for teenagers than for older workers? Sometimes economists are asked to recommend policies to improve economic outcomes. What, for instance, should the government do to improve the economic well-being of teenagers? When economists are trying to explain the world, they are scientists. When they are trying to help improve it, they are policy advisers.

Positive versus Normative Analysis

To help clarify the two roles that economists play, we begin by examining the use of language. Because scientists and policy advisers have different goals, they use language in different ways.

For example, suppose that two people are discussing minimum-wage laws. Here are two statements you might hear:

POLLY: Minimum-wage laws cause unemployment.

NORMA: The government should raise the minimum wage.

Ignoring for now whether you agree with these statements, notice that Polly and Norma differ in what they are trying to do. Polly is speaking like a scientist: She is making a claim about how the world works. Norma is speaking like a policy adviser: She is making a claim about how she would like to change the world.

In general, statements about the world are of two types. One type, such as Polly's, is positive. **Positive statements** are descriptive. They make a claim about how the world *is*. A second type of statement, such as Norma's, is normative. **Normative statements** are prescriptive. They make a claim about how the world *ought to be.*

A key difference between positive and normative statements is how we judge their validity. We can, in principle, confirm or refute positive statements by examining evidence. An economist might evaluate Polly's statement by analyzing data on changes in minimum wages and changes in unemployment over time. By contrast, evaluating normative statements involves values as well as facts. Norma's statement cannot be judged using data alone. Deciding what is good or bad policy is not merely a matter of science. It also involves our views on ethics, religion, and political philosophy.

Of course, positive and normative statements may be related. Our positive views about how the world works affect our normative views about what policies are desirable. Polly's claim that the minimum-wage laws cause unemployment, if true, might lead us to reject Norma's conclusion that the government should raise the minimum wage. Yet our normative conclusions cannot come from positive analysis alone; they involve value judgments as well.

As you study economics, keep in mind the distinction between positive and normative statements. Much of economics just tries to explain how the economy works. Yet often the goal of economics is to improve how the economy works. When you hear economists making normative statements, you know they have crossed the line from scientist to policy adviser.

positive statements
claims that attempt to describe the world as it is

normative statements
claims that attempt to prescribe how the world should be

Economists in Ottawa

U.S. President Harry Truman once said that he wanted to find a one-armed economist. When he asked his economists for advice, they always answered, "On the one hand, . . . On the other hand, ..."

Truman was right in realizing that economists' advice is not always straightforward. This tendency is rooted in one of the ten principles of economics in Chapter 1: People face tradeoffs. Economists are aware that tradeoffs are involved in most policy decisions. A policy might increase efficiency at the cost of equity. It might help future generations but hurt current generations. An economist who says that all policy decisions are easy is an economist not to be trusted.

The Government of Canada, like other governments, relies on the advice of economists. Economists at Finance Canada help design tax policy. Economists at Industry Canada help design and enforce Canada's antimonopoly laws. Economists at the departments of Foreign Affairs Canada and International Trade Canada help negotiate trade agreements with other countries. Economists at Human Resources and Skills Development Canada analyze data on workers and on those looking for work to help formulate labour-market policies. Economists at Environment Canada help design environmental regulations. The Canadian International Development Agency employs economists, both on staff and as consultants, to give advice on overseas development projects. Statistics Canada employs economists to collect the data analyzed by other economists and then give policy advice. The Bank of Canada, the quasi-independent institution that sets Canada's monetary policy, employs more than 200 economists to analyze financial markets and macroeconomic developments.

Economists outside the government also give policy advice. The C.D. Howe Institute, the Fraser Institute, the Institute for Research on Public Policy, the Canadian Centre for Policy Alternatives, and other independent organizations publish reports by economists that analyze current issues such as poverty, unemployment, and the deficit. These reports try to influence public opinion and give advice on government policies. The Internet Resources section just before the appendix to this chapter provides the URLs for the websites of these organizations.

The influence of economists on policy goes beyond their role as advisers: Their research and writings often affect policy indirectly. Economist John Maynard Keynes offered this observation:

> The ideas of economists and political philosophers, both when they are right and when they are wrong, are more powerful than is commonly understood. Indeed, the world is ruled by little else. Practical men, who believe themselves to be quite exempt from intellectual influences, are usually the slaves of some defunct economist. Madmen in authority, who hear voices in the air, are distilling their frenzy from some academic scribbler of a few years back.

Although these words were written in 1935, they remain true today. Indeed, the "academic scribbler" now influencing public policy is often Keynes himself.

QuickQuiz   Give an example of a positive statement and an example of a normative statement. • Name three parts of government that regularly rely on advice from economists.

WHY ECONOMISTS DISAGREE

"If all economists were laid end to end, they would not reach a conclusion." This quip by George Bernard Shaw is revealing. Economists as a group are often criticized for giving conflicting advice to policymakers.

Why do economists so often appear to give conflicting advice to policymakers?

There are two basic reasons:

- Economists may disagree about the validity of alternative positive theories about how the world works.
- Economists may have different values and, therefore, different normative views about what policy should try to accomplish.

Let's discuss each of these reasons.

Differences in Scientific Judgments

Several centuries ago, astronomers debated whether the earth or the sun was at the centre of the solar system. More recently, meteorologists have debated whether the earth is experiencing global warming and, if so, why. Science is a search for understanding about the world around us. It is not surprising that as the search continues, scientists can disagree about the direction in which truth lies.

Economists often disagree for the same reason. Economics is a young science, and there is still much to be learned. Economists sometimes disagree because they have different hunches about the validity of alternative theories or about the size of important parameters.

For example, economists disagree about whether the government should levy taxes based on a household's income or its consumption (spending). Advocates of a switch from the current income tax to a consumption tax believe that the change would encourage households to save more, because income that is saved would not be taxed. Higher saving, in turn, would lead to more rapid growth in productivity and living standards. Advocates of the current income tax system believe that household saving would not respond much to a change in the tax laws. These two groups of economists hold different normative views about the tax system because they have different positive views about the responsiveness of saving to tax incentives.

Differences in Values

Suppose that Peter and Paul both take the same amount of water from the town well. To pay for maintaining the well, the town taxes its residents. Peter has income of $50 000 and is taxed $5000, or 10 percent of his income. Paul has income of $10 000 and is taxed $2000, or 20 percent of his income.

Is this policy fair? If not, who pays too much and who pays too little? Does it matter whether Paul's low income is due to a medical disability or to his decision to pursue a career in acting? Does it matter whether Peter's high income is due to a large inheritance or to his willingness to work long hours at a dreary job?

These are difficult questions on which people are likely to disagree. If the town hired two experts to study how the town should tax its residents to pay for the well, we would not be surprised if they offered conflicting advice.

This simple example shows why economists sometimes disagree about public policy. As we learned earlier in our discussion of normative and positive analysis, policies cannot be judged on scientific grounds alone. Economists give conflicting advice sometimes because they have different values. Perfecting the science of economics will not tell us whether it is Peter or Paul who pays too much.

Perception versus Reality

Because of differences in scientific judgments and differences in values, some disagreement among economists is inevitable. Yet one should not overstate the amount of disagreement. In many cases, economists do offer a united view.

Table 2.1 (p. 34) contains ten propositions about economic policy. In a survey of economists in business, government, and academia, these propositions were endorsed by an overwhelming majority of respondents. Most of these propositions would fail to command a similar consensus among the general public.

The first proposition in the table is about rent control. For reasons we will discuss later, almost all economists believe that rent control adversely affects the availability and quality of housing and is a very costly way of helping the most needy members of society. Nonetheless, some provincial governments choose to ignore the advice of economists and place ceilings on the rents that landlords may charge their tenants.

The second proposition in the table concerns tariffs and import quotas, two policies that restrict trade among nations. For reasons we will discuss more fully in later chapters, almost all economists oppose such barriers to free trade. Nonetheless, over the years, Parliament has often chosen to restrict the import of certain goods.

Why do policies such as rent control and trade barriers persist if the experts are united in their opposition? The reason may be that economists have not yet convinced the general public that these policies are undesirable. One purpose of this book is to make you understand the economist's view of these and other subjects and, perhaps, to persuade you that it is the right one.

QuickQuiz Why might economic advisers to the prime minister disagree about a question of policy?

LET'S GET GOING

The first two chapters of this book have introduced you to the ideas and methods of economics. We are now ready to get to work. In the next chapter we start learning in more detail the principles of economic behaviour and economic policy.

As you proceed through this book, you will be asked to draw on many of your intellectual skills. You might find it helpful to keep in mind some advice from the great economist John Maynard Keynes:

> The study of economics does not seem to require any specialized gifts of an unusually high order. Is it not . . . a very easy subject compared with the higher branches of philosophy or pure science? An easy subject, at which very few excel! The paradox finds its explanation, perhaps, in that the master-economist must possess a rare *combination* of gifts. He must be mathematician, historian, statesman, philosopher—in some degree. He must understand symbols and speak in words. He must contemplate the particular in terms of the general, and touch abstract and concrete in the same flight of thought. He must study the present in the light of the past for the purposes of the future. No part of

TABLE 2.1

Ten Propositions about Which Most Economists Agree

Source: Richard M. Alston, J.R. Kearl, and Michael B. Vaughn, "Is There Consensus among Economists in the 1990s?" *American Economic Review* (May 1992): 203–209. Reprinted by permission.

Proposition (and percentage of economists who agree)
1. A ceiling on rents reduces the quantity and quality of housing available. (93%)
2. Tariffs and import quotas usually reduce general economic welfare. (93%)
3. Flexible and floating exchange rates offer an effective international monetary arrangement. (90%)
4. Fiscal policy (e.g., tax cut and/or government expenditure increase) has a significant stimulative impact on a less than fully employed economy. (90%)
5. If the federal budget is to be balanced, it should be done over the business cycle rather than yearly. (85%)
6. Cash payments increase the welfare of recipients to a greater degree than do transfers-in-kind of equal cash value. (84%)
7. A large federal budget deficit has an adverse effect on the economy. (83%)
8. A minimum wage increases unemployment among young and unskilled workers. (79%)
9. The government should restructure the welfare system along the lines of a "negative income tax." (79%)
10. Effluent taxes and marketable pollution permits represent a better approach to pollution control than imposition of pollution ceilings. (78%)

man's nature or his institutions must lie entirely outside his regard. He must be purposeful and disinterested in a simultaneous mood; as aloof and incorruptible as an artist, yet sometimes as near the earth as a politician.

It is a tall order. But with practice, you will become more and more accustomed to thinking like an economist.

SUMMARY

- Economists try to address their subject with a scientist's objectivity. Like all scientists, they make appropriate assumptions and build simplified models in order to understand the world around them. Two simple economic models are the circular-flow diagram and the production possibilities frontier.

- The field of economics is divided into two subfields: microeconomics and macroeconomics. Microeconomists study decision making by households and firms and the interaction among households and firms in the marketplace. Macroeconomists study the forces and trends that affect the economy as a whole.

- A positive statement is an assertion about how the world *is*. A normative statement is an assertion about how the world *ought to be*. When economists make normative statements, they are acting more as policy advisers than scientists.

- Economists who advise policymakers offer conflicting advice either because of differences in scientific judgments or because of differences in values. At other times, economists are united in the advice they offer, but policymakers may choose to ignore it.

KEY CONCEPTS

circular-flow diagram, p. 24
production possibilities frontier,
   p. 26

microeconomics, p. 28
macroeconomics, p. 28
positive statements, p. 30

normative statements, p. 30

QUESTIONS FOR REVIEW

1. How is economics like a science?

2. Why do economists make assumptions?

3. Should an economic model describe reality exactly?

4. Draw and explain a production possibilities frontier for an economy that produces milk and cookies. What happens to this frontier if disease kills half of the economy's cow population?

5. Use a production possibilities frontier to describe the idea of "efficiency."

6. What are the two subfields into which economics is divided? Explain what each subfield studies.

7. What is the difference between a positive and a normative statement? Give an example of each.

8. What is the Bank of Canada?

9. Why do economists sometimes offer conflicting advice to policymakers?

PROBLEMS AND APPLICATIONS

1. Describe some unusual language used in one of the other fields that you are studying. Why are these special terms useful?

2. One common assumption in economics is that the products of different firms in the same industry are indistinguishable. For each of the following industries, discuss whether this is a reasonable assumption.
   a. steel   c. wheat
   b. novels   d. fast food

3. Draw a circular-flow diagram. Identify the parts of the model that correspond to the flow of goods and services and the flow of dollars for each of the following activities.
   a. Sam pays a storekeeper $1 for a litre of milk.
   b. Sally earns $7 per hour working at a fast-food restaurant.
   c. Serena spends $10 to see a movie.
   d. Stuart earns $10 000 from his 10 percent ownership of Acme Industrial.

4. Imagine a society that produces military goods and consumer goods, which we'll call "guns" and "butter."

   a. Draw a production possibilities frontier for guns and butter. Explain why it most likely has a bowed-out shape.
   b. Show a point that is impossible for the economy to achieve. Show a point that is feasible but inefficient.
   c. Imagine that the society has two political parties, called the Hawks (who want a strong military) and the Doves (who want a smaller military). Show a point on your production possibilities frontier that the Hawks might choose and a point the Doves might choose.
   d. Imagine that an aggressive neighbouring country reduces the size of its military. As a result, both the Hawks and the Doves reduce their desired production of guns by the same amount. Which party would get the bigger "peace dividend," measured by the increase in butter production? Explain.

5. The first principle of economics discussed in Chapter 1 is that people face tradeoffs. Use a production possibilities frontier to illustrate

society's tradeoff between a clean environment and the quantity of industrial output. What do you suppose determines the shape and position of the frontier? Show what happens to the frontier if engineers develop an automobile engine with almost no emissions.

6. Classify the following topics as relating to microeconomics or macroeconomics.
   a. a family's decision about how much income to save
   b. the effect of government regulations on auto emissions
   c. the impact of higher national saving on economic growth
   d. a firm's decision about how many workers to hire
   e. the relationship between the inflation rate and changes in the quantity of money

7. Classify each of the following statements as positive or normative. Explain.
   a. Society faces a short-run tradeoff between inflation and unemployment.
   b. A reduction in the rate of growth of money will reduce the rate of inflation.
   c. The Bank of Canada should reduce the rate of growth of money.
   d. Society ought to require welfare recipients to look for jobs.
   e. Lower tax rates encourage more work and more saving.

8. Classify each of the statements in Table 2.1 as positive, normative, or ambiguous. Explain.

9. If you were prime minister, would you be more interested in your economic advisers' positive views or their normative views? Why?

10. The C.D. Howe Institute, the Fraser Institute, the Institute for Research on Public Policy, and the Canadian Centre for Policy Alternatives regularly publish reports containing economic commentary and policy recommendations. Find a recent publication from one of these organizations at your library (or on its website; see the Internet Resources section at the end of this Problems and Applications section) and read about an issue that interests you. Summarize the discussion of this issue and the author's proposed policy.

11. Who is the current governor of the Bank of Canada? Who is the current minister of Finance Canada? Who are the current ministers of Foreign Affairs Canada and International Trade Canada? Are they economists? Does it matter?

12. Would you expect economists to disagree less about public policy as time goes on? Why or why not? Can their differences be completely eliminated? Why or why not?

13. Look up one of the websites listed in the Internet Resources section on p. 37. What recent economic trends or issues are addressed there?

INTERNET RESOURCES

Here are the websites of some of the organizations that hire economists and influence economic policy.

Bank of Canada	http://www.bankofcanada.ca
Canadian Centre for Policy Alternatives	http://www.policyalternatives.ca
C.D. Howe Institute	http://www.cdhowe.org
Environment Canada	http://www.ec.gc.ca
Finance Canada	http://www.fin.gc.ca
Foreign Affairs Canada	http://www.fac-aec.gc.ca
Fraser Institute	http://www.fraserinstitute.ca
Human Resources and Skills Development Canada	http://www.hrsdc.gc.ca
Industry Canada	http://www.ic.gc.ca
Institute for Research on Public Policy	http://www.irpp.org
International Trade Canada	http://www.itcan-cican.gc.ca
Social Development Canada	http://www.sdc.gc.ca
Statistics Canada	http://www.statcan.ca

 For more study tools, please visit http://www.mankiw3e.nelson.com.

APPENDIX
Graphing: A Brief Review

Many of the concepts that economists study can be expressed with numbers—the price of bananas, the quantity of bananas sold, the cost of growing bananas, and so on. Often these economic variables are related to one another; for example, when the price of bananas rises, people buy fewer bananas. One way of expressing the relationships among variables is with graphs.

Graphs serve two purposes. First, when developing economic theories, graphs offer a way to visually express ideas that might be less clear if described with equations or words. Second, when analyzing economic data, graphs provide a way of finding how variables are in fact related in the world. Whether we are working with theory or with data, graphs provide a lens through which a recognizable forest emerges from a multitude of trees.

Numerical information can be expressed graphically in many ways, just as a thought can be expressed in words in many ways. A good writer chooses words that will make an argument clear, a description pleasing, or a scene dramatic. An effective economist chooses the type of graph that best suits the purpose.

In this appendix we discuss how economists use graphs to study the mathematical relationships among variables. We also discuss some of the pitfalls that can arise in the use of graphical methods.

Graphs of a Single Variable

Three common types of graphs are shown in Figure 2A.1. The *pie chart* in panel (a) shows how total income in Canada is divided among the sources of income, including wages and salaries, corporation profits, and so on. A slice of the pie represents each source's share of the total. The *bar graph* in panel (b) compares income for three countries. The height of each bar represents the average income in each country. The *time-series graph* in panel (c) traces the Canadian unemployment rate over time. The height of the line shows the unemployment rate in each month. You have probably seen similar graphs in newspapers and magazines.

Graphs of Two Variables: The Coordinate System

Although the three graphs in Figure 2A.1 are useful in showing how a variable changes over time or across individuals, such graphs are limited in how much they can tell us. These graphs display information only on a single variable. Economists are often concerned with the relationships between variables. Thus, they need to be able to display two variables on a single graph. The *coordinate system* makes this possible.

Suppose you want to examine the relationship between study time and grade point average. For each student in your class, you could record a pair of numbers: hours per week spent studying and grade point average. These numbers could then be placed in parentheses as an *ordered pair* and appear as a single point on the graph. Albert E., for instance, is represented by the ordered pair (25 hours/week,

Types of Graphs

The pie chart in panel (a) shows how Canadian 2002 national income is derived from various sources. The bar graph in panel (b) compares the average income in three countries. The time-series graph in panel (c) shows the unemployment rate in Canada from January 2000 to August 2003.

Sources: Panel (a): Statistics Canada, http://statcan.ca/Daily/English/030829/d030829a.htm; Panel (b): World Bank; Panel (c): Statistics Canada, "Latest Release from the Labour Force Survey," September 5, 2003, www.statcan.ca/english/Subjects/Labour/LFS/lfs-en.htm.

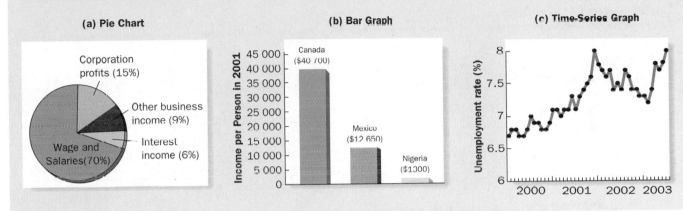

3.5 GPA), while his "what-me-worry?" classmate Alfred E. is represented by the ordered pair (5 hours/week, 2.0 GPA).

We can graph these ordered pairs on a two-dimensional grid. The first number in each ordered pair, called the *x-coordinate*, tells us the horizontal location of the point. The second number, called the *y-coordinate*, tells us the vertical location of the point. The point with both an *x*-coordinate and a *y*-coordinate of zero is known as the *origin*. The two coordinates in the ordered pair tell us where the point is located in relation to the origin: *x* units to the right of the origin and *y* units above it.

Figure 2A.2 (p. 40) graphs grade point average against study time for Albert E., Alfred E., and their classmates. This type of graph is called a *scatterplot* because it plots scattered points. Looking at this graph, we immediately notice that points farther to the right (indicating more study time) also tend to be higher (indicating a better grade point average). Because study time and grade point average typically move in the same direction, we say that these two variables have a *positive correlation*. By contrast, if we were to graph party time and grades, we would likely find that higher party time is associated with lower grades; because these variables typically move in opposite directions, we would call this a *negative correlation*. In either case, the coordinate system makes the correlation between the two variables easy to see.

Curves in the Coordinate System

Students who study more do tend to get higher grades, but other factors also influence a student's grade. Previous preparation is an important factor, for

FIGURE 2A.2

Using the Coordinate System

Grade point average is measured on the vertical axis and study time on the horizontal axis. Albert E., Alfred E., and their classmates are represented by various points. We can see from the graph that students who study more tend to get higher grades.

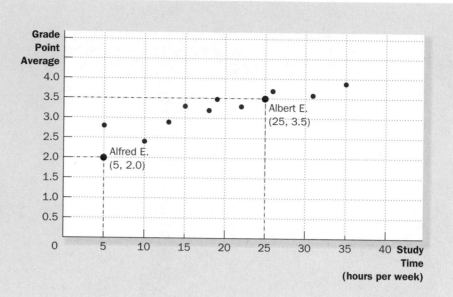

instance, as are talent, attention from teachers, and even eating a good breakfast. A scatterplot like Figure 2A.2 does not attempt to isolate the effect that study has on grades from the effects of other variables. Often, however, economists prefer looking at how one variable affects another holding everything else constant.

To see how this is done, let's consider one of the most important graphs in economics—the *demand curve*. The demand curve traces the effect of a good's price on the quantity of the good consumers want to buy. Before showing a demand curve, however, consider Table 2A.1, which shows how the number of novels that Emma buys depends on her income and on the price of novels. When novels are cheap, Emma buys them in large quantities. As they become more expensive, she borrows books from the library instead of buying them or chooses to go to the movies instead of reading. Similarly, at any given price, Emma buys more novels when she has a higher income. That is, when her income increases, she spends part of the additional income on novels and part on other goods.

We now have three variables—the price of novels, income, and the number of novels purchased—which is more than we can represent in two dimensions. To put the information from Table 2A.1 in graphical form, we need to hold one of the three variables constant and trace the relationship between the other two. Because the demand curve represents the relationship between price and quantity demanded, we hold Emma's income constant and show how the number of novels she buys varies with the price of novels.

Suppose that Emma's income is $30 000 per year. If we place the number of novels Emma purchases on the x-axis and the price of novels on the y-axis, we can graphically represent the middle column of Table 2A.1. When the points that represent these entries from the table—5 novels, $10; 9 novels, $9; and so on—are connected, they form a line. This line, pictured in Figure 2A.3, is known as Emma's demand curve for novels; it tells us how many novels Emma purchases at any

TABLE 2A.1

	Income		
Price	$20 000	$30 000	$40 000
$10	2 novels	5 novels	8 novels
9	6	9	12
8	10	13	16
7	14	17	20
6	18	21	24
5	22	25	28
	Demand curve, D_3	Demand curve, D_1	Demand curve, D_2

Novels Purchased by Emma

This table shows the number of novels Emma buys at various incomes and prices. For any given level of income, the data on price and quantity demanded can be graphed to produce Emma's demand curve for novels, as shown in Figures 2A.3 and 2A.4.

FIGURE 2A.3

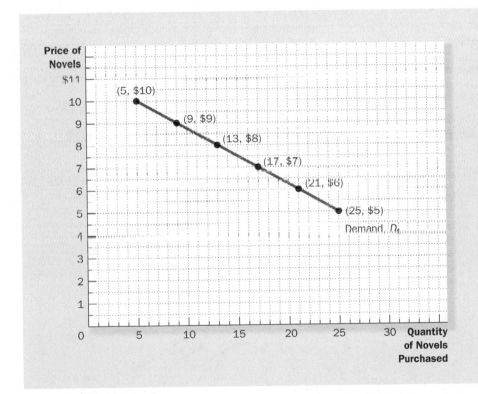

Demand Curve

The line D_1 shows how Emma's purchases of novels depend on the price of novels when her income is held constant. Because the price and the quantity demanded are negatively related, the demand curve slopes downward.

given price. The demand curve is downward sloping, indicating that a higher price reduces the quantity of novels demanded. Because the quantity of novels demanded and the price move in opposite directions, we say that the two variables are *negatively related*. (Conversely, when two variables move in the same direction, the curve relating them is upward sloping, and we say the variables are *positively related*.)

Now suppose that Emma's income rises to $40 000 per year. At any given price, Emma will purchase more novels than she did at her previous level of income. Just as earlier we drew Emma's demand curve for novels using the entries from the middle column of Table 2A.1, we now draw a new demand curve using the entries from the right-hand column of the table. This new demand curve (curve D_2) is pictured alongside the old one (curve D_1) in Figure 2A.4; the new curve is a similar line drawn farther to the right. We therefore say that Emma's demand curve for novels *shifts* to the right when her income increases. Likewise, if Emma's income were to fall to $20 000 per year, she would buy fewer novels at any given price and her demand curve would shift to the left (to curve D_3).

In economics, it is important to distinguish between *movements along a curve* and *shifts of a curve*. As we can see from Figure 2A.3, if Emma earns $30 000 per year and novels cost $8 apiece, she will purchase 13 novels per year. If the price of novels falls to $7, Emma will increase her purchases of novels to 17 per year. The demand curve, however, stays fixed in the same place. Emma still buys the same number of novels *at each price*, but as the price falls she moves along her demand curve from left to right. By contrast, if the price of novels remains fixed at $8 but her income rises to $40 000, Emma increases her purchases of novels from 13 to 16 per year. Because Emma buys more novels *at each price*, her demand curve shifts out, as shown in Figure 2A.4.

There is a simple way to tell when it is necessary to shift a curve. When a variable that is not named on either axis changes, the curve shifts. Income is on neither the x-axis nor the y-axis of the graph, so when Emma's income changes, her

FIGURE 2A.4

Shifting Demand Curves

The location of Emma's demand curve for novels depends on how much income she earns. The more she earns, the more novels she will purchase at any given price, and the farther to the right her demand curve will lie. Curve D_1 represents Emma's original demand curve when her income is $30 000 per year. If her income rises to $40 000 per year, her demand curve shifts to D_2. If her income falls to $20 000 per year, her demand curve shifts to D_3.

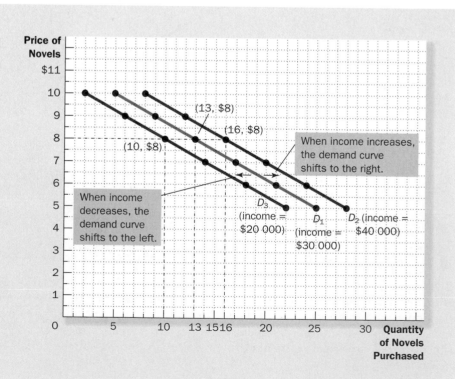

demand curve must shift. Any change that affects Emma's purchasing habits besides a change in the price of novels will result in a shift in her demand curve. If, for instance, the public library closes and Emma must buy all the books she wants to read, she will demand more novels at each price, and her demand curve will shift to the right. Or, if the price of movies falls and Emma spends more time at the movies and less time reading, she will demand fewer novels at each price, and her demand curve will shift to the left. By contrast, when a variable on an axis of the graph changes, the curve does not shift. We read the change as a movement along the curve.

Slope

One question we might want to ask about Emma is how much her purchasing habits respond to price. Look at the demand curve pictured in Figure 2A.5. If this curve is very steep, Emma purchases nearly the same number of novels regardless of whether they are cheap or expensive. If this curve is much flatter, Emma purchases many fewer novels when the price rises. To answer questions about how much one variable responds to changes in another variable, we can use the concept of *slope*.

The slope of a line is the ratio of the vertical distance covered to the horizontal distance covered as we move along the line. This definition is usually written out in mathematical symbols as follows:

$$\text{slope} = \frac{\Delta y}{\Delta x}$$

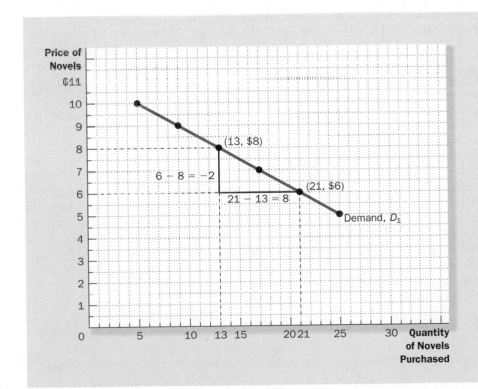

Calculating the Slope of a Line

To calculate the slope of the demand curve, we can look at the changes in the x- and y-coordinates as we move from the point (21 novels, $6) to the point (13 novels, $8). The slope of the line is the ratio of the change in the y-coordinate (−2) to the change in the x-coordinate (+8), which equals −1/4.

where the Greek letter Δ (delta) stands for the change in a variable. In other words, the slope of a line is equal to the "rise" (change in y) divided by the "run" (change in x). The slope will be a small positive number for a fairly flat upward-sloping line, a large positive number for a steep upward-sloping line, and a negative number for a downward-sloping line. A horizontal line has a slope of zero because in this case the y-variable never changes; a vertical line is said to have an infinite slope because the y-variable can take any value without the x-variable changing at all.

What is the slope of Emma's demand curve for novels? First of all, because the curve slopes down, we know the slope will be negative. To calculate a numerical value for the slope, we must choose two points on the line. With Emma's income at $30 000, she will purchase 21 novels at a price of $6 or 13 novels at a price of $8. When we apply the slope formula, we are concerned with the change between these two points; in other words, we are concerned with the difference between them, which lets us know that we will have to subtract one set of values from the other, as follows:

$$\text{slope} = \frac{\Delta y}{\Delta x} = \frac{\text{first } y\text{-coordinate} - \text{second } y\text{-coordinate}}{\text{first } x\text{-coordinate} - \text{second } x\text{-coordinate}} = \frac{6-8}{21-13} = \frac{-2}{8} = \frac{-1}{4}$$

Figure 2A.5 shows graphically how this calculation works. Try computing the slope of Emma's demand curve using two different points. You should get exactly the same result, $-1/4$. One of the properties of a straight line is that it has the same slope everywhere. This is not true of other types of curves, which are steeper in some places than in others.

The slope of Emma's demand curve tells us something about how responsive her purchases are to changes in the price. A small slope (a number close to zero) means that Emma's demand curve is relatively flat; in this case, she adjusts the number of novels she buys substantially in response to a price change. A larger slope (a number farther from zero) means that Emma's demand curve is relatively steep; in this case, she adjusts the number of novels she buys only slightly in response to a price change.

Cause and Effect

Economists often use graphs to advance an argument about how the economy works. In other words, they use graphs to argue about how one set of events *causes* another set of events. With a graph like the demand curve, there is no doubt about cause and effect. Because we are varying price and holding all other variables constant, we know that changes in the price of novels cause changes in the quantity Emma demands. Remember, however, that our demand curve came from a hypothetical example. When graphing data from the real world, it is often more difficult to establish how one variable affects another.

The first problem is that it is difficult to hold everything else constant when measuring how one variable affects another. If we are not able to hold variables constant, we might decide that one variable on our graph is causing changes in the other variable, when actually those changes are caused by a third *omitted variable* not pictured on the graph. Even if we have identified the correct two variables to look at, we might run into a second problem—*reverse causality*. In other words, we might decide that A causes B when in fact B causes A. The omitted-variable and reverse-causality traps require us to proceed with caution when using graphs to draw conclusions about causes and effects.

Omitted Variables   To see how omitting a variable can lead to a deceptive graph, let's consider an example. Imagine that the government, spurred by public concern about the large number of deaths from cancer, commissions an exhaustive study from Big Brother Statistical Services, Inc. Big Brother examines many of the items found in people's homes to see which of them are associated with the risk of cancer. Big Brother reports a strong relationship between two variables: the number of cigarette lighters that a household owns and the probability that someone in the household will develop cancer. Figure 2A.6 shows this relationship.

What should we make of this result? Big Brother advises a quick policy response. It recommends that the government discourage the ownership of cigarette lighters by taxing their sale. It also recommends that the government require warning labels: "Big Brother has determined that this lighter is dangerous to your health."

In judging the validity of Big Brother's analysis, one question is paramount: Has Big Brother held constant every relevant variable except the one under consideration? If the answer is no, the results are suspect. An easy explanation for Figure 2A.6 is that people who own more cigarette lighters are more likely to smoke cigarettes and that cigarettes, not lighters, cause cancer. If Figure 2A.6 does not hold constant the amount of smoking, it does not tell us the true effect of owning a cigarette lighter.

This story illustrates an important principle: When you see a graph being used to support an argument about cause and effect, it is important to ask whether the movements of an omitted variable could explain the results you see.

Reverse Causality   Economists can also make mistakes about causality by misreading its direction. To see how this is possible, suppose the Association of Canadian Anarchists commissions a study of crime in Canada and arrives at Figure 2A.7 (p. 46), which plots the number of violent crimes per thousand people in major cities against the number of police officers per thousand people. The

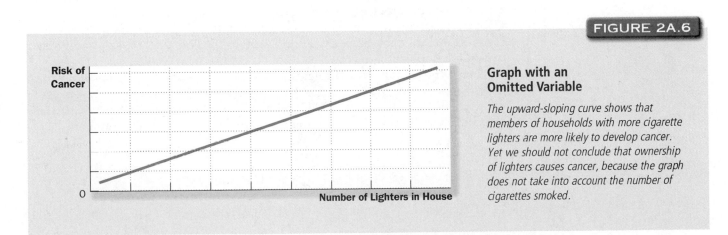

FIGURE 2A.6

Graph with an Omitted Variable

The upward-sloping curve shows that members of households with more cigarette lighters are more likely to develop cancer. Yet we should not conclude that ownership of lighters causes cancer, because the graph does not take into account the number of cigarettes smoked.

Risk of Cancer

0

Number of Lighters in House

FIGURE 2A.7

Graph Suggesting Reverse Causality

The upward-sloping curve shows that cities with a higher concentration of police are more dangerous. Yet the graph does not tell us whether police cause crime or crime-plagued cities hire more police.

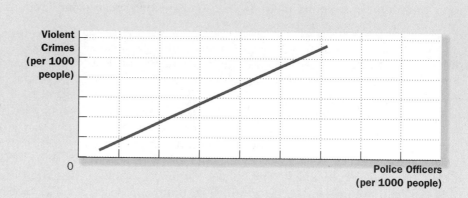

anarchists note the curve's upward slope and argue that because police increase rather than decrease the amount of urban violence, law enforcement should be abolished.

If we could run a controlled experiment, we would avoid the danger of reverse causality. To run an experiment, we would set the number of police officers in different cities randomly and then examine the correlation between police and crime. Figure 2A.7, however, is not based on such an experiment. We simply observe that more dangerous cities have more police officers. The explanation for this may be that more dangerous cities hire more police. In other words, rather than police causing crime, crime may cause police. Nothing in the graph itself allows us to establish the direction of causality.

It might seem that an easy way to determine the direction of causality is to examine which variable moves first. If we see crime increase and then the police force expand, we reach one conclusion. If we see the police force expand and then crime increase, we reach the other. Yet there is also a flaw with this approach: Often people change their behaviour not in response to a change in their present conditions but in response to a change in their *expectations* of future conditions. A city that expects a major crime wave in the future, for instance, might well hire more police now. This problem is even easier to see in the case of babies and minivans. Couples often buy a minivan in anticipation of the birth of a child. The minivan comes before the baby, but we wouldn't want to conclude that the sale of minivans causes the population to grow!

There is no complete set of rules that says when it is appropriate to draw causal conclusions from graphs. Yet just keeping in mind that cigarette lighters don't cause cancer (omitted variable) and minivans don't cause larger families (reverse causality) will keep you from falling for many faulty economic arguments.

3

Learning Objectives

In this chapter, you will ...

- Consider how everyone can benefit when people trade with one another
- Learn the meaning of *absolute advantage* and *comparative advantage*
- See how comparative advantage explains the gains from trade
- Apply the theory of comparative advantage to everyday life and national policy

INTERDEPENDENCE AND THE GAINS FROM TRADE

Consider your typical day. You wake up in the morning, and you pour yourself juice from oranges grown in Florida and coffee from beans grown in Brazil. Over breakfast, you watch a news program broadcast from Toronto on your television made in Japan. You get dressed in clothes made of cotton grown in Georgia and sewn in factories in Thailand. You drive to class in a car made of parts manufactured in more than a dozen countries around the world. Then you open up your economics textbook written by authors living in Massachusetts, Alberta, and Quebec, published by a company located in Ontario, and printed on paper made from trees grown in New Brunswick.

Every day you rely on many people from around the world, most of whom you do not know, to provide you with the goods and services that you enjoy. Such interdependence is possible because people trade with one another. Those people who provide you with goods and services are not acting out of generosity or concern for your welfare. Nor is some government agency directing them to make what you want and to give it to you. Instead, people provide you and other consumers with the goods and services they produce because they get something in return.

In subsequent chapters we will examine how our economy coordinates the activities of millions of people with varying tastes and abilities. As a starting point for this analysis, here we consider the reasons for economic interdependence. One of the ten principles of economics highlighted in Chapter 1 is that trade can make everyone better off. This principle explains why people trade with their neighbours and why nations trade with other nations. In this chapter we examine this principle more closely. What exactly do people gain when they trade with one another? Why do people choose to become interdependent?

A PARABLE FOR THE MODERN ECONOMY

To understand why people choose to depend on others for goods and services and how this choice improves their lives, let's look at a simple economy. Imagine that there are two goods in the world—meat and potatoes. And there are two people in the world—a cattle rancher and a potato farmer—each of whom would like to eat both meat and potatoes.

The gains from trade are most obvious if the rancher can produce only meat and the farmer can produce only potatoes. In one scenario, the rancher and the farmer could choose to have nothing to do with each other. But after several months of eating beef roasted, boiled, broiled, and grilled, the rancher might decide that self-sufficiency is not all it's cracked up to be. The farmer, who has been eating potatoes mashed, fried, baked, and scalloped, would likely agree. It is easy to see that trade would allow them to enjoy greater variety: Each could then have a steak with a baked potato.

Although this scenario illustrates most simply how everyone can benefit from trade, the gains would be similar if the rancher and the farmer were each capable of producing the other good, but only at great cost. Suppose, for example, that the potato farmer is able to raise cattle and produce meat, but that he is not very good at it. Similarly, suppose that the cattle rancher is able to grow potatoes, but that her land is not very well suited for it. In this case, it would be easy to show that the farmer and the rancher can each benefit by specializing in what he or she does best and then trading with the other.

The gains from trade are less obvious, however, when one person is better at producing *every* good. For example, suppose that the rancher is better at raising cattle *and* better at growing potatoes than the farmer. In this case, should the rancher or farmer choose to remain self-sufficient? Or is there still reason for them to trade with each other? To answer this question, we need to look more closely at the factors that affect such a decision.

Production Possibilities

Suppose that the farmer and the rancher each work 8 hours a day and can devote this time to growing potatoes, raising cattle, or a combination of the two. Table 3.1 shows the amount of time each person requires to produce 1 kg of each good. The farmer can produce a kilogram of potatoes in 15 minutes and a kilogram of meat in 60 minutes. The rancher, who is more productive in both activities, can produce a kilogram of potatoes in 10 minutes and a kilogram of meat in 20 minutes. The last columns in Table 3.1 show the amounts of meat or potatoes the farmer and rancher can produce if they work an 8-hour day, producing only that good.

Panel (a) of Figure 3.1 illustrates the amounts of meat and potatoes that the farmer can produce. If the farmer devotes all 8 hours of his time to potatoes, he

TABLE 3.1

	Minutes Needed to Make 1 kg of:		Amount of Meat or Potatoes Produced in 8 Hours	
	Meat	Potatoes	Meat	Potatoes
Farmer	60 min/kg	15 min/kg	8 kg	32 kg
Rancher	20 min/kg	10 min/kg	24 kg	48 kg

The Production Opportunities of the Farmer and the Rancher

FIGURE 3.1

(a) The Farmer's Production Possibilities Frontier

If there is no trade, the farmer chooses this production and consumption.

(b) The Rancher's Production Possibilities Frontier

If there is no trade, the rancher chooses this production and consumption.

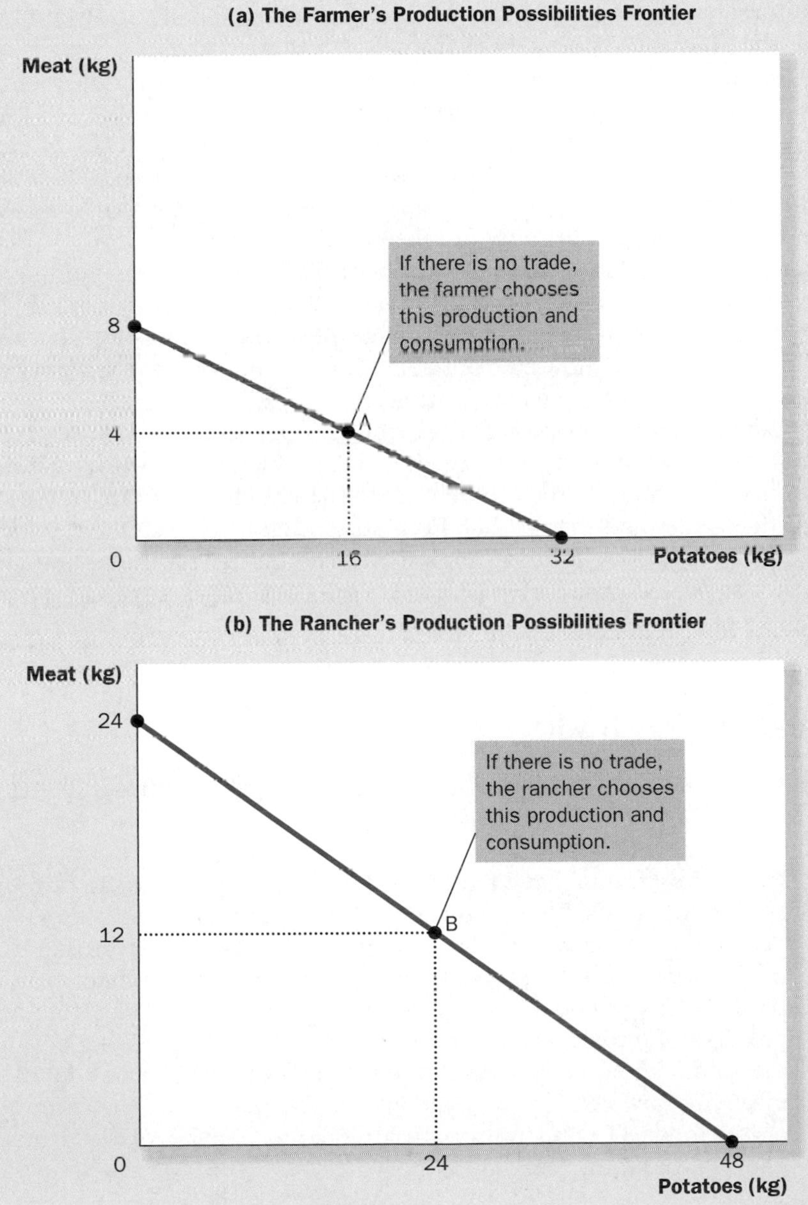

The Production Possibilities Frontier

Panel (a) shows the combinations of meat and potatoes that the farmer can produce. Panel (b) shows the combinations of meat and potatoes that the rancher can produce. Both production possibilities frontiers are derived from Table 3.1 and the assumption that the farmer and rancher each work 8 hours a day.

produces 32 kg of potatoes (measured on the horizontal axis) and no meat. If he devotes all his time to meat, he produces 8 kg of meat (measured on the vertical axis) and no potatoes. If the farmer divides his time equally between the two activities, spending 4 hours on each, he produces 16 kg of potatoes and 4 kg of meat. The figure shows these three possible outcomes and all others in between.

This graph is the farmer's production possibilities frontier. As we discussed in Chapter 2, a production possibilities frontier shows the various mixes of output that an economy can produce. It illustrates one of the ten principles of economics in Chapter 1: People face tradeoffs. Here the farmer faces a tradeoff between producing meat and producing potatoes. You may recall that the production possibilities frontier in Chapter 2 was drawn bowed out; in that case, the tradeoff between the two goods depended on the amounts being produced. Here, however, the farmer's technology for producing meat and potatoes (as summarized in Table 3.1) allows him to switch between one good and the other at a constant rate. In this case, the production possibilities frontier is a straight line.

Panel (b) of Figure 3.1 shows the production possibilities frontier for the rancher. If the rancher devotes all 8 hours of her time to potatoes, she produces 48 kg of potatoes and no meat. If she devotes all her time to meat, she produces 24 kg of meat and no potatoes. If the rancher divides her time equally, spending 4 hours on each activity, she produces 24 kg of potatoes and 12 kg of meat. Once again, the production possibilities frontier shows all the possible outcomes.

If the farmer and rancher choose to be self-sufficient, rather than trade with each other, then each consumes exactly what he or she produces. In this case, the production possibilities frontier is also the consumption possibilities frontier. That is, without trade, Figure 3.1 shows the possible combinations of meat and potatoes that the farmer and rancher can each consume.

Although these production possibilities frontiers are useful in showing the tradeoffs that the farmer and rancher face, they do not tell us what the farmer and rancher will actually choose to do. To determine their choices, we need to know the tastes of the farmer and the rancher. Let's suppose they choose the combinations identified by points A and B in Figure 3.1: The farmer produces and consumes 16 kg of potatoes and 4 kg of meat, while the rancher produces and consumes 24 kg of potatoes and 12 kg of meat.

Specialization and Trade

After several years of eating combination B, the rancher gets an idea and goes to talk to the farmer:

RANCHER: Farmer, my friend, have I got a deal for you! I know how to improve life for both of us. I think you should stop producing meat altogether and devote all your time to growing potatoes. According to my calculations, if you work 8 hours a day growing potatoes, you'll produce 32 kg of potatoes. If you give me 15 of those 32 kg, I'll give you 5 kg of meat in return. In the end, you'll get to eat 17 kg of potatoes and 5 kg of meat, instead of the 16 kg of potatoes and 4 kg of meat you now get. If you go along with my plan, you'll have more of *both* foods. [To illustrate her point, the rancher shows the farmer panel (a) of Figure 3.2.]

FIGURE 3.2

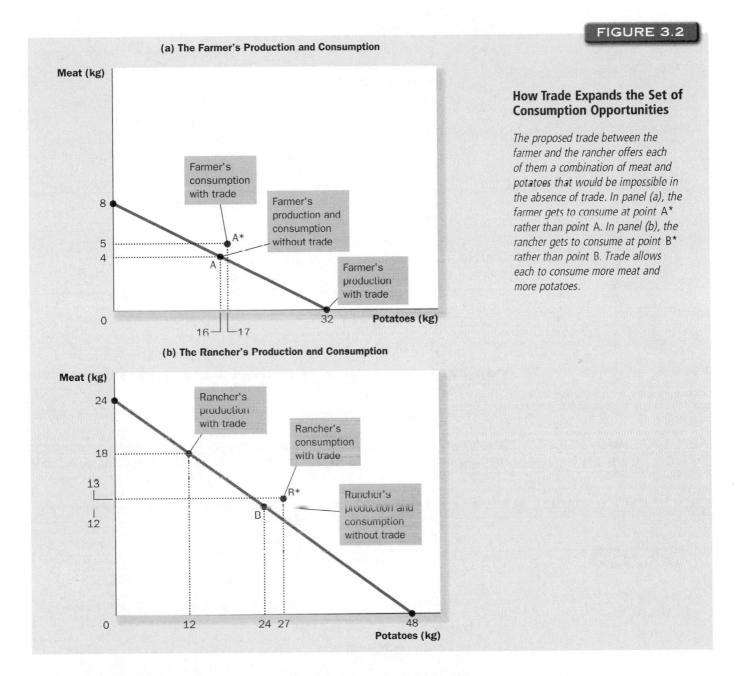

(a) The Farmer's Production and Consumption

Meat (kg)

Farmer's consumption with trade

Farmer's production and consumption without trade

8

5
4

A*

A

Farmer's production with trade

0   32   Potatoes (kg)

16 17

(b) The Rancher's Production and Consumption

Meat (kg)

24

Rancher's production with trade

18

Rancher's consumption with trade

13

12

R*

B

Rancher's production and consumption without trade

0   12   24 27   48

Potatoes (kg)

How Trade Expands the Set of Consumption Opportunities

The proposed trade between the farmer and the rancher offers each of them a combination of meat and potatoes that would be impossible in the absence of trade. In panel (a), the farmer gets to consume at point A* rather than point A. In panel (b), the rancher gets to consume at point B* rather than point B. Trade allows each to consume more meat and more potatoes.

FARMER: *(sounding skeptical)* That seems like a good deal for me. But I don't understand why you are offering it. If the deal is so good for me, it can't be good for you too.

RANCHER: Oh, but it is! Suppose I spend 6 hours a day raising cattle and 2 hours growing potatoes. Then I can produce 18 kg of meat and 12 kg of potatoes. After I give you 5 kg of my meat in exchange for 15 kg of your potatoes, I'll end up with 13 kg of meat and 27 kg of potatoes. So I'll also consume more of both foods than I do now. [She points out panel (b) of Figure 3.2.]

FARMER: I don't know. . . . This sounds too good to be true.

RANCHER: It's really not as complicated as it seems at first. Here—I've summarized my proposal for you in a simple table. [The rancher hands the farmer a copy of Table 3.2.]

FARMER: *(after pausing to study the table)* These calculations seem correct, but I'm puzzled. How can this deal make us both better off?

RANCHER: We can both benefit because trade allows each of us to specialize in doing what we do best. You will spend more time growing potatoes and less time raising cattle. I will spend more time raising cattle and less time growing potatoes. As a result of specialization and trade, each of us can consume more meat and more potatoes without working any more hours.

QuickQuiz Draw an example of a production possibilities frontier for Robinson Crusoe, a shipwrecked sailor who spends his time gathering coconuts and catching fish. Does this frontier limit Crusoe's consumption of coconuts and fish if he lives by himself? Does he face the same limits if he can trade with natives on the island?

THE PRINCIPLE OF COMPARATIVE ADVANTAGE

The rancher's explanation of the gains from trade, though correct, poses a puzzle: If the rancher is better at both raising cattle and growing potatoes, how can the farmer ever specialize in doing what he does best? The farmer doesn't seem to do anything best. To solve this puzzle, we need to look at the principle of *comparative advantage*.

TABLE 3.2

The Gains from Trade: A Summary

	Farmer		Rancher	
	Meat	**Potatoes**	**Meat**	**Potatoes**
Without Trade:				
Production and Consumption	4 kg	16 kg	12 kg	24 kg
With Trade:				
Production	0 kg	32 kg	18 kg	12 kg
Trade	Gets 5 kg	Gives 15 kg	Gives 5 kg	Gets 15 kg
Consumption	5 kg	17 kg	13 kg	27 kg
Gains from Trade:				
Increase in Consumption	+1 kg	+1 kg	+1 kg	+3 kg

As a first step in developing this principle, consider the following question: In our example, who can produce potatoes at lower cost—the farmer or the rancher? There are two possible answers, and in these two answers lie the solution to our puzzle and the key to understanding the gains from trade.

Absolute Advantage

One way to answer the question about the cost of producing potatoes is to compare the inputs required by the two producers. Economists use the term **absolute advantage** when comparing the productivity of one person, firm, or nation to that of another. The producer that requires a smaller quantity of inputs to produce a good is said to have an absolute advantage in producing that good.

In our example, the rancher has an absolute advantage both in producing meat and in producing potatoes, because she requires less time than the farmer to produce a unit of either good. The rancher needs to input only 20 minutes to produce a kilogram of meat, whereas the farmer needs 60 minutes. Similarly, the rancher needs only 10 minutes to produce a kilogram of potatoes, whereas the farmer needs 15 minutes. Based on this information, we can conclude that the rancher has the lower cost of producing potatoes, if we measure cost in terms of the quantity of inputs.

absolute advantage
the comparison among producers of a good according to their productivity

Opportunity Cost and Comparative Advantage

There is another way to look at the cost of producing potatoes. Rather than comparing inputs required, we can compare the opportunity costs. Recall from Chapter 1 that the **opportunity cost** of some item is what we give up to get that item. In our example, we assumed that the farmer and the rancher each spend 8 hours a day working. Time spent producing potatoes, therefore, takes away from time available for producing meat. As the rancher and farmer reallocate time between producing the two goods, they move along their production possibility frontiers; they give up units of one good to produce units of the other. The opportunity cost measures the tradeoff between the two goods that each producer faces.

opportunity cost
whatever must be given up to obtain some item

Let's first consider the rancher's opportunity cost. According to Table 3.1, producing 1 kg of potatoes takes her 10 minutes of work. When the rancher spends that 10 minutes producing potatoes, she spends 10 minutes less producing meat. Because the rancher needs 20 minutes to produce 1 kg of meat, 10 minutes of work would yield 0.5 kg of meat. Hence, the rancher's opportunity cost of producing 1 kg of potatoes is 0.5 kg of meat.

Now consider the farmer's opportunity cost. Producing 1 kg of potatoes takes him 15 minutes. Because he needs 60 minutes to produce 1 kg of meat, 15 minutes of work would yield 0.25 kg of meat. Hence, the farmer's opportunity cost of 1 kg of potatoes is 0.25 kg of meat.

Table 3.3 (p. 54) shows the opportunity costs of meat and potatoes for the two producers. Notice that the opportunity cost of meat is the inverse of the opportunity cost of potatoes. Because 1 kg of potatoes costs the rancher 0.5 kg of meat, 1 kg of meat costs the rancher 2 kg of potatoes. Similarly, because 1 kg of potatoes costs the farmer 0.25 kg of meat, 1 kg of meat costs the farmer 4 kg of potatoes.

TABLE 3.3		Opportunity Cost of:	
The Opportunity Cost of Meat and Potatoes		**1 kg of Meat**	**1 kg of Potatoes**
	Farmer	4 kg potatoes	0.25 kg meat
	Rancher	2 kg potatoes	0.50 kg meat

comparative advantage
the comparison among producers of a good according to their opportunity cost

Economists use the term **comparative advantage** when describing the opportunity cost of two producers. The producer who gives up less of other goods to produce good X has the smaller opportunity cost of producing good X and is said to have a comparative advantage in producing it. In our example, the farmer has a lower opportunity cost of producing potatoes than does the rancher: A kilogram of potatoes costs the farmer only 0.25 kg of meat, while it costs the rancher 0.50 kg of meat. Conversely, the rancher has a lower opportunity cost of producing meat than does the farmer: A kilogram of meat costs the rancher 2 kg of potatoes, while it costs the farmer 4 kg of potatoes. Thus, the farmer has a comparative advantage in growing potatoes, and the rancher has a comparative advantage in producing meat.

Although it is possible for one person to have an absolute advantage in both goods (as the rancher does in our example), it is impossible for one person to have a comparative advantage in both goods. Because the opportunity cost of one good is the inverse of the opportunity cost of the other, if a person's opportunity cost of one good is relatively high, his opportunity cost of the other good must be relatively low. Comparative advantage reflects the relative opportunity cost. Unless two people have exactly the same opportunity cost, one person will have a comparative advantage in one good, and the other person will have a comparative advantage in the other good.

Comparative Advantage and Trade

The rancher has an absolute advantage over the farmer in both meat and potatoes, and will therefore be able to enjoy a higher standard of living than the farmer. Her greater productivity will make the rancher richer than the farmer, but both the rancher and the farmer could improve their standards of living through trade.

Differences in opportunity cost and comparative advantage create the gains from trade. When each person specializes in producing the good for which he or she has a comparative advantage, total production in the economy rises, and this increase in the size of the economic pie can be used to make everyone better off. In other words, as long as two people have different opportunity costs, each can benefit from trade by obtaining a good at a price that is lower than his or her opportunity cost of that good.

Consider the proposed deal from the viewpoint of the farmer. The farmer gets 5 kg of meat in exchange for 15 kg of potatoes. In other words, the farmer buys each kilogram of meat for a price of 3 kg of potatoes. This price of meat is lower than his opportunity cost for 1 kg of meat, which is 4 kg of potatoes. Thus, the farmer benefits from the deal because he gets to buy meat at a good price.

THE LEGACY OF ADAM SMITH AND DAVID RICARDO

Economists have long understood the principle of comparative advantage. Here is how the great economist Adam Smith put the argument:

It is a maxim of every prudent master of a family, never to attempt to make at home what it will cost him more to make than to buy. The tailor does not attempt to make his own shoes, but buys them of the shoemaker. The shoemaker does not attempt to make his own clothes but employs a tailor. The farmer attempts to make neither the one nor the other, but employs those different artificers. All of them find it for their interest to employ their whole industry in a way in which they have some advantage over their neighbors,

and to purchase with a part of its produce, or what is the same thing, with the price of part of it, whatever else they have occasion for.

This quotation is from Smith's 1776 book *An Inquiry into the Nature and Causes of the Wealth of Nations*, which was a landmark in the analysis of trade and economic interdependence.

Smith's book inspired David Ricardo, a millionaire stockbroker, to become an economist. In his 1817 book *Principles of Political Economy and Taxation*, Ricardo developed the principle of comparative advantage as we know it today. His defence of free trade was not a mere academic exercise. Ricardo put his economic beliefs to work as a member of the British Parliament, where he opposed the Corn Laws, which restricted the import of grain.

The conclusions of Adam Smith and David Ricardo on the gains from trade have held up well over time. Although economists often disagree on questions of policy, they are united in their support of free trade. Moreover, the central argument for free trade has not changed much in the past two centuries. Even though the field of economics has broadened its scope and refined its theories since the time of Smith and Ricardo, economists' opposition to trade restrictions is still based largely on the principle of comparative advantage.

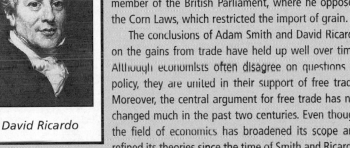
David Ricardo

PHOTO: © BETTMANN/CORBIS/MAGMA

Now consider the deal from the rancher's viewpoint. The rancher buys 15 kg of potatoes for a price of 5 kg of meat. That is, the price of potatoes is one-third of a kilogram of meat. This price of potatoes is lower than her opportunity cost of 1 kg of potatoes, which is 0.5 kg of meat. The rancher benefits because she can buy potatoes at a good price.

These benefits arise because each person concentrates on the activity for which he or she has the lower opportunity cost: The farmer spends more time growing potatoes, and the rancher spends more time producing meat. As a result, the total production of potatoes and the total production of meat both rise. In our example, potato production rises from 40 to 44 kg, and meat production rises from 16 to 18 kg. The farmer and rancher share the benefits of this increased production. The moral of the story of the farmer and the rancher should now be clear: *Trade can benefit everyone in society because it allows people to specialize in activities in which they have a comparative advantage.*

QuickQuiz   Robinson Crusoe can gather 10 coconuts or catch 1 fish per hour. His friend Friday can gather 30 coconuts or catch 2 fish per hour. What is Crusoe's opportunity cost of catching one fish? What is Friday's? Who has an absolute advantage in catching fish? Who has a comparative advantage in catching fish?

APPLICATIONS OF COMPARATIVE ADVANTAGE

The principle of comparative advantage explains interdependence and the gains from trade. Because interdependence is so prevalent in the modern world, the principle of comparative advantage has many applications. Here are two examples, one fanciful and one of great practical importance.

Should Mike Weir Mow His Own Lawn?

Mike Weir spends a lot of time walking around on grass. One of the most talented golfers in the PGA today, he can hit a drive and sink a putt in a way that most casual golfers only dream of doing. Most likely, he is talented at other activities

IN THE NEWS

DOES CANADA HAVE FREE TRADE?

Canada has removed many trade restrictions over the years, especially with our NAFTA partners, the United States and Mexico. But as economics professor William Watson explains in this article, many trade restrictions still remain.

Why Does a Tiger Need Tariffs?

By William Watson

The WTO [World Trade Organization] issued its biennial report on Canadian trade policies last week. Generally speaking, we got a good review. Our trade regime is "amongst the world's most transparent and liberal." The Canadian economy "is generally free from significant policy-induced distortions." We are a shining example of "the benefits for improved living standards of pro-competitive policies that support production based on comparative advantage"—comparative advantage

being the economist's term for specializing in what you do best and buying from other countries what you don't do so well.

As was to be expected, the good news was trumpeted by the folks at the Department of Foreign Affairs and International Trade in their unfailingly self-congratulatory free e-mail service. (One of the more entertaining pastimes for Canadian international trade economists is to try to anticipate what positive spin official e-mail will put on news of another Canadian loss before the WTO dispute settlement panels. Had the DFAIT communications officers been at Pearl Harbor, their communique would

have read: "Warm, sunny Sunday, once smoke cleared.")

In fact, the WTO isn't entirely approving. We still have "barriers to imports in a few … important sectors" and "a number of activities remain subject to interventions, notably in agriculture, textiles and clothing, steel, telecommunications, audiovisual, air and maritime transport, and insurance."

That's just from the executive summary. When you get into the 150 or so pages of detail you're impressed by the number of trade restrictions we still have in place. Take tariffs—in particular, our most-favoured-nation (MFN) tariffs, those paid by all our trading partners too. For example, let's imagine that Weir can mow his lawn faster than anyone else. But just because he *can* mow his lawn fast, does this mean he *should*?

To answer this question, we can use the concepts of opportunity cost and comparative advantage. Let's say that Weir can mow his lawn in 2 hours. In that same 2 hours, he could film a television commercial for Bell Canada and earn $10 000. By contrast, Forrest Gump, the boy next door, can mow Weir's lawn in 4 hours. In that same 4 hours, he could work at McDonald's and earn $20.

In this example, Weir's opportunity cost of mowing the lawn is $10 000 and Forrest's opportunity cost is $20. Weir has an absolute advantage in mowing lawns because he can do the work in less time. Yet Forrest has a comparative advantage in mowing lawns because he has the lower opportunity cost.

The gains from trade in this example are tremendous. Rather than mowing his own lawn, Weir should make the commercial and hire Forrest to mow the lawn.

except the countries we have free trade deals with, who generally don't pay any tariffs, and North Korea and Libya, our very own little axis of evil, who pay the punitive "general" tariff rate.

Half of the items (or "lines," referring to lines of text in our official tariff schedules) covered by our MFN trade are now completely tariff-free. But on the other half, our average tariff was 13.1% in 2002, down from 13.4% in 2000. And on 657 tariff lines, our tariffs exceed 15%. On boats, for example, we charge 25%. We also charge high tariffs on the iron fittings for coffins, of all things, and on pruning shears. Our average tariff on agricultural products is 21.7%, on dairy products a whopping 237.3%. Our tariff on chocolate ice cream is over 200%. What kind of country taxes chocolate ice cream?

Indeed, what kind of country relies on protective tariffs at all? Not us, surely. We're the Northern Tiger, our economy burning bright. We top the world growth charts. We beat the United States at job growth. Our books are balanced, our dollar is rising. Our exports grow and grow. We are Tiger, hear us roar.

But if all that is true, why are we still protecting the dark, backward corners of our world-beating economy?

To be fair, most of our trade is tariff-free. At latest count we have free-trade deals with the United States, Mexico, Chile, Israel, the Palestinian Authority (yes, we do), Costa Rica and 20 Caribbean countries, and we're currently negotiating separate deals with at least five more countries, plus the entire Western hemisphere (minus Cuba) in the Free Trade Area of the Americas initiative.

But that only strengthens the argument for ditching our tariffs entirely. We have survived free trade both with the world's economic colossus and with Mexico, a poor country that was supposed to swallow up our economy with a giant sucking sound. And we haven't just survived. We've thrived—to the point where serious people in Ottawa (there are some) are thinking of ourselves as real economic tigers. Well, real economic tigers don't need tariffs. They give up the sectors they're weak in and focus on their strengths. Maybe if we drop the ice cream tariff to zero we won't have an ice cream industry any more. But we'll still have ice cream. In fact, we'll have even more of it, because we'll be richer focusing on what we do best and trading for all the rest.

Another good argument for putting all our tariffs to zero—right away, unilaterally—is to solve an increasingly complex "rules of origin" problem. At the moment, all our free trade deals include byzantine rules for deciding where a product comes from. Why? Because where it comes from determines what tariff it faces. But if we put all our tariffs to zero, that problem disappears. No matter where you're from (except Libya and North Korea), you'd pay the same tariff. I don't actually know how many of our customs agents spend all their time administering rules of origin, but it must be lots. They could all be moved to more useful work.

This idea is not as strange as it sounds. The United States has announced a goal of zero tariffs in manufacturing by 2015. Unless it gets badly sidetracked, that's where the world is heading.

A tiger, fearless beast, should want to lead the way.

Source: *National Post*, March 19, 2003, p. FP19. Material reprinted with the express permission of "The National Post Company," a CanWest Partnership.

As long as Weir pays Forrest more than $20 and less than $10 000, both of them are better off.

Should Canada Trade with Other Countries?

Just as individuals can benefit from specialization and trade with one another, as the farmer and rancher did, so can populations of people in different countries. Many of the goods that Canadians enjoy are produced abroad, and many of the goods produced in Canada are sold abroad. Goods produced abroad and sold domestically are called **imports**. Goods produced domestically and sold abroad are called **exports**.

imports
goods produced abroad and sold domestically

exports
goods produced domestically and sold abroad

To see how countries can benefit from trade, suppose there are two countries, Canada and Japan, and two goods, food and cars. Imagine that the two countries produce cars equally well: A Canadian worker and a Japanese worker can each produce 1 car per month. By contrast, because Canada has more and better land, it is better at producing food: A Canadian worker can produce 2 tonnes of food per month, whereas a Japanese worker can produce only 1 tonne of food per month.

The principle of comparative advantage states that each good should be produced by the country that has the smaller opportunity cost of producing that good. Because the opportunity cost of a car is 2 tonnes of food in Canada but only 1 tonne of food in Japan, Japan has a comparative advantage in producing cars. Japan should produce more cars than it wants for its own use and export some of them to Canada. Similarly, because the opportunity cost of a tonne of food is 1 car in Japan but only 1/2 car in Canada, Canada has a comparative advantage in producing food. Canada should produce more food than it wants to consume and export some of it to Japan. Through specialization and trade, both countries can have more food and more cars.

In reality, of course, the issues involved in trade among nations are more complex than this example suggests, as we will see in Chapter 9. Most important among these issues is that each country has many citizens with different interests. International trade can make some individuals worse off, even as it makes the country as a whole better off. When Canada exports food and imports cars, the impact on a Canadian farmer is not the same as the impact on a Canadian autoworker. Yet, contrary to the opinions sometimes voiced by politicians and political commentators, international trade is not like war, in which some countries win and others lose. Trade allows all countries to achieve greater prosperity.

QuickQuiz Suppose that the world's fastest typist happens to be trained in brain surgery. Should he do his own typing or hire a secretary? Explain.

CONCLUSION

The principle of comparative advantage shows that trade can make everyone better off. You should now understand more fully the benefits of living in an interdependent economy. But having seen why interdependence is desirable, you might naturally ask how it is possible. How do free societies coordinate the diverse activities of all the people involved in their economies? What ensures that goods and services will get from those who should be producing them to those who should be consuming them?

In a world with only two people, such as the rancher and the farmer, the answer is simple: These two people can directly bargain and allocate resources between themselves. In the real world with billions of people, the answer is less obvious. We take up this issue in the next chapter, where we see that free societies allocate resources through the market forces of supply and demand.

SUMMARY

- Each person consumes goods and services produced by many other people, both in our country and around the world. Interdependence and trade are desirable because they allow everyone to enjoy a greater quantity and variety of goods and services.

- There are two ways to compare the ability of two people in producing a good. The person who can produce the good with the smaller quantity of inputs is said to have an *absolute advantage* in producing the good. The person who has the smaller opportunity cost of producing the good is said to have a *comparative advantage*. The gains from trade are based on comparative advantage, not absolute advantage.

- Trade makes everyone better off because it allows people to specialize in those activities in which they have a comparative advantage.

- The principle of comparative advantage applies to countries as well as to people. Economists use the principle of comparative advantage to advocate free trade among countries.

KEY CONCEPTS

absolute advantage, p. 53
opportunity cost, p. 53

comparative advantage, p. 54
imports, p. 58

exports, p. 58

QUESTIONS FOR REVIEW

1. Explain how absolute advantage and comparative advantage differ.

2. Give an example in which one person has an absolute advantage in doing something but another person has a comparative advantage.

3. Is absolute advantage or comparative advantage more important for trade? Explain your

reasoning using the example in your answer to question 2.

4. Will a nation tend to export or import goods for which it has a comparative advantage? Explain.

5. Why do economists oppose policies that restrict trade among nations?

PROBLEMS AND APPLICATIONS

1. Consider the farmer and the rancher from our example in this chapter. Explain why the farmer's opportunity cost of producing

1 kg of meat is 4 kg of potatoes. Explain why the rancher's opportunity cost of producing 1 kg of meat is 2 kg of potatoes.

2. Maria can read 20 pages of economics in an hour. She can also read 50 pages of sociology in an hour. She spends 5 hours per day studying.
   a. Draw Maria's production possibilities frontier for reading economics and sociology.
   b. What is Maria's opportunity cost of reading 100 pages of sociology?

3. Canadian and Japanese workers can each produce 4 cars per year. A Canadian worker can produce 10 tonnes of grain per year, whereas a Japanese worker can produce 5 tonnes of grain per year. To keep things simple, assume that each country has 100 million workers.
   a. For this situation, construct a table analogous to Table 3.1.
   b. Graph the production possibilities frontier of the Canadian and Japanese economies.
   c. For Canada, what is the opportunity cost of a car? Of grain? For Japan, what is the opportunity cost of a car? Of grain? Put this information in a table analogous to Table 3.3.
   d. Which country has an absolute advantage in producing cars? In producing grain?
   e. Which country has a comparative advantage in producing cars? In producing grain?
   f. Without trade, half of each country's workers produce cars and half produce grain. What quantities of cars and grain does each country produce?
   g. Starting from a position without trade, give an example in which trade makes each country better off.

4. Pat and Kris are roommates. They spend most of their time studying (of course), but they leave some time for their favourite activities: making pizza and brewing root beer. Pat takes 4 hours to brew 5 L of root beer and 2 hours to make a pizza. Kris takes 6 hours to brew 5 L of root beer and 4 hours to make a pizza.
   a. What is each roommate's opportunity cost of making a pizza? Who has the absolute advantage in making pizza? Who has the comparative advantage in making pizza?
   b. If Pat and Kris trade foods with each other, who will trade away pizza in exchange for root beer?

   c. The price of pizza can be expressed in terms of litres of root beer. What is the highest price at which pizza can be traded that would make both roommates better off? What is the lowest price? Explain.

5. Suppose that there are 10 million workers in Canada, and that each of these workers can produce either 2 cars or 30 tonnes of wheat in a year.
   a. What is the opportunity cost of producing a car in Canada? What is the opportunity cost of producing a tonne of wheat in Canada? Explain the relationship between the opportunity costs of the two goods.
   b. Draw Canada's production possibilities frontier. If Canada chooses to consume 10 million cars, how much wheat can it consume without trade? Label this point on the production possibilities frontier.
   c. Now suppose that the United States offers to buy 10 million cars from Canada in exchange for 20 tonnes of wheat per car. If Canada continues to consume 10 million cars, how much wheat does this deal allow Canada to consume? Label this point on your diagram. Should Canada accept the deal?

6. Consider a professor who is writing a book. The professor can both write the chapters and gather the needed data faster than anyone else at his university. Still, he pays a student to collect data at the library. Is this sensible? Explain.

7. England and Scotland both produce scones and sweaters. Suppose that an English worker can produce 50 scones per hour or 1 sweater per hour. Suppose that a Scottish worker can produce 40 scones per hour or 2 sweaters per hour.
   a. Which country has the absolute advantage in the production of each good? Which country has the comparative advantage?
   b. If England and Scotland decide to trade, which commodity will Scotland trade to England? Explain.
   c. If a Scottish worker could produce only 1 sweater per hour, would Scotland still gain

from trade? Would England still gain from trade? Explain.

8. The following table describes the production possibilities of two cities.

	Red Sweaters per Worker per Hour	Blue Sweaters per Worker per Hour
Montreal	3	3
Toronto	2	1

a. Without trade, what is the price of blue sweaters (in terms of red sweaters) in Montreal? What is the price in Toronto?

b. Which city has an absolute advantage in the production of each colour sweater? Which city has a comparative advantage in the production of each colour sweater?

c. If the cities trade with each other, which colour sweater will each export?

d. What is the range of prices at which trade can occur?

9. Suppose that all goods can be produced with fewer worker hours in Germany than in France.

a. In what sense is the cost of all goods lower in Germany than in France?

b. In what sense is the cost of some goods lower in France?

c. If Germany and France traded with each other, would both countries be better off as a result? Explain in the context of your answers to parts (a) and (b).

10. Are the following statements true or false? Explain in each case.

a. "Two countries can achieve gains from trade even if one of the countries has an absolute advantage in the production of all goods."

b. "Certain very talented people have a comparative advantage in everything they do."

c. "If a certain trade is good for one person, it can't be good for the other one."

INTERNET RESOURCES

- To learn more about economist Adam Smith, follow the many links available at http://cepa.newschool.edu/het/profiles/smith.htm.

- You can read Adam Smith's classic book *The Wealth of Nations* (and many other classic texts) at the Liberty Fund's online library at http://oll.libertyfund.org.

- To read more about David Ricardo and his ideas, go to http://cepa.newschool.edu/het/profiles/ricardo.htm.

- If the principle of comparative advantage is such a simple idea that can be taught in first-year college and university textbooks, why do so many educated people reject the argument that there are gains from trade? MIT professor of economics Paul Krugman tries to answer that question in his essay "Ricardo's Difficult Idea": http://web.mit.edu/krugman/www/ricardo.htm.

For more study tools, please visit http://www.mankiw3e.nelson.com.

2

SUPPLY AND DEMAND: HOW MARKETS WORK

© JIM STEINHART

© JIM STEINHART

THE MARKET FORCES OF SUPPLY AND DEMAND

4

Learning Objectives

In this chapter, you will …

- Learn the nature of a competitive market
- Examine what determines the demand for a good in a competitive market
- Examine what determines the supply of a good in a competitive market
- See how supply and demand together set the price of a good and the quantity sold
- Consider the key role of prices in allocating scarce resources in market economies

When a cold snap hits Florida, the price of orange juice rises in supermarkets throughout Canada. When the weather turns warm in Quebec every summer, the price of hotel rooms in the Caribbean plummets. When a war breaks out in the Middle East, the price of gasoline in Canada rises, and the price of a used SUV falls. What do these events have in common? They all show the workings of supply and demand.

Supply and *demand* are the two words that economists use most often—and for good reason. Supply and demand are the forces that make market economies work. They determine the quantity of each good produced and the price at which it is sold. If you want to know how any event or policy will affect the economy, you must think first about how it will affect supply and demand.

This chapter introduces the theory of supply and demand. It considers how buyers and sellers behave and how they interact with one another. It shows how supply and demand determine prices in a market economy and how prices, in turn, allocate the economy's scarce resources.

MARKETS AND COMPETITION

The terms *supply* and *demand* refer to the behaviour of people as they interact with one another in markets. A **market** is a group of buyers and sellers of a particular good or service. The buyers as a group determine the demand for the product, and the sellers as a group determine the supply of the product. Before discussing how buyers and sellers behave, let's first consider more fully what we mean by a "market" and the various types of markets we observe in the economy.

market
a group of buyers and sellers of a particular good or service

Competitive Markets

Markets take many forms. Sometimes markets are highly organized, such as the markets for many agricultural commodities. In these markets, buyers and sellers meet at a specific time and place, where an auctioneer helps set prices and arrange sales.

More often, markets are less organized. For example, consider the market for ice cream in a particular town. Buyers of ice cream do not meet together at any one time. The sellers of ice cream are in different locations and offer somewhat different products. There is no auctioneer calling out the price of ice cream. Each seller posts a price for an ice-cream cone, and each buyer decides how much ice cream to buy at each store.

Even though it is not organized, the group of ice-cream buyers and ice-cream sellers forms a market. Each buyer knows that there are several sellers from which to choose, and each seller is aware that his product is similar to that offered by other sellers. The price of ice cream and the quantity of ice cream sold are not determined by any single buyer or seller. Rather, price and quantity are determined by all buyers and sellers as they interact in the marketplace.

The market for ice cream, like most markets in the economy, is highly competitive. A **competitive market** is a market in which there are many buyers and many sellers so that each has a negligible impact on the market price. Each seller of ice cream has limited control over the price because other sellers are offering similar products. A seller has little reason to charge less than the going price, and if he or she charges more, buyers will make their purchases elsewhere. Similarly, no single buyer of ice cream can influence the price of ice cream because each buyer purchases only a small amount.

competitive market
a market in which there are many buyers and many sellers so that each has a negligible impact on the market price

In this chapter we examine how buyers and sellers interact in competitive markets. We see how the forces of supply and demand determine both the quantity of the good sold and its price.

Competition: Perfect and Otherwise

We assume in this chapter that markets are *perfectly competitive*. Perfectly competitive markets are defined by two primary characteristics: (1) the goods being offered for sale are all the same, and (2) the buyers and sellers are so numerous that no single buyer or seller can influence the market price. Because buyers and sellers in perfectly competitive markets must accept the price the market determines, they are said to be *price takers*.

There are some markets in which the assumption of perfect competition applies almost perfectly. In the wheat market, for example, there are thousands of farmers who sell wheat and millions of consumers who use wheat and wheat products. Because no single buyer or seller can influence the price of wheat, each takes the price as given.

Not all goods and services, however, are sold in perfectly competitive markets. Some markets have only one seller, and this seller sets the price. Such a seller is called a *monopoly*. Your local cable television company, for instance, may be a monopoly. Residents of your town probably have only one cable company from which to buy this service.

Some markets fall between the extremes of perfect competition and monopoly. One such market, called an *oligopoly*, has a few sellers that do not always compete aggressively. Airline routes are an example. If a route between two cities is serviced by only two or three carriers, the carriers may avoid rigorous competition so they can keep prices high. Another type of market is *monopolistically competitive*; it contains many sellers but each offers a slightly different product. Because the products are not exactly the same, each seller has some ability to set the price for its own product. An example is the market for magazines. Magazines compete with one another for readers and anyone can enter the market by starting a new one, but each magazine offers different articles and can set its own price.

Despite the diversity of market types we find in the world, we begin by studying perfect competition. Perfectly competitive markets are the easiest to analyze. Moreover, because some degree of competition is present in most markets, many of the lessons that we learn by studying supply and demand under perfect competition apply in more complicated markets as well.

QuickQuiz What is a market? • What are the characteristics of a competitive market?

DEMAND

We begin our study of markets by examining the behaviour of buyers. To focus our thinking, let's keep in mind a particular good—ice cream.

The Demand Curve: The Relationship between Price and Quantity Demanded

The **quantity demanded** of any good is the amount of the good that buyers are willing to purchase. As we will see, many things determine the quantity demanded of any good, but when analyzing how markets work, one determinant plays a central role—the price of the good. If the price of ice cream rose to $20 per scoop, you would buy less ice cream. You might buy frozen yogurt instead. If the price of ice cream fell to $0.20 per scoop, you would buy more. Because the quantity demanded falls as the price rises and rises as the price falls, we say that the quantity demanded is *negatively related* to the price. This relationship between price and quantity demanded is true for most goods in the economy and, in fact,

quantity demanded
the amount of a good that buyers are willing to purchase

law of demand
the claim that, other things equal, the quantity demanded of a good falls when the price of the good rises

demand schedule
a table that shows the relationship between the price of a good and the quantity demanded

demand curve
a graph of the relationship between the price of a good and the quantity demanded

is so pervasive that economists call it the **law of demand:** Other things equal, when the price of a good rises, the quantity demanded of the good falls, and when the price falls, the quantity demanded rises.

The table in Figure 4.1 shows how many ice-cream cones Catherine buys each month at different prices of ice cream. If ice cream is free, Catherine eats 12 cones. At $0.50 per cone, Catherine buys 10 cones. As the price rises further, she buys fewer and fewer cones. When the price reaches $3.00, Catherine doesn't buy any ice cream at all. This table is a **demand schedule,** a table that shows the relationship between the price of a good and the quantity demanded, holding constant everything else that influences how much consumers of the good want to buy.

The graph in Figure 4.1 uses the numbers from the table to illustrate the law of demand. By convention, the price of ice cream is on the vertical axis, and the quantity of ice cream demanded is on the horizontal axis. The downward-sloping line relating price and quantity demanded is called the **demand curve.**

Market Demand versus Individual Demand

The demand curve in Figure 4.1 shows an individual's demand for a product. To analyze how markets work, we need to determine the *market demand*, which is the sum of all the individual demands for a particular good or service.

FIGURE 4.1

Catherine's Demand Schedule and Demand Curve

The demand schedule shows the quantity demanded at each price. The demand curve, which graphs the demand schedule, shows how the quantity demanded of the good changes as its price varies. Because a lower price increases the quantity demanded, the demand curve slopes downward.

Price of Ice-Cream Cone	Quantity of Cones Demanded
$0.00	12
0.50	10
1.00	8
1.50	6
2.00	4
2.50	2
3.00	0

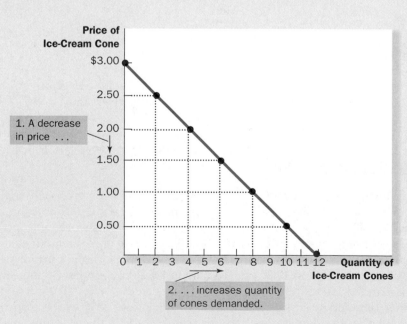

The table in Figure 4.2 shows the demand schedules for ice cream of two individuals—Catherine and Nicholas. At any price, Catherine's demand schedule tells us how much ice cream she buys, and Nicholas's demand schedule tells us how much ice cream he buys. The market demand at each price is the sum of the two individual demands.

The graph in Figure 4.2 shows the demand curves that correspond to these demand schedules. Notice that we sum the individual demand curves *horizontally* to obtain the market demand curve. That is, to find the total quantity demanded at any price, we add the individual quantities found on the horizontal axis of the individual demand curves. Because we are interested in analyzing how markets work, we will work most often with the market demand curve. The market demand curve shows how the total quantity demanded of a good varies as the price of the good varies, while all the other factors that affect how much consumers want to buy are held constant.

Shifts in the Demand Curve

The demand curve for ice cream shows how much ice cream people buy at any given price, holding constant the many other factors beyond price that influence

FIGURE 4.2

Market Demand as the Sum of Individual Demands

The quantity demanded in a market is the sum of the quantities demanded by all the buyers at each price. Thus, the market demand curve is found by adding horizontally the individual demand curves. At a price of $2, Catherine demands 4 ice-cream cones, and Nicholas demands 3 ice-cream cones. The quantity demanded in the market at this price is 7 cones.

Price of Ice-Cream Cone	Catherine		Nicholas		Market
$0.00	12	+	7	-	19
0.50	10		6		16
1.00	8		5		13
1.50	6		4		10
2.00	4		3		7
2.50	2		2		4
3.00	0		1		1

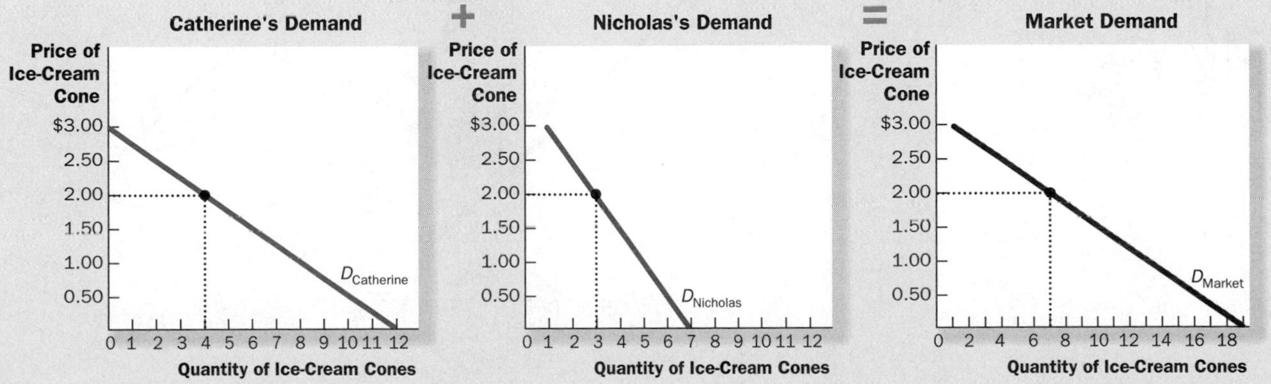

consumers' buying decisions. As a result, this demand curve need not be stable over time. If something happens to alter the quantity demanded at any given price, the demand curve shifts. For example, suppose nutritionists discovered that people who regularly eat ice cream live longer, healthier lives. The discovery would raise the demand for ice cream. At any given price, buyers would now want to purchase a larger quantity of ice cream, and the demand curve for ice cream would shift.

Figure 4.3 illustrates shifts in demand. Any change that increases the quantity demanded at every price, such as our imaginary discovery by nutritionists, shifts the demand curve to the right and is called *an increase in demand*. Any change that reduces the quantity demanded at every price shifts the demand curve to the left and is called *a decrease in demand.*

There are many variables that can shift the demand curve. Here are the most important:

Income What would happen to your demand for ice cream if you lost your job one summer? Most likely, it would fall. A lower income means that you have less to spend in total, so you would have to spend less on some—and probably most—goods. If the demand for a good falls when income falls, the good is called a **normal good.**

Not all goods are normal goods. If the demand for a good rises when income falls, the good is called an **inferior good.** An example of an inferior good might be bus rides. As your income falls, you are less likely to buy a car or take a cab, and more likely to ride the bus.

Prices of Related Goods Suppose that the price of frozen yogurt falls. The law of demand says that you will buy more frozen yogurt. At the same time, you will probably buy less ice cream. Because ice cream and frozen yogurt are both cold, sweet, creamy desserts, they satisfy similar desires. When a fall in the

normal good
a good for which, other things equal, an increase in income leads to an increase in demand

inferior good
a good for which, other things equal, an increase in income leads to a decrease in demand

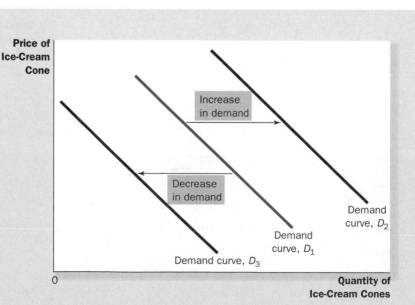

FIGURE 4.3

Shifts in the Demand Curve

Any change that raises the quantity that buyers wish to purchase at a given price shifts the demand curve to the right. Any change that lowers the quantity that buyers wish to purchase at a given price shifts the demand curve to the left.

price of one good reduces the demand for another good, the two goods are called **substitutes.** Substitutes are often pairs of goods that are used in place of each other, such as hot dogs and hamburgers, sweaters and sweatshirts, and movie tickets and video rentals.

Now suppose that the price of hot fudge falls. According to the law of demand, you will buy more hot fudge. Yet, in this case, you will buy more ice cream as well, because ice cream and hot fudge are often used together. When a fall in the price of one good raises the demand for another good, the two goods are called **complements.** Complements are often pairs of goods that are used together, such as gasoline and automobiles, computers and software, and peanut butter and jelly.

Tastes   The most obvious determinant of your demand is your tastes. If you like ice cream, you buy more of it. Economists normally do not try to explain people's tastes because tastes are based on historical and psychological forces that are beyond the realm of economics. Economists do, however, examine what happens when tastes change.

Expectations   Your expectations about the future may affect your demand for a good or service today. For example, if you expect to earn a higher income next month, you may be more willing to spend some of your current savings buying ice cream. As another example, if you expect the price of ice cream to fall tomorrow, you may be less willing to buy an ice-cream cone at today's price.

Number of Buyers   Because market demand is derived from individual demands, it depends on all those factors that determine the demand of individual buyers, including buyers' incomes, tastes, expectations, and the prices of related goods. In addition, it depends on the number of buyers. If Peter, another consumer of ice cream, were to join Catherine and Nicholas, the quantity demanded in the market would be higher at every price and the demand curve would shift to the right.

Summary   The demand curve shows what happens to the quantity demanded of a good when its price varies, holding constant all the other variables that influence buyers. When one of these other variables changes, the demand curve shifts. Table 4.1 lists all the variables that influence how much consumers choose to buy of a good.

substitutes
two goods for which an increase in the price of one leads to an increase in the demand for the other

complements
two goods for which an increase in the price of one leads to a decrease in the demand for the other

---

TABLE 4.1

Variables That Influence Buyers

This table lists the variables that affect how much consumers choose to buy of any good. Notice the special role that the price of the good plays: A change in the good's price represents a movement along the demand curve, whereas a change in one of the other variables shifts the demand curve.

Variable	A Change in This Variable . . .
Price	Represents a movement along the demand curve
Income	Shifts the demand curve
Prices of related goods	Shifts the demand curve
Tastes	Shifts the demand curve
Expectations	Shifts the demand curve
Number of buyers	Shifts the demand curve

Case Study

TWO WAYS TO REDUCE THE QUANTITY OF SMOKING DEMANDED

Public policymakers often want to reduce the amount that people smoke. There are two ways that policy can attempt to achieve this goal.

One way to reduce smoking is to shift the demand curve for cigarettes and other tobacco products. Public service announcements, mandatory health warnings on cigarette packages, and the prohibition of cigarette advertising on television are all policies aimed at reducing the quantity of cigarettes demanded at any given price. If successful, these policies shift the demand curve for cigarettes to the left, as in panel (a) of Figure 4.4.

Alternatively, policymakers can try to raise the price of cigarettes. If the government taxes the manufacture of cigarettes, for example, cigarette companies pass much of this tax on to consumers in the form of higher prices. A higher price encourages smokers to reduce the numbers of cigarettes they smoke. In this case,

FIGURE 4.4

Shifts in the Demand Curve versus Movements along the Demand Curve

If warnings on cigarette packages convince smokers to smoke less, the demand curve for cigarettes shifts to the left. In panel (a), the demand curve shifts from D₁ to D₂. At a price of $2 per pack, the quantity demanded falls from 20 to 10 cigarettes per day, as reflected by the shift from point A to point B. By contrast, if a tax raises the price of cigarettes, the demand curve does not shift. Instead, we observe a movement to a different point on the demand curve. In panel (b), when the price rises from $2 to $4, the quantity demanded falls from 20 to 12 cigarettes per day, as reflected by the movement from point A to point C.

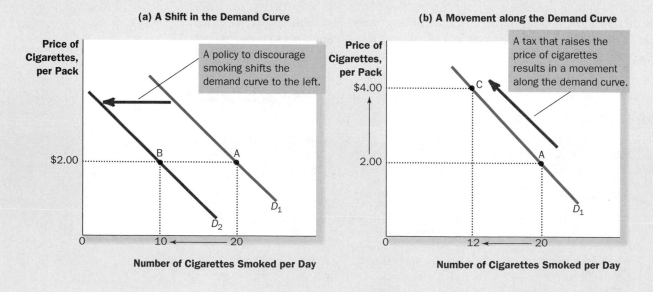

the reduced amount of smoking does not represent a shift in the demand curve. Instead, it represents a movement along the same demand curve to a point with a higher price and lower quantity, as in panel (b) of Figure 4.4.

How much does the amount of smoking respond to changes in the price of cigarettes? Economists have attempted to answer this question by studying what happens when the tax on cigarettes changes. They have found that a 10 percent increase in the price causes a 4 percent reduction in the quantity demanded. Teenagers are found to be especially sensitive to the price of cigarettes: A 10 percent increase in the price causes a 12 percent drop in teenage smoking.

A related question is how the price of cigarettes affects the demand for illicit drugs, such as marijuana. Opponents of cigarette taxes often argue that tobacco and marijuana are substitutes, so that high cigarette prices encourage marijuana use. By contrast, many experts on substance abuse view tobacco as a "gateway drug" leading the young to experiment with other harmful substances. Most studies of the data are consistent with this view: They find that lower cigarette prices are associated with greater use of marijuana. In other words, tobacco and marijuana appear to be complements rather than substitutes. ●

QuickQuiz Make up an example of a demand schedule for pizza, and graph the implied demand curve. • Give an example of something that would shift this demand curve. • Would a change in the price of pizza shift this demand curve?

SUPPLY

We now turn to the other side of the market and examine the behaviour of sellers. Once again, to focus our thinking, let's consider the market for ice cream.

The Supply Curve: The Relationship between Price and Quantity Supplied

The **quantity supplied** of any good or service is the amount that sellers are willing to sell. There are many determinants of quantity supplied, but once again price plays a special role in our analysis. When the price of ice cream is high, selling ice cream is profitable, and so the quantity supplied is large. Sellers of ice cream work long hours, buy many ice-cream machines, and hire many workers. By contrast, when the price of ice cream is low, the business is less profitable, and so sellers produce less ice cream. At a low price, some sellers may even choose to shut down, and their quantity supplied falls to zero. Because the quantity supplied rises as the price rises and falls as the price falls, we say that the quantity supplied is *positively related* to the price of the good. This relationship between price and quantity supplied is called the **law of supply:** Other things equal, when the price of a good rises, the quantity supplied of the good also rises, and when the price falls, the quantity supplied falls as well.

What is the best way to stop this?

quantity supplied
the amount of a good that sellers are willing to sell

law of supply
the claim that, other things equal, the quantity supplied of a good rises when the price of the good rises

supply schedule
a table that shows the relationship between the price of a good and the quantity supplied

supply curve
a graph of the relationship between the price of a good and the quantity supplied

The table in Figure 4.5 shows the quantity supplied by Ben, an ice-cream seller, at various prices of ice cream. At a price below $1.00, Ben does not supply any ice cream at all. As the price rises, he supplies a greater and greater quantity. This is the **supply schedule,** a table that shows the relationship between the price of a good and the quantity supplied, holding constant everything else that influences how much producers of the good want to sell.

The graph in Figure 4.5 uses the numbers from the table to illustrate the law of supply. The curve relating price and quantity supplied is called the **supply curve.** The supply curve slopes upward because, other things equal, a higher price means a greater quantity supplied.

Market Supply versus Individual Supply

Just as market demand is the sum of the demands of all buyers, market supply is the sum of the supplies of all sellers. The table in Figure 4.6 shows the supply schedules for two ice-cream producers—Ben and Jerry. At any price, Ben's supply schedule tells us the quantity of ice cream Ben supplies, and Jerry's supply schedule tells us the quantity of ice cream Jerry supplies. The market supply is the sum of the two individual supplies.

FIGURE 4.5

Ben's Supply Schedule and Supply Curve

The supply schedule shows the quantity supplied at each price. This supply curve, which graphs the supply schedule, shows how the quantity supplied of the good changes as its price varies. Because a higher price increases the quantity supplied, the supply curve slopes upward.

Price of Ice-Cream Cone	Quantity of Cones Supplied
$0.00	0
0.50	0
1.00	1
1.50	2
2.00	3
2.50	4
3.00	5

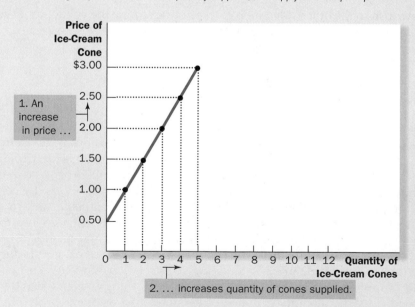

FIGURE 4.6

Market Supply as the Sum of Individual Supplies

The quantity supplied in a market is the sum of the quantities supplied by all the sellers at each price. Thus, the market supply curve is found by adding horizontally the individual supply curves. At a price of $2, Ben supplies 3 ice-cream cones, and Jerry supplies 4 ice-cream cones. The quantity supplied in the market at this price is 7 cones.

Price of Ice-Cream Cone	Ben		Jerry		Market
$0.00	0	+	0	=	0
0.50	0		0		0
1.00	1		0		1
1.50	2		2		4
2.00	3		4		7
2.50	4		6		10
3.00	5		8		13

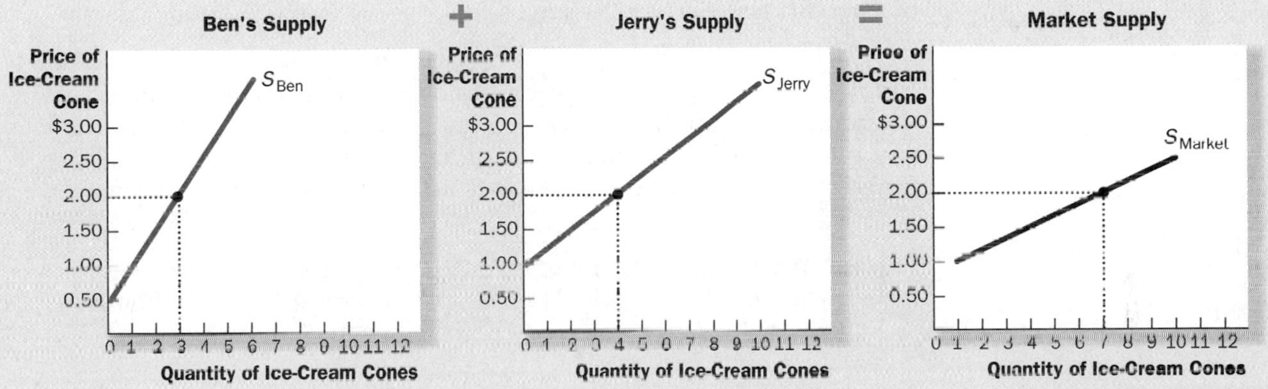

The graph in Figure 4.6 shows the supply curves that correspond to the supply schedules. As with demand curves, we sum the individual supply curves *horizontally* to obtain the market supply curve. That is, to find the total quantity supplied at any price, we add the individual quantities found on the horizontal axis of the individual supply curves. The market supply curve shows how the total quantity supplied varies as the price of the good varies.

Shifts in the Supply Curve

The supply curve for ice cream shows how much ice cream producers offer for sale at any given price, holding constant all the other factors beyond price that influence producers' decisions about how much to sell. This relationship can change over time, which is represented by a shift in the supply curve. For example, suppose the price of sugar falls. Because sugar is an input into producing ice cream, the fall in the price of sugar makes selling ice cream more profitable. This raises the supply of ice cream: At any given price, sellers are now willing to produce a larger quantity. Thus, the supply curve for ice cream shifts to the right.

Figure 4.7 illustrates shifts in supply. Any change that raises quantity supplied at every price, such as a fall in the price of sugar, shifts the supply curve to the right and is called *an increase in supply*. Similarly, any change that reduces the quantity supplied at every price shifts the supply curve to the left and is called *a decrease in supply*.

There are many variables that can shift the supply curve. Here are some of the most important:

Input Prices   To produce their output of ice cream, sellers use various inputs: cream, sugar, flavouring, ice-cream machines, the buildings in which the ice cream is made, and the labour of workers to mix the ingredients and operate the machines. When the price of one or more of these inputs rises, producing ice cream is less profitable, and firms supply less ice cream. If input prices rise substantially, a firm might shut down and supply no ice cream at all. Thus, the supply of a good is negatively related to the price of the inputs used to make the good.

Technology   The technology for turning the inputs into ice cream is yet another determinant of supply. The invention of the mechanized ice-cream machine, for example, reduced the amount of labour necessary to make ice cream. By reducing firms' costs, the advance in technology raised the supply of ice cream.

Expectations   The amount of ice cream a firm supplies today may depend on its expectations of the future. For example, if it expects the price of ice cream to

---

FIGURE 4.7

Shifts in the Supply Curve

Any change that raises the quantity that sellers wish to produce at a given price shifts the supply curve to the right. Any change that lowers the quantity that sellers wish to produce at a given price shifts the supply curve to the left.

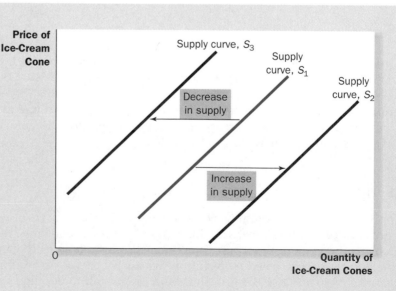

rise in the future, it will put some of its current production into storage and supply less to the market today.

Number of Sellers Market supply depends on all those factors that influence the supply of individual sellers, such as the prices of inputs used to produce the good, the available technology, and expectations. In addition, the supply in a market depends on the number of sellers. If Ben or Jerry were to retire from the ice-cream business, the supply in the market would fall.

Summary The supply curve shows what happens to the quantity supplied of a good when its price varies, holding constant all the other variables that influence sellers. When one of these other variables changes, the supply curve shifts. Table 4.2 lists all the variables that influence how much producers choose to sell of a good.

QuickQuiz Make up an example of a supply schedule for pizza, and graph the implied supply curve. • Give an example of something that would shift this supply curve. • Would a change in the price of pizza shift this supply curve?

SUPPLY AND DEMAND TOGETHER

Having analyzed supply and demand separately, we now combine them to see how they determine the quantity of a good sold in a market and its price.

Equilibrium

Figure 4.8 (p. 78) shows the market supply curve and market demand curve together. Notice that there is one point at which the supply and demand curves intersect. This point is called the market's **equilibrium**. The price at this intersection is called the **equilibrium price**, and the quantity is called the **equilibrium**

equilibrium
a situation in which the price has reached the level where quantity supplied equals quantity demanded

equilibrium price
the price that balances quantity supplied and quantity demanded

equilibrium quantity
the quantity supplied and the quantity demanded at the equilibrium price

---

TABLE 4.2

Variables That Influence Sellers

This table lists the variables that affect how much producers choose to sell of any good. Notice the special role that the price of the good plays: A change in the good's price represents a movement along the supply curve, whereas a change in one of the other variables shifts the supply curve.

Variable	A Change in This Variable . . .
Price	Represents a movement along the supply curve
Input prices	Shifts the supply curve
Technology	Shifts the supply curve
Expectations	Shifts the supply curve
Number of sellers	Shifts the supply curve

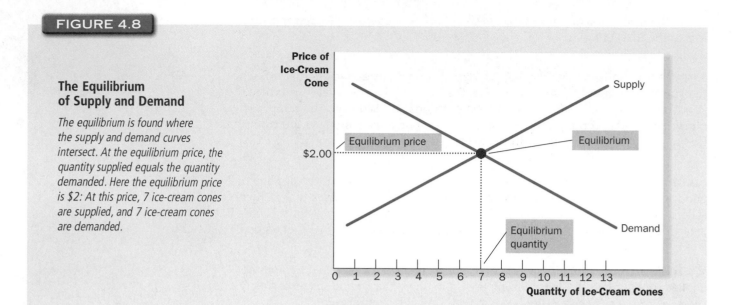

FIGURE 4.8

The Equilibrium of Supply and Demand

The equilibrium is found where the supply and demand curves intersect. At the equilibrium price, the quantity supplied equals the quantity demanded. Here the equilibrium price is $2: At this price, 7 ice-cream cones are supplied, and 7 ice-cream cones are demanded.

quantity. Here the equilibrium price is $2.00 per cone, and the equilibrium quantity is 7 ice-cream cones.

The dictionary defines the word *equilibrium* as a situation in which various forces are in balance—and this also describes a market's equilibrium. *At the equilibrium price, the quantity of the good that buyers are willing to buy exactly balances the quantity that sellers are willing to sell.* The equilibrium price is sometimes called the *market-clearing price* because, at this price, everyone in the market has been satisfied: Buyers can buy all they want to buy, and sellers can sell all they want to sell.

The actions of buyers and sellers naturally move markets toward the equilibrium of supply and demand. To see why, consider what happens when the market price is not equal to the equilibrium price.

Suppose first that the market price is above the equilibrium price, as in panel (a) of Figure 4.9. At a price of $2.50 per cone, the quantity of the good supplied (10 cones) exceeds the quantity demanded (4 cones). There is a **surplus** of the good: Suppliers are unable to sell all they want at the going price. A surplus is sometimes called a situation of *excess supply*. When there is a surplus in the ice-cream market, sellers of ice cream find their freezers increasingly full of ice cream they would like to sell but cannot. They respond to the surplus by cutting their prices. Falling prices, in turn, increase the quantity demanded and decrease the quantity supplied. Prices continue to fall until the market reaches the equilibrium.

Suppose now that the market price is below the equilibrium price, as in panel (b) of Figure 4.9. In this case, the price is $1.50 per cone, and the quantity of the good demanded exceeds the quantity supplied. There is a **shortage** of the good: Demanders are unable to buy all they want at the going price. A shortage is sometimes called a situation of *excess demand*. When a shortage occurs in the ice-cream market, buyers have to wait in long lines for a chance to buy one of the few cones that are available. With too many buyers chasing too few goods, sellers can

surplus
a situation in which quantity supplied is greater than quantity demanded

shortage
a situation in which quantity demanded is greater than quantity supplied

FIGURE 4.9

Markets Not in Equilibrium

In panel (a), there is a surplus. Because the market price of $2.50 is above the equilibrium price, the quantity supplied (10 cones) exceeds the quantity demanded (4 cones). Suppliers try to increase sales by cutting the price of a cone, and this moves the price toward its equilibrium level. In panel (b), there is a shortage. Because the market price of $1.50 is below the equilibrium price, the quantity demanded (10 cones) exceeds the quantity supplied (4 cones). With too many buyers chasing too few goods, suppliers can take advantage of the shortage by raising the price. Hence, in both cases, the price adjustment moves the market toward the equilibrium of supply and demand.

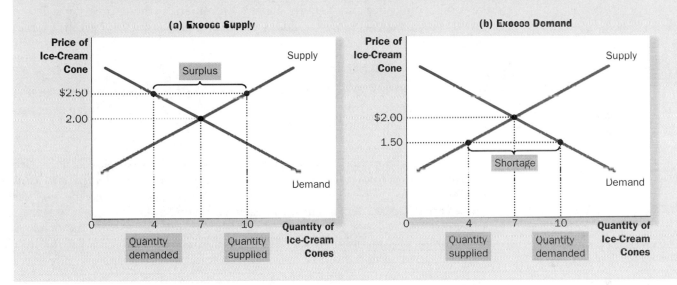

respond to the shortage by raising their prices without losing sales. As the price rises, quantity demanded falls, quantity supplied rises, and the market once again moves toward the equilibrium.

Thus, the activities of the many buyers and sellers automatically push the market price toward the equilibrium price. Once the market reaches its equilibrium, all buyers and sellers are satisfied, and there is no upward or downward pressure on the price. How quickly equilibrium is reached varies from market to market, depending on how quickly prices adjust. In most free markets, surpluses and shortages are only temporary because prices eventually move toward their equilibrium levels. Indeed, this phenomenon is so pervasive that it is called the **law of supply and demand:** The price of any good adjusts to bring the quantity supplied and quantity demanded for that good into balance.

law of supply and demand
the claim that the price of any good adjusts to bring the quantity supplied and the quantity demanded for that good into balance

Three Steps to Analyzing Changes in Equilibrium

So far we have seen how supply and demand together determine a market's equilibrium, which in turn determines the price of the good and the quantity of the good that buyers buy and sellers sell. Of course, the equilibrium price and quantity depend on the position of the supply and demand curves. When some event shifts one of these curves, the equilibrium in the market changes. The analysis of such a change is called *comparative statics* because it involves comparing two unchanging situations—an initial equilibrium and a new equilibrium.

When analyzing how some event affects a market, we proceed in three steps. First, we decide whether the event shifts the supply curve, the demand curve, or in some cases, both curves. Second, we decide whether the curve shifts to the right or to the left. Third, we use the supply-and-demand diagram to compare the initial equilibrium and the new equilibrium, which shows how the shift affects the equilibrium price and quantity. Table 4.3 summarizes these three steps. To see how this recipe is used, let's consider various events that might affect the market for ice cream.

Example: A Change in Demand   Suppose that one summer the weather is very hot. How does this event affect the market for ice cream? To answer this question, let's follow our three steps.

1. The hot weather affects the demand curve by changing people's taste for ice cream. That is, the weather changes the amount of ice cream that people want to buy at any given price. The supply curve is unchanged because the weather does not directly affect the firms that sell ice cream.
2. Because hot weather makes people want to eat more ice cream, the demand curve shifts to the right. Figure 4.10 shows this increase in demand as the shift in the demand curve from D_1 to D_2. This shift indicates that the quantity of ice cream demanded is higher at every price.
3. As Figure 4.10 shows, the increase in demand raises the equilibrium price from $2.00 to $2.50 and the equilibrium quantity from 7 to 10 cones. In other words, the hot weather increases the price of ice cream and the quantity of ice cream sold.

Shifts in Curves versus Movements along Curves   Notice that when hot weather drives up the price of ice cream, the quantity of ice cream that firms supply rises, even though the supply curve remains the same. In this case, economists say there has been an increase in "quantity supplied" but no change in "supply."

TABLE 4.3

A Three-Step Program for Analyzing Changes in Equilibrium

1. Decide whether the event shifts the supply or demand curve (or perhaps both).
2. Decide in which direction the curve shifts.
3. Use the supply-and-demand diagram to see how the shift changes the equilibrium price and quantity.

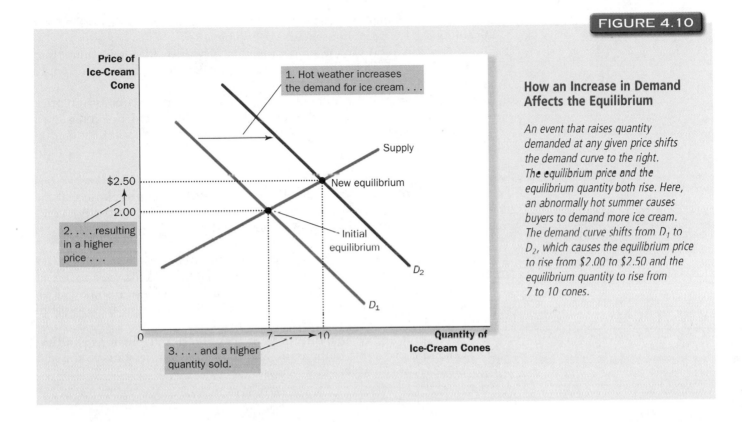

FIGURE 4.10

How an Increase in Demand Affects the Equilibrium

An event that raises quantity demanded at any given price shifts the demand curve to the right. The equilibrium price and the equilibrium quantity both rise. Here, an abnormally hot summer causes buyers to demand more ice cream. The demand curve shifts from D_1 to D_2, which causes the equilibrium price to rise from $2.00 to $2.50 and the equilibrium quantity to rise from 7 to 10 cones.

"Supply" refers to the position of the supply curve, whereas the "quantity supplied" refers to the amount suppliers wish to sell. In this example, supply does not change, because the weather does not alter firms' desire to sell at any given price. Instead, the hot weather alters consumers' desire to buy at any given price and thereby shifts the demand curve. The increase in demand causes the equilibrium price to rise. When the price rises, the quantity supplied rises. This increase in quantity supplied is represented by the movement along the supply curve.

To summarize, a shift *in* the supply curve is called a "change in supply," and a shift *in* the demand curve is called a "change in demand." A movement *along* a fixed supply curve is called a "change in the quantity supplied," and a movement *along* a fixed demand curve is called a "change in the quantity demanded."

Example: A Change in Supply   Suppose that, during another summer, a hurricane destroys part of the sugar cane crop and drives up the price of sugar. How does this event affect the market for ice cream? Once again, to answer this question, we follow our three steps.

1. The change in the price of sugar, an input into making ice cream, affects the supply curve. By raising the costs of production, it reduces the amount of ice cream that firms want to produce and sell at any given price. The demand

curve does not change, because the higher cost of inputs does not directly affect the amount of ice cream households wish to buy.

2. The supply curve shifts to the left because, at every price, the total amount that firms are willing to sell is reduced. Figure 4.11 illustrates this decrease in supply as a shift in the supply curve from S_1 to S_2.

3. As Figure 4.11 shows, the shift in the supply curve raises the equilibrium price from $2.00 to $2.50 and lowers the equilibrium quantity from 7 to 4 cones. As a result of the sugar price increase, the price of ice cream rises, and the quantity of ice cream sold falls.

Example: A Change in Both Supply and Demand   Now suppose that the heat wave and the hurricane occur during the same summer. To analyze this combination of events, we again follow our three steps.

1. We determine that both curves must shift. The hot weather affects the demand curve because it alters the amount of ice cream that households want to buy at any given price. At the same time, when the hurricane drives up sugar prices, it alters the supply curve for ice cream because it changes the amount of ice cream that firms want to sell at any given price.

2. The curves shift in the same directions as they did in our previous analysis: The demand curve shifts to the right, and the supply curve shifts to the left. Figure 4.12 (p. 84) illustrates these shifts.

FIGURE 4.11

How a Decrease in Supply Affects the Equilibrium

An event that reduces quantity supplied at any given price shifts the supply curve to the left. The equilibrium price rises, and the equilibrium quantity falls. Here, an increase in the price of sugar (an input) causes sellers to supply less ice cream. The supply curve shifts from S_1 to S_2, which causes the equilibrium price of ice cream to rise from $2.00 to $2.50 and the equilibrium quantity to fall from 7 to 4 cones.

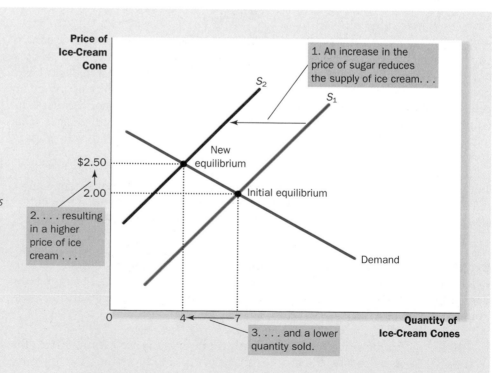

IN THE NEWS

SUPPLY, DEMAND, AND THE PRICE OF LUMBER

This article discusses the impact of forest fires, construction booms, and trade restrictions on the demand, the supply, and the price of Canadian lumber. Notice that expectations of future demand and supply, and hence expectations of the future price of lumber, play an important role.

Lumber Prices Seen Declining

By Peter Kennedy

VANCOUVER — Lumber prices are slipping as fears of supply shortages continue to ease in the wake of damp weather and cooling temperatures in fire-ravaged British Columbia.

Yesterday, the price of lumber for September delivery slipped to $350 (U.S.) for 1,000 board feet from a 2003 high of $366.70 reached last week.

Lumber traders said prices could soon fall below $300 as the market turns its attention from forest fires in B.C. and the northwestern United States to a supply glut that was fuelled in part by U.S. duties on Canadian softwood lumber.

"It's hard to be bullish when prices have been trading near 370," said Graham Dallimore, senior vice-president with Global Futures Corp., a Vancouver-based commodities trader. Analysts say an exceptionally strong residential construction season in the United States has contributed to the rise in futures prices from $285.50 in early July.

But market speculation that prices will continue to retreat are based not only on the waning threat of forest fires but also on the fact that the North American construction season begins to wind down in September.

Prices are expected to come under pressure as the fires die down and the industry gets back to normal business in B.C. and other key forestry regions such as Washington and Oregon.

"There is an expectation that logging [in the B.C. interior] will resume in the coming weeks," Mr. Dallimore said.

Industry officials say forest fires in the interior of B.C. burned through 240,000 hectares, an area that is roughly the equivalent of the annual timber harvest across the entire province.

That in turn led to the closing of nine sawmills in the B.C. interior due to a lack of available logs.

The companies that own those operations include Gorman Bros., Weyerhaeuser Co., Louisiana-Pacific Corp., Tembec Inc. and Slocan Forest Products Ltd. Fire also destroyed ... Tolko Industries Ltd.'s sawmill at Louis Creek, B.C.

"If weather permits, my sense is that in many cases it will take about a week or so for many of them to get enough logs to start up again," said Peter Affleck, vice-president of forestry at the Council of Forest Industries in Kelowna, B.C.

However, Mr. Dallimore said any decline from existing price levels may be gradual because inventories remain relatively low, and the construction sector still needs lumber. He is not alone in taking that view.

"Prices will stay quite high for at least another month and then ease off in the fourth quarter," said Patricia Mohr, vice-president of economics at Bank of Nova Scotia in Toronto.

Some people believe the cash price of western SPF [spruce–pine–fir] two-by-four construction lumber—which traded at $370 for 1,000 board feet yesterday will go as low as $270, Ms. Mohr said.

However, prices may be supported in the near term by fears of how much damage the fires have done to logs, especially in B.C., she said.

Industry officials say it is still too early to determine how much of the damaged wood will turn out to be salvageable. "The actual harvesting of the charred wood is not going to be pleasant," Mr. Affleck said. "The job will be dirty, black and difficult."

Source: *The Globe and Mail,* September 12, 2003.

FIGURE 4.12

A Shift in Both Supply and Demand

Here we observe a simultaneous increase in demand and decrease in supply. Two outcomes are possible. In panel (a), the equilibrium price rises from P_1 to P_2, and the equilibrium quantity rises from Q_1 to Q_2. In panel (b), the equilibrium price again rises from P_1 to P_2, but the equilibrium quantity falls from Q_1 to Q_2.

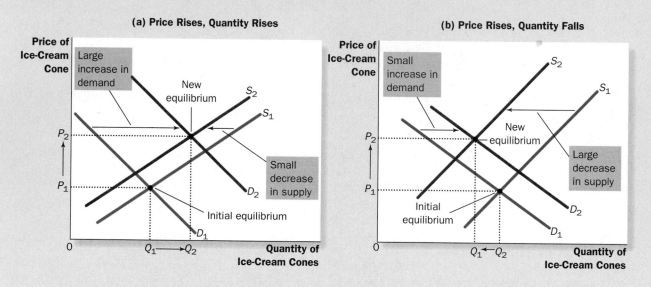

3. As Figure 4.12 shows, there are two possible outcomes that might result, depending on the relative size of the demand and supply shifts. In both cases, the equilibrium price rises. In panel (a), where demand increases substantially while supply falls just a little, the equilibrium quantity also rises. By contrast, in panel (b), where supply falls substantially while demand rises just a little, the equilibrium quantity falls. Thus, these events certainly raise the price of ice cream, but their impact on the amount of ice cream sold is ambiguous (that is, it could go either way).

Summary We have just seen three examples of how to use supply and demand curves to analyze a change in equilibrium. Whenever an event shifts the supply curve, the demand curve, or perhaps both curves, you can use these tools to predict how the event will alter the amount sold in equilibrium and the price at which the good is sold. Table 4.4 shows the predicted outcome for any combination of shifts in the two curves. To make sure you understand how to use the tools of supply and demand, pick a few entries in this table and make sure you can explain to yourself why the table contains the prediction it does.

TABLE 4.4

What Happens to Price and Quantity When Supply or Demand Shifts?

As a quick quiz, make sure you can explain each of the entries in this table using a supply-and-demand diagram.

	No Change in Supply	An Increase in Supply	A Decrease in Supply
No Change in Demand	P same Q same	P down Q up	P up Q down
An Increase in Demand	P up Q up	P ambiguous Q up	P up Q ambiguous
A Decrease in Demand	P down Q down	P down Q ambiguous	P ambiguous Q down

QuickQuiz Analyze what happens to the market for pizza if the price of tomatoes rises. • Analyze what happens to the market for pizza if the price of hamburgers falls.

CONCLUSION: HOW PRICES ALLOCATE RESOURCES

This chapter has analyzed supply and demand in a single market. Although our discussion has centred around the market for ice cream, the lessons learned here apply in most other markets as well. Whenever you go to a store to buy something, you are contributing to the demand for that item. Whenever you look for a job, you are contributing to the supply of labour services. Because supply and demand are such pervasive economic phenomena, the model of supply and demand is a powerful tool for analysis. We will be using this model repeatedly in the following chapters.

One of the ten principles of economics discussed in Chapter 1 is that markets are usually a good way to organize economic activity. Although it is still too early to judge whether market outcomes are good or bad, in this chapter we have begun to see how markets work. In any economic system, scarce resources have to be allocated among competing uses. Market economies harness the forces of supply and demand to serve that end. Supply and demand together determine the prices of the economy's many different goods and services; prices in turn are the signals that guide the allocation of resources.

For example, consider the allocation of beachfront land. Because the amount of this land is limited, not everyone can enjoy the luxury of living by the beach. Who gets this resource? The answer is: whoever is willing to pay the price. The price of beachfront land adjusts until the quantity of land demanded exactly balances the quantity supplied. Thus, in market economies, prices are the mechanism for rationing scarce resources.

Similarly, prices determine who produces each good and how much is produced. For instance, consider farming. Because we need food to survive, it is crucial that some people work on farms. What determines who is a farmer and who is not? In a free society, there is no government planning agency making this decision and ensuring an adequate supply of food. Instead, the allocation of workers to farms is based on the job decisions of millions of workers. This decentralized system works well because these decisions depend on prices. The prices of food and the wages of farmworkers (the price of their labour) adjust to ensure that enough people choose to be farmers.

If a person had never seen a market economy in action, the whole idea might seem preposterous. Economies are large groups of people engaged in many interdependent activities. What prevents decentralized decision making from degenerating into chaos? What coordinates the actions of the millions of people with their varying abilities and desires? What ensures that what needs to be done does in fact get done? The answer, in a word, is *prices*. If market economies are guided by an invisible hand, as Adam Smith famously suggested, then the price system is the baton that the invisible hand uses to conduct the economic orchestra.

SUMMARY

- Economists use the model of supply and demand to analyze competitive markets. In a competitive market, there are many buyers and sellers, each of whom has little or no influence on the market price.

- The demand curve shows how the quantity of a good demanded depends on the price. According to the law of demand, as the price of a good falls, the quantity demanded rises. Therefore, the demand curve slopes downward.

- In addition to price, other determinants of how much consumers want to buy include income, the prices of substitutes and complements, tastes, expectations, and the number of buyers. If one of these factors changes, the demand curve shifts.

- The supply curve shows how the quantity of a good supplied depends on the price. According to the law of supply, as the price of a good rises, the quantity supplied rises. Therefore, the supply curve slopes upward.

- In addition to price, other determinants of how much producers want to sell include input prices, technology, expectations, and the number of sellers. If one of these factors changes, the supply curve shifts.

- The intersection of the supply and demand curves determines the market equilibrium. At the equilibrium price, the quantity demanded equals the quantity supplied.

- The behaviour of buyers and sellers naturally drives markets toward their equilibrium. When the market price is above the equilibrium price, there is a surplus of the good, which causes the market price to fall. When the market price is below the equilibrium price, there is a shortage, which causes the market price to rise.

- To analyze how any event influences a market, we use the supply-and-demand diagram to examine how the event affects the equilibrium price and quantity. To do this we follow three steps. First, we decide whether the event shifts the supply curve or the demand curve (or both). Second, we decide which direction the curve shifts. Third, we compare the new equilibrium with the initial equilibrium.

- In market economies, prices are the signals that guide economic decisions and thereby allocate scarce resources. For every good in the economy, the price ensures that supply and demand are in balance. The equilibrium price then determines how much of the good buyers choose to purchase and how much sellers choose to produce.

KEY CONCEPTS

market, p. 66
competitive market, p. 66
quantity demanded, p. 67
law of demand, p. 68
demand schedule, p. 68
demand curve, p. 68
normal good, p. 70

inferior good, p. 70
substitutes, p. 71
complements, p. 71
quantity supplied, p. 73
law of supply, p. 73
supply schedule, p. 74
supply curve, p. 74

equilibrium, p. 77
equilibrium price, p. 77
equilibrium quantity, p. 77
surplus, p. 78
shortage, p. 78
law of supply and demand, p. 79

QUESTIONS FOR REVIEW

1. What is a competitive market? Briefly describe the types of markets other than perfectly competitive markets.

2. What determines the quantity of a good that buyers demand?

3. What are the demand schedule and the demand curve, and how are they related? Why does the demand curve slope downward?

4. Does a change in consumers' tastes lead to a movement along the demand curve or a shift in the demand curve? Does a change in price lead to a movement along the demand curve or a shift in the demand curve?

5. Popeye's income declines and, as a result, he buys more spinach. Is spinach an inferior or a normal good? What happens to Popeye's demand curve for spinach?

6. What determines the quantity of a good that sellers supply?

7. What are the supply schedule and the supply curve, and how are they related? Why does the supply curve slope upward?

8. Does a change in producers' technology lead to a movement along the supply curve or a shift in the supply curve? Does a change in price lead to a movement along the supply curve or a shift in the supply curve?

9. Define the equilibrium of a market. Describe the forces that move a market toward its equilibrium.

10. Beer and pizza are complements because they are often enjoyed together. When the price of beer rises, what happens to the supply, demand, quantity supplied, quantity demanded, and the price in the market for pizza?

11. Describe the role of prices in market economies.

PROBLEMS AND APPLICATIONS

1. Explain each of the following statements using supply-and-demand diagrams.
   a. When a cold snap hits Florida, the price of orange juice rises in supermarkets throughout Canada.
   b. When the weather turns warm in Quebec every summer, the prices of hotel rooms in Caribbean resorts plummet.
   c. When a war breaks out in the Middle East, the price of gasoline rises, while the price of a used SUV falls.

2. "An increase in the demand for notebooks raises the quantity of notebooks demanded, but not the quantity supplied." Is this statement true or false? Explain.

3. Consider the market for minivans. For each of the events listed here, identify which of the determinants of demand or supply are affected. Also indicate whether demand or supply is increased or decreased. Then show the effect on the price and quantity of minivans.
   a. People decide to have more children.

b. A strike by steelworkers raises steel prices.

c. Engineers develop new automated machinery for the production of minivans.

d. The price of SUVs rises.

e. A stock market crash lowers people's wealth.

4. During the 1990s, technological advances reduced the cost of computer chips. How do you think this affected the market for computers? For computer software? For typewriters?

5. Using supply-and-demand diagrams, show the effect of the following events on the market for sweatshirts.

a. A hurricane in South Carolina damages the cotton crop.

b. The price of leather jackets falls.

c. All colleges require morning calisthenics in appropriate attire.

d. New knitting machines are invented.

6. Suppose that in the year 2005 the number of births is temporarily high. How does this baby boom affect the price of baby-sitting services in 2010 and 2020? (Hint: 5-year-olds need baby-sitters, whereas 15-year-olds can be baby-sitters.)

7. Ketchup is a complement (as well as a condiment) for hot dogs. If the price of hot dogs rises, what happens to the market for ketchup? For tomatoes? For tomato juice? For orange juice?

8. The case study presented in the chapter discussed cigarette taxes as a way to reduce smoking. Now think about the markets for other tobacco products such as cigars and chewing tobacco.

a. Are these goods substitutes or complements for cigarettes?

b. Using a supply-and-demand diagram, show what happens in the markets for cigars and chewing tobacco if the tax on cigarettes is increased.

c. If policymakers wanted to reduce total tobacco consumption, what policies could they combine with the cigarette tax?

9. The market for pizza has the following demand and supply schedules:

Price	Quantity Demanded	Quantity Supplied
$4	135	26
5	104	53
6	81	81
7	68	98
8	53	110
9	39	121

Graph the demand and supply curves. What is the equilibrium price and quantity in this market? If the actual price in this market were *above* the equilibrium price, what would drive the market toward the equilibrium? If the actual price in this market were *below* the equilibrium price, what would drive the market toward the equilibrium?

10. Because bagels and cream cheese are often eaten together, they are complements.

a. We observe that both the equilibrium price of cream cheese and the equilibrium quantity of bagels have risen. What could be responsible for this pattern—a fall in the price of flour or a fall in the price of milk? Illustrate and explain your answer.

b. Suppose instead that the equilibrium price of cream cheese has risen but the equilibrium quantity of bagels has fallen. What could be responsible for this pattern—a rise in the price of flour or a rise in the price of milk? Illustrate and explain your answer.

11. Suppose that the price of basketball tickets at your school is determined by market forces. Currently, the demand and supply schedules are as follows:

Price	Quantity Demanded	Quantity Supplied
$4	10 000	8000
8	8 000	8000
12	6 000	8000
16	4 000	8000
20	2 000	8000

a. Draw the demand and supply curves. What is unusual about this supply curve? Why might this be true?

b. What are the equilibrium price and quantity of tickets?

c. Your school plans to increase total enrollment next year by 5000 students. The additional students will have the following demand schedule:

Price	Quantity Demanded
$4	4000
8	3000
12	2000
16	1000
20	0

Now add the old demand schedule and the demand schedule for the new students to calculate the new demand schedule for the entire school. What will be the new equilibrium price and quantity?

12. An article in *The New York Times* described a successful marketing campaign by the French champagne industry. The article noted that "many executives felt giddy about the stratospheric champagne prices. But they also feared that such sharp price increases would cause demand to decline, which would then cause prices to plunge." What mistake are the executives making in their analysis of the situation? Illustrate your answer with a graph.

13. Market research has revealed the following information about the market for chocolate bars: The demand schedule can be represented by the equation $Q^D = 1600 - 300P$, where Q^D is the quantity demanded and P is the price. The supply schedule can be represented by the equation $Q^S = 1400 + 700P$, where Q^S is the quantity supplied. Calculate the equilibrium price and quantity in the market for chocolate bars.

14. What do we mean by a perfectly competitive market? Do you think that the example of ice cream used in this chapter fits this description? Is there another type of market that better characterizes the market for ice cream?

INTERNET RESOURCES

Economist Alfred Marshall published his *Principles of Economics* in 1890. You can read the entire book online at http://www.econlib.org/library/Marshall/marP.html. Although Marshall's book is over 100 years old, you can still recognize it as an introductory textbook—as the great-great-grandfather of this textbook. Just like modern economists, Marshall thought about demand and supply as schedules or curves, as a relationship between price and quantity. You will find what Marshall has to say about demand and supply in Book V of his *Principles of Economics*.

http://   For more study tools, please visit http://www.mankiw3e.nelson.com.

3

THE DATA OF MACROECONOMICS

© F. HUDEC / FIRSTLIGHT

5

Learning Objectives

In this chapter, you will …

- Consider why an economy's total income equals its total expenditure
- Learn how gross domestic product (GDP) is defined and calculated
- See the breakdown of GDP into its four major components
- Learn the distinction between real GDP and nominal GDP

MEASURING A NATION'S INCOME

When you finish school and start looking for a full-time job, your experience will, to a large extent, be shaped by prevailing economic conditions. In some years, firms throughout the economy are expanding their production of goods and services, employment is rising, and jobs are easy to find. In other years, firms are cutting back on production, employment is declining, and finding a good job takes a long time. Not surprisingly, any college or university graduate would rather enter the labour force in a year of economic expansion than in a year of economic contraction.

Because the condition of the overall economy profoundly affects all of us, changes in economic conditions are widely reported by the media. Indeed, it is hard to pick up a newspaper without seeing some newly reported statistic about the economy. The statistic might measure the total income of everyone in the economy (GDP), the rate at which average prices are rising (inflation), the percentage of the labour force that is out of work (unemployment), total spending at stores (retail sales), or the imbalance of trade between Canada and the rest of the world (the trade deficit). All of these statistics are *macroeconomic*. Rather than

microeconomics
the study of how households and firms make decisions and how they interact in markets

macroeconomics
the study of economy-wide phenomena, including inflation, unemployment, and economic growth

telling us about a particular household or firm, they tell us something about the entire economy.

As you may recall from Chapter 2, economics is divided into two branches: microeconomics and macroeconomics. **Microeconomics** is the study of how individual households and firms make decisions and how they interact with one another in markets. **Macroeconomics** is the study of the economy as a whole. The goal of macroeconomics is to explain the economic changes that affect many households, firms, and markets simultaneously. Macroeconomists address diverse questions: Why is average income high in some countries while it is low in others? Why do prices rise rapidly in some periods of time while they are more stable in other periods? Why do production and employment expand in some years and contract in others? What, if anything, can the government do to promote rapid growth in incomes, low inflation, and stable employment? These questions are all macroeconomic in nature because they concern the workings of the entire economy.

Because the economy as a whole is just a collection of many households and many firms interacting in many markets, microeconomics and macroeconomics are closely linked. The basic tools of supply and demand, for instance, are as central to macroeconomic analysis as they are to microeconomic analysis. Yet studying the economy in its entirety raises some new and intriguing challenges.

In this chapter and the next one, we discuss some of the data that economists and policymakers use to monitor the performance of the overall economy. These data reflect the economic changes that macroeconomists try to explain. This chapter considers *gross domestic product,* or simply GDP, which measures the total income of a nation. GDP is the most closely watched economic statistic because it is thought to be the best single measure of a society's economic well-being.

THE ECONOMY'S INCOME AND EXPENDITURE

If you were to judge how a person is doing economically, you might first look at that person's income. A person with a high income can more easily afford life's necessities and luxuries. It is no surprise that people with higher incomes enjoy higher standards of living—better housing, better food, fancier cars, more opulent vacations, and so on.

The same logic applies to a nation's overall economy. When judging whether the economy is doing well or poorly, it is natural to look at the total income that everyone in the economy is earning. That is the task of gross domestic product.

GDP measures two things at once: the total income of everyone in the economy and the total expenditure on the economy's output of goods and services. The reason that GDP can perform the trick of measuring both total income and total expenditure is that these two things are really the same. *For an economy as a whole, income must equal expenditure.*

Why is this true? An economy's income is the same as its expenditure because every transaction has two parties: a buyer and a seller. Every dollar of spending by some buyer is a dollar of income for some seller. Suppose, for instance, that Karen pays Doug $100 to mow her lawn. In this case, Doug is a seller of a service, and Karen is a buyer. Doug earns $100, and Karen spends $100. Thus, the transaction contributes equally to the economy's income and to its expenditure. GDP, whether measured as total income or total expenditure, rises by $100.

FIGURE 5.1

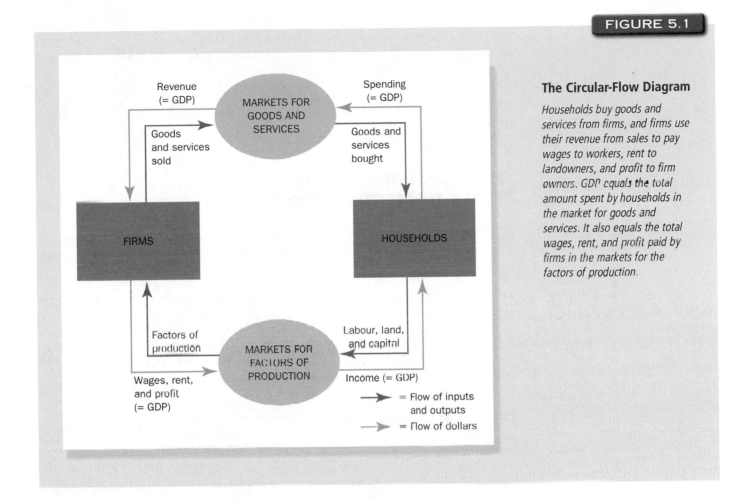

The Circular-Flow Diagram

Households buy goods and services from firms, and firms use their revenue from sales to pay wages to workers, rent to landowners, and profit to firm owners. GDP equals the total amount spent by households in the market for goods and services. It also equals the total wages, rent, and profit paid by firms in the markets for the factors of production.

Another way to see the equality of income and expenditure is with the circular-flow diagram in Figure 5.1. (You may recall this circular-flow diagram from Chapter 2.) The diagram describes all the transactions between households and firms in a simple economy. In this economy, households buy goods and services from firms; these expenditures flow through the markets for goods and services. The firms in turn use the money they receive from sales to pay workers' wages, landowners' rent, and firm owners' profit; this income flows through the markets for the factors of production. In this economy, money flows from households to firms and then back to households.

We can compute GDP for this economy in one of two ways: by adding up the total expenditure by households or by adding up the total income (wages, rent, and profit) paid by firms. Because all expenditure in the economy ends up as someone's income, GDP is the same regardless of how we compute it.

The actual economy is, of course, more complicated than the one illustrated in Figure 5.1. In particular, households do not spend all of their income. They pay some of it to the government in taxes, and they save some for use in the future. In addition, households do not buy all goods and services produced in the economy. Some goods and services are bought by governments, and some are bought by firms that plan to use them in the future to produce their own output. Yet, regardless of whether a household, government, or firm buys a good or service, the transaction has a buyer and seller. Thus, for the economy as a whole, expenditure and income are always the same.

QuickQuiz What two things does gross domestic product measure? How can it measure two things at once?

THE MEASUREMENT OF GROSS DOMESTIC PRODUCT

Now that we have discussed the meaning of gross domestic product in general terms, let's be more precise about how this statistic is measured. Here is a definition of GDP:

gross domestic product (GDP)
the market value of all final goods and services produced within a country in a given period of time

- **Gross domestic product (GDP)** is the market value of all final goods and services produced within a country in a given period of time.

This definition might seem simple enough. But, in fact, many subtle issues arise when computing an economy's GDP. Let's therefore consider each phrase in this definition with some care.

"GDP Is the Market Value . . ."

You have probably heard the adage, "You can't compare apples and oranges." Yet GDP does exactly that. GDP adds together many different kinds of products into a single measure of the value of economic activity. To do this, it uses market prices. Because market prices measure the amount people are willing to pay for different goods, they reflect the value of those goods. If the price of an apple is twice the price of an orange, then an apple contributes twice as much to GDP as does an orange.

". . . Of All . . ."

GDP tries to be comprehensive. It includes all items produced in the economy and sold legally in markets. GDP measures the market value of not just apples and oranges, but also pears and grapefruit, books and movies, haircuts and health care, and on and on.

GDP also includes the market value of the housing services provided by the economy's stock of housing. For rental housing, this value is easy to calculate—the rent equals both the tenant's expenditure and the landlord's income. Yet many people own the place where they live and, therefore, do not pay rent. The government includes this owner-occupied housing in GDP by estimating its rental value. That is, GDP is based on the assumption that the owner, in effect, pays rent to himself, so the rent is included both in his expenditure and in his income.

There are some products, however, that GDP excludes because measuring them is so difficult. GDP excludes most items produced and sold illicitly, such as illegal drugs. It also excludes most items that are produced and consumed at home and, therefore, never enter the marketplace. Vegetables you buy at the grocery store are part of GDP; vegetables you grow in your garden are not.

These exclusions from GDP can at times lead to paradoxical results. For example, when Karen pays Doug to mow her lawn, that transaction is part of GDP. If Karen were to marry Doug, the situation would change. Even though Doug may continue to mow Karen's lawn, the value of the mowing is now left out of GDP because Doug's service is no longer sold in a market. Thus, when Karen and Doug marry, GDP falls.

". . . Final . . ."

When E.B. Eddy makes paper, which Carlton Cards then uses to make a greeting card, the paper is called an *intermediate good,* and the card is called a *final good.* GDP includes only the value of final goods. The reason is that the value of intermediate goods is already included in the prices of the final goods. Adding the market value of the paper to the market value of the card would be double counting. That is, it would (incorrectly) count the paper twice.

An important exception to this principle arises when an intermediate good is produced and, rather than being used, is added to a firm's inventory of goods to be used or sold at a later date. In this case, the intermediate good is taken to be "final" for the moment, and its value as inventory investment is added to GDP. When the inventory of the intermediate good is later used or sold, the firm's inventory investment is negative, and GDP for the later period is reduced accordingly.

". . . Goods and Services . . ."

GDP includes both tangible goods (food, clothing, cars) and intangible services (haircuts, housecleaning, dentist visits). When you buy a CD by your favourite band, you are buying a good, and the purchase price is part of GDP. When you pay to hear a concert by the same band, you are buying a service, and the ticket price is also part of GDP.

". . . Produced . . ."

GDP includes goods and services currently produced. It does not include transactions involving items produced in the past. When General Motors produces and sells a new car, the value of the car is included in GDP. When one person sells a used car to another person, the value of the used car is not included in GDP.

". . . Within a Country . . ."

GDP measures the value of production within the geographic confines of a country. When a British citizen works temporarily in Canada, his production is part of Canadian GDP. When a Canadian citizen owns a factory in Haiti, the production at her factory is not part of Canadian GDP. (It is part of Haiti's GDP.) Thus, items are included in a nation's GDP if they are produced domestically, regardless of the nationality of the producer.

". . . In a Given Period of Time"

GDP measures the value of production that takes place within a specific interval of time. Usually that interval is a year or a quarter (three months). GDP measures the economy's flow of income and expenditure during that interval.

When the government reports the GDP for a quarter, it usually presents GDP "at an annual rate." This means that the figure reported for quarterly GDP is the amount of income and expenditure during the quarter multiplied by 4. The

FYI

OTHER MEASURES OF INCOME

When Statistics Canada computes the nation's GDP every three months, it also computes various other measures of income to get a more complete picture of what's happening in the economy. These other measures differ from GDP by excluding or including certain categories of income. What follows is a brief description of five of these income measures, ordered from largest to smallest.

- *Gross national product (GNP)* is the total income earned by a nation's permanent residents (called *nationals*). It differs from GDP by including income that our citizens earn abroad and excluding income that foreigners earn here. For example, when a British citizen works temporarily in Canada, his production is part of Canadian GDP, but it is not part of Canadian GNP. (It is part of Britain's GNP.) For most countries, including Canada, domestic residents are responsible for most domestic production, so GDP and GNP are quite close.
- *Net national product (NNP)* is the total income of a nation's residents (GNP) minus losses from depreciation. *Depreciation* is the wear and tear on the economy's stock of equipment and structures, such as trucks rusting and computers becoming obsolete.

In the national income accounts prepared by Statistics Canada, depreciation is called the "capital consumption allowance."

- *National income* is the total income earned by a nation's residents in the production of goods and services. It differs from net national product by excluding indirect business taxes (such as sales taxes) and including business subsidies. NNP and national income also differ because of a "statistical discrepancy" that arises from problems in data collection.
- *Personal income* is the income that households and noncorporate businesses receive. Unlike national income, it excludes *retained earnings*, which is income that corporations have earned but have not paid out to their owners. It also subtracts corporate income taxes and contributions for social insurance (mostly Employment Insurance taxes). In addition, personal income includes the interest income that households receive from their holdings of government debt and the income that households receive from government transfer programs, such as welfare, Canada Pension Plan, and Employment Insurance benefits.
- *Disposable personal income* is the income that households and noncorporate businesses have left after satisfying all their obligations to the government. It equals personal income minus personal taxes and certain nontax payments (such as traffic tickets).

Although the various measures of income differ in detail, they almost always tell the same story about economic conditions. When GDP is growing rapidly, these other measures of income are usually growing rapidly. And when GDP is falling, these other measures are usually falling as well. For monitoring fluctuations in the overall economy, it does not matter much which measure of income we use.

government uses this convention so that quarterly and annual figures on GDP can be compared more easily.

In addition, when the government reports quarterly GDP, it presents the data after they have been modified by a statistical procedure called *seasonal adjustment.* The unadjusted data show clearly that the economy produces more goods and services during some times of year than during others. (As you might guess, December's holiday shopping season is a high point.) When monitoring the condition of the economy, economists and policymakers often want to look beyond these regular seasonal changes. Therefore, government statisticians adjust the quarterly data to take out the seasonal cycle. The GDP data reported in the news are always seasonally adjusted.

Now let's repeat the definition of GDP:

- Gross domestic product (GDP) is the market value of all final goods and services produced within a country in a given period of time.

It should be apparent that GDP is a sophisticated measure of the value of economic activity. In advanced courses in macroeconomics, you will learn more about the subtleties that arise in its calculation. But even now you can see that each phrase in this definition is packed with meaning.

QuickQuiz Which contributes more to GDP—the production of a kilogram of hamburger or the production of a kilogram of caviar? Why?

THE COMPONENTS OF GDP

Spending in the economy takes many forms. At any moment, the Smith family may be having breakfast at Tim Horton's, General Motors may be building a car factory; the Canadian Forces may be repairing a submarine; and British Airways may be buying an airplane from Bombardier. GDP includes all of these various forms of spending on domestically produced goods and services.

To understand how the economy is using its scarce resources, economists are often interested in studying the composition of GDP among various types of spending. To do this, GDP (which we denote as Y) is divided into four components: consumption (C), investment (I), government purchases (G), and net exports (NX):

$$Y = C + I + G + NX$$

This equation is an *identity*—an equation that must be true by the way the variables in the equation are defined. In this case, because each dollar of expenditure included in GDP is placed into one of the four components of GDP, the total of the four components must be equal to GDP. Let's look at each of these four components more closely.

Consumption

consumption
spending by households on goods and services, with the exception of purchases of new housing

Consumption is spending by households on goods and services. "Goods" include household spending on durable goods, such as automobiles and appliances, and nondurable goods, such as food and clothing. "Services" include such intangible items as haircuts and dental care. Household spending on postsecondary education is also included in consumption of services (although one might argue that it would fit better in the next component).

Investment

investment
spending on capital equipment, inventories, and structures, including household purchases of new housing

Investment is the purchase of goods that will be used in the future to produce more goods and services. It is the sum of purchases of capital equipment, inventories, and structures. Investment in structures includes expenditure on new housing. By convention, the purchase of a new house is the one form of household spending categorized as investment rather than consumption.

As mentioned earlier in this chapter, the treatment of inventory accumulation is noteworthy. When IBM produces a computer and, instead of selling it, adds it to its inventory, IBM is assumed to have "purchased" the computer for itself. That is, the national income accountants treat the computer as part of IBM's investment spending. (If IBM later sells the computer out of inventory, IBM's inventory investment will then be negative, offseting the positive expenditure of the buyer.) Inventories are treated this way because one aim of GDP is to measure the value of the economy's production, and goods added to inventory are part of that period's production.

Government Purchases

government purchases
spending on goods and services by local, provincial, and federal governments

Government purchases include spending on goods and services by local, provincial, and federal governments. It includes the salaries of government workers and spending on public works.

The meaning of "government purchases" requires a bit of clarification. When the government pays the salary of a Canadian Forces general, that salary is part of government purchases. But what happens when the government pays a Canada Pension Plan benefit to one of the elderly? Such government spending is called a *transfer payment* because it is not made in exchange for a currently produced good or service. Transfer payments alter household income, but they do not reflect the economy's production. (From a macroeconomic standpoint, transfer payments are like negative taxes.) Because GDP is intended to measure income from, and expenditure on, the production of goods and services, transfer payments are not counted as part of government purchases.

Net Exports

net exports
spending on domestically produced goods by foreigners (exports) minus spending on foreign goods by domestic residents (imports)

Net exports equal the purchases of domestically produced goods by foreigners (exports) minus the domestic purchases of foreign goods (imports). A domestic firm's sale to a buyer in another country, such as the Bombardier sale to British Airways, increases net exports.

The "net" in "net exports" refers to the fact that imports are subtracted from exports. This subtraction is made because imports of goods and services are included in other components of GDP. For example, suppose that a household buys a $30 000 car from Volkswagen, the German carmaker. That transaction increases consumption by $30 000 because car purchases are part of consumer spending. It also reduces net exports by $30 000 because the car is an import. In other words, net exports include goods and services produced abroad (with a minus sign) because these goods and services are included in consumption, investment, and government purchases (with a plus sign). Thus, when a domestic household, firm, or government buys a good or service from abroad, the purchase reduces net exports—but because it also raises consumption, investment, or government purchases, it does not affect GDP.

Case Study
THE COMPONENTS OF CANADIAN GDP

Tables 5.1 and 5.2 both show the composition of Canadian GDP in the third quarter of 2003, seasonally adjusted at annual rates. Table 5.1 shows the composition of GDP by category of expenditure, while Table 5.2 shows the composition of GDP by category of income. Remember that there are two ways to calculate GDP. Table 5.1 shows the expenditure approach, and Table 5.2 shows the income approach.

The annual GDP of Canada was about $1216 billion. If we divide this number by the 2003 Canadian population of approximately 31.6 million, we find that GDP per person—the amount of expenditure for the average Canadian—was about $38 481 per year. ●

TABLE 5.1

	Total ($billions/year)	Per Person ($/year)	% of Total
Gross domestic product, Y	$1216	$38 481	100%
Consumption, C	698	22 088	58
Investment, I	200	6 329	16
Government purchases, G	266	8 418	22
Net exports, NX	52	1 646	4
(equals exports	= ($454	= ($14 367	= (37%
minus imports)	− $402)	− $12 721)	− 33%)

GDP: Total Expenditure and Its Components

This table shows total GDP for the Canadian economy in the third quarter of 2003 (at an annual rate) and the breakdown of GDP between different catagories of expenditure. When reading the table, recall the identity $Y = C + I + G + NX$.

Source: Statistics Canada.

TABLE 5.2

GDP: Total Income and Its Components

This table shows total GDP for the Canadian economy in the third quarter of 2003 (at an annual rate) and the breakdown of GDP between different categories of income.

Source: Statistics Canada.

	Total ($billions/year)	Per Person ($/year)	% of Total
Gross domestic product, Y	$1216	$38 481	100%
Wages and salaries	620	19 620	51
Corporation profits before tax	144	4 557	12
Government enterprise profits	10	316	1
Interest and other investment income	52	1 646	4
Other business income	79	2 500	6
Indirect taxes	146	4 620	12
Capital consumption allowance	165	5 222	14

QuickQuiz List the four components of expenditure. Which is the largest?

REAL VERSUS NOMINAL GDP

As we have seen, GDP measures the total spending on goods and services in all markets in the economy. If total spending rises from one year to the next, one of two things must be true: (1) the economy is producing a larger output of goods and services, or (2) goods and services are being sold at higher prices. When studying changes in the economy over time, economists want to separate these two effects. In particular, they want a measure of the total quantity of goods and services the economy is producing that is not affected by changes in the prices of those goods and services.

To do this, economists use a measure called *real GDP*. Real GDP answers a hypothetical question: What would be the value of the goods and services produced this year if we valued these goods and services at the prices that prevailed in some specific year in the past? By evaluating current production using prices that are fixed at past levels, real GDP shows how the economy's overall production of goods and services changes over time.

To see more precisely how real GDP is constructed, let's consider an example.

A Numerical Example

Table 5.3 shows some data for an economy that produces only two goods—hot dogs and hamburgers. The table shows the quantities of the two goods produced and their prices in the years 2001, 2002, and 2003.

To compute total spending in this economy, we would multiply the quantities of hot dogs and hamburgers by their prices. In the year 2001, 100 hot dogs are sold at a price of $1 per hot dog, so expenditure on hot dogs equals $100. In the same year, 50 hamburgers are sold for $2 per hamburger, so expenditure on hamburgers also equals $100. Total expenditure in the economy—the sum of expenditure on hot dogs and expenditure on hamburgers—is $200. This amount, the production of goods and services valued at current prices, is called **nominal GDP.**

nominal GDP
the production of goods and services valued at current prices

TABLE 5.3

Real and Nominal GDP

This table shows how to calculate real GDP, nominal GDP, and the GDP deflator for a hypothetical economy that produces only hot dogs and hamburgers.

Prices and Quantities

Year	Price of Hot Dogs	Quantity of Hot Dogs	Price of Hamburgers	Quantity of Hamburgers
2001	$1	100	$2	50
2002	2	150	3	100
2003	3	200	4	150

Calculating Nominal GDP

Year	
2001	($1 per hot dog × 100 hot dogs) + ($2 per hamburger × 50 hamburgers) = $200
2002	($2 per hot dog × 150 hot dogs) + ($3 per hamburger × 100 hamburgers) = $600
2003	($3 per hot dog × 200 hot dogs) + ($4 per hamburger × 150 hamburgers) = $1200

Calculating Real GDP (base year 2001)

Year	
2001	($1 per hot dog × 100 hot dogs) + ($2 per hamburger × 50 hamburgers) = $200
2002	($1 per hot dog × 150 hot dogs) + ($2 per hamburger × 100 hamburgers) = $350
2003	($1 per hot dog × 200 hot dogs) + ($2 per hamburger × 150 hamburgers) = $500

Calculating the GDP Deflator

Year	
2001	($200/$200) × 100 = 100
2002	($600/$350) × 100 = 171
2003	($1200/$500) × 100 = 240

The table shows the calculation of nominal GDP for these three years. Total spending rises from $200 in 2001 to $600 in 2002 and then to $1200 in 2003. Part of this rise is attributable to the increase in the quantities of hot dogs and hamburgers, and part is attributable to the increase in the prices of hot dogs and hamburgers.

To obtain a measure of the amount produced that is not affected by changes in prices, we use **real GDP**, which is the production of goods and services valued at constant prices. We calculate real GDP by first choosing one year as a *base year*. We then use the prices of hot dogs and hamburgers in the base year to compute the value of goods and services in all of the years. In other words, the prices in the base year provide the basis for comparing quantities in different years.

Suppose that we choose 2001 to be the base year in our example. We can then use the prices of hot dogs and hamburgers in 2001 to compute the value of goods and services produced in 2001, 2002, and 2003. Table 5.3 shows these calculations. To compute real GDP for 2001, we use the prices of hot dogs and hamburgers in 2001 (the base year) and the quantities of hot dogs and hamburgers produced in 2001. (Thus, for the base year, real GDP always equals nominal GDP.) To compute real GDP for 2002, we use the prices of hot dogs and hamburgers in 2001 (the base year) and the quantities of hot dogs and hamburgers produced in 2002. Similarly, to compute real GDP for 2003, we use the prices in 2001 and the quantities in 2003. When we find that real GDP has risen from $200 in 2001 to $350 in 2002 and then to $500 in 2003, we know that the increase is attributable to an increase in the quantities produced, because the prices are being held fixed at base-year levels.

real GDP
the production of goods and services valued at constant prices

To sum up: *Nominal GDP uses current prices to place a value on the economy's production of goods and services. Real GDP uses constant base-year prices to place a value on the economy's production of goods and services.* Because real GDP is not affected by changes in prices, changes in real GDP reflect only changes in the amounts being produced. Thus, real GDP is a measure of the economy's production of goods and services.

Our goal in computing GDP is to gauge how well the overall economy is performing. Because real GDP measures the economy's production of goods and services, it reflects the economy's ability to satisfy people's needs and desires. Thus, real GDP is a better gauge of economic well-being than is nominal GDP. When economists talk about the economy's GDP, they usually mean real GDP rather than nominal GDP. And when they talk about growth in the economy, they measure that growth as the percentage change in real GDP from one period to another.

The GDP Deflator

As we have just seen, nominal GDP reflects both the prices of goods and services and the quantities of goods and services the economy is producing. By contrast, by holding prices constant at base-year levels, real GDP reflects only the quantities produced. From these two statistics, we can compute a third, called the GDP deflator, which reflects the prices of goods and services but not the quantities produced.

The **GDP deflator** is calculated as follows:

GDP deflator
a measure of the price level calculated as the ratio of nominal GDP to real GDP times 100

$$\text{GDP deflator} = \frac{\text{Nominal GDP}}{\text{Real GDP}} \times 100$$

Because nominal GDP and real GDP must be the same in the base year, the GDP deflator for the base year always equals 100. The GDP deflator for subsequent years measures the change in nominal GDP from the base year that cannot be attributable to a change in real GDP.

The GDP deflator measures the current level of prices relative to the level of prices in the base year. To see why this is true, consider a couple of simple examples. First, imagine that the quantities produced in the economy rise over time but prices remain the same. In this case, both nominal and real GDP rise together, so the GDP deflator is constant. Now suppose, instead, that prices rise over time but the quantities produced stay the same. In this second case, nominal GDP rises but real GDP remains the same, so the GDP deflator rises as well. Notice that, in both cases, the GDP deflator reflects what's happening to prices, not quantities.

Let's now return to our numerical example in Table 5.3. The GDP deflator is computed at the bottom of the table. For year 2001, nominal GDP is $200, and real GDP is $200, so the GDP deflator is 100. For the year 2002, nominal GDP is $600, and real GDP is $350, so the GDP deflator is 171. Because the GDP deflator rose in year 2002 from 100 to 171, we can say that the price level increased by 71 percent.

The GDP deflator is one measure that economists use to monitor the average level of prices in the economy. We examine another—the consumer price index—in the next chapter, where we also describe the differences between the two measures.

Case Study
REAL GDP OVER RECENT HISTORY

Now that we know how real GDP is defined and measured, let's look at what this macroeconomic variable tells us about the recent history of Canada. Figure 5.2 shows quarterly data on real GDP for the Canadian economy since 1970.

The most obvious feature of these data is that real GDP grows over time. The real GDP of the Canadian economy in 2001 was more than twice its 1970 level. Put differently, the output of goods and services produced in Canada has grown on average about 3 percent per year since 1970. This continued growth in real GDP enables the typical Canadian to enjoy greater economic prosperity than his or her parents and grandparents did.

A second feature of the GDP data is that growth is not steady. The upward climb of real GDP is occasionally interrupted by periods during which GDP declines, called *recessions*. Figure 5.2 marks recessions with shaded vertical bars. (There is no ironclad rule for when we say that a recession has occurred, but a good rule of thumb is two consecutive quarters of falling real GDP.) Recessions are associated not only with lower incomes but also with other forms of economic distress: rising unemployment, falling profits, increased bankruptcies, and so on.

Much of macroeconomics is aimed at explaining the long-run growth and short-run fluctuations in real GDP. As we will see in the coming chapters, we need different models for these two purposes. Because the short-run fluctuations represent deviations from the long-run trend, we first examine the behaviour of key macroeconomic variables, including real GDP, in the long run. Then in later chapters we build on this analysis to explain short-run fluctuations. ●

QuickQuiz Define real and nominal GDP. Which is a better measure of economic well-being? Why?

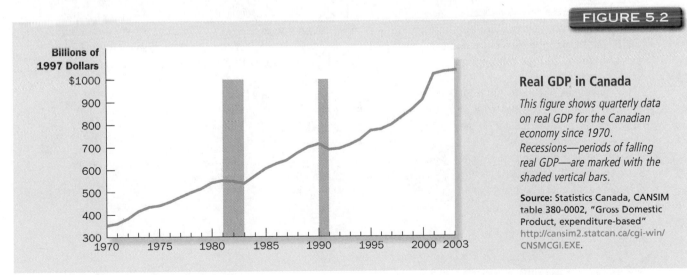

FIGURE 5.2

Real GDP in Canada

This figure shows quarterly data on real GDP for the Canadian economy since 1970. Recessions—periods of falling real GDP—are marked with the shaded vertical bars.

Source: Statistics Canada, CANSIM table 380-0002, "Gross Domestic Product, expenditure-based" http://cansim2.statcan.ca/cgi-win/ CNSMCGI.EXE.

IN THE NEWS

GDP LIGHTENS UP

GDP measures the value of the economy's output of goods and services. What do you think we would learn if, instead, we measured the weight of the economy's output?

From Greenspan, a (Truly) Weighty Idea

By David Wessel

Having weighed the evidence carefully, Federal Reserve Chairman Alan Greenspan wants you to know that the U.S. economy is getting lighter.

Literally.

When he refers to "downsizing" in this instance, Mr. Greenspan means that a dollar's worth of the goods and services produced in the mighty U.S. economy weighs a lot less than it used to, even after adjusting for inflation.

A modern 10-story office building, he says, weighs less than a 10-story building erected in the late 19th century. With synthetic fibers, clothes weigh less. And the electronics revolution has produced televisions so light they can be worn on the wrist.

By conventional measures, the [real] gross domestic product—the value of all goods and services produced in the nation—is five times as great as it was 50 years ago. Yet "the physical weight of our gross domestic product is evidently only modestly higher than it was 50 or 100 years ago," Mr. Greenspan told an audience in Dallas recently.

When you think about it, it's not so surprising that the economy is getting lighter. An ever-growing proportion of the U.S. GDP consists of things that don't weigh anything at all—lawyers' services, psychotherapy, e-mail, online information.

But Mr. Greenspan has a way of making the obvious sound profound. Only "a small fraction" of the nation's economic growth in the past several decades "represents growth in the tonnage of physical materials—oil, coal, ores, wood, raw chemicals," he has observed. "The remainder represents new insights into how to rearrange those physical materials to better serve human needs." . . .

The incredible shrinking GDP helps explain why American workers can produce more for each hour of work than ever before. . . . [It] also helps explain why there is so much international trade these days. "The . . . downsizing of output," Mr. Greenspan said recently, "meant that products were easier and hence less costly to move, and most especially across national borders." . . .

"The world of 1948 was vastly different," Mr. Greenspan observed a few years back. "The quintessential model of industry might in those days was the array of vast, smoke-encased integrated steel mills . . . on the shores of Lake Michigan. Output was things, big physical things."

Today, one exemplar of U.S. economic might is Microsoft Corp., with its almost weightless output. "Virtually unimaginable a half-century ago was the extent to which concepts and ideas would substitute for physical resources and human brawn in the production of goods and services," he has said.

Of course, one thing made in the U.S. is heavier than it used to be: people. The National Institutes of Health says 22.3% of Americans are obese, up from 12.8% in the early 1960s. But Mr. Greenspan doesn't talk about that.

GDP AND ECONOMIC WELL-BEING

Earlier in this chapter, GDP was called the best single measure of the economic well-being of a society. Now that we know what GDP is, we can evaluate this claim.

As we have seen, GDP measures both the economy's total income and the economy's total expenditure on goods and services. Thus, GDP per person tells us the income and expenditure of the average person in the economy. Because most people would prefer to receive higher income and enjoy higher expenditure, GDP per person seems a natural measure of the economic well-being of the average individual.

Yet some people dispute the validity of GDP as a measure of well-being. When Senator Robert Kennedy was running for president of the United States in 1968, he gave a moving critique of such economic measures:

> [Gross domestic product] does not allow for the health of our children, the quality of their education, or the joy of their play. It does not include the beauty of our poetry or the strength of our marriages, the intelligence of our public debate or the integrity of our public officials. It measures neither our courage, nor our wisdom, nor our devotion to our country. It measures everything, in short, except that which makes life worthwhile, and it can tell us everything about America except why we are proud that we are Americans.

Much of what Robert Kennedy said is correct. Why then do we care about GDP?

The answer is that a large GDP does in fact help us to lead a good life. GDP does not measure the health of our children, but nations with larger GDP can afford better health care for their children. GDP does not measure the quality of their education, but nations with larger GDP can afford better educational systems. GDP does not measure the beauty of our poetry, but nations with larger GDP can afford to teach more of their citizens to read and to enjoy poetry. GDP does not take account of our intelligence, integrity, courage, wisdom, or devotion to country, but all of these laudable attributes are easier to foster when people are less concerned about being able to afford the material necessities of life. In short, GDP does not directly measure those things that make life worthwhile, but it does measure our ability to obtain the inputs into a worthwhile life.

GDP is not, however, a perfect measure of well-being. Some things that contribute to a good life are left out of GDP. One is leisure. Suppose, for instance, that everyone in the economy suddenly started working every day of the week, rather than enjoying leisure on weekends. More goods and services would be produced, and GDP would rise. Yet, despite the increase in GDP, we should not conclude that everyone would be better off. The loss from reduced leisure would offset the gain from producing and consuming a greater quantity of goods and services.

Because GDP uses market prices to value goods and services, it excludes the value of almost all activity that takes place outside of markets. In particular, GDP omits the value of goods and services produced at home. When a chef prepares a delicious meal and sells it at his restaurant, the value of that meal is part of GDP. But if the chef prepares the same meal for his spouse, the value he has added to the raw ingredients is left out of GDP. Similarly, child care provided in daycare centres is part of GDP, whereas child care by parents at home is not. Volunteer

GDP reflects the factory's production, but not the harm that it inflicts on the environment.

work also contributes to the well-being of those in society, but GDP does not reflect these contributions.

Another thing that GDP excludes is the quality of the environment. Imagine that the government eliminated all environmental regulations. Firms could then produce goods and services without considering the pollution they create, and GDP might rise. Yet well-being would most likely fall. The deterioration in the quality of air and water would more than offset the gains from greater production.

GDP also says nothing about the distribution of income. A society in which 100 people have annual incomes of $50 000 has GDP of $5 million and, not surprisingly, GDP per person of $50 000. So does a society in which 10 people earn $500 000 and 90 suffer with nothing at all. Few people would look at those two situations and call them equivalent. GDP per person tells us what happens to the average person, but behind the average lies a large variety of personal experiences.

In the end, we can conclude that GDP is a good measure of economic well-being for most—but not all—purposes. It is important to keep in mind what GDP includes and what it leaves out.

Case Study

INTERNATIONAL DIFFERENCES IN GDP AND THE QUALITY OF LIFE

One way to gauge the usefulness of GDP as a measure of economic well-being is to examine international data. Rich and poor countries have vastly different levels of GDP per person. If a large GDP leads to a higher standard of living, then we should observe GDP to be strongly correlated with measures of the quality of life. And, in fact, we do.

Table 5.4 shows Canada and 12 of the world's most populous countries ranked in order of GDP per person. The table also shows life expectancy (the expected life span at birth) and literacy (the percentage of the adult population who can read). These data show a clear pattern. In rich countries, such as Canada, the United States, Germany, and Japan, people can expect to live into their late seventies, and almost all of the population can read. In poor countries, such as Nigeria, Bangladesh, and Pakistan, people typically live only until their fifties or early sixties, and only about half of the population is literate.

Although data on other aspects of the quality of life are less complete, they tell a similar story. Countries with low GDP per person tend to have more infants with low birth weight, higher rates of infant mortality, higher rates of maternal mortality, higher rates of child malnutrition, and less common access to safe drinking water. In countries with low GDP per person, fewer school-age children are actually in school, and those who are in school must learn with fewer teachers per student. These countries also tend to have fewer televisions, fewer telephones, fewer paved roads, and fewer households with electricity. International data leave no doubt that a nation's GDP is closely associated with its citizens' standard of living. ●

TABLE 5.4

Country	Real GDP per Person (2001)	Life Expectancy	Adult Literacy
United States	$34 320	77 years	99%
Canada	27 130	79	99
Germany	25 350	78	99
Japan	25 130	81	99
Mexico	8 430	73	91
Brazil	7 360	68	87
Russia	7 100	67	99
China	4 020	71	86
Indonesia	2 940	66	87
India	2 840	63	58
Pakistan	1 890	60	44
Bangladesh	1 610	60	41
Nigeria	850	52	65

GDP, Life Expectancy, and Literacy

This table shows GDP per person and two measures of the quality of life for 12 major countries.

Source: *Human Development Report 2003*, United Nations.

QuickQuiz Why should policymakers care about GDP?

CONCLUSION

This chapter has discussed how economists measure the total income of a nation. Measurement is, of course, only a starting point. Much of macroeconomics is aimed at revealing the long-run and short-run determinants of a nation's gross domestic product. Why, for example, is GDP higher in Canada, the United States, and Germany than in India and Nigeria? What can the governments of the poorest countries do to promote more rapid growth in GDP? Why does GDP in Canada rise rapidly in some years and fall in others? What can Canadian policymakers do to reduce the severity of these fluctuations in GDP? These are the questions we will take up shortly.

At this point, it is important to acknowledge the importance of just measuring GDP. We all get some sense of how the economy is doing as we go about our lives. But the economists who study changes in the economy and the policymakers who formulate economic policies need more than this vague sense—they need concrete data on which to base their judgments. Quantifying the behaviour of the economy with statistics such as GDP is, therefore, the first step to developing a science of macroeconomics.

SUMMARY

- Every transaction has a buyer and a seller, so the total expenditure in the economy must equal the total income in the economy.

- Gross domestic product (GDP) measures an economy's total expenditure on newly produced goods and services and the total income earned from the production of these goods and services. More precisely, GDP is the market value of all final goods and services produced within a country in a given period of time.

- GDP is divided among four components of expenditure: consumption, investment, government purchases, and net exports. Consumption includes spending on goods and services by households, with the exception of purchases of new housing. Investment includes spending on new equipment and structures, including households' purchases of new housing. Government purchases include

spending on goods and services by local, provincial, and federal governments. Net exports equal the value of goods and services produced domestically and sold abroad (exports) minus the value of goods and services produced abroad and sold domestically (imports).

- Nominal GDP uses current prices to value the economy's production of goods and services. Real GDP uses constant base-year prices to value the economy's production of goods and services. The GDP deflator—calculated from the ratio of nominal to real GDP—measures the level of prices in the economy.

- GDP is a good measure of economic well-being because people prefer higher to lower incomes. But it is not a perfect measure of well-being. For example, GDP excludes the value of leisure and the value of a clean environment.

KEY CONCEPTS

microeconomics, p. 94
macroeconomics, p. 94
gross domestic product (GDP), p. 96

consumption, p. 100
investment, p. 100
government purchases, p. 100
net exports, p. 100

nominal GDP, p. 102
real GDP, p. 103
GDP deflator, p. 104

QUESTIONS FOR REVIEW

1. Explain why an economy's income must equal its expenditure.

2. Which contributes more to GDP—the production of an economy car or the production of a luxury car? Why?

3. A farmer sells wheat to a baker for $2. The baker uses the wheat to make bread, which is sold for $3. What is the total contribution of these transactions to GDP?

4. Many years ago Peggy paid $500 to put together a record collection. Today she sold her albums at a garage sale for $100. How does this sale affect current GDP?

5. List the four components of GDP. Give an example of each.

6. Why do economists use real GDP rather than nominal GDP to gauge economic well-being?

7. In the year 2003, the economy produces 100 loaves of bread that sell for $2 each. In the year 2004, the economy produces 200 loaves of bread that sell for $3 each. Calculate nominal GDP, real GDP, and the GDP deflator for each year. (Use 2003 as the base year.) By what percentage does each of these three statistics rise from one year to the next?

8. Why is it desirable for a country to have a large GDP? Give an example of something that would raise GDP and yet be undesirable.

PROBLEMS AND APPLICATIONS

1. What components of GDP (if any) would each of the following transactions affect? Explain.
   a. A family buys a new refrigerator.
   b. Aunt Jane buys a new house.
   c. Ford sells a Thunderbird from its inventory.
   d. You buy a pizza.
   e. Quebec repaves Highway 50.
   f. Your parents buy a bottle of French wine.
   g. Honda expands its factory in Alliston, Ontario.

2. The "government purchases" component of GDP does not include spending on transfer payments such as Employment Insurance. Thinking about the definition of GDP, explain why transfer payments are excluded.

3. Why do you think households' purchases of new housing are included in the investment component of GDP rather than the consumption component? Can you think of a reason why households' purchases of new cars should also be included in investment rather than in consumption? To what other consumption goods might this logic apply?

4. As the chapter states, GDP does not include the value of used goods that are resold. Why would including such transactions make GDP a less informative measure of economic well-being?

5. Below are some data from the land of milk and honey.

Year	Price of Milk	Quantity of Milk (litres)	Price of Honey	Quantity of Honey (litres)
2001	$1	100	$2	50
2002	1	200	2	100
2003	2	200	4	100

   a. Compute nominal GDP, real GDP, and the GDP deflator for each year, using 2001 as the base year.
   b. Compute the percentage change in nominal GDP, real GDP, and the GDP deflator in 2002 and 2003 from the preceding year. For each year, identify the variable that does not change. Explain in words why your answer makes sense.

   c. Did economic well-being rise more in 2002 or 2003? Explain.

6. Consider the following data on Canadian GDP:

Year	Nominal GDP (in billions)	GDP Deflator (base year 1997)
2000	1075	105
1999	982	101

   a. What was the growth rate of nominal GDP between 1999 and 2000? (Note: The growth rate is the percentage change from one period to the next.)
   b. What was the growth rate of the GDP deflator between 1999 and 2000?
   c. What was real GDP in 1999 measured in 1997 prices?
   d. What was real GDP in 2000 measured in 1997 prices?
   e. What was the growth rate of real GDP between 1999 and 2000?
   f. Was the growth rate of nominal GDP higher or lower than the growth rate of real GDP? Explain.

7. If prices rise, people's income from selling goods increases. The growth of real GDP ignores this gain, however. Why, then, do economists prefer real GDP as a measure of economic well-being?

8. Revised estimates of Canadian GDP are usually released by Statistics Canada near the end of each month. Find a newspaper article that reports on the most recent release, or read the news release yourself at http://www.statcan.ca, the website of Statistics Canada. Discuss the recent changes in real and nominal GDP and in the components of GDP.

9. One day Barry the Barber, Inc., collects $400 for haircuts. Over this day, his equipment depreciates in value by $50. Of the remaining $350, Barry sends $30 to the government in sales taxes, takes home $220 in wages, and retains $100 in his business to add new equipment in the future. From the $220 that Barry takes home, he pays $70 in income taxes. Based on this information, compute Barry's contribution to the following measures of income.

a. gross domestic product
b. net national product
c. national income
d. personal income
e. disposable personal income

10. Goods and services that are not sold in markets, such as food produced and consumed at home, are generally not included in GDP. Can you think of how this might cause the numbers in the second column of Table 5.4 to be misleading in a comparison of the economic well-being of Canada and India? Explain.

11. Until the 1980s, the Canadian government emphasized GNP rather than GDP as a measure of economic well-being. Which measure should the government prefer if it cares about the total income of Canadians?

Which measure should it prefer if it cares about the total amount of economic activity occurring in Canada?

12. The participation of women in the Canadian labour force has risen dramatically since 1970.
a. How do you think this rise affected GDP?
b. Now imagine a measure of well-being that includes time spent working in the home and taking leisure. How would the change in this measure of well-being compare to the change in GDP?
c. Can you think of other aspects of well-being that are associated with the rise in women's labour-force participation? Would it be practical to construct a measure of well-being that includes these aspects?

INTERNET RESOURCES

- Statistics Canada is the main source of information on the Canadian economy. On the Statistics Canada web page (http://www.statcan.ca), you can read the latest press releases, which give data on GDP, unemployment, inflation, and many other topics.

    In the menu at the top of the screen, click on "Canadian Statistics" to access a lot of free data about Canada. For recent data on GDP, click on "Latest Indicators" and then on "System of National Accounts." Notice that GDP is broken down into two types of categories—income-based and expenditure-based.

    If you go back to the "Latest Indicators" page and click on "Prices," you will see a listing for "Implicit chain price indexes, gross domestic product," which is Statistics Canada's name for the GDP deflator.

- You can read the entire United Nations *Human Development Report 2003* at http://hdr.undp.org/reports/global/2003.

- The University of Pennsylvania provides data to compare GDP in different countries around the world in the "Penn World Table": http://pwt.econ.upenn.edu/php_site/pwt_index.php.

- If your college or university is a subscriber, you can easily download a lot of data (both Canadian and international) for free from the University of Toronto's CHASS data centre: http://www.chass.utoronto.ca/chassweb/display.pl?page=index.

For more study tools, please visit http://www.mankiw3e.nelson.com.

© F. HJDEC/FIRESTLIGHT

6

MEASURING THE COST OF LIVING

Learning Objectives

In this chapter, you will …

- Learn how the consumer price index (CPI) is constructed
- Consider why the CPI is an imperfect measure of the cost of living
- Compare the CPI and the GDP deflator as measures of the overall price level
- See how to use a price index to compare dollar figures from different times
- Learn the distinction between real and nominal interest rates

In 1957 the price of gasoline was 43 cents per gallon, or 9.5 cents per litre. In 2003 the average price was around 65 cents per litre. Why did the price of gas increase to nearly seven times the price it was 46 years previously? Do we blame the Organization of Petroleum Exporting Countries (OPEC) for using its monopoly power to force up the price of crude oil? Did the big oil companies that buy the crude oil and sell gas at the pumps increase their markups? Or was this rise in the price of gas the inevitable result of rising demand from more people driving more cars, facing a diminishing supply of a nonrenewable natural resource?

At first sight, the increase in the price of gas might make you think that gas was a more scarce and valuable commodity in 2003 than it was in 1957. But, as everyone knows, the prices of nearly all goods and services have increased over time, and so have people's incomes. So it is not clear whether gas was more or less affordable in 2003 than it was in 1957. Did the value of gas increase or did the value of money decrease?

In the preceding chapter we looked at how economists use gross domestic product (GDP) to measure the quantity of goods and services that the economy is producing. This chapter examines how economists measure the overall cost of living. To compare 1957 prices and incomes with 2003 prices and incomes, we need to find some way of turning dollar figures into meaningful measures of purchasing power. That is exactly the job of a statistic called the *consumer price index.* After seeing how the consumer price index is constructed, we discuss how we can use such a price index to compare dollar figures from different points in time.

The consumer price index is used to monitor changes in the cost of living over time. When the consumer price index rises, the typical family has to spend more dollars to maintain the same standard of living. Economists use the term *inflation* to describe a situation in which the economy's overall price level is rising. The *inflation rate* is the percentage change in the price level from the previous period. As we will see in the coming chapters, inflation is a closely watched aspect of macroeconomic performance and is a key variable guiding macroeconomic policy. This chapter provides the background for that analysis by showing how economists measure the inflation rate using the consumer price index.

THE CONSUMER PRICE INDEX

consumer price index (CPI)
a measure of the overall cost of the goods and services bought by a typical consumer

The **consumer price index (CPI)** is a measure of the overall cost of the goods and services bought by a typical consumer. Each month Statistics Canada computes and reports the consumer price index. In this section we discuss how the consumer price index is calculated and what problems arise in its measurement. We also consider how this index compares to the GDP deflator, another measure of the overall level of prices, which we examined in the preceding chapter.

How the Consumer Price Index Is Calculated

When Statistics Canada calculates the consumer price index and the inflation rate, it uses data on the prices of over 600 different goods and services. To see exactly how these statistics are constructed, let's consider a simple economy in which consumers buy only two goods—hot dogs and hamburgers. Table 6.1 shows the five steps that Statistics Canada follows.

1. *Determine the basket.* The first step in computing the consumer price index is to determine which prices are most important to the typical consumer. If the typical consumer buys more hot dogs than hamburgers, then the price of hot dogs is more important than the price of hamburgers and, therefore, should be given greater weight in measuring the cost of living. Statistics Canada sets these weights by surveying consumers and finding the basket of goods and services that the typical consumer buys. In the example in the table, the typical consumer buys a basket of 4 hot dogs and 2 hamburgers.

2. *Find the prices.* The second step in computing the consumer price index is to find the prices of each of the goods and services in the basket for each point in time. The table shows the prices of hot dogs and hamburgers for three different years.

3. *Compute the basket's cost.* The third step is to use the data on prices to calculate the cost of the basket of goods and services at different times. The table shows

TABLE 6.1

Step 1: Survey Consumers to Determine a Fixed Basket of Goods

4 hot dogs, 2 hamburgers

Step 2: Find the Price of Each Good in Each Year

Year	Price of Hot Dogs	Price of Hamburgers
2001	$1	$2
2002	2	3
2003	3	4

Step 3: Compute the Cost of the Basket of Goods in Each Year

2001	($1 per hot dog × 4 hot dogs) + ($2 per hamburger × 2 hamburgers) = $8
2002	($2 per hot dog × 4 hot dogs) + ($3 per hamburger × 2 hamburgers) = $14
2003	($3 per hot dog × 4 hot dogs) + ($4 per hamburger × 2 hamburgers) = $20

Step 4: Choose One Year as a Base Year (2001) and Compute the Consumer Price Index in Each Year

2001	($8/$8) × 100 = 100
2002	($14/$8) × 100 = 175
2003	($20/$8) × 100 = 250

Step 5: Use the Consumer Price Index to Compute the Inflation Rate from Previous Year

2002	(175 − 100)/100 × 100 = 75%
2003	(250 − 175)/175 × 100 = 43%

Calculating the Consumer Price Index and the Inflation Rate: An Example

This table shows how to calculate the consumer price index and the inflation rate for a hypothetical economy in which consumers buy only hot dogs and hamburgers.

this calculation for each of the three years. Notice that only the prices in this calculation change. By keeping the basket of goods the same (4 hot dogs and 2 hamburgers), we are isolating the effects of price changes from the effect of any quantity changes that might be occurring at the same time.

4. *Choose a base year and compute the index.* The fourth step is to designate one year as the base year, which is the benchmark against which other years are compared. To calculate the index, the price of the basket of goods and services in each year is divided by the price of the basket in the base year, and this ratio is then multiplied by 100. The resulting number is the consumer price index.

   In the example in the table, the year 2001 is the base year. In this year, the basket of hot dogs and hamburgers costs $8. Therefore, the price of the basket in all years is divided by $8 and multiplied by 100. The consumer price index is 100 in 2001. (The index is always 100 in the base year.) The consumer price index is 175 in 2002. This means that the price of the basket in 2002 is 175 percent of its price in the base year. Put differently, a basket of goods that costs $100 in the base year costs $175 in 2002. Similarly, the consumer price index is 250 in 2003, indicating that the price level in 2003 is 250 percent of the price level in the base year.

inflation rate
the percentage change in the price index from the preceding period

5. *Compute the inflation rate.* The fifth and final step is to use the consumer price index to calculate the **inflation rate,** which is the percentage change in the price index from the preceding period. That is, the inflation rate between two consecutive years is computed as follows:

$$\text{Inflation rate in year 2} = \frac{\text{CPI in year 2} - \text{CPI in year 1}}{\text{CPI in year 1}} \times 100$$

In our example, the inflation rate is 75 percent in 2002 and 43 percent in 2003.

Although this example simplifies the real world by including only two goods, it shows how Statistics Canada computes the consumer price index and the inflation rate. Statistics Canada collects and processes data on the prices of hundreds of goods and services every month and, by following the five forgoing steps, determines how quickly the cost of living for the typical consumer is rising. When

FYI

WHAT IS IN THE CPI'S BASKET?

When constructing the consumer price index, Statistics Canada tries to include all the goods and services that the typical consumer buys. Moreover, it tries to weight these goods and services according to how much consumers buy of each item.

Figure 6.1 shows the breakdown of consumer spending into the major categories of goods and services. The numbers show the percentage of expenditure on each category of goods and services for the average consumer in 2001, when the CPI basket was last updated. The largest category is shelter, which makes up 28.4 percent of the typical consumer's budget. This category includes the cost of renting an apartment or making mortgage payments on a house (which means that a rise in interest rates can directly affect the CPI).

The next largest category, at 19 percent, is transportation, which includes spending on cars, gasoline, airfares, buses, and so on. The next category, at 16.4 percent, is food; this includes both food eaten at home and restaurant meals. Next is the recreation, education, and reading category, which includes your university tuition fees and the price of this book. This category makes up 11.8 percent of the typical consumer's budget, but probably makes up a much larger percentage of your budget.

Unless you happen to buy exactly the same goods and services that the typical consumer bought in 2001, changes in the CPI can never perfectly measure changes in your personal cost of living.

FIGURE 6.1

The Basket of Goods and Services

This figure shows how the typical Canadian consumer in 2001 divided his or her spending among various goods and services. These percentages are the weights that Statistics Canada uses to compute the CPI.

Source: Statistics Canada, *The Consumer Price Index,* January 2003, Catalogue No. 62-001.

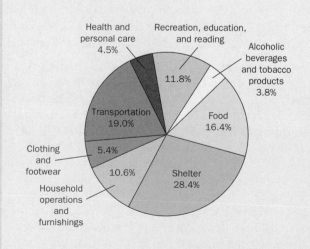

Statistics Canada makes its monthly announcement of the consumer price index, you can usually hear the number on the evening television news or see it in the next day's newspaper.

In addition to the consumer price index for the overall economy, Statistics Canada calculates several other price indexes. It reports the index for each province and for 16 cities across Canada, as well as for some narrow categories of goods and services (such as food, clothing, and shelter). It also calculates the rate of "core" inflation, which excludes the most volatile components from the CPI basket of goods and services. **Core inflation** is often thought to be useful in predicting the underlying trend of changes in the consumer price index.

core inflation
the measure of the underlying trend of inflation

Problems in Measuring the Cost of Living

The goal of the consumer price index is to measure changes in the cost of living. In other words, the consumer price index tries to gauge how much incomes must rise in order to maintain a constant standard of living. The consumer price index, however, is not a perfect measure of the cost of living. Three problems with the index are widely acknowledged but difficult to solve.

The first problem is called *substitution bias*. When prices change from one year to the next, they do not all change proportionately: Some prices rise more than others. Consumers respond to these differing price changes by buying less of the goods whose prices have risen by large amounts and by buying more of the goods whose prices have risen less or perhaps even have fallen. That is, consumers substitute toward goods that have become relatively less expensive. If a price index is computed assuming a fixed basket of goods, it ignores the possibility of consumer substitution and, therefore, overstates the increase in the cost of living from one year to the next.

Let's consider a simple example. Imagine that in the base year, apples are cheaper than pears, and so consumers buy more apples than pears. When Statistics Canada constructs the basket of goods, it will include more apples than pears. Suppose that next year pears are cheaper than apples. Consumers will naturally respond to the price changes by buying more pears and fewer apples. Yet, when computing the consumer price index, Statistics Canada uses a fixed basket, which in essence assumes that consumers continue buying the now expensive apples in the same quantities as before. For this reason, the index will measure a much larger increase in the cost of living than consumers actually experience.

The second problem with the consumer price index is the *introduction of new goods*. When a new good is introduced, consumers have more variety from which to choose. Greater variety, in turn, makes each dollar more valuable, so consumers need fewer dollars to maintain any given standard of living. Yet because the consumer price index is based on a fixed basket of goods and services, it does not reflect this change in the purchasing power of the dollar.

Again, let's consider an example. When VCRs were introduced, consumers were able to watch their favourite movies at home. Compared with going to a movie theatre, the convenience was greater and the cost was less. A perfect cost-of-living index would have reflected the introduction of the VCR with a decrease in the cost of living. The consumer price index, however, did not decrease in response to the introduction of the VCR. Eventually, Statistics Canada did revise the basket of goods to include VCRs, and subsequently the index reflected changes in VCR prices. But the reduction in the cost of living associated with the initial introduction of the VCR never showed up in the index.

The third problem with the consumer price index is *unmeasured quality change.* If the quality of a good deteriorates from one year to the next, the value of a dollar falls, even if the price of the good stays the same. Similarly, if the quality rises from one year to the next, the value of a dollar rises. Statistics Canada does its best to account for quality change. When the quality of a good in the basket changes—for example, when a car model has more horsepower or uses less gas from one year to the next—Statistics Canada adjusts the price of the good to account for the quality change. It is, in essence, trying to compute the price of a basket of goods of constant quality. Despite these efforts, changes in quality remain a problem, because quality is so hard to measure.

There is still much debate among economists about how severe these measurement problems are and what should be done about them. Several studies written during the 1990s concluded that the consumer price index overstated inflation by about half a percentage point per year. The issue is important because many government programs use the consumer price index to adjust for changes in the overall level of prices. Recipients of Canada Pension Plan benefits, for instance, get annual increases in benefits that are tied to the consumer price index. Some economists have suggested modifying these programs to correct for the measurement problems, such as by reducing the magnitude of the automatic benefit increases.

The GDP Deflator versus the Consumer Price Index

In the preceding chapter, we examined another measure of the overall level of prices in the economy—the GDP deflator. The GDP deflator is the ratio of nominal GDP to real GDP. Because nominal GDP is current output valued at current prices and real GDP is current output valued at base-year prices, the GDP deflator reflects the current level of prices relative to the level of prices in the base year.

Economists and policymakers monitor both the GDP deflator and the consumer price index to gauge how quickly prices are rising. Usually, these two statistics tell a similar story. Yet there are two important differences that can cause them to diverge.

The first difference is that the GDP deflator reflects the prices of all goods and services *produced domestically,* whereas the consumer price index reflects the prices of all goods and services *bought by consumers.* For example, suppose that the price of an airplane produced by Bombardier and sold to the Canadian Forces rises. Even though the plane is part of GDP, it is not part of the basket of goods and services bought by a typical consumer. Thus, the price increase shows up in the GDP deflator but not in the consumer price index.

As another example, suppose that Volkswagen raises the price of its cars. Because Volkswagens are made in Germany, the car is not part of Canada's GDP. But Canadian consumers buy Volkswagens, so the car is part of the typical consumer's basket of goods. Hence, a price increase in an imported consumption good, such as a Volkswagen, shows up in the consumer price index but not in the GDP deflator.

The second and more subtle difference between the GDP deflator and the consumer price index concerns how various prices are weighted to yield a single number for the overall level of prices. The consumer price index compares the price of a *fixed* basket of goods and services to the price of the basket in the base year. Only occasionally does Statistics Canada change the basket of goods. By contrast, the GDP deflator compares the price of *currently produced* goods and services to the price of the same goods and services in the base year. Thus, the group of goods and services used to compute the GDP deflator changes automatically over time. This difference is not important when all prices are changing proportionately. But if the prices of different goods and services are changing by varying amounts, the way we weight the various prices matters for the overall inflation rate.

Figure 6.2 shows the inflation rate as measured by both the GDP deflator and the consumer price index for each year since 1965. You can see that sometimes the two measures diverge. When they do diverge, it is possible to go behind these numbers and explain the divergence with the two differences we have discussed. The figure shows, however, that divergence between these two measures is the exception rather than the rule. In the late 1970s, both the GDP deflator and the consumer price index show high rates of inflation. In the late 1980s and 1990s, both measures show low rates of inflation.

QuickQuiz Explain briefly what the consumer price index is trying to measure and how it is constructed.

CORRECTING ECONOMIC VARIABLES FOR THE EFFECTS OF INFLATION

The purpose of measuring the overall level of prices in the economy is to permit comparison between dollar figures from different points in time. Now that we

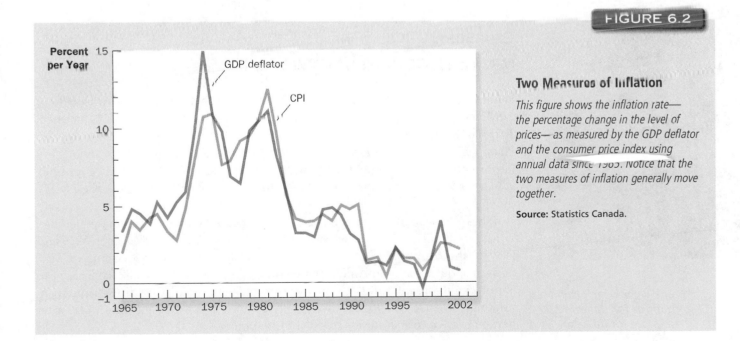

FIGURE 6.2

Two Measures of Inflation

This figure shows the inflation rate— the percentage change in the level of prices— as measured by the GDP deflator and the consumer price index using annual data since 1965. Notice that the two measures of inflation generally move together.

Source: Statistics Canada.

know how price indexes are calculated, let's see how we might use such an index to compare a dollar figure from the past to a dollar figure in the present.

Dollar Figures from Different Times

We return to the issue of the price of gasoline. Was the 1957 price of 9.5 cents per litre high or low compared with the 2003 price of gas?

To answer this question, we need to know the level of prices in 1957 and the level of prices in 2003. How much of the rise in the price of gas is simply a reflection of the general rise in prices? In other words, how much of the rise in the price of gas is due to a fall in the value of money? To compare the 1957 price of gas with the 2003 price, we need to inflate the price of 9.5 cents per litre to turn 1957 dollars into 2003 dollars. A price index shows us the size of this inflation correction.

Statistics Canada gives a CPI of 17.6 for 1957 and 122 for the year 2003. (The base year is 1992.) Thus, the overall level of prices rose by a factor of 6.93 (which equals 122/17.6). We can use these numbers to measure the 1957 price of gas in year 2003 dollars. The calculation is:

$$\text{1957 gas price in 1997 dollars} = \text{1957 gas price} \times (\text{CPI in 2003/CPI in 1957})$$
$$= 9.5 \text{ cents} \times (122/17.6)$$
$$= 65.8 \text{ cents}$$

We find that the 1957 price of gas is equivalent to a price of 65.8 cents per litre in 2003. This is about the same as the 2003 price of gas—so, adjusting for inflation, the price of gas was no higher in 2003 than it was 46 years earlier! The price of gas increased by about the same percentage as the average increase in the price of goods and services. A litre of gas was not more valuable in 2003 than it was in 1957—money was a lot less valuable.

"Frankly, my dear, I don't care much for the effects of inflation."

Case Study

MR. INDEX GOES TO HOLLYWOOD

What was the most popular movie of all time? The answer might surprise you.

Movie popularity is usually gauged by box office receipts. By that measure, *Titanic* is the #1 movie of all time, followed by *Star Wars, ET: The Extra-Terrestrial, Star Wars: The Phantom Menace,* and *Spiderman.* But this ranking ignores an obvious but important fact: Prices, including those of movie tickets, have been rising over time. When we correct box office receipts for the effects of inflation, the story is very different.

Table 6.2 shows the top ten movies of all time ranked by inflation-adjusted box office receipts. The #1 movie is *Gone with the Wind,* which was released in 1939 and is well ahead of *Titanic.* In the 1930s, before everyone had televisions in their homes, about 90 million Americans went to the cinema each week, compared to about 25 million today. But the movies from that era rarely show up in popularity rankings because ticket prices were only a quarter. Scarlett and Rhett fare a lot better once we correct for the effects of inflation. ●

Film	Year of Release	Total Domestic Gross (in millions of 2001 U.S. dollars)
1. *Gone with the Wind*	1939	$1002
2. *Star Wars*	1977	866
3. *The Sound of Music*	1965	695
4. *E.T.: The Extra-Terrestrial*	1982	687
5. *Titanic*	1997	640
6. *The Ten Commandments*	1956	639
7. *Jaws*	1975	625
8. *Doctor Zhivago*	1965	591
9. *The Jungle Book*	1967	519
10. *Snow White and the Seven Dwarfs*	1937	518

TABLE 6.2

The Most Popular Movies of All Time, Inflation Adjusted

Source: *The Movie Times,* online website (http://www.the-movie-times.com).

Indexation

As we have just seen, price indexes are used to correct for the effects of inflation when comparing dollar figures from different times. This type of correction shows up in many places in the economy. When some dollar amount is automatically corrected for inflation by law or contract, the amount is said to be **indexed** for inflation.

For example, many long-term contracts between firms and unions include partial or complete indexation of the wage to the consumer price index. Such a provision is called a *cost-of-living allowance,* or COLA. A COLA automatically raises the wage when the consumer price index rises.

Indexation is also a feature of many laws. Canada Pension Plan and Old Age Security benefits, for example, are adjusted every year to compensate the elderly for increases in prices. The brackets of the federal income tax—the income levels at which the tax rates change—are also indexed for inflation. There are, however, many ways in which the tax system is not indexed for inflation, even when perhaps it should be. We discuss these issues more fully when we discuss the costs of inflation later in this book.

indexation
the automatic correction of a dollar amount for the effects of inflation by law or contract

Real and Nominal Interest Rates

Correcting economic variables for the effects of inflation is particularly important—and somewhat tricky—when we look at data on interest rates. When you deposit your savings into a bank account, you will earn interest on your deposit. Conversely, when you borrow from a bank to buy a car, you will pay interest on your car loan. Interest represents a payment in the future for a transfer of money in the past. As a result, interest rates always involve comparing amounts of money at different points in time. To fully understand interest rates, we need to know how to correct for the effects of inflation.

Let's consider an example. Suppose that Sally Saver deposits $1000 in a bank account that pays an annual interest rate of 10 percent. After a year passes, Sally has accumulated $100 in interest. Sally then withdraws her $1100. Is Sally $100 richer than she was when she made the deposit a year earlier?

The answer depends on what we mean by "richer." Sally does have $100 more than she had before. In other words, the number of dollars has risen by 10 percent. But if prices have risen at the same time, each dollar now buys less than it did a year ago. Thus, her purchasing power has not risen by 10 percent. If the inflation rate was 4 percent, then the amount of goods she can buy has increased by only 6 percent. And if the inflation rate was 15 percent, then the price of goods has increased proportionately more than the number of dollars in her account. In that case, Sally's purchasing power has actually fallen by 5 percent.

The interest rate that the bank pays is called the **nominal interest rate,** and the interest rate corrected for inflation is called the **real interest rate.** We can write the relationship among the nominal interest rate, the real interest rate, and inflation as follows:

$$\text{Real interest rate} = \text{Nominal interest rate} - \text{Inflation rate}$$

nominal interest rate
the interest rate as usually reported without a correction for the effects of inflation

real interest rate
the interest rate corrected for the effects of inflation

The real interest rate is the difference between the nominal interest rate and the rate of inflation. The nominal interest rate tells you how fast the number of dollars in your bank account rises over time. The real interest rate tells you how fast the purchasing power of your bank account rises over time.

Figure 6.3 shows real and nominal interest rates since 1965. The nominal interest rate is the interest rate on three-month corporate bonds. The real interest rate is computed by subtracting inflation—the percentage change in the consumer price index—from this nominal interest rate.

You can see that real and nominal interest rates do not always move together. For example, in the late 1970s, nominal interest rates were high, but because inflation was very high, real interest rates were low. Indeed, in some years, real interest rates were negative, because inflation eroded people's savings more quickly than nominal interest payments increased them. By contrast, in the 1990s, nominal interest rates were low, but because inflation was also low, real interest rates were relatively high. In the coming chapters, when we study the causes and effects of changes in interest rates, it will be important for us to keep in mind the distinction between real and nominal interest rates.

QuickQuiz Henry Ford paid his workers $5 a day in 1914. If the U.S. consumer price index was 10 in 1914 and 177 in 2001, how much is the Ford paycheque worth in 2001 dollars?

CONCLUSION

"A nickel ain't worth a dime anymore," baseball player Yogi Berra once observed. Indeed, throughout recent history, the real values behind the nickel, the dime, and the dollar have not been stable. Persistent increases in the overall level of prices have been the norm. Such inflation reduces the purchasing power of each unit of money over time. When comparing dollar figures from different times, it is important to keep in mind that a dollar today is not the same as a dollar 20 years ago or, most likely, 20 years from now.

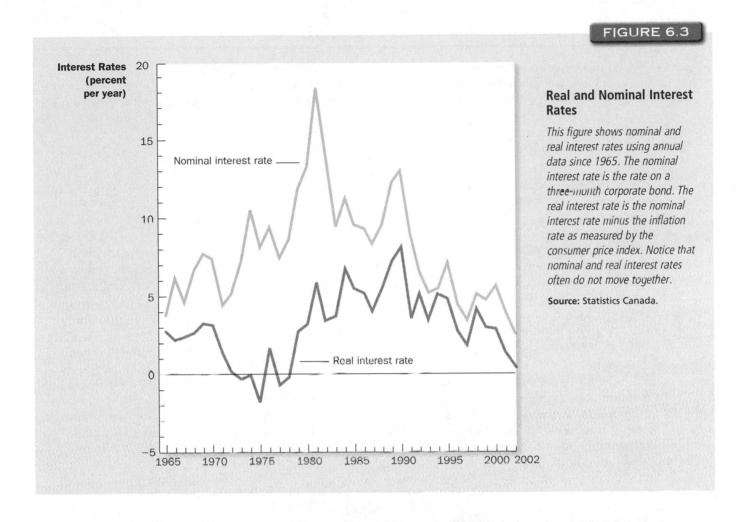

FIGURE 6.3

Real and Nominal Interest Rates

This figure shows nominal and real interest rates using annual data since 1965. The nominal interest rate is the rate on a three-month corporate bond. The real interest rate is the nominal interest rate minus the inflation rate as measured by the consumer price index. Notice that nominal and real interest rates often do not move together.

Source: Statistics Canada.

This chapter has discussed how economists measure the overall level of prices in the economy and how they use price indexes to correct economic variables for the effects of inflation. This analysis is only a starting point. We have not yet examined the causes and effects of inflation or how inflation interacts with other economic variables. To do that, we need to go beyond issues of measurement. Indeed, that is our next task. Having explained how economists measure macroeconomic quantities and prices in the past two chapters, we are now ready to develop the models that explain long-run and short-run movements in these variables.

SUMMARY

- The consumer price index shows the cost of a basket of goods and services relative to the cost of the same basket in the base year. The index is used to measure the overall level of prices in the economy. The percentage change in the consumer price index measures the inflation rate.

- The consumer price index is an imperfect measure of the cost of living for three reasons. First, it does not take into account consumers' ability to substitute toward goods that become relatively cheaper over time. Second, it does not take into account increases in the purchasing power of the dollar due to the introduction of new goods. Third, it is distorted by unmeasured changes in the quality of goods and services. Because of these measurement problems, the CPI overstates true inflation.

- Although the GDP deflator also measures the overall level of prices in the economy, it differs from the consumer price index because it includes goods and services produced rather than goods and services consumed. As a result, imported goods affect the consumer price index but not the GDP deflator. In addition, while the consumer price index uses a fixed basket of goods, the GDP deflator automatically changes the group of goods and services over time as the composition of GDP changes.

- Dollar figures from different points in time do not represent a valid comparison of purchasing power. To compare a dollar figure from the past to a dollar figure today, the older figure should be inflated using a price index.

- Various laws and private contracts use price indexes to correct for the effects of inflation. The tax laws, however, are only partially indexed for inflation.

- A correction for inflation is especially important when looking at data on interest rates. The nominal interest rate is the interest rate usually reported; it is the rate at which the number of dollars in a savings account increases over time. By contrast, the real interest rate takes into account changes in the value of the dollar over time. The real interest rate equals the nominal interest rate minus the rate of inflation.

KEY CONCEPTS

consumer price index (CPI), p. 114

inflation rate, p. 116

core inflation, p. 117

indexation, p. 121

nominal interest rate, p. 122

real interest rate, p. 122

QUESTIONS FOR REVIEW

1. Which do you think has a greater effect on the consumer price index: a 10 percent increase in the price of chicken or a 10 percent increase in the price of caviar? Why?

2. Describe the three problems that make the consumer price index an imperfect measure of the cost of living.

3. If the price of a military aircraft rises, is the consumer price index or the GDP deflator affected more? Why?

4. Over a long period of time, the price of a candy bar rose from $0.10 to $0.60. Over the same period, the consumer price index rose from 150 to 300. Adjusted for overall inflation, how much did the price of the candy bar change?

5. Explain the meaning of *nominal interest rate* and *real interest rate*. How are they related?

PROBLEMS AND APPLICATIONS

1. Suppose that people consume only three goods, as shown in this table:

	Tennis Balls	Tennis Racquets	Gatorade
2003 price	$2	$40	$1
2003 quantity	100	10	200
2004 price	$2	$60	$2
2004 quantity	100	10	200

   a. What is the percentage change in the price of each of the three goods? What is the percentage change in the overall price level?
   b. Do tennis racquets become more or less expensive relative to Gatorade? Does the well-being of some people change relative to the well-being of others? Explain.

2. Suppose that the residents of Vegopia spend all of their income on cauliflower, broccoli, and carrots. In 2003 they buy 100 heads of cauliflower for $200, 50 bunches of broccoli for $75, and 500 carrots for $50. In 2004 they buy 75 heads of cauliflower for $225, 80 bunches of broccoli for $120, and 500 carrots for $100. If the base year is 2003, what is the CPI in both years? What is the inflation rate in 2004?

3. Go to the website of Statistics Canada (http://www.statcan.ca) and find data on the consumer price index. By how much has the index including all items risen over the past year? For which categories of spending have prices risen the most? The least? Have any categories experienced price declines? Can you explain any of these facts?

4. Beginning in 1994, U.S. environmental regulations have required that gasoline contain a new additive to reduce air pollution. This requirement raised the cost of gasoline. The U.S. Bureau of Labor Statistics (BLS) decided that this increase in cost represented an improvement in quality.
   a. Given this decision, did the increased cost of gasoline raise the CPI?
   b. What is the argument in favour of the BLS's decision? What is the argument for a different decision?

5. Which of the problems in the construction of the CPI might be illustrated by each of the following situations? Explain.
   a. the invention of the Sony Walkman
   b. the introduction of air bags in cars
   c. increased personal computer purchases in response to a decline in the price
   d. more scoops of raisins in each package of Raisin Bran
   e. greater use of fuel-efficient cars after gasoline prices increase

6. The *Ottawa Citizen* cost $0.10 in 1970 and $0.50 in 1990. The average wage in manufacturing was $3.01 per hour in 1970 and $14.19 in 1990.
   a. By what percentage did the price of a newspaper rise?
   b. By what percentage did the wage rise?
   c. In each year, how many minutes does a worker have to work to earn enough to buy a newspaper?
   d. Did workers' purchasing power in terms of newspapers rise or fall?

7. The chapter explains that Canada Pension Plan benefits are increased each year in proportion to the increase in the CPI, even though most economists believe that the CPI overstates actual inflation.
   a. If the elderly consume the same market basket as other people, does Canada Pension Plan provide the elderly with an improvement in their standard of living each year? Explain.
   b. In fact, the elderly consume more medicine than younger people, and medicine costs have risen faster than overall inflation. What would you do to determine whether the elderly are actually better off from year to year?

8. How do you think the basket of goods and services you buy differs from the basket bought by the typical Canadian household? Do you think you face a higher or lower inflation rate than is indicated by the CPI? Why?

9. Income tax brackets were not indexed until 2000. When inflation pushed up people's nominal incomes during the 1970s, what do

you think happened to real tax revenue? (Hint: This phenomenon was known as "bracket creep.")

10. When deciding how much of their income to save for retirement, should workers consider the real or the nominal interest rate that their savings will earn? Explain.

11. Suppose that a borrower and a lender agree on the nominal interest rate to be paid on a loan. Then inflation turns out to be higher than they both expected.

a. Is the real interest rate on this loan higher or lower than expected?
b. Does the lender gain or lose from this unexpectedly high inflation? Does the borrower gain or lose?
c. Inflation during the 1970s was much higher than most people had expected when the decade began. How did this affect homeowners who obtained fixed-rate mortgages during the 1960s? How did it affect the banks who lent the money?

INTERNET RESOURCES

- To see the latest data on Canadian inflation, go to the Statistics Canada website at http://www.statcan.ca and click on "Consumer Price Index" in the Infomat "Latest Indicators" table.

   You can also click on "Canadian Statistics" in the menu at the top of the screen to access a lot of free data about Canada. Recent data on various measures of prices, such as the consumer price index for various cities and provinces, as well as industrial product and raw materials price indexes, can be accessed by clicking on "Latest Indicators" (under "Economy") and then "Prices" in the menu on this page.

- The Bank of Canada also provides data on various measures of inflation on its website at http://www.bankofcanada.ca; just click on "Inflation" in the menu. The page on inflation also has a link to an easy-to-use inflation calculator. To obtain historical data on interest rates, go to http://www.bankofcanada.ca/en/sel_hist.htm.

http://   For more study tools, please visit http://www.mankiw3e.nelson.com.

4

THE REAL ECONOMY IN THE LONG RUN

PRODUCTION AND GROWTH

Learning Objectives

In this chapter, you will …

- See how economic growth differs around the world
- Consider why productivity is the key determinant of a country's standard of living
- Analyze the factors that determine a country's productivity
- Examine how a country's policies influence its productivity growth

When you travel around the world, you see tremendous variation in the standard of living. The average person in a rich country, such as Canada, the United States, or Germany, has an income more than ten times as high as the average person in a poor country, such as India, Indonesia, or Nigeria. These large differences in income are reflected in large differences in the quality of life. Richer countries have more automobiles, more telephones, more televisions, better nutrition, safer housing, better health care, and longer life expectancy.

Even within a country, there are large changes in the standard of living over time. In Canada over the past century, average income as measured by real GDP per person has grown by about 2 percent per year. Although 2 percent might seem small, this rate of growth implies that average income doubles every 35 years. Because of this growth, average income today is about eight times as high as average income a century ago. As a result, the typical Canadian enjoys much greater economic prosperity than did his or her parents, grandparents, and great-grandparents.

Growth rates vary substantially from country to country. In some East Asian countries, such as Singapore, South Korea, and Taiwan, average income has risen about 7 percent per year in recent decades. At this rate, average income doubles every ten years. These countries have, in the length of one generation, gone from being among the poorest in the world to being among the richest. By contrast, in some African countries, such as Chad, Ethiopia, and Nigeria, average income has been stagnant for many years.

What explains these diverse experiences? How can the rich countries ensure that they maintain their high standard of living? What policies should the poor countries pursue to promote more rapid growth in order to join the developed world? These are among the most important questions in macroeconomics. As economist Robert Lucas put it, "The consequences for human welfare in questions like these are simply staggering: Once one starts to think about them, it is hard to think about anything else."

In the previous two chapters we discussed how economists measure macroeconomic quantities and prices. In this chapter we start studying the forces that determine these variables. As we have seen, an economy's gross domestic product (GDP) measures both the total income earned in the economy and the total expenditure on the economy's output of goods and services. The level of real GDP is a good gauge of economic prosperity, and the growth of real GDP is a good gauge of economic progress. Here we focus on the long-run determinants of the level and growth of real GDP. Later in this book we study the short-run fluctuations of real GDP around its long-run trend.

We proceed here in three steps. First, we examine international data on real GDP per person. These data will give you some sense of how much the level and growth of living standards vary around the world. Second, we examine the role of *productivity*—the amount of goods and services produced for each hour of a worker's time. In particular, we see that a nation's standard of living is determined by the productivity of its workers, and we consider the factors that determine a nation's productivity. Third, we consider the link between productivity and the economic policies that a nation pursues.

ECONOMIC GROWTH AROUND THE WORLD

As a starting point for our study of long-run growth, let's look at the experiences of some of the world's economies. Table 7.1 shows data on real GDP per person for 13 countries. For each country, the data cover about a century of history. The first and second columns of the table present the countries and time periods. (The time periods differ somewhat from country to country because of differences in data availability.) The third and fourth columns show estimates of real GDP per person about a century ago and for a recent year.

The data on real GDP per person show that living standards vary widely from country to country. Income per person in Canada, for instance, is about 7 times that in China and about 11 times that in India. The poorest countries have average levels of income that have not been seen in the developed world for many decades. The typical citizen of China in 2000 had about as much real income as the typical resident of England in 1870. The typical person in Pakistan in 2000 had almost the same real income as a typical Canadian 130 years previously.

TABLE 7.1

The Variety of Growth Experiences

Sources: Robert J. Barro and Xavier Sala-i-Martin, *Economic Growth* (New York: McGraw-Hill, 1995), Tables 10.2 and 10.3; World Bank, *World Development Report 2002: Building Institutions for Markets* (New York: World Bank and Oxford University Press, 2001), Table 1; and author's calculations.

Country	Period	Real GDP per Person at Beginning of Period*	Real GDP per Person at End of Period*	Growth Rate (per Year)
Japan	1890–2000	$1865	$39 298	2.81%
Brazil	1900–2000	965	10 872	2.45
Mexico	1900–2000	1438	13 085	2.23
Canada	1870–2000	2947	40 591	2.04
Germany	1870–2000	2710	37 145	2.03
China	1900–2000	888	5 852	1.90
Argentina	1900–2000	2844	17 956	1.86
United States	1870–2000	4971	50 883	1.81
India	1900–2000	838	3 550	1.45
Indonesia	1900–2000	1104	4 218	1.35
United Kingdom	1870–2000	6100	34 977	1.35
Pakistan	1900–2000	915	2 911	1.16
Bangladesh	1900–2000	772	2 451	1.16

*Real GDP is measured in 2000 Canadian dollars.

The last column of the table shows each country's growth rate. The growth rate measures how rapidly real GDP per person grew in the typical year. In Canada, for example, real GDP per person was $2947 in 1870 and $40 591 in 2000. The growth rate was 2.04 percent per year. This means that if real GDP per person, beginning at $2947, were to increase by 2.04 percent for each of 130 years, it would end up at $40 591. Of course, real GDP per person did not actually rise exactly 2.04 percent every year. Some years it rose by more and other years by less. The growth rate of 2.04 percent per year ignores short-run fluctuations around the long-run trend and represents an average rate of growth for real GDP per person over many years.

The countries in Table 7.1 are ordered by their growth rate from the most to the least rapid. Japan tops the list, with a growth rate of 2.81 percent per year. In 1890, Japan was not a rich country. Japan's average income was only somewhat higher than Mexico's, and it was well behind Argentina's. To put the issue another way, Japan's income in 1890 was less than India's income in 2000. But because of its spectacular growth, Japan is now an economic superpower, with average income only slightly behind that of Canada. At the bottom of the list of countries are Bangladesh and Pakistan, which experienced growth of only 1.16 percent per year over the century. As a result, the typical resident of these countries continues to live in abject poverty.

Because of differences in growth rates, the ranking of countries by income changes substantially over time. As we have seen, Japan is a country that has risen relative to others. One country that has fallen behind is the United Kingdom. In 1870, the United Kingdom was the richest country in the world, with average income about 20 percent higher than that of the United States and more than twice that of Canada. Today, average income in the United Kingdom is below the average income in its two former colonies.

These data show that the world's richest countries have no guarantee they will stay the richest and that the world's poorest countries are not doomed forever to remain in poverty. But what explains these changes over time? Why do some

ARE YOU RICHER THAN THE RICHEST AMERICAN?

In October 1998 the magazine *American Heritage* published a list of the richest Americans of all time. The #1 spot went to John D. Rockefeller, the oil entrepreneur who lived from 1839 to 1937. According to the magazine's calculations, his wealth would today be the equivalent of $200 billion, significantly more than that of Bill Gates, the software entrepreneur who is today's richest American.

Despite his great wealth, Rockefeller did not enjoy many of the conveniences that we now take for granted. He couldn't watch television, play video games, surf the Internet, or send an e-mail. During

John D. Rockefeller

the heat of summer, he couldn't cool his home with air conditioning. For much of his life, he couldn't travel by car or plane, and he couldn't use a telephone to call friends or family. If he became ill, he couldn't take advantage of many medicines, such as antibiotics, that doctors today routinely use to prolong and enhance life.

Now consider: How much money would someone have to pay you to give up for the rest of your life all the modern conveniences that Rockefeller lived without? Would you do it for $200 billion? Perhaps not. And if you wouldn't, is it fair to say that you are better off than John D. Rockefeller, allegedly the richest American ever?

The preceding chapter discussed how standard price indexes, which are used to compare sums of money from different points in time, fail to fully reflect the introduction of new goods in the economy. As a result, the rate of inflation is overestimated. The flip side of this observation is that the rate of real economic growth is underestimated. Pondering Rockefeller's life shows how significant this problem might be. Because of tremendous technological advances, the average American today is arguably "richer" than the richest American a century ago, even if that fact is lost in standard economic statistics.

countries zoom ahead while others lag behind? These are precisely the questions that we take up next.

QuickQuiz What is the approximate growth rate of real GDP per person in Canada? Name a country that has had faster growth and a country that has had slower growth.

PRODUCTIVITY: ITS ROLE AND DETERMINANTS

Explaining the large variation in living standards around the world is, in one sense, very easy. As we will see, the explanation can be summarized in a single word—*productivity*. But, in another sense, the international variation is deeply puzzling. To explain why incomes are so much higher in some countries than in others, we must look at the many factors that determine a nation's productivity.

Why Productivity Is So Important

Let's begin our study of productivity and economic growth by developing a simple model based loosely on Daniel Defoe's famous novel *Robinson Crusoe*.

Robinson Crusoe, as you may recall, is a sailor stranded on a desert island. Because Crusoe lives alone, he catches his own fish, grows his own vegetables, and makes his own clothes. We can think of Crusoe's activities—his production and consumption of fish, vegetables, and clothing—as being a simple economy. By examining Crusoe's economy, we can learn some lessons that also apply to more complex and realistic economies.

What determines Crusoe's standard of living? The answer is obvious. If Crusoe is good at catching fish, growing vegetables, and making clothes, he lives well. If he is bad at doing these things, he lives poorly. Because Crusoe gets to consume only what he produces, his living standard is tied to his productive ability.

The term **productivity** refers to the quantity of goods and services that a worker can produce for each hour of work. In the case of Crusoe's economy, it is easy to see that productivity is the key determinant of living standards and that growth in productivity is the key determinant of growth in living standards. The more fish Crusoe can catch per hour, the more he eats at dinner. If Crusoe finds a better place to catch fish, his productivity rises. This increase in productivity makes Crusoe better off: He could eat the extra fish, or he could spend less time fishing and devote more time to making other goods he enjoys.

productivity
the amount of goods and services produced from each hour of a worker's time

The key role of productivity in determining living standards is as true for nations as it is for stranded sailors. Recall that an economy's gross domestic product (GDP) measures two things at once: the total income earned by everyone in the economy and the total expenditure on the economy's output of goods and services. The reason why GDP can measure these two things simultaneously is that, for the economy as a whole, they must be equal. Put simply, an economy's income is the economy's output.

Like Crusoe, a nation can enjoy a high standard of living only if it can produce a large quantity of goods and services. Canadians live better than Nigerians because Canadian workers are more productive than Nigerian workers. The Japanese have enjoyed more rapid growth in living standards than Argentineans because Japanese workers have experienced more rapidly growing productivity. Indeed, one of the ten principles of economics in Chapter 1 is that a country's standard of living depends on its ability to produce goods and services.

Hence, to understand the large differences in living standards we observe across countries or over time, we must focus on the production of goods and services. But seeing the link between living standards and productivity is only the first step. It leads naturally to the next question: Why are some economies so much better at producing goods and services than others?

How Productivity Is Determined

Although productivity is uniquely important in determining Robinson Crusoe's standard of living, many factors determine Crusoe's productivity. Crusoe will be better at catching fish, for instance, if he has more fishing poles, if he has been trained in the best fishing techniques, if his island has a plentiful fish supply, and if he invents a better fishing lure. Each of these determinants of Crusoe's productivity—which we can call *physical capital, human capital, natural resources,* and *technological knowledge*—has a counterpart in more complex and realistic economies. Let's consider each of these factors in turn.

Physical Capital

physical capital
the stock of equipment and structures that are used to produce goods and services

Workers are more productive if they have tools with which to work. The stock of equipment and structures that are used to produce goods and services is called **physical capital,** or just *capital.* For example, when woodworkers make furniture, they use saws, lathes, and drill presses. More tools allow work to be done more quickly and more accurately. That is, a worker with only basic hand tools can make less furniture each week than a worker with sophisticated and specialized woodworking equipment.

As you may recall from Chapter 2, the inputs used to produce goods and services—labour, capital, and so on—are called the *factors of production.* An important feature of capital is that it is a *produced* factor of production. That is, capital is an input into the production process that in the past was an output from the production process. The woodworker uses a lathe to make the leg of a table. Earlier the lathe itself was the output of a firm that manufactures lathes. The lathe manufacturer in turn used other equipment to make its product. Thus, capital is a factor of production used to produce all kinds of goods and services, including more capital.

Human Capital

human capital
the knowledge and skills that workers acquire through education, training, and experience

A second determinant of productivity is human capital. **Human capital** is the economist's term for the knowledge and skills that workers acquire through education, training, and experience. Human capital includes the skills accumulated in early childhood programs, grade school, high school, college or university, and on-the-job training for adults in the labour force.

Although education, training, and experience are less tangible than lathes, bulldozers, and buildings, human capital is like physical capital in many ways. Like physical capital, human capital raises a nation's ability to produce goods and services. Also like physical capital, human capital is a produced factor of production. Producing human capital requires inputs in the form of teachers, libraries, and student time. Indeed, students can be viewed as "workers" who have the important job of producing the human capital that will be used in future production.

Natural Resources

natural resources
the inputs into the production of goods and services that are provided by nature, such as land, rivers, and mineral deposits

A third determinant of productivity is **natural resources.** Natural resources are inputs into production that are provided by nature, such as land, rivers, and mineral deposits. Natural resources take two forms: renewable and nonrenewable. A forest is an example of a renewable resource. When one tree is cut down, a seedling can be planted in its place to be harvested in the future. Oil is an example of a nonrenewable resource. Because oil is produced by nature over many thousands of years, there is only a limited supply. Once the supply of oil is depleted, it is impossible to create more.

Differences in natural resources are responsible for some of the differences in standards of living around the world. The historical success of Canada was driven in part by the large supply of land well suited for agriculture and by an abundance of minerals, forests, and pools of oil and natural gas. Today, some countries in the Middle East, such as Kuwait and Saudi Arabia, are rich simply because they happen to be on top of some of the largest pools of oil in the world.

Although natural resources can be important, they are not necessary for an economy to be highly productive in producing goods and services. Japan, for instance, is one of the richest countries in the world, despite having few natural resources. International trade makes Japan's success possible. Japan imports many of the natural resources it needs, such as oil, and exports its manufactured goods to economies rich in natural resources.

Technological Knowledge   A fourth determinant of productivity is **technological knowledge**—the understanding of the best ways to produce goods and services. A hundred years ago, most Canadians worked on farms, because farm technology required a high input of labour in order to feed the entire population. Today, thanks to advances in the technology of farming, a small fraction of the population can produce enough food to feed the entire country. This technological change made labour available to produce other goods and services.

Technological knowledge takes many forms. Some technology is common knowledge—after it becomes used by one person, everyone becomes aware of it. For example, once Henry Ford successfully introduced production in assembly lines, other carmakers quickly followed suit. Other technology is proprietary—it is known only by the company that discovers it. Only the Coca-Cola Company, for instance, knows the secret recipe for making its famous soft drink. Still other technology is proprietary for a short time. When a pharmaceutical company discovers a new drug, the patent system gives that company a temporary right to be its exclusive manufacturer. When the patent expires, however, other companies are allowed to make the drug. All these forms of technological knowledge are important for the economy's production of goods and services.

It is worthwhile to distinguish between technological knowledge and human capital. Although they are closely related, there is an important difference. Technological knowledge refers to society's understanding about how the world works.

technological knowledge
society's understanding of the best ways to produce goods and services

THE PRODUCTION FUNCTION

Economists often use a *production function* to describe the relationship between the quantity of inputs used in production and the quantity of output from production. For example, suppose Y denotes the quantity of output, L the quantity of labour, K the quantity of physical capital, H the quantity of human capital, and N the quantity of natural resources. Then we might write

$$Y = A F(L, K, H, N)$$

where $F(\ )$ is a function that shows how the inputs are combined to produce output. A is a variable that reflects the available production technology. As technology improves, A rises, so the economy produces more output from any given combination of inputs.

Many production functions have a property called *constant returns to scale*. If a production function has constant returns to scale, then a doubling of all the inputs causes the amount of output to double as well. Mathematically, we write that a production function has constant returns to scale if, for any positive number x,

$$xY = A F(xL, xK, xH, xN)$$

A doubling of all inputs is represented in this equation by $x = 2$. The right-hand side shows the inputs doubling, and the left-hand side shows output doubling.

Production functions with constant returns to scale have an interesting implication. To see what it is, set $x = 1/L$. Then the equation above becomes

$$Y/L = A F(1, K/L, H/L, N/L)$$

Notice that Y/L is output per worker, which is a measure of productivity. This equation says that productivity depends on physical capital per worker (K/L), human capital per worker (H/L), and natural resources per worker (N/L). Productivity also depends on the state of technology, as reflected by the variable A. Thus, this equation provides a mathematical summary of the four determinants of productivity we have just discussed.

Human capital refers to the resources expended transmitting this understanding to the labour force. To use a relevant metaphor, knowledge is the quality of society's textbooks, whereas human capital is the amount of time that the population has devoted to reading them. Workers' productivity depends on both the quality of textbooks they have available and the amount of time they have spent studying them.

Case Study

ARE NATURAL RESOURCES A LIMIT TO GROWTH?

The world's population is far larger today than it was a century ago, and many people are enjoying a much higher standard of living. A perennial debate concerns whether this growth in population and living standards can continue in the future.

Many commentators have argued that natural resources provide a limit to how much the world's economies can grow. At first, this argument might seem hard to ignore. If the world has only a fixed supply of nonrenewable natural resources, how can population, production, and living standards continue to grow over time? Eventually, won't supplies of oil and minerals start to run out? When these shortages start to occur, won't they stop economic growth and, perhaps, even force living standards to fall?

Despite the apparent appeal of such arguments, most economists are less concerned about such limits to growth than one might guess. They argue that technological progress often yields ways to avoid these limits. If we compare the economy today to the economy of the past, we see various ways in which the use of natural resources has improved. Modern cars have better gas consumption. New houses have better insulation and require less energy to heat and cool them. Technological advances have also allowed us to access resources previously thought to be too difficult to extract. Such advances have, for example, made it possible to extract much more oil from the oil sands in Alberta than once was thought possible. Other technological advances have resulted in recycling, causing some nonrenewable resources to be reused. Finally, the development of alternative fuels, such as ethanol instead of gasoline, allows us to substitute renewable for nonrenewable resources.

Fifty years ago, some conservationists were concerned about the excessive use of tin and copper. At the time, these were crucial commodities: Tin was used to make many food containers and copper was used to make telephone wire. Some people advocated mandatory recycling and rationing of tin and copper so that supplies would be available for future generations. Today, however, plastic has replaced tin as a material for making many food containers, and phone calls often travel over fibre-optic cables, which are made from sand. Technological progress has made once crucial natural resources less necessary.

But are all these efforts enough to permit continued economic growth? One way to answer this question is to look at the prices of natural resources. In a market economy, scarcity is reflected in market prices. If the world were running out of natural resources, then the prices of those resources would be rising over time. But, in fact, the opposite is more nearly true. The prices of most natural resources (adjusted for overall inflation) are stable or falling. It appears that our ability to conserve these resources is growing more rapidly than their supplies are dwindling. Market prices give no reason to believe that natural resources are a limit to economic growth. ●

QuickQuiz List and describe four determinants of a country's productivity.

ECONOMIC GROWTH AND PUBLIC POLICY

So far, we have determined that a society's standard of living depends on its ability to produce goods and services and that its productivity depends on physical capital, human capital, natural resources, and technological knowledge. Let's now turn to the question faced by policymakers around the world: What can government policy do to raise productivity and living standards?

The Importance of Saving and Investment

Because capital is a produced factor of production, a society can change the amount of capital it has. If today the economy produces a large quantity of new capital goods, then tomorrow it will have a larger stock of capital and be able to produce more of all types of goods and services. Thus, one way to raise future productivity is to invest more current resources in the production of capital.

One of the ten principles of economics presented in Chapter 1 is that people face tradeoffs. This principle is especially important when considering the accumulation of capital. Because resources are scarce, devoting more resources to producing capital requires devoting fewer resources to producing goods and services for current consumption. That is, for society to invest more in capital, it must consume less and save more of its current income. The growth that arises from capital accumulation is not a free lunch: It requires that society sacrifice consumption of goods and services in the present in order to enjoy higher consumption in the future.

The next chapter examines in more detail how the economy's financial markets coordinate saving and investment. It also examines how government policies influence the amount of saving and investment that takes place. At this point it is important to note that encouraging saving and investment is one way that a government can encourage growth and, in the long run, raise the economy's standard of living.

To see the importance of investment for economic growth, consider Figure 7.1 (p. 138), which displays data on 15 countries. Panel (a) shows each country's growth rate over a 31-year period. The countries are ordered by their growth rates, from most to least rapid. Panel (b) shows the percentage of GDP that each country

FIGURE 7.1

Growth and Investment

Panel (a) shows the growth rate of GDP per person for 15 countries over the period 1960–1991. Panel (b) shows the percentage of GDP that each country devoted to investment over this period. The figure shows that investment and growth are positively correlated.

Source: Robert Summers and Alan Heston, *The Penn World Tables,* and author's calculations.

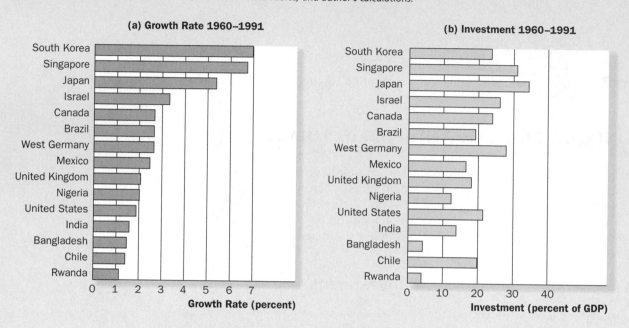

devotes to investment. The correlation between growth and investment, although not perfect, is strong. Countries that devote a large share of GDP to investment, such as Singapore and Japan, tend to have high growth rates. Countries that devote a small share of GDP to investment, such as Rwanda and Bangladesh, tend to have low growth rates. Studies that examine a more comprehensive list of countries confirm this strong correlation between investment and growth.

There is, however, a problem in interpreting these data. As the appendix to Chapter 2 discussed, a correlation between two variables does not establish which variable is the cause and which is the effect. It is possible that high investment causes high growth, but it is also possible that high growth causes high investment. (Or, perhaps, high growth and high investment are both caused by a third variable that has been omitted from the analysis.) The data by themselves cannot tell us the direction of causation. Nonetheless, because capital accumulation affects productivity so clearly and directly, many economists interpret these data as showing that high investment leads to more rapid economic growth.

Diminishing Returns and the Catch-Up Effect

Suppose that a government, convinced by the evidence in Figure 7.1, pursues policies that raise the nation's saving rate—the percentage of GDP devoted to saving rather than consumption. What happens? With the nation saving more, fewer resources are needed to make consumption goods, and more resources are available to make capital goods. As a result, the capital stock increases, leading to rising productivity and more rapid growth in GDP. But how long does this higher rate of growth last? Assuming that the saving rate remains at its new higher level, does the growth rate of GDP stay high indefinitely or only for a period of time?

The traditional view of the production process is that capital is subject to **diminishing returns:** As the stock of capital rises, the extra output produced from an additional unit of capital falls. In other words, when workers already have a large quantity of capital to use in producing goods and services, giving them an additional unit of capital increases their productivity only slightly. Because of diminishing returns, an increase in the saving rate leads to higher growth only for a while. As the higher saving rate allows more capital to be accumulated, the benefits from additional capital become smaller over time, and so growth slows down. *In the long run, the higher saving rate leads to a higher level of productivity and income, but not to higher growth in these variables.* Reaching this long run, however, can take quite a while. According to studies of international data on economic growth, increasing the saving rate can lead to substantially higher growth for a period of several decades.

The diminishing returns to capital has another important implication: Other things equal, it is easier for a country to grow fast if it starts out relatively poor. This effect of initial conditions on subsequent growth is sometimes called the **catch-up effect.** In poor countries, workers lack even the most rudimentary tools and, as a result, have low productivity. Small amounts of capital investment would substantially raise these workers' productivity. By contrast, workers in rich countries have large amounts of capital with which to work, and this partly explains their high productivity. Yet with the amount of capital per worker already so high, additional capital investment has a relatively small effect on productivity. Studies of international data on economic growth confirm this catch-up effect: Controlling for other variables, such as the percentage of GDP devoted to investment, poor countries do tend to grow at a faster rate than rich countries.

This catch-up effect can help explain some of the puzzling results in Figure 7.1. Over this 31-year period, Canada and South Korea devoted a similar share of GDP to investment. Yet Canada experienced only mediocre growth of about 2.5 percent, while Korea experienced spectacular growth of more than 7 percent. The explanation is the catch-up effect. In 1960, Korea had GDP per person less than one-tenth of the Canadian level, in part because previous investment had been so low. With a small initial capital stock, the benefits to capital accumulation were much greater in Korea, and this gave Korea a higher subsequent growth rate.

This catch-up effect shows up in other aspects of life. When a school gives an end-of-year award to the "Most Improved" student, that student is usually one who began the year with relatively poor performance. Students who began the year not studying find improvement easier than students who always worked hard. Note that it is good to be "Most Improved," given the starting point, but it is even better to be "Best Student." Similarly, economic growth over the last several decades has been much more rapid in South Korea than in Canada, but GDP per person is still higher in Canada.

diminishing returns
the property whereby the benefit from an extra unit of an input declines as the quantity of the input increases

catch-up effect
the property whereby countries that start off poor tend to grow more rapidly than countries that start off rich

Investment from Abroad

So far we have discussed how policies aimed at increasing a country's saving rate can increase investment and, thereby, long-term economic growth. Yet saving by domestic residents is not the only way for a country to invest in new capital. The other way is investment by foreigners.

Investment from abroad takes several forms. Nortel might build a plant to assemble telecommunications equipment in Mexico. A capital investment that is owned and operated by a foreign entity is called *foreign direct investment.* Alternatively, a Canadian might buy stock in a Mexican corporation (that is, buy a share in the ownership of the corporation); the Mexican corporation can use the proceeds from the stock sale to build a new factory. An investment that is financed with foreign money but operated by domestic residents is called *foreign portfolio investment.* In both cases, Canadians provide the resources necessary to increase the stock of capital in Mexico. That is, Canadian saving is being used to finance Mexican investment.

When foreigners invest in a country, they do so because they expect to earn a return on their investment. Nortel's assembly plant increases the Mexican capital stock and, therefore, increases Mexican productivity and Mexican GDP. Yet Nortel takes some of this additional income back to Canada in the form of profit. Similarly, when a Canadian investor buys Mexican stock, the investor has a right to a portion of the profit that the Mexican corporation earns.

Investment from abroad, therefore, does not have the same effect on all measures of economic prosperity. Recall that gross domestic product (GDP) is the income earned within a country by both residents and nonresidents, whereas gross national product (GNP) is the income earned by residents of a country both at home and abroad. When Nortel opens its assembly plant in Mexico, some of the income the plant generates accrues to people who do not live in Mexico. As a result, foreign investment in Mexico raises the income of Mexicans (measured by GNP) by less than it raises the production in Mexico (measured by GDP).

Nonetheless, investment from abroad is one way for a country to grow. Even though some of the benefits from this investment flow back to the foreign owners, this investment does increase the economy's stock of capital, leading to higher productivity and higher wages. Moreover, investment from abroad is one way for poor countries to learn the state-of-the-art technologies developed and used in richer countries. For these reasons, many economists who advise governments in less developed economies advocate policies that encourage investment from abroad. Often this means removing restrictions that governments have imposed on foreign ownership of domestic capital.

An organization that tries to encourage the flow of capital to poor countries is the World Bank. This international organization obtains funds from the world's advanced countries, such as Canada and the United States, and uses these resources to make loans to less developed countries so that they can invest in roads, sewer systems, schools, and other types of capital. It also offers the countries advice about how the funds might best be used. The World Bank, together with its sister organization, the International Monetary Fund, was set up after World War II. One lesson from the war was that economic distress often leads to political turmoil, international tensions, and military conflict. Thus, every country has an interest in promoting economic prosperity around the world. The World Bank and the International Monetary Fund are aimed at achieving that common goal.

Education

Education—investment in human capital—is at least as important as investment in physical capital for a country's long-run economic success. In Canada, each year of schooling has historically raised a person's wage on average by about 10 percent. In less developed countries, where human capital is especially scarce, the gap between the wages of educated and uneducated workers is even larger. Thus, one way in which government policy can enhance the standard of living is to provide good schools and to encourage the population to take advantage of them.

Investment in human capital, like investment in physical capital, has an opportunity cost. When students are in school, they forgo the wages they could have earned. In less developed countries, children often drop out of school at an early age, even though the benefit of additional schooling is very high, simply because their labour is needed to help support the family.

Some economists have argued that human capital is particularly important for economic growth because human capital conveys positive externalities. An *externality* is the effect of one person's actions on the well-being of a bystander. An educated person, for instance, might generate new ideas about how best to produce goods and services. If these ideas enter society's pool of knowledge, so everyone can use them, then the ideas are an external benefit of education. In this case, the return to schooling for society is even greater than the return for the individual. This argument would justify the large subsidies to human-capital investment that we observe in the form of public education.

One problem facing some poor countries is the *brain drain*—the emigration of many of the most highly educated workers to rich countries, where these workers can enjoy a higher standard of living. If human capital does have positive externalities, then this brain drain makes those people left behind poorer than they otherwise would be. But it is not only poor countries that experience the economic effects of the brain drain. Canada is a rich country with a good system of higher education that attracts many of the best students from poor countries. In this way, Canada benefits from the brain drain suffered by poor countries. However Canada also suffers a brain drain of its own as highly educated workers are attracted to high-paying jobs in the United States. Concern over the size of the brain drain to the United States has prompted many analysts to stress the need for Canada to cut taxes. This is deemed necessary in order to make the after-tax incomes of skilled workers more comparable to those in the United States and in this way stem the flow of human capital out of Canada. However not all analysts are convinced that the brain drain to the United States is so large as to justify such a response.

Property Rights and Political Stability

Another way in which policymakers can foster economic growth is by protecting property rights and promoting political stability. As we first noted when we discussed economic interdependence in Chapter 3, production in market economies arises from the interactions of millions of individuals and firms. When you buy a car, for instance, you are buying the output of a car dealer, a car manufacturer, a steel company, an iron ore mining company, and so on. This division of production among many firms allows the economy's factors of production to be used as effectively as possible. To achieve this outcome, the economy has to coordinate

IN THE NEWS

PROMOTING HUMAN CAPITAL

Gary Becker won the Nobel Prize in Economic Sciences in part because of his pioneering work on human capital. For many countries, he argues, it is the key to economic growth.

Bribe Third World Parents to Keep Their Kids in School

By Gary Becker

Many well-meaning Americans, including college students and religious organizations, have attacked Nike Inc. and other companies accused of using child labor in their overseas plants in poor nations. I agree that something should be done to save the children from dismal long-term economic prospects. However, effective policies must recognize that the fundamental cause of child labor is poverty, not greedy foreign and domestic employers. To combat the effects of poverty, poor mothers should be "bribed" to keep their children in school longer.

Really poor families in Brazil, Mexico, Zaire, India, and many other nations put their children to work because their meager earnings help provide basic food and medicine for themselves and younger siblings. Although parents may recognize that schooling would improve their children's marketable labor skills later in life, they cannot afford the "luxury" of taking them out of the labor market. In essence, child labor is the result of a conflict between short-term parental economic interests and the long-term interests of the children.

Adequate economic growth always eliminates child labor even without laws against it. But poor nations needn't wait until they grow richer. There are short-term solutions. Many nations have compulsory schooling laws up to age 15 or so, but they are often hard to enforce, especially in rural areas and poor sections of large cities. Families who want their children to work simply do not send them to school, or the children have very high absenteeism rates. Officials are reluctant

transactions among these firms, as well as between firms and consumers. Market economies achieve this coordination through market prices. That is, market prices are the instrument with which the invisible hand of the marketplace brings supply and demand into balance.

An important prerequisite for the price system to work is an economy-wide respect for *property rights*: the ability of people to exercise authority over the resources they own. A mining company will not make the effort to mine iron ore if it expects the ore to be stolen. The company mines the ore only if it is confident that it will benefit from the ore's subsequent sale. For this reason, courts serve an important role in a market economy: They enforce property rights. Through the criminal justice system, the courts discourage direct theft. In addition, through the civil justice system, the courts ensure that buyers and sellers live up to their contracts.

Although those of us in developed countries tend to take property rights for granted, those living in less developed countries understand that lack of property rights can be a major problem. In many countries, the system of justice does not work well. Contracts are hard to enforce, and fraud often goes unpunished. In to punish parents of working children, perhaps because they recognize that the problem is not selfishness but poverty.

I propose a better way: Give parents a financial incentive to keep their children in school longer. Poor mothers should be paid if schools certify that their children attend classes regularly. Parents would be strongly motivated to send their children to school—even when the children do not want to go—if these payments were not much below what the children could earn. Most poor parents would happily contribute something to improve their children's long-run chances, but they are reluctant to bear the entire burden.

I have been proposing this for some time, and the Mexican government has begun such a program, called Progresa, that covers over 2 million very poor families in Chiapas and other rural areas. Mothers whose children attend classes regularly, succeed in getting promoted, and get regular medical checkups are paid every month by the central government. These payments average about $25 per family. Most poor Mexican families earn only about $100 a month. That

large a percentage increase should have a noticeable effect on their behavior.

Poor families in less developed nations whose children do go to school are likely to withdraw their daughters when they become teenagers. This tends to perpetuate economic inequalities, since the children of women who receive little schooling also tend to be badly educated. Progresa tries to combat this tendency to favor education of older sons by paying a little more to families that keep teenage daughters enrolled.

This pioneering Mexican approach appears to be highly successful. An evaluation prepared for an October economics conference in Chile shows that after only a couple of years, Progresa significantly raised the schooling of children in very poor Mexican families. It has also narrowed the education gap between girls and boys and reduced the labor force participation of boys.

Of course, governments need to find the tax revenue to finance programs like Progresa. A good start would be to recognize that Mexico and many other less developed nations typically spend

disproportionately on universities and other education of their elites. Redistributing some of this spending to the poor would both reduce inequality and stimulate faster economic growth. Widespread basic education is more effective in promoting economic development than generous subsidies to the richer students who attend universities.

Child-labor critics could spend their time more fruitfully by attacking not the overseas employment policies of multinationals but the social policies of governments in poor nations that are really responsible for the prevalence of child labor there. These governments, and perhaps international organizations such as the World Bank, should follow Mexico's example and introduce programs that pay poor mothers to keep their teenage and younger sons and daughters in school and out of the labor force.

Source: *Business Week*, November 22, 1999, p. 15. © Business Week, November 22, 1999. Reprinted with permission of McGraw-Hill Companies, Inc. All rights reserved.

more extreme cases, the government not only fails to enforce property rights but actually infringes on them. To do business in some countries, firms are expected to bribe powerful government officials. Such corruption impedes the coordinating power of markets. It also discourages domestic saving and investment from abroad.

One threat to property rights is political instability. When revolutions and coups are common, there is doubt about whether property rights will be respected in the future. If a revolutionary government might confiscate the capital of some businesses, as was often true after communist revolutions, domestic residents have less incentive to save, invest, and start new businesses. At the same time, foreigners have less incentive to invest in the country. Even the threat of revolution can act to depress a nation's standard of living.

Thus, economic prosperity depends in part on political prosperity. A country with an efficient court system, honest government officials, and a stable constitution will enjoy a higher economic standard of living than a country with a poor court system, corrupt officials, and frequent revolutions and coups.

Free Trade

Some of the world's poorest countries have tried to achieve more rapid economic growth by pursuing *inward-oriented policies*. These policies are aimed at raising productivity and living standards within the country by avoiding interaction with the rest of the world. This approach gets support from some domestic firms, which claim that they need protection from foreign competition in order to compete and grow. This infant-industry argument, together with a general distrust of foreigners, has at times led policymakers in less developed countries to impose tariffs and other trade restrictions.

Most economists today believe that poor countries are better off pursuing *outward-oriented policies* that integrate these countries into the world economy. When we studied international trade earlier in the book, we showed how international trade can improve the economic well-being of a country's citizens. Trade is, in some ways, a type of technology. When a country exports wheat and imports steel, the country benefits in the same way as if it had invented a technology for turning wheat into steel. A country that eliminates trade restrictions will, therefore, experience the same kind of economic growth that would occur after a major technological advance.

The adverse impact of inward orientation becomes clear when one considers the small size of many less developed economies. The total GDP of Argentina, for instance, is about that of Toronto. Imagine what would happen if the Toronto city council were to prohibit city residents from trading with people living outside the city limits. Without being able to take advantage of the gains from trade, Toronto would need to produce all the goods it consumes. It would also have to produce all its own capital goods, rather than importing state-of-the-art equipment from other cities. Living standards in Toronto would fall immediately, and the problem would likely only get worse over time. This is precisely what happened when Argentina pursued inward-oriented policies throughout much of the twentieth century. By contrast, countries pursuing outward-oriented policies, such as South Korea, Singapore, and Taiwan, have enjoyed high rates of economic growth.

The amount that a nation trades with others is determined not only by government policy but also by geography. Countries with good natural seaports find trade easier than countries without this resource. It is not a coincidence that many of the world's major cities, such as New York, San Francisco, and Hong Kong, are located next to oceans. Similarly, because landlocked countries find international trade more difficult, they tend to have lower levels of income than countries with easy access to the world's waterways.

Research and Development

The primary reason that living standards are higher today than they were a century ago is that technological knowledge has advanced. The telephone, the transistor, the computer, and the internal combustion engine are among the thousands of innovations that have improved the ability to produce goods and services.

Although most technological advance comes from private research by firms and individual inventors, there is also a public interest in promoting these efforts. To a large extent, knowledge is a *public good*: Once one person discovers an idea, the idea enters society's pool of knowledge, and other people can freely use it. Just as government has a role in providing a public good such as national defence, it also has a role in encouraging the research and development of new technologies.

The Canadian government has long played a role in creating and disseminating technological knowledge. Research at the Dominion Experimental Farms led to the introduction of the Marquis strain of wheat to western Canada in 1911. Marquis matured earlier than other strains of wheat, making it feasible to cultivate much more of the Prairies than would otherwise have been possible. This research was therefore a significant contributor to Canada's early economic growth.

More recently, the Canadian government funded research that led to the development of the CANDU nuclear reactor. The government continues to encourage advances in knowledge with research grants from agencies such as the Natural Sciences and Engineering Research Council of Canada, the Medical Research Council, and the Social Sciences and Humanities Research Council of Canada. The federal and provincial governments also encourage advances in knowledge by offering tax breaks to firms that engage in research and development.

Yet another way in which government policy encourages research is through the patent system. When a person or firm invents a new product, such as a new drug, the inventor can apply for a patent. If the product is deemed truly original, the government awards the patent, which gives the inventor the exclusive right to make the product for a specified number of years. In essence, the patent gives the inventor a property right over his invention, turning his new idea from a public good into a private good. By allowing inventors to profit from their inventions—even if only temporarily—the patent system enhances the incentive for individuals and firms to engage in research.

Case Study

THE PRODUCTIVITY SLOWDOWN AND SPEEDUP

The rate of productivity growth is not at all steady and reliable. As measured by real output per worker, productivity in Canada grew at a rate of 2.3 percent per year from 1962 to 1973. From 1974 to 1982, productivity slowed, growing by only 0.3 percent per year before speeding up to 1.7 percent per year over the 1983–88 period. Another productivity slowdown occurred during 1909–96 (0.9 percent per year) before another spurt of 2.0 percent annual growth was enjoyed from 1997 to 2000.

The effects of these changes in productivity growth are easy to see. Productivity is reflected in real wages and family incomes. When productivity growth slowed, the typical worker received smaller inflation-adjusted raises, and many people experienced a general sense of economic anxiety. Accumulated over many years, even a small change in productivity growth has a large effect. For example, over the entire period of 1962 to 2000, output per worker grew at an average rate of 1.4 percent per year. If output per worker had continued to grow at the average rate enjoyed from 1962 to 1973, the income of the average Canadian would today be about 50 percent higher than it is currently.

The causes of these changes in productivity growth are more elusive. One fact is well established: These changes cannot be traced to the factors of production that are most easily measured. Economists can measure directly the quantity of physical capital that workers have available. They can also measure human capital in the form of years of schooling. It appears that the slowdown and speedup in

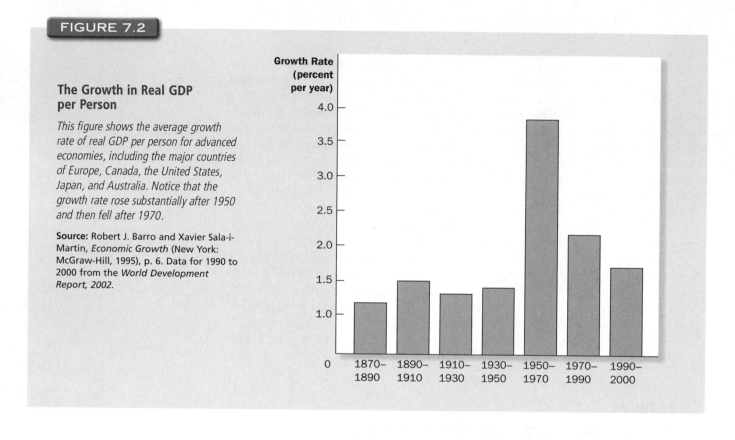

FIGURE 7.2

The Growth in Real GDP per Person

This figure shows the average growth rate of real GDP per person for advanced economies, including the major countries of Europe, Canada, the United States, Japan, and Australia. Notice that the growth rate rose substantially after 1950 and then fell after 1970.

Source: Robert J. Barro and Xavier Sala-i-Martin, *Economic Growth* (New York: McGraw-Hill, 1995), p. 6. Data for 1990 to 2000 from the *World Development Report, 2002.*

productivity growth are not due primarily to changes in the growth of these inputs.

Technology is one of the few remaining culprits. That is, having ruled out other explanations, many economists attribute the slowdown and speedup in economic growth to changes in the creation of new ideas about how to produce goods and services. This explanation is difficult to confirm or refute, because the quantity of "ideas" is hard to measure, but the hypothesis is plausible.

What does the future hold for technological progress and economic growth? History gives us little reason to be confident in any prediction. Neither the productivity slowdown nor the productivity speedup was foreseen by many forecasters before it arrived.

History can, however, give us a sense of what is the normal rate of technological progress. Figure 7.2 shows the average growth of real GDP per person in the developed world, going back to 1870. This figure shows an important lesson: Compared to most of history, the anomaly is the rapid growth that occurred between 1950 and 1970. Perhaps the decades after World War II were a period of unusually rapid technological advance, and growth slowed down in 1973 simply because technological progress was returning to a more normal rate. ●

Population Growth

Economists and other social scientists have long debated how population growth affects a society. The most direct effect is on the size of the labour force: A large population means more workers to produce goods and services. At the same time, it means more people to consume those goods and services. Beyond these obvious effects, population growth interacts with the other factors of production in ways that are less obvious and more open to debate.

Stretching Natural Resources Thomas Robert Malthus (1766–1834), an English minister and early economic thinker, is famous for his book called *An Essay on the Principle of Population as It Affects the Future Improvement of Society*. In it, Malthus offered what may be history's most chilling forecast. Malthus argued that an ever-increasing population would continually strain society's ability to provide for itself. As a result, mankind was doomed to forever live in poverty.

Malthus's logic was simple. He began by noting that "food is necessary to the existence of man" and that "the passion between the sexes is necessary and will remain nearly in its present state." He concluded that "the power of population is infinitely greater than the power in the earth to produce subsistence for man." According to Malthus, the only check on population growth was "misery and vice." Attempts by charities or governments to alleviate poverty were counterproductive, he argued, because they merely allowed the poor to have more children, placing even greater strains on society's productive capabilities.

Fortunately, Malthus's dire forecast was far off the mark. Although the world population has increased about sixfold over the past two centuries, living standards around the world are on average much higher. As a result of economic growth, chronic hunger and malnutrition are less common now than they were in Malthus's day. Famines occur from time to time, but they are more often the result of an unequal income distribution or political instability than an inadequate production of food.

Where did Malthus go wrong? As we discussed in a case study earlier in this chapter, growth in mankind's ingenuity has offset the effects of a larger population. Pesticides, fertilizers, mechanized farm equipment, new crop varieties, and other technological advances that Malthus never imagined have allowed each farmer to feed ever-greater numbers of people. Even with more mouths to feed, fewer farmers are necessary because each farmer is so productive.

Thomas Robert Malthus

Diluting the Capital Stock Whereas Mathus worried about the effects of population on the use of natural resources, some modern theories of economic growth emphasize its effects on capital accumulation. According to these theories, high population growth reduces GDP per worker because rapid growth in the number of workers forces the capital stock to be spread more thinly. In other words, when population growth is rapid, each worker is equipped with less capital. A smaller quantity of capital per worker leads to lower productivity and lower GDP per worker.

This problem is most apparent in the case of human capital. Countries with high population growth have large numbers of school-age children. This places a larger burden on the educational system. It is not surprising, therefore, that educational attainment tends to be low in countries with high population growth.

IN THE NEWS

A SOLUTION TO AFRICA'S PROBLEMS

In 2000 the average income in sub-Saharan Africa was $480. Why? Here is the analysis of Jeffrey Sachs, an adviser to governments around the world and a critic of the World Bank and the International Monetary Fund (IMF), the international policy organizations that dispense advice and money to struggling countries.

Growth in Africa: It Can Be Done

By Jeffrey Sachs

In the old story, the peasant goes to the priest for advice on saving his dying chickens. The priest recommends prayer, but the chickens continue to die. The priest then recommends music for the chicken coop, but the deaths continue unabated. Pondering again, the priest recommends repainting the chicken coop in bright colors. Finally, all the chickens die. "What a shame," the priest tells the peasant. "I had so many more good ideas."

Since independence, African countries have looked to donor nations—often their former colonial rulers—and to the international finance institutions for guidance on growth. Indeed, since the onset of the African debt crises of the 1980s, the guidance has become a kind of economic receivership, with the policies of many African nations decided in a seemingly endless cycle of meetings with the IMF, the World Bank, donors, and creditors.

What a shame. So many good ideas, so few results. . . .

The IMF and World Bank would be absolved of shared responsibility for slow growth if Africa were structurally incapable of growth rates seen in other parts of the world or if the continent's low growth were an impenetrable mystery. But Africa's growth rates are not huge mysteries. . . . Studies of cross-country growth show that per capita growth is related to:

- the initial income level of the country, with poorer countries tending to grow faster than richer countries;
- the extent of overall market orientation, including openness to trade, domestic market liberalization, private rather than state ownership, protection of private property rights, and low marginal tax rates;
- the national saving rate, which in turn is strongly affected by the government's own saving rate; and
- the geographic and resource structure of the economy. . . .

These four factors can account broadly for Africa's long-term growth predicament. While it should have grown faster than other developing areas because of relatively low income per head (and hence larger opportunity for "catch-up" growth), Africa grew more

The differences in population growth rates around the world are large. In many poor African countries, population grows at about 3 percent per year. At this rate, the population doubles every 23 years. This rapid population growth makes it harder to provide workers with the tools and skills they need to achieve high levels of productivity. By contrast, in developed countries, such as Canada, the United States, and Western Europe, the population growth rate has been only about 1 percent per year in recent decades. This rate of growth is below the rate necessary to maintain population at current levels. Policymakers in these countries are concerned that a shrinking population of working-age people will be slowly. This was mainly because of much higher trade barriers; excessive tax rates; lower saving rates; and adverse structural conditions, including an unusually high incidence of inaccessibility to the sea (15 of 53 countries are landlocked). . . .

If the policies are largely to blame, why, then, were they adopted? The historical origins of Africa's antimarket orientation are not hard to discern. After almost a century of colonial depredations, African nations understandably if erroneously viewed open trade and foreign capital as a threat to national sovereignty. As in Sukarno's Indonesia, Nehru's India, and Peron's Argentina, "self sufficiency" and "state leadership," including state ownership of much of industry, became the guideposts of the economy. As a result, most of Africa went into a largely self-imposed economic exile. . . .

Adam Smith in 1755 famously remarked that "little else is requisite to carry a state to the highest degrees of opulence from the lowest barbarism, but peace, easy taxes, and tolerable administration of justice." A growth agenda need not be long and complex. Take his points in turn.

Peace, of course, is not so easily guaranteed, but the conditions for peace on the continent are better than today's ghastly headlines would suggest. Several of the large-scale conflicts that have ravaged the continent are over or nearly so. . . . The ongoing disasters, such as in Liberia, Rwanda and Somalia, would be better contained if the West were willing to provide modest support to African-based peacekeeping efforts.

"Easy taxes" are well within the ambit of the IMF and World Bank. But here, the IMF stands guilty of neglect, if not malfeasance. African nations need simple, low taxes, with modest revenue targets as a share of GDP. Easy taxes are most essential in international trade, since successful growth will depend, more than anything else, on economic integration with the rest of the world. Africa's largely self-imposed exile from world markets can end quickly by cutting import tariffs and ending export taxes on agricultural exports. Corporate tax rates should be cut. . . .

Adam Smith spoke of a "tolerable" administration of justice, not perfect justice. Market liberalization is the primary key to strengthening the rule of law. Free trade, currency convertibility and automatic incorporation of business vastly reduce the scope for official corruption and allow the government to focus on the real public goods—internal public order, the judicial system, basic public health and education, and monetary stability. . . .

All of this is possible only if the government itself has held its own spending

© TOM VAN SANT/CORBIS/MAGMA

to the necessary minimum. . . . Subsidies to publicly owned companies or marketing boards should be scrapped. Food and housing subsidies for urban workers cannot be financed. And, notably, interest payments on foreign debt are not budgeted for. This is because most bankrupt African states need a fresh start based on deep debt-reduction, which should be implemented in conjunction with far-reaching domestic reforms.

Source: *The Economist,* June 29, 1996, pp. 19–21. © 1996 The Economist Newspaper Ltd. All rights reserved. Reprinted with permission. Further reproduction prohibited. http://www.economist.com.

unable to maintain economic growth rates. The result may be tax revenue that is insufficient to support a growing share of the population that is retired, hoping to collect public pensions, and expecting to be cared for in publicly funded hospitals.

Although rapid population growth is not the main reason that less developed countries are poor, some analysts believe that reducing the rate of population growth would help these countries raise their standards of living. In some countries, this goal is accomplished directly with laws that regulate the number of children families may have. China, for instance, allows only one child per family; couples who violate this rule are subject to substantial fines. In countries with greater freedom, the goal of reduced population growth is accomplished less directly by increasing awareness of birth control techniques.

Another way in which a country can influence population growth is to apply one of the ten principles of economics: People respond to incentives. Bearing a child, like any decision, has an opportunity cost. When the opportunity cost rises, people will choose to have smaller families. In particular, women with the opportunity to receive good education and desirable employment tend to want fewer children than those with fewer opportunities outside the home. Hence, policies that foster equal treatment of women are one way for less developed economies to reduce the rate of population growth and, perhaps, raise their standards of living.

Promoting Technological Progress Although rapid population growth may depress economic prosperity by reducing the amount of capital each worker has, it may also have some benefits. Some economists have suggested that world population growth has been an engine of technological progress and economic prosperity. The mechanism is simple: If there are more people, then there are more scientists, inventors, and engineers to contribute to technological advance, which benefits everyone.

Economist Michael Kremer has provided some support for this hypothesis in an article titled "Population Growth and Technological Change: 1 000 000 B.C. to 1990," which was published in the *Quarterly Journal of Economics* in 1993. Kremer begins by noting that over the broad span of human history, world growth rates have increased as world population has. For example, world growth was more rapid when the world population was 1 billion (which occurred around the year 1800) than it was when the population was only 100 million (around 500 B.C.). This fact is consistent with the hypothesis that having more people induces more technological progress.

Kremer's second piece of evidence comes from comparing regions of the world. The melting of the polar icecaps at the end of the ice age around 10 000 B.C. flooded the land bridges and separated the world into several distinct regions that could not communicate with one another for thousands of years. If technological progress is more rapid when there are more people to discover things, then larger regions should have experienced more rapid growth.

According to Kremer, that is exactly what happened. The most successful region of the world in 1500 (when Columbus reestablished technological contact) comprised the "Old World" civilizations of the large Eurasia-Africa region. Next in technological development were the Aztec and Mayan civilizations in the Americas, followed by the hunter–gatherers of Australia, and then the primitive people of Tasmania, who lacked even fire-making and most stone and bone tools.

The smallest isolated region was Flinders Island, a tiny island between Tasmania and Australia. With the smallest population, Flinders Island had the fewest opportunities for technological advance and, indeed, seemed to regress. Around 3000 B.C., human society on Flinders Island died out completely. A large population, Kremer concludes, is a prequisite for technological advance.

QuickQuiz Describe three ways in which a government policymaker can try to raise the growth in living standards in a society. Are there any drawbacks to these policies?

CONCLUSION: THE IMPORTANCE OF LONG-RUN GROWTH

In this chapter we have discussed what determines the standard of living in a nation and how policymakers can endeavour to raise the standard of living through policies that promote economic growth. Most of this chapter is summarized in one of the ten principles of economics: A country's standard of living depends on its ability to produce goods and services. Policymakers who want to encourage growth in standards of living must aim to increase their nations' productive ability by encouraging rapid accumulation of the factors of production and ensuring that these factors are employed as effectively as possible.

Economists differ in their views of the role of government in promoting economic growth. At the very least, government can lend support to the invisible hand by maintaining property rights and political stability. More controversial is whether government should target and subsidize specific industries that might be especially important for technological progress. There is no doubt that these issues are among the most important in economics. The success of one generation's policymakers in learning and heeding the fundamental lessons about economic growth determines what kind of world the next generation will inherit.

SUMMARY

- Economic prosperity, as measured by GDP per person, varies substantially around the world. The average income in the world's richest countries is more than ten times that in the world's poorest countries. Because growth rates of real GDP also vary substantially, the relative positions of countries can change dramatically over time.

- The standard of living in an economy depends on the economy's ability to produce goods and services. Productivity, in turn, depends on the amounts of physical capital, human capital, natural resources, and technological knowledge available to workers.

- Government policies can try to influence the economy's growth rate in many ways: by encouraging saving and investment, encouraging investment from abroad, fostering education, maintaining property rights and political stability, allowing free trade, promoting the research and development of new technologies, and controlling population growth.

- The accumulation of capital is subject to diminishing returns: The more capital an economy has, the less additional output the economy gets from an extra unit of capital. Because of diminishing returns, higher saving leads to higher growth for a period of time, but growth eventually slows down as the economy approaches a higher level of capital, productivity, and income. Also because of diminishing returns, the return to capital is especially high in poor countries. Other things equal, these countries can grow faster because of the catch-up effect.

KEY CONCEPTS

productivity, p. 133
physical capital, p. 134
human capital, p. 134

natural resources, p. 134
technological knowledge, p. 135
diminishing returns, p. 139

catch-up effect, p. 139

QUESTIONS FOR REVIEW

1. What does the level of a nation's GDP measure? What does the growth rate of GDP measure? Would you rather live in a nation with a high level of GDP and a low growth rate, or in a nation with a low level of GDP and a high growth rate?

2. List and describe four determinants of productivity.

3. In what way is a university or college degree a form of capital?

4. Explain how higher saving leads to a higher standard of living. What might deter a policymaker from trying to raise the rate of saving?

5. Does a higher rate of saving lead to higher growth temporarily or indefinitely?

6. Why would removing a trade restriction, such as a tariff, lead to more rapid economic growth?

7. How does the rate of population growth influence the level of GDP per person?

8. Describe two ways in which the Canadian government tries to encourage advances in technological knowledge.

PROBLEMS AND APPLICATIONS

1. Most countries, including Canada, import substantial amounts of goods and services from other countries. Yet this chapter says that a nation can enjoy a high standard of living only if it can produce a large quantity of goods and services itself. Can you reconcile these two facts?

2. List the capital inputs necessary to produce each of the following.
   a. cars
   b. high-school educations
   c. plane travel
   d. fruits and vegetables

3. Canadian income per person today is many times what it was a century ago. Many other countries have also experienced significant growth over that period. What are some specific ways in which your standard of living differs from that of your great-grandparents?

4. This chapter discusses how employment has declined relative to output in the farm sector. Can you think of another sector of the economy where the same phenomenon has occurred more recently? Would you consider the change in employment in this sector to represent a success or a failure from the standpoint of society as a whole?

5. Suppose that society decided to reduce consumption and increase investment.
   a. How would this change affect economic growth?
   b. What groups in society would benefit from this change? What groups might be hurt?

6. Societies choose what share of their resources to devote to consumption and what share to devote to investment. Some of these decisions involve private spending; others involve government spending.
   a. Describe some forms of private spending that represent consumption, and some forms that represent investment.
   b. Describe some forms of government spending that represent consumption, and some forms that represent investment.

7. What is the opportunity cost of investing in capital? Do you think a country can "over-invest" in capital? What is the opportunity cost of investing in human capital? Do you think a country can "over-invest" in human capital? Explain.

8. Suppose that an auto company owned entirely by German citizens opens a new factory in Quebec.
   a. What sort of foreign investment would this represent?
   b. What would be the effect of this investment on Canadian GDP? Would the effect on Canadian GNP be larger or smaller?

9. In the 1960s American investors made significant direct and portfolio investments in Canada. At the time, many Canadians were unhappy that this investment was occurring.
   a. In what way was it better for Canada to receive this American investment than not to receive it?
   b. In what way would it have been better still for Canadians to have done this investment?

10. In the countries of South Asia in 1992, only 56 young women were enrolled in secondary school for every 100 young men. Describe several ways in which greater educational opportunities for young women could lead to faster economic growth in these countries.

11. How large will Canada's GDP be 25 years from now? The answer depends on what the rate of growth in GDP will be over that 25-year period.

A mathematical formula we can use for this calculation is the following:

$$GDP_{2030} = GDP_{2005} \,(1 + g)^{25}$$

where GDP_{2030} is the level of GDP in the year 2030, GDP_{2005} is the level of GDP in the year 2005, and g is the rate of growth in GDP. Assume that GDP in 2005 is $1000 million and assume that the value of g is 0.035 (3.5 percent per year). What will be the value of GDP in 2030? Now suppose that the value of g is 0.040 (4.0 percent per year). What will be the value of GDP in 2030 given this slightly larger rate of growth? What does this result say about the importance of policies that promote even slightly faster rates of growth in GDP?

INTERNET RESOURCES

- The World Bank (http://www.worldbank.org) and the International Monetary Fund (http://www.imf.org) both maintain websites that explain the roles they play in trying to promote economic prosperity around the world.

- Industry Canada provides an interesting and useful discussion of the importance of productivity for economic growth and the economic well-being of Canadians at http://strategis.ic.gc.ca/epic/internet/inpro-pro.nsf/vwGeneratedInterE/home.

 For more study tools, please visit http://www.mankiw3e.nelson.com.

© CP PICTURE ARCHIVE/BILL BECKER

SAVING, INVESTMENT, AND THE FINANCIAL SYSTEM

Learning Objectives

In this chapter, you will …

- Learn about some of the important financial institutions in the Canadian economy
- Consider how the financial system is related to key macroeconomic variables
- Develop a model of the supply and demand for loanable funds in financial markets
- Use a model to analyze various government policies
- Consider how government budget deficits and surpluses affect the Canadian economy

Imagine that you have just graduated from university or college (with a degree in economics, of course) and you decide to start your own business—an economic forecasting firm. Before you make any money selling your forecasts, you have to incur substantial costs to set up your business. You have to buy computers with which to make your forecasts, as well as desks, chairs, and filing cabinets to furnish your new office. Each of these items is a type of capital that your firm will use to produce and sell its services.

How do you obtain the funds to invest in these capital goods? Perhaps you are able to pay for them out of your past savings. More likely, however, like most entrepreneurs, you do not have enough money of your own to finance the start of your business. As a result, you have to get the money you need from other sources.

There are various ways for you to finance these capital investments. You could borrow the money, perhaps from a bank or from a friend or relative. In this case, you would promise not only to return the money at a later date but also to pay interest for the use of the money. Alternatively, you could convince someone to provide the money you need for your business in exchange for a share of your future profits, whatever they might happen to be. In either case, your investment in computers and office equipment is being financed by someone else's saving.

The **financial system** consists of those institutions in the economy that help to match one person's saving with another person's investment. As we discussed in the previous chapter, saving and investment are key ingredients to long-run economic growth: When a country saves a large portion of its GDP, more resources are available for investment in capital, and higher capital raises a country's productivity and living standard. The previous chapter, however, did not explain how the economy coordinates saving and investment. At any time, some people want to save some of their income for the future, and others want to borrow in order to finance investments in new and growing businesses. What brings these two groups of people together? What ensures that the supply of funds from those who want to save balances the demand for funds from those who want to invest?

This chapter examines how the financial system works. First, we discuss the large variety of institutions that make up the financial system in our economy. Second, we discuss the relationship between the financial system and some key macroeconomic variables—notably saving and investment. Third, we develop a model of the supply and demand for funds in financial markets. In the model, the interest rate is the price that adjusts to balance supply and demand. The model shows how various government policies affect the interest rate and, thereby, society's allocation of scarce resources.

FINANCIAL INSTITUTIONS IN THE CANADIAN ECONOMY

At the broadest level, the financial system moves the economy's scarce resources from savers (people who spend less than they earn) to borrowers (people who spend more than they earn). Savers save for various reasons—to put a child through college or university in several years or to retire comfortably in several decades. Similarly, borrowers borrow for various reasons—to buy a house in which to live or to start a business with which to make a living. Savers supply their money to the financial system with the expectation that they will get it back with interest at a later date. Borrowers demand money from the financial system with the knowledge that they will be required to pay it back with interest at a later date.

The financial system is made up of various financial institutions that help coordinate savers and borrowers. As a prelude to analyzing the economic forces that drive the financial system, let's discuss the most important of these institutions. Financial institutions can be grouped into two categories—financial markets and financial intermediaries. We consider each category in turn.

Financial Markets

financial markets
financial institutions through which savers can directly provide funds to borrowers

Financial markets are the institutions through which a person who wants to save can directly supply funds to a person who wants to borrow. The two most important financial markets in our economy are the bond market and the stock market.

financial system
the group of institutions in the economy that help to match one person's saving with another person's investment

The Bond Market   When Intel, the giant maker of computer chips, wants to borrow to finance construction of a new factory, it can borrow directly from the public. It does this by selling bonds. A **bond** is a certificate of indebtedness that specifies the obligations of the borrower to the holder of the bond. Put simply, a bond is an IOU. It identifies the time at which the loan will be repaid, called the *date of maturity,* and the rate of interest that will be paid periodically until the loan matures. The buyer of a bond gives his or her money to Intel in exchange for this promise of interest and eventual repayment of the amount borrowed (called the *principal*). The buyer can hold the bond until maturity or can sell the bond at an earlier date to someone else.

bond
a certificate of indebtedness

There are literally millions of different bonds in the Canadian economy. When large corporations, the federal government, or provincial governments need to borrow to finance the purchase of a new factory, a new jet fighter, or a new school, they usually do so by issuing bonds. If you look at the business section of your local newspaper, you will find a listing of the prices and interest rates of some of the most important bond issues. Although these bonds differ in many ways, two characteristics of bonds are most important.

The first characteristic is a bond's *term*—the length of time until the bond matures. Some bonds have short terms, such as a few months, while others have terms as long as 30 years. (The British government has even issued a bond that never matures, called a *perpetuity.* This bond pays interest forever, but the principal is never repaid.) The interest rate on a bond depends, in part, on its term. Long-term bonds are riskier than short-term bonds because holders of long-term bonds have to wait longer for repayment of principal. If a holder of a long-term bond needs his money earlier than the distant date of maturity, he has no choice but to sell the bond to someone else, perhaps at a reduced price. To compensate for this risk, long-term bonds usually pay higher interest rates than short-term bonds.

The second important characteristic of a bond is its *credit risk*—the probability that the borrower will fail to pay some of the interest or principal. Such a failure to pay is called a *default.* Borrowers can (and sometimes do) default on their loans by declaring bankruptcy. When bond buyers perceive that the probability of default is high, they demand a higher interest rate to compensate them for this credit risk.

Credit risk is affected by such things as the level of debt carried by the issuer of the bond, recent changes in the amount of debt carried, and the stability of the issuer's revenues. The Canadian government is considered a relatively safe credit risk because (as we'll see shortly) although it carries a lot of debt, the amount of debt it carries is falling and its tax revenues are fairly stable.

Provincial governments also issue bonds, but provinces are considered to be a somewhat greater credit risk than the federal government because provincial economies tend to be less diverse than the national economy and, as such, their tax revenues are more volatile. Since a sudden fall in tax revenue might cause a province difficulty in paying its debts, the rate of interest paid on provincial bonds is somewhat higher than that paid on federal bonds with a similar term to maturity. The rate of interest paid on provincial bonds varies by province, reflecting provincial differences in revenue volatility and provincial government debt.

Corporate bonds tend to pay higher rates of interest than provincial bonds because corporate revenues are likely to be more volatile than provincial tax revenues. Financially shaky corporations raise money by issuing *junk bonds*, which as the name suggests, pay considerably higher interest rates than the bonds issued by more secure corporations and by governments.

Some idea of the role of credit risk in determining the interest rate paid on bonds is suggested by the fact that on July 31, 2003, the interest rate paid on bonds maturing in 2012 was 4.8 percent on federal government bonds, 5.1 percent on Government of Ontario bonds, and 5.5 percent on bonds issued by Bell Canada. Buyers of bonds can judge credit risk by checking with various private agencies, such as Standard & Poor's, that rate the credit risk of different bonds.

The Stock Market   Another way for Intel to raise funds to build a new semiconductor factory is to sell stock in the company. **Stock** represents ownership in a firm and is, therefore, a claim to the profits that the firm makes. For example, if Intel sells a total of 1 000 000 shares of stock, then each share represents ownership of 1/1 000 000 of the business.

stock
a claim to partial ownership in a firm

The sale of stock to raise money is called *equity finance,* whereas the sale of bonds is called *debt finance.* Although corporations use both equity and debt finance to raise money for new investments, stocks and bonds are very different. The owner of shares of Intel stock is a part owner of Intel; the owner of an Intel bond is a creditor of the corporation. If Intel is very profitable, the shareholders enjoy the benefits of these profits, whereas the bondholders get only the interest on their bonds. And if Intel runs into financial difficulty, the bondholders are paid what they are due before stockholders receive anything at all. Compared to bonds, stocks offer the holder both higher risk and potentially higher return.

After a corporation issues stock by selling shares to the public, these shares trade among stockholders on organized stock exchanges. In these transactions, the corporation itself receives no money when its stock changes hands. The most important stock exchanges in the U.S. economy are the New York Stock Exchange, the American Stock Exchange, and NASDAQ (National Association of Securities Dealers Automated Quotation system). In Canada, the Toronto Stock Exchange (TSX) is the most important. A more speculative stock exchange that raises money for junior companies is the Canadian Venture Exchange, located in Calgary. Most of the world's countries have their own stock exchanges on which the shares of local companies trade.

The prices at which shares trade on stock exchanges are determined by the supply and demand for the stock in these companies. Because stock represents ownership in a corporation, the demand for a stock (and thus its price) reflects people's perception of the corporation's future profitability. When people become optimistic about a company's future, they raise their demand for its stock and thereby bid up the price of a share of stock. Conversely, when people come to expect a company to have little profit or even losses, the price of a share falls.

Various stock indexes are available to monitor the overall level of stock prices. A *stock index* is computed as an average of a group of stock prices. The most famous stock index is the Dow Jones Industrial Average, which has been computed regularly since 1896. It is now based on the prices of the stocks of 30 major U.S. companies, such as General Motors, General Electric, Microsoft, Coca-Cola, AT&T, and IBM. The best-known and most closely watched stock index in Canada is the TSX 300, which is based on the prices of 300 major firms listed on the TSX. Because stock prices reflect expected profitability, these stock indexes are watched closely as possible indicators of future economic conditions.

HOW TO READ THE NEWSPAPER'S STOCK TABLES

Most daily newspapers include stock tables, which contain information about recent trading in the stocks of several thousand companies. Here is the kind of information these tables usually provide:

- *Price.* The single most important piece of information about a stock is the price of a share. The newspaper usually presents several prices. The "last" or "closing" price is the price of the last transaction that occurred before the stock exchange closed the previous day. Many newspapers also give the "high" and "low" prices over the past day of trading and, sometimes, over the past year as well.
- *Volume.* Most newspapers present the number of shares sold during the past day of trading. This figure is called the *daily volume.*
- *Dividend.* Corporations pay out some of their profits to their shareholders; this amount is called the *dividend.* (Profits not paid out are called *retained earnings* and are used by the corporation

for additional investment.) Newspapers often report the dividend paid over the previous year for each share of stock. They sometimes report the *dividend yield,* which is the dividend expressed as a percentage of the stock's price.
- *Price/earnings ratio.* A corporation's earnings, or profit, is the amount of revenue it receives for the sale of its products minus its costs of production as measured by its accountants. *Earnings per share* is the company's total earnings divided by the number of shares of stock outstanding. Companies use some of their earnings to pay dividends to shareholders; the rest is kept in the firm to make new investments. The price/earnings ratio, often called the P/E, is the price of a corporation's stock divided by the amount the corporation earned per share over the past year. Historically, the typical price/earnings ratio is about 15. A higher P/E indicates that a corporation's stock is expensive relative to its recent earnings; this might indicate either that people expect earnings to rise in the future or that the stock is overvalued. Conversely, a lower P/E indicates that a corporation's stock is cheap relative to its recent earnings; this might indicate either that people expect earnings to fall or that the stock is undervalued.

Why does the newspaper report all these data every day? Many people who invest their savings in stock follow these numbers closely when deciding which stocks to buy and sell. By contrast, other shareholders follow a buy-and-hold strategy: They buy the stock of well-run companies, hold it for long periods of time, and do not respond to the daily fluctuations reported in the paper.

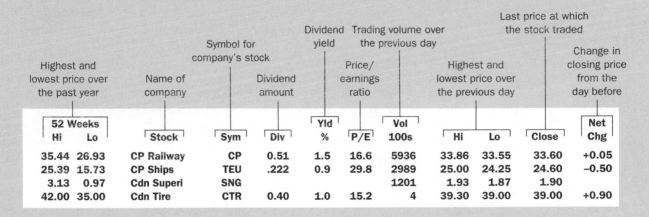

52 Weeks		Stock	Sym	Div	Yld %	P/E	Vol 100s	Hi	Lo	Close	Net Chg
Hi	Lo										
35.44	26.93	CP Railway	CP	0.51	1.5	16.6	5936	33.86	33.55	33.60	+0.05
25.39	15.73	CP Ships	TEU	.222	0.9	29.8	2989	25.00	24.25	24.60	−0.50
3.13	0.97	Cdn Superi	SNG				1201	1.93	1.87	1.90	
42.00	35.00	Cdn Tire	CTR	0.40	1.0	15.2	4	39.30	39.00	39.00	+0.90

Financial Intermediaries

Financial intermediaries are financial institutions through which savers can indirectly provide funds to borrowers. The term *intermediary* reflects the role of these

financial intermediaries
financial institutions through which savers can indirectly provide funds to borrowers

institutions in standing between savers and borrowers. Here we consider two of the most important financial intermediaries—banks and mutual funds.

Banks   If the owner of a small grocery store wants to finance an expansion of his business, he probably takes a strategy quite different from Intel. Unlike Intel, a small grocer would find it difficult to raise funds in the bond and stock markets. Most buyers of stocks and bonds prefer to buy those issued by larger, more familiar companies. The small grocer, therefore, most likely finances his business expansion with a loan from a local bank.

Banks are the financial intermediaries with which people are most familiar. A primary job of banks is to take in deposits from people who want to save and use these deposits to make loans to people who want to borrow. Banks pay depositors interest on their deposits and charge borrowers slightly higher interest on their loans. The difference between these rates of interest covers the banks' costs and returns some profit to the owners of the banks.

Besides being financial intermediaries, banks play a second important role in the economy: They facilitate purchases of goods and services by allowing people to write cheques against their deposits. In other words, banks help create a special asset that people can use as a *medium of exchange*. A medium of exchange is an item that people can easily use to engage in transactions. A bank's role in providing a medium of exchange distinguishes it from many other financial institutions. Stocks and bonds, like bank deposits, are a possible *store of value* for the wealth that people have accumulated in past saving, but access to this wealth is not as easy, cheap, and immediate as just writing a cheque. For now, we ignore this second role of banks, but we will return to it when we discuss the monetary system later in the book.

Mutual Funds   A financial intermediary of increasing importance in the Canadian economy is the mutual fund. A **mutual fund** is an institution that sells shares to the public and uses the proceeds to buy a selection, or *portfolio*, of various types of stocks, bonds, or both stocks and bonds. The shareholder of the mutual fund accepts all the risk and return associated with the portfolio. If the value of the portfolio rises, the shareholder benefits; if the value of the portfolio falls, the shareholder suffers the loss.

mutual fund
an institution that sells shares to the public and uses the proceeds to buy a portfolio of stocks and bonds

The primary advantage of mutual funds is that they allow people with small amounts of money to diversify. Buyers of stocks and bonds are well advised to heed the adage: Don't put all your eggs in one basket. Because the value of any single stock or bond is tied to the fortunes of one company, holding a single kind of stock or bond is very risky. By contrast, people who hold a diverse portfolio of stocks and bonds face less risk because they have only a small stake in each company. Mutual funds make this diversification easy. With only a few hundred dollars, a person can buy shares in a mutual fund and, indirectly, become the part owner or creditor of hundreds of major companies. For this service, the company operating the mutual fund charges shareholders a fee, usually between 0.5 and 3.0 percent of assets each year.

A second advantage claimed by mutual fund companies is that mutual funds give ordinary people access to the skills of professional money managers. The managers of most mutual funds pay close attention to the developments and prospects of the companies in which they buy stock. These managers buy the stock of those

IN THE NEWS

FINANCE IN CHINA

The importance of free financial markets is most apparent when a country doesn't have them.

Sharp Shift for China's Economy as Entrepreneurs Woo Investors

By Craig S. Smith

Wang Shuxian, a former farmer who now drives a Cadillac, built his successful textile company with money from friends and family. As a private businessman, he could never sell shares on the country's state-run stock market. Now he can, in a change signaling that China's economy is preparing to take a sudden turn. . . .

New rules are allowing privately owned companies access to the country's capital markets, which so far have been effectively off limits for nearly

all of them. . . . With easier access to capital, private companies have a chance at becoming the main engine of China's economy for the first time since a brief period earlier this century and otherwise since the Song Dynasty nearly 1,000 years ago.

The change also has political implications: As China's ranks of private businesses grow in number and wealth, their owners will become an increasingly powerful constituency whose demands the government will not be able to easily ignore.

"The rule of law and access to finance are the two things that will make China's private companies independent from political power," said Andy Xie, an

economist for Morgan Stanley Dean Witter in Hong Kong.

Under the existing system, the government, not the market, decides which companies can sell stock to the public. That system puts the power over which concerns get investment money in the hands of local Communist Party bureaucrats, who are most concerned with helping state enterprises in their province survive. The system also encourages bribery and crams the markets with lower-quality state companies that would otherwise never be able to list their shares.

Source: *The New York Times,* December 28, 2000, p. A1. Copyright © 2000 by The New York Times Co. Reprinted with permission.

---

companies that they view as having a profitable future and sell the stock of companies with less promising prospects. This professional management, it is argued, should increase the return that mutual fund depositors earn on their savings.

Financial economists, however, are often skeptical of this second argument. With thousands of money managers paying close attention to each company's prospects, the price of a company's stock is usually a good reflection of the company's true value. As a result, it is hard to "beat the market" by buying good stocks and selling bad ones. In fact, mutual funds called *index funds,* which buy all the stocks in a given stock index, perform somewhat better on average than mutual funds that take advantage of active management by professional money managers. The explanation for the superior performance of index funds is that they keep costs low by buying and selling very rarely and by not having to pay the salaries of the professional money managers.

Summing Up

The Canadian economy contains a large variety of financial institutions. In addition to the bond market, the stock market, banks, and mutual funds, there are also pension funds, credit unions and caisses populaires, insurance companies, and even the local loan shark. These institutions differ in many ways. When analyzing the macroeconomic role of the financial system, however, it is more important to keep in mind the similarity of these institutions than the differences. These financial institutions all serve the same goal—directing the resources of savers into the hands of borrowers.

QuickQuiz What is stock? What is a bond? How are they different? How are they similar?

SAVING AND INVESTMENT IN THE NATIONAL INCOME ACCOUNTS

Events that occur within the financial system are central to understanding developments in the overall economy. As we have just seen, the institutions that make up this system—the bond market, the stock market, banks, and mutual funds—have the role of coordinating the economy's saving and investment. And as we saw in the previous chapter, saving and investment are important determinants of long-run growth in GDP and living standards. As a result, macroeconomists need to understand how financial markets work and how various events and policies affect them.

As a starting point for an analysis of financial markets, we discuss in this section the key macroeconomic variables that measure activity in these markets. Our emphasis here is not on behaviour but on accounting. *Accounting* refers to how various numbers are defined and added up. A personal accountant might help an individual add up her income and expenses. A national income accountant does the same thing for the economy as a whole. The national income accounts include, in particular, GDP and the many related statistics.

The rules of national income accounting include several important identities. Recall that an *identity* is an equation that must be true because of the way the variables in the equation are defined. Identities are useful to keep in mind, because they clarify how different variables are related to one another. Here we consider some accounting identities that shed light on the macroeconomic role of financial markets.

Some Important Identities

Recall that gross domestic product (GDP) is both total income in an economy and the total expenditure on the economy's output of goods and services. GDP (denoted as Y) is divided into four components of expenditure: consumption (C), investment (I), government purchases (G), and net exports (NX). We write

$$Y = C + I + G + NX$$

This equation is an identity because every dollar of expenditure that shows up on the left-hand side also shows up in one of the four components on the right-hand side. Because of the way each of the variables is defined and measured, this equation must always hold.

In this chapter, we simplify our analysis by assuming that the economy we are examining is closed. A *closed economy* is one that does not interact with other economies. In particular, a closed economy does not engage in international trade in goods and services, nor does it engage in international borrowing and lending. Of course, actual economies are *open economies*—that is, they interact with other economies around the world. Nonetheless, assuming a closed economy is a useful simplification with which we can learn some lessons that apply to all economies. Moreover, this assumption applies perfectly to the world economy (because interplanetary trade is not yet common).

Because a closed economy does not engage in international trade, imports and exports are exactly zero. Therefore, net exports (NX) are also zero. In this case, we can write

$$Y = C + I + G$$

This equation states that GDP is the sum of consumption, investment, and government purchases. Each unit of output sold in a closed economy is consumed by a household, invested by a firm or a household, or bought by government.

To see what this identity can tell us about financial markets, subtract C and G from both sides of this equation. We obtain

$$Y - C - G = I$$

The left-hand side of this equation ($Y - C - G$) is the total income in the economy that remains after paying for consumption and government purchases: This amount is called **national saving**, or just **saving**, and is denoted S. Substituting S for $Y - C - G$, we can write the last equation as

national saving (saving)
the total income in the economy that remains after paying for consumption and government purchases

$$S = I$$

This equation states that saving equals investment.

To understand the meaning of national saving, it is helpful to manipulate the definition a bit more. Let T denote the amount that the government collects from households in taxes minus the amount it pays back to households in the form of transfer payments (such as Employment Insurance and welfare). We can then write national saving in either of two ways:

$$S = Y - C - G$$

or

$$S = (Y - T - C) + (T - G)$$

These equations are the same, because the two T's in the second equation cancel each other, but each reveals a different way of thinking about national saving. In

private saving
the income that households have left after paying for taxes and consumption

public saving
the tax revenue that the government has left after paying for its spending

budget surplus
an excess of tax revenue over government spending

budget deficit
a shortfall of tax revenue from government spending

particular, the second equation separates national saving into two pieces: private saving $(Y - T - C)$ and public saving $(T - G)$.

Consider each of these two pieces. **Private saving** is the amount of income that households have left after paying their taxes and paying for their consumption. In particular, because households receive income of Y, pay taxes of T, and spend C on consumption, private saving is $Y - T - C$. **Public saving** is the amount of tax revenue that the government has left after paying for its spending. The government receives T in tax revenue and spends G on goods and services. If T exceeds G, the government runs a **budget surplus** because it receives more money than it spends. This surplus of $T - G$ represents public saving. If the government spends more than it receives in tax revenue, then G is larger than T. In this case, the government runs a **budget deficit,** and public saving $T - G$ is a negative number.

Now consider how these accounting identities are related to financial markets. The equation $S = I$ reveals an important fact: *For the economy as a whole, saving must be equal to investment.* Yet this fact raises some important questions: What mechanisms lie behind this identity? What coordinates those people who are deciding how much to save and those people who are deciding how much to invest? The answer is the financial system. The bond market, the stock market, banks, mutual funds, and other financial markets and intermediaries stand between the two sides of the $S = I$ equation. They take in the nation's saving and direct it to the nation's investment.

The Meaning of Saving and Investment

The terms *saving* and *investment* can sometimes be confusing. Most people use these terms casually and sometimes interchangeably. By contrast, the macroeconomists who put together the national income accounts use these terms carefully and distinctly.

Consider an example. Suppose that Larry earns more than he spends and deposits his unspent income in a bank or uses it to buy a bond or some stock from a corporation. Because Larry's income exceeds his consumption, he adds to the nation's saving. Larry might think of himself as "investing" his money, but a macroeconomist would call Larry's act saving rather than investment.

In the language of macroeconomics, investment refers to the purchase of new capital, such as equipment or buildings. When Moe borrows from the bank to build himself a new house, he adds to the nation's investment. Similarly, when the Curly Corporation sells some stock and uses the proceeds to build a new factory, it also adds to the nation's investment.

Although the accounting identity $S = I$ shows that saving and investment are equal for the economy as a whole, this does not have to be true for every individual household or firm. Larry's saving can be greater than his investment, and he can deposit the excess in a bank. Moe's saving can be less than his investment, and he can borrow the shortfall from a bank. Banks and other financial institutions make these individual differences between saving and investment possible by allowing one person's saving to finance another person's investment.

QuickQuiz Define *private saving, public saving, national saving,* and *investment.* How are they related?

THE MARKET FOR LOANABLE FUNDS

Having discussed some of the important financial institutions in our economy and the macroeconomic role of these institutions, we are ready to build a model of financial markets. Our purpose in building this model is to explain how financial markets coordinate the economy's saving and investment. The model also gives us a tool with which we can analyze various government policies that influence saving and investment.

To keep things simple, we assume that the economy has only one financial market, called the **market for loanable funds.** All savers go to this market to deposit their saving, and all borrowers go to this market to get their loans. Thus, the term *loanable funds* refers to all income that people have chosen to save and lend out, rather than use for their own consumption. In the market for loanable funds, there is one interest rate, which is both the return to saving and the cost of borrowing.

The assumption of a single financial market, of course, is not literally true. As we have seen, the economy has many types of financial institutions. But, as we discussed in Chapter 2, the art in building an economic model is simplifying the world in order to explain it. For our purposes here, we can ignore the diversity of financial institutions and assume that the economy has a single financial market.

market for loanable funds
the market in which those who want to save supply funds and those who want to borrow to invest demand funds

Supply and Demand for Loanable Funds

The economy's market for loanable funds, like other markets in the economy, is governed by supply and demand. To understand how the market for loanable funds operates, therefore, we first look at the sources of supply and demand in that market.

The supply of loanable funds comes from those people who have some extra income they want to save and lend out. This lending can occur directly, such as when a household buys a bond from a firm, or it can occur indirectly, such as when a household makes a deposit in a bank, which in turn uses the funds to make loans. In both cases, *saving is the source of the supply of loanable funds.*

The demand for loanable funds comes from households and firms who wish to borrow to make investments. This demand includes families taking out mortgages to buy homes. It also includes firms borrowing to buy new equipment or build factories. In both cases, *investment is the source of the demand for loanable funds.*

The interest rate is the price of a loan. It represents the amount that borrowers pay for loans and the amount that lenders receive on their saving. Because a high interest rate makes borrowing more expensive, the quantity of loanable funds demanded falls as the interest rate rises. Similarly, because a high interest rate makes saving more attractive, the quantity of loanable funds supplied rises as the interest rate rises. In other words, the demand curve for loanable funds slopes downward, and the supply curve for loanable funds slopes upward.

Figure 8.1 (p. 166) shows the interest rate that balances the supply and demand for loanable funds. In the equilibrium shown, the interest rate is 5 percent, and the quantity of loanable funds demanded and the quantity of loanable funds supplied both equal $120 billion.

FIGURE 8.1

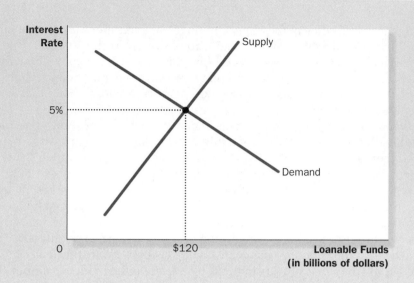

The Market for Loanable Funds

The interest rate in the economy adjusts to balance the supply and demand for loanable funds. The supply of loanable funds comes from national saving, including both private saving and public saving. The demand for loanable funds comes from firms and households that want to borrow for purposes of investment. Here the equilibrium interest rate is 5 percent, and $120 billion of loanable funds are supplied and demanded.

The adjustment of the interest rate to the equilibrium level occurs for the usual reasons. If the interest rate were lower than the equilibrium level, the quantity of loanable funds supplied would be less than the quantity of loanable funds demanded. The resulting shortage of loanable funds would encourage lenders to raise the interest rate they charge. A higher interest rate would encourage saving (thereby increasing the quantity of loanable funds supplied) and discourage borrowing for investment (thereby decreasing the quantity of loanable funds demanded). Conversely, if the interest rate were higher than the equilibrium level, the quantity of loanable funds supplied would exceed the quantity of loanable funds demanded. As lenders competed for the scarce borrowers, interest rates would be driven down. In this way, the interest rate approaches the equilibrium level at which the supply and demand for loanable funds exactly balance.

Recall that economists distinguish between the real interest rate and the nominal interest rate. The nominal interest rate is the interest rate as usually reported—the monetary return to saving and cost of borrowing. The real interest rate is the nominal interest rate corrected for inflation; it equals the nominal interest rate minus the inflation rate. Because inflation erodes the value of money over time, the real interest rate more accurately reflects the real return to saving and cost of borrowing. Therefore, the supply and demand for loanable funds depend on the real (rather than nominal) interest rate, and the equilibrium in Figure 8.1 should be interpreted as determining the real interest rate in the economy. For the rest of this chapter, when you see the term *interest rate,* you should remember that we are talking about the real interest rate.

This model of the supply and demand for loanable funds shows that financial markets work much like other markets in the economy. In the market for milk, for instance, the price of milk adjusts so that the quantity of milk supplied balances the quantity of milk demanded. In this way, the invisible hand coordinates the behaviour of dairy farmers and the behaviour of milk drinkers. Once we realize that saving represents the supply of loanable funds and investment represents the demand, we can see how the invisible hand coordinates saving and investment. When the interest rate adjusts to balance supply and demand in the market for loanable funds, it coordinates the behaviour of people who want to save (the suppliers of loanable funds) and the behaviour of people who want to invest (the demanders of loanable funds).

We can now use this analysis of the market for loanable funds to examine various government policies that affect the economy's saving and investment. Because this model is just supply and demand in a particular market, we analyze any policy using the three steps discussed in Chapter 4. First, we decide whether the policy shifts the supply curve or the demand curve. Second, we determine the direction of the shift. Third, we use the supply-and-demand diagram to see how the equilibrium changes.

Policy 1: Saving Incentives

Canadian families save a smaller fraction of their incomes than their counterparts in many other countries, such as Japan and Germany, but they save slightly more than families in the United States. Although the reasons for these international differences are unclear, many policymakers view the relatively low level of savings in Canada as a major problem. One of the ten principles of economics in Chapter 1 is that a country's standard of living depends on its ability to produce goods and services. And, as we discussed in the preceding chapter, saving is an important long-run determinant of a nation's productivity. If Canada could somehow raise its saving rate to the level that prevails in other countries, the growth rate of GDP would increase, and over time, Canadian citizens would enjoy a higher standard of living.

Another of the ten principles of economics is that people respond to incentives. Many economists have used this principle to suggest that the low saving rate in Canada is at least partly attributable to tax laws that discourage saving. The federal government, as well as all of the provincial governments, collects revenue by taxing income, including interest and dividend income. To see the effects of this policy, consider a 25-year-old who saves $1000 and buys a 30-year bond that pays an interest rate of 9 percent. In the absence of taxes, the $1000 grows to $13 268 when the individual reaches age 55. Yet if that interest is taxed at a rate of, say, 33 percent, then the after-tax interest rate is only 6 percent. In this case, the $1000 grows to only $5743 after 30 years. The tax on interest income substantially reduces the future payoff from current saving and, as a result, reduces the incentive for people to save.

In response to this problem, economists favour changes to the tax system that encourage greater saving. An important change to the Canadian tax system that most economists supported was the introduction of the federal Goods and Services Tax (GST) in 1991. The GST is a consumption tax. Under a consumption tax, income that is saved is not taxed, so the tax clearly encourages greater saving. The sales tax that provinces use to collect revenue is another example of a consumption tax. The only province not currently collecting a sales tax is Alberta, but the evidence in favour of collecting more revenue from a sales tax and less from the income taxes as a way of encouraging greater savings is so strong that tax economists have recently urged the province to introduce such a tax.

Another change to the tax system that would encourage saving is an increase in the amount that people can contribute to registered retirement savings plans (RRSPs). By buying an RRSP, people reduce the amount of their income that is subject to income tax. In this way, saving is encouraged. Let's consider the effect of such saving incentives on the market for loanable funds, as illustrated in Figure 8.2.

First, which curve would these policies affect? Because the tax change would alter the incentive for households to save *at any given interest rate*, it would affect the quantity of loanable funds supplied at each interest rate. Thus, the supply of loanable funds would shift. The demand for loanable funds would remain the same, because the tax change would not directly affect the amount that borrowers want to borrow at any given interest rate.

Second, which way would the supply curve shift? Because saving would be taxed less heavily than under current law, households would increase their saving by consuming a smaller fraction of their income. Households would use this additional saving to increase their deposits in banks or to buy more bonds. The supply of loanable funds would increase, and the supply curve would shift to the right from S_1 to S_2, as shown in Figure 8.2.

Finally, we can compare the old and new equilibria. In the figure, the increased supply of loanable funds reduces the interest rate from 5 percent to 4 percent. The lower interest rate raises the quantity of loanable funds demanded from $120 billion to $160 billion. That is, the shift in the supply curve moves the market equilibrium along the demand curve. With a lower cost of borrowing, households and firms are motivated to borrow more to finance greater investment. Thus, *if a reform of the tax laws encouraged greater saving, the result would be lower interest rates and greater investment.*

FIGURE 8.2

An Increase in the Supply of Loanable Funds

A change in the tax laws to encourage Canadians to save more would shift the supply of loanable funds to the right from S_1 to S_2. As a result, the equilibrium interest rate would fall, and the lower interest rate would stimulate investment. Here the equilibrium interest rate falls from 5 percent to 4 percent, and the equilibrium quantity of loanable funds saved and invested rises from $120 billion to $160 billion.

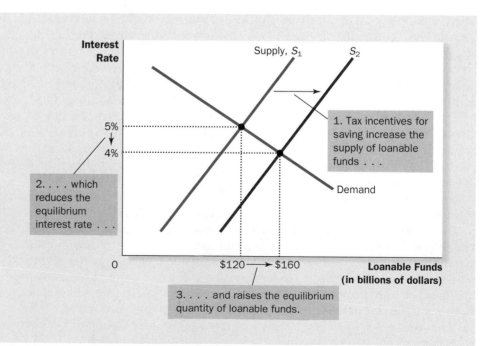

Although this analysis of the effects of increased saving is widely accepted among economists, there is less consensus about what kinds of tax changes should be enacted. Many economists endorse tax reform aimed at increasing saving in order to stimulate investment and growth. Yet others are skeptical that these tax changes would have much effect on national saving. These skeptics also doubt the equity of the proposed reforms. They argue that, in many cases, the benefits of the tax changes would accrue primarily to the wealthy, who are least in need of tax relief. This argument would hold true, for example, with respect to increasing allowable RRSP contributions, because most RRSP contributions are made by those who are relatively wealthy. We examine this debate more fully in the final chapter of this book.

Policy 2: Investment Incentives

Suppose that Parliament passed a tax reform aimed at making investment more attractive. In essence, this is what Parliament does when it institutes an *investment tax credit*, which it does from time to time. An investment tax credit gives a tax advantage to any firm building a new factory or buying a new piece of equipment. Let's consider the effect of such a tax reform on the market for loanable funds, as illustrated in Figure 8.3.

First, would the law affect supply or demand? Because the tax credit would reward firms that borrow and invest in new capital, it would alter investment at any given interest rate and, thereby, change the demand for loanable funds. By contrast, because the tax credit would not affect the amount that households save at any given interest rate, it would not affect the supply of loanable funds.

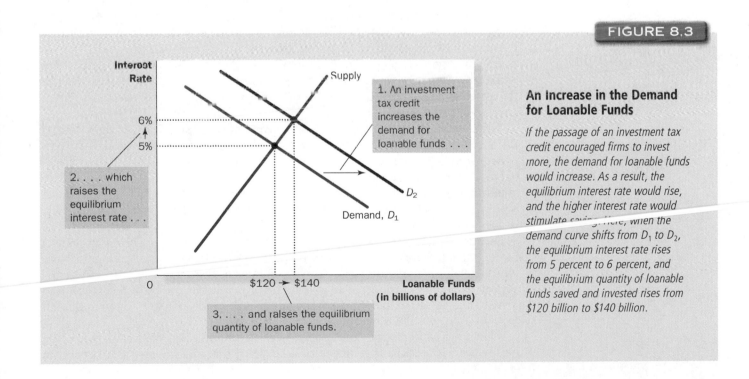

FIGURE 8.3

An Increase in the Demand for Loanable Funds

If the passage of an investment tax credit encouraged firms to invest more, the demand for loanable funds would increase. As a result, the equilibrium interest rate would rise, and the higher interest rate would stimulate saving. Here, when the demand curve shifts from D_1 to D_2, the equilibrium interest rate rises from 5 percent to 6 percent, and the equilibrium quantity of loanable funds saved and invested rises from $120 billion to $140 billion.

Interest Rate

Supply

1. An investment tax credit increases the demand for loanable funds . . .

6%

5%

D_2

2. . . . which raises the equilibrium interest rate . . .

Demand, D_1

0    $120 → $140   Loanable Funds (in billions of dollars)

3. . . . and raises the equilibrium quantity of loanable funds.

Second, which way would the demand curve shift? Because firms would have an incentive to increase investment at any interest rate, the quantity of loanable funds demanded would be higher at any given interest rate. Thus, the demand curve for loanable funds would move to the right, as shown by the shift from D_1 to D_2 in the figure.

Third, consider how the equilibrium would change. In Figure 8.3, the increased demand for loanable funds raises the interest rate from 5 percent to 6 percent, and the higher interest rate in turn increases the quantity of loanable funds supplied from $120 billion to $140 billion, as households respond by increasing the amount they save. This change in household behaviour is represented here as a movement along the supply curve. Thus, *if a reform of the tax laws encouraged greater investment, the result would be higher interest rates and greater saving.*

Policy 3: Government Budget Deficits and Surpluses

Many of the most pressing policy issues that have arisen over the past 25 years in Canada have either directly or indirectly resulted from large government budget deficits and the debt that accumulated as a result of these deficits. When a government spends more than it receives in tax revenue, the shortfall is called the government's budget deficit. When a government spends less than it receives in tax revenue, the excess is called the government's budget surplus. When a government spends exactly what it receives in tax revenue it is said to have a balanced budget. The sum of all past budget deficits minus the sum of all past budget surpluses is called the government's debt.

From 1975 to 1997, the federal government ran very large budget deficits, resulting in a rapidly growing federal government debt. During the same period, many provincial governments also ran large deficits, resulting in rapidly growing provincial government debts. Much public debate over the past 20 years has centred on the effects of these deficits, both on the allocation of the economy's scarce resources and on long-term economic growth.

Imagine that the government starts with a balanced budget and then, because of a tax cut or a spending increase, starts running a budget deficit. We can analyze the effects of the budget deficit by following our three steps in the market for loanable funds, as illustrated in Figure 8.4.

First, which curve shifts when the government starts running a budget deficit? Recall that national saving—the source of the supply of loanable funds—is composed of private saving and public saving. A change in the government budget balance represents a change in public saving and, thereby, in the supply of loanable funds. Because the budget deficit does not influence the amount that households and firms want to borrow to finance investment at any given interest rate, it does not alter the demand for loanable funds.

Second, which way does the supply curve shift? When the government runs a budget deficit, public saving is negative, and this reduces national saving. In other words, when the government borrows to finance its budget deficit, it reduces the supply of loanable funds available to finance investment by households and firms. Thus, a budget deficit shifts the supply curve for loanable funds to the left from S_1 to S_2, as shown in Figure 8.4.

Third, we can compare the old and new equilibria. In the figure, when the budget deficit reduces the supply of loanable funds, the interest rate rises from

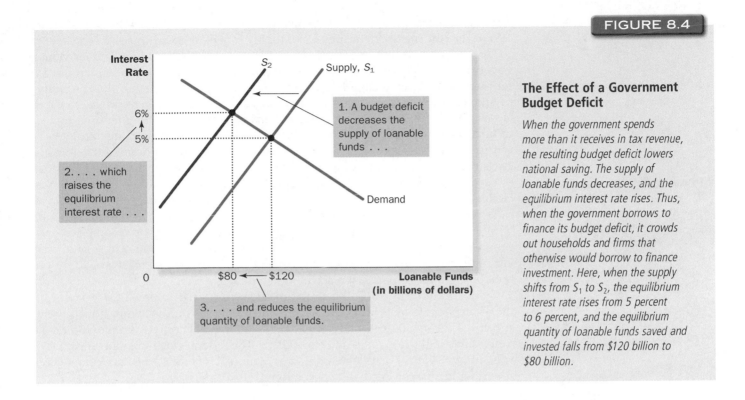

FIGURE 8.4

The Effect of a Government Budget Deficit

When the government spends more than it receives in tax revenue, the resulting budget deficit lowers national saving. The supply of loanable funds decreases, and the equilibrium interest rate rises. Thus, when the government borrows to finance its budget deficit, it crowds out households and firms that otherwise would borrow to finance investment. Here, when the supply shifts from S_1 to S_2, the equilibrium interest rate rises from 5 percent to 6 percent, and the equilibrium quantity of loanable funds saved and invested falls from $120 billion to $80 billion.

5 percent to 6 percent. This higher interest rate then alters the behaviour of the households and firms that participate in the loan market. In particular, many demanders of loanable funds are discouraged by the higher interest rate. Fewer families buy new homes, and fewer firms choose to build new factories. The fall in investment because of government borrowing is called **crowding out** and is represented in the figure by the movement along the demand curve from a quantity of $120 billion in loanable funds to a quantity of $80 billion. That is, when the government borrows to finance its budget deficit, it crowds out private borrowers who are trying to finance investment.

crowding out
a decrease in investment that results from government borrowing

Thus, the most basic lesson about budget deficits follows directly from their effects on the supply and demand for loanable funds: *When the government reduces national saving by running a budget deficit, the interest rate rises, and investment falls.* Because investment is important for long-run economic growth, government budget deficits reduce the economy's growth rate.

Long strings of government deficits such as those Canada experienced from 1975 to 1997 can push the economy into a **vicious circle** where deficits cause lower economic growth that in turn lead to lower tax revenue and higher spending on Employment Insurance and other income-support programs. Lower tax revenue and higher government spending lead to higher deficits and even slower economic growth. The only way to break out of this vicious circle is to raise tax rates and cut spending on government programs to eliminate the deficit and halt the circle of deficits, but this leads to slower economic growth and even higher deficits.

vicious circle
cycle that results when deficits reduce the supply of loanable funds, increase interest rates, discourage investment, and result in slower economic growth; slower growth leads to lower tax revenue and higher spending on income-support programs, and the result can be even higher budget deficits

Most analysts believe that the long string of deficits incurred by Canadian governments from 1975 to 1997 caused Canada to become trapped in such a vicious circle. The rapid run-up in tax rates and the large cuts to government spending on health care, defence, social services, and education during the late 1980s and early 1990s were the inevitable responses of highly indebted governments.

Government budget surpluses work just the opposite as budget deficits. When government collects more in tax revenue than it spends, it saves the difference by retiring some of the outstanding government debt. This budget surplus, or public saving, contributes to national saving. Thus, *a budget surplus increases the supply of loanable funds, reduces the interest rate, and stimulates investment.* Higher investment, in turn, means greater capital accumulation and more rapid economic growth.

Just as long strings of government deficits can push the economy into a vicious circle of higher deficits leading to slower growth leading to even higher deficits, so can strings of government budget surpluses push the economy into a **virtuous circle**. In this case, by increasing the supply of loanable funds, reducing interest rates, and stimulating investment, surpluses encourage faster economic growth. Because this leads to higher tax revenues and lower spending on income-support programs, the government surplus grows over time. A virtuous circle produces very attractive choices: Should government cut tax rates, increase spending on social programs, or pay down accumulated debt?

By the end of the 1990s, the strong medicine required to break Canada out of the vicious circle had borne fruit in the form of large and growing government surpluses. Many analysts believe that the Canadian economy was enjoying a virtuous circle in the late 1990s and early 2000s. The federal election in the fall of 2000 was fought over the very choices that a virtuous circle provides: tax cuts versus spending increases versus debt reduction.

virtuous circle

cycle that results when surpluses increase the supply of loanable funds, reduce interest rates, stimulate investment, and result in faster economic growth; faster growth leads to higher tax revenue and lower spending on income-support programs, and the result can be even higher budget surpluses

Case Study

THE ACCUMULATION OF GOVERNMENT DEBT IN CANADA

Budget deficits became a chronic problem in Canada only in the mid-1970s. From 1950 to 1974, the federal government ran budget surpluses as often as it ran budget deficits. These budget imbalances were generally small. In 1975, the federal government posted a large deficit and did so in every year until 1997. Between 1975 and 1997, the federal government accumulated about $550 billion in debt. In 1998 the string of deficits was broken and the federal government reported a budget surplus of $3.5 billion—the first time in 28 years that the federal government has actually paid down a portion of its debt. Between 1998 and 2003, the federal government ran a string of surpluses that enabled it to reduce its debt by about $50 billion.

Figure 8.5 shows the debt of the federal government and the combined debts of the ten provinces as a percentage of GDP. Throughout the 1950s and until 1975, the federal government's debt-to-GDP ratio declined. Although the federal government ran budget deficits during many of these years, the deficits were small enough that the government's debt grew less rapidly than the overall economy. Because GDP is a rough measure of the government's ability to raise tax revenue, a declining debt-to-GDP ratio indicates that the economy is, in some sense, living within its means. By contrast, in the years following 1975 when the federal

"Our debt-reduction plan is simple, but it will require a great deal of money."

FIGURE 8.5

Federal and Provincial Debt in Canada

The debt of the federal government and the combined debt of the ten provincial governments are expressed here as a percentage of GDP. Data on provincial government debt are available only from 1970. The federal government debt fell dramatically following World War II, but then started to increase quickly in 1975 when the government began to run large and persistent deficits. Since 1980 the provincial governments have also seen their debts increase relative to GDP.

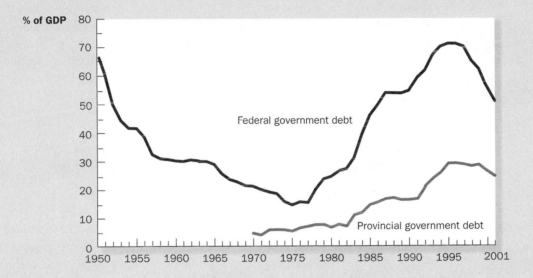

Sources: Authors' calculations, based on Statistics Canada information. Net debt is measured as the difference between financial assets and direct liabilities. Federal net debt is from CANSIM series D469420. Data on assets and liabilities of the provincial government sector are from CANSIM matrices 3202–3211. Calculation of Quebec's net debt requires an adjustment for the Quebec Pension Plan. The data for this adjustment are contained in CANSIM series D151784. Data on GDP is from CANSIM series D16439.

government's budget deficit ballooned, the debt started rising more rapidly than the overall economy. As a result, the debt-to-GDP ratio quickly increased. On three occasions—1982, 1989, and 1996—the federal government managed to halt the rise in its debt-to-GDP ratio. The first two efforts managed to halt the rise only temporarily. On both occasions, an economic slowdown caused government spending to increase and tax revenues to fall so that debt began to accumulate again. The last effort, in 1996, proved more successful, and the federal government has actually managed to reduce its debt-to-GDP ratio from its high of 72 percent in 1996 to 51 percent in 2001. In recent budgets, the federal government has indicated its intention to reduce the debt-to-GDP ratio still further.

Until 1982, the provincial governments together maintained a fairly constant level of debt relative to the economy. Although the provinces ran budget deficits, these were not large enough to cause the combined debt of the provinces to grow faster than the overall economy. As a result, the provincial debt-to-GDP ratio stayed at roughly 6 percent of GDP from 1970 to 1982. In 1982, a major recession caused the provinces to run larger deficits and caused the provincial debt-to-GDP ratio to begin to climb. By 1995, the ratio reached its maximum of 29 percent. Since then the debt-to-GDP ratio of the aggregate provincial government sector has slowly fallen.

As we saw in the previous chapter, national saving is a key ingredient in long-run economic growth. By using some of the private sector's saving to finance budget deficits, governments pull resources away from investment in new capital and, by doing so, depress the living standard of future generations. In recent years, all political parties in Canada have come to recognize this basic argument and now view persistent budget deficits as an important policy problem. As a result, Canadians have over the past decade seen governments of all political stripes—from an NDP government in Saskatchewan to a Progressive Conservative government in Alberta to a Parti Québécois government in Quebec to a Liberal government in Ottawa—introduce policies to reduce their respective deficits. No major political party in Canada advocates a return to large and persistent government deficits. ●

Case Study
THE DEBATE OVER BUDGET SURPLUSES

Since 1993, the federal government has taken forceful measures to reduce the size of its deficit. This effort has been so successful that the federal government now regularly reports budget surpluses and makes regular payments to reduce its outstanding debt. Many provincial governments have also been reducing their budget deficits, and many have reported budget surpluses for the past few years. As a result of these changes to government finances, public debate in Canada has recently shifted from the effects of large and growing budget deficits to the effects of deficit reduction and budget surpluses on the allocation of the economy's scarce resources and on long-term economic growth.

Many policymakers favour leaving the budget surpluses alone rather than reducing them with spending increases or tax cuts. These people base their conclusions on what was discussed above: Using the surplus to pay down government debt will stimulate private investment and economic growth.

Other policymakers take a different view. Some believe budget surpluses should be used to increase government spending on infrastructure, health care, and education. They base their conclusions on the belief that government investment in these areas receives a higher rate of return than is received on private investment in new factories and housing. Other people want to see tax cuts, arguing that lower tax rates distort decision making less and lead to a more efficient allocation of resources. These analysts also caution that without tax cuts, governments will be tempted to spend the surplus on government projects of dubious value.

The debate over what to do with current and projected budget surpluses is an ongoing one. All of the views discussed above are reasonable. The right policy depends on how much value you place on public versus private investment, how distortionary you view taxation, and how likely it is that the political process will avoid wasteful spending. ●

BUDGET RULES

Recent efforts to reduce and even eliminate their budget deficits have caused many provincial governments to legislate *budget rules*. Budget rules are limits on the size of a government's deficit, the level of taxes it levies, its level of spending, the size of its outstanding debt, or any combination of these. The purpose of legislating budget rules is to reduce the possibility that the government will now, or in the future, allow its deficit and its accumulated debt to grow to an unmanageable size.

Many state governments in the United States use tax and expenditure limits and balanced budget rules to constrain state budget choices. In California, for example, per capita state tax revenue must be held constant. In Arizona, state taxes are limited to no more than 7 percent of personal income. Most states have long had budget rules that limit the ability of the state to run a budget deficit.

Many Canadian governments have introduced budget rules. New Brunswick was first off the mark with legislation introduced in 1993 that restricted the size of a budget deficit. In 1995, Alberta passed the Debt Retirement Act, which prohibited a budget deficit and established a schedule for the elimination of the province's net debt. Manitoba passed similar legislation in 1995, with the additional provision of financial penalties to be incurred by members of the provincial Cabinet should a deficit occur. Also in 1995, Saskatchewan passed its Balanced Budget Act, which required each newly elected government to publish a four-year fiscal plan; these plans cannot allow spending to exceed revenue. While the imposition of budget rules has been widespread among provincial governments, the federal government has been noticeably reticent about committing itself to any such rule.

One problem with a budget rule that is imposed on a government by legislation is that the rule can be repealed by the next government that is elected. This happened in British Columbia in 1992 when the newly elected government repealed legislation, passed in the previous year, that called for limits on spending growth. It is for this reason that economists prefer budget rules that are difficult to repeal. The government of Alberta has made one of its budget rules difficult to repeal by requiring a referendum to do so. According to the Alberta Taxpayer Protection Act, no Alberta government can introduce a provincial sales tax without first obtaining the approval of a majority of voters in a referendum.

The effectiveness of budget rules has been the subject of a number of recent studies by economists. In general, these studies find that budget rules limit the size of government deficits and cause unexpected deficits to be eliminated more quickly than they would otherwise. Budget rules also seem to increase the probability that a government will have a low debt-to-GDP ratio. Unfortunately, these favourable results come at a price: Budget rules limit the flexibility of governments to respond to changes in economic circumstances not foreseen by the designers of the budget rules. Suppose, for example, a new fuel technology makes Alberta's oil and gas reserves worthless and results in the government losing billions of dollars of energy royalties. With a rule prohibiting deficits, how could the government cope?

Studies of the effects of budget rules have been based on the experiences of U.S. state governments, but the spending responsibilities and revenue sources of Canadian provinces are substantially different from those of U.S. states. As a result, it is uncertain how effective budget rules will be at controlling provincial government budgets. Economists must wait a number of years to determine whether the existing budget rules do, in fact, achieve their goals. Economists will also need to assess whether the benefits of these rules outweigh their costs.

QuickQuiz   If more Canadians adopted a "live for today" approach to life, how would this affect saving, investment, and the interest rate?

CONCLUSION

"Neither a borrower nor a lender be," Polonius advises his son in Shakespeare's *Hamlet*. If everyone followed this advice, this chapter would have been unnecessary.

Few economists would agree with Polonius. In our economy, people borrow and lend often, and usually for good reason. You may borrow one day to start your own business or to buy a home. And people may lend to you in the hope that the interest you pay will allow them to enjoy a more prosperous retirement. The financial system has the job of coordinating all this borrowing and lending activity.

In many ways, financial markets are like other markets in the economy. The price of loanable funds—the interest rate—is governed by the forces of supply and demand, just as other prices in the economy are. And we can analyze shifts in supply or demand in financial markets as we do in other markets. One of the ten principles of economics introduced in Chapter 1 is that markets are usually a good way to organize economic activity. This principle applies to financial markets as well. When financial markets bring the supply and demand for loanable funds into balance, they help allocate the economy's scarce resources to their most efficient use.

In one way, however, financial markets are special. Financial markets, unlike most other markets, serve the important role of linking the present and the future. Those who supply loanable funds—savers—do so because they want to convert some of their current income into future purchasing power. Those who demand loanable funds—borrowers—do so because they want to invest today in order to have additional capital in the future to produce goods and services. Thus, well-functioning financial markets are important not only for current generations but also for future generations who will inherit many of the resulting benefits.

SUMMARY

- The Canadian financial system is made up of many types of financial institutions, such as the bond market, the stock market, banks, and mutual funds. All these institutions act to direct the resources of households who want to save some of their income into the hands of households and firms who want to borrow.

- National income accounting identities reveal some important relationships among macroeconomic variables. In particular, for a closed economy, national saving must equal investment. Financial institutions are the mechanism through which the economy matches one person's saving with another person's investment.

- The interest rate is determined by the supply and demand for loanable funds. The supply of loanable funds comes from households who want to save some of their income and lend it out. The demand for loanable funds comes from households and firms who want to borrow for investment. To analyze how any policy or event affects the interest rate, one must consider how it affects the supply and demand for loanable funds.

- National saving equals private saving plus public saving. A government budget deficit represents negative public saving and, therefore, reduces national saving and the supply of loanable funds available to finance investment. When a government budget deficit crowds out investment, it reduces the growth of productivity and GDP.

KEY CONCEPTS

financial system, p. 156
financial markets, p. 156
bond, p. 157
stock, p. 158
financial intermediaries, p. 159

mutual fund, p. 160
national saving (saving), p. 163
private saving, p. 164
public saving, p. 164
budget surplus, p. 164

budget deficit, p. 164
market for loanable funds, p. 165
crowding out, p. 171
vicious circle, p. 171
virtuous circle, p. 172

QUESTIONS FOR REVIEW

1. What is the role of the financial system? Name and describe two markets that are part of the financial system in our economy. Name and describe two financial intermediaries.

2. Why is it important for people who own stocks and bonds to diversify their holdings? What type of financial institution makes diversification easier?

3. What is national saving? What is private saving? What is public saving? How are these three variables related?

4. What is investment? How is it related to national saving?

5. Describe a change in the tax code that might increase private saving. If this policy were implemented, how would it affect the market for loanable funds?

6. What is a government budget deficit? How does it affect interest rates, investment, and economic growth?

PROBLEMS AND APPLICATIONS

1. For each of the following pairs, which bond would you expect to pay a higher interest rate? Explain.
   a. a bond of the Canadian government or a bond of an East European government
   b. a bond that repays the principal in year 2005 or a bond that repays the principal in year 2025
   c. a bond from Coca-Cola or a bond from a software company you run in your garage
   d. a bond issued by the federal government or a bond issued by Prince Edward Island

2. Check a newspaper or the Internet for the stock listings of two companies you know something about (perhaps as a customer). What is the price/earnings ratio for each company? Why do you think they differ? If you were to buy one of these stocks, which would you choose? Why?

3. Theodore Roosevelt once said, "There is no moral difference between gambling at cards or in lotteries or on the race track and gambling in the stock market." What social purpose do you think is served by the existence of the stock market?

4. Declines in stock prices are sometimes viewed as harbingers of future declines in real GDP. Why do you suppose that might be true?

5. When the Russian government defaulted on its debt to foreigners in 1998, interest rates rose on bonds issued by many other developing countries. Why do you suppose this happened?

6. Many workers hold large amounts of stock issued by the firms for which they work. Why do you suppose companies encourage this behaviour? Why might a person *not* want to hold stock in the company where he works?

7. Explain the difference between saving and investment as defined by a macroeconomist. Which of the following situations represent investment? Saving? Explain.
   a. Your family takes out a mortgage and buys a new house.
   b. You use your $200 paycheque to buy stock in Bombardier.
   c. Your roommate earns $100 and deposits it in her account at a bank.
   d. You borrow $1000 from a bank to buy a car to use in your pizza delivery business.

8. Suppose GDP is $800 billion, taxes are $150 billion, private saving is $50 billion, and public saving is $20 billion. Assuming this economy is closed, calculate consumption, government purchase, national saving, and investment.

9. Suppose that Intel is considering building a new chip-making factory.
   a. Assuming that Intel needs to borrow money in the bond market, why would an increase in interest rates affect Intel's decision about whether to build the factory?
   b. If Intel has enough of its own funds to finance the new factory without borrowing, would an increase in interest rates still affect Intel's decision about whether to build the factory? Explain.

10. Suppose the government borrows $20 billion more next year than this year.
   a. Use a supply-and-demand diagram to analyze this policy. Does the interest rate rise or fall?
   b. What happens to investment? To private saving? To public saving? To national saving? Compare the size of the changes to the $20 billion of extra government borrowing.

   c. How does the elasticity of supply of loanable funds affect the size of these changes?
   d. How does the elasticity of demand for loanable funds affect the size of these changes?
   e. Suppose households believe that greater government borrowing today implies higher taxes to pay off the government debt in the future. What does this belief do to private saving and the supply of loanable funds today? Does it increase or decrease the effects you discussed in parts (a) and (b)?

11. Over the past ten years, new computer technology has enabled firms to reduce substantially the amount of inventories they hold for each dollar of sales. Illustrate the effect of this change on the market for loanable funds. (Hint: Expenditure on inventories is a type of investment.) What do you think has been the effect on investment in factories and equipment?

12. "Some economists worry that the aging populations of industrial countries are going to start running down their savings just when the investment appetite of emerging economies is growing" (*The Economist,* May 6, 1995). Illustrate the effect of these phenomena on the world market for loanable funds.

13. This chapter explains that investment can be increased both by reducing taxes on private saving and by reducing the government budget deficit.
   a. Why is it difficult to implement both of these policies at the same time?
   b. What would you need to know about private saving in order to judge which of these two policies would be a more effective way to raise investment?

INTERNET RESOURCES

- To learn more about the deficits and debts of Canadian governments, visit the Finance Canada website at http://www.fin.gc.ca. Links to information about the provincial and territorial government budgets are also provided on this site.

- The Government of Canada also maintains a useful website called *Economic Concepts* (http://www.canadianeconomy.gc.ca/english/economy/ concepts.html) that offers definitions of deficits and debt and discusses their economic implications.

- To learn more about financial markets, visit the Financial Consumer Agency of Canada website at http://www.fcac-acfc.gc.ca.

 For more study tools, please visit http://www.mankiw3e.nelson.com.

© CP PICTURE ARCHIVE/BILL BECKER

9

Learning Objectives

In this chapter, you will ...

- Measure the value of money at different points in time
- Learn how to manage risk
- Examine what determines the value of an asset

THE BASIC TOOLS OF FINANCE

Sometime in your life, you will have to deal with the economy's financial system. You will deposit your savings into a bank account, or you will take out a mortgage to buy a house. After you take a job, you will decide whether to invest your retirement account in stocks, bonds, or other financial instruments. You may try to put together your own stock portfolio, and then you will have to decide between betting on established companies such as Canadian Pacific Railway or newer ones such as Nortel Networks. And whenever you watch the evening news, you will hear reports about whether the stock market is up or down, together with the often feeble attempts to explain why the market behaves as it does.

If you reflect for a moment on the many financial decisions you will make throughout your life, you will see two related elements in almost all of them—time and risk. As we saw in the preceding chapter, the financial system coordinates the economy's saving and investment. Thus, it concerns decisions we make today that will affect our lives in the future. But the future is unknown. When a person decides to allocate some saving, or a firm decides to undertake an investment, the decision is based on a guess about the likely future result—but the actual result could end up being very different.

finance
the field that studies how people make decisions regarding the allocation of resources over time and the handling of risk

This chapter introduces some tools that help us understand the decisions that people make as they participate in financial markets. The field of **finance** develops these tools in great detail, and you may choose to take courses that focus on this topic. But because the financial system is so important to the functioning of the economy, many of the basic insights of finance are central to understanding how the economy works. The tools of finance may also help you think through some of the decisions that you will make in your own life.

This chapter takes up three topics. First, we discuss how to compare sums of money at different points in time. Second, we discuss how to manage risk. Third, we build on our analysis of time and risk to examine what determines the value of an asset, such as a share of stock.

PRESENT VALUE: MEASURING THE TIME VALUE OF MONEY

Imagine that someone offered to give you $100 today or $100 in ten years. Which would you choose? This is an easy question. Getting $100 today is better, because you can always deposit the money in a bank, still have it in ten years, and earn interest on the $100 along the way. The lesson: Money today is more valuable than the same amount of money in the future.

Now consider a harder question: Imagine that someone offered you $100 today or $200 in ten years. Which would you choose? To answer this question, you need some way to compare sums of money from different points in time. Economists do this with a concept called *present value.* The **present value** of any future sum of money is the amount today that would be needed, at current interest rates, to produce that future sum.

present value
the amount of money today that would be needed to produce, using prevailing interest rates, a given future amount of money

To learn how to use the concept of present value, let's work through a couple of simple examples:

Question: If you put $100 into a bank account today, how much will it be worth in N years? That is, what will be the **future value** of this $100?

future value
the amount of money in the future that an amount of money today will yield, given prevailing interest rates

Answer: Let's use r to denote the interest rate expressed in decimal form (so an interest rate of 5 percent means $r = 0.05$). Suppose that interest is paid annually and that the interest paid remains in the bank account to earn more interest—a process called **compounding.** Then the $100 will become

compounding
the accumulation of a sum of money in, say, a bank account, where the interest earned remains in the account to earn additional interest in the future

$(1 + r) \times \$100$	after one year
$(1 + r) \times (1 + r) \times \$100$	after two years
$(1 + r) \times (1 + r) \times (1 + r) \times \$100$	after three years…
$(1 + r)^N \times \$100$	after N years.

For example, if you are investing at an interest rate of 5 percent for 10 years, then the future value of the $100 will be $(1.05)^{10} \times \$100$, which is $163.

Question: Now suppose you are going to be paid $200 in N years. What is the *present value* of this future payment? That is, how much would you have to deposit in a bank right now to yield $200 in N years?

Answer: To answer this question, just turn the previous answer on its head. In the first question, we computed a future value from a present value by *multiplying* by the factor $(1 + r)^N$. To compute a present value from a future value, we *divide* by the factor $(1 + r)^N$. Thus, the present value of $200 in N years is $200/(1 + r)^N$. If that amount is deposited in a bank today, after N years it would become $(1 + r)^N \times [\$200/(1 + r)^N]$, which is $200. For instance, if the interest rate is 5 percent, the present value of $200 in 10 years is $200/(1.05)^{10}$, which is $123.

This illustrates the general formula: *If r is the interest rate, then an amount X to be received in N years has present value of X/(1 + r)^N.*

Let's now return to our earlier question: Should you choose $100 today or $200 in 10 years? We can infer from our calculation of present value that if the interest rate is 5 percent, you should prefer the $200 in 10 years. The future $200 has a present value of $123, which is greater than $100. You are better off waiting for the future sum.

Notice that the answer to our question depends on the interest rate. If the interest rate were 8 percent, then the $200 in 10 years would have a present value of $200/(1.08)^{10}$, which is only $93. In this case, you should take the $100 today.

THE MAGIC OF COMPOUNDING AND THE RULE OF 70

Suppose you observe that one country has an average growth rate of 1 percent per year while another has an average growth rate of 3 percent per year. At first, this might not seem like a big deal. What difference can 2 percent make?

The answer is: a big difference. Even growth rates that seem small when written in percentage terms seem large after they are compounded for many years.

Consider an example. Suppose that two university graduates—Jerry and Elaine—both take their first jobs at the age of 22 earning $30 000 a year. Jerry lives in an economy where all incomes grow at 1 percent per year, while Elaine lives in one where incomes grow at 3 percent per year. Straightforward calculations show what happens. Forty years later, when both are 62 years old, Jerry earns $45 000 per year, while Elaine earns $98 000. Because of that difference of 2 percentage points in the growth rate, Elaine's salary is more than twice Jerry's.

An old rule of thumb, called the *rule of 70*, is helpful in understanding growth rates and the effects of compounding. According to the rule of 70, if some variable grows at a rate of x percent per year, then that variable doubles in approximately 70/x years. In Jerry's economy, incomes grow at 1 percent per year, so it takes about 70 years for incomes to double. In Elaine's economy, incomes grow at 3 percent per year, so it takes about 70/3, or 23, years for incomes to double.

The rule of 70 applies not only to a growing economy but also to a growing savings account. Here is an example: In 1791, Ben Franklin died and left $5000 to be invested for a period of 200 years to benefit medical students and scientific research. If this money had earned 7 percent per year (which would, in fact, have been possible to do), the investment would have doubled in value every 10 years. Over 200 years, it would have doubled 20 times. At the end of 200 years of compounding, the investment would have been worth $2^{20} \times \$5000$, which is about $5 billion. (In fact, Franklin's $5000 grew to only $2 million over 200 years because some of the money was spent along the way.)

As these examples show, growth rates and interest rates compounded over many years can lead to some spectacular results. That is probably why Albert Einstein once called compounding "the greatest mathematical discovery of all time."

Why should the interest rate matter for your choice? The answer is that the higher the interest rate, the more you can earn by depositing your money at the bank, so the more attractive getting $100 today becomes.

The concept of present value is useful in many applications, including the decisions that companies face when evaluating investment projects. For instance, imagine that Petro-Canada is thinking about building a new refinery. Suppose that the refinery will cost $100 million today and will yield the company $200 million in ten years. Should Petro-Canada undertake the project? You can see that this decision is exactly like the one we have been studying. To make its decision, the company will compare the present value of the $200 million return to the $100 million cost.

The company's decision, therefore, will depend on the interest rate. If the interest rate is 5 percent, then the present value of the $200 million return from the refinery is $123 million, and the company will choose to pay the $100 million cost. By contrast, if the interest rate is 8 percent, then the present value of the return is only $93 million, and the company will decide to forgo the project. Thus, the concept of present value helps explain why investment—and thus the quantity of loanable funds demanded—declines when the interest rate rises.

Here is another application of present value: Suppose you win a million-dollar lottery and are given a choice between $20 000 per year for 50 years (totalling $1 000 000) or an immediate payment of $400 000. Which would you choose? To make the right choice, you need to calculate the present value of the stream of payments. After performing 50 calculations similar to those above (one calculation for each payment) and adding up the results, you would learn that the present value of this million-dollar prize at a 7 percent interest rate is only $276 000. You are better off picking the immediate payment of $400 000. The million dollars may seem like more money, but the future cash flows, once discounted to the present, are worth far less.

QuickQuiz   The interest rate is 7 percent. What is the present value of $150 to be received in 10 years?

MANAGING RISK

Life is full of gambles. When you go skiing, you risk breaking your leg in a fall. When you drive to work, you risk a car accident. When you put some of your savings in the stock market, you risk a fall in prices. The rational response to this risk is not necessarily to avoid it at any cost, but to take it into account in your decision making. Let's consider how a person might do that.

Risk Aversion

risk averse
exhibiting a dislike of uncertainty

Most people are **risk averse.** This means more than that people dislike bad things happening to them. It means that they dislike bad things more than they like comparable good things.

For example, suppose a friend offers you the following opportunity. He will flip a coin. If it comes up heads, he will pay you $1000. But if it comes up tails, you will have to pay him $1000. Would you accept the bargain? You wouldn't if you were risk averse. For a risk-averse person, the pain from losing the $1000 would exceed the gain from winning $1000.

Economists have developed models of risk aversion using the concept of *utility*, which is a person's subjective measure of well-being or satisfaction. Every level of wealth provides a certain amount of utility, as shown by the utility function in Figure 9.1. But the function exhibits the property of diminishing marginal utility: The more wealth a person has, the less utility he gets from an additional dollar. Thus, in the figure, the utility function gets flatter as wealth increases. Because of diminishing marginal utility, the utility lost from losing the $1000 bet is more than the utility gained from winning it. As a result, people are risk averse.

Risk aversion provides the starting point for explaining various things we observe in the economy. Let's consider three of them: insurance, diversification, and the risk–return tradeoff.

The Markets for Insurance

One way to deal with risk is to buy insurance. The general feature of insurance contracts is that a person facing a risk pays a fee to an insurance company, which in return agrees to accept all or part of the risk. There are many types of insurance. Car insurance covers the risk of your being in an auto accident, fire insurance

FIGURE 9.1

The Utility Function

This utility function shows how utility, a subjective measure of satisfaction, depends on wealth. As wealth rises, the utility function becomes flatter, reflecting the property of diminishing marginal utility. Because of diminishing marginal utility, a $1000 loss decreases utility by more than a $1000 gain increases it.

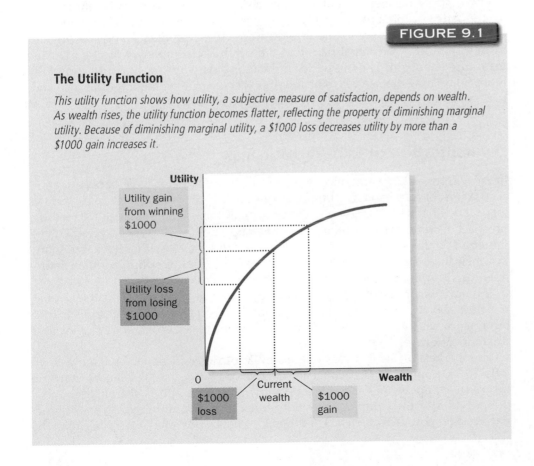

covers the risk that your house will burn down, health insurance covers the risk that you might need expensive medical treatment, and life insurance covers the risk that you will die and leave your family without your income. There is also insurance against the risk of living too long: For a fee paid today, an insurance company will pay you an *annuity*—a regular income every year until you die.

In a sense, every insurance contract is a gamble. It is possible that you will not be in an auto accident, that your house will not burn down, and that you will not need expensive medical treatment. In most years, you will pay the insurance company the premium and get nothing in return except peace of mind. Indeed, the insurance company is counting on the fact that most people will not make claims on their policies; otherwise, it couldn't pay out the large claims to those few who are unlucky and still stay in business.

From the standpoint of the economy as a whole, the role of insurance is not to eliminate the risks inherent in life but to spread them around more efficiently. Consider fire insurance, for instance. Owning fire insurance does not reduce the risk of losing your home in a fire. But if that unlucky event occurs, the insurance company compensates you. The risk, rather than being borne by you alone, is shared among the thousands of insurance company shareholders. Because people are risk averse, it is easier for 10 000 people to bear 1/10 000 of the risk than for one person to bear the entire risk himself.

The markets for insurance suffer from two types of problems that impede their ability to spread risk. One problem is *adverse selection:* A high-risk person is more likely to apply for insurance than a low-risk person. A second problem is *moral hazard:* After people buy insurance, they have less incentive to avoid their risky behaviour. Insurance companies are aware of these problems, and the price of insurance reflects the actual risks that the insurance company will face after the insurance is bought. The high price of insurance is why some people, especially those who know themselves to be low-risk, decide against buying insurance and, instead, endure some of life's uncertainty on their own.

Diversification of Idiosyncratic Risk

In 2002 Enron, a large and once widely respected company, went bankrupt amid accusations of fraud and accounting irregularities. The company's top executives were called before the U.S. Congress to explain their actions, and they faced the prospect of criminal prosecution. The saddest part of the story, however, involved thousands of lower-level employees. Not only did they lose their jobs, but many lost their life savings as well. The employees had about two-thirds of their retirement funds in Enron stock, which was now worthless.

If there is one piece of practical advice that finance offers to risk-averse people, it is this: "Don't put all your eggs in one basket." You may have heard this before, but finance has turned this traditional wisdom into a science. It goes by the name **diversification.**

diversification
the reduction of risk achieved by replacing a single risk with a large number of smaller unrelated risks

The market for insurance is one example of diversification. Imagine a town with 10 000 homeowners, each facing the risk of a house fire. If someone starts an insurance company and each person in town becomes both a shareholder and a policyholder of the company, they all reduce their risk through diversification. Each person now faces 1/10 000 of the risk of 10 000 possible fires, rather than the entire risk of a single fire in his own home. Unless the entire town catches fire at the same time, the downside that each person faces is much smaller.

When people use their savings to buy financial assets, they can also reduce risk through diversification. A person who buys stock in a company is placing a bet on the future profitability of that company. That bet is often quite risky because companies' fortunes are hard to predict. Microsoft evolved from a start-up by some geeky teenagers into one of the world's most valuable companies in only a few years; Enron went from one of the world's most respected companies to an almost worthless one in only a few months. Fortunately, a shareholder need not tie his own fortune to that of any single company. Risk can be reduced by placing a large number of small bets, rather than a small number of large ones.

Figure 9.2 shows how the risk of a portfolio of stocks depends on the number of stocks in the portfolio. Risk is measured here with a statistic called *standard deviation,* which you may have learned about in a math or statistics class. Standard deviation measures the volatility of a variable—that is, how much the variable is likely to fluctuate. The higher the standard deviation of a portfolio's return, the riskier it is.

FIGURE 9.2

Diversification Reduces Risk

This figure shows how the risk of a portfolio, measured here with a statistic called standard deviation, *depends on the number of stocks in the portfolio. The investor is assumed to put an equal percentage of her portfolio in each of the stocks. Increasing the number of stocks reduces the amount of risk in a stock portfolio, but it does not eliminate it.*

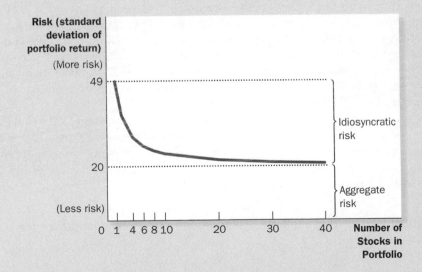

Source: Adapted from Meir Statman, "How Many Stocks Make a Diversified Portfolio?" *Journal of Financial and Quantitative Analysis* 22 (September 1987): 353–364. Reprinted by permission of School of Business Administration/University of Washington.

The figure shows that the risk of a stock portfolio falls substantially as the number of stocks increase. For a portfolio with a single stock, the standard deviation is 49 percent. Going from 1 stock to 10 stocks eliminates about half the risk. Going from 10 to 20 stocks reduces the risk by another 13 percent. As the number of stocks continues to increase, risk continues to fall, although the reductions in risk after 20 or 30 stocks are small.

idiosyncratic risk
risk that affects only a single economic actor

aggregate risk
risk that affects all economic actors at once

Notice that it is impossible to eliminate all risk by increasing the number of stocks in the portfolio. Diversification can eliminate **idiosyncratic risk**—the uncertainty associated with the specific companies. But diversification cannot eliminate **aggregate risk**—the uncertainty associated with the entire economy, which affects all companies. For example, when the economy goes into a recession, most companies experience falling sales, reduced profit, and low stock returns. Diversification reduces the risk of holding stocks, but it does not eliminate it.

The Tradeoff between Risk and Return

One of the ten principles of economics in Chapter 1 is that people face tradeoffs. The tradeoff that is most relevant for understanding financial decisions is the tradeoff between risk and return.

As we have seen, there are risks inherent in holding stocks, even in a diversified portfolio. But risk-averse people are willing to accept this uncertainty because they are compensated for doing so. Historically, stocks have offered much higher rates of return than alternative financial assets, such as bonds and bank savings accounts. Over the past two centuries, stocks offered an average real return of 8.3 percent per year, while short-term government bonds paid a real return of only 3.1 percent per year.

When deciding how to allocate their savings, people have to decide how much risk they are willing to undertake to earn the higher return. Figure 9.3 illustrates the risk–return tradeoff for a person choosing between risky stock, with an average return of 8.3 percent and a standard deviation of 20 percent, and a safe alternative, with a return of 3.1 percent and a standard deviation of zero. The safe alternative can be either a bank savings account or a government bond. Each point in this figure represents a particular allocation of a portfolio between risky stocks and the safe asset. The figure shows that the more a person puts into stock, the greater both the risk and the return.

Acknowledging the risk–return tradeoff does not, by itself, tell us what a person should do. The choice of a particular combination of risk and return depends on a person's risk aversion, which reflects a person's own preferences. But it is important for stockholders to realize that the higher average return that they enjoy comes at the price of higher risk.

QuickQuiz Describe three ways that a risk-averse person might reduce the risk she faces.

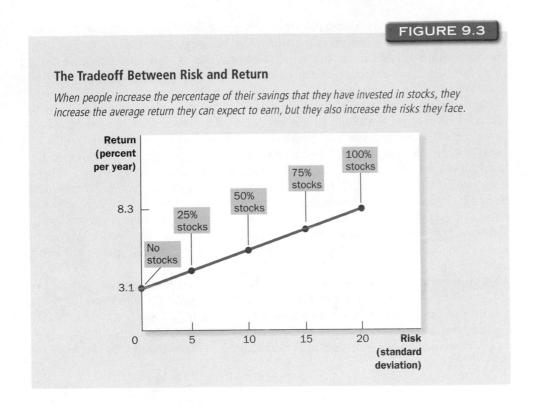

FIGURE 9.3

The Tradeoff Between Risk and Return

When people increase the percentage of their savings that they have invested in stocks, they increase the average return they can expect to earn, but they also increase the risks they face.

ASSET VALUATION

Now that we have developed a basic understanding of the two building blocks of finance—time and risk—let's apply this knowledge. This section considers a simple question: What determines the price of a share of stock? Like most prices, the answer is supply and demand. But that is not the end of the story. To understand stock prices, we need to think more deeply about what determines a person's willingness to pay for a share of stock.

Fundamental Analysis

Let's imagine that you have decided to put 60 percent of your savings into stock and, to achieve diversification, you have decided to buy 20 different stocks. If you open the newspaper, you will find thousands of stocks listed. How should you pick the 20 for your portfolio?

When you buy stock, you are buying shares in a business. When deciding which businesses you want to own, it is natural to consider two things: the value of the business and the price at which the shares are being sold. If the price is less than the value, the stock is said to be *undervalued*. If the price is more than the value, the stock is said to be *overvalued*. If the price and the value are equal, the stock is said to be *fairly valued*. When choosing 20 stocks for your portfolio, you should prefer undervalued stocks. In these cases, you are getting a bargain by paying less than the business is worth.

This is easier said than done. Learning the price is easy: You can just look it up in the newspaper. Determining the value of the business is the hard part. The term **fundamental analysis** refers to the detailed analysis of a company to determine its value. Many investment firms hire stock analysts to conduct such fundamental analysis and offer advice about which stocks to buy.

fundamental analysis
the study of a company's accounting statements and future prospects to determine its value

The value of a stock to a stockholder is what he gets out of owning it, which includes the present value of the stream of dividend payments and the final sale price. Recall that *dividends* are the cash payments that a company makes to its shareholders. A company's ability to pay dividends, as well as the value of the stock when the stockholder sells his shares, depends on the company's ability to earn profits. Its profitability, in turn, depends on a large number of factors—the demand for its product, how much competition it faces, how much capital it has in place, whether its workers are unionized, how loyal its customers are, what kinds of government regulations and taxes it faces, and so on. The job of fundamental analysts is to take all these factors into account to determine how much a share of stock in the company is worth.

If you want to rely on fundamental analysis to pick a stock portfolio, there are three ways to do it. One way is to do all the necessary research yourself, by reading through companies' annual reports and so forth. A second way is to rely on the advice of investment analysts. A third way is to buy a mutual fund, which has a manager who conducts fundamental analysis and makes the decision for you.

The Efficient Markets Hypothesis

There is another way to choose 20 stocks for your portfolio: Pick them randomly by, for instance, putting the stock pages on your bulletin board and throwing darts at the page. This may sound crazy, but there is reason to believe that it won't lead you too far astray. That reason is called the **efficient markets hypothesis.**

efficient markets hypothesis
the theory that asset prices reflect all publicly available information about the value of an asset

To understand this theory, the starting point is to acknowledge that each company listed on a major stock exchange is followed closely by many money managers, such as the individuals who run mutual funds. Every day, these managers monitor news stories and conduct fundamental analysis to try to determine the stock's value. Their job is to buy a stock when its price falls below its value, and to sell it when its price rises above its value.

The second piece to the efficient markets hypothesis is that the equilibrium of supply and demand sets the market price. This means that, at the market price, the number of shares being offered for sale exactly equals the number of shares that people want to buy. In other words, at the market price, the number of people who think the stock is overvalued exactly balances the number of people who think it's undervalued. As judged by the typical person in the market, all stocks are fairly valued all the time.

informationally efficient
reflecting all available information in a rational way

According to this theory, the stock market is **informationally efficient:** It reflects all available information about the value of the asset. Stock prices change when information changes. When the good news about the company's prospects becomes public, the value and the stock price both rise. When the company's prospects deteriorate, the value and price both fall. But at any moment in time, the market price is the best guess of the company's value based on available information.

One implication of the efficient markets hypothesis is that stock prices should follow a **random walk.** This means that the changes in stock prices are impossible to predict from available information. If, based on publicly available information, a person could predict that a stock price would rise by 10 percent tomorrow, then the stock market must be failing to incorporate that information today. According to this theory, the only thing that can move stock prices is news that changes the market's perception of the company's value. But news must be unpredictable—otherwise, it wouldn't really be news. For the same reason, changes in stock prices should be unpredictable.

If the efficient markets hypothesis is correct, then there is little point in spending many hours studying the business page to decide which 20 stocks to add to your portfolio. If prices reflect all available information, no stock is a better buy than any other. The best you can do is buy a diversified portfolio.

random walk
the path of a variable whose changes are impossible to predict

Case Study
RANDOM WALKS AND INDEX FUNDS

The efficient markets hypothesis is a theory about how financial markets work. The theory is probably not completely true: As we discuss in the next section, there is reason to doubt that stockholders are always rational and that stock prices are informationally efficient at every moment. Nonetheless, the efficient markets hypothesis does much better as a description of the world than you might think.

There is much evidence that stock prices, even if not exactly a random walk, are very close to it. For example, you might be tempted to buy stocks that have recently risen and avoid stocks that have recently fallen (or perhaps just the opposite). But statistical studies have shown that following such trends (or bucking them) fails to outperform the market. The correlation between how well a stock does one year and how well it does the following year is almost exactly zero.

Some of the best evidence in favour of the efficient markets hypothesis comes from the performance of index funds. An index fund is a mutual fund that buys all the stocks in a given stock index. The performance of these funds can be compared with that of actively managed mutual funds, where a professional portfolio manager picks stocks based on extensive research and alleged expertise. In essence, an index fund buys all stocks, whereas active funds are supposed to buy only the best stocks.

In practice, active managers usually fail to beat index funds, and in fact, most of them do worse. For example, in the ten years ending February 2002, 82 percent of stock mutual funds failed to beat an index fund holding all 500 stocks in the Standard & Poor's 500 Index. Most active portfolio managers give a lower return than index funds because they trade more frequently, incurring more trading costs, and because they charge greater fees as compensation for their alleged expertise.

What about those 18 percent of managers who did beat the market? Perhaps they are smarter than average, or perhaps they were more lucky. If you have 5000

IN THE NEWS

SOME LESSONS FROM ENRON

When many investors lost their life savings in the wake of the collapse of Enron, the rationality of stock market investors was called into question.

Investor Behavior Clouds the Wisdom of Offering Wider Choice in 401(k)'s

By Hal R. Varian

After the Enron collapse, Congress is debating whether to limit the amount of their own company's stock that employees can put into their own 401(k) retirement plans.

Those in favor of such caps, like Senators Barbara Boxer and Jon S. Corzine, see them as a way to encourage diversification and reduce risk. Those opposed, like Labor Secretary Elaine L. Chao, say such caps violate freedom of choice.

Economists generally believe that more choice is better, but even economists acknowledge that there are plenty of exceptions in real life. Offering a cigarette to someone trying to quit, a drink to a recovering alcoholic, or a candy bar to a dieter isn't doing that person a favor.

To most economists, the problems illustrated by these examples are anomalies. But to one group, behavioral economists, the examples are central.

Clearly, more choice is not better when people have problems with self-control. . . . In some investment situations, more choice can be downright

people flipping coins ten times, on average about five will flip ten heads; these five might claim exceptional coin-flipping skill, but they would have trouble replicating the feat. Similarly, studies have shown that mutual fund managers with a history of superior performance usually fail to maintain it in subsequent periods.

The efficient markets hypothesis says that it is impossible to beat the market. The accumulation of many studies in financial markets confirms that beating the market is, at best, extremely difficult. Even if the efficient markets hypothesis is not an exact description of the world, it contains a large element of truth. ●

Market Irrationality

The efficient markets hypothesis assumes that people buying and selling stock rationally process the information they have about the stock's underlying value. But is the stock market really that rational? Or do stock prices sometimes deviate from reasonable expectations of their true value?

There is a long tradition suggesting that fluctuations in stock prices are partly psychological. In the 1930s, economist John Maynard Keynes suggested that asset dangerous. Two finance professors, Brad Barber and Terrance Odean, studied the performance of 66,465 households with discount brokerage accounts. Households that traded infrequently received an 18 percent return on their investments, while the return for households that traded most actively was 11.3 percent.

In the words of Mr. Barber and Mr. Odean: "Trading can be hazardous to your wealth."

In later work, these two financial economists investigated who it was that traded too much. They found that one important determinant of excessive trading was gender.

Psychologists consistently find that men tend to have excessive confidence in their own abilities. . . . Mr. Barber and Mr. Odean find that on average, men trade 45 percent more than women. They also find that this excessive trading reduces men's net returns by almost a full percentage point.

Psychologists find that men tend to suffer from "self-serving attribution bias." In plain language: men tend to think their successes are the result of their own skill, rather than dumb luck, and so become overconfident.

It is not hard to see how overconfidence might lead to bubbles: Though frequent traders lose on average, sometimes they luck out. If many happen to get lucky at the same time, they will attribute this success to their superior abilities and double their bets. This pushes up the value of stocks even more, leading to more excessive confidence and an unsustainable boom in stock prices.

If we accept this evidence that investors have problems with self-control, poor decision making, and overconfidence, what can we say about the regulation of financial markets and pensions? . . . The findings from behavioral economics suggest that mandated saving plans, like conventional defined-benefit pension plans and social security, are pretty good programs. The tendency in the last several years has been to offer employees more choice of retirement options. But if individuals do not make good choices when left to their own devices, this may not be appropriate. . . .

Many employees of Enron, Global Crossing, Lucent, and Nortel have seen their pensions evaporate when the price of their company stock dropped. If these investors had held more diversified portfolios, they would be sleeping a lot more soundly today.

markets are driven by the "animal spirits" of investors—irrational waves of optimism and pessimism. In the 1990s, as the stock market soared to new heights, U.S. Federal Reserve chairman Alan Greenspan questioned whether the boom reflected "irrational exuberance." Stock prices did subsequently fall, but whether the exuberance of the 1990s was irrational given the information available at the time remains debatable.

The possibility of such speculative bubbles arises in part because the value of the stock to a stockholder depends not only on the stream of dividend payments but also on the final sale price. Thus, a person might be willing to pay more than a stock is worth today if he expects another person to pay even more for it tomorrow. When you evaluate a stock, you have to estimate not only the value of the business but also what other people will think the business is worth in the future.

There is much debate among economists about whether departures from rational pricing are important or rare. Believers in market irrationality point out (correctly) that the stock market often moves in ways that are hard to explain on the basis of news that might alter a rational valuation. Believers in the efficient markets hypothesis point out (correctly) that it is impossible to know the correct, rational valuation of a company, so one should not quickly jump to the conclusion that any particular valuation is irrational. Moreover, if the market were irrational, a rational person should be able to take advantage of this fact; yet, as the previous case study discussed, beating the market is nearly impossible.

QuickQuiz *Fortune* magazine regularly publishes a list of the "most respected" companies. According to the efficient markets hypothesis, if you restrict your stock portfolio to these companies, would you earn a better than average return? Explain.

CONCLUSION

This chapter has developed some of the basic tools that people should (and often do) use as they make financial decisions. The concept of present value reminds us that a dollar in the future is less valuable than a dollar today, and it gives us a way to compare sums of money at different points in time. The theory of risk management reminds us that the future is uncertain and that risk-averse people can take precautions to guard against this uncertainty. The study of asset valuation tells us that the stock price of any company should reflect its expected future profitability.

Although most of the tools of finance are well established, there is more controversy about the validity of the efficient markets hypothesis and whether stock prices are, in practice, rational estimates of a company's true worth. Rational or not, the large movements in stock prices that we observe have important macroeconomic implications. Stock market fluctuations often go hand in hand with fluctuations in the economy more broadly. We will see the stock market again when we study economic fluctuations later in the book.

SUMMARY

- Because savings can earn interest, a sum of money today is more valuable than the same sum of money in the future. A person can compare sums from different times using the concept of present value. The present value of any future sum is the amount that would be needed today, given prevailing interest rates, to produce that future sum.

- Because of diminishing marginal utility, most people are risk averse. Risk-averse people can reduce risk using insurance, through diversification, and by choosing a portfolio with lower risk and lower return.

- The value of an asset, such as a share of stock, equals the present value of the cash flows the owner of the share will receive, including the stream of dividends and the final sale price. According to the efficient markets hypothesis, financial markets process available information rationally, so a stock price always equals the best estimate of the value of the underlying business. Some economists question the efficient markets hypothesis, however, and believe that irrational psychological factors also influence asset prices.

KEY CONCEPTS

finance, p. 182
present value, p. 182
future value, p. 182
compounding, p. 182
risk averse, p. 184

diversification, p. 186
idiosyncratic risk, p. 188
aggregate risk, p. 188
fundamental analysis, p. 190

efficient markets
    hypothesis, p. 190
informationally efficient, p. 190
random walk, p. 191

QUESTIONS FOR REVIEW

1. The interest rate is 7 percent. Use the concept of present value to compare $200 to be received in 10 years and $300 to be received in 20 years.

2. What benefit do people get from the market for insurance? What two problems impede the insurance company from working perfectly?

3. What is diversification? Does a stockholder get more diversification going from 1 to 10 stocks or going from 100 to 120 stocks?

4. Comparing stocks and government bonds, which has more risk? Which pays a higher average return?

5. What factors should a stock analyst think about in determining the value of a share of stock?

6. Describe the efficient markets hypothesis, and give a piece of evidence consistent with this theory.

7. Explain the view of those economists who are skeptical of the efficient markets hypothesis.

PROBLEMS AND APPLICATIONS

1. About 400 years ago, native Americans sold the island of Manhattan for $24. If they had invested this money at an interest rate of 7 percent per year, how much would they have today?

2. A company has an investment project that would cost $10 million today and yield a payoff of $15 million in four years.
   a. Should the firm undertake the project if the interest rate is 11 percent? 10 percent? 9 percent? 8 percent?
   b. Can you figure out the exact cutoff for the interest rate between profitability and nonprofitability?

3. For each of the following kinds of insurance, give an example of behaviour that can be called *moral hazard* and another example of behaviour that can be called *adverse selection*.
   a. health insurance
   b. car insurance

4. Imagine that you intend to buy a portfolio of ten stocks with some of your savings. Should the stocks be of companies in the same industry? Should the stocks be of companies located in the same country? Explain.

5. Which kind of stock would you expect to pay the higher average return: stock in an industry that is very sensitive to economic conditions (such as an automaker) or stock in an industry that is relatively insensitive to economic conditions (such as a water company). Why?

6. A company faces two kinds of risk. An idiosyncratic risk is that a competitor might enter its market and take some of its customers. An aggregate risk is that the economy might enter a recession, reducing sales. Which of these two risks would more likely cause the company's shareholders to demand a higher return? Why?

7. You have two roommates who invest in the stock market.
   a. One roommate says she buys stock only in companies that everyone believes will experience big increases in profits in the future. How do you suppose the price/earnings ratios of these companies compare to the price/earnings ratios of other companies? What might be the disadvantage of buying stock in these companies?
   b. Another roommate says she buys stock only in companies that are cheap, which she measures by a low price/earnings ratio. How do you suppose the earnings prospects of these companies compare to those of other companies? What might be the disadvantage of buying stock in these companies?

8. When company executives buy and sell stock based on private information they obtain as part of their jobs, they are engaged in *insider trading*.
   a. Give an example of inside information that might be useful for buying or selling stock.
   b. Those who trade stocks based on inside information usually earn very high rates of return. Does this fact violate the efficient market hypothesis?
   c. Insider trading is illegal. Why do you suppose that is?

INTERNET RESOURCES

The Globe and Mail provides a wide variety of stock market information on its website at http://www.globeinvestor.com.

http://   For more study tools, please visit http://www.mankiw3e.nelson.com.

© CP PICTURE ARCHIVE/BILL BECKER

UNEMPLOYMENT AND ITS NATURAL RATE

10

Learning Objectives

In this chapter, you will ...

- Learn about the data used to measure the amount of unemployment

- Consider how unemployment arises from the process of job search

- Consider how unemployment can result from minimum-wage laws

- See how unemployment can arise from bargaining between firms and unions

- Examine how unemployment results when firms choose to pay efficiency wages

Losing a job can be the most distressing economic event in a person's life. Most people rely on their labour earnings to maintain their standard of living, and many people get from their work not only income but also a sense of personal accomplishment. A job loss means a lower living standard in the present, anxiety about the future, and reduced self-esteem. It is not surprising, therefore, that politicians campaigning for office often speak about how their proposed policies will help create jobs.

In previous chapters we have seen some of the forces that determine the level and growth of a country's standard of living. A country that saves and invests a high fraction of its income, for instance, enjoys more rapid growth in its capital stock and its GDP than a similar country that saves and invests less. An even more obvious determinant of a country's standard of living is the amount of unemployment it typically experiences. People who would like to work but cannot find jobs are not contributing to the economy's production of goods and services. Although some degree of unemployment is inevitable in a complex economy with thousands of firms and millions of workers, the amount of unemployment varies substantially over time and across countries. When a country keeps its workers as fully employed as possible, it achieves a higher level of GDP than it would if it left many of its workers idle.

This chapter begins our study of unemployment. The problem of unemployment is usefully divided into two categories—the long-run problem and the short-run problem. The economy's *natural rate of unemployment* refers to the amount of unemployment that the economy normally experiences. *Cyclical unemployment* refers to the year-to-year fluctuations in unemployment around its natural rate, and it is closely associated with the short-run ups and downs of economic activity. Cyclical unemployment has its own explanation, which we will defer until we study short-run economic fluctuations later in this book. In this chapter we discuss the determinants of an economy's natural rate of unemployment. As we will see, the designation *natural* does not imply that this rate of unemployment is desirable. Nor does it imply that it is constant over time or impervious to economic policy. It merely means that this unemployment does not go away on its own even in the long run.

We begin the chapter by looking at some of the relevant facts that describe unemployment. In particular, we examine three questions: How does the government measure the economy's rate of unemployment? What problems arise in interpreting the unemployment data? How long are the unemployed typically without work?

We then turn to the reasons why economies always experience some unemployment and the ways in which policymakers can help the unemployed. We discuss four explanations for the economy's natural rate of unemployment: job search, minimum-wage laws, unions, and efficiency wages. As we will see, long-run unemployment does not arise from a single problem that has a single solution. Instead, it reflects a variety of related problems. As a result, there is no easy way for policymakers to reduce the economy's natural rate of unemployment and, at the same time, to alleviate the hardships experienced by the unemployed.

IDENTIFYING UNEMPLOYMENT

We begin this chapter by examining more precisely what the term *unemployment* means. We consider how the government measures unemployment, what problems arise in interpreting the unemployment data, how long the typical spell of unemployment lasts, and why there will always be some people unemployed.

How Is Unemployment Measured?

Measuring unemployment is the job of Statistics Canada. Every month Statistics Canada produces data on unemployment and on other aspects of the labour market, such as types of employment, length of the average workweek, and the duration of unemployment. These data come from a regular survey of about 50 000 households, called the Labour Force Survey.

Based on the answers to survey questions, Statistics Canada places each adult (aged 15 and older) in each surveyed household into one of three categories:

- Employed
- Unemployed
- Not in the labour force

A person is considered employed if he or she spent some of the previous week working at a paid job. A person is unemployed if he or she is on temporary layoff or is looking for a job. A person who fits neither of the first two categories, such as a full-time student, homemaker, or retiree, is not in the labour force. Figure 10.1 shows this breakdown for 2002.

Once Statistics Canada has placed all the individuals covered by the survey in a category, it computes various statistics to summarize the state of the labour market. Statistics Canada defines the **labour force** as the sum of the employed and the unemployed:

$$\text{Labour force} = \text{Number of employed} + \text{Number of unemployed}$$

labour force
the total number of workers, including both the employed and the unemployed

Statistics Canada defines the **unemployment rate** as the percentage of the labour force that is unemployed:

$$\text{Unemployment rate} = \frac{\text{Number of unemployed}}{\text{Labour force}} \times 100$$

unemployment rate
the percentage of the labour force that is unemployed

Statistics Canada computes unemployment rates for the entire adult population and for more narrowly defined groups—young, old, men, women, and so on.

Statistics Canada uses the same survey to produce data on labour-force participation. The **labour-force participation rate** measures the percentage of the total adult population of Canada that is in the labour force:

$$\text{Labour-force participation rate} = \frac{\text{Labour force}}{\text{Adult population}} \times 100$$

labour-force participation rate
the percentage of the adult population that is in the labour force

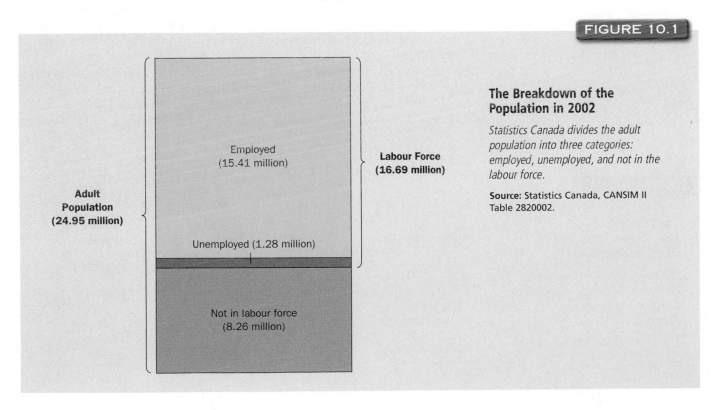

FIGURE 10.1

The Breakdown of the Population in 2002

Statistics Canada divides the adult population into three categories: employed, unemployed, and not in the labour force.

Source: Statistics Canada, CANSIM II Table 2820002.

Employed (15.41 million)

Labour Force (16.69 million)

Adult Population (24.95 million)

Unemployed (1.28 million)

Not in labour force (8.26 million)

This statistic tells us the fraction of the population that has chosen to participate in the labour market. The labour-force participation rate, like the unemployment rate, is computed both for the entire adult population and for more specific groups.

To see how these data are computed, consider the figures for 2002. In that year, 15.41 million people were employed, and 1.28 million people were unemployed. The labour force was

$$\text{Labour force} = 15.41 + 1.28 = 16.69 \text{ million.}$$

The unemployment rate was

$$\text{Unemployment rate} = (1.28/16.69) \times 100 = 7.7 \text{ percent.}$$

Because the adult population was 24.95 million, the labour-force participation rate was

$$\text{Labour-force participation rate} = (16.69/24.95) \times 100 = 66.9 \text{ percent.}$$

Hence, in 2002, two-thirds of Canada's adult population were participating in the labour market, and 7.7 percent of those labour-market participants were without work.

Table 10.1 shows the statistics on unemployment and labour-force participation for various groups within the Canadian population. Two comparisons are most apparent. First, women have lower rates of labour-force participation than men in the same age group. However, once in the labour force, similarly aged men and women have similar rates of unemployment. Second, young people aged 15 to 24 have much higher rates of unemployment than older people. More generally, these data show that labour-market experiences vary widely among groups within the labour force.

Labour-force data also allow economists and policymakers to monitor changes in the economy over time. Figure 10.2 shows the unemployment rate for Canada and for groupings of provinces: Atlantic Canada (Newfoundland and Labrador, Prince Edward Island, Nova Scotia, and New Brunswick), Central Canada

---

TABLE 10.1

The Labour-Market Experiences of Various Demographic Groups

This table shows the unemployment rate and the labour-force participation rate of various groups in the population for 2002.

Source: Statistics Canada, CANSIM II Table 2820002.

Demographic Group	Unemployment Rate	Labour-Force Participation Rate
Both Sexes, 15 years and over	7.7%	66.9%
Males, 15–24 years	15.3	67.7
Males, 25–44 years	7.3	92.4
Males, 45–64 years	6.1	79.4
Females, 15–24 years	11.8	64.9
Females, 25–44 years	6.7	81.2
Females, 45–64 years	5.5	64.2

FIGURE 10.2

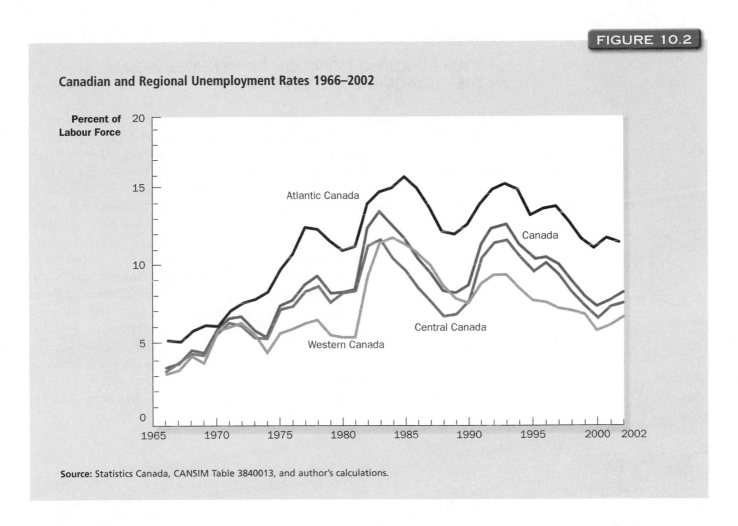

Canadian and Regional Unemployment Rates 1966–2002

Source: Statistics Canada, CANSIM Table 3840013, and author's calculations.

(Ontario and Quebec), and Western Canada (Manitoba, Saskatchewan, Alberta, and British Columbia). The figure shows that the economy always has some unemployment and that the amount changes from year to year.

Figure 10.2 also shows that both the unemployment rate and the amount by which it changes from year to year vary widely for different regions of the country. The unemployment rate in Atlantic Canada is consistently higher than in the rest of the country. Furthermore, the difference between the unemployment rate in Atlantic Canada and that in the rest of the country, while quite small in 1970, has grown since then. The unemployment rate in Western Canada has generally been lower than in the rest of the country. During the mid- to late 1980s, however, Western Canada's unemployment rate increased to become roughly equal to the Canadian average. This was mainly due to a fall in oil and natural gas prices—an event that harmed the economies in Western Canada but benefited those in the rest of the country. Finally, the unemployment rate in Central Canada closely follows the national unemployment rate. This is to be expected, since Central Canada comprises more than 60 percent of the Canadian labour force.

Case Study

LABOUR-FORCE PARTICIPATION OF MEN AND WOMEN IN THE CANADIAN ECONOMY

Women's role in Canadian society has changed dramatically over the past century. Social commentators have pointed to many causes for this change. In part, it is attributable to new technologies, such as the washing machine, clothes dryer, refrigerator, freezer, and dishwasher, which have reduced the amount of time required to complete routine household tasks. In part, it is attributable to improved birth control, which has reduced the number of children born to the typical family. And, of course, this change in women's role is also partly attributable to changing political and social attitudes. Together these developments have had a profound impact on society in general and on the economy in particular.

Nowhere is that impact more obvious than in data on labour-force participation. Figure 10.3 shows the labour-force participation rates of men and women in Canada since 1951. Just after World War II, men and women had very different roles in society. Only 24 percent of women were working or looking for work, in contrast to 84 percent of men. Over the past several decades, the difference between the participation rates of men and women has gradually diminished, as growing numbers of women have entered the labour force and some men have left it. Data for 2002 show that 61 percent of women were in the labour force, in

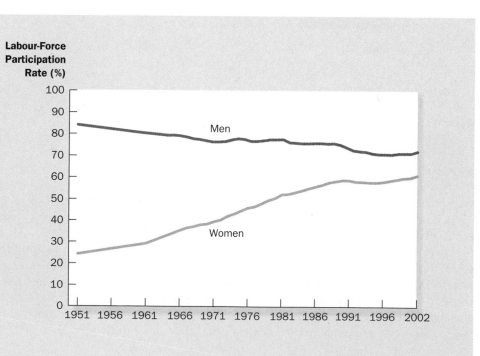

FIGURE 10.3

Labour-Force Participation Rates for Men and Women since 1951

This figure shows the percentage of adult men and women who are members of the labour force. It shows that over the past several decades, women have entered the labour force, and men have left it.

Sources: Data for 1966–2002 are from Statistics Canada. Observations for 1951 and 1961 are from F.H. Leacy, ed., *Historical Statistics of Canada*, 2nd ed. (Ottawa: Statistics Canada, 1983). Values for 1952–60 and 1962–65 are linear interpolations from the 1951, 1961, and 1966 observations.

contrast to 73 percent of men. As measured by labour-force participation, men and women are now playing a more equal role in the economy.

The increase in women's labour-force participation is easy to understand, but the fall in men's may seem puzzling. There are several reasons for this decline. First, young men now stay in school longer than their fathers and grandfathers did. Second, older men now retire earlier and live longer. Third, with more women employed, more fathers now stay at home to raise their children. Full-time students, retirees, and stay-at-home fathers are all counted as out of the labour force. ●

Does the Unemployment Rate Measure What We Want It To?

Measuring the amount of unemployment in the economy might seem straight-forward. In fact, it is not. While it is easy to distinguish between a person with a full-time job and a person who is not working at all, it is much harder to distinguish between a person who is unemployed and a person who is not in the labour force.

Movements into and out of the labour force are, in fact, very common. More than one-third of the unemployed are recent entrants into the labour force. These entrants include young workers looking for their first jobs, such as recent university and college graduates. They also include, in greater numbers, older workers who had previously left the labour force but have now returned to look for work. Moreover, not all unemployment ends with the job seeker finding a job. Almost half of all spells of unemployment end when the unemployed person leaves the labour force.

Because people move into and out of the labour force so often and for such a variety of reasons, statistics on unemployment can be difficult to interpret. On the one hand, some of those who report being unemployed may not, in fact, be trying hard to find a job; for example, they might be on temporary layoff and are waiting to be recalled to work. Or perhaps they are calling themselves unemployed because they want to qualify for Employment Insurance or because they are actually working and being paid "under the table." It may be more realistic to view these individuals as out of the labour force or, in some cases, employed.

On the other hand, some of those who report being out of the labour force may, in fact, want to work. These individuals may have tried to find a job but have given up after an unsuccessful search. Such individuals, labelled **discouraged searchers** by Statistics Canada, do not show up in unemployment statistics, even though they are truly workers without jobs. Similarly, some workers may be working part-time when in fact they want to work full-time. Although such workers are working less than they want to and so are underemployed, they do not show up in unemployment statistics.

The bottom part of Table 10.2, which provides 2002 data, shows the official unemployment rate for Canada as well as several alternative measures of labour underutilization calculated by Statistics Canada. The table shows that these alternative measures can paint quite a different picture of the unemployment situation. In the end, it is best to view the official unemployment rate as a useful but imperfect measure of joblessness.

discouraged searchers
individuals who would like to work but have given up looking for a job

TABLE 10.2

Alternative Measures of Labour Underutilization

This table shows various measures of joblessness for the Canadian economy. The data are averages for 2002. Figures may fail to sum exactly due to rounding.

Source: Statistics Canada, CANSIM II Tables 2820048 and 2820086, and author's calculations.

Measure and Description	Percentage of the Labour Force
Unemployed 1 to 4 weeks	2.7%
Unemployed 5 to 13 weeks	2.2
Unemployed 14 to 25 weeks	1.1
Unemployed 26 to 52 weeks	1.0
Unemployed more than 52 weeks	0.7
Official Unemployment Rate	**7.7**
Discouraged searchers	0.2
Those awaiting recall	0.6
Involuntary part-time workers	2.4
Official rate + discouraged searchers + those awaiting recall + involuntary part-time workers	10.8

How Long Are the Unemployed without Work?

In 2002 the average spell of unemployment in Canada lasted 16.2 weeks. Unfortunately, averages can hide a lot of interesting variation. For example, the Canadian average hides the fact that the average spell of unemployment varied widely across the country. In 2002, the average spell of unemployment ranged from a low of 9.9 weeks in Alberta to a high of 20.2 weeks in Newfoundland and Labrador. Average values also hide the fact that there may be a wide dispersion of unemployment experiences across individuals. Consider a simple example: Suppose that Bart experiences an unemployment spell lasting 51 weeks while Lisa, Otto, Edna, and Willy all experience spells of unemployment lasting just one week. While it is true that in this example the average unemployed person suffered 11 weeks of unemployment, this summary statistic seems inadequate for describing the true picture. In particular, by looking only at the average we would fail to learn that unemployment is a short-term and a relatively minor problem for Lisa, Otto, Edna, and Willy, while unemployment is a long-term and much more serious problem for Bart.

In our simple example, most spells of unemployment were quite short; for four of the five people in the example, unemployment lasted just one week. The figures in the top part of Table 10.2 indicate this is also true in Canada: One-third of those suffering through a spell of unemployment are unemployed for a month or less and two-thirds are unemployed for less than three months. While being unemployed for up to three months is by no means a minor problem, it is a far less serious problem than that faced by those suffering unemployment spells lasting longer than three months and certainly a less serious problem than that faced by those suffering unemployment spells lasting more than a year.

The figures in Table 10.2 suggest that economists and policymakers must be careful when interpreting data on unemployment and when designing policies to help the unemployed. Most people who become unemployed will soon find jobs. Policy solutions directed toward fixing the unemployment problem should be directed toward those suffering prolonged spells of unemployment.

Why Are There Always Some People Unemployed?

We have discussed how the government measures the amount of unemployment, the problems that arise in interpreting unemployment statistics, and the findings of labour economists on the duration of unemployment. You should now have a good idea about what unemployment is.

This discussion, however, has not explained why economies experience unemployment. In most markets in the economy, prices adjust to bring quantity supplied and quantity demanded into balance. In an ideal labour market, wages would adjust to balance the quantity of labour supplied and the quantity of labour demanded. This adjustment of wages would ensure that all workers are always fully employed.

Of course, reality does not resemble this ideal. There are always some workers without jobs, even when the overall economy is doing well. Figure 10. 4 shows Canada's observed unemployment rate and an estimate of Canada's natural unemployment rate. The **natural rate of unemployment** is what economists judge to be the rate of unemployment to which the economy tends to return in the long run. The exact value of the natural unemployment rate is unknown, but most economists estimate the rate in Canada to be currently 6 to 8 percent. Economists form estimates of the natural unemployment rate based on those variables they believe are the underlying determinants of the natural rate of unemployment. We will discuss these underlying determinants in the remainder of this chapter.

The values of the natural unemployment rate shown in Figure 10.4 represent the authors' opinions. Because the natural unemployment rate is only an estimate, there may be some dispute about the level of the rate at any particular time. However, the movements shown in the figure represent a fairly widespread view

natural rate of unemployment
the rate of unemployment to which the economy tends to return in the long run

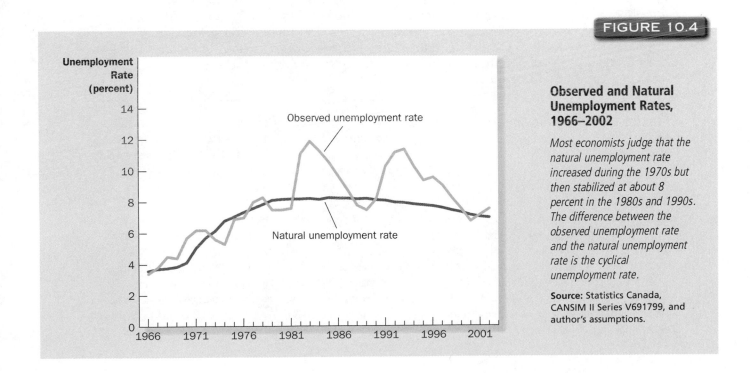

FIGURE 10.4

Observed and Natural Unemployment Rates, 1966–2002

Most economists judge that the natural unemployment rate increased during the 1970s but then stabilized at about 8 percent in the 1980s and 1990s. The difference between the observed unemployment rate and the natural unemployment rate is the cyclical unemployment rate.

Source: Statistics Canada, CANSIM II Series V691799, and author's assumptions.

among economists about what has happened to Canada's natural unemployment rate since 1966. During the 1970s and 1980s, the natural unemployment rate roughly doubled from about 4 percent to over 8 percent, and began falling in the mid-1990s. By 2000, the prevailing opinion was that the natural rate was very close to being equal to the observed unemployment rate.

Figure 10.4 also shows that the observed unemployment rate fluctuates around the natural rate. The observed unemployment rate differs from the natural rate due to the existence of **cyclical unemployment.** Cyclical unemployment arises due to short-run economic fluctuations. Later in this book we discuss short-run economic fluctuations, including the year-to-year fluctuations in unemployment around its natural rate. In the rest of this chapter, however, we ignore the short-run fluctuations and examine why unemployment is a chronic problem for market economies. That is, we will examine the determinants of the natural unemployment rate.

cyclical unemployment
the deviation of unemployment from its natural rate

IN THE NEWS

PROVINCIAL NATURAL UNEMPLOYMENT RATES

Many of the factors that affect the size of the natural unemployment rate differ in importance, depending on the province in which one lives. As a result, we might expect natural unemployment rates to differ across provinces. The following article presents estimates of the level of provincial natural unemployment rates in 1997 and relates these differences to how minimum wages, unionization, and the design of the Employment Insurance program differ across provinces.

Prairies Hit Full Employment: Study

By Bruce Little

Canada's national unemployment rate is still stuck at more than 9 percent, but the three Prairie provinces have already arrived at what many economists regard as full employment, according to a new study by Nesbitt Burns Inc.

Sherry Cooper, Nesbitt's chief economist, said the jobless rate in Alberta, Saskatchewan, and Manitoba has fallen below what she called the natural unemployment rate and, as a result, widespread labour shortages and strong wage pressures have emerged.

Ms Cooper said the strong showing by the Prairie trio is evidence that governments in other parts of Canada should not try to cure their unemployment problems by increasing government spending.

"Manitoba, Alberta, and Saskatchewan were the first [provinces] to eliminate their fiscal deficits, launch debt repayment programs, and implement tax relief measures," she said in the report, jointly written with Nesbitt economist Alex Araujo. "Low unemployment rates have not been the result of government make-work projects—quite the contrary."

The economists said Canada's natural unemployment rate—which they defined as the lowest rate consistent with stable inflation—has fallen to about 7.5 percent in the 1990s from 8.5 in the 1980s, but added that there are huge variations across the country.

Using a technique developed by analysts at the U.S. Federal Reserve Board, they calculated that the natural jobless

To preview our conclusions, we will find that there are four ways to explain unemployment in the long run. The first explanation is that it takes time for workers to search for the jobs that are best suited for them. The unemployment that results from the process of matching workers and jobs is sometimes called **frictional unemployment,** and it is often thought to explain relatively short spells of unemployment.

The next three explanations for unemployment suggest that the number of jobs available in some labour markets may be insufficient to give a job to everyone who wants one. This occurs when the quantity of labour supplied exceeds the quantity demanded. Unemployment of this sort is sometimes called **structural unemployment,** and it is often thought to explain longer spells of unemployment. As we will see, this kind of unemployment results when wages are, for some reason, set above the level that brings supply and demand into equilibrium. We will examine three possible reasons for an above-equilibrium wage: minimum-wage laws, unions, and efficiency wages.

frictional unemployment
unemployment that results because it takes time for workers to search for the jobs that best suit their tastes and skills

structural unemployment
unemployment that results because the number of jobs available in some labour markets is insufficient to provide a job for everyone who wants one

---

rate ranges from 5.5 percent in Ontario to 16.5 in Newfoundland.

Ontario, with an actual unemployment rate of 8.2 percent in the third quarter, is still a long way—2.7 percentage points—from the point at which the province would begin to generate inflation pressures.

In the late 1980s, Ontario's booming—and eventually overheated economy—was blamed by many Westerners as a major cause of the Bank of Canada's decision to raise interest rates to levels that tipped the economy into recession. At the time, British Columbia and Alberta were still in the early stages of recovery from prolonged recessions.

Ms Cooper said the natural unemployment rate "is a true measure of the degree of structural unemployment in a particular region." High structural unemployment in some regions is caused by age demographics, education levels, worker mobility, and reliance on seasonal employment.

The study said Quebec and the four Atlantic provinces all have natural unemployment rates of more than 10 percent, partly because university graduates make up a smaller share of the region's work force than they do elsewhere. The Atlantic provinces also rely heavily on seasonal jobs and have relatively more young people (whose jobless rate is higher) than other parts of Canada. Quebec's high rate also reflects "its relatively immobile labour force," which stays put "mainly because of language barriers."

Ontario's low rate is the result of a well-diversified economy, a highly educated labour force, and high-technology hotbeds of activity in Ottawa and southwestern Ontario.

In the Prairies, Alberta's tight job market has already "led to substantial upward pressure on wages and large net in-migration," the report said. In the past year, average wages have increased 5 percent in the three Prairie provinces, but only 3 percent in the rest of Canada. Because the three provinces account for only one-fifth of Canada's economy, however, there is "no risk of a nationwide wage runup."

British Columbia's 7.5 percent natural jobless rate is higher than neighbouring Alberta's 6 percent rate because of its "greater economic reliance on seasonal industry and relatively militant unions" and because of government policies that are seen as "business-unfriendly," the report said.

At a news conference, Ms Cooper said B.C.'s minimum wage has increased 40 percent since the province's NDP government took power in 1991. When the latest rise takes effect next April, it will be $7.15 an hour, compared with $5.00 in Alberta. She noted that the unemployment rate among young people, many of whom work for minimum wages, is 16.5 percent in B.C. and 10.7 in Alberta.

Despite a high rate of unemployment in many parts of Canada, the study said, "insufficient job creation is not the coast-to-coast problem that many are led to believe. Skilled labour is in short supply in many sectors, most notably marketing, design, engineering, [computer] programming, and oil and gas technology."

Source: *The Globe and Mail,* November 15, 1997, p. B3.

JOB SEARCH

job search
the process by which workers find appropriate jobs given their tastes and skills

One reason why economies always experience some unemployment is job search. **Job search** is the process of matching workers with appropriate jobs. If all workers and all jobs were the same, so that all workers were equally well suited for all jobs, job search would not be a problem. Laid-off workers would quickly find new jobs that were well suited for them. But, in fact, workers differ in their tastes and skills, jobs differ in their attributes, and information about job candidates and job vacancies is disseminated slowly among the many firms and households in the economy.

Why Some Frictional Unemployment Is Inevitable

Frictional unemployment is often the result of changes in the demand for labour among different firms. When consumers decide that they prefer Compaq over Dell computers, Compaq increases employment, and Dell lays off workers. The former Dell workers must now search for new jobs, and Compaq must decide which new workers to hire for the various jobs that have opened up. The result of this transition is a period of unemployment.

Similarly, because different regions of the country produce different goods, employment can rise in one region while it falls in another. Consider, for instance, what happens when the world price of oil falls. Oil-producing firms in Alberta respond to the lower price by cutting back on production and employment. At the same time, cheaper gasoline stimulates car sales, so auto-producing firms in Ontario raise production and employment. Changes in the composition of demand among industries or regions are called *sectoral shifts*. Because it takes time for workers to search for jobs in the new sectors, sectoral shifts temporarily cause unemployment.

Frictional unemployment is inevitable simply because the economy is always changing. Only 90 years ago, car manufacturing, petroleum, and aircraft manufacturing industries were very minor sources of employment in Canada. Today, these are three of the largest employers in the Canadian economy. At the same time, agriculture has fallen from being the largest single source of employment in Canada in 1911 to being only a minor source of employment today. As this transition took place, jobs were created in some industries and destroyed in others. The end result of this process has been higher productivity and higher living standards. But, along the way, workers in declining industries found themselves out of work and searching for new jobs.

Data show that, on average, Canadian companies that are expanding increase employment by roughly 10 percent each year. Companies that are contracting typically decrease employment by a somewhat smaller amount. The implication is that each year there is a very large transition of workers from contracting firms to expanding firms. This churning of the labour force is normal in a well-functioning and dynamic market economy, but it is inevitable that the labour market will have difficulty matching available jobs with available workers. The result is some amount of frictional unemployment. Recent estimates for Canada indicate that the mismatch between available jobs and people seeking employment explains why roughly one out of every eight unemployed workers is unemployed.

Public Policy and Job Search

Even if some frictional unemployment is inevitable, the precise amount is not. The faster information spreads about job openings and worker availability, the more rapidly the economy can match workers and firms. The Internet, for instance, may help facilitate job search and reduce frictional unemployment. In addition, public policy may play a role. If policy can reduce the time it takes unemployed workers to find new jobs, it can reduce the economy's natural rate of unemployment.

Government programs try to facilitate job search in various ways. One way is through government-run employment agencies, which give out information about job vacancies. Another way is through public training programs, which aim to ease the transition of workers from declining to growing industries and to help disadvantaged groups escape poverty. Government training programs in Canada are, for the most part, conducted through the federal government's Employment Insurance program. Recent reforms to this program have reallocated funds away from the payment of benefits to unemployed people and toward the funding of training programs.

Advocates of government programs designed to facilitate job search believe that the programs make the economy operate more efficiently by keeping the labour force more fully employed, and reduce the inequities inherent in a constantly changing market economy. These supporters also stress that in certain circumstances the private sector is incapable of helping those who lose their jobs. This is the case when job loss is the result of disasters, such as the collapse of the cod fishery in Newfoundland. It is argued that the virtual disappearance of an industry that is central to the economy of an entire region demands government involvement. In such cases, the solution is not simply for workers to find a similar job in the next company down the street, but rather to retrain for a new job in a new industry in a new area of the country. Government retraining and relocation programs may play a useful role in these cases, one that the private sector may be incapable of playing.

Critics of these programs question whether the government should get involved with the process of job search. They argue that it is better to let the private market match workers and jobs. In fact, most job search in our economy takes place without intervention by the government. Newspaper ads, Internet job sites, university and college placement offices, headhunters, and word of mouth all help spread information about job openings and job candidates. Similarly, much worker education is done privately, either through schools or through on-the-job training. These critics contend that the government is no better—and most likely worse—at disseminating the right information to the right workers and deciding what kinds of worker training would be most valuable. They claim that these decisions are best made privately by workers and employers.

Employment Insurance

Employment Insurance (EI)
a government program that partially protects workers' incomes when they become unemployed

In Canada, the federal government maintains an **Employment Insurance (EI)** program. This program is intended to ease the burden of those who find themselves unemployed, by temporarily providing them with income. Canada's EI program is expensive (in 2003, the government budgeted over $15 billion for the EI program) and controversial. Many economists believe that, while EI eases the burden of being unemployed, it may also cause the unemployment rate to be higher than it would be otherwise. Thus, the program may increase the amount of frictional unemployment without intending to do so.

Since 1971, two considerations have determined when and for how long someone can collect EI benefits: the number of hours worked in the past year and the unemployment rate in the area of residence. More hours of work make a claimant eligible to collect EI benefits for a longer period of time. The higher the local unemployment rate, the longer a claimant can collect and the fewer hours the claimant must work in order to become eligible. The details of the program have changed a great deal since 1971, and revisions to the program occur frequently.

As of 2003, EI regulations require that workers who live in a region where the unemployment rate exceeds 16 percent have to work only 420 hours (for example, 12 weeks of full-time, 35-hours-per-week employment) to become eligible for 32 weeks of benefits. Workers who live in a region where the unemployment rate is 6 percent or less have to work a minimum of 700 hours (for example, 20 weeks of full-time employment) to become eligible for benefits, and this minimum amount of work makes claimants eligible for just 14 weeks of insurance. In regions of the country with high unemployment rates, therefore, relatively few hours of work are needed to be eligible for EI, and EI benefits can be collected for a long time. In regions of the country with low unemployment rates, many more hours of work are needed to be eligible for EI, and EI benefits can be collected for a much shorter time.

These features of the program suggest that while EI reduces the hardship of unemployment, it can also increase the amount of unemployment. The explanation is based on one of the ten principles of economics in Chapter 1: People respond to incentives. Because EI benefits stop when a worker takes a new job, we might expect that the unemployed would devote less effort to job search and be more likely to turn down unattractive job offers. In addition, the design of the program provides an incentive for people to enter the labour force when they might not otherwise have done so. The reason is that the EI program increases the total income people receive by working: They not only earn a wage while working, but also become eligible to collect EI benefits should they leave the job.

Many studies by labour economists have examined the incentive effects of Employment Insurance. A federal government department, Human Resources and Skills Development Canada (HRSDC), has released, and continues to release, studies that attempt to measure the impact of the EI program on the labour market, the distribution of income, and living standards in Canada. The results of the studies released so far confirm economists' expectations of the program's effects. In one study it was found that job duration is affected by the length of time required to become eligible to collect EI benefits. In particular, the study found that those who collect EI tend to quit their jobs much sooner than they would otherwise have done if not for the availability of EI. The same study found that employers also respond to incentives of the EI program. Employers initiate layoffs only after workers become eligible for EI benefits. This is presumably done as a benefit to workers who in return accept lower wages.

Other studies have found that success at finding employment while collecting EI benefits is affected by the number of weeks of benefits remaining on the individual's claim: The likelihood of finding new employment increases as EI recipients near the end of their benefits. Finally, many studies have confirmed that joining the labour force is significantly influenced by the availability and generosity of EI benefits. These results all suggest that the design of the EI program influences behaviour in ways that increase the unemployment rate.

Even though Employment Insurance increases the unemployment rate, we should not necessarily conclude that the program is a bad one. EI does achieve its primary goal of reducing the income uncertainty faced by unemployed people. What's more, one of the HRSDC studies found that Employment Insurance allows unemployed people to conduct a more thorough job search, resulting in a higher wage in their new job than would otherwise have been the case. On the basis of such results, some economists have argued that Employment Insurance improves the ability of the economy to match each worker with the most appropriate job.

As mentioned above, the design of Canada's EI program has changed considerably over time. Changes introduced in 1971 made it substantially easier to become eligible to collect EI benefits and to collect it for a long time. Most economists believe these changes were responsible for a large increase in Canada's natural unemployment rate. Since 1990, many changes introduced to the program have had the opposite effect. The conditions under which one is eligible to collect EI benefits, and the length of time one is able to collect them, are now more stringent than they were in 1971. Economists believe these changes have contributed to a fall in Canada's natural unemployment rate from a peak reached in the late 1980s.

The study of Employment Insurance shows that the unemployment rate is an imperfect measure of a nation's overall level of economic well-being. Most economists agree that eliminating Employment Insurance would reduce the amount of unemployment in the economy. Yet economists disagree on whether economic well-being would be enhanced or diminished by this change in policy.

QuickQuiz How would an increase in the world price of oil affect the amount of frictional unemployment? Is this unemployment undesirable? What public policies might affect the amount of unemployment caused by this price change?

MINIMUM-WAGE LAWS

Having seen how frictional unemployment results from the process of matching workers and jobs, let's now examine how structural unemployment results when the number of jobs is insufficient for the number of workers.

To understand structural unemployment, we begin by reviewing how unemployment arises from minimum-wage laws. Although minimum wages are not the predominant reason for unemployment in our economy, they have an important effect on certain groups with particularly high unemployment rates. Moreover, the analysis of minimum wages is a natural place to start because, as we will see, it can be used to understand some of the other reasons for structural unemployment.

Figure 10.5 reviews the basic economics of a minimum wage. When a minimum-wage law forces the wage to remain above the level that balances supply and demand, it raises the quantity of labour supplied and reduces the quantity of labour demanded compared to the equilibrium level. There is a surplus of labour. Because there are more workers willing to work than there are jobs, some workers are unemployed.

It is important to note that minimum-wage laws are not a predominant reason for unemployment in the economy, because most workers in the economy earn wages well above the legal minimum. Minimum-wage laws are binding most often for the least skilled and least experienced members of the labour force, such as teenagers. It is only among these workers that minimum-wage laws explain the existence of unemployment.

Although Figure 10.5 is drawn to show the effects of a minimum-wage law, it also illustrates a more general lesson: *If the wage is kept above the equilibrium level for any reason, the result is unemployment.* Minimum-wage laws are just one reason why wages may be "too high." In the remaining two sections of this chapter, we consider two other reasons why wages may be kept above the equilibrium level—unions and efficiency wages. The basic economics of unemployment in these cases is the same as that shown in Figure 10.5, but these explanations of unemployment can apply to many more of the economy's workers.

At this point, however, we should stop and notice that the structural unemployment that arises from an above-equilibrium wage is, in an important sense,

FIGURE 10.5

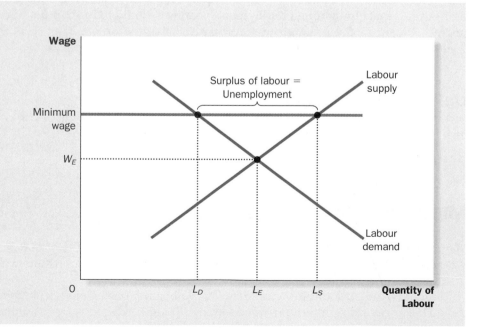

Unemployment from a Wage above the Equilibrium Level

In this labour market, the wage at which supply and demand balance is W_E. At this equilibrium wage, the quantity of labour supplied and the quantity of labour demanded both equal L_E. By contrast, if the wage is forced to remain above the equilibrium level, perhaps because of a minimum-wage law, the quantity of labour supplied rises to L_S, and the quantity of labour demanded falls to L_D. The resulting surplus of labour, $L_S - L_D$, represents unemployment.

different from the frictional unemployment that arises from the process of job search. The need for job search is not due to the failure of wages to balance labour supply and labour demand. When job search is the explanation for unemployment, workers are *searching* for the jobs that best suit their tastes and skills. By contrast, when the wage is above the equilibrium level, the quantity of labour supplied exceeds the quantity of labour demanded, and workers are unemployed because they are *waiting* for jobs to open up.

QuickQuiz Draw the supply curve and the demand curve for a labour market in which the wage is fixed above the equilibrium level. Show the quantity of labour supplied, the quantity demanded, and the amount of unemployment.

UNIONS AND COLLECTIVE BARGAINING

A **union** is a worker association that bargains with employers over wages and working conditions. As of 2002, 26 percent of all Canadian workers belonged to unions. The level of labour-force unionization has fallen slowly but steadily over the past 15 years: In 1989, 29 percent of workers were members of unions. In the 1940s and 1950s, union membership as a fraction of the labour force was considerably smaller, at just 10 percent in 1941 and 20 percent in 1951. While union membership in Canada is larger now than it was 50 years ago, the opposite is true in the United States. Union membership in the United States peaked in the 1950s at about one-third of the labour force and has fallen ever since. Today, only about 16 percent of U.S. workers are union members. In contrast to North American rates, European union membership rates are quite high. For example, in Sweden and Denmark, more than 75 percent of all workers belong to unions.

Union membership as a fraction of the labour force varies by province and by occupation. Union membership is highest in Quebec, where about 40 percent of the labour force is unionized, and lowest in Alberta, where only 24 percent of the labour force is unionized. In the public sector, 70 percent of workers are unionized, while only 19 percent in the private sector are unionized. Unionization is highest in industries in the public sector (education, public administration, and health care) and lowest in the food and accommodation industry.

union
a worker association that bargains with employers over wages and working conditions

The Economics of Unions

A union is a type of cartel. Like any cartel, a union is a group of sellers acting together in the hope of exerting their joint market power. Most workers in the Canadian economy discuss their wages, benefits, and working conditions with their employers as individuals. By contrast, workers in a union do so as a group. The process by which unions and firms agree on the terms of employment is called **collective bargaining.**

When a union bargains with a firm, it asks for higher wages, better benefits, and better working conditions than the firm would offer in the absence of a union. If the union and the firm do not reach agreement, the union can organize a withdrawal of labour from the firm, called a **strike.** Because a strike reduces production, sales, and profit, a firm facing a strike threat is likely to agree to pay higher

collective bargaining
the process by which unions and firms agree on the terms of employment

strike
the organized withdrawal of labour from a firm by a union

wages than it otherwise would. Economists who study the effects of unions typically find that union workers earn about 10 to 20 percent more than similar workers who do not belong to unions.

When a union raises the wage above the equilibrium level, it raises the quantity of labour supplied and reduces the quantity of labour demanded, resulting in unemployment. Those workers who remain employed are better off, but those who were previously employed and are now unemployed at the higher wage are worse off. Indeed, unions are often thought to cause conflict between different groups of workers—between the *insiders* who benefit from high union wages and the *outsiders* who do not get the union jobs.

The outsiders can respond to their status in one of two ways. Some of them remain unemployed and wait for the chance to become insiders and earn the high union wage. Others take jobs in firms that are not unionized. Thus, when unions raise wages in one part of the economy, the supply of labour increases in other parts of the economy. This increase in labour supply, in turn, reduces wages in industries that are not unionized. In other words, workers in unions reap the benefit of collective bargaining, while workers not in unions bear some of the cost.

The role of unions in the economy depends in part on the laws that govern union organization and collective bargaining. Normally, explicit agreements among members of a cartel are illegal. If firms that sell a common product were to agree to set a high price for that product, the agreement would be a "conspiracy to unduly limit competition." The government would prosecute these firms in civil and criminal court for violating Canada's competition laws. By contrast, unions are exempt from these laws. The policymakers who wrote Canada's competition laws believed that workers needed greater market power as they bargained with employers. Indeed, various laws are designed to encourage the formation of unions. In particular, the National War Labour Order of 1944 provided private sector employees with the right to union representation and collective bargaining. The Public Service Staff Relations Act of 1967 extended these rights to federal public sector employees. Similar acts of provincial legislatures have extended these rights to provincial public sector employees. Given these pieces of legislation, it is not surprising that 70 percent of public sector employees are unionized.

In the private sector, unions must approach workers in nonunionized companies and try to convince a majority of those workers of the benefits of union membership. While these membership drives are often unsuccessful, the very threat of such attempts at unionization likely have the effect of causing firms to increase wages and improve working conditions as a way of discouraging workers from joining a union.

Are Unions Good or Bad for the Economy?

Economists disagree about whether unions are good or bad for the economy as a whole. Let's consider both sides of the debate.

Critics of unions argue that unions are merely a type of cartel. When unions raise wages above the level that would prevail in competitive markets, they reduce the quantity of labour demanded, cause some workers to be unemployed, and reduce the wages in the rest of the economy. The resulting allocation of labour is, critics argue, both inefficient and inequitable. It is inefficient because high union wages reduce employment in unionized firms below the efficient, competitive level. It is inequitable because some workers benefit at the expense of other workers.

Advocates of unions contend that unions are a necessary antidote to the market power of the firms that hire workers. The extreme case of this market power is the "company town," where a single firm does most of the hiring in a geographic region. In a company town, if workers do not accept the wages and working conditions that the firm offers, they have little choice but to move or stop working. In the absence of a union, therefore, the firm could use its market power to pay lower wages and offer worse working conditions than would prevail if it had to compete with other firms for the same workers. In this case, a union may balance the firm's market power and protect the workers from being at the mercy of the firm owners.

Advocates of unions also claim that unions are important for helping firms respond efficiently to workers' concerns. Whenever a worker takes a job, the worker and the firm must agree on many attributes of the job in addition to the wage: hours of work, overtime, vacations, sick leave, health benefits, promotion schedules, job security, and so on. By representing workers' views on these issues, unions allow firms to provide the right mix of job attributes. Even if unions have the adverse effect of pushing wages above the equilibrium level and causing unemployment, they have the benefit of helping firms keep a happy and productive work force.

In the end, there is no consensus among economists about whether unions are good or bad for the economy. Like many institutions, their influence is probably beneficial in some circumstances and adverse in others.

QuickQuiz How does a union in the auto industry affect wages and employment at General Motors and Ford? How does it affect wages and employment in other industries?

THE THEORY OF EFFICIENCY WAGES

A fourth reason why economies always experience some unemployment—in addition to job search, minimum-wage laws, and unions—is suggested by the theory of **efficiency wages**. According to this theory, firms operate more efficiently if wages are above the equilibrium level. Therefore, it may be profitable for firms to keep wages high even in the presence of a surplus of labour.

In some ways, the unemployment that arises from efficiency wages is similar to the unemployment that arises from minimum-wage laws and unions. In all three cases, unemployment is the result of wages above the level that balances the quantity of labour supplied and the quantity of labour demanded. Yet there is also an important difference. Minimum-wage laws and unions prevent firms from lowering wages in the presence of a surplus of workers. Efficiency-wage theory states that such a constraint on firms is unnecessary in many cases because firms may be better off keeping wages above the equilibrium level.

Why should firms want to keep wages high? This decision may seem odd at first, because wages are a large part of firms' costs. Normally, we expect profit-maximizing firms to want to keep costs—and therefore wages—as low as possible. The novel insight of efficiency-wage theory is that paying high wages might be profitable because they might raise the efficiency of a firm's workers.

efficiency wages
above-equilibrium wages paid by firms in order to increase worker productivity

There are several types of efficiency-wage theory. Each type suggests a different explanation for why firms may want to pay high wages. Let's now consider four of these types.

Worker Health

The first and simplest type of efficiency-wage theory emphasizes the link between wages and worker health. Better paid workers eat a more nutritious diet, and workers who eat a better diet are healthier and more productive. A firm may find it more profitable to pay high wages and have healthy, productive workers than to pay lower wages and have less healthy, less productive workers.

This type of efficiency-wage theory is not relevant for firms in rich countries such as Canada. In these countries, the equilibrium wages for most workers are well above the level needed for an adequate diet. Firms are not concerned that paying equilibrium wages would place their workers' health in jeopardy.

This type of efficiency-wage theory is more relevant for firms in less developed countries where inadequate nutrition is a more common problem. Unemployment is high in the cities of many poor African countries, for example. In these countries, firms may fear that cutting wages would, in fact, adversely influence their workers' health and productivity. In other words, concern over nutrition may explain why firms do not cut wages despite a surplus of labour.

Worker Turnover

A second type of efficiency-wage theory emphasizes the link between wages and worker turnover. Workers quit jobs for many reasons—to take jobs in other firms, to move to other parts of the country, to leave the labour force, and so on. The frequency with which they quit depends on the entire set of incentives they face, including the benefits of leaving and the benefits of staying. The more a firm pays its workers, the less often its workers will choose to leave. Thus, a firm can reduce turnover among its workers by paying them a high wage.

Why do firms care about turnover? The reason is that it is costly for firms to hire and train new workers. Moreover, even after they are trained, newly hired workers are not as productive as experienced workers. Firms with higher turnover, therefore, will tend to have higher production costs. Firms may find it profitable to pay wages above the equilibrium level in order to reduce worker turnover.

Worker Effort

A third type of efficiency-wage theory emphasizes the link between wages and worker effort. In many jobs, workers have some discretion over how hard to work. As a result, firms monitor the efforts of their workers, and workers caught shirking their responsibilities are fired. But not all shirkers are caught immediately because monitoring workers is costly and imperfect. A firm can respond to this problem by paying wages above the equilibrium level. High wages make workers more eager to keep their jobs and, thereby, give workers an incentive to put forward their best effort.

This particular type of efficiency-wage theory is similar to the old Marxist idea of the "reserve army of the unemployed." Marx thought that employers benefited from unemployment because the threat of unemployment helped to discipline those workers who had jobs. In the worker-effort variant of efficiency-wage theory, unemployment fills a similar role. If the wage were at the level that balanced supply and demand, workers would have less reason to work hard because if they were fired, they could quickly find new jobs at the same wage. Therefore, firms raise wages above the equilibrium level, causing unemployment and providing an incentive for workers not to shirk their responsibilities.

Worker Quality

A fourth and final type of efficiency-wage theory emphasizes the link between wages and worker quality. When a firm hires new workers, it cannot perfectly gauge the quality of the applicants. By paying a high wage, the firm attracts a better pool of workers to apply for its jobs.

To see how this might work, consider a simple example. Waterwell Company owns one well and needs one worker to pump water from the well. Two workers, Bill and Ted, are interested in the job. Bill, a proficient worker, is willing to work for $10 per hour. Below that wage, he would rather start his own lawn-mowing business. Ted, a complete incompetent, is willing to work for anything above $2 per hour. Below that wage, he would rather sit on the beach. Economists say that Bill's *reservation wage*—the lowest wage he would accept—is $10, and Ted's reservation wage is $2.

What wage should the firm set? If the firm were interested in minimizing labour costs, it would set the wage at $2 per hour. At this wage, the quantity of workers supplied (one) would balance the quantity demanded. Ted would take the job, and Bill would not apply for it. Yet suppose Waterwell knows that only one of these two applicants is competent, but it does not know whether it is Bill or Ted. If the firm hires the incompetent worker, he may damage the well, causing the firm huge losses. In this case, the firm has a better strategy than paying the equilibrium wage of $2 and hiring Ted: It can offer $10 per hour, inducing both Bill and Ted to apply for the job. By choosing randomly between these two applicants and turning the other away, the firm has a fifty-fifty chance of hiring the competent one. By contrast, if the firm offers any lower wage, it is sure to hire the incompetent worker.

This story illustrates a general phenomenon. When a firm faces a surplus of workers, it might seem profitable to reduce the wage it is offering. But by reducing the wage, the firm induces an adverse change in the mix of workers. In this case, at a wage of $10, Waterwell has two workers applying for one job. But if Waterwell responds to this labour surplus by reducing the wage, the competent worker (who has better alternative opportunities) will not apply. Thus, it is profitable for the firm to pay a wage above the level that balances supply and demand.

Case Study

HENRY FORD AND THE VERY GENEROUS $5-A-DAY WAGE

Henry Ford was an industrial visionary. As founder of the Ford Motor Company, he was responsible for introducing modern techniques of production. Rather than building cars with small teams of skilled craftsmen, Ford built cars on assembly lines in which unskilled workers were taught to perform the same simple tasks over and over again. The output of this assembly process was the Model T Ford, one of the most famous early automobiles.

In 1914, Ford introduced another innovation: the $5 workday. This might not seem like much today, but back then $5 was about twice the going wage. It was also far above the wage that balanced supply and demand. When the new $5-a-day wage was announced, long lines of job seekers formed outside the Ford factories. The number of workers willing to work at this wage far exceeded the number of workers Ford needed.

Ford's high-wage policy had many of the effects predicted by efficiency-wage theory. Turnover fell, absenteeism fell, and productivity rose. Workers were so much more efficient that Ford's production costs were lower even though wages were higher. Thus, paying a wage above the equilibrium level was profitable for the firm. Henry Ford himself called the $5-a-day wage "one of the finest cost-cutting moves we ever made."

Historical accounts of this episode are also consistent with efficiency-wage theory. A historian of the early Ford Motor Company wrote, "Ford and his associates freely declared on many occasions that the high-wage policy turned out to be good business. By this they meant that it had improved the discipline of the workers, given them a more loyal interest in the institution, and raised their personal efficiency."

Why did it take Henry Ford to introduce this efficiency wage? Why were other firms not already taking advantage of this seemingly profitable business strategy? According to some analysts, Ford's decision was closely linked to his use of the assembly line. Workers organized in an assembly line are highly interdependent. If one worker is absent or works slowly, other workers are less able to complete their own tasks. Thus, while assembly lines made production more efficient, they also raised the importance of low worker turnover, high worker quality, and high worker effort. As a result, paying efficiency wages may have been a better strategy for the Ford Motor Company than for other businesses at the time. ●

QuickQuiz   Give four explanations for why firms might find it profitable to pay wages above the level that balances quantity of labour supplied and quantity of labour demanded.

CONCLUSION

In this chapter we discussed the measurement of unemployment and the reasons why economies always experience some degree of unemployment. We have seen how job search, minimum-wage laws, unions, and efficiency wages can all help explain why some workers do not have jobs. Which of these four explanations for the natural rate of unemployment are the most important for the Canadian economy and other economies around the world? Unfortunately, there is no easy way to tell. Economists differ in which of these explanations of unemployment they consider most important.

The analysis of this chapter yields an important lesson: Although the economy will always have some unemployment, its natural rate is not immutable. Many events and policies can change the amount of unemployment the economy typically experiences. As the information revolution changes the process of job search, as governments adjust the minimum wage and alter the eligibility requirements for Employment Insurance, as workers form or quit unions, and as firms alter their reliance on efficiency wages, the natural rate of unemployment evolves. Unemployment is not a simple problem with a simple solution. But how we choose to organize our society can profoundly influence how prevalent a problem it is.

SUMMARY

- The unemployment rate is the percentage of those who would like to work but do not have jobs. Statistics Canada calculates this statistic monthly based on a survey of thousands of households.

- The unemployment rate is an imperfect measure of joblessness. Some people who call themselves unemployed may actually not want to work, and some people who would like to work have left the labour force after an unsuccessful search.

- In the Canadian economy, most people who become unemployed find work within a fairly short period of time. The fraction of those who find themselves unemployed for periods longer than six months is relatively small. Public policy solutions to the unemployment problem should be directed toward providing help to those experiencing long bouts of unemployment.

- One reason for unemployment is the time it takes for workers to search for jobs that best suit their tastes and skills. Employment Insurance is

a government policy that, while protecting workers' incomes, increases the amount of frictional unemployment.

- A second reason why our economy always has some unemployment is minimum-wage laws. By raising the wage of unskilled and inexperienced workers above the equilibrium level, minimum-wage laws raise the quantity of labour supplied and reduce the quantity demanded. The resulting surplus of labour represents unemployment.

- A third reason for unemployment is the market power of unions. When unions push the wages in unionized industries above the equilibrium level, they create a surplus of labour.

- A fourth reason for unemployment is suggested by the theory of efficiency wages. According to this theory, firms find it profitable to pay wages above the equilibrium level. High wages can improve worker health, lower worker turnover, increase worker effort, and raise worker quality.

KEY CONCEPTS

labour force, p. 199
unemployment rate, p. 199
labour-force participation
    rate, p. 199
discouraged searchers, p. 203

natural rate of
    unemployment, p. 205
cyclical unemployment, p. 206
frictional unemployment, p. 207
structural unemployment, p. 207
job search, p. 208

Employment Insurance, p. 210
union, p. 213
collective bargaining, p. 213
strike, p. 213
efficiency wages, p. 215

QUESTIONS FOR REVIEW

1. What are the three categories into which Statistics Canada divides everyone? How does Statistics Canada compute the labour force, the unemployment rate, and the labour-force participation rate?

2. Employment Insurance provides an economic incentive that encourages people to enter the labour force. Explain.

3. Why is frictional unemployment inevitable? How might the government reduce the amount of frictional unemployment?

4. Are minimum-wage laws a better explanation for structural unemployment among teenagers or among postsecondary graduates? Why?

5. How do unions affect the natural rate of unemployment?

6. What claims do advocates of unions make to argue that unions are good for the economy?

7. Explain four ways in which a firm might increase its profits by raising the wages it pays.

PROBLEMS AND APPLICATIONS

1. Statistics Canada announced that in June 2003, of all Canadians aged 15 years and older, 16 074 600 were employed, 1 244 700 were unemployed, and 7 920 000 were not in the labour force. How big was the labour force? What was the labour-force participation rate? What was the unemployment rate?

2. As shown in Figure 10.3, the overall labour-force participation rate of men declined between 1976 and 1997. This overall decline reflects different patterns for different age groups, however, as shown in the following table.

	All Men	Men 15–24	Men 25–54	Men 55 and over
1976	78%	68%	95%	48%
1997	72	63	91	33

Which group experienced the largest decline? Given this information, what factor may have played an important role in the decline in overall male labour-force participation over this period?

3. The labour-force participation rate of women increased sharply between 1976 and 1997, as shown in Figure 10.3. As with men, however, there were different patterns for different age groups, as shown in this table:

	Women 55	All Women	Women 15–24	Women 25–54 and Over
1976	46%	58%	52%	18%
1997	57	59	76	17

Why do you think that younger women experienced a bigger increase in labour-force participation than older women?

4. Between 1999 and 2000, total employment in Canada increased by 378 000 workers, but the number of unemployed workers declined by only 100 000. How are these numbers consistent with each other? Why might one expect a reduction in the number of people counted as unemployed to be smaller than the increase in the number of people employed?

5. Go to the Human Resources and Skills Development Canada website at http://www.hrsdc.gc.ca and, under "Individuals," click on "Financial Benefits" and then on "Employment Insurance." There you will find information about Employment Insurance eligibility and entitlement for various regions of Canada. What is the unemployment rate in the area in which you live? For how long would you need to work in order to become eligible for Employment Insurance? Once eligible, for how long would you be able to collect Employment Insurance? Compare these eligibility and entitlement periods to those appropriate for someone living in an area of the country with a much different unemployment rate than the one that exists where you live. How might these differences be reflected in labour-market behaviour in one region versus the other?

6. Are the following workers more likely to experience short-term or long-term unemployment? Explain.
   a. a construction worker laid off because of bad weather
   b. a manufacturing worker who loses her job at a plant in an isolated area
   c. a stagecoach-industry worker laid off because of competition from railroads
   d. a short-order cook who loses his job when a new restaurant opens across the street
   e. an expert welder with little formal education who loses her job when the company installs automatic welding machinery

7. Using a diagram of the labour market, show the effect of an increase in the minimum wage on the wage paid to workers, the number of workers supplied, the number of workers demanded, and the amount of unemployment.

8. Do you think that firms in small towns or in cities have more market power in hiring? Do you think that firms generally have more market power in hiring today than 50 years ago, or less? How do you think this change over time has affected the role of unions in the economy? Explain.

9. Consider an economy with two labour markets, neither of which is unionized. Now suppose a union is established in one market.
   a. Show the effect of the union on the market in which it is formed. In what sense is the quantity of labour employed in this market an inefficient quantity?
   b. Show the effect of the union on the nonunionized market. What happens to the equilibrium wage in this market?

10. It can be shown that an industry's demand for labour will become more elastic when the demand for the industry's product becomes more elastic. Let's consider the implications of this fact for the Canadian automobile industry and the Canadian Auto Workers union (CAW).
    a. What happened to the elasticity of demand for Canadian cars when the Japanese developed a strong auto industry? What happened to the elasticity of demand for Canadian autoworkers? Explain.
    b. As the chapter explains, a union generally faces a tradeoff in deciding how much to raise wages, because a larger increase is better for workers who remain employed but also results in a greater reduction in employment. How did the rise in auto imports from Japan affect the wage–employment tradeoff faced by the CAW?
    c. Do you think the growth of the Japanese auto industry increased or decreased the gap between the competitive wage and the wage chosen by the CAW? Explain.

11. Some workers in the economy are paid a flat salary and some are paid by commission. Which compensation scheme would require more monitoring by supervisors? In which case do firms have an incentive to pay more than the equilibrium level (as in the worker-effort variant of efficiency-wage theory)?

What factors do you think determine the type of compensation firms choose?

12. (This problem is challenging.) Suppose that Parliament passes a law requiring employers to provide employees some benefit (such as dental care) that raises the cost of an employee by $4 per hour.

a. What effect does this employer mandate have on the demand for labour? (In answering this and the following questions, be quantitative when you can.)

b. If employees place a value on this benefit exactly equal to its cost, what effect does this employer mandate have on the supply of labour?

c. If the wage is free to balance supply and demand, how does this law affect the wage and the level of employment? Are employers better or worse off? Are employees better or worse off?

d. If a minimum-wage law prevents the wage from balancing supply and demand, how does the employer mandate affect the wage, the level of employment, and the level of unemployment? Are employers better or worse off? Are employees better or worse off?

e. Now suppose that workers do not value the mandated benefit at all. How does this alternative assumption change your answers to parts (b), (c), and (d) above?

INTERNET RESOURCES

- To learn how the unemployment rate is calculated and to download a copy of the Labour Force Survey questionnaire that is used to determine the size of the labour force, the level of employment, and the level of unemployment, visit the Statistics Canada website at http://www.statcan.ca/english/sdds/3701.htm.

- On the Human Resources and Skills Development Canada (HRSDC) website (http://www.hrsdc.gc.ca), under "Individuals," click on "Labour and Workplace" to access a great deal of information related to the Canadian labour market.

    From the "Labour and Workplace" menu, select "Labour Standards," which will take you to a link to the "Employment Standards Legislation in Canada" page, where you can find out the current level of the minimum wage paid in your province, plus information on many other workplace topics.

    To learn more about the regulations governing the provision of Employment Insurance, on the HRSDC website, under "Individuals," click on "Financial Benefits," then on "Employment Insurance," and then on "Employment Insurance Legislation."

- Information on union membership in Canada can be found at http://www.jobquality.ca/indicator_e/uni001.stm.

For more study tools, please visit http://www.mankiw3e.nelson.com.

5

MONEY AND PRICES IN THE LONG RUN

THE MONETARY SYSTEM

11

Learning Objectives

In this chapter, you will ...

- Consider the nature of money and its functions in the economy
- Learn about the Bank of Canada
- Study how the banking system helps determine the supply of money
- Examine the tools used by the Bank of Canada to alter the supply of money

When you walk into a restaurant to buy a meal, you get something of value—a full stomach. To pay for this service, you might hand the restaurateur several worn-out pieces of coloured paper decorated with strange symbols, birds, government buildings, and the portraits of the Queen or a dead prime minister. Or you might hand him a piece of paper with the name of a bank and your signature, or a plastic card. Whether you pay by cash, cheque, or debit card, the restaurateur is happy to work hard to satisfy your gastronomical desires in exchange for these pieces of paper and plastic that, in and of themselves, are worthless.

To anyone who has lived in a modern economy, this social custom is not at all odd. Even though paper money has no intrinsic value, the restaurateur is confident that, in the future, some third person will accept it in exchange for something that the restaurateur does value. And that third person is confident that some fourth person will accept the money, with the knowledge that yet a fifth person will accept the money . . . and so on. To the restaurateur and to other people in our society, your cash, cheque, or debit card represents a claim to goods and services in the future.

The social custom of using money for transactions is extraordinarily useful in a large, complex society. Imagine, for a moment, that there was no item in the economy widely accepted in exchange for goods and services. People would have to rely on *barter*—the exchange of one good or service for another—to obtain the things they need. To get your restaurant meal, for instance, you would have to offer the restaurateur something of immediate value. You could offer to wash some dishes, clean his car, or give him your family's secret recipe for meat loaf. An economy that relies on barter will have trouble allocating its scarce resources efficiently. In such an economy, trade is said to require the *double coincidence of wants*—the unlikely occurrence that two people each have a good or service that the other wants.

The existence of money makes trade easier. The restaurateur does not care whether you can produce a valuable good or service for him. He is happy to accept your money, knowing that other people will do the same for him. Such a convention allows trade to be roundabout. The restaurateur accepts your money and uses it to pay his chef; the chef uses her paycheque to send her child to day care; the daycare centre uses this tuition to pay a teacher; and the teacher hires you to mow his lawn. As money flows from person to person in the economy, it facilitates production and trade, thereby allowing each person to specialize in what he or she does best and raising everyone's standard of living.

In this chapter we begin to examine the role of money in the economy. We discuss what money is, the various forms that money takes, how the banking system helps create money, and how the government controls the quantity of money in circulation. Because money is so important in the economy, we devote much effort in the rest of this book to learning how changes in the quantity of money affect various economic variables, including inflation, interest rates, production, and employment. Consistent with our long-run focus in the previous three chapters, in the next chapter we will examine the long-run effects of changes in the quantity of money. The short-run effects of monetary changes are a more complex topic, which we will take up later in the book. This chapter provides the background for all of this further analysis.

THE MEANING OF MONEY

What is money? This might seem like an odd question. When you read that billionaire Bill Gates has a lot of money, you know what that means: He is so rich that he can buy almost anything he wants. In this sense, the term *money* is used to mean *wealth*.

money
the set of assets in an economy that people regularly use to buy goods and services from other people

Economists, however, use the word in a more specific sense: **Money** is the set of assets in the economy that people regularly use to buy goods and services from other people. The cash in your wallet is money because you can use it to buy a meal at a restaurant or a shirt at a clothing store. By contrast, if you happened to own most of Microsoft Corporation, as Bill Gates does, you would be wealthy, but this asset is not considered a form of money. You could not buy a meal or a shirt with this wealth without first obtaining some cash. According to the economist's definition, money includes only those few types of wealth that are regularly accepted by sellers in exchange for goods and services.

The Functions of Money

Money has three functions in the economy: It is a *medium of exchange*, a *unit of account*, and a *store of value*. These three functions together distinguish money from other assets in the economy, such as stocks, bonds, real estate, art, and even hockey cards. Let's examine each of these functions of money in turn.

A **medium of exchange** is an item that buyers give to sellers when they purchase goods and services. When you buy a shirt at a clothing store, the store gives you the shirt, and you give the store your money. This transfer of money from buyer to seller allows the transaction to take place. When you walk into a store, you are confident that the store will accept your money for the items it is selling because money is the commonly accepted medium of exchange.

A **unit of account** is the yardstick people use to post prices and record debts. When you go shopping, you might observe that a shirt costs $20 and a hamburger costs $2. Even though it would be accurate to say that the price of a shirt is 10 hamburgers and the price of a hamburger is 1/10 of a shirt, prices are never quoted in this way. Similarly, if you take out a loan from a bank, the size of your future loan repayments will be measured in dollars, not in a quantity of goods and services. When we want to measure and record economic value, we use money as the unit of account.

A **store of value** is an item that people can use to transfer purchasing power from the present to the future. When a seller accepts money today in exchange for a good or service, that seller can hold the money and become a buyer of another good or service at another time. Of course, money is not the only store of value in the economy, because a person can also transfer purchasing power from the present to the future by holding other assets. The term *wealth* is used to refer to the total of all stores of value, including both money and nonmonetary assets.

Economists use the term **liquidity** to describe the ease with which an asset can be converted into the economy's medium of exchange. Because money is the economy's medium of exchange, it is the most liquid asset available. Other assets vary widely in their liquidity. Most stocks and bonds can be sold easily with small cost, so they are relatively liquid assets. By contrast, selling a house, a Rembrandt painting, or a 1964 Bobby Orr hockey card requires more time and effort, so these assets are less liquid.

When people decide in what form to hold their wealth, they have to balance the liquidity of each possible asset against the asset's usefulness as a store of value. Money is the most liquid asset, but it is far from perfect as a store of value. When prices rise, the value of money falls. In other words, when goods and services become more expensive, each dollar in your wallet can buy less. This link between the price level and the value of money will turn out to be important for understanding how money affects the economy.

The Kinds of Money

When money takes the form of a commodity with intrinsic value, it is called **commodity money.** The term *intrinsic value* means that the item would have value even if it were not used as money. One example of commodity money is gold. Gold has intrinsic value because it is used in industry and in the making of jewellery. Although today we no longer use gold as money, historically gold has been

medium of exchange
an item that buyers give to sellers when they want to purchase goods and services

unit of account
the yardstick people use to post prices and record debts

store of value
an item that people can use to transfer purchasing power from the present to the future

liquidity
the ease with which an asset can be converted into the economy's medium of exchange

commodity money
money that takes the form of a commodity with intrinsic value

a common form of money because it is relatively easy to carry, measure, and verify for impurities. When an economy uses gold as money (or uses paper money that is convertible into gold on demand), it is said to be operating under a *gold standard.*

Another example of commodity money is cigarettes. In prisoner-of-war camps during World War II, prisoners traded goods and services with one another using cigarettes as the store of value, unit of account, and medium of exchange. Similarly, as the Soviet Union was breaking up in the late 1980s, cigarettes started replacing the ruble as the preferred currency in Moscow. In both cases, even non-smokers were happy to accept cigarettes in an exchange, knowing that they could use the cigarettes to buy other goods and services.

Money without intrinsic value is called **fiat money.** A *fiat* is simply an order or decree, and fiat money is established as money by government decree. For example, compare the paper dollars in your wallet (printed by the Canadian government) and the paper dollars from a game of Monopoly (printed by the Parker Brothers game company). Why can you use the first to pay your bill at a restaurant but not the second? The answer is that the Canadian government has decreed its dollars to be valid money. Each paper dollar in your wallet reads: "This note is legal tender."

fiat money
money without intrinsic value that is used as money because of government decree

IN THE NEWS

MONEY ON THE ISLAND OF YAP

The role of social custom in the monetary system is most apparent in foreign cultures with customs very different from our own. The following article describes the money on the island of Yap. As you read the article, ask yourself whether Yap is using a type of commodity money, a type of fiat money, or something in between.

Fixed Assets, or Why a Loan in Yap Is Hard to Roll Over
By Art Pine

YAP, MICRONESIA—On this tiny South Pacific island, life is easy and the currency is hard.

Elsewhere, the world's troubled monetary system creaks along; floating exchange rates wreak havoc on currency markets, and devaluations are commonplace. But on Yap the currency is as solid as a rock. In fact, it *is* rock. Limestone to be precise.

For nearly 2,000 years the Yapese have used large stone wheels to pay for major purchases, such as land, canoes and permissions to marry. Yap is a U.S. trust territory, and the dollar is used in grocery stores and gas stations. But reliance on stone money, like the island's ancient caste system and the traditional dress of loincloths and grass skirts, continues.

Buying property with stones is "much easier than buying it with U.S. dollars," says John Chodad, who recently purchased a building lot with a 30-inch stone wheel. "We don't know the value of the U.S. dollar.". . .

Stone wheels don't make good pocket money, so for small transactions, Yapese use other forms of currency, such as beer. Beer is proffered as payment for all sorts of odd jobs, including construction. The 10,000 people on Yap consume

Although the government is central to establishing and regulating a system of fiat money (by prosecuting counterfeiters, for example), other factors are also required for the success of such a monetary system. To a large extent, the acceptance of fiat money depends as much on expectations and social convention as on government decree. The Soviet government in the 1980s never abandoned the ruble as the official currency. Yet the people of Moscow preferred to accept cigarettes (or even American dollars) in exchange for goods and services, because they were more confident that these alternative monies would be accepted by others in the future.

Money in the Canadian Economy

As we will see, the quantity of money circulating in the economy, called the *money stock*, has a powerful influence on many economic variables. But before we consider why that is true, we need to ask a preliminary question: What is the quantity of money? In particular, suppose you were given the task of measuring how much money there is in the Canadian economy. What would you include in your measure?

Money on the island of Yap: Not exactly pocket change.

40,000 to 50,000 cases a year, mostly of Budweiser. . . .

The people of Yap have been using stone money ever since a Yapese warrior named Anagumang first brought the huge stones from limestone caverns on neighboring Palau, some 1,500 to 2,000 years ago. Inspired by the moon, he fashioned the stone into large circles. The rest is history.

Yapese lean the stone wheels against their houses or prop up rows of them in village "banks." Most of the stones are 2 1/2 to 5 feet in diameter, but some are as much as 12 feet across. Each has a hole in the center so it can be slipped onto the trunk of a fallen betel nut tree and carried. It takes 20 men to lift some stones.

By custom, the stones are worthless when broken. You never hear people on Yap musing about wanting a piece of the rock. Rather than risk a broken stone—or back—Yapese tend to leave the larger stones where they are and make a mental accounting that the ownership has been transferred—much as gold bars used in international transactions change hands without leaving the vaults of the New York Federal Reserve Bank. . . .

There are some decided advantages to using massive stones for money. They are immune to black-market trading, for one thing, and they pose formidable obstacles to pickpockets. In addition, there aren't any sterile debates about how to stabilize the Yapese monetary system. With only 6,600 stone wheels remaining on the island, the money supply stays put. . . .

Meanwhile, Yap's stone money may be about to take on international significance. Just yesterday, Washington received notice that Tosiho Nakayama, the president of Micronesia, plans to bring a stone disk when he visits the United States next month. It will be flown by Air Force jet.

Officials say Mr. Nakayama intends the stone as Micronesia's symbolic contribution toward reducing the U.S. budget deficit.

Source: *The Wall Street Journal*, March 29, 1984, p. A1. © 1984 by Dow Jones & Co. Inc. Reproduced with permission of DOW JONES & CO INC in the format Textbook via Copyright Clearance Center.

currency
the paper bills and coins in the hands of the public

demand deposits
balances in bank accounts that depositors can access on demand by writing a cheque or using a debit card

The most obvious asset to include is **currency**—the paper bills and coins in the hands of the public. Currency is clearly the most widely accepted medium of exchange in our economy. There is no doubt that it is part of the money stock.

Yet currency is not the only asset that you can use to buy goods and services. Many stores also accept personal cheques and debit cards. Wealth held in your chequing account is almost as convenient for buying things as wealth held in your wallet. To measure the money stock, therefore, you might want to include **demand deposits**—balances in bank accounts that depositors can access on demand simply by writing a cheque or using a debit card.

Once you start to consider balances in chequing accounts as part of the money stock, you are led to consider the large variety of other accounts that people hold at banks and other financial institutions. Bank depositors can often write cheques against the balances in their savings accounts, and they can easily transfer funds from savings into chequing accounts. In addition, depositors in money market mutual funds can sometimes write cheques against their balances. Thus, these other accounts should plausibly be part of the Canadian money stock.

In a complex economy such as ours, it is not easy to draw a line between assets that can be called "money" and assets that cannot. The coins in your pocket are clearly part of the money stock, and the CN Tower clearly is not, but there are many assets in between these extremes for which the choice is less clear. Therefore, various measures of the money stock are available for the Canadian economy. Figure 11.1 shows the two most important, designated M1 and M2. Each of these measures uses a slightly different criterion for distinguishing monetary and nonmonetary assets.

CREDIT CARDS, DEBIT CARDS, AND MONEY

It might seem natural to include credit cards as part of the economy's stock of money. After all, people use credit cards to make many of their purchases. Aren't credit cards, therefore, a medium of exchange?

Although at first this argument may seem persuasive, credit cards are excluded from all measures of the quantity of money. The reason is that credit cards are not really a method of payment but a method of *deferring* payment. When you buy a meal with a credit card, the bank that issued the card pays the restaurant what it is due. At a later date, you will have to repay the bank (perhaps with interest). When the time comes to pay your credit card bill, you will probably do so by writing a cheque against your chequing account. The balance in this chequing account is part of the economy's stock of money.

Notice that credit cards are very different from debit cards, which automatically withdraw funds from a bank account to pay for items bought. Rather than allowing the user to postpone payment for a purchase, a debit card allows the user immediate access to deposits in a bank account. In this sense, a debit card is more similar to a cheque than to a credit card. The account balances that lie behind debit cards are included in measures of the quantity of money.

Even though credit cards are not considered a form of money, they are nonetheless important for analyzing the monetary system. People who have credit cards can pay many of their bills all at once at the end of the month, rather than sporadically as they make purchases. As a result, people who have credit cards probably hold less money on average than people who do not have credit cards. Thus, the introduction and increased popularity of credit cards may reduce the amount of money that people choose to hold.

FIGURE 11.1

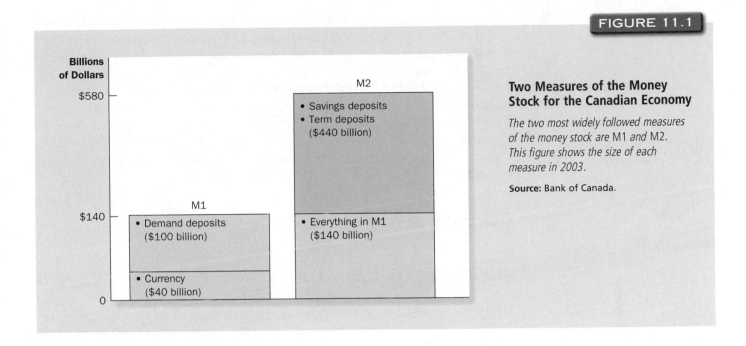

Two Measures of the Money Stock for the Canadian Economy

The two most widely followed measures of the money stock are M1 and M2. This figure shows the size of each measure in 2003.

Source: Bank of Canada.

For our purposes in this book, we need not dwell on the differences between the various measures of money. The important point is that the money stock for the Canadian economy includes not just currency but also deposits in banks and other financial institutions that can be readily accessed and used to buy goods and services.

Case Study

WHERE IS ALL THE CURRENCY?

One puzzle about the money stock of the Canadian economy concerns the amount of currency. In 2003 there was about $40 billion of currency outstanding. To put this number in perspective, we can divide it by 25.8 million, the number of adults (aged 15 and over) in Canada. This calculation implies that the average adult holds about $1550 of currency. Most people are surprised to learn that our economy has so much currency because they carry far less than this in their wallets.

Who is holding all this currency? No one knows for sure. Some of the currency is held by banks and companies, but a plausible explanation is that much of the currency is being held by tax evaders, drug dealers, and other criminals. For most people in the Canadian economy, currency is not a particularly good way to hold large amounts of wealth. Currency can be lost or stolen. Moreover, currency does not earn interest, whereas money in a bank account does. Thus, most people hold only small amounts of currency. By contrast, criminals may prefer not to hold their wealth in banks. A bank deposit would give police a paper trail with which to trace illegal activities. For criminals, currency may be the best store of value available.

A similar calculation for the United States economy gives about $2900 in U.S. currency per adult, which is even more surprising. Perhaps there is more criminal activity in the United States than in Canada? But a more plausible explanation is that much of the U.S. currency is held outside the United States. In countries without a stable monetary system, people often prefer U.S. dollars to domestic assets. It is, in fact, not unusual to see U.S. dollars being used around the world as a medium of exchange, unit of account, and store of value. The Canadian dollar, in contrast, is rarely used outside Canada. ●

QuickQuiz   List and describe the three functions of money.

THE BANK OF CANADA

Bank of Canada
the central bank of Canada

central bank
an institution designed to regulate the quantity of money in the economy

Whenever an economy relies on a system of fiat money, as the Canadian economy does, some organization must be responsible for controlling the stock of money. In Canada, that organization is the **Bank of Canada**. If you look at a Canadian bank note, you will see on it the words "Bank of Canada" and the signatures of the governor and the deputy governor of the Bank of Canada. The Bank of Canada is an example of a **central bank**—an institution designed to control the quantity of money in the economy. Other major central banks around the world include the Bank of England, the Bank of Japan, the European Central Bank, and the Federal Reserve of the United States.

The Bank of Canada Act

Until the Great Depression of the 1930s, Canada had no central bank. Bank notes were issued by the Department of Finance and by the large commercial banks, like the Bank of Montreal. The monetary system was regulated by the Department of Finance, acting in concert with those large commercial banks. The gold standard ensured that bank notes could normally be exchanged for a fixed quantity of gold. The economic problems of the Great Depression, and the need to control the quantity of fiat money when the gold standard collapsed, led the government to set up a royal commission to study the issues. The commission recommended that a central bank be established. As a result, in 1934 Parliament enacted the Bank of Canada Act, which laid down the responsibilities of the Bank of Canada. The Bank was established in 1935 and nationalized in 1938, so it is now owned by the Canadian government.

The Bank of Canada is managed by a board of directors composed of the governor, the senior deputy governor, and 12 directors, including the deputy minister of Finance. The current governor of the Bank of Canada, David Dodge, was appointed in 2001. All members of the board of directors are appointed by the minister of Finance, with seven-year terms for the governor and senior deputy governor and three-year terms for the other directors.

The significance of this management structure is that ultimately the Bank of Canada is controlled by the Canadian government; the government not only appoints the board of directors but can, as a last resort, issue a written directive to the governor with which he or she must comply. In practice, however, the Bank of Canada is largely independent of the Canadian government. Just as Supreme Court judges are appointed for life to insulate them from politics, the seven-year term of the governor of the Bank of Canada provides insulation from short-term political pressures when the governor formulates monetary policy. And it is generally accepted that the governor would immediately resign if issued with a written directive from the minister of Finance. The threat of the turmoil in financial markets that would follow the governor's resignation means that the Finance minister would use this weapon only as a last resort.

Commercial banks, like the "Big 5"—the Bank of Montreal, the Royal Bank, the Toronto-Dominion Bank, the Canadian Imperial Bank of Commerce, and the Bank of Nova Scotia—are owned by their individual shareholders. The primary responsibility of these commercial banks is to maximize the profits they earn on behalf of these shareholders. Central banks like the Bank of Canada are owned by the government and hand over to the government any profits they earn. Their primary responsibility however, is not to maximize profits but to act in the national interest. The preamble to the Bank of Canada Act reads:

> "Whereas it is desirable to establish a central bank in Canada to regulate credit and currency in the best interests of the economic life of the nation, to control and protect the external value of the national monetary unit and to mitigate by its influence fluctuations in the general level of production, trade, prices and employment, so far as may be possible within the scope of monetary action, and generally to promote the economic and financial welfare of Canada...."

The Bank of Canada has four related jobs. The first is to issue currency. The Bank of Canada Act gives the Bank a monopoly over the right to issue notes for circulation in Canada. The second job is to act as banker to the commercial banks. Just as you may have a demand deposit at the Bank of Montreal, so the Bank of Montreal (and the other large commercial banks) has a demand deposit at the Bank of Canada. These deposits at the Bank of Canada enable the commercial banks to make payments to each other. The Bank of Canada makes daily loans to banks when banks themselves need to borrow money to make payments to other banks. Also, when financially troubled banks find themselves short of cash, the Bank of Canada may occasionally act as a lender of last resort—a lender to those who cannot borrow anywhere else—in order to maintain stability in the overall banking system. The third job is to act as banker to the Canadian government. The Government of Canada has a demand deposit at the Bank of Canada as well as demand deposits at the large commercial banks. The Bank of Canada manages the government's bank accounts, and also manages Canada's foreign exchange reserves and national debt on behalf of the government.

The Bank of Canada's fourth and most important job is to control the quantity of money that is made available to the economy, called the **money supply**. Decisions by policymakers concerning the money supply constitute **monetary policy**.

money supply
the quantity of money available in the economy

monetary policy
the setting of the money supply by policymakers in the central bank

Monetary Policy

The Bank of Canada has the power to increase or decrease the number of dollars in the economy. In simple metaphorical terms, you can imagine the Bank of Canada printing up $20 bills and dropping them around the country by helicopter. Similarly, you can imagine the Bank of Canada using a giant vacuum cleaner to suck $20 bills out of people's wallets. Although in practice the Bank of Canada's methods of controlling the money supply are more complex and subtle than this, the helicopter–vacuum metaphor is a good first approximation of the meaning of *monetary policy*. We discuss later how the Bank of Canada actually changes the money supply.

The Bank of Canada is an important institution because changes in the money supply can profoundly affect the economy. One of the ten principles of economics identified in Chapter 1 is that prices rise when the government prints too much money. Another of these ten principles is that society faces a short-run tradeoff between inflation and unemployment. The power of the Bank of Canada rests on these principles.

For reasons we discuss more fully in coming chapters, the Bank of Canada's policy decisions have an important influence on the economy's rate of inflation in the long run and the economy's employment and production in the short run. Indeed, the governor of the Bank of Canada might be called the second most powerful person in Canada. To learn more about the Bank of Canada, check out its website at http://www.bankofcanada.ca.

QuickQuiz What is the difference between a central bank like the Bank of Canada and a commercial bank like the Bank of Montreal?

COMMERCIAL BANKS AND THE MONEY SUPPLY

So far we have introduced the concept of "money" and discussed the role of the Bank of Canada. Although the Bank of Canada alone is responsible for Canadian monetary policy, the central bank can control the supply of money only through its influence on the entire banking system. We now look at the role played by commercial banks (which include credit unions, caisses populaires, and trust companies) in the monetary system.

The Simple Case of 100-Percent-Reserve Banking

To see how banks influence the money supply, it is useful to imagine first a world without any banks at all. In this simple world, currency is the only form of money. To be concrete, let's suppose that the total quantity of currency is $100. The supply of money is, therefore, $100.

Now suppose that someone opens a bank, appropriately called First National Bank. First National Bank is only a depository institution—that is, it accepts deposits but does not make loans. The purpose of the bank is to give depositors a safe place to keep their money. Whenever a person deposits some money, the bank keeps the money in its vault until the depositor comes to withdraw it or writes a cheque against his or her balance. Deposits that banks have received but have not loaned out are called **reserves.** In this imaginary economy, all deposits are held as reserves, so this system is called *100-percent-reserve banking.*

We can express the financial position of First National Bank with a *T-account,* which is a simplified accounting statement that shows changes in a bank's assets and liabilities. Here is the T-account for First National Bank if the economy's entire $100 of money is deposited in the bank:

reserves
deposits that banks have received but have not loaned out

FIRST NATIONAL BANK

Assets		Liabilities	
Reserves	$100.00	Deposits	$100.00

On the left-hand side of the T-account are the bank's assets of $100 (the reserves it holds in its vaults). On the right-hand side of the T-account are the bank's liabilities of $100 (the amount it owes to its depositors). Notice that the assets and liabilities of First National Bank exactly balance.

Now consider the money supply in this imaginary economy. Before First National Bank opens, the money supply is the $100 of currency that people are holding. After the bank opens and people deposit their currency, the money supply is the $100 of demand deposits. (There is no longer any currency outstanding, because it is all in the bank vault.) Each deposit in the bank reduces currency and raises demand deposits by exactly the same amount, leaving the money supply unchanged. Thus, *if banks hold all deposits in reserve, banks do not influence the supply of money.*

Money Creation with Fractional-Reserve Banking

Eventually, the bankers at First National Bank may start to reconsider their policy of 100-percent-reserve banking. Leaving all that money sitting idle in their vaults seems unnecessary. Why not use some of it to make loans? Families buying houses and firms building new factories would be happy to pay interest to borrow some of that money for a while. Of course, First National Bank has to keep some reserves so that currency is available if depositors want to make withdrawals. But if the flow of new deposits is roughly the same as the flow of withdrawals, First National needs to keep only a fraction of its deposits in reserve. Thus, First National adopts a system called **fractional-reserve banking.**

The fraction of total deposits that a bank holds as reserves is called the **reserve ratio.** This ratio is determined by a combination of government regulation and bank policy. As we discuss more fully later in the chapter, some central banks place a minimum on the amount of reserves that banks hold, called a *reserve requirement.* In addition, banks may hold reserves above the legal minimum, called *excess reserves,* so they can be more confident that they will not run short of cash. For our purpose here, we just take the reserve ratio as given and examine what fractional-reserve banking means for the money supply.

fractional-reserve banking
a banking system in which banks hold only a fraction of deposits as reserves

reserve ratio
the fraction of deposits that banks hold as reserves

Let's suppose that First National has a reserve ratio of 10 percent. This means that it keeps 10 percent of its deposits in reserve and loans out the rest. Now let's look again at the bank's T-account:

FIRST NATIONAL BANK

Assets		Liabilities	
Reserves	$10.00	Deposits	$100.00
Loans	90.00		

First National still has $100 in liabilities because making the loans did not alter the bank's obligation to its depositors. But now the bank has two kinds of assets: It has $10 of reserves in its vault, and it has loans of $90. (These loans are liabilities of the people taking out the loans but they are assets of the bank making the loans, because the borrowers will later repay the bank.) In total, First National's assets still equal its liabilities.

Once again consider the supply of money in the economy. Before First National makes any loans, the money supply is the $100 of deposits in the bank. Yet when First National makes these loans, the money supply increases. The depositors still have demand deposits totalling $100, but now the borrowers hold $90 in currency. The money supply (which equals currency plus demand deposits) equals $190. Thus, *when banks hold only a fraction of deposits in reserve, banks create money.*

At first, this creation of money by fractional-reserve banking may seem too good to be true because it appears that the bank has created money out of thin air. To make this creation of money seem less miraculous, note that when First National Bank loans out some of its reserves and creates money, it does not create any wealth. Loans from First National give the borrowers some currency and thus the ability to buy goods and services. Yet the borrowers are also taking on debts, so the loans do not make them any richer. In other words, as a bank creates the asset of money, it also creates a corresponding liability for its borrowers. At the end of this process of money creation, the economy is more liquid in the sense that there is more of the medium of exchange, but the economy is no wealthier than before.

The Money Multiplier

The creation of money does not stop with First National Bank. Suppose the borrower from First National uses the $90 to buy something from someone who then deposits the currency in Second National Bank. Here is the T-account for Second National Bank:

SECOND NATIONAL BANK

Assets		Liabilities	
Reserves	$ 9.00	Deposits	$90.00
Loans	81.00		

After the deposits, this bank has liabilities of $90. If Second National also has a reserve ratio of 10 percent, it keeps assets of $9 in reserve and makes $81 in loans. In this way, Second National Bank creates an additional $81 of money. If this $81 is eventually deposited in Third National Bank, which also has a reserve ratio of 10 percent, this bank keeps $8.10 in reserve and makes $72.90 in loans. Here is the T-account for Third National Bank:

THIRD NATIONAL BANK

Assets		Liabilities	
Reserves	$ 8.10	Deposits	$81.00
Loans	72.90		

The process goes on and on. Each time that money is deposited and a bank loan is made, more money is created.

How much money is eventually created in this economy? Let's add it up:

Original deposit	= $	100.00
First National lending	= $	90.00 [= .9 × $100.00]
Second National lending	= $	81.00 [= .9 × $90.00]
Third National lending	= $	72.90 [= .9 × $81.00]
⋮		⋮
Total money supply		= $1000.00

It turns out that even though this process of money creation can continue forever, it does not create an infinite amount of money. If you laboriously add the infinite sequence of numbers in the forgoing example, you find the $100 of reserves generates $1000 of money. The amount of money the banking system generates with each dollar of reserves is called the **money multiplier.** In this imaginary economy, where the $100 of reserves generates $1000 of money, the money multiplier is 10.

What determines the size of the money multiplier? It turns out that the answer is simple: *The money multiplier is the reciprocal of the reserve ratio.* If R is the reserve ratio for all banks in the economy, then each dollar of reserves generates $1/R$ dollars of money. In our example, $R = 1/10$, so the money multiplier is 10.

This reciprocal formula for the money multiplier makes sense. If a bank holds $1000 in deposits, then a reserve ratio of 1/10 (10 percent) means that the bank must hold $100 in reserves. The money multiplier just turns this idea around: If the banking system as a whole holds a total of $100 in reserves, it can have only $1000 in deposits. In other words, if R is the ratio of reserves to deposits at each bank (that is, the reserve ratio), then the ratio of deposits to reserves in the banking system (that is, the money multiplier) must be $1/R$.

This formula shows how the amount of money banks create depends on the reserve ratio. If the reserve ratio were only 1/20 (5 percent), then the banking system would have 20 times as much in deposits as in reserves, implying a money multiplier of 20. Each dollar of reserves would generate $20 of money. Similarly, if the reserve ratio were 1/5 (20 percent), deposits would be 5 times reserves, the money multiplier would be 5, and each dollar of reserves would generate $5 of money. *Thus, the higher the reserve ratio, the less of each deposit banks loan out, and the smaller the money multiplier.* In the special case of 100-percent-reserve banking, the reserve ratio is 1, the money multiplier is 1, and banks do not make loans or create money.

money multiplier
the amount of money the banking system generates with each dollar of reserves

ZERO RESERVE RATIOS

Over the years, Canadian banks have chosen to hold smaller and smaller ratios of reserves to deposits. The main reason for this decline is that Canadian banks are no longer legally required to hold reserves, and since they can quickly borrow currency from the Bank of Canada if they need it, they hold only enough currency for their customers' daily needs. Currently the reserve ratio is about 2 percent, which makes the money multiplier about 50! What would happen to the money supply if banks' reserve ratios became zero?

With a zero reserve ratio, all currency would be in people's wallets, rather than in banks' reserves. For a given amount of currency, the size of the money supply depends on the *currency ratio*—the fraction of the total money supply that people want to hold in the form of currency. If the currency ratio is 100 percent, meaning that people want to hold all their money in the form of currency, there will be no bank deposits at all and the money supply will equal the quantity of currency. If the currency ratio is 50 percent, meaning that people want to keep $1 in currency for every $1 they hold in bank deposits, the total money supply (currency plus deposits) in equilibrium will equal 2 times the quantity of currency. (If people held excess currency, they would deposit the excess currency in the banks, which would then expand loans, deposits, and the money supply until the equilibrium is reached.) If the currency ratio is 10 percent, meaning that people want to keep $1 in currency for every $9 they hold in bank deposits, the total money supply in equilibrium would equal 10 times the quantity of currency.

In an economy where banks hold zero reserves against deposits, the money supply will be the reciprocal of the currency ratio times the quantity of currency. For example, if the currency ratio is 50 percent (equals 1/2), the money supply will be 2 times the quantity of currency in circulation.

In Canada's monetary system today, where banks' reserve ratios are very small, the reserve ratio is much less important than the currency ratio.

The Bank of Canada's Tools of Monetary Control

As we have already discussed, the Bank of Canada is responsible for controlling the supply of money in the economy. Now that we understand how fractional-reserve banking works, we are in a better position to understand how the Bank of Canada can carry out this job. Because banks create money in a system of fractional-reserve banking, the Bank of Canada's control of the money supply is indirect. When the Bank of Canada decides to change the money supply, it must consider how its actions will work through the banking system.

Over its history, the Bank of Canada has used different methods of controlling the money supply. Different central banks around the world likewise use different tools of monetary control. Central banks have three main tools in their toolbox: open-market operations, changes in reserve requirements, and changes in the overnight rate. The Bank of Canada currently uses open-market operations and changes in the overnight rate to control the money supply.

Open-Market Operations Central banks can increase the supply of money in circulation by buying something. They can decrease the supply of money by selling something. It really doesn't matter what the Bank of Canada buys or sells. For example, if the Bank of Canada buys a new computer for its researchers with $1000 of newly printed currency, the firm that sold the computer to the Bank of Canada now holds an extra $1000 cash, so the money supply increases by $1000 immediately. If the Bank of Canada sells a used computer for $200 cash, the quantity of currency in circulation will immediately decrease by $200.

Since the Bank of Canada does not buy or sell a large quantity of computers, any changes in the money supply from buying or selling computers are small enough to be ignored. But the Bank of Canada does buy from and sell to the public a large quantity of Canadian government bonds; these transactions are called **open-market operations.** To increase the money supply, the Bank of Canada can buy government bonds or Treasury bills (a Treasury bill is just a short-term government bond). The dollars the Bank of Canada pays for the bonds increase the number of dollars in circulation. Some of these new dollars are held as currency, some are deposited in banks. Each new dollar held as currency increases the money supply by exactly $1. Each new dollar deposited in a bank increases the money supply by a greater extent because it increases reserves and, thereby, the amount of money that a fractional-reserve banking system can create.

To reduce the money supply, the Bank of Canada can do just the opposite: It can sell government bonds to the public. The public pays for these bonds with its holdings of currency and bank deposits, directly reducing the amount of money in circulation. In addition, as people make withdrawals from banks, banks find themselves with a smaller quantity of reserves. In response, banks reduce the amount of lending, and the process of money creation reverses itself.

Another important market in which the Bank of Canada buys and sells things is the foreign exchange market, where its purchases and sales of foreign moneys are called **foreign exchange market operations**. If the Bank of Canada buys $100 million U.S. dollars in the foreign exchange market for $150 million Canadian, the Canadian money supply increases immediately by $150 million. If the Bank of Canada sells foreign currency from its foreign exchange reserves, it gets Canadian dollars in exchange. Those Canadian dollars are withdrawn from circulation, so the Canadian money supply is reduced.

Sometimes the Bank of Canada wants to sell foreign currency in the foreign exchange market to support the Canadian dollar's exchange rate, but does not want the money supply to fall. To do this, it uses the Canadian dollars it acquires in the foreign exchange market to buy Canadian government bonds, thus putting the Canadian dollars back into circulation. This process of offsetting a foreign exchange market operation with an open-market operation is called **sterilization**. Currently, the Bank of Canada routinely sterilizes foreign exchange market operations.

When we discussed the role of the Bank of Canada in controlling the money supply, we introduced the helicopter–vacuum metaphor. Of course, the Bank of Canada does not literally hand out freshly printed money for free, nor does it literally vacuum money out of our wallets. But if the Government of Canada borrows money by selling a government bond and gives that money away as transfer payments, and if the Bank of Canada buys that government bond in an open-market operation with newly printed money, the net result is that the public has more money and the same amount of bonds. This is the same as if the Bank of Canada had printed some money and loaned it to the government to drop out of a helicopter. And if the Government of Canada increases taxes and uses the money to buy back a government bond and so reduce its debt, and if the Bank of Canada sells a government bond in an open-market operation, the net result is that the public has less money and the same amount of government bonds. This is the same as if the Bank of Canada had vacuumed money out of our wallets. The helicopter–vacuum metaphor is a lot more realistic than it first appeared!

open-market operations
the purchase or sale of government bonds by the Bank of Canada

foreign exchange market operations
the purchase or sale of foreign money by the Bank of Canada

sterilization
the process of offsetting foreign exchange market operations with open-market operations, so that the effect on the money supply is cancelled out

reserve requirements
regulations on the minimum amount of reserves that banks must hold against deposits

Changing Reserve Requirements   Some central banks around the world (but not the Bank of Canada) also influence the money supply with **reserve requirements**, which are regulations on the minimum amount of reserves that banks must hold against deposits. Reserve requirements influence how much money the banking system can create with each dollar of reserves. An increase in reserve requirements means that banks must hold more reserves and, therefore, can loan out less of each dollar that is deposited; as a result, it raises the reserve ratio, lowers the money multiplier, and decreases the money supply. Conversely, a decrease in reserve requirements lowers the reserve ratio, raises the money multiplier, and increases the money supply.

The Bank of Canada has rarely used changes in reserve requirements to control the money supply, because frequent changes would disrupt the business of banking. Indeed, since 1994 the Bank of Canada has phased out reserve requirements altogether to give banks a level playing field with other financial institutions, which are not required to hold reserves. This means that the Bank of Canada does not currently use changes in reserve requirements to change the money supply. All that the Bank of Canada now requires is that banks that run out of reserves, and are forced to borrow from the Bank of Canada to cover withdrawals, pay a penalty to discourage them from doing so. With zero required reserves, Canadian banks choose a very low reserve ratio (currently around 2 percent), so the Canadian money multiplier is very large.

Changing the Overnight Rate   Central banks like the Bank of Canada act as bankers to the commercial banks. These banks hold demand deposits at the Bank of Canada, which are part of their reserves.

If Muriel, who has a chequing account at the Bank of Montreal, buys a car for $5000 from Julia, who has a chequing account at the Bank of Nova Scotia, the Bank of Montreal will deduct $5000 from Muriel's chequing account and pay $5000 to the Bank of Nova Scotia so that the Bank of Nova Scotia in turn can credit Julia's chequing account. Transfers between banks are done by the Bank of Canada. The Bank of Canada will deduct $5000 from the Bank of Montreal's demand deposit and add $5000 to the Bank of Nova Scotia's demand deposit. What happens if the Bank of Montreal doesn't have $5000 in its demand deposit at the Bank of Canada? The Bank of Montreal may then borrow from the Bank of Canada—in effect, it must get an overdraft. The rate of interest that central banks charge commercial banks for these loans is called the discount rate in some countries. In Canada it is called the **bank rate**.

bank rate
the interest rate charged by the Bank of Canada on loans to the commercial banks

Since 1998 the Bank of Canada has allowed commercial banks to borrow freely at the bank rate, and has paid commercial banks the bank rate, minus half a percent, on their deposits at the Bank of Canada. For example, if the bank rate is 5 percent, this means the Bank of Montreal must pay 5 percent interest if it needs to borrow from the Bank of Canada. And the Bank of Canada would pay 4.5 percent interest if the Bank of Montreal had a positive balance in its demand deposit at the Bank of Canada. What is called the operating band is then from 4.5 to 5 percent, which sets the pattern for all short-term interest rates in Canada.

Commercial banks never need to pay more than the bank rate for short-term loans, because they can always borrow from the Bank of Canada instead. Conversely, commercial banks never need to accept less than the bank rate, minus half a percent, when they make short-term loans, because they can always lend to the

Bank of Canada instead. In practice, the **overnight rate**, which is the rate of interest on very short-term loans between commercial banks, stays very close to the middle of the operating band, so the overnight rate will always be about one-quarter of a percent below the bank rate.

overnight rate
the interest rate on very short-term loans between commercial banks

The Bank of Canada can alter the money supply by changing the bank rate, which in turn causes an equal change in the overnight rate. A higher overnight rate discourages banks from borrowing reserves from the Bank of Canada. Thus, an increase in the overnight rate reduces the quantity of reserves in the banking system, which in turn reduces the money supply. Conversely, a lower overnight rate encourages banks to borrow from the Bank of Canada, increases the quantity of reserves, and increases the money supply.

The Bank of Canada currently uses open-market operations for long-run control of the money supply and changes in the overnight rate for short-run control of the money supply. It lowers the overnight rate whenever it wants the money supply to expand, and raises the overnight rate whenever it wants the money supply to contract. Because the overnight rate not only affects the money supply but also sets the pattern for all Canadian interest rates, changes in the overnight rate are a closely watched indicator of the Bank of Canada's views about the sort of monetary policy the Canadian economy needs. Since November 2000, the Bank of Canada has fixed eight dates each year, roughly six weeks apart, on which it announces whether it will raise the overnight rate, lower the overnight rate, or leave the overnight rate unchanged. It can also change the overnight rate at any time, if extraordinary action is needed.

Problems in Controlling the Money Supply

The Bank of Canada's tools—open-market operations and changes in the overnight rate—have powerful effects on the money supply. Yet the Bank of Canada's control of the money supply is not precise. The Bank of Canada must wrestle with two problems, each of which arises because much of the money supply is created by our system of fractional-reserve banking.

The first problem is that the Bank of Canada does not control the amount of money that households choose to hold as deposits in banks. The more money that households deposit, the more reserves banks have, and the more money the banking system can create. And the less money that households deposit, the less reserves banks have, and the less money the banking system can create. To see why this is a problem, suppose that one day people begin to lose confidence in the banking system and, therefore, decide to withdraw deposits and hold more currency. When this happens, the banking system loses reserves and creates less money. The money supply falls, even without any Bank of Canada action.

The second problem with monetary control is that the Bank of Canada does not control the amount that commercial bankers choose to lend. Once money is deposited in a bank, it creates more money only when the bank loans it out. Yet banks can choose simply to hold the money as extra reserves. Since 1994 the Bank of Canada has abandoned legal reserve requirements, so commercial banks can choose to hold any ratio of reserves to deposits they want. Even if there were a legal minimum reserve ratio, banks could choose to hold excess reserves above the required minimum. To see why excess reserves complicate control of the money supply, suppose that one day bankers become more cautious about economic conditions and decide to make fewer loans and hold greater reserves. When this happens, the banking system creates less money than it otherwise would. Because of the bankers' decision, the money supply falls.

Hence, in a system of fractional-reserve banking, the amount of money in the economy depends in part on the behaviour of depositors and bankers. Because the Bank of Canada cannot control or perfectly predict this behaviour, it cannot perfectly control the money supply. But these problems need not be large. The Bank of Canada collects data on deposits every week, so it is quickly aware of any changes in the money supply caused by changes in depositor or banker behaviour. If the Bank of Canada discovers that the money supply is growing too fast, it can raise the overnight rate to slow it down. If the Bank of Canada discovers that the money supply is growing too slowly, or falling, it can lower the overnight rate to increase the money supply. The Bank of Canada is like the driver of a car using the gas pedal to control her speed. Many things may cause the car to speed up or slow down, but by watching the speedometer and adjusting the gas pedal accordingly, the driver can keep her speed close to the level she chooses.

Case Study

BANK RUNS AND THE MONEY SUPPLY

Although you have probably never witnessed a bank run in real life, you may have seen one depicted in movies such as *Mary Poppins* or *It's a Wonderful Life*. A bank run occurs when depositors suspect that a bank may go bankrupt and, therefore, "run" to the bank to withdraw their deposits.

Bank runs are a problem for banks under fractional-reserve banking. Because a bank holds only a fraction of its deposits in reserve, it cannot satisfy withdrawal requests from all depositors. Even if the bank is in fact solvent (meaning that its assets exceed its liabilities), it will not have enough cash on hand to allow all depositors immediate access to all of their money. When a run occurs, the bank is forced to close its doors until some bank loans are repaid or until some lender of last resort (such as the Bank of Canada) provides it with the currency it needs to satisfy depositors.

Bank runs complicate the control of the money supply. An important example of this problem occurred in the United States during the Great Depression in the early 1930s. After a wave of bank runs and bank closings, households and bankers became more cautious. Households withdrew their deposits from banks, preferring to hold their money in the form of currency. This decision reversed the process of money creation, as bankers responded to falling reserves by reducing bank loans. At the same time, bankers increased their reserve ratios so that they would have enough cash on hand to meet their depositors' demands in any future bank runs. The higher reserve ratio reduced the money multiplier, which also reduced the money supply. From 1929 to 1933, the U.S. money supply fell by 28 percent, even without the Federal Reserve (the U.S. central bank) taking any deliberate contractionary action. Many economists point to this massive fall in the U.S. money supply to explain the high unemployment and falling prices that prevailed during this period. (In future chapters we examine the mechanisms by which changes in the money supply affect unemployment and prices.)

Canadian banks in the 1930s were larger, more diversified, and safer than American banks. Canada did not experience the wave of bank runs and bank failures that happened in the United States. In Canada, banks' reserve ratios increased only slightly, and the decline in the Canadian money supply was much smaller. But the Great Depression was as bad in Canada as it was in the United States, perhaps because the Canadian economy was more dependent on international trade and exports of primary products, whose value dropped considerably during the Great Depression.

Today, bank runs are not a major problem for the banking system or the Bank of Canada. A few small banks did fail in the 1980s, but there were no major bank runs. The Office of the Superintendent of Financial Institutions monitors financial institutions in Canada to try to prevent bankruptcies. Also, the federal government now guarantees the safety of deposits up to $60 000 at Canadian banks through the Canada Deposit Insurance Corporation (CDIC). Small depositors do not run on their banks, because they are confident that, even if their banks go bankrupt, the CDIC will make good on the deposits. As a result, most people see bank runs only in the movies. ●

QuickQuiz Describe how banks create money. ● If the Bank of Canada wanted to use all three of its policy tools to decrease the money supply, what would it do?

CONCLUSION

Whenever we buy or sell anything, we are relying on the extraordinarily useful social convention called "money." Now that we know what money is and what determines its supply, we can discuss how changes in the quantity of money affect the economy. We begin to address that topic in the next chapter.

SUMMARY

- The term *money* refers to assets that people regularly use to buy goods and services.
- Money serves three functions. As a medium of exchange, it provides the item used to make transactions. As a unit of account, it provides the way in which prices and other economic values are recorded. As a store of value, it provides a way of transferring purchasing power from the present to the future.

- Commodity money, such as gold, is money that has intrinsic value: It would be valued even if it were not used as money. Fiat money, such as paper dollars, is money without intrinsic value: It would be worthless if it were not used as money.
- In the Canadian economy, money takes the form of currency and various types of bank deposits, such as chequing accounts.

- The Bank of Canada, Canada's central bank, is responsible for controlling the supply of money in Canada. The governor and senior deputy governor of the Bank of Canada are appointed for seven-year terms, and the other directors are appointed for three-year terms. All these appointments are made by the Canadian government, which owns the Bank of Canada.

- The Bank of Canada controls the supply of money primarily through changes in the overnight rate. Lowering the overnight rate increases the money supply, and raising the overnight rate reduces the money supply. The Bank of Canada also controls the money supply through open-market operations. The purchase of government bonds increases the money supply, and the sale of government bonds reduces the money supply.

- When banks loan out some of their deposits, they increase the quantity of money in the economy. Because of this role of banks in determining the money supply, the Bank of Canada's control of the money supply is imperfect.

KEY CONCEPTS

money, p. 226
medium of exchange, p. 227
unit of account, p. 227
store of value, p. 227
liquidity, p. 227
commodity money, p. 227
fiat money, p. 228
currency, p. 230

demand deposits, p. 230
Bank of Canada, p. 232
central bank, p. 232
money supply, p. 233
monetary policy, p. 233
reserves, p. 235
fractional-reserve banking, p. 235
reserve ratio, p. 235

money multiplier, p. 237
open-market operations, p. 239
foreign exchange market
    operations, p. 239
sterilization, p. 239
reserve requirements, p. 240
bank rate, p. 240
overnight rate, p. 241

QUESTIONS FOR REVIEW

1. What distinguishes money from other assets in the economy?

2. What is commodity money? What is fiat money? Which kind do we use?

3. What are demand deposits, and why should they be included in the stock of money?

4. Who is responsible for setting monetary policy in Canada?

5. If the Bank of Canada wants to increase the money supply with open-market operations, what does it do?

6. Why don't banks hold 100 percent reserves? How is the amount of reserves banks hold related to the amount of money the banking system creates?

7. What is the overnight rate? What happens to the money supply when the Bank of Canada raises the overnight rate?

8. What are reserve requirements? What happens to the money supply when the Bank of Canada raises reserve requirements?

9. Why can't the Bank of Canada control the money supply perfectly?

PROBLEMS AND APPLICATIONS

1. Which of the following are money in the Canadian economy? Which are not? Explain your answers by discussing each of the three functions of money.
   a. a Canadian penny
   b. a Mexican peso
   c. a Picasso painting
   d. a plastic credit card

2. Every month *Yankee* magazine includes a "Swopper's [*sic*] Column" of offers to barter goods and services. Here is an example: "Will swop custom-designed wedding gown and up to 6 bridesmaids' gowns for 2 round-trip plane tickets and 3 nights' lodging in the countryside of England." Why would it be difficult to run our economy using a "Swopper's Column" instead of money? In light of your answer, why might the *Yankee* "Swopper's Column" exist?

3. What characteristics of an asset make it useful as a medium of exchange? As a store of value?

4. Consider how the following situations would affect the economy's monetary system.
   a. Suppose that the people on Yap discovered an easy way to make limestone wheels. How would this development affect the usefulness of stone wheels as money? Explain.
   b. Suppose that someone in Canada discovered an easy way to counterfeit $100 bills. How would this development affect the Canadian monetary system? Explain.

5. Go to the website of the Bank of Canada at http://www.bankofcanada.ca and find the following information:
   a. data on the recent history of the overnight rate, and the growth rates of money supply M1 and M2
   b. the next fixed announcement date
   c. the Bank's latest press release about overnight rates and explain why the Bank decided to change, or not change, its target for the overnight rate

6. Your uncle repays a $100 loan from Tenth National Bank by writing a $100 cheque on his TNB chequing account. Use T-accounts to show the effect of this transaction on your uncle and on TNB. Has your uncle's wealth changed? Explain.

7. Beleaguered State Bank (BSB) holds $250 million in deposits and maintains a reserve ratio of 10 percent.
   a. Show a T-account for BSB.
   b. Now suppose that BSB's largest depositor withdraws $10 million in cash from her account. If BSB decides to restore its reserve ratio by reducing the amount of loans outstanding, show its new T-account.
   c. Explain what effect BSB's action will have on other banks.
   d. Why might it be difficult for BSB to take the action described in part (b)? Discuss another way for BSB to return to its original reserve ratio.

8. You take $100 you had kept under your mattress and deposit it in your bank account. If this $100 stays in the banking system as reserves and if banks hold reserves equal to 10 percent of deposits, by how much does the total amount of deposits in the banking system increase? By how much does the money supply increase?

9. The Bank of Canada conducts a $10 million open-market purchase of government bonds. If the required reserve ratio is 10 percent, what is the largest possible increase in the money supply that could result? Explain. What is the smallest possible increase? Explain.

10. Suppose that the T-account for First National Bank is as follows:

Assets		Liabilities	
Reserves	$100 000	Deposits	$500 000
Loans	400 000		

   a. If the Bank of Canada requires banks to hold 5 percent of deposits as reserves, how much in excess reserves does First National now hold?
   b. Assume that all other banks hold only the required amount of reserves. If First National decides to reduce its reserves to

only the required amount, by how much would the economy's money supply increase?

11. Suppose that the Bank of Canada sells 100 million pounds sterling from its foreign exchange reserves, and that the exchange rate is $2.40 Canadian per pound sterling.
    a. Explain what happens to the Canadian money supply.
    b. Now suppose that the Bank of Canada does not want the money supply to change. What would it need to do to sterilize its foreign exchange market operation?

12. Assume that the reserve ratio is zero, and that the currency ratio is 25 percent, so that people hold $1 in currency for every $3 they have in deposit accounts.
    a. If the Bank of Canada buys $1 million of government bonds, what will be the effect on the amount of currency, the amount of deposits, and the total money supply?
    b. If the Bank of Canada sells $1 million worth of foreign currency, what will be the effect on the amount of Canadian currency, the amount of deposits, and the total Canadian money supply?

13. (This problem is challenging.) The economy of Elmendyn contains 2000 $1 bills.
    a. If people hold all money as currency, what is the quantity of money?
    b. If people hold all money as demand deposits and banks maintain 100 percent reserves, what is the quantity of money?
    c. If people hold equal amounts of currency and demand deposits and banks maintain 100 percent reserves, what is the quantity of money?
    d. If people hold all money as demand deposits and banks maintain a reserve ratio of 10 percent, what is the quantity of money?
    e. If people hold equal amounts of currency and demand deposits and banks maintain a reserve ratio of 10 percent, what is the quantity of money?

INTERNET RESOURCES

The best website for learning about the Canadian monetary system is the Bank of Canada's website: http://www.bankofcanada.ca. For a history of the Canadian dollar, click on "Currency" on the main menu, and for many links related to the Bank's inflation target for monetary policy, "backgrounders" for the general audience, and even a module giving the Bank's view on how monetary policy works, click on "Monetary Policy."

http://   For more study tools, please visit http://www.mankiw3e.nelson.com.

© GARY RHIJNSBURGER/MASTERFILE

MONEY GROWTH AND INFLATION

Learning Objectives

In this chapter, you will ...

- See why inflation results from rapid growth in the money supply
- Learn the meaning of the classical dichotomy and monetary neutrality
- See why some countries print so much money that they experience hyperinflation
- Examine how the nominal interest rate responds to the inflation rate
- Consider the various costs that inflation imposes on society

Although today you need a dollar or two to buy yourself an ice-cream cone, life was very different 60 years ago. In one Trenton, New Jersey, candy store (run, incidentally, by one author's grandmother in the 1930s), ice-cream cones came in two sizes. A cone with a small scoop of ice cream cost three cents. Hungry customers could buy a large scoop for a nickel.

You are probably not surprised at the increase in the price of ice cream. In our economy, most prices tend to rise over time. This increase in the overall level of prices is called *inflation*. Earlier in the book we examined how economists measure the inflation rate as the percentage change in the consumer price index, the GDP deflator, or some other index of the overall price level. These price indexes show that, over the past 60 years, prices have risen on average about 4 percent per year. Accumulated over so many years, a 4 percent annual inflation rate leads to a 12-fold increase in the price level.

Inflation may seem natural and inevitable to a person who grew up in Canada during the second half of the twentieth century, but in fact it is not inevitable at all. There were long periods in the nineteenth century during which most prices fell—a phenomenon called *deflation*. The average level of prices in the Canadian economy was 37 percent lower in 1933 than in 1920, and this deflation was a major problem. Farmers, who had accumulated large debts, were suffering when the fall in crop prices reduced their incomes and thus their ability to pay off their debts. They advocated government policies to reverse the deflation. Japan has also experienced some deflation in recent years.

Although inflation has been the norm in more recent history, there has been substantial variation in the rate at which prices rise. During the 1990s, prices rose at an average rate of about 2 percent per year. By contrast, in the 1970s, prices rose by 7 percent per year, which meant a doubling of the price level over the decade. The public often views such high rates of inflation as a major economic problem.

International data show an even broader range of inflation experiences. Germany after World War I experienced a spectacular example of inflation. The price of a newspaper rose from 0.3 marks in January 1921 to 70 000 000 marks less than two years later. Other prices rose by similar amounts. An extraordinarily high rate of inflation such as this is called *hyperinflation*. The German hyperinflation had such an adverse effect on the German economy that it is often viewed as one contributor to the rise of Nazism and, as a result, World War II. Over the past 50 years, with this episode still in mind, German policymakers have been extraordinarily averse to inflation, and Germany has had much lower inflation than Canada.

What determines whether an economy experiences inflation and, if so, how much? This chapter answers this question by developing the *quantity theory of money*. Chapter 1 summarized this theory as one of the ten principles of economics: Prices rise when the government prints too much money. This insight has a long and venerable tradition among economists. The quantity theory was discussed by the famous eighteenth-century philosopher David Hume and has been advocated more recently by the prominent economist Milton Friedman. This theory of inflation can explain both moderate inflations, such as those we have experienced in Canada, and hyperinflations, such as those experienced in interwar Germany and, more recently, in some Latin American countries.

After developing a theory of inflation, we turn to a related question: Why is inflation a problem? At first glance, the answer to this question may seem obvious: Inflation is a problem because people don't like it. In the 1970s, when Canada experienced a relatively high rate of inflation, opinion polls placed inflation as the most important issue facing the nation.

But what, exactly, are the costs that inflation imposes on a society? The answer may surprise you. Identifying the various costs of inflation is not as straightforward as it first appears. As a result, although all economists decry hyperinflation, some economists argue that the costs of moderate inflation are not nearly as large as the general public believes.

THE CLASSICAL THEORY OF INFLATION

We begin our study of inflation by developing the quantity theory of money. This theory is often called "classical" because it was developed by some of the earliest thinkers about economic issues. Most economists today rely on this theory to explain the long-run determinants of the price level and the inflation rate.

The Level of Prices and the Value of Money

Suppose we observe over some period of time the price of an ice-cream cone rising from a nickel to a dollar. What conclusion should we draw from the fact that people are willing to give up so much more money in exchange for a cone? It is possible that people have come to enjoy ice cream more (perhaps because some chemist has developed a miraculous new flavour). Yet that is probably not the case. It is more likely that people's enjoyment of ice cream has stayed roughly the same and that, over time, the money used to buy ice cream has become less valuable. Indeed, the first insight about inflation is that it is more about the value of money than about the value of goods.

This insight helps point the way toward a theory of inflation. When the consumer price index and other measures of the price level rise, commentators are often tempted to look at the many individual prices that make up these price indexes: "The CPI rose by 3 percent last month, led by a 20 percent rise in the price of coffee and a 30 percent rise in the price of heating oil." Although this approach does contain some interesting information about what's happening in the economy, it also misses a key point: Inflation is an economy-wide phenomenon that concerns, first and foremost, the value of the economy's medium of exchange.

The economy's overall price level can be viewed in two ways. So far, we have viewed the price level as the price of a basket of goods and services. When the price level rises, people have to pay more for the goods and services they buy. Alternatively, we can view the price level as a measure of the value of money. A rise in the price level means a lower value of money because each dollar in your wallet now buys a smaller quantity of goods and services.

It may help to express these ideas mathematically. Suppose P is the price level as measured, for instance, by the consumer price index or the GDP deflator. Then P measures the number of dollars needed to buy a basket of goods and services. Now turn this idea around: The quantity of goods and services that can be bought with \$1 equals $1/P$. In other words, if P is the price of goods and services measured in terms of money, $1/P$ is the value of money measured in terms of goods and services. Thus, when the overall price level rises, the value of money falls.

Money Supply, Money Demand, and Monetary Equilibrium

What determines the value of money? The answer to this question, like many in economics, is supply and demand. Just as the supply and demand for bananas determines the price of bananas, the supply and demand for money determines the value of money. Thus, our next step in developing the quantity theory of money is to consider the determinants of money supply and money demand.

First consider money supply. In the preceding chapter we discussed how the Bank of Canada, together with the banking system, determines the supply of money. When the Bank of Canada sells bonds in open-market operations, it receives dollars in exchange and contracts the money supply. When the Bank of Canada buys government bonds, it pays out dollars and expands the money supply. In addition, if any of these dollars are deposited in banks which then hold them as reserves, the money multiplier swings into action, and these open-market operations can have an even greater effect on the money supply. For our purposes in this chapter, we ignore the complications introduced by the banking system and simply take the quantity of money supplied as a policy variable that the Bank of Canada controls.

Now consider money demand. Most fundamentally, the demand for money reflects how much wealth people want to hold in liquid form. Many factors influence the quantity of money demanded. The amount of currency that people hold in their wallets, for instance, depends on how much they rely on credit cards and on whether an automated teller machine is easy to find. And, as we will emphasize in Chapter 16, the quantity of money demanded depends on the interest rate that a person could earn by using the money to buy an interest-bearing bond rather than leaving it in a wallet or low-interest chequing account.

Although many variables affect the demand for money, one variable stands out in importance: the average level of prices in the economy. People hold money because it is the medium of exchange. Unlike other assets, such as bonds or stocks, people can use money to buy the goods and services on their shopping lists. How much money they choose to hold for this purpose depends on the prices of those goods and services. The higher prices are, the more money the typical transaction requires, and the more money people will choose to hold in their wallets and chequing accounts. That is, a higher price level (a lower value of money) increases the quantity of money demanded.

What ensures that the quantity of money the Bank of Canada supplies balances the quantity of money people demand? The answer, it turns out, depends on the time horizon being considered. Later in this book we will examine the short-run answer, and we will see that interest rates play a key role. In the long run, however, the answer is different and much simpler. *In the long run, the overall level of prices adjusts to the level at which the demand for money equals the supply.* If the price level is above the equilibrium level, people will want to hold more money than the Bank of Canada has created, so the price level must fall to balance supply and demand. If the price level is below the equilibrium level, people will want to hold less money than the Bank of Canada has created, and the price level must rise to balance supply and demand. At the equilibrium price level, the quantity of money that people want to hold exactly balances the quantity of money supplied by the Bank of Canada.

Figure 12.1 illustrates these ideas. The horizontal axis of this graph shows the quantity of money. The left-hand vertical axis shows the value of money $1/P$, and the right-hand vertical axis shows the price level P. Notice that the price-level axis on the right is inverted: A low price level is shown near the top of this axis, and a high price level is shown near the bottom. This inverted axis illustrates that when the value of money is high (as shown near the top of the left axis), the price level is low (as shown near the top of the right axis).

The two curves in this figure are the supply and demand curves for money. The supply curve is vertical because the Bank of Canada has fixed the quantity of money available. The demand curve for money is downward sloping, indicating that when the value of money is low (and the price level is high), people demand a larger quantity of it to buy goods and services. At the equilibrium, shown in the figure as point A, the quantity of money demanded balances the quantity of money supplied. This equilibrium of money supply and money demand determines the value of money and the price level.

FIGURE 12.1

How the Supply and Demand for Money Determine the Equilibrium Price Level

The horizontal axis shows the quantity of money. The left vertical axis shows the value of money, and the right vertical axis shows the price level. The supply curve for money is vertical because the quantity of money supplied is fixed by the Bank of Canada. The demand curve for money is downward sloping because people want to hold a larger quantity of money when each dollar buys less. At the equilibrium, point A, the value of money (on the left axis) and the price level (on the right axis) have adjusted to bring the quantity of money supplied and the quantity of money demanded into balance.

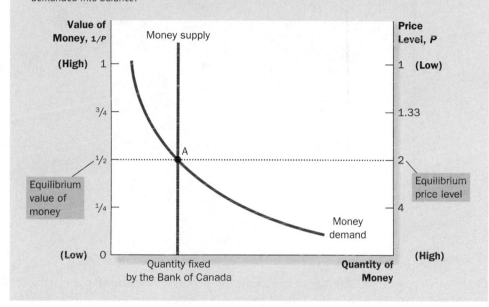

The Effects of a Monetary Injection

Let's now consider the effects of a change in monetary policy. To do so, imagine that the economy is in equilibrium and then, suddenly, the Bank of Canada doubles the supply of money by printing some dollar bills and dropping them around the country from helicopters. (Or, less dramatically and more realistically, the Bank of Canada could inject money into the economy by buying some government bonds from the public in open-market operations.) What happens after such a monetary injection? How does the new equilibrium compare to the old one?

Figure 12.2 (p. 252) shows what happens. The monetary injection shifts the supply curve to the right from MS_1 to MS_2, and the equilibrium moves from point A to point B. As a result, the value of money (shown on the left axis) decreases from 1/2 to 1/4, and the equilibrium price level (shown on the right axis) increases from 2 to 4. In other words, when an increase in the money supply makes dollars more plentiful, the result is an increase in the price level that makes each dollar less valuable.

This explanation of how the price level is determined and why it might change over time is called the **quantity theory of money.** According to the quantity

quantity theory of money
a theory asserting that the quantity of money available determines the price level and that the growth rate in the quantity of money available determines the inflation rate

FIGURE 12.2

An Increase in the Money Supply

When the Bank of Canada increases the supply of money, the money supply curve shifts from MS$_1$ to MS$_2$. The value of money (on the left axis) and the price level (on the right axis) adjust to bring supply and demand back into balance. The equilibrium moves from point A to point B. Thus, when an increase in the money supply makes dollars more plentiful, the price level increases, making each dollar less valuable.

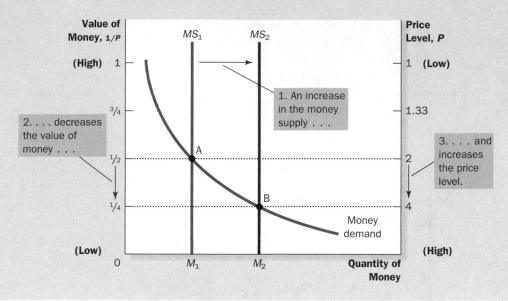

theory, the quantity of money available in the economy determines the value of money, and growth in the quantity of money is the primary cause of inflation. As economist Milton Friedman once put it, "Inflation is always and everywhere a monetary phenomenon."

A Brief Look at the Adjustment Process

So far we have compared the old equilibrium and the new equilibrium after an injection of money. How does the economy get from the old to the new equilibrium? A complete answer to this question requires an understanding of short-run fluctuations in the economy, which we examine later in this book. Yet, even now, it is instructive to consider briefly the adjustment process that occurs after a change in money supply.

The immediate effect of a monetary injection is to create an excess supply of money. Before the injection, the economy was in equilibrium (point A in Figure 12.2). At the prevailing price level, people had exactly as much money as they wanted. But after the helicopters drop the new money and people pick it up off the streets, people have more dollars in their wallets than they want. At the prevailing price level, the quantity of money supplied now exceeds the quantity demanded.

People try to get rid of this excess supply of money in various ways. They might buy goods and services with their excess holdings of money. Or they might use this excess money to make loans to others by buying bonds or by depositing the money into a bank savings account. These loans allow other people to buy goods and services. In either case, the injection of money increases the demand for goods and services.

The economy's ability to supply goods and services, however, has not changed. As we saw in the chapter on production and growth, the economy's output of goods and services is determined by the available labour, physical capital, human capital, natural resources, and technological knowledge. None of these is altered by the injection of money.

Thus, the greater demand for goods and services causes the prices of goods and services to increase. The increase in the price level, in turn, increases the quantity of money demanded because people are using more dollars for every transaction. Eventually, the economy reaches a new equilibrium (point B in Figure 12.2) at which the quantity of money demanded again equals the quantity of money supplied. In this way, the overall price level for goods and services adjusts to bring money supply and money demand into balance.

The Classical Dichotomy and Monetary Neutrality

We have seen how changes in the money supply lead to changes in the average level of prices of goods and services. How do these monetary changes affect other important macroeconomic variables, such as production, employment, real wages, and real interest rates? This question has long intrigued economists. Indeed, the great philosopher David Hume wrote about it in the eighteenth century. The answer we give today owes much to Hume's analysis.

Hume and his contemporaries suggested that all economic variables should be divided into two groups. The first group consists of **nominal variables**—variables measured in monetary units. The second group consists of **real variables**—variables measured in physical units. For example, the income of corn farmers is a nominal variable because it is measured in dollars, whereas the quantity of corn they produce is a real variable because it is measured in tonnes. Similarly, nominal GDP is a nominal variable because it measures the dollar value of the economy's output of goods and services; real GDP is a real variable because it measures the total quantity of goods and services produced and is not influenced by the current prices of those goods and services. This separation of variables into these groups is now called the **classical dichotomy**. (A *dichotomy* is a division into two groups, and *classical* refers to the earlier economic thinkers.)

Application of the classical dichotomy is somewhat tricky when we turn to prices. Prices in the economy are normally quoted in terms of money and, therefore, are nominal variables. For instance, when we say that the price of corn is $200 per tonne or that the price of wheat is $100 per tonne, both prices are nominal variables. But what about a *relative* price—the price of one thing compared to another? In our example, we could say that the price of a tonne of corn is two tonnes of wheat. Notice that this relative price is no longer measured in terms of money. When comparing the prices of any two goods, the dollar signs cancel, and the resulting number is measured in physical units. The lesson is that dollar prices are nominal variables, whereas relative prices are real variables.

nominal variables
variables measured in monetary units

real variables
variables measured in physical units

classical dichotomy
the theoretical separation of nominal and real variables

This lesson has several important applications. For instance, the real wage (the dollar wage adjusted for inflation) is a real variable because it measures the rate at which the economy exchanges goods and services for each unit of labour. Similarly, the real interest rate (the nominal interest rate adjusted for inflation) is a real variable because it measures the rate at which the economy exchanges goods and services produced today for goods and services produced in the future.

Why bother separating variables into these two groups? Hume suggested that the classical dichotomy is useful in analyzing the economy because different forces influence real and nominal variables. In particular, he argued, nominal variables are heavily influenced by developments in the economy's monetary system, whereas the monetary system is largely irrelevant for understanding the determinants of important real variables.

Notice that Hume's idea was implicit in our earlier discussions of the real economy in the long run. In previous chapters, we examined how real GDP, saving, investment, real interest rates, and unemployment are determined without any mention of the existence of money. As explained in that analysis, the economy's production of goods and services depends on productivity and factor supplies, the real interest rate adjusts to balance the supply and demand for loanable funds, the real wage adjusts to balance the supply and demand for labour, and unemployment results when the real wage is for some reason kept above its equilibrium level. These important conclusions have nothing to do with the quantity of money supplied.

Changes in the supply of money, according to Hume, affect nominal variables but not real variables. When the central bank doubles the money supply, the price level doubles, the dollar wage doubles, and all other dollar values double. Real variables, such as production, employment, real wages, and real interest rates, are unchanged. This irrelevance of monetary changes for real variables is called **monetary neutrality.**

monetary neutrality
the proposition that changes in the money supply do not affect real variables

An analogy sheds light on the meaning of monetary neutrality. Recall that, as the unit of account, money is the ruler we use to measure economic transactions. When a central bank doubles the money supply, all prices double, and the value of the unit of account falls by half. A similar change would occur if the government were to reduce the length of the metre from 100 to 50 cm: As a result of the new unit of measurement, all *measured* distances (nominal variables) would double, but the *actual* distances (real variables) would remain the same. The dollar, like the metre, is merely a unit of measurement, so a change in its value should not have important real effects.

Is this conclusion of monetary neutrality a realistic description of the world in which we live? The answer is: not completely. A change in the length of the metre from 100 to 50 cm would not matter much in the long run, but in the short run it would certainly lead to confusion and various mistakes. Similarly, most economists today believe that over short periods of time—within the span of a year or two—there is reason to think that monetary changes do have important effects on real variables. Hume himself also doubted that monetary neutrality would apply in the short run. (We will turn to the study of short-run nonneutrality later in the book, and this topic will shed light on the reasons why the Bank of Canada changes the supply of money over time.)

Most economists today accept Hume's conclusion as a description of the economy in the long run. Over the course of a decade, for instance, monetary changes have important effects on nominal variables (such as the price level) but only negligible effects on real variables (such as real GDP). When studying long-run changes in the economy, the neutrality of money offers a good description of how the world works.

Velocity and the Quantity Equation

We can obtain another perspective on the quantity theory of money by considering the following question: How many times per year is the typical dollar bill used to pay for a newly produced good or service? The answer to this question is given by a variable called the **velocity of money.** In physics, the term *velocity* refers to the speed at which an object travels. In economics, the velocity of money refers to the speed at which the typical dollar travels around the economy from pocket to pocket.

velocity of money
the rate at which money changes hands

To calculate the velocity of money, we divide the nominal value of output (nominal GDP) by the quantity of money. If P is the price level (the GDP deflator), Y the quantity of output (real GDP), and M the quantity of money, then velocity is

$$V = (P \times Y)/M$$

To see why this makes sense, imagine a simple economy that produces only pizza. Suppose that the economy produces 100 pizzas in a year, that a pizza sells for $10, and that the quantity of money in the economy is $50. Then the velocity of money is

$$V = (\$10 \times 100)/\$50$$
$$= 20$$

In this economy, people spend a total of $1000 per year on pizza. For this $1000 of spending to take place with only $50 of money, each dollar must change hands on average 20 times per year.

With slight algebraic rearrangement, this equation can be rewritten as

$$M \times V = P \times Y$$

This equation states that the quantity of money (M) times the velocity of money (V) equals the price of output (P) times the amount of output (Y). It is called the **quantity equation** because it relates the quantity of money (M) to the nominal value of output ($P \times Y$). The quantity equation shows that an increase in the quantity of money in an economy must be reflected in one of the other three variables: The price level must rise, the quantity of output must rise, or the velocity of money must fall.

quantity equation
the equation $M \times V = P \times Y$, which relates the quantity of money, the velocity of money, and the dollar value of the economy's output of goods and services

In many cases, it turns out that the velocity of money is relatively stable. For example, Figure 12.3 (p. 256) shows nominal GDP, the quantity of money (as measured by M2), and the velocity of money for the Canadian economy since 1961. Although the velocity of money is not exactly constant, it has not changed dramatically. By contrast, the money supply and nominal GDP during this period have increased more than tenfold. Thus, for some purposes, the assumption of constant velocity may be a good approximation.

FIGURE 12.3

Nominal GDP, the Quantity of Money, and the Velocity of Money

This figure shows the nominal value of output as measured by nominal GDP, the quantity of money as measured by M2, and the velocity of money as measured by their ratio. For comparability, all three series have been scaled to equal 100 in 1961. Notice that nominal GDP and the quantity of money have grown dramatically over this period, while velocity has been relatively stable.

Source: Statistics Canada.

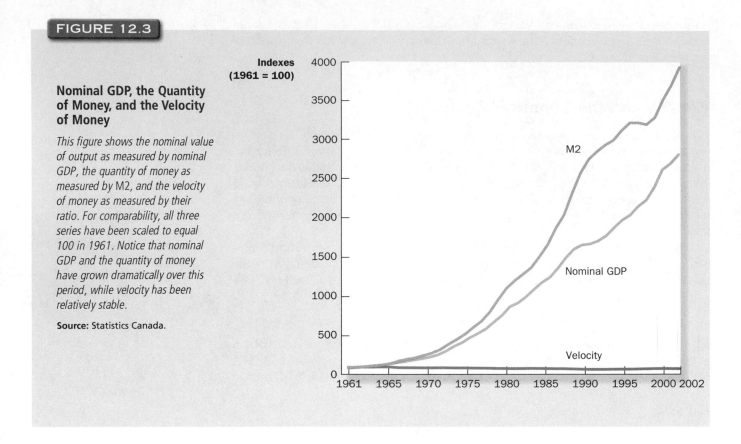

We now have all the elements necessary to explain the equilibrium price level and inflation rate. Here they are:

1. The velocity of money is relatively stable over time.
2. Because velocity is stable, when the central bank changes the quantity of money (M), it causes proportionate changes in the nominal value of output ($P \times Y$).
3. The economy's output of goods and services (Y) is primarily determined by factor supplies (labour, physical capital, human capital, and natural resources) and the available production technology. In particular, because money is neutral, money does not affect output.
4. With output (Y) determined by factor supplies and technology, when the central bank alters the money supply (M) and induces proportional changes in the nominal value of output ($P \times Y$), these changes are reflected in changes in the price level (P).
5. Therefore, when the central bank increases the money supply rapidly, the result is a high rate of inflation.

These five steps are the essence of the quantity theory of money.

Case Study

MONEY AND PRICES DURING FOUR HYPERINFLATIONS

Although earthquakes can wreak havoc on a society, they have the beneficial by-product of providing much useful data for seismologists. These data can shed light on alternative theories and, thereby, help society predict and deal with future threats. Similarly, hyperinflations offer monetary economists a natural experiment they can use to study the effects of money on the economy.

Hyperinflations are interesting in part because the changes in the money supply and price level are so large. Indeed, hyperinflation is generally defined as inflation that exceeds 50 percent *per month*. This means that the price level increases more than 100-fold over the course of a year.

The data on hyperinflation show a clear link between the quantity of money and the price level. Figure 12.4 (p. 258) graphs data from four classic hyperinflations that occurred during the 1920s in Austria, Hungary, Germany, and Poland. Each graph shows the quantity of money in the economy and an index of the price level. The slope of the money line represents the rate at which the quantity of money was growing, and the slope of the price line represents the inflation rate. The steeper the lines, the higher the rates of money growth or inflation.

Notice that in each graph the quantity of money and the price level are almost parallel. In each instance, growth in the quantity of money is moderate at first, and so is inflation. But over time, the quantity of money in the economy starts growing faster and faster. At about the same time, inflation also takes off. Then when the quantity of money stabilizes, the price level stabilizes as well. These episodes illustrate well one of the ten principles of economics: Prices rise when the government prints too much money. ●

The Inflation Tax

If inflation is so easy to explain, why do countries experience hyperinflation? That is, why do the central banks of these countries choose to print so much money that its value is certain to fall rapidly over time?

The answer is that the governments of these countries are using money creation as a way to pay for their spending. When the government wants to build roads, pay salaries to police officers, or give transfer payments to the poor or elderly, it first has to raise the necessary funds. Normally, the government does this by levying taxes, such as income and sales taxes, and by borrowing from the public by selling government bonds. Yet the government can also pay for spending by simply printing the money it needs.

When the government raises revenue by printing money, it is said to levy an **inflation tax.** The inflation tax is not exactly like other taxes, however, because no one receives a bill from the government for this tax. Instead, the inflation tax is more subtle. When the government prints money, the price level rises, and the dollars in your pocket are less valuable. Thus, *the inflation tax is like a tax on everyone who holds money.*

inflation tax
the revenue the government raises by creating money

FIGURE 12.4

Money and Prices during Four Hyperinflations

This figure shows the quantity of money and the price level during four hyperinflations. (Note that these variables are graphed on logarithmic scales. This means that equal vertical distances on the graph represent equal percentage changes in the variable.) In each case, the quantity of money and the price level move closely together. The strong association between these two variables is consistent with the quantity theory of money, which states that growth in the money supply is the primary cause of inflation.

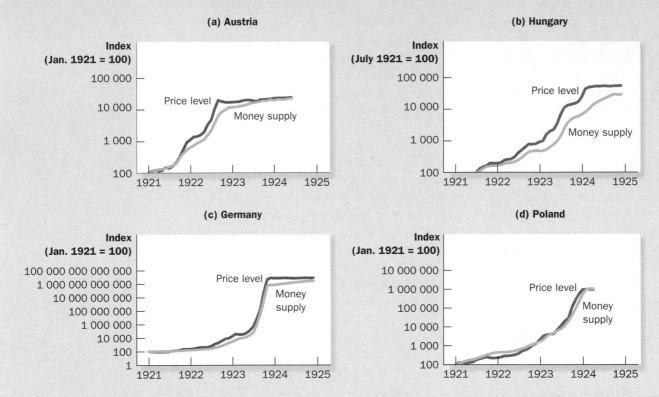

Source: Adapted from Thomas J. Sargent, "The End of Four Big Inflations," in Robert Hall, ed., *Inflation* (Chicago: University of Chicago Press, 1983), pp. 41–93. Reprinted with permission.

The importance of the inflation tax varies from country to country and over time. In Canada, the inflation tax is now a trivial source of revenue: It currently accounts for less than 1 percent of government revenue. During the 1770s, however, the Continental Congress of the fledgling United States relied heavily on the inflation tax to pay for military spending. Because the new government had a limited ability to raise funds through regular taxes or borrowing, printing dollars was the easiest way to pay the American soldiers. As the quantity theory predicts, the result was a high rate of inflation: Prices measured in terms of the continental dollar rose more than 100-fold over a few years.

IN THE NEWS

RUSSIA TURNS TO THE INFLATION TAX

Whenever governments find themselves short of cash, they are tempted to solve the problem simply by printing some more. In 1998, Russian policymakers found this temptation hard to resist, and the inflation rate rose to more than 100 percent per year.

Russia's New Leaders Plan to Pay Debts by Printing Money

By Michael Wines

Moscow—Russia's new Communist-influenced Government indicated today that it plans to satisfy old debts and bail out old friends by printing new rubles, a decision that drew a swift and strong reaction from President Boris N. Yeltsin's old capitalist allies.

The deputy head of the central bank said today that the bank intends to bail out many of the nation's bankrupt financial institutions by buying back their multibillion-ruble portfolios of Government bonds and Treasury bills. The Government temporarily froze $40 billion worth of notes when the fiscal crisis erupted last month because it lacked the money to pay investors who hold them.

Asked by the Reuters news service how the near-broke Government would find the money to pay off the banks, the deputy, Andrei Kozlov, replied, "Emissions, of course, emissions." "Emissions" is a euphemism for printing money.

Hours later in Washington, Deputy Treasury Secretary Lawrence H. Summers told a House subcommittee that Russia was heading toward a return of the four-digit inflation rates that savaged consumers and almost toppled Mr. Yeltsin's Government in 1993.

Russia's new leaders cannot repeal "basic economic laws," he said.

Source: *The New York Times,* September 18, 1998, p. A3. © 1998 by The New York Times Co. Reprinted with permission.

Almost all hyperinflations follow the same pattern as the hyperinflation during the American Revolution. The government has high spending, inadequate tax revenue, and limited ability to borrow. As a result, it turns to the printing press to pay for its spending. The massive increases in the quantity of money lead to massive inflation. The inflation ends when the government institutes fiscal reforms—such as cuts in government spending—that eliminate the need for the inflation tax.

The Fisher Effect

According to the principle of monetary neutrality, an increase in the rate of money growth raises the rate of inflation but does not affect any real variable. An important application of this principle concerns the effect of money on interest rates. Interest rates are important variables for macroeconomists to understand because they link the economy of the present and the economy of the future through their effects on saving and investment.

To understand the relationship between money, inflation, and interest rates, recall the distinction between the nominal interest rate and the real interest rate. The *nominal interest rate* is the interest rate you hear about at your bank. If you have a savings account, for instance, the nominal interest rate tells you how fast the number of dollars in your account will rise over time. The *real interest rate* corrects the nominal interest rate for the effect of inflation in order to tell you how fast the purchasing power of your savings account will rise over time. The real interest rate is the nominal interest rate minus the inflation rate:

$$\text{Real interest rate} = \text{Nominal interest rate} - \text{Inflation rate}$$

For example, if the bank posts a nominal interest rate of 7 percent per year and the inflation rate is 3 percent per year, then the real value of the deposits grows by 4 percent per year.

We can rewrite this equation to show that the nominal interest rate is the sum of the real interest rate and the inflation rate:

$$\text{Nominal interest rate} = \text{Real interest rate} + \text{Inflation rate}$$

This way of looking at the nominal interest rate is useful because different economic forces determine each of the two terms on the right-hand side of this equation. As we discussed earlier in the book, the supply and demand for loanable funds determine the real interest rate. And, according to the quantity theory of money, growth in the money supply determines the inflation rate.

Let's now consider how the growth in the money supply affects interest rates. In the long run over which money is neutral, a change in money growth should not affect the real interest rate. The real interest rate is, after all, a real variable. For the real interest rate not to be affected, the nominal interest rate must adjust one-for-one to changes in the inflation rate. Thus, *when the Bank of Canada increases the rate of money growth, the result is both a higher inflation rate and a higher nominal interest rate.* This adjustment of the nominal interest rate to the inflation rate is called the **Fisher effect,** after economist Irving Fisher (1867–1947), who first studied it.

Keep in mind that our analysis of the Fisher effect has maintained a long-run perspective. The Fisher effect does not hold in the short run to the extent that inflation is unanticipated. A nominal interest rate is a payment on a loan, and it is typically set when the loan is first made. If inflation catches the borrower and lender by surprise, the nominal interest rate they set will fail to reflect the rise in prices. To be precise, the Fisher effect states that the nominal interest rate adjusts to expected inflation. Expected inflation moves with actual inflation in the long run but not necessarily in the short run.

The Fisher effect is crucial for understanding changes over time in the nominal interest rate. Figure 12.5 shows the nominal interest rate and the inflation rate in the Canadian economy since 1962. The close association between these two variables is clear. The nominal interest rate rose from the early 1960s through the 1970s because inflation was also rising during this time. Similarly, the nominal interest rate fell from the early 1980s through the 1990s because the Bank of Canada got inflation under control.

Fisher effect
the one-for-one adjustment of the nominal interest rate to the inflation rate

FIGURE 12.5

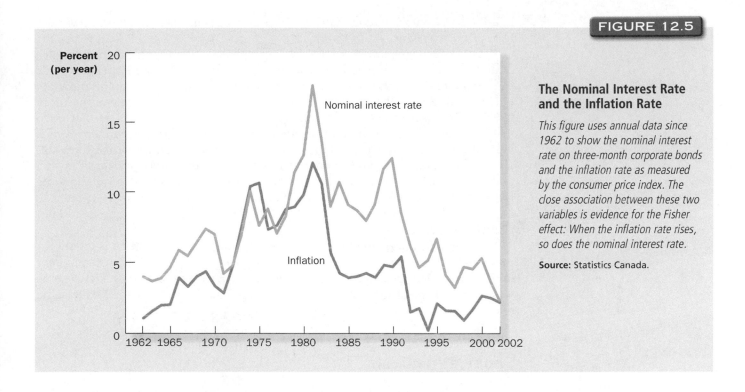

The Nominal Interest Rate and the Inflation Rate

This figure uses annual data since 1962 to show the nominal interest rate on three-month corporate bonds and the inflation rate as measured by the consumer price index. The close association between these two variables is evidence for the Fisher effect: When the inflation rate rises, so does the nominal interest rate.

Source: Statistics Canada.

QuickQuiz   The government of a country increases the growth rate of the money supply from 5 percent per year to 50 percent per year. What happens to prices? What happens to nominal interest rates? Why might the government be doing this?

THE COSTS OF INFLATION

In the late 1970s, when the Canadian inflation rate reached about 10 percent per year, inflation dominated debates over economic policy. And even though inflation was low during the 1990s, it remained a closely watched macroeconomic variable. Inflation is closely watched and widely discussed because it is thought to be a serious economic problem. But is that true? And if so, why?

A Fall in Purchasing Power? The Inflation Fallacy

If you ask the typical person why inflation is bad, he will tell you that the answer is obvious: Inflation robs him of the purchasing power of his hard-earned dollars. When prices rise, each dollar of income buys fewer goods and services. Thus, it might seem that inflation directly lowers living standards.

Yet further thought reveals a fallacy in this answer. When prices rise, buyers of goods and services pay more for what they buy. At the same time, however, sellers of goods and services get more for what they sell. Because most people earn their incomes by selling their services, such as their labour, inflation in incomes goes hand in hand with inflation in prices. Thus, *inflation does not in itself reduce people's real purchasing power.*

People believe the inflation fallacy because they do not appreciate the principle of monetary neutrality. A worker who receives an annual raise of 10 percent tends to view that raise as a reward for her own talent and effort. When an inflation rate of 6 percent reduces the real value of that raise to only 4 percent, the worker might feel that she has been cheated of what is rightfully her due. In fact, as we discussed in the chapter on production and growth, real incomes are determined by real variables, such as physical capital, human capital, natural resources, and the available production technology. Nominal incomes are determined by those factors and the overall price level. If the Bank of Canada were to lower the inflation rate from 6 percent to zero, our worker's annual raise would fall from 10 percent to 4 percent. She might feel less robbed by inflation, but her real income would not rise more quickly.

If nominal incomes tend to keep pace with rising prices, why then is inflation a problem? It turns out that there is no single answer to this question. Instead, economists have identified several costs of inflation. Each of these costs shows some way in which persistent growth in the money supply does, in fact, have some effect on real variables.

Shoeleather Costs

As we have discussed, inflation is like a tax on the holders of money. The tax itself is not a cost to society: It is only a transfer of resources from households to the government. Yet most taxes give people an incentive to alter their behaviour to avoid paying the tax, and this distortion of incentives causes deadweight losses for society as a whole. Like other taxes, the inflation tax also causes deadweight losses because people waste scarce resources trying to avoid it.

How can a person avoid paying the inflation tax? Because inflation erodes the real value of the money in your wallet, you can avoid the inflation tax by holding less money. One way to do this is to go to the bank more often. For example, rather than withdrawing $200 every four weeks, you might withdraw $50 once a week. By making more frequent trips to the bank, you can keep more of your wealth in your interest-bearing savings account and less in your wallet, where inflation erodes its value.

shoeleather costs
the resources wasted when inflation encourages people to reduce their money holdings

The cost of reducing your money holdings is called the **shoeleather cost** of inflation because making more frequent trips to the bank causes your shoes to wear out more quickly. Of course, this term is not to be taken literally: The actual cost of reducing your money holdings is not the wear and tear on your shoes but the time and convenience you must sacrifice to keep less money on hand than you would if there were no inflation.

The shoeleather costs of inflation may seem trivial. And, in fact, they are in the Canadian economy, which has had only moderate inflation in recent years. But this cost is magnified in countries experiencing hyperinflation. Here is a description of one person's experience in Bolivia during its hyperinflation (as reported in the August 13, 1985, issue of *The Wall Street Journal*, p. 1):

When Edgar Miranda gets his monthly teacher's pay of 25 million pesos, he hasn't a moment to lose. Every hour, pesos drop in value. So, while his wife rushes to market to lay in a month's supply of rice and noodles, he is off with the rest of the pesos to change them into black-market dollars.

Mr. Miranda is practicing the First Rule of Survival amid the most out-of-control inflation in the world today. Bolivia is a case study of how runaway inflation undermines a society. Price increases are so huge that the figures build up almost beyond comprehension. In one six-month period, for example, prices soared at an annual rate of 38,000 percent. By official count, however, last year's inflation reached 2,000 percent, and this year's is expected to hit 8,000 percent—though other estimates range many times higher. In any event, Bolivia's rate dwarfs Israel's 370 percent and Argentina's 1,100 percent—two other cases of severe inflation.

It is easier to comprehend what happens to the thirty-eight-year-old Mr. Miranda's pay if he doesn't quickly change it into dollars. The day he was paid 25 million pesos, a dollar cost 500,000 pesos. So he received $50. Just days later, with the rate at 900,000 pesos, he would have received $27.

As this story shows, the shoeleather costs of inflation can be substantial. With the high inflation rate, Mr. Miranda does not have the luxury of holding the local money as a store of value. Instead, he is forced to convert his pesos quickly into goods or into U.S. dollars, which offer a more stable store of value. The time and effort that Mr. Miranda expends to reduce his money holdings are a waste of resources. If the monetary authority pursued a low-inflation policy, Mr. Miranda would be happy to hold pesos, and he could put his time and effort to more productive use. In fact, shortly after this article was written, the Bolivian inflation rate was reduced substantially with more restrictive monetary policy.

Menu Costs

Most firms do not change the prices of their products every day. Instead, firms often announce prices and leave them unchanged for weeks, months, or even years. The typical Canadian firm changes its prices about once a year.

Firms change prices infrequently because there are costs of changing prices. Costs of price adjustment are called **menu costs**, a term derived from a restaurant's cost of printing a new menu. Menu costs include the cost of deciding on new prices, the cost of printing new price lists and catalogues, the cost of sending these new price lists and catalogues to dealers and customers, the cost of advertising the new prices, and even the cost of dealing with customer annoyance over price changes.

menu costs
the costs of changing prices

Inflation increases the menu costs that firms must bear. In the current Canadian economy, with its low inflation rate, annual price adjustment is an appropriate business strategy for many firms. But when high inflation makes firms' costs rise rapidly, annual price adjustment is impractical. During hyperinflations, for example, firms must change their prices daily or even more often just to keep up with all the other prices in the economy.

Relative-Price Variability and the Misallocation of Resources

Suppose that the Eatabit Eatery prints a new menu with new prices every January and then leaves its prices unchanged for the rest of the year. If there is no inflation,

Eatabit's relative prices—the prices of its meals compared to other prices in the economy—would be constant over the course of the year. By contrast, if the inflation rate is 12 percent per year, Eatabit's relative prices will automatically fall by 1 percent each month. The restaurant's relative prices (that is, its prices compared with others in the economy) will be high in the early months of the year, just after it has printed a new menu, and low in the later months. And the higher the inflation rate, the greater is this automatic variability. Thus, because prices change only once in a while, inflation causes relative prices to vary more than they otherwise would.

Why does this matter? The reason is that market economies rely on relative prices to allocate scarce resources. Consumers decide what to buy by comparing the quality and prices of various goods and services. Through these decisions, they determine how the scarce factors of production are allocated among industries and firms. When inflation distorts relative prices, consumer decisions are distorted, and markets are less able to allocate resources to their best use.

Inflation-Induced Tax Distortions

Almost all taxes distort incentives, cause people to alter their behaviour, and lead to a less efficient allocation of the economy's resources. Many taxes, however, become even more problematic in the presence of inflation. The reason is that lawmakers often fail to take inflation into account when writing the tax laws. Economists who have studied the tax code conclude that inflation tends to raise the tax burden on income earned from savings.

One example of how inflation discourages saving is the tax treatment of *capital gains*—the profits made by selling an asset for more than its purchase price. Suppose that in 1980 you used some of your savings to buy stock in Microsoft Corporation for $10 and that in 2000 you sold the stock for $50. According to the tax law, you have earned a capital gain of $40, which you must include in your income when computing how much income tax you owe. But suppose the overall price level doubled from 1980 to 2000. In this case, the $10 you invested in 1980 is equivalent (in terms of purchasing power) to $20 in 2000. When you sell your stock for $50, you have a real gain (an increase in purchasing power) of only $30. The tax code, however, does not take account of inflation and assesses you a tax on a gain of $40. Thus, inflation exaggerates the size of capital gains and inadvertently increases the tax burden on this type of income.

Another example is the tax treatment of interest income. The income tax treats the *nominal* interest earned on savings as income, even though part of the nominal interest rate merely compensates for inflation. To see the effects of this policy, consider the numerical example in Table 12.1. The table compares two economies, both of which tax interest income at a rate of 25 percent. In economy A, inflation is zero, and the nominal and real interest rates are both 4 percent. In this case, the 25 percent tax on interest income reduces the real interest rate from 4 percent to 3 percent. In economy B, the real interest rate is again 4 percent, but the inflation rate is 8 percent. As a result of the Fisher effect, the nominal interest rate is 12 percent. Because the income tax treats this entire 12 percent interest as income, the government takes 25 percent of it, leaving an after-tax nominal interest rate of only 9 percent and an after-tax real interest rate of only 1 percent. In this case, the 25 percent tax on interest income reduces the real interest rate from 4 percent to

TABLE 12.1

	Economy A (price stability)	Economy B (inflation)
Real interest rate	4%	4%
Inflation rate	0	8
Nominal interest rate (real interest rate + inflation rate)	4	12
Reduced interest due to 25 percent tax (.25 × nominal interest rate)	1	3
After-tax nominal interest rate (.75 × nominal interest rate)	3	9
After-tax real interest rate (after-tax nominal interest rate − inflation rate)	3	1

How Inflation Raises the Tax Burden on Saving

In the presence of zero inflation, a 25 percent tax on interest income reduces the real interest rate from 4 percent to 3 percent. In the presence of 8 percent inflation, the same tax reduces the real interest rate from 4 percent to 1 percent.

1 percent. Because the after-tax real interest rate provides the incentive to save, saving is much less attractive in the economy with inflation (economy B) than in the economy with stable prices (economy A).

The taxes on nominal capital gains and on nominal interest income are two examples of how the tax code interacts with inflation. There are many others. Because of these inflation-induced tax changes, higher inflation tends to discourage people from saving. Recall that the economy's saving provides the resources for investment, which in turn is a key ingredient to long-run economic growth. Thus, when inflation raises the tax burden on saving, it tends to depress the economy's long-run growth rate. There is, however, no consensus among economists about the size of this effect.

One solution to this problem, other than eliminating inflation, is to index the tax system. That is, the tax laws could be rewritten to take account of the effects of inflation. In the case of capital gains, for example, the tax code could adjust the purchase price using a price index and assess the tax only on the real gain. In the case of interest income, the government could tax only real interest income by excluding that portion of the interest income that merely compensates for inflation. To some extent, the tax laws have moved in the direction of indexation. For example, the income levels at which income tax rates change are adjusted automatically each year based on changes in the consumer price index. Yet many other aspects of the tax laws—such as the tax treatment of capital gains and interest income—are not indexed.

In an ideal world, the tax laws would be written so that inflation would not alter anyone's real tax liability. In the world in which we live, however, tax laws are far from perfect. More complete indexation would probably be desirable, but it would further complicate a tax code that many people already consider too complex.

Confusion and Inconvenience

Imagine that we took a poll and asked people the following question: "This year the metre is 100 cm. How long do you think it should be next year?" Assuming we

IN THE NEWS

THE HYPERINFLATION IN SERBIA

Whenever governments turn to the printing press to finance substantial amounts of spending, the result is hyperinflation. As residents of Serbia learned in the early 1990s, life under such circumstances is far from easy.

Special, Today Only: 6 Million Dinars for a Snickers Bar

By Roger Thurow

BELGRADE, YUGOSLAVIA—At the Luna boutique, a Snickers bar costs 6 million dinars. Or at least it does until manager Tihomir Nikolic reads the overnight fax from his boss.

"Raise prices 99 percent," the document tersely orders. It would be an even 100 percent except that the computers at the boutique, which would be considered a dime store in other parts of the world, can't handle three-digit changes.

So for the second time in three days, Mr. Nikolic sets about raising prices. He jams a mop across the door frame to keep customers from getting away with a bargain. The computer spits out the new prices on perforated paper. The manager and two assistants rip the paper into tags and tape them to the shelves. They used to put the prices directly on the goods, but there were so many stickers it was getting difficult to read the labels.

could get people to take us seriously, they would tell us that the metre should stay the same length—100 cm. Anything else would just complicate life needlessly.

What does this finding have to do with inflation? Recall that money, as the economy's unit of account, is what we use to quote prices and record debts. In other words, money is the ruler with which we measure economic transactions. The job of the Bank of Canada is a bit like the job of Measurement Canada—to ensure the reliability of a commonly used unit of measurement. When the Bank of Canada increases the money supply and creates inflation, it erodes the real value of the unit of account.

It is difficult to judge the costs of the confusion and inconvenience that arise from inflation. Earlier we discussed how the tax code incorrectly measures real incomes in the presence of inflation. Similarly, accountants incorrectly measure firms' earnings when prices are rising over time. Because inflation causes dollars at different times to have different real values, computing a firm's profit—the difference between its revenue and costs—is more complicated in an economy with inflation. Therefore, to some extent, inflation makes investors less able to sort out successful from unsuccessful firms, which in turn impedes financial markets in their role of allocating the economy's saving to alternative types of investment.

After four hours, the mop is removed from the door. The customers wander in, rub their eyes and squint at the tags, counting the zeros. Mr. Nikolic himself squints as the computer prints another price, this one for a video recorder.

"Is that billions?" he asks himself. It is: 20,391,560,223 dinars, to be precise. He points to his T-shirt, which is emblazoned with the words "Far Out," the name of a fruit juice he once sold. He suggests it is an ideal motto for Serbia's bizarre economic situation. "It fits the craziness," he says.

How else would you describe it? Since the international community imposed economic sanctions, the inflation rate has been at least 10 percent *daily*. This translates to an annual rate in the quadrillions—so high as to be meaningless. In Serbia, one U.S. dollar will get you 10 million dinars at the Hyatt hotel, 12 million from the shady money changers on Republic Square, and 17 million from a bank run by Belgrade's underworld. Serbs complain that the dinar is as worthless as toilet paper. But for the moment, at least, there is plenty of toilet paper to go around.

The government mint, hidden in the park behind the Belgrade racetrack, is said to be churning out dinars 24 hours a day, furiously trying to keep up with the inflation that is fueled, in turn, by its own nonstop printing. The government, which believes in throwing around money to damp dissent, needs dinars to pay workers for not working at closed factories and offices. It needs them to buy the harvest from the farmers. It needs them to finance its smuggling forays and other ways to evade the sanctions, bringing in everything from oil to Mr. Nikolic's Snickers bars. It also needs them to supply brother Serbs fighting in Bosnia-Herzegovina and Croatia.

The money changers, whose fingertips detect the slightest change in paper quality, insist that the mint is even contracting out to private printers to meet demand.

"We're experts. They can't fool us," says one of the changers as he hands over 800 million worth of 5-million-dinar bills. "These," he notes confidently, "are fresh from the mint." He says he got them from a private bank, which got them from the central bank, which got them from the mint—an unholy circuit linking the black market with the Finance Ministry. "It's collective lunacy," the money changer says, laughing wickedly.

Source: *The Wall Street Journal*, August 4, 1993, p. A1. © 1993 by Dow Jones & Co. Inc. Reproduced with permission of DOW JONES & CO INC in the format Textbook via Copyright Clearance Center.

A Special Cost of Unexpected Inflation: Arbitrary Redistributions of Wealth

So far, the costs of inflation we have discussed occur even if inflation is steady and predictable. Inflation has an additional cost, however, when it comes as a surprise. Unexpected inflation redistributes wealth among the population in a way that has nothing to do with either merit or need. These redistributions occur because many loans in the economy are specified in terms of the unit of account—money.

Consider an example. Suppose that Peter Plumber takes out a $20 000 loan at a 7 percent interest rate from Bigbank to expand his business. In ten years, the loan will come due. After his debt has compounded for ten years at 7 percent, Sam will owe Bigbank $40 000. The real value of this debt will depend on inflation over the decade. If Sam is lucky, the economy will have a hyperinflation. In this case, wages and prices will rise so high that Sam will be able to pay the $40 000 debt out of pocket change. By contrast, if the economy goes through a major deflation, then wages and prices will fall, and Sam will find the $40 000 debt a greater burden than he anticipated.

This example shows that unexpected changes in prices redistribute wealth among debtors and creditors. A hyperinflation enriches Sam at the expense of Bigbank because it diminishes the real value of the debt; Sam can repay the loan in less valuable dollars than he anticipated. Deflation enriches Bigbank at Sam's expense because it increases the real value of the debt; in this case, Sam has to repay the loan in more valuable dollars than he anticipated. If inflation were predictable, then Bigbank and Sam could take inflation into account when setting the nominal interest rate. (Recall the Fisher effect.) But if inflation is hard to predict, it imposes risk on Sam and Bigbank that both would prefer to avoid.

This cost of unexpected inflation is important to consider together with another fact: Inflation is especially volatile and uncertain when the average rate of inflation is high. This is seen most simply by examining the experience of different countries. Countries with low average inflation, such as Germany in the late twentieth century, tend to have stable inflation. Countries with high average inflation, such as many countries in Latin America, tend also to have unstable inflation. There are no known examples of economies with high, stable inflation. This relationship between the level and volatility of inflation points to another cost of inflation. If a country pursues a high-inflation monetary policy, it will have to bear not

IN THE NEWS

HOW TO PROTECT YOUR SAVINGS FROM INFLATION

As we have seen, unexpected changes in the price level redistribute wealth among debtors and creditors. This would no longer be true if debt contracts were written in real, rather than nominal, terms. In 1997 the U.S. Treasury started issuing bonds with a return indexed to the price level. In the following article, written a few months before the policy was implemented, two prominent economists discuss the merits of this policy.

Inflation Fighters for the Long Term

By John Y. Campbell and Robert J. Shiller

Treasury Secretary Robert Rubin announced on Thursday that the government plans to issue inflation-indexed bonds—that is, bonds whose interest and principal payments are adjusted upward for inflation, guaranteeing their real purchasing power in the future.

This is a historic moment. Economists have been advocating such bonds for many long and frustrating years. Index bonds were first called for in 1822 by the economist Joseph Lowe. In the 1870s, they were championed by the British economist William Stanley Jevons. In the early part of this century, the legendary Irving Fisher made a career of advocating them.

In recent decades, economists of every political stripe—from Milton Friedman to James Tobin, Alan Blinder to Alan Greenspan—have supported them. Yet, because there was little public clamor for such an investment, the government never issued indexed bonds.

Let's hope this lack of interest does not continue now that they will become available. The success of the indexed bonds depends on whether the public understands them—and buys them. Until now, inflation has made government bonds a risky investment. In 1966, when the inflation rate was only 3 percent, if someone had bought a 30-year government bond yielding 5 percent, he would have expected that by now his investment would be worth 180 percent of its original value. However, after years of higher-than-expected inflation, the only the costs of high expected inflation but also the arbitrary redistributions of wealth associated with unexpected inflation.

Case Study

MONEY GROWTH, INFLATION, AND THE BANK OF CANADA

In the early 1970s, Canada had a quickly growing money supply, and the inflation rate rose to over 10 percent. At the same time, an economic viewpoint known as "monetarism" was becoming increasingly influential. One of the main recommendations of monetarists was that central banks should keep the supply of money growing at a slow, constant rate.

investment is worth only 85 percent of its original value.

Because inflation has been modest in recent years, many people today are not worried about how it will affect their savings. This complacency is dangerous: Even a low rate of inflation can seriously erode savings over long periods of time.

Imagine that you retire today with a pension invested in Treasury bonds that pay a fixed $10,000 each year, regardless of inflation. If there is no inflation, in 20 years the pension will have the same purchasing power that it does today. But if there is an inflation rate of only 3 percent per year, in 20 years your pension will be worth only $5,540 in today's dollars. Five percent inflation over 20 years will cut your purchasing power to $3,770, and 10 percent will reduce it to a pitiful $1,390. Which of these scenarios is likely? No one knows. Inflation ultimately depends on the people who are elected and appointed as guardians of our money supply.

At a time when Americans are living longer and planning for several decades of retirement, the insidious effects of inflation should be of serious concern. For this reason alone, the creation of inflation-indexed bonds, with their guarantee of a safe return over long periods of time, is a welcome development.

No other investment offers this kind of safety. Conventional government bonds make payments that are fixed in dollar terms; but investors should be concerned about purchasing power, not about the number of dollars they receive. Money market funds make dollar payments that increase with inflation to some degree, since short-term interest rates tend to rise with inflation. But many other factors also influence interest rates, so the real income from a money market fund is not secure.

The stock market offers a high rate of return on average, but it can fall as well as rise. Investors should remember the bear market of the 1970s as well as the bull market of the 1980s and 1990s.

Inflation-indexed government bonds have been issued in Britain for 15 years, in Canada for 5 years, and in many other countries, including Australia, New Zealand, and Sweden. In Britain, which has the world's largest indexed-bond market, the bonds have offered a yield 3 to 4 percent higher than the rate of inflation. In the United States, a safe long-term return of this sort should make indexed bonds an important part of retirement savings.

We expect that financial institutions will take advantage of the new inflation-indexed bonds and offer innovative new products. Indexed-bond funds will probably appear first, but indexed annuities and even indexed mortgages—monthly payments would be adjusted for inflation—should also become available. [Author's note: Since this article was written, some of these indexed products have been introduced, but their use is not yet widespread.]

Although the Clinton administration may not get much credit for it today, the decision to issue inflation-indexed bonds is an accomplishment that historians decades hence will single out for special recognition.

Source: *The New York Times,* May 18, 1996, p. 19. © 1996 by The New York Times Co. Reprinted with permission.

In response to the problem of inflation and influenced by the monetarist perspective, the Bank of Canada adopted a policy of "monetary gradualism." The central bank announced a target path for the future supply of money, along which the growth rate of M1 would gradually be reduced. It hoped that the inflation rate would also gradually fall. The results were not as expected. At first inflation stayed high, despite the slowdown in money growth. Then in the early 1980s, inflation fell much more quickly than money growth. The link between money growth and inflation was seen as not precise enough to rely on, so the central bank abandoned its policy of monetary gradualism. In the words of the then governor of the Bank of Canada, Gerald Bouey: "We did not abandon M1. M1 abandoned us."

When we look at different countries over long periods of time, we see great variation in the growth rates of money supply. Variations in velocity are small in comparison, so the link between money growth and inflation can be seen clearly. This is especially true during periods of hyperinflation. But in any one country, over a few years, if the money supply does not vary much, variations in velocity become relatively more important. Fluctuations in velocity mean that the Canadian inflation rate could fluctuate in the short run even if the Bank of Canada kept the money growth rate constant.

Since 1992, the Bank of Canada has explicitly rejected targeting the supply of money and has instead announced a target rate of inflation, currently 2 percent. Under this policy of inflation targeting, which is now the policy of many of the world's central banks, the Bank of Canada adjusts monetary policy, by changing the overnight rate of interest, to try to ensure that inflation will stay at or near the 2 percent target.

The money supply is just one of many sources of information the Bank of Canada considers when setting the overnight rate. After looking at all of its information, if the central bank thinks that there is a danger of inflation rising above the 2 percent target, it raises the overnight rate, which reduces the growth rate of the money supply and also reduces future inflation. If the central bank thinks there is a danger of inflation falling below the 2 percent target, it lowers the overnight rate, which increases the growth rate of the money supply and also increases future inflation.

The Bank of Canada has successfully used monetary policy over the last ten years to keep inflation close to its 2 percent target. But the central bank looks at a very wide range of information when deciding whether to raise or lower the overnight rate, and there has been little or no relation between money growth and inflation during that time. Does this mean that money growth is not very important as a cause of inflation? And if money growth is not very important as a cause of inflation, how has the Bank of Canada, using only monetary policy, been able to keep inflation so close to target?

Milton Friedman, one of the founders of monetarism, offers an analogy to help us better understand the relation between money growth and inflation. In a house with a good thermostat, set at a constant 20°C, we will see fluctuations in the outside temperature and compensating fluctuations in the amount of oil burned in the furnace, but very small fluctuations in the temperature inside the house and little or no relation between the amount of oil burned in the furnace and the inside temperature. Similarly, in a country with a good inflation-targeting central bank, we will see fluctuations in velocity and compensating fluctuations in money growth, but very small fluctuations in inflation and little or no relation between money growth and inflation.

Other things equal, an increase in the amount of oil burned in the furnace will cause an increase in the inside temperature. Similarly, other things equal, an increase in money growth will cause an increase in inflation. But a good thermostat will never increase the quantity of oil burned in the furnace except when other things (like the outside temperature) are *not* equal. Similarly, a good inflation-targeting central bank will never increase money growth except when the other things (like velocity) are *not* equal. You could observe the true relation between oil consumption and inside temperature only by random experiments with the thermostat. Similarly, you could observe the true relation between money growth and inflation only by random experiments with monetary policy. Although economists might love to learn the results by conducting random experiments with monetary policy, the Bank of Canada is understandably reluctant! ●

QuickQuiz   List and describe six costs of inflation.

CONCLUSION

This chapter discussed the causes and costs of inflation. The primary cause of inflation is simply growth in the quantity of money. When the central bank creates money in large quantities, the value of money falls quickly. To maintain stable prices, the central bank must maintain strict control over the money supply.

The costs of inflation are more subtle. They include shoeleather costs, menu costs, increased variability of relative prices, unintended changes in tax liabilities, confusion and inconvenience, and arbitrary redistributions of wealth. Are these costs, in total, large or small? All economists agree that they become huge during hyperinflation. But their size for moderate inflation—when prices rise by less than 10 percent per year—is more open to debate.

Although this chapter presented many of the most important lessons about inflation, the discussion is incomplete. When the central bank reduces the rate of money growth, prices rise less rapidly, as the quantity theory suggests. Yet as the economy makes the transition to this lower inflation rate, the change in monetary policy will have disruptive effects on production and employment. That is, even though monetary policy is neutral in the long run, it has profound effects on real variables in the short run. Later in this book we will examine the reasons for short-run monetary nonneutrality in order to enhance our understanding of the causes and costs of inflation.

SUMMARY

- The overall level of prices in an economy adjusts to bring money supply and money demand into balance. When the central bank increases the supply of money, it causes the price level to rise. Persistent growth in the quantity of money supplied leads to continuing inflation.

- The principle of monetary neutrality asserts that changes in the quantity of money influence nominal variables but not real variables. Most economists believe that monetary neutrality approximately describes the behaviour of the economy in the long run.

- A government can pay for some of its spending simply by printing money. When countries rely heavily on this "inflation tax," the result is hyperinflation.

- One application of the principle of monetary neutrality is the Fisher effect. According to the Fisher effect, when the inflation rate rises, the nominal interest rate rises by the same amount, so that the real interest rate remains the same.

- Many people think that inflation makes them poorer because it raises the cost of what they buy. This view is a fallacy, however, because inflation also raises nominal incomes.

- Economists have identified six costs of inflation: shoeleather costs associated with reduced money holdings, menu costs associated with more frequent adjustment of prices, increased variability of relative prices, unintended changes in tax liabilities due to nonindexation of the tax code, confusion and inconvenience resulting from a changing unit of account, and arbitrary redistributions of wealth between debtors and creditors. Many of these costs are large during hyperinflation, but the size of these costs for moderate inflation is less clear.

KEY CONCEPTS

quantity theory of money, p. 251
nominal variables, p. 253
real variables, p. 253
classical dichotomy, p. 253

monetary neutrality, p. 254
velocity of money, p. 255
quantity equation, p. 255
inflation tax, p. 257

Fisher effect, p. 260
shoeleather costs, p. 262
menu costs, p. 263

QUESTIONS FOR REVIEW

1. Explain how an increase in the price level affects the real value of money.

2. According to the quantity theory of money, what is the effect of an increase in the quantity of money?

3. Explain the difference between nominal and real variables, and give two examples of each. According to the principle of monetary neutrality, which variables are affected by changes in the quantity of money?

4. In what sense is inflation like a tax? How does thinking about inflation as a tax help explain hyperinflation?

5. According to the Fisher effect, how does an increase in the inflation rate affect the real interest rate and the nominal interest rate?

6. What are the costs of inflation? Which of these costs do you think are most important for the Canadian economy?

7. If inflation is less than expected, who benefits— debtors or creditors? Explain.

PROBLEMS AND APPLICATIONS

1. Suppose that this year's money supply is $50 billion, nominal GDP is $1 trillion, and real GDP is $500 billion.
   a. What is the price level? What is the velocity of money?
   b. Suppose that velocity is constant and the economy's output of goods and services rises by 5 percent each year. What will happen to nominal GDP and the price level next year if the Bank of Canada keeps the money supply constant?
   c. What money supply should the Bank of Canada set next year if it wants to keep the price level stable?
   d. What money supply should the Bank of Canada set next year if it wants inflation of 10 percent?

2. Suppose that changes in bank regulations expand the availability of credit cards, so that people need to hold less cash.
   a. How does this event affect the demand for money?
   b. If the Bank of Canada does not respond to this event, what will happen to the price level?
   c. If the Bank of Canada wants to keep the price level stable, what should it do?

3. It is often suggested that the Bank of Canada try to achieve zero inflation. If we assume that velocity is constant, does this zero-inflation goal require that the rate of money growth equal zero? If yes, explain why. If no, explain what the rate of money growth should equal.

4. The economist John Maynard Keynes wrote: "Lenin is said to have declared that the best way to destroy the capitalist system was to debauch the currency. By a continuing process of inflation, governments can confiscate, secretly and unobserved, an important part of the wealth of their citizens." Justify Lenin's assertion.

5. Suppose that a country's inflation rate increases sharply. What happens to the inflation tax on the holders of money? Why is wealth that is held in savings accounts *not* subject to a change in the inflation tax? Can you think of any way in which holders of savings accounts are hurt by the increase in the inflation rate?

6. Hyperinflations are extremely rare in countries whose central banks are independent of the rest of the government. Why might this be so?

7. Let's consider the effects of inflation in an economy composed only of two people: Bob, a bean farmer, and Rita, a rice farmer. Bob and Rita both always consume equal amounts of rice and beans. In year 2000, the price of beans was $1, and the price of rice was $3.
   a. Suppose that in 2001 the price of beans was $2 and the price of rice was $6. What was inflation? Was Bob better off, worse off, or unaffected by the changes in prices? What about Rita?
   b. Now suppose that in 2001 the price of beans was $2 and the price of rice was $4. What was inflation? Was Bob better off, worse off, or unaffected by the changes in prices? What about Rita?
   c. Finally, suppose that in 2001 the price of beans was $2 and the price of rice was $1.50. What was inflation? Was Bob better off, worse off, or unaffected by the changes in prices? What about Rita?
   d. What matters more to Bob and Rita—the overall inflation rate or the relative price of rice and beans?

8. If the tax rate is 40 percent, compute the before-tax real interest rate and the after-tax real interest rate in each of the following cases.
   a. The nominal interest rate is 10 percent and the inflation rate is 5 percent.
   b. The nominal interest rate is 6 percent and the inflation rate is 2 percent.
   c. The nominal interest rate is 4 percent and the inflation rate is 1 percent.

9. What are your shoeleather costs of going to the bank? How might you measure these costs in dollars? How do you think the shoeleather costs of the president of your school differ from your own?

10. Recall that money serves three functions in the economy. What are those functions? How does

inflation affect the ability of money to serve each of these functions?

11. Suppose that people expect inflation to equal 3 percent, but in fact prices rise by 5 percent. Describe how this unexpectedly high inflation rate would help or hurt the following:
    a. the government
    b. a homeowner with a fixed-rate mortgage
    c. a union worker in the second year of a labour contract
    d. a college or university that has invested some of its endowment in government bonds

12. Explain one harm associated with unexpected inflation that is *not* associated with expected inflation. Then explain one harm associated with both expected and unexpected inflation.

13. Explain whether the following statements are true, false, or uncertain.
    a. "Inflation hurts borrowers and helps lenders, because borrowers must pay a higher rate of interest."
    b. "If prices change in a way that leaves the overall price level unchanged, then no one is made better or worse off."
    c. "Inflation does not reduce the purchasing power of most workers."

INTERNET RESOURCES

- The Bank of Canada provides free data on money supply growth and inflation in Canada on its website at http://www.bankofcanada.ca. Click on "Monetary Policy" and then on "Summary of Key Monetary Policy Variables."

- A brief history of monetary theory, including the quantity theory of money, can be found at http://cepa.newschool.edu/het/essays/money/moneycont.htm.

- You can read about some historical episodes of hyperinflation at http://www2.sjsu.edu/faculty/watkins/hyper.htm.

http://   For more study tools, please visit http://www.mankiw3e.nelson.com.

6

THE MACROECONOMICS OF OPEN ECONOMIES

© JOSON/ZEFA

13

OPEN-ECONOMY MACROECONOMICS: BASIC CONCEPTS

When you decide to buy a car, you may compare the latest models offered by Ford and Toyota. When you take your next vacation, you may consider spending it on a ski hill in British Columbia or on a beach in Mexico. When you start saving for your retirement, you may choose between a mutual fund that buys stock in Canadian companies and one that buys stock in foreign companies. In all of these cases, you are participating not just in the Canadian economy but in economies around the world.

There are clear benefits to being open to international trade: Trade allows people to produce what they produce best and to consume the great variety of goods and services produced around the world. Indeed, one of the ten principles of economics highlighted in Chapter 1 is that trade can make everyone better off. As we saw in Chapter 3, international trade can raise living standards in all countries by allowing each country to specialize in producing those goods and services in which it has a comparative advantage.

So far our development of macroeconomics has largely ignored the economy's interaction with other economies around the world. For most questions in macroeconomics, international issues are peripheral. For instance, when we discussed the natural rate of unemployment in Chapter 10 and the causes of inflation in Chapter 12, the effects of international trade could safely be ignored. Indeed, to keep their analysis simple, macroeconomists often assume a **closed economy**—an economy that does not interact with other economies.

Yet some new macroeconomic issues arise in an **open economy**—an economy that interacts freely with other economies around the world. This chapter and the next one, therefore, provide an introduction to open-economy macroeconomics. We begin in this chapter by discussing the key macroeconomic variables that describe an open economy's interactions in world markets. You may have noticed mention of these variables—exports, imports, the trade balance, and exchange rates—when reading the newspaper or watching the nightly news. Our first job is to understand what these data mean. In the next chapter we develop a model to explain how these variables are determined and how they are affected by various government policies.

THE INTERNATIONAL FLOWS OF GOODS AND CAPITAL

An open economy interacts with other economies in two ways: It buys and sells goods and services in world product markets, and it buys and sells capital assets such as stocks and bonds in world financial markets. Here we discuss these two activities and the close relationship between them.

The Flow of Goods: Exports, Imports, and Net Exports

As we first noted in Chapter 3, **exports** are domestically produced goods and services that are sold abroad, and **imports** are foreign-produced goods and services that are sold domestically. When Bombardier, the Canadian aircraft manufacturer, builds a plane and sells it to Air France, the sale is an export for Canada and an import for France. When Volvo, the Swedish car manufacturer, makes a car and sells it to a Canadian resident, the sale is an import for Canada and an export for Sweden.

The **net exports** of any country are the value of its exports minus the value of its imports. The Bombardier sale raises Canada's net exports, and the Volvo sale reduces Canada's net exports. Because net exports tell us whether a country is, in total, a seller or a buyer in world markets for goods and services, net exports are also called the **trade balance.** If net exports are positive, exports are greater than imports, indicating that the country sells more goods and services abroad than it buys from other countries. In this case, the country is said to run a **trade surplus.** If net exports are negative, exports are less than imports, indicating that the country sells fewer goods and services abroad than it buys from other countries. In this case, the country is said to run a **trade deficit.** If net exports are zero, its exports and imports are exactly equal, and the country is said to have **balanced trade.**

In the next chapter we develop a theory that explains an economy's trade balance, but even at this early stage it is easy to think of many factors that might influence a country's exports, imports, and net exports. Those factors include the following:

closed economy
an economy that does not interact with other economies in the world

open economy
an economy that interacts freely with other economies around the world

exports
goods and services that are produced domestically and sold abroad

imports
goods and services that are produced abroad and sold domestically

net exports
the value of a nation's exports minus the value of its imports; also called the trade balance

trade balance
the value of a nation's exports minus the value of its imports; also called net exports

trade surplus
an excess of exports over imports

trade deficit
an excess of imports over exports

balanced trade
a situation in which exports equal imports

- tastes of consumers for domestic and foreign goods
- prices of goods at home and abroad
- exchange rates at which people can use domestic currency to buy foreign currencies
- incomes of consumers at home and abroad
- cost of transporting goods from country to country
- policies of the government toward international trade

As these variables change over time, so does the amount of international trade.

Case Study

THE INCREASING OPENNESS OF THE CANADIAN ECONOMY

Perhaps the most dramatic change in the Canadian economy over the past four decades has been the increasing importance of international trade and finance. This change is illustrated in Figure 13.1, which shows the total value of goods and services exported to other countries and imported from other countries expressed as a percentage of gross domestic product. In the 1960s, exports of goods and services averaged less than 20 percent of GDP. Today they are more than twice that level. Imports of goods and services have risen by a similar amount.

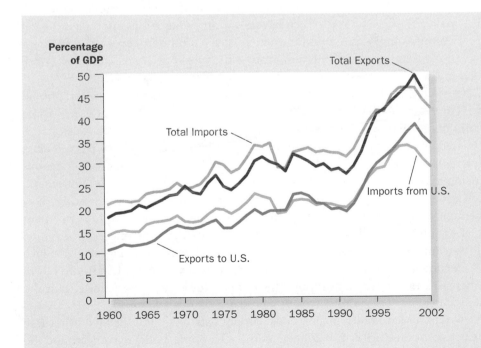

FIGURE 13.1

The Internationalization of the Canadian Economy

This figure shows the value of Canada's exports and imports as a percentage of GDP since 1960. It shows the value of exports and imports to the whole world and the value of exports and imports to the United States. The substantial increase over time shows the increasing importance of international trade, particularly with the United States. The dramatic increase in trade since the signing of the Canada–U.S. Free Trade Agreement in 1989 is especially noteworthy.

Source: Statistics Canada. (The values of exports and imports are defined as including transfer and investment income receipts and payments, respectively.)

Figure 13.1 also shows the value of Canadian exports to and imports from the United States as a percentage of gross domestic product. Clearly, Canada's trade with the United States is the largest part of Canada's total trade. What's more, fluctuations in Canada's total exports and imports over time are mainly due to fluctuations in Canadian exports to and imports from the United States.

This increase in international trade is partly due to improvements in transportation. In 1950 the average merchant ship carried less than 10 000 tonnes of cargo; today, many ships carry more than 100 000 tonnes. The long-distance jet was introduced in 1958 and the wide-body jet in 1967, making air transport far cheaper. Because of these developments, goods that once had to be produced locally can now be traded around the world. Cut flowers, for instance, are now grown in Israel and flown to Canada to be sold. Fresh fruits and vegetables that can grow only in summer can now be consumed in winter as well, because they can be shipped to Canada from countries in the southern hemisphere.

The increase in international trade has also been influenced by advances in telecommunications, which have allowed businesses to reach overseas customers more easily. For example, the first transatlantic telephone cable was not laid until 1956. As recently as 1966, the technology allowed only 138 simultaneous conversations between North America and Europe. Today, communications satellites permit more than 1 million conversations to occur at the same time.

Technological progress has also fostered international trade by changing the kinds of goods that economies produce. When bulky raw materials (such as steel) and perishable goods (such as foodstuffs) were a large part of the world's output, transporting goods was often costly and sometimes impossible. By contrast, goods produced with modern technology are often light and easy to transport. Consumer electronics, for instance, have low weight for every dollar of value, which makes them easy to produce in one country and sell in another. An even more extreme example is the film industry. Once a studio in Hollywood makes a movie, it can send copies of the film around the world at almost zero cost. And, indeed, movies are a major export of the United States.

Government trade policies have also been a factor in increasing international trade. For example, the Canada–U.S. Auto Pact, signed in 1965, made it possible for automobile manufacturers to move auto parts and finished automobiles across the Canada–U.S. border without having to pay import duties. The Auto Pact is largely responsible for the establishment in Canada of a large automobile manufacturing industry. In 1989 Canada signed the Canada–U.S. Free Trade Agreement, which called for the gradual elimination of tariffs on a much larger scale. This agreement was followed in 1994 by the North American Free Trade Agreement (NAFTA) among Canada, the United States, and Mexico. The effect of these free trade agreements on Canadian exports and imports is clear from Figure 13.1. Since 1989, Canada's exports and imports have dramatically increased. Virtually all of the increases in exports and imports have been due to increased trade with the United States.

As we discussed earlier in this book, economists have long believed that free trade between countries is mutually beneficial. Over time, policymakers around the world have come to accept these conclusions. International agreements, such as the NAFTA and those negotiated with the World Trade Organization, have gradually lowered tariffs, import quotas, and other trade barriers. The pattern of increasing trade illustrated in Figure 13.1 is a phenomenon that most economists and policy-makers endorse and encourage. ●

The Flow of Financial Resources: Net Capital Outflow

So far we have been discussing how residents of an open economy participate in world markets for goods and services. In addition, residents of an open economy participate in world financial markets. A Canadian resident with $20 000 could use that money to buy a car from Toyota, but he could instead use that money to buy stock in the Toyota corporation. The first transaction would represent a flow of goods, whereas the second would represent a flow of capital.

The term **net capital outflow** refers to the purchase of foreign assets by domestic residents minus the purchase of domestic assets by foreigners. (It is sometimes called *net foreign investment*.) When a Canadian resident buys stock in Telmex, the Mexican phone company, the purchase raises Canadian net capital outflow. When a Japanese resident buys a bond issued by the Canadian government, the purchase reduces Canadian net capital outflow.

Recall that the flow of capital abroad takes two forms. If Tim Hortons opens a fast food outlet in Russia, that is an example of *foreign direct investment*. Alternatively, if a Canadian buys stock in a Russian corporation, that is an example of *foreign portfolio investment*. In the first case, the Canadian owner is actively managing the investment, whereas in the second case the Canadian owner has a more passive role. In both cases, Canadian residents are buying assets located in another country, so both purchases increase Canadian net capital outflow.

We develop a theory to explain net capital outflow in the next chapter. Here, let's consider briefly some of the more important variables that influence net capital outflow:

- real interest rates being paid on foreign assets
- real interest rates being paid on domestic assets
- perceived economic and political risks of holding assets abroad
- government policies that affect foreign ownership of domestic assets

For example, consider Canadian investors deciding whether to buy Mexican government bonds or Canadian government bonds. (Recall that a bond is, in effect, an IOU of the issuer.) To make this decision, Canadian investors compare the real interest rates offered on the two bonds. The higher a bond's real interest rate, the more attractive it is. While making this comparison, however, Canadian investors must also take into account the risk that one of these governments might *default* on its debt (that is, not pay interest or principal when it is due), as well as any restrictions that the Mexican government has imposed, or might impose in the future, on foreign investors in Mexico.

net capital outflow
the purchase of foreign assets by domestic residents minus the purchase of domestic assets by foreigners

The Equality of Net Exports and Net Capital Outflow

We have seen that an open economy interacts with the rest of the world in two ways—in world markets for goods and services and in world financial markets. Net exports and net capital outflow each measure a type of imbalance in these markets. Net exports measure an imbalance between a country's exports and its imports. Net capital outflow measures an imbalance between the amount of foreign assets bought by domestic residents and the amount of domestic assets bought by foreigners.

An important but subtle fact of accounting states that, for an economy as a whole, these two imbalances must offset each other. That is, net capital outflow (*NCO*) always equals net exports (*NX*):

$$NCO = NX$$

This equation holds because every transaction that affects one side of this equation must also affect the other side by exactly the same amount. This equation is an *identity*—an equation that must hold because of the way the variables in the equation are defined and measured.

To see why this accounting identity is true, consider an example. Suppose that Bombardier, the Canadian aircraft maker, sells some planes to a Japanese airline. In this sale, a Canadian company gives planes to a Japanese company, and a Japanese company gives yen to a Canadian company. Notice that two things have occurred simultaneously. Canada has sold to a foreigner some of its output (the planes), and this sale increases Canadian net exports. In addition, Canada has acquired some foreign assets (the yen), and this acquisition increases Canada's net capital outflow.

Although Bombardier most likely will not hold on to the yen it has acquired in this sale, any subsequent transaction will preserve the equality of net exports and net capital outflow. For example, Bombardier may exchange its yen for dollars with a Canadian mutual fund that wants the yen to buy stock in Sony Corporation, the Japanese maker of consumer electronics. In this case, Boeing's net export of planes equals the mutual fund's net capital outflow in Sony stock. Hence, *NX* and *NCO* rise by an equal amount.

Alternatively, Bombardier may exchange its yen for dollars with another Canadian company that wants to buy computers from Toshiba, the Japanese computer maker. In this case, Canada's imports (of computers) exactly offset Canada's exports (of planes). The sales by Bombardier and Toshiba together affect neither Canada's net exports nor Canada's net capital outflow. That is, *NX* and *NCO* are the same as they were before these transactions took place.

The equality of net exports and net capital outflow follows from the fact that every international transaction is an exchange. When a seller country transfers a good or service to a buyer country, the buyer country gives up some asset to pay for this good or service. The value of that asset equals the value of the good or service sold. When we add everything up, the net value of goods and services sold by a country (*NX*) must equal the net value of assets acquired (*NCO*). The international flow of goods and services and the international flow of capital are two sides of the same coin.

Saving, Investment, and Their Relationship to the International Flows

A nation's saving and investment are, as we have seen in earlier chapters, crucial to its long-run economic growth. Let's therefore consider how these variables are related to the international flows of goods and capital as measured by net exports and net capital outflow. We can do this most easily with the help of some simple mathematics.

As you may recall, the term *net exports* first appeared earlier in the book when we discussed the components of gross domestic product. The economy's gross domestic product (Y) is divided among four components: consumption (C), investment (I), government purchases (G), and net exports (NX). We write this as

$$Y = C + I + G + NX$$

Total expenditure on the economy's output of goods and services is the sum of expenditure on consumption, investment, government purchases, and net exports. Because each dollar of expenditure is placed into one of these four components, this equation is an accounting identity: It must be true because of the way the variables are defined and measured.

Recall that national saving is the income of the nation that is left after paying for current consumption and government purchases. National saving (S) equals $Y - C - G$. If we rearrange the above equation to reflect this fact, we obtain

$$Y - C - G = I + NX$$

$$S = I + NX$$

Because net exports (NX) also equal net capital outflow (NCO), we can write this equation as

$$S \quad = \quad I \quad + \quad NCO$$

$$\text{Saving} \quad = \quad \begin{array}{c}\text{Domestic}\\\text{investment}\end{array} \quad + \quad \begin{array}{c}\text{Net capital}\\\text{outflow}\end{array}$$

This equation shows that a nation's saving must equal its domestic investment plus its net capital outflow. In other words, when Canadian citizens save a dollar of their income for the future, that dollar can be used to finance accumulation of domestic capital or it can be used to finance the purchase of capital abroad.

This equation should look somewhat familiar. Earlier in the book, when we analyzed the role of the financial system, we considered this identity for the special case of a closed economy. In a closed economy, net capital outflow is zero ($NCO = 0$), so saving equals investment ($S = I$). By contrast, an open economy has two uses for its saving: domestic investment and net capital outflow.

As before, we can view the financial system as standing between the two sides of this identity. For example, suppose the Smith family decides to save some of its income for retirement. This decision contributes to national saving, the left-hand side of our equation. If the Smiths deposit their saving in a mutual fund, the mutual fund may use some of the deposit to buy stock issued by Stelco, which uses the proceeds to build a new steel plant in Ontario. In addition, the mutual fund may use some of the Smiths' deposit to buy stock issued by Toyota, which uses the proceeds to build a steel plant in Osaka. These transactions show up on the right-hand side of the equation. From the standpoint of Canadian accounting, the Stelco expenditure on a new steel plant is domestic investment, and the purchase of Toyota stock by a Canadian resident is net capital outflow. Thus, all saving in the Canadian economy shows up as investment in the Canadian economy or as Canadian net capital outflow.

Summing Up

Table 13.1 summarizes many of the ideas presented so far in this chapter. It describes the three possibilities for an open economy: a country with a trade deficit, a country with balanced trade, and a country with a trade surplus.

Consider first a country with a trade surplus. By definition, a trade surplus means that the value of exports exceeds the value of imports. Because net exports are exports minus imports, net exports (NX) are greater than zero. As a result, income ($Y = C + I + G + NX$) must be greater than domestic spending ($C + I + G$). But if Y is more than $C + I + G$, then $Y - C - G$ must be more than I. That is, saving ($S = Y - C - G$) must exceed investment. Because the country is saving more than it is investing, it must be sending some of its saving abroad. That is, the net capital outflow must be greater than zero.

The converse logic applies to a country with a trade deficit. By definition, a trade deficit means that the value of exports is less than the value of imports. Because net exports are exports minus imports, net exports (NX) are negative. Thus, income ($Y = C + I + G + NX$) must be less than domestic spending ($C + I + G$). But if Y is less than $C + I + G$, then $Y - C - G$ must be less than I. That is, saving must be less than investment. The net capital outflow must be negative.

A country with balanced trade is between these cases. Exports equal imports, so net exports are zero. Income equals domestic spending, and saving equals investment. The net capital outflow equals zero.

TABLE 13.1

International Flows of Goods and Capital: Summary

This table shows the three possible outcomes for an open economy.

	Trade Deficit	Balanced Trade	Trade Surplus
	Exports < Imports	Exports = Imports	Exports > Imports
	Net exports < 0	Net exports = 0	Net exports > 0
	$Y < C + I + G$	$Y = C + I + G$	$Y > C + I + G$
	Saving < Investment	Saving = Investment	Saving > Investment
	Net capital outflow < 0	Net capital outflow = 0	Net capital outflow > 0

Case Study

SAVING, INVESTMENT, AND NET CAPITAL OUTFLOW OF CANADA

Canada is a net debtor in world financial markets. This means that foreigners own more Canadian assets than Canadians own foreign assets. In the 1960s and 1970s, much concern was expressed about the extent of foreign investment in Canada. At the time, many people advocated restrictions on foreign ownership of Canadian assets. Was this a sensible policy to recommend? Is the fact that Canada is a net debtor a legitimate source of concern?

To answer these questions, let's see what these macroeconomic accounting identities tell us about the Canadian economy. Panel (a) of Figure 13.2 shows national saving and domestic investment as a percentage of GDP since 1961. Panel (b) shows net capital outflow as a percentage of GDP. Notice that, as the identities require, net capital outflow always equals national saving minus domestic investment.

Panel (b) shows that over the period 1961 to 1998, Canada typically experienced negative net capital outflow (NCO). That is, it was typically true that each year foreigners purchased more Canadian assets than Canadians purchased foreign assets. This net purchase of Canadian assets by foreigners allowed domestic investment in Canada to exceed Canada's national saving by an average of 2.3 percent of GDP over the period 1961 to 1998. Because net exports must equal net foreign investment, net exports in Canada were also typically negative over this period, as we saw in Figure 13.1.

Since 1999, a significant change has occurred in Canada's net capital outflow: It has turned positive. Although this had occurred previously for short periods in 1970, 1982, and 1996, since 1999 the change has proven to be longer lasting and the size of the net capital outflow is much larger than in those earlier periods. What has happened to cause this change?

National saving has increased from 14 percent of GDP in 1993 to 22 percent in 2002. In large part this has been the result of efforts by the federal government and most provincial governments to eliminate their deficits. Since 1999, the resulting increase in national saving has been sufficiently large that, despite a significant increase in domestic investment, Canadians' savings have been more than sufficient to meet the demands of firms for investment funds. As a result, Canadians' savings have been made available for lending to foreigners.

Were the trade deficits and their counterpart—negative amounts of net capital outflow— problems for the Canadian economy during the period 1961 to 1999? Most economists argue that they were not a problem in themselves but were a symptom of a problem: reduced national saving. Reduced national saving is potentially a problem because it means that the nation is putting away less to provide for its future. However, there is less reason to be concerned if the result is a trade deficit. As our accounting identities teach us, a fall in national saving must result in either a larger trade deficit or a fall in domestic investment. If national saving falls without inducing a trade deficit, domestic investment in Canada must

FIGURE 13.2

National Saving, Domestic Investment, and Net Capital Outflow

Panel (a) shows national saving and domestic investment as a percentage of GDP. Panel (b) shows net capital outflow as a percentage of GDP. In all but three years from 1961 to 1998, net capital outflow was negative and large in absolute value. Since 1999, net capital outflow has been positive and large in value. The recent situation indicates that national saving is more than sufficient to satisfy the demand of domestic firms for investment funds. The excess saving is being used to purchase foreign assets.

Source: Statistics Canada, and author's calculations.

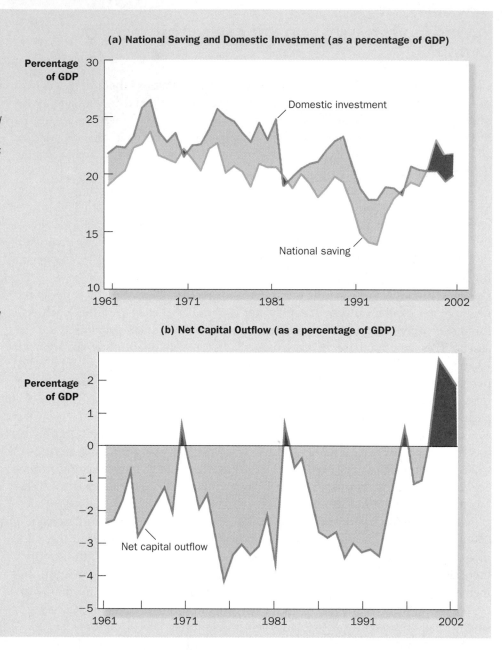

(a) National Saving and Domestic Investment (as a percentage of GDP)

(b) Net Capital Outflow (as a percentage of GDP)

fall instead. This fall in investment, in turn, would adversely affect growth in the capital stock, labour productivity, and real wages. If national saving falls and the trade deficit increases as well, then the savings of foreigners are being used to finance Canadian investment. In other words, given the fact that Canadians were not saving much, it is better to have had foreigners invest in the Canadian economy than no one at all. Had it not been for a willingness on the part of foreigners to put their savings into Canada, the fall in national saving brought about by large government deficits in the 1980s would have resulted in a much larger reduction in domestic investment than otherwise. The trade deficits, and their counterpart negative amounts of net capital outflow, were thus simply a sign that foreigners were making their savings available to Canadian firms that were looking to finance new investment but were finding Canadian savings to be insufficient to provide those funds.

Have the trade surpluses and their counterpart—positive amounts of net capital outflow—been problems for the Canadian economy since 1999? To answer this question, it is again important to keep an eye on the nation's saving and investment. Had the increase in net capital outflow been the result of a reduction in domestic investment, this might have signalled an inability of Canadian firms to develop profitable investment opportunities. In fact, however, the positive net capital outflow has been the result of an increase in national saving. As this reflects the fact that Canadians are putting away more of their incomes for the future, rather than being a sign of trouble, the positive net capital outflow indicates a healthy supply of domestic saving available to finance new investment and growth. ●

QuickQuiz Define *net exports* and *net capital outflow*. Explain how they are related.

THE PRICES FOR INTERNATIONAL TRANSACTIONS: REAL AND NOMINAL EXCHANGE RATES

So far we have discussed measures of the flow of goods and services and the flow of capital across a nation's border. In addition to these quantity variables, macroeconomists also study variables that measure the prices at which these international transactions take place. Just as the price in any market serves the important role of coordinating buyers and sellers in that market, international prices help coordinate the decisions of consumers and producers as they interact in world markets. Here we discuss the two most important international prices—the nominal and real exchange rates.

Nominal Exchange Rates

The **nominal exchange rate** is the rate at which a person can trade the currency of one country for the currency of another. For example, if you go to a bank, you might see a posted exchange rate of 80 yen per dollar. If you give the bank one Canadian dollar, it will give you 80 Japanese yen; and if you give the bank 80 Japanese yen, it will give you one Canadian dollar. (In actuality, the bank will post slightly different prices for buying and selling yen. The difference gives the bank some profit for offering this service. For our purposes here, we can ignore these differences.)

An exchange rate can always be expressed in two ways. If the exchange rate is 80 yen per dollar, it is also 1/80 (= 0.0125) dollar per yen. Throughout this book,

nominal exchange rate
the rate at which a person can trade the currency of one country for the currency of another

appreciation
an increase in the value of a currency as measured by the amount of foreign currency it can buy

depreciation
a decrease in the value of a currency as measured by the amount of foreign currency it can buy

we always express the nominal exchange rate as units of foreign currency per Canadian dollar, such as 80 yen per dollar.

If the exchange rate changes so that a dollar buys more foreign currency, that change is called an **appreciation** of the dollar. If the exchange rate changes so that a dollar buys less foreign currency, that change is called a **depreciation** of the dollar. For example, when the exchange rate rises from 80 to 90 yen per dollar, the dollar is said to appreciate. At the same time, because a Japanese yen now buys less of the Canadian currency, the yen is said to depreciate. When the exchange rate falls from 80 to 70 yen per dollar, the dollar is said to depreciate, and the yen is said to appreciate.

At times you may have heard the media report that the dollar is either "strong" or "weak." These descriptions usually refer to recent changes in the nominal exchange rate. When a currency appreciates, it is said to *strengthen* because it can then buy more foreign currency. Similarly, when a currency depreciates, it is said to *weaken*.

For any country, there are many nominal exchange rates. The Canadian dollar can be used to buy Japanese yen, British pounds, Mexican pesos, U.S. dollars, and so on. When economists study changes in the exchange rate, they often use indexes that average these many exchange rates. Just as the consumer price index turns the many prices in the economy into a single measure of the price level, an exchange rate index turns these many exchange rates into a single measure of the international value of the currency. So when economists talk about the dollar appreciating or depreciating, they often are referring to an exchange rate index that takes into account many individual exchange rates.

FYI

THE VALUE OF THE CANADIAN DOLLAR

When Canadians think about the value of the Canadian dollar, they typically compare it with the U.S. dollar. This is not surprising, given that when they leave Canada on holiday or on business, the vast majority of Canadians go to the United States. The value of the Canadian dollar relative to the U.S. dollar is therefore foremost in the minds of Canadians.

It is important to remember, however, that there is a nominal exchange rate between the Canadian dollar and the currency of every other country. What's more, Canada trades with many countries other than the United States. There are, then, many ways of defining the value of the Canadian dollar. We can compare it with the U.S. dollar, the British pound, or any other currency in the world.

The four graphs in Figure 13.3 show how the exchange rate has changed recently between the Canadian dollar and four currencies: the U.S. dollar, the British pound, the Japanese yen, and the Australian dollar. The graph in panel (a) shows that from August 1996 to August 2003, the Canadian dollar first fell in value relative to the U.S. dollar but then reversed direction and regained most of its value against the U.S. dollar during 2003. The opposite occurred in relation to the Australian dollar (panel d), with the Canadian dollar first rising in value before reversing direction and falling in value since 2001. Since 1996 the value of the Canadian dollar has fallen, increased, fallen, and increased again relative to the British pound. Finally, after a precipitous fall in value relative to the Japanese yen between 1998 and 2001, the Canadian dollar has gained in value relative to the Japanese currency.

Information on exchange rates is useful to Canadians wondering where to go on their next holiday. These graphs indicate that a holiday in Florida became considerably less expensive in 2003, while a trip to Australia would now be more expensive than it was in 2001.

FIGURE 13.3

The Value of the Canadian Dollar

These graphs show how the value of the Canadian dollar has changed relative to the values of other currencies from August 1996 to August 2003.

Source: Statistics Canada.

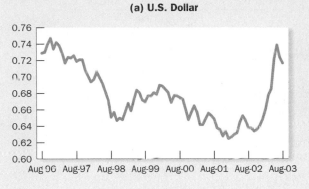

(a) U.S. Dollar

(b) British Pound

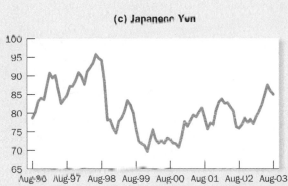

(c) Japanese Yen

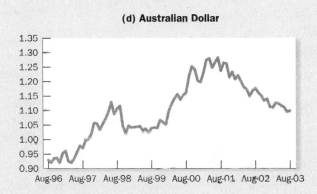

(d) Australian Dollar

Real Exchange Rates

The **real exchange rate** is the rate at which a person can trade the goods and services of one country for the goods and services of another. For example, suppose you go shopping and find that a case of German beer is twice as expensive as a case of Canadian beer. We would then say that the real exchange rate is half of a case of German beer per case of Canadian beer. Notice that, like the nominal exchange rate, we express the real exchange rate as units of the foreign item per unit of the domestic item. But in this instance the item is a good rather than a currency.

Real and nominal exchange rates are closely related. To see how, consider an example. Suppose that a bushel of Canadian wheat sells for $200, and a bushel of Russian wheat sells for 1600 rubles. What is the real exchange rate between

real exchange rate
the rate at which a person can trade the goods and services of one country for the goods and services of another

Canadian and Russian wheat? To answer this question, we must first use the nominal exchange rate to convert the prices into a common currency. If the nominal exchange rate is 4 rubles per dollar, then a price for Canadian wheat of $200 per bushel is equivalent to 800 rubles per bushel. Canadian wheat is half as expensive as Russian wheat. The real exchange rate is 1/2 bushel of Russian wheat per bushel of Canadian wheat.

We can summarize this calculation for the real exchange rate with the following formula:

$$\text{Real exchange rate} = \frac{\text{Nominal exchange rate} \times \text{Domestic price}}{\text{Foreign price}}$$

Using the numbers in our example, the formula applies as follows:

$$\text{Real exchange rate} = \frac{(4 \text{ rubles per dollar}) \times (\$200 \text{ per bushel of Canadian wheat})}{1600 \text{ rubles per bushel of Russian wheat}}$$

$$= \frac{800 \text{ rubles per bushel of Canadian wheat}}{1600 \text{ rubles per bushel of Russian wheat}}$$

$$= 1/2 \text{ bushel of Russian wheat per bushel of Canadian wheat}$$

Thus, the real exchange rate depends on the nominal exchange rate and on the prices of goods in the two countries measured in the local currencies.

Why does the real exchange rate matter? As you might guess, the real exchange rate is a key determinant of how much a country exports and imports. When Five Roses Inc. is deciding whether to buy Canadian wheat or Russian wheat to make flour, for example, it will ask which wheat is cheaper. The real exchange rate gives the answer. As another example, imagine that you are deciding whether to take a seaside vacation in Tofino, British Columbia, or in Cancun, Mexico. You might ask your travel agent the price of a hotel room in Tofino (measured in dollars), the price of a hotel room in Cancun (measured in pesos), and the exchange rate between pesos and dollars. If you decide where to vacation by comparing costs, you are basing your decision on the real exchange rate.

When studying an economy as a whole, macroeconomists focus on overall prices rather than the prices of individual items. That is, to measure the real exchange rate, they use price indexes, such as the consumer price index, which measure the price of a basket of goods and services. By using a price index for a Canadian basket (P), a price index for a foreign basket (P^*), and the nominal exchange rate between the Canadian dollar and foreign currencies (e), we can compute the overall real exchange rate between Canada and other countries as follows:

$$\text{Real exchange rate} = (e \times P)/P^*$$

This real exchange rate measures the price of a basket of goods and services available domestically relative to a basket of goods and services available abroad.

FYI

THE EURO

You may have once heard of, or perhaps even seen, currencies such as the French franc, the German mark, or the Italian lira. These types of money no longer exist. During the 1990s, many European nations decided to give up their national currencies and use a common currency called the *euro*. The euro started circulating on January 1, 2002. Monetary policy for the euro area is now set by the European Central Bank (ECB), with representatives from all of the participating countries. The ECB issues the euro and controls the supply of this money, much as the Bank of Canada controls the supply of dollars in the Canadian economy.

Why did these countries adopt a common currency? One benefit of a common currency is that it makes trade easier. Imagine that each

of the ten Canadian provinces and three territories had a different currency. Every time you crossed a provincial or territorial border you would need to change your money and perform the kind of exchange-rate calculations discussed in the text. This would be inconvenient, and it might deter you from buying goods and services outside your own province or territory. The countries of Europe decided that as their economies became more integrated, it would be better to avoid this inconvenience.

To some extent, the adoption of a common currency in Europe was a political decision based on concerns beyond the scope of standard economics. Some advocates of the euro wanted to reduce nationalistic feelings and to make Europeans appreciate more fully their shared history and destiny. A single money for most of the continent, they argued, would help achieve this goal.

There are, however, costs of choosing a common currency. If the nations of Europe have only one money, they can have only one monetary policy. If they disagree about what monetary policy is best, they will have to reach some kind of agreement, rather than each going its own way. Because adopting a single money has both benefits and costs, there is debate among economists about whether Europe's adoption of the euro was a good decision. Only time will tell what effects the decision will have.

As we examine more fully in the next chapter, a country's real exchange rate is a key determinant of its net exports of goods and services. A depreciation (fall) in Canada's real exchange rate means that Canadian goods have become cheaper relative to foreign goods. This change encourages consumers both at home and abroad to buy more Canadian goods and fewer goods from other countries. As a result, Canada's exports rise, and Canada's imports fall, and both of these changes raise Canada's net exports. Conversely, an appreciation (rise) in Canada's real exchange rate means that Canadian goods have become more expensive compared to foreign goods, so Canada's net exports fall.

QuickQuiz Define *nominal exchange rate* and *real exchange rate,* and explain how they are related. • If the nominal exchange rate goes from 100 to 120 yen per dollar, has the dollar appreciated or depreciated?

A FIRST THEORY OF EXCHANGE-RATE DETERMINATION: PURCHASING-POWER PARITY

Exchange rates vary substantially over time. In 1970, a Canadian dollar could be used to buy 3.49 German marks or 600 Italian lira. In 2000, a Canadian dollar bought 1.43 German marks or 1413 Italian lira. In other words, over this period the value of the dollar fell compared with the mark and rose compared with the lira.

What explains these large and opposite changes? Economists have developed many models to explain how exchange rates are determined, each emphasizing just some of the many forces at work. Here we develop the simplest theory of exchange rates, called **purchasing-power parity.** This theory states that a unit of any given currency should be able to buy the same quantity of goods in all countries. Many economists believe that purchasing-power parity describes the forces that determine exchange rates in the long run. We now consider the logic on which this long-run theory of exchange rates is based, as well as the theory's implications and limitations.

purchasing-power parity
a theory of exchange rates whereby a unit of any given currency should be able to buy the same quantity of goods in all countries

The Basic Logic of Purchasing-Power Parity

The theory of purchasing-power parity is based on a principle called the *law of one price.* This law asserts that a good must sell for the same price in all locations. Otherwise, opportunities for profit would be left unexploited. For example, suppose that coffee beans sold for less in Vancouver than in Halifax. A person could buy coffee in Vancouver for, say, $4 a kilo and then sell it in Halifax for $5 per kilo, making a profit of $1 per kilo from the difference in price. The process of taking advantage of differences in prices in different markets is called *arbitrage.* In our example, as people took advantage of this arbitrage opportunity, they would increase the demand for coffee in Vancouver and increase the supply in Halifax. The price of coffee would rise in Vancouver (in response to greater demand) and fall in Halifax (in response to greater supply). This process would continue until, eventually, the prices were the same in the two markets.

Now consider how the law of one price applies to the international marketplace. If a dollar (or any other currency) could buy more coffee in Canada than in Japan, international traders could profit by buying coffee in Canada and selling it in Japan. This export of coffee from Canada to Japan would drive up the Canadian price of coffee and drive down the Japanese price. Conversely, if a dollar could buy more coffee in Japan than in Canada, traders could buy coffee in Japan and sell it in Canada. This import of coffee into Canada from Japan would drive down the Canadian price of coffee and drive up the Japanese price. In the end, the law of one price tells us that a dollar must buy the same amount of coffee in all countries.

This logic leads us to the theory of purchasing-power parity. According to this theory, a currency must have the same purchasing power in all countries. That is, a Canadian dollar must buy the same quantity of goods in Canada and Japan, and a Japanese yen must buy the same quantity of goods in Japan and Canada. Indeed, the name of this theory describes it well. *Parity* means equality, and *purchasing power* refers to the value of money. *Purchasing-power parity* states that a unit of all currencies must have the same real value in every country.

Implications of Purchasing-Power Parity

What does the theory of purchasing-power parity say about exchange rates? It tells us that the nominal exchange rate between the currencies of two countries depends on the price levels in those countries. If a dollar buys the same quantity of goods in Canada (where prices are measured in dollars) as in Japan (where prices are measured in yen), then the number of yen per dollar must reflect the prices of goods in Canada and Japan. For example, if a kilo of coffee costs 500 yen in Japan and $5 in Canada, then the nominal exchange rate must be 100 yen per dollar (500 yen/$5 = 100 yen per dollar). Otherwise, the purchasing power of the dollar would not be the same in the two countries.

To see more fully how this works, it is helpful to use just a bit of mathematics. Suppose that P is the price of a basket of goods in Canada (measured in dollars), P^* is the price of a basket of goods in Japan (measured in yen), and e is the nominal exchange rate (the number of yen a dollar can buy). Now consider the quantity of goods a dollar can buy at home and abroad. At home, the price level is P, so the purchasing power of $1 at home is $1/P$. Abroad, a dollar can be exchanged into e units of foreign currency, which in turn have purchasing power e/P^*. For the purchasing power of a dollar to be the same in the two countries, it must be the case that

$$1/P = e/P^*$$

With rearrangement, this equation becomes

$$1 = eP/P^*$$

Notice that the left-hand side of this equation is a constant, and the right-hand side is the real exchange rate. Thus, *if the purchasing power of the dollar is always the same at home and abroad, then the real exchange rate—the relative price of domestic and foreign goods—cannot change.*

To see the implication of this analysis for the nominal exchange rate, we can rearrange the last equation to solve for the nominal exchange rate:

$$e = P^*/P$$

That is, the nominal exchange rate equals the ratio of the foreign price level (measured in units of the foreign currency) to the domestic price level (measured in units of the domestic currency). *According to the theory of purchasing-power parity, the nominal exchange rate between the currencies of two countries must reflect the different price levels in those countries.*

A key implication of this theory is that nominal exchange rates change when price levels change. As we saw in the preceding chapter, the price level in any country adjusts to bring the quantity of money supplied and the quantity of money demanded into balance. Because the nominal exchange rate depends on the price levels, it also depends on the money supply and money demand in each country. When a central bank in any country increases the money supply and causes the price level to rise, it also causes that country's currency to depreciate relative to other currencies in the world. In other words, *when the central bank prints large quantities of money, that money loses value both in terms of the goods and services it can buy and in terms of the amount of other currencies it can buy.*

We can now answer the question that began this section: Why did the Canadian dollar lose value compared to the German mark and gain value compared to the Italian lira? The answer is that Germany pursued a less inflationary monetary policy than Canada, and Italy pursued a more inflationary monetary policy. From 1970 to 1998, inflation in Canada was 5.4 percent per year. By contrast, inflation was 3.5 percent in Germany, and 9.6 percent in Italy. As Canadian prices rose relative to German prices, the value of the dollar fell relative to the mark. Similarly, as Canadian prices fell relative to Italian prices, the value of the dollar rose relative to the lira.

Germany and Italy now have a common currency—the euro. This means that the two countries share a single monetary policy and that the inflation rates in the two countries will be closely linked. But the historical lessons of the lira and the mark will apply to the euro as well. Whether the Canadian dollar buys more or fewer euros 20 years from now than it does today depends on whether the European Central Bank produces more or less inflation in Europe than the Bank of Canada does in Canada.

Case Study

THE NOMINAL EXCHANGE RATE DURING A HYPERINFLATION

Macroeconomists can only rarely conduct controlled experiments. Most often, they must glean what they can from the natural experiments that history gives them. One natural experiment is hyperinflation—the high inflation that arises when a government turns to the printing press to pay for large amounts of government spending. Because hyperinflations are so extreme, they illustrate some basic economic principles with clarity.

Consider the German hyperinflation of the early 1920s. Figure 13.4 shows the German money supply, the German price level, and the nominal exchange rate (measured as U.S. cents per German mark) for that period. Notice that these series move closely together. When the supply of money starts growing quickly, the price level also takes off, and the German mark depreciates. When the money supply stabilizes, so does the price level and the exchange rate.

The pattern shown in this figure appears during every hyperinflation. It leaves no doubt that there is a fundamental link among money, prices, and the nominal exchange rate. The quantity theory of money discussed in the previous chapter explains how the money supply affects the price level. The theory of purchasing-power parity discussed here explains how the price level affects the nominal exchange rate. ●

Limitations of Purchasing-Power Parity

Purchasing-power parity provides a simple model of how exchange rates are determined. For understanding many economic phenomena, the theory works well. In particular, it can explain many long-term trends, such as the depreciation of the Canadian dollar against the German mark and the appreciation of the

FIGURE 13.4

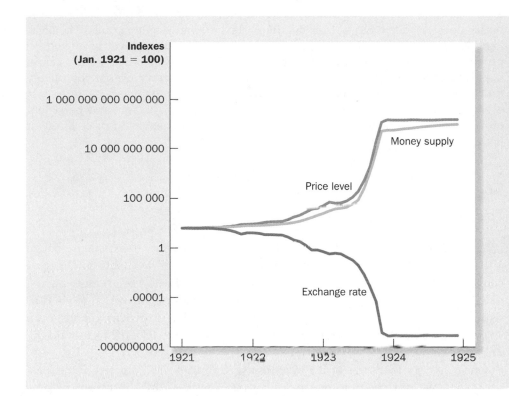

Money, Prices, and the Nominal Exchange Rate during the German Hyperinflation

This figure shows the money supply, the price level, and the exchange rate (measured as U.S. cents per mark) for the German hyperinflation from January 1921 to December 1924. Notice how similarly these three variables move. When the quantity of money started growing quickly, the price level followed, and the mark depreciated relative to the dollar. When the German central bank stabilized the money supply, the price level and exchange rate stabilized as well.

Source: Adapted from Thomas J. Sargent, "The End of Four Big Inflations," in Robert Hall, ed., *Inflation* (Chicago: University of Chicago Press, 1983), pp. 41–93. Reprinted with permission.

Canadian dollar against the Italian lira discussed earlier. It can also explain the major changes in exchange rates that occur during hyperinflations.

Yet the theory of purchasing-power parity is not completely accurate. That is, exchange rates do not always move to ensure that a dollar has the same real value in all countries all the time. There are two reasons why the theory of purchasing-power parity does not always hold in practice.

The first reason is that many goods are not easily traded. Imagine, for instance, that haircuts are more expensive in Paris than in Montreal. International travellers might avoid getting their haircuts in Paris, and some haircutters might move from Montreal to Paris. Yet such arbitrage would probably be too limited to eliminate the differences in prices. Thus, the deviation from purchasing power parity might persist, and a dollar (or euro) would continue to buy less of a haircut in Paris than in Montreal.

The second reason that purchasing-power parity does not always hold is that even tradable goods are not always perfect substitutes when they are produced in different countries. For example, some consumers prefer German beer, and others prefer Canadian beer. Moreover, consumer tastes can change over time. If German beer suddenly becomes more popular, the increase in demand will drive up the price of German beer compared to Canadian beer. But despite this difference in prices in the two markets, there might be no opportunity for profitable arbitrage because consumers do not view the two beers as equivalent.

Thus, both because some goods are not tradable and because some tradable goods are not perfect substitutes with their foreign counterparts, purchasing-power parity is not a perfect theory of exchange-rate determination. For these reasons, real exchange rates fluctuate over time. Nonetheless, the theory of purchasing-power parity does provide a useful first step in understanding exchange rates. The basic logic is persuasive: As the real exchange rate drifts from the level predicted by purchasing-power parity, people have greater incentive to move goods across national borders. Even if the forces of purchasing-power parity do not completely fix the real exchange rate, they provide a reason to expect that changes in the real exchange rate are most often small or temporary. As a result, large and persistent movements in nominal exchange rates typically reflect changes in price levels at home and abroad.

Case Study

THE HAMBURGER STANDARD

When economists apply the theory of purchasing-power parity to explain exchange rates, they need data on the prices of a basket of goods available in different countries. One analysis of this sort is conducted by *The Economist,* an international newsmagazine. The magazine occasionally collects data on a basket of goods consisting of "two all-beef patties, special sauce, lettuce, cheese, pickles, onions, on a sesame seed bun." It's called the "Big Mac" and is sold by McDonald's around the world.

Once we have the prices of Big Macs in two countries denominated in the local currencies, we can compute the exchange rate predicted by the theory of purchasing-power parity. The predicted exchange rate is the one that makes the cost of the Big Mac the same in the two countries. For instance, if the price of a Big Mac is $2 in the United States and 200 yen in Japan, purchasing-power parity would predict an exchange rate of 100 yen per dollar.

How well does purchasing-power parity work when applied using Big Mac prices? Here are some examples from an *Economist* article published on April 24, 2003, when the price of a Big Mac was $2.71 in the United States:

Country	Price of a Big Mac	Predicted Exchange Rate	Actual Exchange Rate
Canada	3.20 $CDN	1.18 $CDN/$US	1.45 $CDN /$US
South Korea	3300 won	1218 won/$US	1220 won/$US
Japan	262 yen	96.7 yen/$US	120 yen/$US
Sweden	30 kronor	11.1 kronor/$US	8.34 kronor/$US
Mexico	23 peso	8.49 peso/$US	10.53 peso/$US
Euro area	2.71 euro	1.00 euro/$US	1.10 euro/$US
Britain	1.99 pounds	1.36 pounds/$US	1.58 pounds/$US

Source: ©April 24, 2003, The Economist Newspaper Ltd. All rights reserved. Reprinted with permission. Further reproduction prohibited. (http://www.economist.com; under "Data Bank," click on "Big Mac Index")

You can see that the predicted and actual exchange rates are not always exactly the same. After all, international arbitrage in Big Macs is not easy. Yet the predicted and the actual exchange rates are usually in the same ballpark. Indeed, for the South Korean won, they are almost identical. Purchasing-power parity is not a precise theory of exchange rates, but it often provides a reasonable first approximation. ●

In Canada the 2003 price of a Big Mac was $3.20; in Japan it was 262 yen.

QuickQuiz Over the past 20 years, Spain has had high inflation and Japan has had low inflation. What do you predict has happened to the number of Spanish pesetas a person can buy with a Japanese yen?

INTEREST RATE DETERMINATION IN A SMALL OPEN ECONOMY WITH PERFECT CAPITAL MOBILITY

When they want to predict whether Canadian interest rates will rise or fall, Canadian economists tend to pay a lot of attention to anticipated changes in U.S. interest rates. They do so because interest rates in Canada tend to increase when interest rates in the United States increase and fall when interest rates in the United States fall.

Why do interest rates in Canada and the United States tend to move up and down together? Recall our earlier discussion of the market for loanable funds, which we used to explain the determination of the real interest rate. That discussion assumed a closed economy—one that does not trade goods and services with other economies. This assumption is not appropriate for describing the Canadian economy. As we saw earlier in this chapter, Canada is an open economy in which trade with other countries makes up a very large part of GDP. For this reason, economists prefer to use a model of the Canadian economy that takes into consideration these trade flows. The model most economists prefer to use is one that describes Canada as a *small open economy with perfect capital mobility*.

In this section, we take a first step toward modifying our description of the market for loanable funds in a small open economy with perfect capital mobility. We will see that determining the real interest rate in such an economy is pretty straightforward. In the next chapter we will make use of this discussion to modify our discussion of the market for loanable funds in a way that is appropriate for a small open economy.

A Small Open Economy

What do we mean when we say Canada is a **small open economy** with perfect capital mobility? By "small" we mean an economy that is a small part of the world economy. In particular, we are describing an economy that, by itself, has only a negligible effect on the prices of goods and services and on interest rates in the rest of the world. Thus, for example, an increase in demand for computer chips by Canadians is unlikely to have an effect on the world price for computer chips. Canada's share of the total world demand for computer chips is too small for such a change to have anything but a negligible effect on the world price. Canadian financial markets are also "small" in this sense. An increase in the supply of Canadian bonds has a negligible effect on the total world supply of bonds. Changes in Canadian financial markets therefore have negligible effects on world interest rates.

small open economy
an economy that trades goods and services with other economies and, by itself, has a negligible effect on world prices and interest rates

Perfect Capital Mobility

perfect capital mobility
full access to world financial markets

By **perfect capital mobility** we mean that Canadians have full access to world financial markets and that people in the rest of the world have full access to the Canadian financial market.

The implication of perfect capital mobility for a small open economy like Canada's is that the real interest rate in Canada should equal the real interest rate prevailing in world financial markets. In simple mathematical terms, if r is the Canadian real interest rate and r^w is the world real interest rate, then

$$r = r^w$$

Why should this be so? Some examples will illustrate. If $r^w = 8$ percent and $r = 5$ percent, this situation cannot persist. The reason is simple: With full access to world financial markets, Canadian savers would prefer to buy foreign assets that pay an interest rate of 8 percent than Canadian assets that pay an interest rate of just 5 percent. We would expect to see savers sell their Canadian assets and buy foreign assets instead. The sale of Canadian assets then forces Canadian borrowers to offer a more attractive interest rate. Indeed, we would expect them to offer an interest rate of 8 percent, the world interest rate.

Similarly, if $r^w = 5$ percent and $r = 8$ percent, this situation cannot persist either. With full access to world financial markets, Canadian borrowers would prefer to borrow from foreigners at an interest rate of 5 percent than from Canadians at an interest rate of 8 percent. In order to find someone to whom to lend money, Canadian savers would have to offer to lend their savings at 5 percent, the world interest rate. As long as the Canadian and the foreign assets are close substitutes, the difference in interest rates provides an arbitrage opportunity for either borrowers or savers.

interest rate parity
a theory of interest rate determination whereby the real interest rate on comparable financial assets should be the same in all economies with full access to world financial markets

The logic by which the real interest rates in Canada should adjust to equal the real interest rate in the rest of the world should remind you of our discussion of the law of one price and purchasing-power parity. This is because the concepts are closely related. Just as we discussed earlier in the context of the prices of goods, people taking advantage of arbitrage opportunities will ensure that price differentials disappear. The only difference is that here the price we are talking about is the price of borrowing: the real interest rate. The theory that the real interest rate in Canada should equal that in the rest of the world is known as **interest rate parity.**

Limitations to Interest Rate Parity

Just as there are limitations to purchasing-power parity explaining how exchange rates are determined, there are also limitations to interest rate parity explaining how real interest rates are determined. The real interest rate in Canada is not always equal to the real interest rate in the rest of the world, for two key reasons.

The first reason is that financial assets carry with them the possibility of default. That is, while the seller of a financial asset promises to repay the buyer at some future date, the possibility always exists that the seller may not do so. If the seller does in fact renege on this agreement, the seller is said to be in default of the loan. Buyers of financial assets are therefore said to incur a *default risk*. Buyers of financial assets try to learn about relative levels of default risk in order to better evaluate the relative attractiveness of different financial assets. The higher the default risk, the higher the interest rate asset that buyers (savers) demand from asset sellers (borrowers). If the seller of one financial asset is perceived to be more likely to default than the seller of another otherwise similar asset, the difference in the rate of interest paid on these assets may not necessarily represent an arbitrage opportunity. For this reason, interest rate differences may persist.

The second reason why interest rate parity does not always hold in practice is because financial assets offered for sale in different countries are not necessarily perfect substitutes for one another. For example, the manner in which governments tax the returns earned on financial assets differs across countries. While similar assets in two countries may pay the same rate of pre-tax return, different tax regimes in these two countries may result in different after-tax returns. Those seeking arbitrage opportunities look only at after-tax returns. Thus, while after-tax returns will be equalized internationally, differences in pre-tax rates of return will persist

Because of the differences in default risk and in tax treatments, interest rate parity is not a perfect theory of real interest rate determination in a small open economy. For this reason, we do not expect real interest rates in Canada to exactly equal those in the rest of the world. Nonetheless, interest rate parity does offer a persuasive argument for believing that the difference in real interest rates in Canada versus the rest of the world will be relatively small, and that Canadian interest rates will fluctuate with those in the rest of the world.

The data bear this out. Over the 19-year period of 1984–2002, the real interest rates paid on long-term government debt in Canada and the United States have tended to move up and down together. The average real interest rate over this period was 5.2 percent in Canada and 4.4 percent in the United States. The 0.8 percentage-point difference is a measure of how much more, on average, Canadian lenders had to offer to compensate borrowers for higher default risk and higher tax rates in Canada. This difference grew wider during the 1980s and early 1990s as Canadian tax rates increased relative to those in the United States and as frequent constitutional crises and growing levels of government debt raised concerns in the minds of lenders about the possibility of the Canadian government defaulting on its debt.

Since 1996 the difference in interest rates has grown much smaller. Over the period 1996–2002, the difference in real interest rates averaged just 0.4 percentage points and the difference continues to shrink. This change reflects less frequent constitutional crises over this period and the fact that Canadian governments reined in their deficits and began to reduce their debt loads. If we interpret the U.S. interest rate as the "world" interest rate, r^w, then these data provide support for our imposing the interest rate parity condition on our model. That will be our strategy when we turn to the macroeconomic theory of the open economy.

CONCLUSION

The purpose of this chapter has been to develop some basic concepts that macroeconomists use to study open economies. You should now understand why a nation's net imports must equal its net capital outflow, and why national saving must equal domestic investment plus net capital outflow. You should also understand the meaning of the nominal and real exchange rates, as well as the implications and limitations of purchasing-power parity as a theory of how exchange rates are determined. Finally, you should understand why real interest rates in Canada tend to rise and fall with interest rates in the rest of the world.

The macroeconomic variables defined here offer a starting point for analyzing an open economy's interactions with the rest of the world. In the next chapter we develop a model that can explain what determines these variables. We can then discuss how various events and policies affect a country's trade balance and the rate at which nations make exchanges in world markets.

SUMMARY

- Net exports are the value of domestic goods and services sold abroad minus the value of foreign goods and services sold domestically. Net capital outflow is the acquisition of foreign assets by domestic residents minus the acquisition of domestic assets by foreigners. Because every international transaction involves an exchange of an asset for a good or service, an economy's net capital outflow always equals its net exports.

- An economy's saving can be used either to finance investment at home or to buy assets abroad. Thus, national saving equals domestic investment plus net capital outflow.

- The nominal exchange rate is the relative price of the currency of two countries, and the real exchange rate is the relative price of the goods and services of two countries. When the nominal exchange rate changes so that each dollar buys more foreign currency, the dollar is said to *appreciate* or *strengthen*. When the nominal exchange rate changes so that each dollar buys less foreign currency, the dollar is said to *depreciate* or *weaken*.

- According to the theory of purchasing-power parity, a dollar (or a unit of any other currency) should be able to buy the same quantity of goods in all countries. This theory implies that the nominal exchange rate between the currencies of two countries should reflect the price levels in those countries. As a result, countries with relatively high inflation should have depreciating currencies, and countries with relatively low inflation should have appreciating currencies.

- Most economists prefer to use a model that describes Canada as a small open economy with perfect capital mobility. In such economies, interest rate parity is expected to hold. Interest rate parity is a theory that predicts interest rates in Canada will equal those in the rest of the world. Due to differences in tax rates and concerns about default risk, interest rates in Canada are not expected to exactly equal those in the rest of the world, but we do expect Canadian interest rates to rise and fall with increases and decreases in world interest rates.

KEY CONCEPTS

QUESTIONS FOR REVIEW

1. Define net exports and net capital outflow. Explain how and why they are related.

2. Explain the relationship among saving, investment, and net capital outflow.

3. If a car in Japan costs 500 000 yen, a similar car in Canada costs $10 000, and a dollar can buy 100 yen, what are the nominal and real exchange rates?

4. Describe the economic logic behind the theory of purchasing-power parity.

5. If the Bank of Canada started printing large quantities of Canadian dollars, what would happen to the number of Japanese yen a dollar could buy?

6. Describe the economic logic behind the theory of interest rate parity.

PROBLEMS AND APPLICATIONS

1. How would the following transactions affect Canada's exports, imports, and net exports?
   a. A Canadian art professor spends the summer touring museums in Europe.
   b. Students in Paris flock to see the latest Diana Krall concert.
   c. Your uncle buys a new Volvo.
   d. The student bookstore at Oxford University sells a pair of Bauer hockey skates.
   e. A Canadian citizen shops at a store in northern Vermont to avoid Canadian sales taxes.

2. International trade in each of the following products has increased over time. Suggest some reasons why this might be so.
   a. wheat
   b. banking services
   c. computer software
   d. automobiles

3. Describe the difference between foreign direct investment and foreign portfolio investment. Who is more likely to engage in foreign direct investment—a corporation or an individual investor? Who is more likely to engage in foreign portfolio investment?

4. How would the following transactions affect Canada's net capital outflow? Also, state whether each involves direct investment or portfolio investment.
   a. A Canadian cellular phone company establishes an office in the Czech Republic.
   b. Harrod's of London sells stock to the Ontario Teachers' Pension Plan.
   c. Honda expands its factory in Alliston, Ontario.
   d. An Altamira mutual fund sells its Volkswagen stock to a French investor.

5. Holding national saving constant, does an increase in net capital outflow increase, decrease, or have no effect on a country's accumulation of domestic capital?

6. The business section of most major newspapers contains a table showing Canadian exchange rates. Find such a table and use it to answer the following questions.
   a. Does this table show nominal or real exchange rates? Explain.
   b. What are the exchange rates between the United States and Canada and between Canada and Japan? Calculate the exchange rate between the United States and Japan.
   c. If Canadian inflation exceeds Japanese inflation over the next year, would you expect the Canadian dollar to appreciate or depreciate relative to the Japanese yen?

7. Would each of the following groups be happy or unhappy if the Canadian dollar appreciated? Explain.
   a. Dutch pension funds holding Canadian government bonds
   b. Canadian manufacturing industries
   c. Australian tourists planning a trip to Canada

d. A Canadian firm trying to purchase property overseas

8. What is happening to Canada's real exchange rate in each of the following situations? Explain.
   a. Canada's nominal exchange rate is unchanged, but prices rise faster in Canada than abroad.
   b. Canada's nominal exchange rate is unchanged, but prices rise faster abroad than in Canada.
   c. Canada's nominal exchange rate declines, and prices are unchanged in Canada and abroad.
   d. Canada's nominal exchange rate declines, and prices rise faster abroad than in Canada.

9. List three goods for which the law of one price is likely to hold, and three goods for which it is not. Justify your choices.

10. A can of pop costs $0.75 in Canada and 12 pesos in Mexico. What would the peso–dollar exchange rate be if purchasing-power parity holds? If a monetary expansion caused all prices in Mexico to double, so that the price of pop rose to 24 pesos, what would happen to the peso–dollar exchange rate?

11. Assume that Canadian wheat sells for $100 per bushel, Russian wheat sells for 1600 rubles per bushel, and the nominal exchange rate is 4 rubles per dollar.
    a. Explain how you could make a profit from this situation. What would be your profit per bushel of wheat? If other people exploit the same opportunity, what would happen to the price of wheat in Russia and the price of wheat in Canada?
    b. Suppose that wheat is the only commodity in the world. What would happen to the real exchange rate between Canada and Russia?

12. A case study in the chapter analyzed purchasing-power parity for several countries using the price of Big Macs. Here are data for a few more countries:

Country	Price of a Big Mac	Predicted Exchange Rate	Actual Exchange Rate
Indonesia	16 100 rupiah	_____ rupiah/$US	8740 rupiah/$US
Hungary	490 forint	_____ forint/$US	224 forint/$US
Czech Republic	56.57 koruna	_____ koruna/$US	28.9 koruna/$US
Thailand	59.0 baht	_____ baht/$US	42.7 baht/$US
China	9.90 yuan	_____ yuan/$US	8.28 yuan/$US

a. For each country, compute the predicted exchange rate of the local currency per U.S. dollar. (Recall that the U.S. price of a Big Mac was $2.71.) How well does the theory of purchasing-power parity explain exchange rates?
b. According to purchasing-power parity, what is the predicted exchange rate between the Hungarian forint and the Chinese yuan? What is the actual exchange rate?

INTERNET RESOURCES

- Data on Canadian exports and imports are available from the Statistics Canada website at http://www.statcan.ca. From the main menu at the top of the screen, choose "Canadian Statistics," then, under "The Economy," select "International Trade." There you will find information on exports and imports by type of good and service (automotive products versus forestry products, etc.) and by the country with which Canada is trading.

- For a list of all international trade agreements that Canada has signed with other countries, visit the Government of Canada website at http://canadianeconomy.gc.ca/english/economy/issues.html. Follow the links at that site to learn about the North American Free Trade Agreement (NAFTA), the Canada–World Trade Organization (WTO) agreement, and many more.

- If you're planning a trip abroad and want to know the latest value of the exchange rate between the Canadian dollar and the currency of the country you plan to visit, use the currency converter available at the Bank of Canada website at http://www.bankofcanada.ca/en/exchange.htm.

http://   For more study tools, please visit http://www.mankiw3e.nelson.com.

© JOSON.ZEFA

14

Learning Objectives

In this chapter, you will ...

- Build a model to explain an open economy's trade balance and exchange rate
- Use the model to analyze the effects of government budget deficits
- Use the model to analyze the macroeconomic effects of trade policies
- Use the model to analyze political instability and capital flight

A MACROECONOMIC THEORY OF THE OPEN ECONOMY

Issues related to international trade are of constant concern to Canadians. In part this is because many Canadians are employed in industries that depend on international trade, and because all Canadians consume goods and services that are available only because of trade. Trade issues are also of concern to Canadians because these issues are often the sources of conflict with our trading partners. For example, softwood lumber producers in the United States have claimed that Canadian softwood lumber producers receive an unfair competitive advantage due to the nature of certain government policies. These claims have led to conflict and spawned a prolonged process of negotiation to resolve the issue.

Canadians have often expressed concern about the purchase of Canadian assets by foreigners. As we have seen, Canada's net capital outflow (NCO) has been negative for much of the past 40 years. Over that period, foreigners purchased more Canadian assets than Canadians purchased foreign assets. As a result, many firms located in Canada are owned by foreigners. In the past, this situation has prompted the government to introduce legislation designed to limit the extent of foreign ownership. Quite recently, however, Canada's NCO has become quite large and positive, indicating that Canadians are now buying more foreign assets than foreigners are buying Canadian assets. To some, this situation is also indicative of economic problems: Canadians' savings are going abroad to purchase foreign assets.

Imagine that you are the prime minister and some people are demanding that you do something about the fact that Canada's net capital outflow is positive, while others are ready to criticize if net capital outflow returns to negative values. What should you do? Should you try to place limits on international trade? Should you discourage or encourage foreigners to buy Canadian oil and gas firms?

To understand what factors determine a country's trade balance and how government policies can affect it, we need a macroeconomic theory of the open economy. The preceding chapter introduced some of the key macroeconomic variables that describe an economy's relationship with other economies—including net exports, net capital outflow, and the real and nominal exchange rates. This chapter develops a model that identifies the forces that determine these variables and shows how these variables are related to one another.

To develop this macroeconomic model of an open economy, we build on our previous analysis in three important ways. First, the model takes the economy's GDP as given. We assume that the economy's output of goods and services, as measured by real GDP, is determined by the supplies of the factors of production and by the available production technology that turns these inputs into output. Second, the model takes the economy's price level as given. We assume that the price level adjusts to bring the supply and demand for money into balance. Third, the model takes the real interest rate as given. The real interest rate is assumed to equal the world interest rate because of perfect capital mobility. In other words, this chapter takes as a starting point the lessons learned in previous chapters about the determination of the economy's output, interest rate, and price level.

The goal of the model in this chapter is to highlight the forces that determine the economy's trade balance and exchange rate. In one sense, the model is simple: It applies the tools of supply and demand to an open economy. Yet the model is also more complicated than others we have seen because it involves looking simultaneously at two related markets—the market for loanable funds and the market for foreign-currency exchange. After we develop this model of the open economy, we use it to examine how various events and policies affect the economy's trade balance and exchange rate.

SUPPLY AND DEMAND FOR LOANABLE FUNDS AND FOR FOREIGN-CURRENCY EXCHANGE

To understand the forces at work in an open economy, we focus on supply and demand in two markets. The first is the market for loanable funds, which coordinates the economy's saving, investment, and the flow of loanable funds abroad (called the net capital outflow). The second is the market for foreign-currency exchange, which coordinates people who want to exchange the domestic currency for the currency of other countries. In this section we discuss supply and demand in each of these markets. In the next section we put these markets together to explain the overall equilibrium for an open economy.

The Market for Loanable Funds

When we first analyzed the role of the financial system in Chapter 8, we made the simplifying assumption that the financial system consists of only one market, called the *market for loanable funds*. All savers go to this market to deposit their saving, and all borrowers go to this market to get their loans. In this market, there is one interest rate, which is both the return to saving and the cost of borrowing.

To understand the market for loanable funds in an open economy, the place to start is the identity discussed in the preceding chapter:

$$S = I + NCO$$

$$\text{Saving} = \text{Domestic investment} + \text{Net capital outflow}$$

This identity emphasizes that in an open economy the amount that a nation saves does not have to equal the amount it spends to purchase domestic capital. If the amount of national saving exceeds the amount needed to finance the purchase of domestic capital, the amount left over can be used to finance the purchase of an asset abroad. In this case, net capital outflow (NCO) is a positive number. If national saving is insufficient to finance the purchase of domestic capital, the shortfall can be met by the savings of foreigners. In this case, NCO is a negative number. The equation identifies the three components of the market for loanable funds in an open economy and shows how they are related. The demand for loanable funds comes from domestic investment (I).

In Canada the supply of loanable funds from national saving (S) has at times not been sufficient to satisfy the demand for loanable funds for investment (I), so we have had $S < I$. In those cases, the shortfall has been met by the savings of foreigners and *net capital outflow* has been negative. For much of the past 40 years, that situation described the Canadian experience. At other times in Canada, the supply of loanable funds from national saving (S) has been more than sufficient to satisfy the demand for loanable funds from investment (I), so $S > I$. In those cases, Canadian savings have been used to purchase foreign assets and NCO has been positive. That situation has described the Canadian experience since 1999. In both of these cases, the identity relating values of national saving (S), domestic investment (I), and net capital outflow (NCO) has been satisfied.

As we learned in our earlier discussion of the market for loanable funds, the quantity of loanable funds supplied and the quantity of loanable funds demanded depend on the real interest rate. A higher real interest rate encourages people to save and, therefore, raises the quantity of loanable funds made available by national saving. A higher interest rate also makes borrowing to finance capital projects more costly; thus, it discourages investment and reduces the quantity of loanable funds demanded.

The next step in understanding the market for loanable funds in a small open economy is to recall our discussion from the preceding chapter on interest rate determination. We found that in a small open economy with perfect capital mobility, like Canada, if we ignore differences in tax treatments and default risk, the domestic interest rate will equal the world interest rate. The reason for this is simple. Suppose that the Canadian interest rate is 5 percent and the world interest rate is 8 percent. This situation cannot persist because with full access to world financial markets, Canadian savers would prefer to buy foreign assets that pay the higher interest rate. We would expect to see savers sell their holdings of Canadian assets and buy foreign assets instead. To halt the sale of Canadian assets, Canadian borrowers would have to offer to pay the more attractive world interest rate of 8 percent. Similarly, if the world interest rate is 5 percent and the Canadian interest rate is 8 percent, Canadian borrowers would prefer to borrow from foreigners. In order to find someone to whom to lend money, Canadian savers would have to offer to lend their savings at 5 percent, the world interest rate.

The market for loanable funds is represented in the familiar supply-and-demand diagram in Figure 14.1. As in our earlier analysis of the financial system, the demand curve slopes downward because a higher interest rate decreases the quantity of loanable funds demanded, and the supply curve slopes upward because a higher interest rate increases the quantity of loanable funds supplied. Unlike the situation in our previous discussion, however, in a small open economy with perfect capital mobility, the supply curve represents only part of the supply of loanable funds available. The supply curve shows the amount of national saving—the savings of Canadians—available at every real interest rate. It shows, then, that a higher interest rate increases the quantity of loanable funds made available by Canadians. If, we were discussing a closed economy, we would need to consider only the supply of loanable funds made available by the savings of Canadians. In that case we would conclude that the real rate of interest would be determined by the intersection of the demand and supply curves for loanable funds. In a small open economy with perfect capital mobility, however, the interest rate is equal to the world interest rate, and we need to also consider the role played by the savings of foreigners.

In panel (a) of Figure 14.1, the world interest rate is greater than the Canadian interest rate would be if this were a closed economy. Because there is perfect capital mobility, the Canadian interest rate is given by the world interest rate. At this interest rate, the demand for loanable funds in Canada (*I*) is $100 billion, and the supply of loanable funds that Canadians make available (*S*) is $150 billion. At this world interest rate, the supply of Canadians' savings is more than enough to satisfy the demand for loanable funds in Canada. The excess supply of loanable funds, $50 billion, is therefore available to purchase foreign assets. In this situation, net capital outflow (*NCO*) is $50 billion. Note that *S* = *I* + *NCO*, as required by our accounting identity.

In panel (b) of Figure 14.1, the world interest rate is shown as being less than the interest rate would be if this were a closed economy. At this world interest rate, the demand for loanable funds in Canada (*I*) is now $130 billion, and the supply of loanable funds that Canadians make available (*S*) is $90 billion. At this world interest rate, the supply of Canadians' savings is not enough to satisfy the demand for loanable funds in Canada. The excess demand for loanable funds, $40 billion, must therefore be satisfied by the savings of foreigners. In this situation, *NCO* takes on a negative value: –$40 billion. (Don't be confused by the negative number. We have defined net capital outflow as the amount of foreign assets that Canadians purchase minus the amount of Canadian assets that foreigners buy. A negative value simply indicates a net purchase of Canadian assets by foreigners.) Note that, once again, *S* = *I* + *NCO* as required by our accounting identity.

These two diagrams show that the market for loanable funds in a small open economy with perfect capital mobility is different from that in a closed economy. In particular, the interest rate is no longer determined by the demand and supply of loanable funds. Instead, the interest rate is equal to the world interest rate. As

FIGURE 14.1

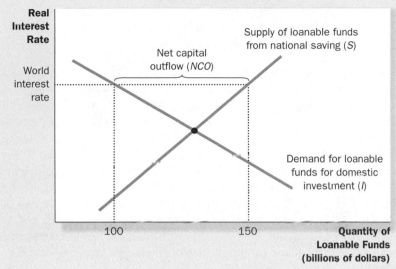

(a) Positive Net Capital Outflow

Real Interest Rate

World interest rate

Supply of loanable funds from national saving (S)

Net capital outflow (NCO)

Demand for loanable funds for domestic investment (I)

100   150   Quantity of Loanable Funds (billions of dollars)

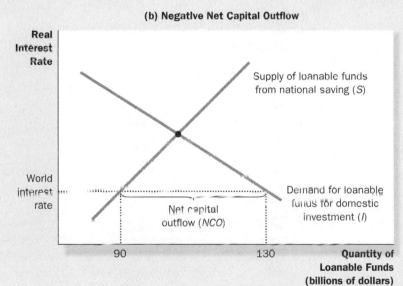

(b) Negative Net Capital Outflow

Real Interest Rate

Supply of loanable funds from national saving (S)

World interest rate

Demand for loanable funds for domestic investment (I)

Net capital outflow (NCO)

90   130   Quantity of Loanable Funds (billions of dollars)

The Market for Loanable Funds

In a small open economy with perfect capital mobility, like Canada, the domestic real interest rate is equal to the world real interest rate. Domestic investment determines the demand for loanable funds. National saving determines the supply of loanable funds provided by Canadians. In panel (a), at the world interest rate domestic investment is $100 billion and Canadians save $150 billion. The difference between domestic investment and national saving, $50 billion, is net capital outflow. It measures the value of foreign assets purchased by Canadians. In panel (b), at the world interest rate domestic investment is $130 billion and Canadians save only $90 billion. The shortfall of national saving relative to domestic investment, $40 billion, is made up by the savings of foreigners. In this case, net capital outflow is negative, indicating that foreigners are purchasing more Canadian assets than Canadians are purchasing foreign assets.

a result, the quantity of loanable funds made available by the savings of Canadians does not have to equal the quantity of loanable funds demanded for domestic investment. The difference between these two amounts is net capital outflow. Net capital outflow is determined by the difference between the supply of loanable funds due to national saving (S) and the demand for loanable funds (I) at the world interest rate. If we recall another identity from the preceding chapter,

$$NCO = NX$$
$$\text{Net capital outflow} = \text{Net exports}$$

we can also state this result as follows: Net exports are determined by the difference between the supply of loanable funds due to national saving (S) and the demand for loanable funds (I) at the world interest rate. These two statements are equivalent because net exports must equal net capital outflow.

The Market for Foreign-Currency Exchange

The second market in our model of the open economy is the market for foreign-currency exchange. The market for foreign exchange exists because people want to trade goods, services, and financial assets with people in other countries, but they want to be paid for these things in their own currency. This means that, for a Canadian to purchase a good, service, or financial asset from someone in another country, the Canadian must purchase the other country's currency as well. Similarly, for a foreigner to purchase a good, service, or financial asset from someone in Canada, the foreigner must purchase Canadian dollars. The need to make these currency exchanges means that a market must exist where the exchanges can take place. This is the foreign-currency exchange market. In this section we will describe the market in which Canadian dollars are traded for foreign currencies.

To understand the market for foreign-currency exchange, we begin with the accounting identity we just discussed:

$$NCO = NX$$

Net capital outflow = Net exports

If we combine this identity with the identity we discussed earlier,

$$S = I + NCO$$

Saving = Domestic investment + Net capital outflow

we see that

$$S - I = NX$$

Saving − Domestic investment = Net exports

Each of these statements is an identity and, as such, each describes a relationship that must be true. The last identity is useful for describing the market for foreign-currency exchange. This identity states that the imbalance between the domestic supply of loanable funds that is due to national saving (S) and the demand for loanable funds for domestic investment (I) must equal the imbalance between exports and imports (NX). This must be true because, as we have just seen, the imbalance between the domestic supply and demand for loanable funds must equal net capital outflow (NCO), which in turn must equal net exports.

We can view the two sides of this identity as representing the two sides of the market for foreign-currency exchange. The difference between national saving and domestic investment represents net capital outflow. This difference, then, represents the quantity of dollars supplied in the market for foreign-currency exchange for the purpose of buying foreign assets. For example, when a Canadian mutual fund wants to buy a Japanese government bond, it needs to exchange dollars for yen, so it *supplies* dollars in a market for foreign-currency exchange. Net exports represent the quantity of dollars demanded in that market for the purpose of buying Canadian net exports of goods and services. For example, when a

Japanese airline wants to buy a plane made by Bombardier, it needs to exchange its yen for dollars, so it *demands* dollars in the market for foreign-currency exchange.

What price balances the supply and demand in the market for foreign-currency exchange? The answer is the real exchange rate. As we saw in the preceding chapter, the real exchange rate is the relative price of domestic and foreign goods and, therefore, is a key determinant of net exports. When Canada's real exchange rate appreciates, Canadian goods become more expensive relative to foreign goods, making Canadian goods less attractive to consumers both at home and abroad. As a result, exports from Canada fall, and imports into Canada rise. For both reasons, net exports fall. Hence, an appreciation of the real exchange rate reduces the quantity of dollars demanded in the market for foreign currency exchange.

Figure 14.2 shows supply and demand in the market for foreign-currency exchange. The demand curve slopes downward for the reason we just discussed: A higher real exchange rate makes Canadian goods more expensive and reduces the quantity of dollars demanded to buy those goods. The supply curve is vertical

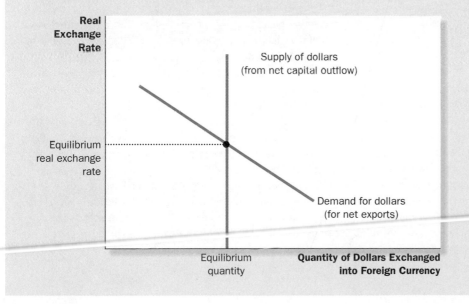

FIGURE 14.2

The Market for Foreign-Currency Exchange

The real exchange rate is determined by the supply and demand for foreign-currency exchange. The supply of dollars to be exchanged into foreign currency comes from net capital outflow. Net capital outflow, in turn, equals the difference between the demand for loanable funds (domestic investment) and the supply of loanable funds made available by the savings of Canadians. Because neither domestic savings nor domestic investment depends on the real exchange rate, the supply curve is vertical. The demand for dollars comes from net exports. Because a lower real exchange rate stimulates net exports (and thus increases the quantity of dollars demanded to pay for these net exports), the demand curve is downward sloping. At the equilibrium real exchange rate, the number of dollars people supply to buy foreign assets exactly balances the number of dollars people demand to buy net exports.

Real Exchange Rate

Supply of dollars
(from net capital outflow)

Equilibrium
real exchange
rate

Demand for dollars
(for net exports)

Equilibrium
quantity

**Quantity of Dollars Exchanged
into Foreign Currency**

because the quantity of dollars supplied for net capital outflow does not depend on the real exchange rate. (As discussed earlier, net capital outflow depends on the real interest rate. When discussing the market for foreign-currency exchange, we take the real interest rate and net capital outflow as given.)

The real exchange rate adjusts to balance the supply and demand for dollars just as the price of any good adjusts to balance supply and demand for that good. If the real exchange rate were below the equilibrium level, the quantity of dollars supplied would be less than the quantity demanded. The resulting shortage of dollars would push the value of the dollar upward. Conversely, if the real exchange rate were above the equilibrium level, the quantity of dollars supplied would exceed the quantity demanded. The surplus of dollars would drive the value of the dollar downward. *At the equilibrium real exchange rate, the demand for dollars to buy net exports exactly balances the supply of dollars to be exchanged into foreign currency to buy assets abroad.*

At this point, it is worth noting that the division of transactions between "supply" and "demand" in this model is somewhat artificial. In our model, net exports are the source of the demand for dollars, and net capital outflow is the source of the supply. Thus, when a Canadian resident imports a car made in Japan, our model treats that transaction as a decrease in the quantity of dollars demanded (because net exports fall) rather than an increase in the quantity of dollars supplied. Similarly, when a Japanese citizen buys a Canadian government bond, our model treats that transaction as a decrease in the quantity of dollars supplied (because net capital outflow falls) rather than an increase in the quantity

FYI

PURCHASING-POWER PARITY AS A SPECIAL CASE

An alert reader of this book might ask: Why are we developing a theory of the exchange rate here? Didn't we already do that in the preceding chapter?

As you may recall, the preceding chapter developed a theory of the exchange rate called *purchasing-power parity*. This theory asserts that a dollar (or any other currency) must buy the same quantity of goods and services in every country. As a result, the real exchange rate is fixed, and all changes in the nominal exchange rate between two currencies reflect changes in the price levels in the two countries.

The model of the exchange rate developed here is related to the theory of purchasing-power parity. According to the theory of

purchasing-power parity, international trade responds quickly to international price differences. If goods were cheaper in one country than in another, they would be exported from the first country and imported into the second until the price difference disappeared. In other words, the theory of purchasing-power parity assumes that net exports are highly responsive to small changes in the real exchange rate. If net exports were in fact so responsive, the demand curve in Figure 14.2 would be horizontal.

Thus, the theory of purchasing-power parity can be viewed as a special case of the model considered here. In that special case, the demand curve for foreign-currency exchange, rather than being downward sloping, is horizontal at the level of the real exchange rate that ensures parity of purchasing power at home and abroad. That special case is a good place to start when studying exchange rates, but it is far from the end of the story.

This chapter, therefore, concentrates on the more realistic case in which the demand curve for foreign-currency exchange is downward sloping. This allows for the possibility that the real exchange rate changes over time, as in fact it sometimes does in the real world.

of dollars demanded. This use of language may seem somewhat unnatural at first, but it will prove useful when analyzing the effects of various policies.

QuickQuiz Describe the sources of supply and demand in the market for loanable funds and the market for foreign-currency exchange.

EQUILIBRIUM IN THE OPEN ECONOMY

So far we have discussed supply and demand in two markets—the market for loanable funds and the market for foreign-currency exchange. Let's now consider how these markets are related to each other.

Net Capital Outflow: The Link between the Two Markets

We begin by recapping what we've learned so far in this chapter. We have been discussing how the economy coordinates four important macroeconomic variables: national saving (S), domestic investment (I), net capital outflow (NCO), and net exports (NX). Keep in mind the following identities:

$$S = I + NCO$$

and

$$NCO = NX$$

In the market for loanable funds, national saving provides the domestic supply, demand comes from domestic investment, and net capital outflow is the difference between the two at the world interest rate. In the market for foreign-currency exchange, supply comes from net capital outflow, demand comes from net exports, and the real exchange rate balances supply and demand.

Net capital outflow is the variable that links these two markets. In the market for loanable funds, net capital outflow is the difference between domestic investment and national saving at the world interest rate. A change in domestic investment, national saving, or the world interest rate will cause net capital outflow to change. A change in net capital outflow means a Canadian is buying or selling foreign assets. Because a person who wants to buy an asset in another country must supply dollars in order to exchange them for the currency of that country, a change in net capital outflow affects the market for foreign-currency exchange.

The key determinant of net capital outflow, as we have discussed, is the world interest rate. When the world interest rate is higher than the interest rate that equates the demand for loanable funds in Canada to the supply of loanable funds coming from the savings of Canadians, as in panel (a) of Figure 14.1, net capital outflow is positive and is equal to the difference between national saving and the demand for loanable funds. When the world interest rate is lower than the interest rate that equates the demand for loanable funds in Canada to the supply of loanable funds coming from the savings of Canadians, as in panel (b) of Figure 14.1, net capital outflow is negative and is equal to the difference between national saving and the demand for loanable funds.

Simultaneous Equilibrium in Two Markets

We can now put all the pieces of our model together in Figure 14.3. This figure shows how the market for loanable funds and the market for foreign-currency exchange jointly determine the important macroeconomic variables of an open economy.

Panel (a) of Figure 14.3 shows the market for loanable funds (taken from Figure 14.1). As before, national saving measures the supply of loanable funds made available by the savings of Canadians. Domestic investment is the source of

FIGURE 14.3

The Real Equilibrium in a Small Open Economy

In panel (a), the real interest rate is determined by the world real interest rate. At the world interest rate, national saving (S) exceeds the demand for loanable funds for domestic investment (I). The difference (S – I) measures net capital outflow. In panel (b), net capital outflow determines the supply of Canadian dollars offered for sale in the market for foreign-currency exchange. The demand for foreign-currency exchange is determined by Canada's net exports. The equilibrium real exchange rate (E_1) brings into balance the quantity of dollars supplied and the quantity of dollars demanded in the market for foreign-currency exchange.

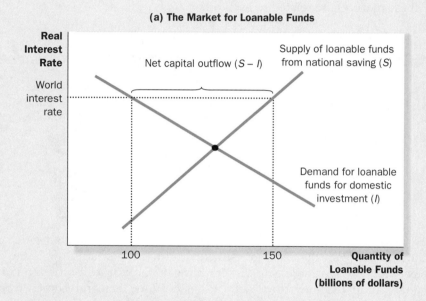

(a) The Market for Loanable Funds

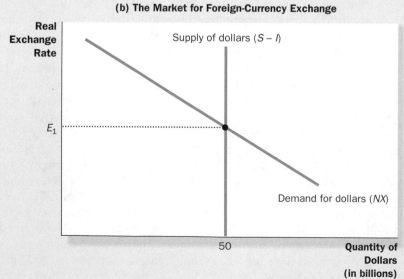

(b) The Market for Foreign-Currency Exchange

the demand for loanable funds. The world interest rate determines the quantity of loanable funds demanded ($100 billion) and the quantity of loanable funds supplied by the savings of Canadians ($150 billion). The difference between these amounts, $50 billion, measures the amount of national saving available to purchase foreign assets. Because national saving is more than sufficient to provide loanable funds for domestic investment, the excess is used to buy foreign assets. This is net capital outflow.

Panel (b) of the figure shows the market for foreign-currency exchange (taken from Figure 14.2). Because national saving is more than enough to provide for domestic investment, Canadians are purchasing foreign assets. Since to do so they must purchase foreign currency, they must sell Canadian dollars in the market for foreign exchange. For this reason, the quantity of net capital outflow from panel (a) determines the supply of dollars to be exchanged into foreign currencies. The real exchange rate does not affect net capital outflow, so the supply curve is vertical. The demand for dollars comes from net exports. Because a depreciation of the real exchange rate increases net exports, the demand curve for foreign-currency exchange slopes downward. The equilibrium real exchange rate (E_1) brings into balance the quantity of dollars supplied and the quantity of dollars demanded in the market for foreign-currency exchange.

The two markets shown in Figure 14.3 determine the real exchange rate, national saving, domestic investment, and the size of net foreign investment. National saving, domestic investment, and net foreign investment are determined in panel (a). National saving and domestic investment are determined by the world interest rate. Net foreign investment is the difference between these amounts. The real exchange rate determined in panel (b) is the price of domestic goods and services relative to foreign goods and services. We will use this model soon to see how all of these variables change when some policy or event causes one of these curves to shift.

QuickQuiz In the model of the open economy just developed, two markets determine one price and the value of three variables. What are the markets? What three variables are determined? What price is determined?

HOW POLICIES AND EVENTS AFFECT AN OPEN ECONOMY

Having developed a model to explain how key macroeconomic variables are determined in an open economy, we can now use the model to analyze how changes in policy and other events alter the economy's equilibrium. As we proceed, keep in mind that our model is just supply and demand in two markets—the market for loanable funds and the market for foreign-currency exchange. When using the model to analyze any event, we can apply the three steps outlined in Chapter 4. First, we determine which of the supply and demand curves the event affects. Second, we determine which way the curves shift. Third, we use the supply-and-demand diagrams to examine how these shifts alter the economy's equilibrium.

NEGATIVE VALUES OF NET CAPITAL OUTFLOW

In this section we use our model to analyze how policy changes and economic events alter the economy's equilibrium. Throughout this section we will be considering a small open economy such as the one described in Figure 14.3, an economy in which net capital outflow is a positive amount. Earlier, we saw evidence that in the past Canada's NCO has often been negative. How would our analyses in this section change for this case?

The answer is: very little. The difference is that now national saving is insufficient to provide for domestic investment, and Canada must rely on the savings of foreigners to make up the difference. This is net capital outflow again, but this time it is a negative number. Since NCO must equal net exports, net exports must be negative too. This means that foreigners are seeking to buy Canadian assets and therefore want to purchase Canadian dollars in the foreign-currency exchange market. On the goods side, Canadians are buying more foreign goods than foreigners are buying Canadian goods. Thus, Cana-dians want to purchase foreign currencies and to do so they must sell Canadian dollars in the foreign-currency exchange market. Now the demand for dollars is coming from net capital outflow, while the supply is coming from net exports.

It is worth repeating what we noted earlier—the division of transactions between "supply" and "demand" in the market for foreign-currency exchange is somewhat artificial. Whether net capital outflow is a source of supply to this market or a source of demand depends on whether it takes on a positive or a negative value. Similarly, whether the value of net exports is a source of supply or demand in this market depends on whether net exports are positive or negative. It is essential to understand that the real exchange rate is determined by the supply and demand for foreign-currency exchange and that the supply and demand of foreign-currency exchange come from net capital outflow and net exports.

Fortunately for our purposes in this section, whether net capital outflow and net exports are positive or negative is not relevant. All that matters is the *direction of change* in these values. For this reason, we rely on presentations that involve positive values of net capital outflow and net exports because this makes for an easier discussion and because it describes the current situation in Canada. However, the results we derive in this section would be exactly the same whether we assumed positive or negative values of net capital outflow and net exports.

Increase in World Interest Rates

We have seen that in a small open economy with perfect capital mobility, the real interest rate is equal to the world real interest rate. One implication of this fact is that events outside Canada that cause the world interest rate to change can have important effects on the Canadian economy. This explains why Canadian newspapers so often report changes to interest rates in the United States. Because the United States is the largest economy in the world, movements in U.S. interest rates are responsible in large part for movements in the world interest rate. Indeed, it is not unreasonable to treat the U.S. interest rate as the world interest rate. Changes in U.S. interest rates therefore have important implications for Canada.

Figure 14.4 shows the effect of an increase in the world interest rate on a small open economy with perfect capital mobility. In panel (a), which shows the market for loanable funds, no curves shift. Instead, the increase in the world interest rate causes a slide up the supply and demand curves for loanable funds. The quantity of loanable funds made available by the savings of Canadians rises. The quantity of loanable funds demanded for domestic investment falls. Both of these changes cause an increase in the amount by which the savings of Canadians exceed the demand for loanable funds in Canada. This excess is net capital outflow, and it measures the amount of Canadian saving that is available to purchase foreign assets.

FIGURE 14.4

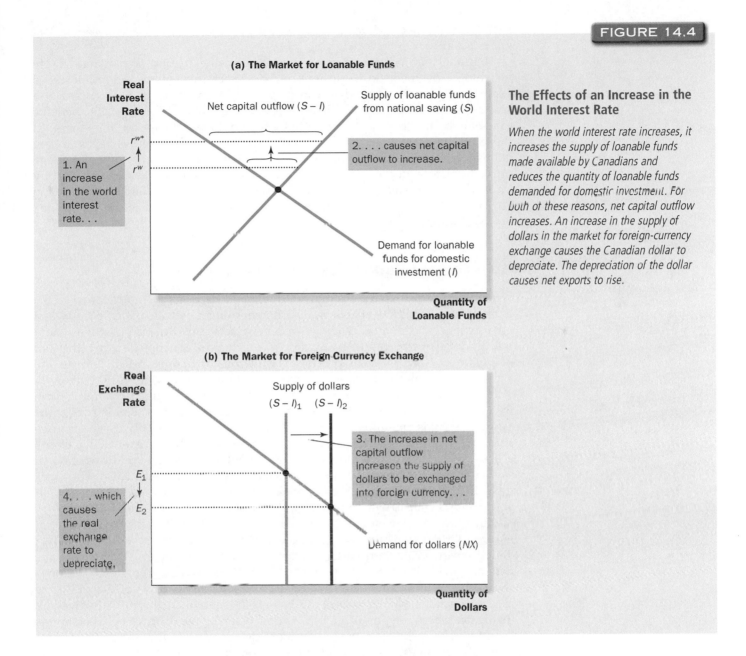

(a) The Market for Loanable Funds

Real Interest Rate

Net capital outflow (S − I)

Supply of loanable funds from national saving (S)

r^{w*}
r^w

2. . . . causes net capital outflow to increase.

1. An increase in the world interest rate. . .

Demand for loanable funds for domestic investment (I)

Quantity of Loanable Funds

(b) The Market for Foreign-Currency Exchange

Real Exchange Rate

Supply of dollars

$(S − I)_1$ $(S − I)_2$

E_1

E_2

3. The increase in net capital outflow increases the supply of dollars to be exchanged into foreign currency. . .

4. . . . which causes the real exchange rate to depreciate,

Demand for dollars (NX)

Quantity of Dollars

The Effects of an Increase in the World Interest Rate

When the world interest rate increases, it increases the supply of loanable funds made available by Canadians and reduces the quantity of loanable funds demanded for domestic investment. For both of these reasons, net capital outflow increases. An increase in the supply of dollars in the market for foreign-currency exchange causes the Canadian dollar to depreciate. The depreciation of the dollar causes net exports to rise.

In panel (b), the increase in net capital outflow shifts the curve that measures the supply of dollars to be exchanged in the market for foreign-currency exchange to the right, from $(S − I)_1$ to $(S − I)_2$. The increased supply of dollars causes the real exchange rate to depreciate from E_1 to E_2. That is, the dollar becomes less valuable relative to other currencies. This depreciation, in turn, makes Canadian goods less expensive compared with foreign goods. Because people both at home and abroad switch their purchases toward the less expensive Canadian goods, exports from Canada rise and imports into Canada fall. For both reasons, Canada's net exports rise. Hence, *in a small open economy with perfect capital mobility, an increase in the world interest rate crowds out domestic investment, causes the dollar to depreciate, and causes net exports to rise.*

This analysis indicates why it is not surprising to find Canadians closely watching movements in world interest rates. Such movements are of interest to exporters, importers, Canadian consumers, and Canadian firms. An increase in world interest rates, by causing the Canadian dollar to depreciate, benefits exporters by making goods priced in Canadian dollars cheaper to foreigners. At the same time, the depreciation of the dollar hurts Canadian importers by making goods priced in foreign currencies more expensive to Canadians. Given the large quantity of foreign goods they purchase, Canadian consumers are also hurt by increases in world interest rates. Finally, of course, those Canadian firms planning new investment projects must now pay a higher rate of interest on funds they borrow for that purpose.

Government Budget Deficits and Surpluses

When we first discussed the supply and demand for loanable funds earlier in the book, we examined the effects of government budget deficits, which occur when government spending exceeds government revenue. Because a government budget deficit represents *negative* public saving, it reduces national saving (the sum of public and private saving). Thus, a government budget deficit reduces the supply of loanable funds, drives up the interest rate, and crowds out investment.

Now let's consider the effects of a budget deficit in an open economy. First, which curve in our model shifts? As in a closed economy, the initial impact of the budget deficit is on national saving and, therefore, on the supply curve for loanable funds. Second, which way does this supply curve shift? Again as in a closed economy, a budget deficit represents *negative* public saving, so it reduces national saving and shifts the supply curve for loanable funds to the left. This is shown as the shift to the left of the curve that measures the supply of loanable funds available from national saving in panel (a) of Figure 14.5.

Our third and final step is to compare the old and new equilibria. Panel (a) of Figure 14.5 shows the impact of an increase in a Canadian government budget deficit on the Canadian market for loanable funds. At the world interest rate, national saving is less now than it was before. This decrease in national saving is shown by the movement from point A to point B. As a result of this shift, the excess of national saving over domestic investment, which was initially given by the distance between points A and C, is now given by the distance between points B and C. The increase in the government deficit reduces the excess of national saving over domestic investment and therefore causes net capital outflow to fall.

Panel (b) shows how the increase in the budget deficit affects the market for foreign-currency exchange. Because net capital outflow is reduced, the supply of Canadian dollars offered for sale in the market for foreign-currency exchange is reduced. This decrease in the supply of dollars is shown by the movement of the supply curve from $(S-I)_1$ to $(S-I)_2$. The reduced supply of dollars causes the real exchange rate to appreciate from E_1 to E_2. That is, the dollar becomes more valuable relative to foreign currencies. This appreciation, in turn, makes Canadian goods more expensive compared with foreign goods. Because people both at home and abroad switch their purchases away from more expensive Canadian goods, exports from Canada fall and imports to Canada rise. For both reasons,

FIGURE 14.5

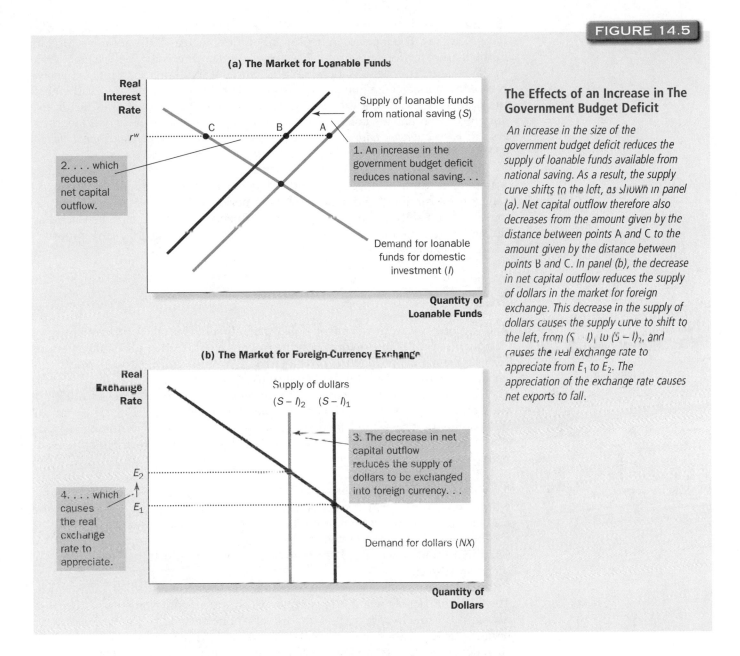

(a) The Market for Loanable Funds

Real Interest Rate

Supply of loanable funds from national saving (S)

r^w

C   B   A

1. An increase in the government budget deficit reduces national saving. . .

2. . . . which reduces net capital outflow.

Demand for loanable funds for domestic investment (I)

Quantity of Loanable Funds

(b) The Market for Foreign-Currency Exchange

Real Exchange Rate

Supply of dollars

$(S - I)_2$ $(S - I)_1$

3. The decrease in net capital outflow reduces the supply of dollars to be exchanged into foreign currency. . .

E_2

4. . . . which causes the real exchange rate to appreciate.

E_1

Demand for dollars (NX)

Quantity of Dollars

The Effects of an Increase in The Government Budget Deficit

An increase in the size of the government budget deficit reduces the supply of loanable funds available from national saving. As a result, the supply curve shifts to the left, as shown in panel (a). Net capital outflow therefore also decreases from the amount given by the distance between points A and C to the amount given by the distance between points B and C. In panel (b), the decrease in net capital outflow reduces the supply of dollars in the market for foreign exchange. This decrease in the supply of dollars causes the supply curve to shift to the left, from $(S - I)_1$ to $(S - I)_2$, and causes the real exchange rate to appreciate from E_1 to E_2. The appreciation of the exchange rate causes net exports to fall.

Canada's net exports fall. Hence, *in a small open economy with perfect capital mobility, an increase in government budget deficits causes the dollar to appreciate and causes net exports to fall.*

This analysis shows how decisions made in the past that caused government deficits to increase have affected Canada's real exchange rate and net exports. Since the mid-1990s, more and more Canadian governments have adopted policies to eliminate deficits and even introduce budget surpluses. We can understand the implications of these policies by reversing the movements described in Figure 14.5 and discussed above. A decrease in government budget deficits increases national saving. At the world interest rate, the excess of national saving over domestic investment increases, which is equivalent to saying that net capital out-flow increases. The increase in net capital outflow increases the supply of dollars in the market for foreign-currency exchange, which causes the real exchange rate to depreciate. This depreciation, in turn, makes Canadian goods less expensive compared with foreign goods. Because people both at home and abroad switch their purchases toward less expensive Canadian goods, exports from Canada rise and imports to Canada fall. For both reasons, Canada's net exports rise. Hence, *in a small open economy with perfect capital mobility, a decrease in government budget deficits causes the dollar to depreciate and causes net exports to rise.*

This analysis indicates why it is not surprising to find Canadians closely watching movements in government budget balances. The change in government policy from running large deficits over the period 1975 to 1995 to running large surpluses currently, has had a depressing influence on the value of the Canadian dollar. While benefiting Canadian exporters, the lower dollar has hurt importers and Canadian consumers of imported goods.

Trade Policy

trade policy
a government policy that directly influences the quantity of goods and services that a country imports or exports

A **trade policy** is a government policy that directly influences the quantity of goods and services that a country imports or exports. Trade policy takes various forms. One common trade policy is a **tariff,** a tax on imported goods. Another is an **import quota,** a limit on the quantity of a good that can be produced abroad and sold domestically. Trade policies are common throughout the world, although sometimes they are disguised. For example, the Canadian and U.S. governments have sometimes pressured Japanese automakers to reduce the number of cars they sell in North America. These so-called "voluntary export restrictions" are not really voluntary and, in essence, are a form of import quota.

tariff
a tax on goods produced abroad and sold domestically

Let's consider the macroeconomic impact of trade policy. Suppose that the North American auto industry, concerned about competition from Japanese automakers, convinces the Canadian government to impose a quota on the number of cars that can be imported from Japan. In making their case, lobbyists for the auto industry assert that the trade restriction would shrink the size of the Canadian trade deficit. Are they right? Our model, as illustrated in Figure 14.6, offers an answer.

import quota
a limit on the quantity of a good that is produced abroad and sold domestically

The first step in analyzing the trade policy is to determine which curve shifts. The initial impact of the import restriction is, not surprisingly, on imports. Because net exports equal exports minus imports, the policy also affects net exports. And because net exports are the source of demand for dollars in the market for foreign-currency exchange, the policy affects the demand curve in this market.

The second step is to determine which way this demand curve shifts. Because the quota restricts the number of Japanese cars sold in Canada, it reduces imports at any given real exchange rate. Net exports, which equal exports minus imports, will therefore *rise* for any given real exchange rate. Because foreigners need dollars to buy Canada's net exports, there is an increased demand for dollars in the market for foreign-currency exchange. This increase in the demand for dollars is shown in panel (b) of Figure 14.6 as the shift to the right of the demand curve.

The third step is to compare the old and new equilibria. As we can see in panel (b), the increase in the demand for dollars causes the real exchange rate to appreciate from E_1 to E_2. Because nothing has happened in the market for loanable

FIGURE 14.6

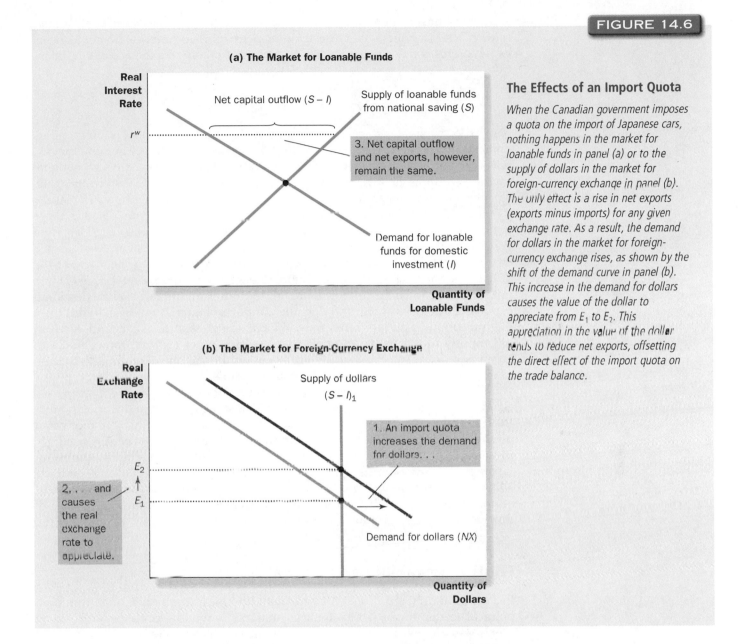

(a) The Market for Loanable Funds

Real Interest Rate

Net capital outflow (S – I)

Supply of loanable funds from national saving (S)

r^w

3. Net capital outflow and net exports, however, remain the same.

Demand for loanable funds for domestic investment (I)

Quantity of Loanable Funds

(b) The Market for Foreign-Currency Exchange

Real Exchange Rate

Supply of dollars

$(S – I)_1$

1. An import quota increases the demand for dollars. . .

E_2

2. . . . and causes the real exchange rate to appreciate.

E_1

Demand for dollars (NX)

Quantity of Dollars

The Effects of an Import Quota

When the Canadian government imposes a quota on the import of Japanese cars, nothing happens in the market for loanable funds in panel (a) or to the supply of dollars in the market for foreign-currency exchange in panel (b). The only effect is a rise in net exports (exports minus imports) for any given exchange rate. As a result, the demand for dollars in the market for foreign-currency exchange rises, as shown by the shift of the demand curve in panel (b). This increase in the demand for dollars causes the value of the dollar to appreciate from E_1 to E_2. This appreciation in the value of the dollar tends to reduce net exports, offsetting the direct effect of the import quota on the trade balance.

funds in panel (a), there is no change in net capital outflow. And because there is no change in net capital outflow, there can be no change in net exports, even though the import quota has reduced imports.

The reason why net exports can stay the same while imports fall is explained by the change in the real exchange rate: When the dollar appreciates in value in the market for foreign-currency exchange, domestic goods become more expensive relative to foreign goods. This appreciation encourages imports and discourages exports—and both of these changes work to offset the direct increase in net exports due to the import quota. In the end, an import quota reduces both imports and exports, but net exports (exports minus imports) are unchanged.

We have thus come to a surprising implication: *Trade policies do not affect the trade balance.* That is, policies that directly influence exports or imports do not alter net exports. This conclusion seems less surprising if one recalls the accounting identity:

$$NX = NCO = S - I$$

Net exports equal net capital outflow, which equals national saving minus domestic investment. Trade policies do not alter the trade balance because they do not alter national saving or domestic investment. For given levels of national saving and domestic investment, the real exchange rate adjusts to keep the trade balance the same, regardless of the trade policies the government puts in place.

Although trade policies do not affect a country's overall trade balance, these policies do affect specific firms, industries, and countries. When the Canadian government imposes an import quota on Japanese cars, General Motors has less competition from abroad and will sell more cars. At the same time, because the dollar has appreciated in value, Bombardier, the Canadian aircraft maker, will find it harder to compete with Embraer, the Brazilian aircraft maker. Canadian exports of aircraft will fall, and Canadian imports of aircraft will rise. In this case, the import quota on Japanese cars will increase net exports of cars and decrease net exports of planes. In addition, it will increase net exports from Canada to Japan and decrease net exports from Canada to Brazil. The overall trade balance of the Canadian economy, however, stays the same.

The effects of trade policies are, therefore, more microeconomic than macroeconomic. Although advocates of trade policies sometimes claim (incorrectly) that these policies can alter a country's trade balance, they are usually more motivated by concerns about particular firms or industries. One should not be surprised, for instance, to hear an executive from General Motors advocating import quotas for Japanese cars. Economists almost always oppose such trade policies. Free trade allows economies to specialize in doing what they do best—making residents of all countries better off. Trade restrictions interfere with these gains from trade and, thus, reduce overall economic well-being.

Political Instability and Capital Flight

In 1994 political instability in Mexico, including the assassination of a prominent political leader, made world financial markets nervous. People began to view Mexico as a much less stable country than they had previously thought. They decided to pull some of their assets out of Mexico in order to move these funds to the United States and other "safe havens." Such a large and sudden movement of funds out of a country is called **capital flight.** To see the implications of capital flight for the Mexican economy, we again follow our three steps for analyzing a change in equilibrium, but this time we apply our model of the open economy from the perspective of Mexico rather than Canada.

Panel (a) of Figure 14.7 shows the market for loanable funds in Mexico before the flight of capital. At the world interest rate, r^w, the supply of loanable funds made available by the savings of Mexicans is greater than the demand for loanable funds for investment in Mexico. The difference is the amount of Mexican saving that is available to purchase foreign assets—in other words, Mexico's net

capital flight
a large and sudden reduction in the demand for assets located in a country

FIGURE 14.7

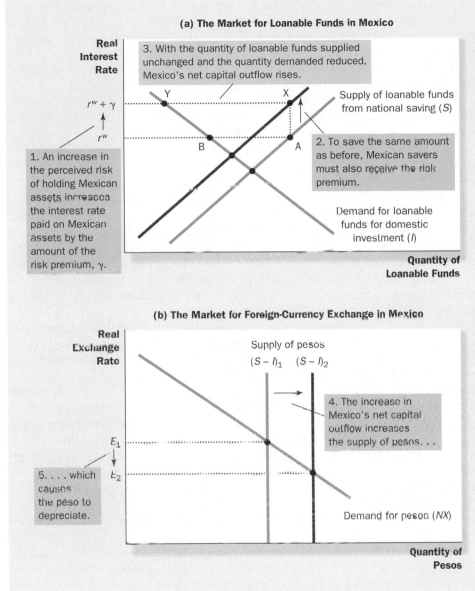

(a) The Market for Loanable Funds in Mexico

3. With the quantity of loanable funds supplied unchanged and the quantity demanded reduced, Mexico's net capital outflow rises.

$r^w + \gamma$

r^w

1. An increase in the perceived risk of holding Mexican assets increases the interest rate paid on Mexican assets by the amount of the risk premium, γ.

Supply of loanable funds from national saving (S)

2. To save the same amount as before, Mexican savers must also receive the risk premium.

Demand for loanable funds for domestic investment (I)

Real Interest Rate

Quantity of Loanable Funds

(b) The Market for Foreign-Currency Exchange in Mexico

Real Exchange Rate

Supply of pesos

$(S - I)_1$ $(S - I)_2$

4. The increase in Mexico's net capital outflow increases the supply of pesos. . .

E_1

E_2

5. . . . which causes the peso to depreciate.

Demand for pesos (NX)

Quantity of Pesos

The Effects of Capital Flight

If Mexico is judged to be a risky place to keep savings, savers in Mexico and elsewhere will demand that they receive a risk premium if they are to continue to hold Mexican assets. The response of Mexican savers is shown in panel (a) by the upward shift in the curve that represents the supply of loanable funds available from the savings of Mexicans. Because borrowers in Mexico must now pay a higher interest rate, $r^w + \gamma$, than they paid before the crisis of confidence, the quantity of loanable funds demanded for domestic investment falls. The increase in the interest rate paid by Mexican borrowers and the shift of the supply curve causes an increase in the net capital outflow of Mexico. Net capital outflow increases from an amount measured by the distance between points A and B to an amount measured by the distance between points X and Y. The increase in net capital outflow means that the supply of pesos in the market for foreign-currency exchange increases. This is shown in panel (b) by the shift to the right of the supply curve from $(S - I)_1$ to $(S - I)_2$. This increase in the supply of pesos causes the peso to depreciate from E_1 to E_2, so the peso becomes less valuable compared with other currencies.

capital outflow. Mexico's net capital outflow is shown in panel (a) by the distance between points A and B. The level of net capital outflow determines the supply of pesos in the market for foreign-currency exchange. This is shown in panel (b) by the curve $(S - I)_1$. The point at which the demand and supply of pesos are in equilibrium determines the real exchange rate, E_1.

Now consider which curves are affected, and which way the affected curves shift, if the world financial community suddenly loses confidence in the Mexican economy. As we have seen previously, if lenders lose confidence in the ability of a borrower to repay debts, they will demand that that borrower pay them a higher interest rate. Lenders, then, by receiving a higher interest rate, are compensated for the greater default risk that they incur. If the world financial community begins to question the ability of Mexico to repay its debts, lenders will hold Mexican debt only if they receive a higher interest rate than they can receive in other countries. In a small open economy like Mexico, this requires that Mexican borrowers offer to pay an interest rate greater than the world interest rate.

Let's define γ as the extra amount lenders need to receive from Mexican borrowers if they are to hold Mexican debt. This amount is commonly referred to as the *risk premium* that risky borrowers must pay. To prevent the sale of all Mexican assets, borrowers in Mexico must now pay the world interest rate, r^w, plus the risk premium, γ. To save the same quantity of loanable funds as before the confidence crisis, Mexican savers also demand that they receive $r^w + \gamma$. This response of Mexican savers is shown in panel (a) by a shift upward of the curve that represents the supply of loanable funds made available by Mexicans. The curve shifts up by the amount of the risk premium to indicate that Mexicans will choose to contribute the same quantity of their savings to the Mexican market for loanable funds only if they are compensated for the greater risk they incur by doing so. After all, Mexican savers could otherwise put their savings into Canada's, Japan's, or some other country's market for loanable funds. Paying the risk premium enables Mexican borrowers to halt the sale of Mexican assets, and receiving the risk premium causes Mexicans to save the same quantity of loanable funds as they did before the capital flight. Thus, the capital flight stops.

However, as we can see from panel (a), the addition of the risk premium also reduces domestic investment. The net effect of these changes is that net capital outflow has increased by the time the sale of Mexican assets has been halted. In panel (a), Mexico's net capital outflow is now represented by the distance between points X and Y. In panel (b), the increase in net capital outflow increases the supply of pesos in the market for foreign-currency exchange from $(S - I)_1$ to $(S - I)_2$. That is, the rush to sell Mexican assets causes a large increase in the supply of pesos to be converted into dollars. This increase in supply causes the peso to depreciate from E_1 to E_2. Thus, *capital flight from Mexico increases Mexican interest rates and decreases the value of the Mexican peso in the market for foreign-currency exchange.* This is exactly what was observed in 1994. From November 1994 to March 1995, the interest rate on short-term Mexican government bonds rose from 14 percent to 70 percent, and the peso depreciated in value from 40 to 21 Canadian cents per peso.

These price changes that result from capital flight influence some key macroeconomic quantities. The depreciation of the currency makes exports cheaper and imports more expensive, thus causing net exports to increase. Most importantly, and most damaging, is the effect of the increase in the interest rate. By reducing domestic investment, the increase in the interest rate caused by capital flight slows capital accumulation and economic growth.

The events that we have been describing in Mexico could happen to any economy in the world, and in fact they do from time to time. In 1997, the world learned that the banking systems of several Asian economies, including Thailand, South Korea, and Indonesia, were at or near the point of bankruptcy, and this news induced capital to flee from these nations. In 1998, the Russian government defaulted on its debt, inducing international investors to take whatever money they could and run. A similar (but more complicated) set of events unfolded in Argentina in 2002. In each of these cases of capital flight, the results were much as our model predicts: rising interest rates and a falling currency.

Could the events that occurred in Mexico, Southeast Asia, and Russia ever happen in Canada? Although the Canadian economy has long been viewed as a safe place in which to invest, political developments in Canada have at times induced small amounts of capital flight. For example, past referendums held on the question of Quebec separation, and the possibility of future referendums, are generally acknowledged to have caused interest rates to be higher in Canada than they would otherwise have been. Because the issue of Quebec separation has led some international investors to wonder whether Canada will continue to exist as a country, Canadian borrowers have had to pay a risk premium to Canadian and international lenders. In addition to causing Canadian interest rates to be higher, the uncertainty about Canada's political future has caused domestic investment and the value of the Canadian dollar to be lower, as our model has predicted.

Economic developments in Canada have also been the source of capital flight. High levels of government debt have at times caused international investors to express concern about the wisdom of placing their savings in Canada. Their concern has forced Canadian borrowers to offer a risk premium to international investors and this has resulted in all of the effects described above; an increase in net capital outflow, a lower value for the Canadian dollar, higher interest rates, and slower economic growth.

Even a large economy like the United States has suffered small amounts of capital flight. For example, the September 22, 1995, issue of *The New York Times* reported that on the previous day, "House Speaker Newt Gingrich threatened to send the United States into default on its debt for the first time in the nation's history, to force the Clinton administration to balance the budget on Republican terms" (p. A1). Even though most people believed such a default was unlikely, the effect of the announcement was, in a small way, similar to that experienced by Mexico in 1994. Over the course of that single day, the interest rate on a 30-year U.S. government bond rose from 6.46 percent to 6.55 percent, and the exchange rate fell from 102.7 to 99.0 yen per dollar. Thus, even the stable U.S. economy is potentially susceptible to the effects of capital flight.

QuickQuiz Suppose that Canadians decided to spend a smaller fraction of their incomes. What would be the effect on saving, domestic investment, net capital outflow, the real exchange rate, and the trade balance?

CONCLUSION

International economics is a topic of increasing importance. More and more, Canadian citizens are buying goods produced abroad and producing goods to be sold overseas. Through mutual funds and other financial institutions, they borrow and lend in world financial markets. As a result, a full analysis of the Canadian economy requires an understanding of how the Canadian economy interacts with other economies in the world. This chapter has provided a basic model for thinking about the macroeconomics of open economies.

It is worth noting, however, that the model that has been presented in this chapter is just that—a model. As such, it relies on a number of assumptions and simplifications. These assumptions and simplifications produce answers that need to be modified when these assumptions and simplifications are relaxed. There is nothing unusual about this. (Recall our discussion in Chapter 2 when we talked about the scientific method and the role of models.) The model presented in this chapter dispenses with various details that, for some purposes, are significant. More complex models of the type you will see in future courses in macroeconomics will include, for example, the role of people's expectations in relation to the future and the longer-run implications of capital flows. More complex models may also allow for a relaxation of our assumption of perfectly mobile capital. Having said that, it is nonetheless true that the basic model presented in this chapter provides a very useful way of thinking about the macroeconomics of a small open economy.

Although the study of international economics is valuable, we should be careful not to exaggerate its importance. Policymakers and commentators are often quick to blame foreigners for problems facing the Canadian economy. By contrast, economists more often view these problems as homegrown. For example, politicians often discuss foreign competition as a threat to Canadian living standards. Economists are more likely to lament the low level of national saving. Low saving impedes growth in capital, productivity, and living standards, regardless of whether the economy is open or closed. Foreigners are a convenient target for politicians because blaming foreigners provides a way to avoid responsibility without insulting any domestic constituency. Whenever you hear popular discussions of international trade and finance, therefore, it is especially important to try to separate myth from reality. The tools you have learned in the past two chapters should help in that endeavour.

SUMMARY

- Most economists prefer to use a model that describes Canada as a small open economy with perfect capital mobility. This means that borrowers must pay, and lenders demand that they receive, the world interest rate. In the analysis of the macroeconomics of such an economy, two markets are central—the market for loanable funds and the market for foreign-currency exchange. In the market for loanable funds, the world interest rate determines the quantity of loanable funds demanded for domestic investment and the quantity of loanable funds made available from national saving. The difference between the quantity of loanable funds demanded and the quantity of loanable funds supplied at the world interest rate is net capital outflow. In the market for foreign-currency exchange, the real exchange rate adjusts to balance the supply of dollars (from net capital outflow) and the demand for

dollars (from net exports). Because net capital outflow is determined in the market for loanable funds and provides the supply of dollars for foreign-currency exchange, it is the variable that connects these two markets.

- An increase in a government budget deficit reduces the supply of loanable funds available from national saving. This reduces net capital outflow and in turn reduces the supply of dollars in the market for foreign-currency exchange. The fall in the supply of dollars causes the real exchange rate to appreciate and therefore causes net exports to fall. A decrease in a government deficit, or an increase in a government surplus, increases the supply of loanable funds and increases net capital outflow. The increase in the supply of dollars in the market for foreign-currency exchange causes the real exchange rate to depreciate and net exports to rise.

- Although restrictive trade policies, such as tariffs or quotas on imports, are sometimes advocated as a way to alter the trade balance, they do not necessarily have that effect. A trade restriction increases net exports for a given exchange rate and, therefore, increases the demand for dollars in the market for foreign-currency exchange. As a result, the dollar appreciates in value, making domestic goods more expensive relative to foreign goods. This appreciation offsets the initial impact of the trade restriction on net exports.

- When investors change their attitudes about holding assets of a country, the ramifications for the country's economy can be profound. In particular, political instability can lead to capital flight, which tends to increase interest rates and cause the currency to depreciate.

KEY CONCEPTS

trade policy, p. 320
tariff, p. 320

import quota, p. 320

capital flight, p. 322

QUESTIONS FOR REVIEW

1. Describe supply and demand in the market for loanable funds and the market for foreign-currency exchange. How are these markets linked?

2. How would a fall in U.S. interest rates affect Canadian investment, saving, and net capital outflow, and the Canadian real exchange rate?

3. Suppose that a textile workers' union encourages people to buy only Canadian-made clothes. What would this policy do to the trade balance and the real exchange rate? What is the impact on the textile industry? What is the impact on the auto industry?

4. What is capital flight? When a country experiences capital flight, what is the effect on its interest rate and exchange rate?

PROBLEMS AND APPLICATIONS

1. Japan generally runs a significant trade surplus. Do you think this is most related to high foreign demand for Japanese goods, low Japanese demand for foreign goods, a high Japanese saving rate relative to Japanese investment, or structural barriers against imports into Japan? Explain your answer.

2. How would an increase in foreigners' incomes affect Canada's net exports curve? How would this affect the value of the dollar in the market for foreign-currency exchange?

3. Suppose that Parliament passes an investment tax credit, which subsidizes domestic investment. How does this policy affect national saving, domestic investment, net capital outflow, the interest rate, the exchange rate, and the trade balance?

4. Economists generally favour reductions in trade restrictions. Many policymakers, however, insist that any lowering of Canadian import restrictions must be accompanied by reductions in other countries' import quotas on Canadian

exports. Only in this way, these policymakers believe, can Canadian exporters benefit from a lowering of Canadian import quotas. Explain how a reduction in import restrictions will benefit exporters even if other countries do not follow Canada's example and reduce their import quotas on Canadian exports.

5. In fiscal year 1996–97, the government of Ontario ran a budget deficit of $7.5 billion. At this size, the deficit was only slightly smaller than the federal government's budget deficit of $8.9 billion, and larger than the combined deficits of all of the other provinces. The Ontario government has taken steps to reduce its provincial budget deficit since that time. What effect has this reduction had on the economies of the other provinces?

6. Economists often lament the low level of national saving. Low saving impedes capital growth, productivity, and living standards. For this reason, economists tend to favour policies designed to increase saving. Suppose that all Canadians choose to increase their saving. What would be the effect of increased saving on the value of the dollar and on net exports?

7. Changes in government deficits are closely related to changes in net exports. In particular, increases in government deficits lead to reductions in net exports, while reductions in government deficits lead to increases in net exports. Use a two-panel diagram to explain this important relationship.

8. Suppose the French suddenly develop a strong taste for British Columbia wines. Answer the following questions in words and using a diagram:
   a. What happens to the demand for dollars in the market for foreign-currency exchange?
   b. What happens to the value of dollars in the market for foreign-currency exchange?
   c. What happens to the quantity of net exports?

9. A Member of Parliament renounces her past support for protectionism: "Canada's trade deficit must be reduced, but import quotas only annoy our trading partners. If we subsidize Canadian exports instead, we can reduce the trade deficit by increasing our competitiveness."

Using a two-panel diagram, show the effect of an export subsidy on net exports and the real exchange rate. Do you agree with the MP?

10. Suppose that the federal government increases the tax on corporate profits. Such a tax has the effect of reducing domestic investment. What effect would this tax increase have on Canada's real exchange rate and net exports?

11. Suppose that the world interest rate rises.
    a. If the elasticity of national saving in relation to the world interest rate is very high, will this rise in the world interest rate have a large or small effect on Canada's net capital outflow?
    b. If the elasticity of Canada's exports in relation to the real exchange rate is very low, will this rise in the world interest rate have a large or small effect on Canada's real exchange rate?

12. Suppose that Europeans suddenly become very interested in investing in Canada.
    a. What happens to Canadian net capital outflow?
    b. What effect does this have on Canadian private saving and Canadian domestic investment?
    c. What is the long-run effect on the Canadian capital stock?

13. During the 1960s, a commonly held concern among Canadians was that Americans were "buying Canada." This concern stemmed from the fact that Canada's net capital outflow during the 1960s was consistently negative. As a result, foreigners, particularly Americans, were buying more Canadian assets than Canadians were buying foreign assets. Because many of these assets were firms operating in Canada, Canadians were concerned that eventually all of Canada would be owned by Americans. In response to this concern, the federal government of the time passed legislation limiting the amount that foreigners could invest in certain sectors of the economy. How do you think this legislation affected investment in Canada? What do you think happened to Canada's real exchange rate and net exports as a result?

14. Figure 14.4 (p. 317) shows the effect of an increase in the world interest rate on a small open economy with perfect capital mobility. In the figure, we assumed that net capital outflow (NCO) was positive. For most of the past 40 years, however, Canada's NCO has been negative. Redraw the two panels of Figure 14.4, but this time assume that NCO is negative at the world interest rate. Now suppose that the world interest rate increases. What happens to national saving (S)? What happens to domestic investment (I)? What happens to NCO and the real exchange rate? Does the conclusion we reached in our discussion of Figure 14.4—that an increase in world interest rates causes the Canadian dollar to depreciate and net exports to increase—still hold?

INTERNET RESOURCES

- The Industry Canada website at http://strategis.ic.gc.ca offers a wealth of information and data on Canadian trade and capital flows and exchange rates.

- The Organisation for Economic Co-Operation and Development website (http://www.oecd.org) presents similar data for its 30 members.

- The World Trade Organization (http://www.wto.org) offers an even wider range of information, data, and discussion on issues pertaining to international trade.

- The Bank of Canada provides current data on exchange rates between the Canadian dollar and other world currencies on its website at http://www.bankofcanada.ca/en/exchange.htm. A currency converter on that page quickly calculates how many Canadian dollars are required to buy any currency in the world.

 For more study tools, please visit http://www.mankiw3e.nelson.com.

7

SHORT-RUN ECONOMIC FLUCTUATIONS

© IMAGES C-3/CORBIS-MAGMA

AGGREGATE DEMAND AND AGGREGATE SUPPLY

Learning Objectives

In this chapter, you will …

- Learn three key facts about short-run economic fluctuations
- Consider how the economy in the short run differs from the economy in the long run
- Use the model of aggregate demand and aggregate supply to explain economic fluctuations
- See how shifts in aggregate demand or aggregate supply can cause booms and recessions

Economic activity fluctuates from year to year. In most years, the production of goods and services rises. Because of increases in the labour force, increases in the capital stock, and advances in technological knowledge, the economy can produce more and more over time. This growth allows everyone to enjoy a higher standard of living. On average over the past 130 years, the production of the Canadian economy as measured by real GDP per person has grown by about 2 percent per year.

In some years, however, this normal growth does not occur. Firms find themselves unable to sell all of the goods and services they have to offer, so they cut back on production. Workers are laid off, unemployment rises, and factories are left idle. With the economy producing fewer goods and services, real GDP and other measures of income fall. Such a period of falling incomes and rising unemployment is called a **recession** if it is relatively mild and a **depression** if it is more severe.

What causes short-run fluctuations in economic activity? What, if anything, can public policy do to prevent periods of falling incomes and rising unemployment? When recessions and depressions occur, how can policymakers reduce their length and severity? These are the questions that we take up now.

recession
a period of declining real incomes and rising unemployment

depression
a severe recession

The variables that we study are largely those we have already seen in previous chapters. They include GDP, unemployment, interest rates, exchange rates, and the price level. Also familiar are the policy instruments of government spending, taxes, and the money supply. What differs from our earlier analysis is the time horizon. So far, our focus has been on the behaviour of the economy in the long run. Our focus now is on the economy's short-run fluctuations around its long-run trend.

Although there remains some debate among economists about how to analyze short-run fluctuations, most economists use the *model of aggregate demand and aggregate supply*. Learning how to use this model for analyzing the short-run effects of various events and policies is the primary task ahead. This chapter introduces the model's two key pieces—the aggregate-demand curve and the aggregate-supply curve. But before turning to the model, let's look at the facts.

THREE KEY FACTS ABOUT ECONOMIC FLUCTUATIONS

Short-run fluctuations in economic activity occur in all countries and in all times throughout history. As a starting point for understanding these year-to-year fluctuations, let's discuss some of their most important properties.

Fact 1: Economic Fluctuations Are Irregular and Unpredictable

Fluctuations in the economy are often called *the business cycle*. As this term suggests, economic fluctuations correspond to changes in business conditions. When real GDP grows rapidly, business is good. During such periods of economic expansion, firms find that customers are plentiful and that profits are growing. On the other hand, when real GDP falls during recessions, businesses have trouble. During such periods of economic contraction, most firms experience declining sales and dwindling profits.

The term *business cycle* is somewhat misleading, however, because it seems to suggest that economic fluctuations follow a regular, predictable pattern. In fact, economic fluctuations are not at all regular, and they are almost impossible to predict with much accuracy. Panel (a) of Figure 15.1 shows the real GDP of the Canadian economy since 1966. The shaded areas represent times of recession. As the figure shows, recessions do not come at regular intervals. Sometimes recessions are close together, such as the recessions of 1980 and 1982. Sometimes the economy goes many years without a recession. From 1991 to the fall of 2003, Canada enjoyed a recession-free period of economic growth.

Fact 2: Most Macroeconomic Quantities Fluctuate Together

Real GDP is the variable that is most commonly used to monitor short-run changes in the economy because it is the most comprehensive measure of

FIGURE 15.1

(a) Real GDP

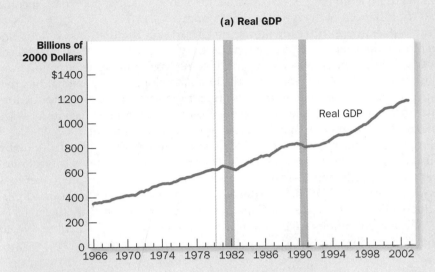

A Look at Short-Run Economic Fluctuations

This figure shows real GDP in panel (a), investment spending in panel (b), and unemployment in panel (c) for the Canadian economy using quarterly data since 1966. Recessions, defined here as two or more quarters of negative real GDP growth, are shown as the shaded areas. Notice that real GDP and investment spending decline during recessions, while unemployment rises.

Source: Statistics Canada, CANSIM II database.

(b) Investment Spending

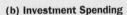
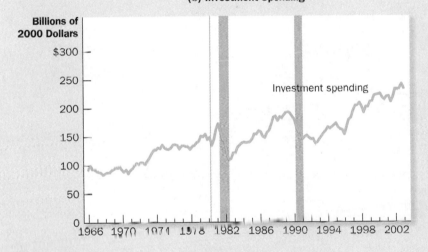

(c) Unemployment Rate

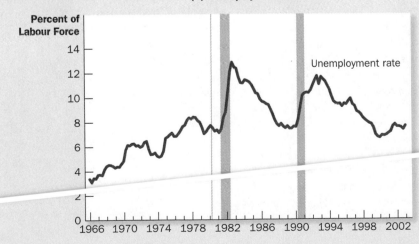

economic activity. Real GDP measures the value of all final goods and services produced within a given period of time. It also measures the total income (adjusted for inflation) of everyone in the economy.

It turns out, however, that for monitoring short-run fluctuations, it does not really matter which measure of economic activity you choose. Most macroeconomic variables that measure some type of income, spending, or production fluctuate closely together. When real GDP falls in a recession, so do personal income, corporate profits, consumer spending, investment spending, industrial production, retail sales, home sales, auto sales, and so on. Because recessions are economy-wide phenomena, they show up in many sources of macroeconomic data.

Although many macroeconomic variables fluctuate together, they fluctuate by different amounts. In particular, as panel (b) of Figure 15.1 shows, investment spending varies greatly over the business cycle. Even though investment averages only about one-fifth of GDP, declines in investment accounted for about 80 percent of the declines in GDP during Canada's last two recessions. In other words, when economic conditions deteriorate, much of the decline is attributable to reductions in spending on new factories, housing, and inventories.

IN THE NEWS

THE TRASH INDICATOR

When the economy goes into a recession, many economic variables fall together. Here's an offbeat example from the recession of 2001.

Economy Is in the Dumper— That's Not a Lot of Garbage

By John Keilman

When people say the economy is in the trash can, they're not exaggerating.

The stalling fortunes of many businesses and families in the Chicago area show up in the smaller volume of garbage they are throwing away, according to refuse collectors and experts.

Trash as an economic indicator is not exactly an established science. But recent statistics have the unmistakable whiff of a downward trend. In Chicago,

the total waste stream dropped 6 percent from 1999 to 2000. Across 23 northwestern suburbs, annual 2 to 10 percent increases in household trash during the bull market have been replaced by a yearlong slide approaching 1 percent. . . .

"It doesn't sound like a lot, but in this business, it's a lot," said C. Brooke Beal, executive director of the Solid Waste Agency of Northern Cook County. "The increase and decrease is directly tied to how the economy is going. . . ."

Residential trash goes up notably when the economy is good, thanks mostly to purchases of furniture or items

such as televisions or computers that come with lots of packaging.

Kathy Cisco, co-director of the University of Arizona's Garbage Project, a think tank that explores what trash says about culture, said the flip side comes when times are hard. We can expect to see less big-purchase debris—large cardboard boxes, hunks of Styrofoam and tangles of cellophane—enter the waste stream.

Source: *The Chicago Tribune*, November 10, 2001, p. 1. Reprinted by permission.

Fact 3: As Output Falls, Unemployment Rises

Changes in the economy's output of goods and services are strongly correlated with changes in the economy's utilization of its labour force. In other words, when real GDP declines, the rate of unemployment rises. This fact is hardly surprising: When firms choose to produce a smaller quantity of goods and services, they lay off workers, expanding the pool of unemployed.

Panel (c) of Figure 15.1 shows the unemployment rate in the Canadian economy since 1966. Once again, recessions are shown as the shaded areas in the figure. The figure shows clearly the impact of recessions on unemployment. In each of the recessions, the unemployment rate rises substantially. When the recession ends and real GDP starts to expand, the unemployment rate gradually declines. The unemployment rate never approaches zero; instead, it fluctuates around its natural rate. As we discussed ealier when reviewing the determinants of unemployment, because the value of the natural rate is only an estimate, there may be some dispute about the level of the rate at any particular time. However, most economists believe that the natural unemployment rate in Canada increased during the 1970s, peaked at about 8 percent in the 1980s, and has fallen slowly since the mid-1990s to some value between 6 and 8 percent.

QuickQuiz List and discuss three key facts about economic fluctuations

EXPLAINING SHORT-RUN ECONOMIC FLUCTUATIONS

Describing the patterns that economies experience as they fluctuate over time is easy. Explaining what causes these fluctuations is more difficult. Indeed, compared to the topics we have studied in previous chapters, the theory of economic fluctuations remains controversial. In this chapter and the next two chapters, we develop the model that most economists use to explain short-run fluctuations in economic activity.

How the Short Run Differs from the Long Run

In previous chapters we developed theories to explain what determines most important macroeconomic variables in the long run. Chapter 7 explained the level and growth of productivity and real GDP. Chapters 8 and 9 explained how the financial system works and how the real interest rate adjusts to balance saving and investment in a closed economy. Chapter 10 explained why there is always some unemployment in the economy. Chapters 11 and 12 explained the monetary system and how changes in the money supply affect the price level, the inflation rate, and the nominal interest rate. Chapters 13 and 14 extended this analysis to open economies in order to explain the trade balance and the exchange rate. There we learned that, as a result of perfect capital mobility the real interest rate in Canada must increase and decrease with increases and decreases in the value of the world real interest rate.

All of this previous analysis was based on two related ideas—the classical dichotomy and monetary neutrality. Recall that the classical dichotomy is the separation of variables into real variables (those that measure quantities or relative prices) and nominal variables (those measured in terms of money). According to classical macroeconomic theory, changes in the money supply affect nominal variables but not real variables. As a result of this monetary neutrality, Chapters 7 through 10 were able to examine the determinants of real variables (real GDP, the real interest rate, and unemployment) without introducing nominal variables (the money supply and the price level).

Do these assumptions of classical macroeconomic theory apply to the world in which we live? The answer to this question is of central importance to understanding how the economy works: *Most economists believe that classical theory describes the world in the long run but not in the short run.* Beyond a period of several years, changes in the money supply affect prices and other nominal variables but do not affect real GDP, unemployment, or other real variables. When studying year-to-year changes in the economy, however, the assumption of monetary neutrality is no longer appropriate. Most economists believe that, in the short run, real and nominal variables are highly intertwined. In particular, changes in the money supply can temporarily push output away from its long-run trend.

To understand the economy in the short run, therefore, we need a new model. To build this new model, we rely on many of the tools we have developed in previous chapters, but we have to abandon the classical dichotomy and the neutrality of money.

The Basic Model of Economic Fluctuations

Our model of short-run economic fluctuations focuses on the behaviour of two variables. The first variable is the economy's output of goods and services, as measured by real GDP. The second variable is the overall price level, as measured by the CPI or the GDP deflator. Notice that output is a real variable, whereas the price level is a nominal variable. Hence, by focusing on the relationship between these two variables, we are highlighting the breakdown of the classical dichotomy.

We analyze fluctuations in the economy as a whole with the **model of aggregate demand and aggregate supply,** which is illustrated in Figure 15.2. On the vertical axis is the overall price level in the economy. On the horizontal axis is the overall quantity of goods and services. The **aggregate-demand curve** shows the quantity of goods and services that households, firms, and the government want to buy at each price level. The **aggregate-supply curve** shows the quantity of goods and services that firms produce and sell at each price level. According to this model, the price level and the quantity of output adjust to bring aggregate demand and aggregate supply into balance.

It may be tempting to view the model of aggregate demand and aggregate supply as nothing more than a large version of the model of market demand and market supply, which we introduced in Chapter 4. Yet in fact this model is quite different. When we consider demand and supply in a particular market—ice cream, for instance—the behaviour of buyers and sellers depends on the ability of resources to move from one market to another. When the price of ice cream rises, the quantity demanded falls because buyers will use their incomes to buy products other than ice cream. Similarly, a higher price of ice cream raises the quantity

model of aggregate demand and aggregate supply
the model that most economists use to explain short-run fluctuations in economic activity around its long-run trend

aggregate-demand curve
a curve that shows the quantity of goods and services that households, firms, and the government want to buy at each price level

aggregate-supply curve
a curve that shows the quantity of goods and services that firms choose to produce and sell at each price level

FIGURE 15.2

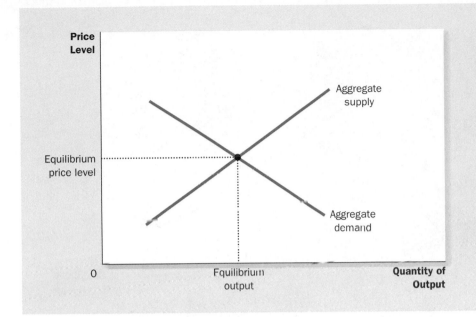

Aggregate Demand and Aggregate Supply

Economists use the model of aggregate demand and aggregate supply to analyze economic fluctuations. On the vertical axis is the overall level of prices. On the horizontal axis is the economy's total output of goods and services. Output and the price level adjust to the point at which the aggregate-supply and aggregate-demand curves intersect.

supplied because firms that produce ice cream can increase production by hiring workers away from other parts of the economy. This *microeconomic* substitution from one market to another is impossible when we are analyzing the economy as a whole. After all, the quantity that our model is trying to explain—real GDP— measures the total quantity produced in all of the economy's markets. To understand why the aggregate-demand curve is downward sloping and why the aggregate-supply curve is upward sloping, we need a *macroeconomic* theory. Developing such a theory is our next task.

QuickQuiz   How does the economy's behaviour in the short run differ from its behaviour in the long run? • Draw the model of aggregate demand and aggregate supply. What variables are on the two axes?

THE AGGREGATE-DEMAND CURVE

The aggregate-demand curve tells us the quantity of all goods and services demanded in the economy at any given price level. As Figure 15.3 (p. 340) illustrates, the aggregate-demand curve is downward sloping. This means that, other things equal, a fall in the economy's overall level of prices (from, say, P_1 to P_2) tends to raise the quantity of goods and services demanded (from Y_1 to Y_2).

Why the Aggregate-Demand Curve Slopes Downward

Why does a fall in the price level raise the quantity of goods and services demanded? To answer this question, it is useful to recall that GDP (which we

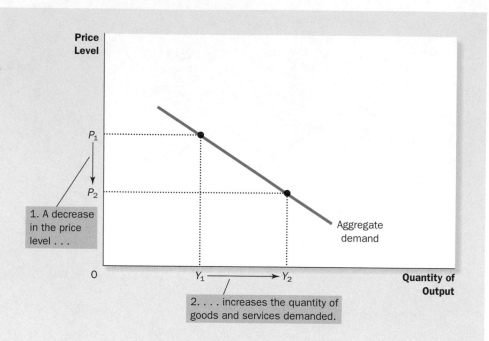

FIGURE 15.3

The Aggregate-Demand Curve

A fall in the price level from P_1 to P_2 increases the quantity of goods and services demanded from Y_1 to Y_2. There are three reasons for this negative relationship. As the price level falls, real wealth rises, interest rates fall, and the exchange rate depreciates. These effects stimulate spending on consumption, investment, and net exports. Increased spending on these components of output means a larger quantity of goods and services demanded.

denote as Y) is the sum of consumption (C), investment (I), government purchases (G), and net exports (NX):

$$Y = C + I + G + NX$$

Each of these four components contributes to the aggregate demand for goods and services. For now, we assume that government spending is fixed by policy. The other three components of spending—consumption, investment, and net exports—depend on economic conditions and, in particular, on the price level. To understand the downward slope of the aggregate-demand curve, therefore, we must examine how the price level affects the quantity of goods and services demanded for consumption, investment, and net exports.

The Price Level and Consumption: The Wealth Effect Consider the money that you hold in your wallet and your bank account. The nominal value of this money is fixed, but its real value is not. When prices fall, these dollars are more valuable because then they can be used to buy more goods and services. Thus, *a decrease in the price level makes consumers wealthier, which in turn encourages them to spend more. The increase in consumer spending means a larger quantity of goods and services demanded.*

The Price Level and Investment: The Interest-Rate Effect As we discussed in Chapter 12, the price level is one determinant of the quantity of money demanded. The lower the price level, the less money households need to hold to buy the goods and services they want. When the price level falls, therefore, households try to reduce their holdings of money by lending some of it out. For instance, a household might use its excess money to buy interest-bearing bonds. Or it might deposit its excess money in an interest-bearing savings account, and the bank would use these funds to make more loans. In either case, as households try to convert some of their money into interest-bearing assets, they drive down interest rates. Lower interest rates, in turn, encourage borrowing by firms that want to invest in new plants and equipment and by households who want to invest in new housing. Thus, *a lower price level reduces the interest rate, encourages greater spending on investment goods, and thereby increases the quantity of goods and services demanded.*

The Price Level and Net Exports: The Real Exchange-Rate Effect The real exchange rate measures the rate at which a person can trade Canadian-produced goods and services for the goods and services of other countries. For a given nominal exchange rate, a lower price level reduces the real exchange rate. This depreciation makes Canadian-produced goods and services cheaper relative to foreign-produced goods and services. As a result, Canadians and foreigners substitute away from foreign-produced goods and services in favour of Canadian-produced goods and services. Thus, *a fall in the Canadian price level causes the real exchange rate to depreciate, and this depreciation stimulates Canadian net exports and thereby increases the quantity of goods and services demanded.*

Summary There are, therefore, three distinct but related reasons why a fall in the price level increases the quantity of goods and services demanded: (1) Consumers are wealthier, which stimulates the demand for consumption goods. (2) Interest rates fall, which stimulates the demand for investment goods. (3) The exchange rate depreciates, which stimulates the demand for net exports. For all three reasons, the aggregate-demand curve slopes downward.

It is important to keep in mind that the aggregate-demand curve (like all demand curves) is drawn holding "other things equal." In particular, our three explanations of the downward-sloping aggregate-demand curve assume that the money supply is fixed. That is, we have been considering how a change in the price level affects the demand for goods and services, holding the amount of money in the economy constant. As we will see, a change in the quantity of money shifts the aggregate-demand curve. At this point, just keep in mind that the aggregate-demand curve is drawn for a given quantity of money.

Why the Aggregate-Demand Curve Might Shift

The downward slope of the aggregate-demand curve shows that a fall in the price level raises the overall quantity of goods and services demanded. Many other factors, however, affect the quantity of goods and services demanded at a given price level. When one of these other factors changes, the aggregate-demand curve shifts.

Let's consider some examples of events that shift aggregate demand. We can categorize them according to which component of spending is most directly affected.

Shifts Arising from Consumption   Suppose Canadians suddenly become more concerned about saving for retirement and, as a result, reduce their current consumption. This concern about retirement savings might arise because of a fall in stock prices that makes people feel less wealthy. Because the quantity of goods and services demanded at any price level is lower, the aggregate-demand curve shifts to the left. Conversely, imagine that a stock market boom makes people wealthier and less concerned about saving. The resulting increase in consumer spending means a greater quantity of goods and services demanded at any given price level, so the aggregate-demand curve shifts to the right.

Thus, any event that changes how much people want to consume at a given price level shifts the aggregate-demand curve. One policy variable that has this effect is the level of taxation. When the government cuts taxes, it encourages people to spend more, so the aggregate-demand curve shifts to the right. When the government raises taxes, people cut back on their spending, and the aggregate-demand curve shifts to the left.

Shifts Arising from Investment   Any event that changes how much firms want to invest at a given price level also shifts the aggregate-demand curve. For instance, imagine that the computer industry introduces a faster line of computers, and many firms decide to invest in new computer systems. Because the quantity of goods and services demanded at any price level is higher, the aggregate-demand curve shifts to the right. Conversely, if firms become pessimistic about future business conditions, they may cut back on investment spending, shifting the aggregate-demand curve to the left.

Tax policy can also influence aggregate demand through investment. As we saw in Chapter 8, an investment tax credit (a tax rebate tied to a firm's investment spending) increases the quantity of investment goods that firms demand at any given interest rate. It therefore shifts the aggregate-demand curve to the right. The repeal of an investment tax credit reduces investment and shifts the aggregate-demand curve to the left.

Another policy variable that can influence investment and aggregate demand is the money supply. As we discuss more fully in the next chapter, an increase in the money supply lowers the interest rate in the short run. This makes borrowing less costly, which stimulates investment spending and thereby shifts the aggregate-demand curve to the right. Conversely, a decrease in the money supply raises the interest rate, discourages investment spending, and thereby shifts the aggregate-demand curve to the left. Many economists believe that throughout Canada's history, changes in monetary policy have been an important source of shifts in aggregate demand.

Shifts Arising from Government Purchases   The most direct way that policymakers shift the aggregate-demand curve is through government purchases. For example, suppose Parliament decides to increase purchases of new equipment for Canada's armed forces. Because the quantity of goods and services demanded at any price level is higher, the aggregate-demand curve shifts to the right. Conversely, if provincial governments choose to spend less on highway construction, the result is a smaller quantity of goods and services demanded at any price level, so the aggregate-demand curve shifts to the left.

Shifts Arising from Net Exports Any event that changes net exports for a given price level also shifts aggregate demand. For instance, when the United States experiences a recession, it buys fewer goods from Canada. This reduces Canada's net exports and shifts the aggregate-demand curve for the Canadian economy to the left. When the United States recovers from its recession, it starts buying Canadian goods again, shifting the aggregate-demand curve to the right.

Net exports sometimes change because of movements in the exchange rate. Suppose, for instance, that international speculators bid up the value of the Canadian dollar in the market for foreign-currency exchange. This appreciation of the dollar would make Canadian goods more expensive compared to foreign goods, which would depress net exports and shift the aggregate-demand curve to the left. Conversely, a depreciation of the dollar stimulates net exports and shifts the aggregate-demand curve to the right.

Summary In the next chapter we analyze the aggregate-demand curve in more detail. There we examine more precisely how the tools of monetary and fiscal policy can shift aggregate demand and whether policymakers should use these tools for that purpose. At this point, however, you should have some idea about why the aggregate-demand curve slopes downward and what kinds of events and policies can shift this curve. Table 15.1 summarizes what we have learned so far.

TABLE 15.1

The Aggregate-Demand Curve: Summary

Why Does the Aggregate-Demand Curve Slope Downward?

1. *The Wealth Effect:* A lower price level increases real wealth, which encourages spending on consumption.
2. *The Interest-Rate Effect:* A lower price level reduces the interest rate, which encourages spending on investment.
3. *The Real Exchange-Rate Effect:* A lower price level causes the real exchange rate to depreciate, which encourages spending on net exports.

Why Might the Aggregate-Demand Curve Shift?

1. *Shifts Arising from Consumption:* An event that makes consumers spend more at a given price level (a tax cut, a stock market boom) shifts the aggregate-demand curve to the right. An event that makes consumers spend less at a given price level (a tax hike, a stock market decline) shifts the aggregate-demand curve to the left.
2. *Shifts Arising from Investment:* An event that makes firms invest more at a given price level (optimism about the future, a fall in interest rates due to an increase in the money supply) shifts the aggregate-demand curve to the right. An event that makes firms invest less at a given price level (pessimism about the future, a rise in interest rates due to a decrease in the money supply) shifts the aggregate-demand curve to the left.
3. *Shifts Arising from Government Purchases:* An increase in government purchases of goods and services (greater spending on defence or highway construction) shifts the aggregate-demand curve to the right. A decrease in government purchases of goods and services (a cutback in defence or highway spending) shifts the aggregate-demand curve to the left.
4. *Shifts Arising from Net Exports:* An event that raises spending on net exports at a given price level (a boom experienced by a major trading partner, an exchange-rate depreciation) shifts the aggregate-demand curve to the right. An event that reduces spending on net exports at a given price level (a recession experienced by a major trading partner, an exchange-rate appreciation) shifts the aggregate-demand curve to the left.

QuickQuiz Explain the three reasons why the aggregate-demand curve slopes downward. • Give an example of an event that would shift the aggregate-demand curve. Which way would this event shift the curve?

THE AGGREGATE-SUPPLY CURVE

The aggregate-supply curve tells us the total quantity of goods and services that firms produce and sell at any given price level. Unlike the aggregate-demand curve, which is always downward sloping, the aggregate-supply curve shows a relationship that depends crucially on the time horizon being examined. *In the long run, the aggregate-supply curve is vertical, whereas in the short run, the aggregate-supply curve is upward sloping.* To understand short-run economic fluctuations, and how the short-run behaviour of the economy deviates from its long-run behaviour, we need to examine both the long-run aggregate-supply curve and the short-run aggregate-supply curve.

Why the Aggregate-Supply Curve Is Vertical in the Long Run

What determines the quantity of goods and services supplied in the long run? We implicitly answered this question earlier in the book when we analyzed the process of economic growth. *In the long run, an economy's production of goods and services (its real GDP) depends on its supplies of labour, capital, and natural resources and on the available technology used to turn these factors of production into goods and services.* Because the price level does not affect these long-run determinants of real GDP, the long-run aggregate-supply curve is vertical, as in Figure 15.4. In other

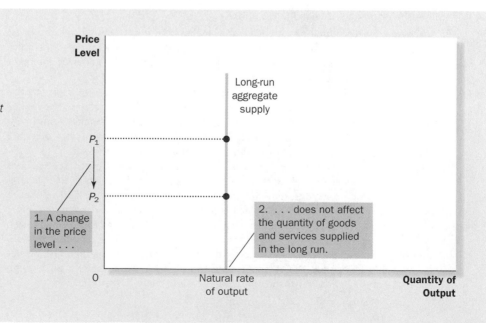

FIGURE 15.4

The Long-Run Aggregate-Supply Curve

In the long run, the quantity of output supplied depends on the economy's quantities of labour, capital, and natural resources and on the technology for turning these inputs into output. The quantity supplied does not depend on the overall price level. As a result, the long-run aggregate-supply curve is vertical at the natural rate of output.

Price Level

Long-run aggregate supply

P_1

P_2

1. A change in the price level . . .

2. . . . does not affect the quantity of goods and services supplied in the long run.

0

Natural rate of output

Quantity of Output

words, in the long run, the economy's labour, capital, natural resources, and technology determine the total quantity of goods and services supplied, and this quantity supplied is the same regardless of what the price level happens to be.

The vertical long-run aggregate-supply curve is, in essence, just an application of the classical dichotomy and monetary neutrality. As we have already discussed, classical macroeconomic theory is based on the assumption that real variables do not depend on nominal variables. The long-run aggregate-supply curve is consistent with this idea because it implies that the quantity of output (a real variable) does not depend on the level of prices (a nominal variable). As noted earlier, most economists believe that this principle works well when studying the economy over a period of many years, but not when studying year-to-year changes. Thus, the aggregate-supply curve is vertical only in the long run.

One might wonder why supply curves for specific goods and services can be upward sloping if the long-run aggregate-supply curve is vertical. The reason is that the supply of specific goods and services depends on *relative prices*—the prices of those goods and services compared to other prices in the economy. For example, when the price of ice cream rises, holding other prices in the economy constant, suppliers of ice cream can increase their production by taking labour, milk, chocolate, and other inputs away from the production of other goods, such as frozen yogurt. By contrast, the economy's overall production of goods and services is limited by its labour, capital, natural resources, and technology. Thus, when all prices in the economy rise together, there is no change in the overall quantity of goods and services supplied.

Why the Long-Run Aggregate-Supply Curve Might Shift

The position of the long-run aggregate-supply curve shows the quantity of goods and services predicted by classical macroeconomic theory. This level of production is sometimes called *potential output* or *full-employment output*. To be more accurate, we call it the *natural rate of output* because it shows what the economy produces when unemployment is at its natural, or normal, rate. The natural rate of output is the level of production toward which the economy gravitates in the long run.

Any change in the economy that alters the natural rate of output shifts the long-run aggregate-supply curve. Because output in the classical model depends on labour, capital, natural resources, and technological knowledge, we can categorize shifts in the long-run aggregate-supply curve as arising from these sources.

Shifts Arising from Labour   Imagine that an economy experiences an increase in immigration from abroad. Because there would be a greater number of workers, the quantity of goods and services supplied would increase. As a result, the long-run aggregate-supply curve would shift to the right. Conversely, if many workers left the economy to go abroad, the long-run aggregate-supply curve would shift to the left.

The position of the long-run aggregate-supply curve also depends on the natural rate of unemployment, so any change in the natural rate of unemployment shifts the long-run aggregate-supply curve. For example, if provincial governments were to raise the minimum wage substantially, the natural rate of unemployment would rise, and the economy would produce a smaller quantity of goods and services. As a result, the long-run aggregate-supply curve would shift to the left. Conversely, if a reform of the Employment Insurance system were to encourage unemployed workers to search harder for new jobs, the natural rate of unemployment would fall, and the long-run aggregate-supply curve would shift to the right.

Shifts Arising from Capital

An increase in the economy's capital stock increases productivity and, thereby, the quantity of goods and services supplied. As a result, the long-run aggregate-supply curve shifts to the right. Conversely, a decrease in the economy's capital stock decreases productivity and the quantity of goods and services supplied, shifting the long-run aggregate-supply curve to the left.

Notice that the same logic applies regardless of whether we are discussing physical capital or human capital. An increase either in the number of machines or in the number of college and university degrees will raise the economy's ability to produce goods and services. Thus, either would shift the long-run aggregate-supply curve to the right.

Shifts Arising from Natural Resources

An economy's production depends on its natural resources, including its land, minerals, and weather. A discovery of a new mineral deposit shifts the long-run aggregate-supply curve to the right. A change in weather patterns that makes farming more difficult shifts the long-run aggregate-supply curve to the left.

In many countries, important natural resources are imported from abroad. A change in the availability of these resources can also shift the aggregate-supply curve. As we discuss later in this chapter, events occurring in the world oil market have historically been an important source of shifts in aggregate supply.

Shifts Arising from Technological Knowledge

Perhaps the most important reason that the economy today produces more than it did a generation ago is that our technological knowledge has advanced. The invention of the computer, for instance, has allowed us to produce more goods and services from any given amounts of labour, capital, and natural resources. As a result, it has shifted the long-run aggregate-supply curve to the right.

Although not literally technological, there are many other events that act like changes in technology. For example, opening up international trade has effects similar to inventing new production processes, so it also shifts the long-run aggregate-supply curve to the right. Conversely, if the government passed new regulations preventing firms from using some production methods, perhaps because they produced too much pollution, the result would be a leftward shift in the long-run aggregate-supply curve.

Summary

The long-run aggregate-supply curve reflects the classical model of the economy we developed in previous chapters. Any policy or event that raised real GDP in previous chapters can now be viewed as increasing the quantity of goods and services supplied and shifting the long-run aggregate-supply curve to the right. Any policy or event that lowered real GDP in previous chapters can now be viewed as decreasing the quantity of goods and services supplied and shifting the long-run aggregate-supply curve to the left.

A New Way to Depict Long-Run Growth and Inflation

Having introduced the economy's aggregate-demand curve and the long-run aggregate-supply curve, we now have a new way to describe the economy's long-run trends. Figure 15.5 illustrates the changes that occur in the economy from decade to decade. Notice that both curves are shifting. Although there are many forces that govern the economy in the long run and can in principle cause such

FIGURE 15.5

Long-Run Growth and Inflation in the Model of Aggregate Demand and Aggregate Supply

As the economy becomes better able to produce goods and services over time, primarily because of technological progress, the long-run aggregate-supply curve shifts to the right. At the same time, as the Bank of Canada increases the money supply, the aggregate-demand curve also shifts to the right. In this figure, output grows from Y_{1980} to Y_{1990} and then to Y_{2000}, and the price level rises from P_{1980} to P_{1990} and then to P_{2000}. Thus, the model of aggregate demand and aggregate supply offers a new way to describe the classical analysis of growth and inflation.

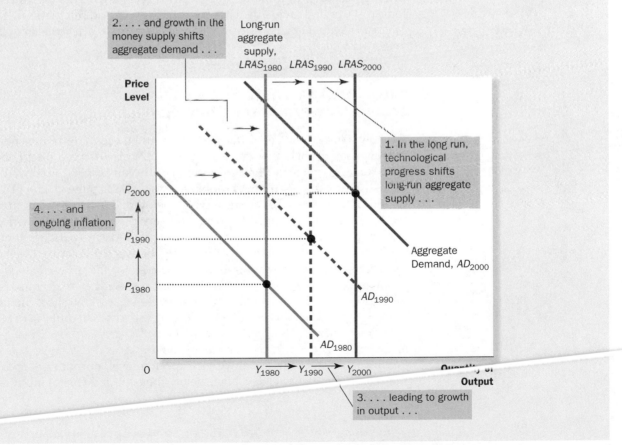

shifts, the two most important in practice are technology and monetary policy. Technological progress enhances the economy's ability to produce goods and services, and this continually shifts the long-run aggregate-supply curve to the right. At the same time, because the Bank of Canada increases the money supply over time, the aggregate-demand curve also shifts to the right.

Figure 15.5 illustrates the aggregate-demand curve shifting farther to the right than the aggregate-supply curve. The result is trend growth in output (as shown by increasing Y) and inflation (as shown by increasing P). If the Bank of Canada introduced smaller increases in the money supply, the shifts to the right in the aggregate-demand curve would also be smaller. The result would be lower inflation (as shown by smaller increases in P) but no change in the trend growth in output. This is just another way of representing the classical analysis of growth and inflation we conducted in Chapters 7 and 12. It also effectively summarizes what we learned previously about inflation and one of our ten principles of economics: Prices rise when the government prints too much money. In particular, as we illustrate in Figure 15.5, the primary cause of inflation is simply growth in the quantity of money that is faster than growth in output.

The purpose of developing the model of aggregate demand and aggregate supply, however, is not to dress our long-run conclusions in new clothing. Instead, it is to provide a framework for short-run analysis, as we will see soon. As we develop the short-run model, we keep the analysis simple by not showing the continuing growth and inflation depicted in Figure 15.5. But always remember that long-run trends provide the background for short-run fluctuations. *Short-run fluctuations in output and the price level should be viewed as deviations from the continuing long-run trends.*

Why the Aggregate-Supply Curve Slopes Upward in the Short Run

We now come to the key difference between the economy in the short run and in the long run: the behaviour of aggregate supply. As we have already discussed, the long-run aggregate-supply curve is vertical. By contrast, in the short run, the aggregate-supply curve is upward sloping, as shown in Figure 15.6. That is, over a period of a year or two, an increase in the overall level of prices in the economy tends to raise the quantity of goods and services supplied, and a decrease in the level of prices tends to reduce the quantity of goods and services supplied.

What causes this positive relationship between the price level and output? Macroeconomists have proposed three theories for the upward slope of the short-run aggregate-supply curve. In each theory, a specific market imperfection causes the supply side of the economy to behave differently in the short run than it does in the long run. Although each of the following theories will differ in detail, they share a common theme: *The quantity of output supplied deviates from its long-run, or "natural," level when the price level deviates from the price level that people expected to prevail.* When the price level rises above the expected level, output rises above its natural rate, and when the price level falls below the expected level, output falls below its natural rate.

The Sticky-Wage Theory The first and simplest explanation of the upward slope of the short-run aggregate-supply curve is the sticky-wage theory.

FIGURE 15.6

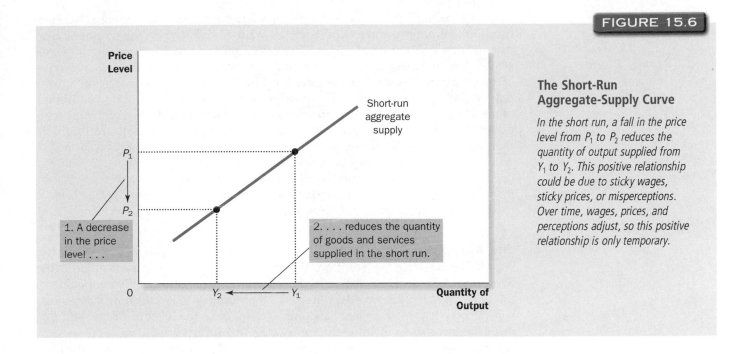

The Short-Run Aggregate-Supply Curve

In the short run, a fall in the price level from P_1 to P_2 reduces the quantity of output supplied from Y_1 to Y_2. This positive relationship could be due to sticky wages, sticky prices, or misperceptions. Over time, wages, prices, and perceptions adjust, so this positive relationship is only temporary.

According to this theory, the short-run aggregate-supply curve slopes upward because nominal wages are slow to adjust, or are "sticky," in the short run. To some extent, the slow adjustment of nominal wages is attributable to long-term contracts between workers and firms that fix nominal wages, sometimes for as long as three years. In addition, this slow adjustment may be attributable to social norms and notions of fairness that influence wage setting and that change only slowly over time.

To see what sticky nominal wages mean for aggregate supply, imagine that a firm has agreed in advance to pay its workers a certain nominal wage based on what it expected the price level to be. If the price level P falls below the level that was expected and the nominal wage remains stuck at W, then the real wage W/P rises above the level the firm planned to pay. Because wages are a large part of a firm's production costs, a higher real wage means that the firm's real costs have risen. The firm responds to these higher costs by hiring less labour and producing a smaller quantity of goods and services. In other words, *because nominal wages do not adjust immediately to the price level, a lower price level makes employment and production less profitable, so firms reduce the quantity of goods and services they supply.*

The Sticky-Price Theory Some economists have advocated another approach to the short-run aggregate-supply curve, called the sticky-price theory. As we just discussed, the sticky-wage theory emphasizes that nominal wages adjust slowly over time. The sticky-price theory emphasizes that the prices of some goods and services also adjust sluggishly in response to changing economic conditions. This slow adjustment of prices occurs in part because there are costs to adjusting prices, called *menu costs*. These menu costs include the cost of printing and distributing catalogues and the time required to change price tags. As a result of these costs, prices as well as wages may be sticky in the short run.

To see the implications of sticky prices for aggregate supply, suppose that each firm in the economy announces its prices in advance based on the economic conditions it expects to prevail. Then, after prices are announced, the economy experiences an unexpected contraction in the money supply, which (as we have learned) will reduce the overall price level in the long run. Although some firms reduce their prices immediately in response to changing economic conditions, other firms may not want to incur additional menu costs and, therefore, may temporarily lag behind. Because these lagging firms have prices that are too high, their sales decline. Declining sales, in turn, cause these firms to cut back on production and employment. In other words, *because not all prices adjust instantly to changing conditions, an unexpected fall in the price level leaves some firms with higher-than-desired prices, and these higher-than-desired prices depress sales and induce firms to reduce the quantity of goods and services they produce.*

The Misperceptions Theory   A third approach to the short-run aggregate-supply curve is the misperceptions theory. According to this theory, changes in the overall price level can temporarily mislead suppliers about what is happening in the individual markets in which they sell their output. As a result of these short-run misperceptions, suppliers respond to changes in the level of prices, and this response leads to an upward-sloping aggregate-supply curve.

To see how this might work, suppose the overall price level falls below the level that people expected. When suppliers see the prices of their products fall, they may mistakenly believe that their *relative* prices have fallen. For example, wheat farmers may notice a fall in the price of wheat before they notice a fall in the prices of the many items they buy as consumers. They may infer from this observation that the reward to producing wheat is temporarily low, and they may respond by reducing the quantity of wheat they supply. Similarly, workers may notice a fall in their nominal wages before they notice a fall in the prices of the goods they buy. They may infer that the reward to working is temporarily low and respond by reducing the quantity of labour they supply. In both cases, *a lower price level causes misperceptions about relative prices, and these misperceptions induce suppliers to respond to the lower price level by decreasing the quantity of goods and services supplied.*

Summary   There are three alternative explanations for the upward slope of the short-run aggregate-supply curve: (1) sticky wages, (2) sticky prices, and (3) misperceptions. Economists debate which of these theories is correct, and it is very possible that each contains an element of truth. For our purposes in this book, the similarities of the theories are more important than the differences. All three theories suggest that output deviates from its natural rate when the price level deviates from the price level that people expected. We can express this mathematically as follows:

$$\text{Quantity of output supplied} = \text{Natural rate of output} + a\left(\text{Actual price level} - \text{Expected price level}\right)$$

where a is a number that determines how much output responds to unexpected changes in the price level.

Notice that each of the three theories of short-run aggregate supply emphasizes a problem that is likely to be only temporary. Whether the upward slope of the aggregate-supply curve is attributable to sticky wages, sticky prices, or mispercep-tions, these conditions will not persist forever. Eventually, as people adjust their expectations, nominal wages adjust, prices become unstuck, and misperceptions are corrected. In other words, the expected and actual price levels are equal in the long run. In the long run, then, our mathematical statement becomes

Quantity of output supplied = Natural level of output

which indicates that the aggregate-supply curve is vertical rather than upward sloping. This is the mathematical description of the long-run aggregate-supply curve drawn in Figure 15.4.

Why the Short-Run Aggregate-Supply Curve Might Shift

The short-run aggregate-supply curve tells us the quantity of goods and services supplied in the short run for any given level of prices. We can think of this curve as similar to the long-run aggregate-supply curve but made upward sloping by the presence of sticky wages, sticky prices, and misperceptions. Thus, when thinking about what shifts the short-run aggregate-supply curve, we have to con-sider all those variables that shift the long-run aggregate-supply curve plus a new variable—the expected price level—that influences sticky wages, sticky prices, and misperceptions.

Let's start with what we know about the long-run aggregate-supply curve. As we discussed earlier, shifts in the long-run aggregate-supply curve normally arise from changes in labour, capital, natural resources, or technological knowledge. These same variables shift the short-run aggregate-supply curve. For example, when an increase in the economy's capital stock increases productivity, both the long-run and short-run aggregate-supply curves shift to the right. When an increase in the minimum wage raises the natural rate of unemployment, both the long-run and short-run aggregate-supply curves shift to the left.

The important new variable that affects the position of the short-run aggregate-supply curve is people's expectation of the price level. As we have discussed, the quantity of goods and services supplied depends, in the short run, on sticky wages, sticky prices, and misperceptions. Yet wages, prices, and perceptions are set on the basis of expectations of the price level. So when expectations change, the short-run aggregate-supply curve shifts.

To make this idea more concrete, let's consider a specific theory of aggregate supply—the sticky-wage theory. According to this theory, when workers and firms expect the price level to be high, they are more likely to negotiate high nom-inal wages. High wages raise firms' costs and, for any given actual price level, reduce the quantity of goods and services that firms supply. Thus, when the expected price level rises, wages are higher, costs increase, and firms supply a smaller quantity of goods and services at any given actual price level. Thus, the short-run aggregate-supply curve shifts to the left. Conversely, when the expected price level falls, wages are lower, costs decline, firms increase production at any given price level, and the short-run aggregate-supply curve shifts to the right.

A similar logic applies in each theory of aggregate supply. The general lesson is the following: *An increase in the expected price level reduces the quantity of goods and services supplied and shifts the short-run aggregate-supply curve to the left. A decrease in the expected price level raises the quantity of goods and services supplied and shifts the short-run aggregate-supply curve to the right.* As we will see in the next section, this influence of expectations on the position of the short-run aggregate-supply curve plays a key role in reconciling the economy's behaviour in the short run with its behaviour in the long run. In the short run, expectations are fixed, and the economy finds itself at the intersection of the aggregate-demand curve and the short-run aggregate-supply curve. In the long run, expectations adjust, and the short-run aggregate-supply curve shifts. This shift ensures that the economy eventually finds itself at the intersection of the aggregate-demand curve and the long-run aggregate-supply curve.

You should now have some understanding about why the short-run aggregate-supply curve slopes upward and what events and policies can cause this curve to shift. Table 15.2 summarizes our discussion.

QuickQuiz Explain why the long-run aggregate-supply curve is vertical. • Explain three theories for why the short-run aggregate-supply curve is upward sloping.

TABLE 15.2

The Short-Run Aggregate-Supply Curve: Summary

Why Does the Short-Run Aggregate-Supply Curve Slope Upward?

1. *The Sticky-Wage Theory:* An unexpectedly low price level raises the real wage, which causes firms to hire fewer workers and produce a smaller quantity of goods and services.
2. *The Sticky-Price Theory:* An unexpectedly low price level leaves some firms with higher-than-desired prices, which depresses their sales and leads them to cut back production.
3. *The Misperceptions Theory:* An unexpectedly low price level leads some suppliers to think their relative prices have fallen, which induces a fall in production.

Why Might the Short-Run Aggregate-Supply Curve Shift?

1. *Shifts Arising from Labour:* An increase in the quantity of labour available (perhaps due to a fall in the natural rate of unemployment) shifts the aggregate-supply curve to the right. A decrease in the quantity of labour available (perhaps due to a rise in the natural rate of unemployment) shifts the aggregate-supply curve to the left.
2. *Shifts Arising from Capital:* An increase in physical or human capital shifts the aggregate-supply curve to the right. A decrease in physical or human capital shifts the aggregate-supply curve to the left.
3. *Shifts Arising from Natural Resources:* An increase in the availability of natural resources shifts the aggregate-supply curve to the right. A decrease in the availability of natural resources shifts the aggregate-supply curve to the left.
4. *Shifts Arising from Technology:* An advance in technological knowledge shifts the aggregate-supply curve to the right. A decrease in the available technology (perhaps due to government regulation) shifts the aggregate-supply curve to the left.
5. *Shifts Arising from the Expected Price Level:* A decrease in the expected price level shifts the short-run aggregate-supply curve to the right. An increase in the expected price level shifts the short-run aggregate-supply curve to the left.

TWO CAUSES OF ECONOMIC FLUCTUATIONS

Now that we have introduced the model of aggregate demand and aggregate supply, we have the basic tools we need to analyze fluctuations in economic activity. In particular, we can use what we have learned about aggregate demand and aggregate supply to examine the two basic causes of short-run fluctuations.

To keep things simple, we assume the economy begins in long-run equilibrium, as shown in Figure 15.7. Equilibrium output and the price level are determined by the intersection of the aggregate-demand curve and the long-run aggregate-supply curve, shown as point A in the figure. At this point, output is at its natural rate. The short-run aggregate-supply curve passes through this point as well, indicating that wages, prices, and perceptions have fully adjusted to this long-run equilibrium. That is, when an economy is in its long-run equilibrium, wages, prices, and perceptions must have adjusted so that the intersection of aggregate demand with short-run aggregate supply is the same as the intersection of aggregate demand with long-run aggregate supply.

The Effects of a Shift in Aggregate Demand

Suppose that for some reason a wave of pessimism suddenly overtakes the economy. The cause might be a crash in the stock market or the outbreak of war overseas. Because of this event, many people lose confidence in the future and alter their plans. Households cut back on their spending and delay major purchases, and firms put off buying new equipment.

What is the impact of such a wave of pessimism on the economy? Such an event reduces the aggregate demand for goods and services. That is, for any given price

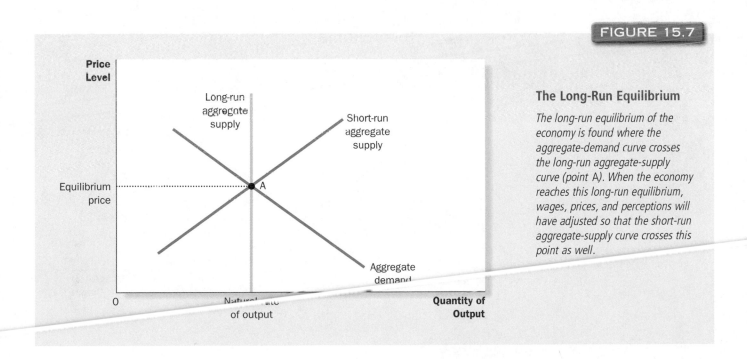

FIGURE 15.7

The Long-Run Equilibrium

The long-run equilibrium of the economy is found where the aggregate-demand curve crosses the long-run aggregate-supply curve (point A). When the economy reaches this long-run equilibrium, wages, prices, and perceptions will have adjusted so that the short-run aggregate-supply curve crosses this point as well.

level, households and firms now want to buy a smaller quantity of goods and services. As Figure 15.8 shows, the aggregate-demand curve shifts to the left from AD_1 to AD_2.

In this figure we can examine the effects of the fall in aggregate demand. In the short run, the economy moves along the initial short-run aggregate-supply curve AS_1, going from point A to point B. As the economy moves from point A to point B, output falls from Y_1 to Y_2, and the price level falls from P_1 to P_2. The falling level of output indicates that the economy is in a recession. Although not shown in the figure, firms respond to lower sales and production by reducing employment. Thus, the pessimism that caused the shift in aggregate demand is, to some extent, self-fulfilling: Pessimism about the future leads to falling incomes and rising unemployment.

What should policymakers do when faced with such a recession? One possibility is to take action to increase aggregate demand. As we noted earlier, an increase in government spending or an increase in the money supply would increase the quantity of goods and services demanded at any price and, therefore, would shift the aggregate-demand curve to the right. If policymakers can act with sufficient speed and precision, they can offset the initial shift in aggregate demand, return the aggregate-demand curve back to AD_1, and bring the economy back to point A. (The next chapter discusses in more detail the ways in which monetary and fiscal policy influence aggregate demand, as well as some of the practical difficulties in using these policy instruments.)

Even without action by policymakers, the recession will remedy itself over a period of time. Because of the reduction in aggregate demand, the price level falls.

FIGURE 15.8

A Contraction in Aggregate Demand

A fall in aggregate demand, which might be due to a wave of pessimism in the economy, is represented with a leftward shift in the aggregate-demand curve from AD_1 to AD_2. The economy moves from point A to point B. Output falls from Y_1 to Y_2, and the price level falls from P_1 to P_2. Over time, as wages, prices, and perceptions adjust, the short-run aggregate-supply curve shifts to the right from AS_1 to AS_2, and the economy reaches point C, where the new aggregate-demand curve crosses the long-run aggregate-supply curve. The price level falls to P_3, and output returns to its natural rate, Y_1.

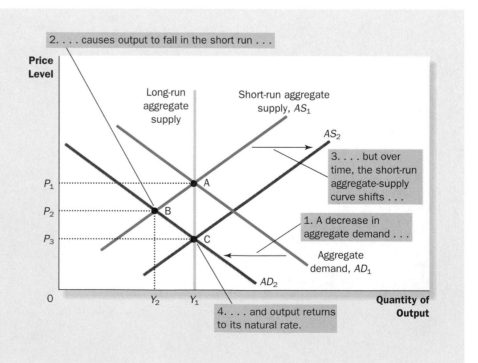

2. . . . causes output to fall in the short run . . .

3. . . . but over time, the short-run aggregate-supply curve shifts . . .

1. A decrease in aggregate demand . . .

4. . . . and output returns to its natural rate.

Eventually, expectations catch up with this new reality, and the expected price level falls as well. Because the fall in the expected price level alters wages, prices, and perceptions it shifts the short-run aggregate-supply curve to the right from AS_1 to AS_2 in Figure 15.8. This adjustment of expectations allows the economy over time to approach point C, where the new aggregate-demand curve (AD_2) crosses the long-run aggregate-supply curve.

In the new long-run equilibrium, point C, output is back to its natural rate. Even though the wave of pessimism has reduced aggregate demand, the price level has fallen sufficiently (to P_3) to offset the shift in the aggregate-demand curve. Thus, in the long run, the shift in aggregate demand is reflected fully in the price level and not at all in the level of output. In other words, the long-run effect of a shift in aggregate demand is a nominal change (the price level is lower) but not a real change (output is the same).

To sum up, this story about shifts in aggregate demand has two important lessons:

1. In the short run, shifts in aggregate demand cause fluctuations in the economy's output of goods and services.
2. In the long run, shifts in aggregate demand affect the overall price level but do not affect output.

Case Study

BIG SHIFTS IN AGGREGATE DEMAND: TWO DEPRESSIONS AND WORLD WAR II

At the beginning of this chapter we established three key facts about economic fluctuations by looking at data since 1966. Let's now take a much longer look at Canadian economic history. Figure 15.9 shows data on real GDP per person going back to 1870. Most short-run economic fluctuations are hard to see in this figure; they are dwarfed by the fourteen-fold increase in GDP per person over the past 130 years. The figure also shows a trend line, which indicates how GDP per person would have grown over time if it had increased by a steady 2 percent per year (the average rate of growth in real GDP per person since 1870). Clearly, the rate of growth in GDP has at times varied quite considerably from the average. Three episodes stand out as being particularly significant—the large drop in real GDP following World War I, another large drop in the early 1930s, and the rapid increase in real GDP in the 1940s. All three of these events are attributable to shifts in aggregate demand.

In what was until then the most severe recession in Canada's history, real GDP per person fell by 27 percent between 1917 and 1921. The view of economic historians is that the 1917–21 depression was the result of two key events. One was the end of an investment and export boom. From 1900 to 1914, huge investments were made in settling Western Canada, mainly in the form of railway construction. This investment and the settlement that accompanied it, both of which were driven by a rapid increase in wheat prices, sparked a tremendous increase in Canadian

FIGURE 15.9

Canadian Real GDP per Person since 1870

Over the course of Canadian economic history, three fluctuations stand out as being especially large. Between World War I and World War II, the economy suffered through the two worst depressions in Canadian history. During World War II the economy experienced rapid economic growth. These major fluctuations are usually explained as resulting from large shifts in aggregate demand.

Note: Real GDP per person is graphed here using a proportional scale. This means that equal distances on the vertical axis represent equal percentage changes. For example, the distance between 5000 and 10 000 (a 100 percent increase) is the same as the distance between 10 000 and 20 000 (a 100 percent increase). With such a scale, stable growth shows as an upward-sloping straight line. Thus the trend line shows the average rate of growth in real GDP per person since 1870: 2 percent per year.

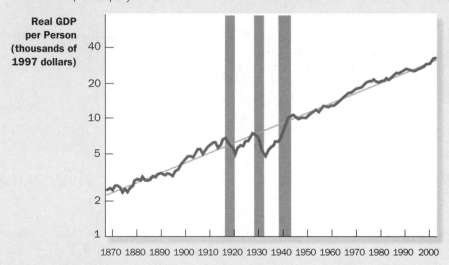

Sources: Data for 1870–1925 from M.C. Urquhart, "New Estimates of Gross National Product, Canada, 1870–1926: Some Implications for Canadian Development," in S. Engerman and R. Gallman, eds., *Long-Term Factors in American Economic Growth* (Chicago: University of Chicago Press, 1986); data for 1926–1960 from F.H. Leacy, ed., *Historical Statistics of Canada*, 2nd ed. (Ottawa: Statistics Canada, 1983); data for 1961–2002 from Statistics Canada, CANSIM II database.

exports. By 1914 this boom was ending, but by then a second source of increase in aggregate demand arose: World War I. The war brought with it a tremendous expansion of industry, which enabled growth in per capita GDP to continue. The end of the war, however, meant an end to war production. Now the industrial expansion of the war years was mirrored by industrial contraction following them. The end of the war and the end of the earlier investment and export boom resulted in a major contraction of aggregate demand and fall in GDP.

The economic calamity of the early 1930s is called the Great Depression, and as Figure 15.9 indicates, it was the largest economic downturn in Canadian history. Real GDP per person fell by 30 percent from 1929 to 1933, and unemployment rose from 4 percent to 25 percent. At the same time, the price level fell by 19 percent

NATIONAL ARCHIVES OF CANADA/PA 68220

Wars: One way to stimulate aggregate demand.

over these four years. Many other countries experienced similar declines in output and prices during this period.

Economic historians continue to debate the causes of the Great Depression in Canada, but most explanations centre on a large decline in aggregate demand. What caused this decline is still the subject of disagreement.

Many economists emphasize the decline in the money supply, which from 1929 to 1933 fell by 16 percent. As households' savings fell and bankers became more cautious and started holding greater reserves, the process of money creation under fractional-reserve banking went into reverse. Many economists suggest that the Great Depression was so severe because Canada did not have a central bank (the Bank of Canada was not created until 1935) that could have offset this fall in the money supply with expansionary open-market operations. Indeed, it was the economic problems of the Great Depression that led the government to establish the Bank of Canada.

Other economists emphasize that Canada's exposure to the U.S. economy because of the large amount of trade Canada has with the United States was an important cause of the Great Depression. Thus, a fall in aggregate demand arising from a fall in net exports is also a likely contributor.

Finally, still other economists suggest the collapse of the stock market in 1929 as an explanation for the Great Depression. Stock prices fell by 90 percent during this period, depressing household wealth and thereby consumer spending. The collapse in stock prices may also have made it difficult for firms to finance new investment projects, leading to a fall in investment spending. Of course, all of these forces may have acted together to contract aggregate demand during the Great Depression.

The third significant episode indicated in Figure 15.9—the economic boom of the 1940s—is easier to explain. The obvious cause of this boom was World War II. As Canada entered the war in 1939, the federal government had to devote more resources to the military. Government spending dramatically increased from 1939 to 1944. The huge expansion of aggregate demand increased real GDP per person by 60 percent over this period, and the unemployment rate fell from 15 percent to under 2 percent, the lowest in Canada's history. ●

The Effects of a Shift in Aggregate Supply

Imagine once again an economy in its long-run equilibrium. Now suppose that suddenly some firms experience an increase in their costs of production. For example, bad weather might destroy some crops, driving up the cost of producing food products. Or a war in the Middle East might interrupt the shipping of crude oil, driving up the cost of producing oil products.

What is the macroeconomic impact of such an increase in production costs? For any given price level, firms now want to supply a smaller quantity of goods and services. Thus, as Figure 15.10 shows, the short-run aggregate-supply curve shifts to the left from AS_1 to AS_2. (Depending on the event, the long-run aggregate-supply curve might also shift. To keep things simple, however, we will assume that it does not.)

FIGURE 15.10

An Adverse Shift in Aggregate Supply

When some event increases firms' costs, the short-run aggregate-supply curve shifts to the left from AS_1 to AS_2. The economy moves from point A to point B. The result is stagflation: Output falls from Y_1 to Y_2, and the price level rises from P_1 to P_2.

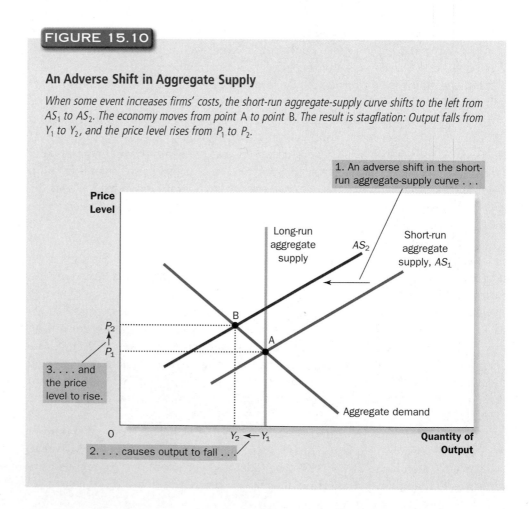

In this figure we can trace the effects of the leftward shift in aggregate supply. In the short run, the economy moves along the existing aggregate-demand curve, going from point A to point B. The output of the economy falls from Y_1 to Y_2, and the price level rises from P_1 to P_2. Because the economy is experiencing both *stagnation* (falling output) and *inflation* (rising prices), such an event is sometimes called **stagflation.**

What should policymakers do when faced with stagflation? There are no easy choices. One possibility is to do nothing. In this case, the output of goods and services remains depressed at Y_2 for a while. Eventually, however, the recession will remedy itself as wages, prices, and perceptions adjust to the higher production costs. A period of low output and high unemployment, for instance, puts downward pressure on workers' wages. Lower wages, in turn, increase the quantity of output supplied. Over time, as the short-run aggregate-supply curve shifts back toward AS_1, the price level falls, and the quantity of output approaches its natural rate. In the long run, the economy returns to point A, where the aggregate-demand curve crosses the long-run aggregate-supply curve. In this case, policymakers make the choice of maintaining a low price level at the cost of temporarily lower output and employment.

Alternatively, policymakers who control monetary and fiscal policy might attempt to offset some of the effects of the shift in the short-run aggregate-supply curve by shifting the aggregate-demand curve. This possibility is shown in Figure 15.11. In this case, changes in policy shift the aggregate-demand curve to the right from AD_1 to AD_2—exactly enough to prevent the shift in aggregate supply from affecting output. The economy moves directly from point A to point C. Output remains at its natural rate, and the price level rises from P_1 to P_3. In this

stagflation
a period of falling output and rising prices

FIGURE 15.11

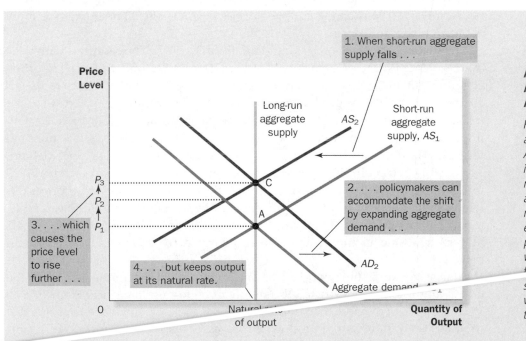

1. When short-run aggregate supply falls . . .

2. . . . policymakers can accommodate the shift by expanding aggregate demand . . .

3. . . . which causes the price level to rise further . . .

4. . . . but keeps output at its natural rate.

Accommodating an Adverse Shift in Aggregate Supply

Faced with an adverse shift in aggregate supply from AS_1 to AS_2, policymakers who can influence aggregate demand might try to shift the aggregate-demand curve to the right from AD_1 to AD_2. The economy would move from point A to point C. This policy would prevent the supply shift from reducing output in the short run, but the price level would permanently rise from P_1 to P_3.

case, policymakers are said to *accommodate* the shift in aggregate supply because they allow the increase in costs to permanently affect the level of prices. Policymakers make the choice of maintaining a constant level of real output and employment at the cost of a permanently higher price level.

To sum up, this story about shifts in aggregate supply has two important lessons:

1. Shifts in aggregate supply can cause stagflation—a combination of recession (falling output) and inflation (rising prices).
2. Policymakers who can influence aggregate demand cannot offset both of these adverse effects simultaneously.

Case Study

OIL AND THE ECONOMY

Some of the largest economic fluctuations in the Canadian economy since 1970 have originated in the oil fields of the Middle East. Crude oil is a key input into the production of many goods and services, and much of the world's oil comes from Saudi Arabia, Kuwait, and other Middle Eastern countries. When some event (usually political in origin) reduces the supply of crude oil flowing from this region, the price of oil rises around the world. Canadian firms that produce gasoline, tires, and many other products experience rising costs. The result is a leftward shift in the aggregate-supply curve, which in turn leads to stagflation. In major oil-producing provinces like Alberta and Saskatchewan, increases in oil prices also cause an increase in aggregate demand because provincial income and net exports rise. For Canada as a whole, however, the effect on aggregate supply is the dominant influence.

The first episode of this sort occurred in the mid-1970s. The countries with large oil reserves got together as members of the Organization of Petroleum Exporting Countries (OPEC). OPEC was a *cartel*—a group of sellers that attempts to thwart competition and reduce production in order to raise prices. And, indeed, oil prices rose substantially. From 1973 to 1975, the world price of oil almost tripled. Oil-importing countries around the world experienced simultaneous inflation and recession. In Canada, the inflation rate as measured by the GDP price deflator exceeded 14 percent in 1974. The unemployment rate rose from 5.5 percent in 1973 to 7.0 percent in 1975. Not surprisingly, the effects of the increase in oil prices differed considerably across oil-exporting and oil-importing provinces. For example, from 1973 to 1975, the unemployment rate in Alberta fell from 5.3 percent to 4.1 percent, while the unemployment rate in Ontario increased from 4.3 percent to 6.3 percent.

Almost the same thing happened again a few years later. In the late 1970s, the OPEC countries again restricted the supply of oil to raise the price. From 1978 to 1981, the price of oil more than doubled. Once again, costs increased for firms that used oil as an input in the production process. This second shock to oil prices prompted the federal government to introduce the National Energy Program

THE ORIGINS OF AGGREGATE DEMAND AND AGGREGATE SUPPLY

Now that we have a preliminary understanding of the model of aggregate demand and aggregate supply, it is worthwhile to step back from it and consider its history. How did this model of short-run fluctuations develop? The answer is that this model, to a large extent, is a byproduct of the Great Depression of the 1930s. Economists and policymakers at the time were puzzled about what had caused this calamity and were uncertain about how to deal with it.

In 1936, economist John Maynard Keynes published a book entitled *The General Theory of Employment, Interest, and Money*, which attempted to explain short-run economic fluctuations in general and the Great Depression in particular. Keynes's primary message was that recessions and depres-

John Maynard Keynes

sions can occur because of inadequate aggregate demand for goods and services.

Keynes had long been a critic of classical economic theory—the theory we examined earlier in the book—because it could explain only the long-run effects of policies. A few years before offering *The General Theory*, Keynes had written the following about classical economics:

The long run is a misleading guide to current affairs. In the long run we are all dead. Economists set themselves too easy, too useless a task if in tempestuous seasons they can only tell us when the storm is long past, the ocean will be flat.

Keynes's message was aimed at policymakers as well as economists. As the world's economies suffered with high unemployment, Keynes advocated policies to increase aggregate demand, including government spending on public works.

In the next chapter we examine in detail how policymakers can try to use the tools of monetary and fiscal policy to influence aggregate demand. The analysis in the next chapter, as well as in this one, owes much to the legacy of John Maynard Keynes.

(NEP) in 1980. The NEP was intended to slow the growth in oil prices in Canada to below the rate of growth in world markets, and thereby minimize the stagflation effects of the most recent jump in oil prices. The NEP helped industries that used oil as an input, but it also harmed industries that produced oil. As a result, although this policy response to the OPEC price shock reduced the stagflation effects for Canada on average, it did so by favouring some industries over others and, in oil-producing provinces, caused a great deal of bitterness toward the federal government.

The world market for oil can also be a source of favourable shifts in aggregate supply. In 1986 squabbling broke out among members of OPEC. Member countries reneged on their agreements to restrict oil production. In the world market for crude oil, prices fell by about half. This fall in oil prices reduced costs to firms that used oil as an input in the production process. As a result, Canada's aggregate-supply curve shifted to the right and the Canadian economy experienced the opposite of stagflation: Output grew rapidly, and the Canadian unemployment rate fell from 10.5 percent in 1985 to 7.5 percent in 1989. Once again, however, the effects of the decrease in oil prices differed considerably across oil-exporting and oil-importing provinces. For example, from 1985 to 1987, the unemployment rate

Changes in Middle East oil production are one source of Canadian economic fluctuations.

in Alberta remained constant at about 10.0 percent, while the unemployment rate in Ontario fell from 8.0 percent to 6.1 percent.

Clearly, the world market for crude oil is often very volatile. This volatility is in part a reflection of the inherent instability of cartels. Members of cartels have an incentive to undercut the agreed-upon price and, in doing so, increase their share of the market. Because all members of the cartel face this incentive, the price agreed on by the cartel occasionally collapses. The volatility of crude oil prices also reflects the political turmoil associated with the Middle East in recent years. Both of these influences were behind the collapse of world oil prices in early 1998. Between October 1997 and December 1998, the price of crude oil fell by 41 percent. Soon after this collapse in prices, however, OPEC met and decided to restrict output. The result was that from December 1998 to November 2000 the price of crude oil *increased* by 200 percent.

In recent years, the world market for oil has not been as important a source of economic fluctuations. Part of the reason is that OPEC has been less effective as a cartel: The real price of oil has never again come close to the levels reached in the early 1980s. In addition, conservation efforts and changes in technology have reduced the economy's dependence on oil. For each dollar of real GDP produced, Canada uses only about half the amount of oil that it did before the first OPEC price shock in 1973. As a result, changes in the price of oil now have a smaller impact on Canada's aggregate-supply curve. Nonetheless, it would be premature to conclude that Canada no longer needs to worry about oil prices. Political troubles in the Middle East (or greater cooperation among the members of OPEC) could always send oil prices higher. If the rise in oil prices were large enough, the macroeconomic result would most likely resemble the stagflation of the 1970s. ●

QuickQuiz Suppose that the election of a popular prime minister suddenly increases people's confidence in the future. Use the model of aggregate demand and aggregate supply to analyze the effect on the economy.

CONCLUSION

This chapter has achieved two goals. First, we have discussed some of the important facts about short-run fluctuations in economic activity. Second, we have introduced a basic model to explain those fluctuations, called the model of aggregate demand and aggregate supply. We continue our study of this model in the next chapter in order to understand more fully what causes fluctuations in the economy and how policymakers might respond to these fluctuations.

SUMMARY

- All societies experience short-run economic fluctuations around long-run trends. These fluctuations are irregular and largely unpredictable. When recessions do occur, real GDP and other measures of income, spending, and production fall, and unemployment rises.

- Economists analyze short-run economic fluctuations using the model of aggregate demand and aggregate supply. According to this model, the output of goods and services and the overall level of prices adjust to balance aggregate demand and aggregate supply.

- The aggregate-demand curve slopes downward for three reasons. First, a lower price level raises the real value of households' money holdings, which stimulates consumer spending. Second, a lower price level reduces the quantity of money households demand; as households try to convert money into interest-bearing assets, interest rates fall, which stimulates investment spending. Third, a lower price level reduces the real exchange rate. This depreciation makes Canadian produced goods and services cheaper relative to foreign-produced goods and services, and in this way stimulates net exports.

- Any event or policy that raises consumption, investment, government purchases, or net exports at a given price level increases aggregate demand. Any event or policy that reduces consumption, investment, government purchases, or net exports at a given price level decreases aggregate demand.

- The long-run aggregate-supply curve is vertical. In the long run, the quantity of goods and services supplied depends on the economy's labour, capital, natural resources, and technology, but not on the overall level of prices.

- Three theories have been proposed to explain the upward slope of the short-run aggregate-supply curve. According to the sticky-wage theory, an unexpected fall in the price level temporarily raises real wages, which induces firms to reduce employment and production. According to the sticky-price theory, an unexpected fall in the price level leaves some firms with prices that are temporarily too high, which reduces their sales and causes them to cut back production. According to the misperceptions theory, an unexpected fall in the price level leads suppliers to mistakenly believe that their relative prices have fallen, which induces them to reduce production. All three theories imply that output deviates from its natural rate when the price level deviates from the price level that people expected.

- Events that alter the economy's ability to produce output, such as changes in labour, capital, natural resources, or technology, shift the short-run aggregate-supply curve (and may shift the long-run aggregate-supply curve as well). In addition, the position of the short-run aggregate-supply curve depends on the expected price level.

- One possible cause of economic fluctuations is a shift in aggregate demand. When the aggregate-demand curve shifts to the left, for instance, output and prices fall in the short run. Over time, as a change in the expected price level causes wages, prices, and perceptions to adjust, the short-run aggregate-supply curve shifts to the right, and the economy returns to its natural rate of output at a new, lower price level.

- A second possible cause of economic fluctuations is a shift in aggregate supply. When the aggregate-supply curve shifts to the left, the short-run effect is falling output and rising prices—a combination called stagflation. Over time, as wages, prices, and perceptions adjust, the price level falls back to its original level, and output recovers.

KEY CONCEPTS

recession, p. 333
depression, p. 333

model of aggregate demand and
  aggregate supply, p. 338

aggregate-demand curve, p. 338
aggregate-supply curve, p. 338
stagflation, p. 359

QUESTIONS FOR REVIEW

1. Name two macroeconomic variables that decline when the economy goes into a recession. Name one macroeconomic variable that rises during a recession.

2. Draw a diagram with aggregate demand, short-run aggregate supply, and long-run aggregate supply. Be careful to label the axes correctly.

3. List and explain the three reasons why the aggregate-demand curve is downward sloping.

4. Explain why the long-run aggregate-supply curve is vertical.

5. List and explain the three theories for why the short-run aggregate-supply curve is upward sloping.

6. What might shift the aggregate-demand curve to the left? Use the model of aggregate demand and aggregate supply to trace through the effects of such a shift.

7. What might shift the aggregate-supply curve to the left? Use the model of aggregate demand and aggregate supply to trace through the effects of such a shift.

PROBLEMS AND APPLICATIONS

1. Why do you think that investment is more variable over the business cycle than consumer spending? Which category of consumer spending do you think would be most volatile: durable goods (such as furniture and car purchases), nondurable goods (such as food and clothing), or services (such as haircuts and dental care)? Why?

2. Suppose that the economy is in a long-run equilibrium.
   a. Use a diagram to illustrate the state of the economy. Be sure to show aggregate demand, short-run aggregate supply, and long-run aggregate supply.
   b. Now suppose that a stock market crash causes aggregate demand to fall. Use your diagram to show what happens to output and the price level in the short run. What happens to the unemployment rate?
   c. Use the sticky-wage theory of aggregate supply to explain what will happen to output and the price level in the long run

(assuming there is no change in policy). What role does the expected price level play in this adjustment? Be sure to illustrate your analysis in a graph.

3. Explain whether each of the following events will increase, decrease, or have no effect on long-run aggregate supply.
   a. Canada experiences a wave of immigration.
   b. Provincial governments raise the minimum wage to $10 per hour.
   c. Intel invents a new and more powerful computer chip.
   d. A severe hurricane damages factories along the east coast.

4. In Figure 15.8, how does the unemployment rate at points B and C compare to the unemployment rate at point A? Under the sticky-wage explanation of the short-run aggregate-supply curve, how does the real wage at points B and C compare to the real wage at point A?

5. Explain why the following statements are false.
   a. "The aggregate-demand curve slopes downward because it is the horizontal sum of the demand curves for individual goods."
   b. "The long-run aggregate-supply curve is vertical because economic forces do not affect long-run aggregate supply."
   c. "If firms adjusted their prices every day, then the short-run aggregate-supply curve would be horizontal."
   d. "Whenever the economy enters a recession, its long-run aggregate-supply curve shifts to the left."

6. For each of the three theories for the upward slope of the short-run aggregate-supply curve, carefully explain the following.
   a. how the economy recovers from a recession and returns to its long-run equilibrium without any policy intervention
   b. what determines the speed of that recovery

7. Suppose the Bank of Canada expands the money supply, but because the public expects this action, it simultaneously raises the public's expectation of the price level. What will happen to output and the price level in the short run? Compare this result to the outcome if the Bank of Canada expanded the money supply but the public didn't change its expectation of the price level.

8. Suppose that the economy is currently in a recession. If policymakers take no action, how will the economy evolve over time? Explain in words and using an aggregate-demand/aggregate-supply diagram.

9. Suppose workers and firms suddenly believe that inflation will be quite high over the coming year. Suppose also that the economy begins in long-run equilibrium, and the aggregate-demand curve does not shift.
   a. What happens to nominal wages? What happens to real wages?
   b. Using an aggregate-demand/aggregate-supply diagram, show the effect of the change in expectations on both the short-run and long-run levels of prices and output.
   c. Were the expectations of high inflation accurate? Explain.

10. For each of the following events explain the effect, if any, on the position of the short- and long-run aggregate-supply curves and the aggregate-demand curve.
    a. In the summer of 2003, a single cow in Alberta was found to suffer from BSE, or mad cow disease. As a consequence, many countries stopped importing Canadian beef and Canadian ranchers found that, at any price, they could sell much less beef than they could previously.
    b. Over the past decade, prospectors have discovered diamonds in Canada. The development of these diamond mines has progressed to the point that today Canada produces roughly 10 percent of the world's diamonds.
    c. Ongoing crises in the Middle East and the high price of oil have encouraged firms to significantly expand plants for the extraction of oil from the oil sands region of Alberta.
    d. In 2003, an outbreak of severe acute respiratory syndrome (SARS) in the Toronto region resulted in a significant reduction in the number of tourists visiting Canada.

11. Explain whether each of the following events shifts the short-run aggregate-supply curve, the aggregate-demand curve, both, or neither. For each event that does shift a curve, use a diagram to illustrate the effect on the economy.
    a. Households decide to save a larger share of their income.
    b. Okanagan peach orchards suffer a prolonged period of below-freezing temperatures.
    c. Increased job opportunities overseas cause many people to leave the country.

12. For each of the following events, explain the short-run and long-run effects on output and the price level, assuming policymakers take no action.
    a. The stock market declines sharply, reducing consumers' wealth.
    b. The federal government increases spending on national defence.
    c. A technological improvement raises productivity.
    d. A recession overseas causes foreigners to buy fewer Canadian goods.

13. Suppose that firms become very optimistic about future business conditions and invest heavily in new capital equipment.
   a. Use an aggregate-demand/aggregate-supply diagram to show the short-run effect of this optimism on the economy. Label the new levels of prices and real output. Explain in words why the aggregate quantity of output *supplied* changes.
   b. Now use the diagram from part (a) to show the new long-run equilibrium of the economy. (For now, assume there is no change in the long-run aggregate-supply curve.) Explain in words why the aggregate quantity of output *demanded* changes between the short run and the long run.
   c. How might the investment boom affect the long-run aggregate-supply curve? Explain.

INTERNET RESOURCES

- As noted in the text, the Great Depression that struck Canada beginning in 1930 was the most severe economic contraction ever experienced in Canada. It had a profound effect on the economy and on Canadians. The federal government's Canadian Economy website provides information on the economic and social impacts of the Great Depression. Go to http://canadianeconomy.gc.ca and click on "Key Economic Events" and then on "1929–1939: Great Depression."

- We also explained in the text how fluctuations in the price of crude oil have in the past played an important role in affecting the Canadian economy. Everything you ever wanted to know about the economics, politics, and production aspects of oil in Canada and around the world can be found on the World News Network Web page *Oil.com:* http://www.oilsite.com.

- More recent data on economic conditions in Canada can be found on Finance Canada's website at http://www.fin.gc.ca/purl/econbr-e.html. This site also offers an up-to-date commentary on current macroeconomic conditions.

http:// For more study tools, please visit http://www.mankiw3e.nelson.com.

© IMAGES CO./CORBIS/MAGMA

THE INFLUENCE OF MONETARY AND FISCAL POLICY ON AGGREGATE DEMAND

Learning Objectives

In this chapter, you will …

- Learn the theory of liquidity preference as a short-run theory of the interest rate
- Analyze how monetary policy affects interest rates and aggregate demand in open and closed economies
- Analyze how fiscal policy affects interest rates and aggregate demand in open and closed economies
- Discuss the debate over whether policymakers should try to stabilize the economy

Imagine that you are the governor of the Bank of Canada and therefore are in charge of setting monetary policy. You observe that the economy is slowing down and unemployment is rising. What should the Bank of Canada do? Imagine now that you are the federal government's minister of finance in charge of setting fiscal policy. What should you do given the evidence of an economic slowdown? Does the choice of the governor of the Bank of Canada depend on the choice made by the minister of finance?

To answer these questions, you need to consider the impact of monetary and fiscal policy on the economy. In the preceding chapter we saw how to explain short-run economic fluctuations using the model of aggregate demand and aggregate supply. When the aggregate-demand curve or the aggregate-supply curve shifts, the result is fluctuations in the economy's overall output of goods and services and in its overall level of prices. As we noted in the previous chapter, monetary and fiscal policy can each influence aggregate demand. Thus, a change in one of these policies can lead to short-run fluctuations in output and prices. Policymakers will want to anticipate this effect and, perhaps, adjust the other policy in response.

In this chapter we examine in more detail how the government's tools of monetary and fiscal policy influence the position of the aggregate-demand curve. We have previously discussed the long-run effects of these policies. In Chapters 7 and 8 we saw how fiscal policy affects saving, investment, and long-run economic growth. In Chapters 11 and 12 we saw how the Bank of Canada controls the money supply and how the money supply affects the price level in the long run. In Chapters 13 and 14 we looked at macroeconomic relationships in open economies and saw how the real exchange rate, net exports, and net foreign investment are determined.

In this chapter we will also see how the tools of monetary and fiscal policy can shift the aggregate-demand curve and, in doing so, affect short-run economic fluctuations. We will also see that the effect of policy tools on the position of the aggregate-demand curve depends on the degree to which the economy is closed or open to trade in goods, services, and financial capital. We begin our discussion of the influence of monetary and fiscal policy on aggregate demand by assuming a closed economy. This approach simplifies the analysis and puts us on the road to understanding what will happen in a small open economy. We will then show the implications for fiscal and monetary policy of Canada's being a small open economy.

As we have already learned, many factors influence aggregate demand besides monetary and fiscal policy. In particular, desired spending by households and firms determines the overall demand for goods and services. When desired spending changes, aggregate demand shifts. If policymakers do not respond, such shifts in aggregate demand cause short-run fluctuations in output and employment. As a result, monetary and fiscal policymakers sometimes use the policy levers at their disposal to try to offset these shifts in aggregate demand and thereby stabilize the economy. Here we discuss the theory behind these policy actions and some of the difficulties that arise in using this theory.

HOW MONETARY POLICY INFLUENCES AGGREGATE DEMAND

The aggregate-demand curve shows the total quantity of goods and services demanded in the economy for any price level. As you may recall from the preceding chapter, the aggregate-demand curve slopes downward for three reasons:

1. *The wealth effect:* A lower price level raises the real value of households' money holdings, and higher real wealth stimulates consumer spending.
2. *The interest-rate effect:* A lower price level lowers the interest rate as people try to lend out their excess money holdings, and the lower interest rate stimulates investment spending.
3. *The real exchange-rate effect:* A lower price level reduces the real exchange rate. This depreciation makes Canadian-produced goods and services cheaper relative to foreign-produced goods and services. As a result, Canadian net exports rise.

These three effects should not be viewed as alternative theories. Instead, they occur simultaneously to increase the quantity of goods and services demanded when the price level falls and to decrease it when the price level rises.

Although all three effects work together in explaining the downward slope of the aggregate-demand curve, they are not of equal importance. Because money holdings are a small part of household wealth, the wealth effect is the least important of the three. In a closed economy, the real exchange-rate effect is nonexistent, leaving the interest rate effect as the most important reason for the downward slope of the aggregate-demand curve. Since it is our goal to begin our discussion of the influence of monetary and fiscal policy on aggregate demand by first assuming a closed economy, we examine the interest rate effect in more detail. When thinking about Canada, however, we need to keep in mind that exports and imports make up a large proportion of the Canadian economy and that over the past 15 years their share of the economy has grown steadily. As a result, the real exchange-rate effect is an increasingly important explanation for why Canada's aggregate-demand curve slopes downward.

To begin developing an understanding of how policy influences aggregate demand, we examine the interest rate effect in more detail. This will involve discussing the **theory of liquidity preference.** After we develop this theory, we use it to understand the downward slope of the aggregate-demand curve and how monetary policy shifts this curve in a closed economy. We will then turn our attention to how monetary policy shifts the aggregate-demand curve in a small open economy.

theory of liquidity preference
Keynes's theory that the interest rate adjusts to bring money supply and money demand into balance

The Theory of Liquidity Preference

In his classic book *The General Theory of Employment, Interest, and Money*, John Maynard Keynes proposed the theory of liquidity preference to explain what factors determine the economy's interest rate. The theory is, in essence, just an application of supply and demand. According to Keynes, the interest rate adjusts to balance the supply and demand for money.

You may recall that economists distinguish between two interest rates: The *nominal interest rate* is the interest rate as usually reported, and the *real interest rate* is the interest rate corrected for the effects of inflation. Which interest rate are we now trying to explain? The answer is both. In the analysis that follows, we hold constant the expected rate of inflation. (This assumption is reasonable for studying the economy in the short run, as we are now doing.) Thus, when the nominal interest rate rises or falls, the real interest rate that people expect to earn rises or falls as well. For the rest of this chapter, when we refer to changes in the interest rate, you should envision the real and nominal interest rates moving in the same direction.

Let's now develop the theory of liquidity preference by considering the supply and demand for money and how each depends on the interest rate.

Money Supply   The first piece of the theory of liquidity preference is the supply of money. As we first discussed in Chapter 11, the money supply in the Canadian economy is controlled by the Bank of Canada. The Bank of Canada alters the money supply using two methods. The first is to change the quantity of reserves in the banking system through what is known as an open-market operation. One form that open-market operations take involves the Bank of Canada buying and selling federal government bonds in the bond market. When the Bank of Canada buys government bonds, the dollars it pays for the bonds are typically deposited in banks, and these dollars are added to bank reserves. When the Bank of Canada sells government bonds, the dollars it receives for the bonds are withdrawn from the banking system, and bank reserves fall. These changes in bank reserves, in turn, lead to changes in banks' ability to make loans and create money.

A different form of open-market operation involves the Bank of Canada buying and selling foreign currencies in the market for foreign-currency exchange. These sales and purchases are referred to as foreign exchange market operations. As we discussed in Chapter 11, if the Bank of Canada buys US$100 million in the market for foreign-currency exchange for CDN$150 million, the Canadian money supply increases immediately by $150 million. If the Bank of Canada sells foreign currency from its foreign exchange reserves, it receives Canadian dollars in exchange. Those Canadian dollars are withdrawn from circulation, so the Canadian money supply is reduced.

The second method the Bank of Canada uses to alter the money supply is by changing the bank rate. The bank rate is the interest rate on the loans that the Bank of Canada makes to commercial banks. Commercial banks may borrow from the Bank of Canada if they find that their reserves are inadequate. By increasing the bank rate, the Bank of Canada makes such loans more expensive and thus discourages commercial banks from borrowing reserves. Therefore, an increase in the bank rate effectively reduces the quantity of reserves in the banking system, which in turn reduces the money supply. Similarly, a decrease in the bank rate makes it less expensive for banks to borrow from the Bank of Canada and thus effectively increases the quantity of reserves in the banking system, which in turn increases the money supply.

Open-market operations and changing the bank rate are the most important methods used by the Bank of Canada for changing the money supply. As we will see, the Bank of Canada's decision on whether or not to buy and sell dollars in the market for foreign-currency exchange has important implications for the effect of monetary and fiscal policy on aggregate demand.

The relationship between money demand and money supply is shown in Figure 16.1, with the quantity of money on the horizontal axis and the interest rate on the vertical axis. We assume that the Bank of Canada controls the money supply directly. In particular, we assume that the supply of money is not affected at all by changes in the interest rate. For this reason, the money-supply curve is a vertical line.

Money Demand   The second piece of the theory of liquidity preference is the demand for money. As a starting point for understanding money demand, recall that any asset's *liquidity* refers to the ease with which that asset is converted into the economy's medium of exchange. Money is the economy's medium of exchange, so it is by definition the most liquid asset available. The liquidity of money explains the demand for it: People choose to hold money instead of other assets that offer higher rates of return because money can be used to buy goods and services.

Although many factors determine the quantity of money demanded, the one emphasized by the theory of liquidity preference is the interest rate. The reason is that the interest rate is the opportunity cost of holding money. That is, when you hold wealth as cash in your wallet, instead of as an interest-bearing bond, you lose the interest you could have earned. An increase in the interest rate raises the cost

FIGURE 16.1

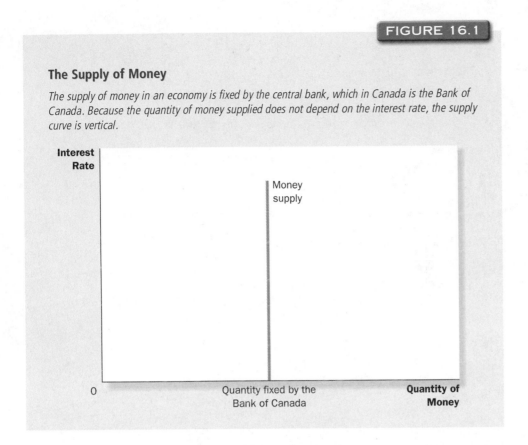

The Supply of Money

The supply of money in an economy is fixed by the central bank, which in Canada is the Bank of Canada. Because the quantity of money supplied does not depend on the interest rate, the supply curve is vertical.

of holding money and, as a result, reduces the quantity of money demanded. A decrease in the interest rate reduces the cost of holding money and raises the quantity demanded. Thus, as shown in Figure 16.2 (page 372), the money-demand curve slopes downward.

The other key determinant of the quantity of money demanded is the fact that money is used to buy goods and services. As a result, when either the quantity or the price of goods and services increases, people need to hold more of their assets in the form of money. The quantity of goods and services that people buy is simply equal to real GDP. The price of goods and services in the economy is represented by a price index such as the consumer price index or the GDP deflator. The product of these two measures is the dollar value of all transactions in the economy. Figure 16.3 (page 373) shows the influence on money demand of an increase in either the price level or the level of real GDP. For a given interest rate, an increase in the dollar value of transactions causes the demand for money to increase. As a result, the money-demand curve shifts to the right. For a given interest rate, a decrease in the dollar value of transactions causes the demand for money to decrease. As a result, the money-demand curve shifts to the left.

Equilibrium in the Money Market   According to the theory of liquidity preference, the interest rate adjusts to balance the supply and demand for money. There is one interest rate, called the *equilibrium interest rate*, at which the quantity of money demanded exactly balances the quantity of money supplied. If the

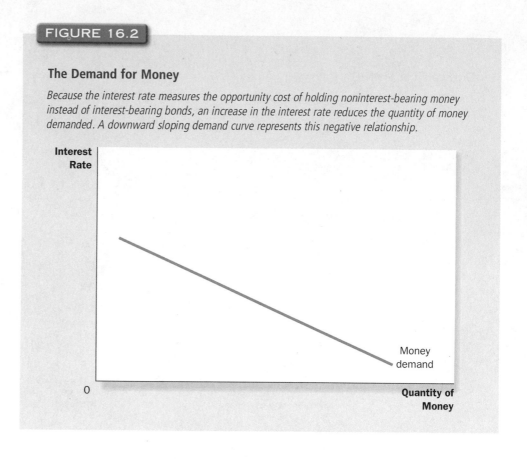

FIGURE 16.2

The Demand for Money

Because the interest rate measures the opportunity cost of holding noninterest-bearing money instead of interest-bearing bonds, an increase in the interest rate reduces the quantity of money demanded. A downward sloping demand curve represents this negative relationship.

interest rate is at any other level, people will try to adjust their portfolios of assets and, as a result, drive the interest rate toward the equilibrium.

For example, suppose that the interest rate is above the equilibrium level, such as r_1 in Figure 16.4 (page 374). In this case, the quantity of money that people want to hold, M_1^d, is less than the quantity of money that the Bank of Canada has supplied. Those people who are holding the surplus of money will try to get rid of it by buying interest-bearing bonds or by depositing it in an interest-bearing bank account. Because bond issuers and banks prefer to pay lower interest rates, they respond to this surplus of money by lowering the interest rates they offer. As the interest rate falls, people become more willing to hold money until, at the equilibrium interest rate, people are happy to hold exactly the amount of money the Bank of Canada has supplied.

Conversely, at interest rates below the equilibrium level, such as r_2 in Figure 16.4, the quantity of money that people want to hold, M_2^d, is greater than the quantity of money that the Bank of Canada has supplied. As a result, people try to increase their holdings of money by reducing their holdings of bonds and other interest-bearing assets. As people cut back on their holdings of bonds, bond issuers find that they have to offer higher interest rates to attract buyers. Thus, the interest rate rises and approaches the equilibrium level.

FIGURE 16.3

Shifts in the Demand for Money

People hold money in order to buy goods and services. If the dollar value of transactions increases because of an increase in either prices or GDP, then for any interest rate (r_1), people will hold more of their assets as money (increasing from M_1^d to M_3^d). As a result, the money-demand curve shifts to the right. If the dollar value of transactions decreases because of a decrease in either price or GDP, then for any interest rate (r_1) people will hold less of their assets as money (decreasing from M_1^d to M_2^d). As a result, the money-demand curve shifts to the left.

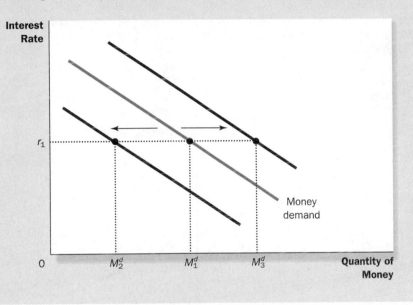

The Downward Slope of the Aggregate-Demand Curve

Having seen how the theory of liquidity preference explains the economy's equilibrium interest rate, we now consider its implications for the aggregate demand for goods and services. As a warm-up exercise, let's begin by using the theory to reexamine a topic we already understand—the interest-rate effect and the downward slope of the aggregate-demand curve. In particular, suppose that the overall level of prices in the economy rises. What happens to the interest rate that balances the supply and demand for money, and how does that change affect the quantity of goods and services demanded?

As we have just discussed, the price level is one determinant of the quantity of money demanded. At higher prices, more money is exchanged every time a good or service is sold. As a result, people will choose to hold a larger quantity of money. That is, a higher price level increases the quantity of money demanded for any given interest rate. Thus, an increase in the price level from P_1 to P_2 shifts the money-demand curve to the right from MD_1 to MD_2, as shown in panel (a) of Figure 16.5 (page 375).

Notice how this shift in money demand affects the equilibrium in the money market. For a fixed money supply, the interest rate must rise to balance money

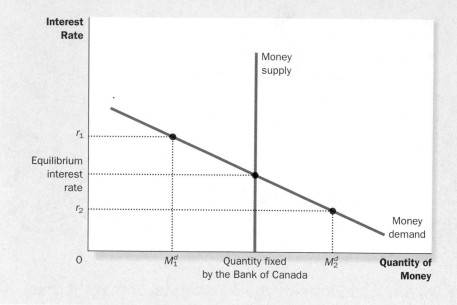

FIGURE 16.4

Equilibrium in the Money Market

According to the theory of liquidity preference, the interest rate adjusts to bring the quantity of money supplied and the quantity of money demanded into balance. If the interest rate is above the equilibrium level (such as at r_1), the quantity of money people want to hold (M_1^d) is less than the quantity the Bank of Canada has created, and this surplus of money puts downward pressure on the interest rate. Conversely, if the interest rate is below the equilibrium level (such as at r_2), the quantity of money people want to hold (M_2^d) is greater than the quantity the Bank of Canada has created, and this shortage of money puts upward pressure on the interest rate. Thus, the forces of supply and demand in the market for money push the interest rate toward the equilibrium interest rate, at which people are content holding the quantity of money the Bank of Canada has created.

supply and money demand. The higher price level has increased the amount of money people want to hold and has shifted the money demand curve to the right. Yet the quantity of money supplied is unchanged, so the interest rate must rise from r_1 to r_2 to discourage the additional demand.

This increase in the interest rate has ramifications not only for the money market but also for the quantity of goods and services demanded, as shown in panel (b). At a higher interest rate, the cost of borrowing and the return to saving are greater. Fewer households choose to borrow to buy a new house, and those who do buy smaller houses, so the demand for residential investment falls. Fewer firms choose to borrow to build new factories and buy new equipment, so business investment falls. Thus, when the price level rises from P_1 to P_2, increasing money demand from MD_1 to MD_2 and raising the interest rate from r_1 to r_2, the quantity of goods and services demanded falls from Y_1 to Y_2.

Hence, this analysis of the interest-rate effect can be summarized in three steps: (1) A higher price level raises money demand. (2) Higher money demand leads to a higher interest rate. (3) A higher interest rate reduces the quantity of goods and

FIGURE 16.5

The Money Market and the Slope of the Aggregate-Demand Curve

An increase in the price level from P_1 to P_2 shifts the money-demand curve to the right, as in panel (a). This increase in money demand causes the interest rate to rise from r_1 to r_2. Because the interest rate is the cost of borrowing, the increase in the interest rate reduces the quantity of goods and services demanded from Y_1 to Y_2. This negative relationship between the price level and quantity demanded is represented with a downward-sloping aggregate-demand curve, as in panel (b).

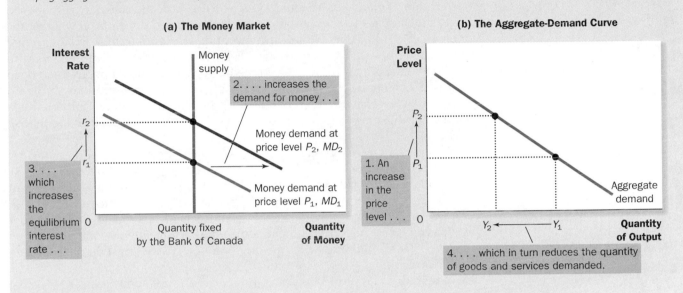

services demanded. Of course, the same logic works in reverse as well: A lower price level reduces money demand, which leads to a lower interest rate, and this in turn increases the quantity of goods and services demanded. The end result of this analysis is a negative relationship between the price level and the quantity of goods and services demanded, which is illustrated with a downward-sloping aggregate-demand curve.

In an open economy, the other important influence is the real exchange-rate effect. An increase in the price level causes the real exchange rate to increase. Because this makes Canadian-produced goods more expensive relative to foreign-produced goods, both foreigners and Canadians substitute away from Canadian-produced goods. As a result, Canada's net exports fall. For this additional reason, then, in a small open economy an increase in the price level causes the quantity of Canadian-produced goods and services demanded to fall. Whether it is due primarily to the interest rate effect or to the real exchange-rate effect, the end result of this analysis is a negative relationship between the price level and the quantity of goods and services demanded. This relationship is illustrated with a downward sloping aggregate-demand curve.

Changes in the Money Supply

So far we have used the theory of liquidity preference to explain more fully how the total quantity demanded of goods and services in the economy changes as the price level changes. That is, we have examined movements along the downward-sloping aggregate-demand curve. The theory also sheds light, however, on some of the other events that alter the quantity of goods and services demanded. Whenever the quantity of goods and services demanded changes *for a given price level*, the aggregate-demand curve shifts. As we will see, how the economy responds to changes in the quantity of goods and services demanded depends on whether the economy is closed or open. It is worth repeating that our strategy will be to first show what happens in a closed economy. We will then turn to open-economy considerations. This is a useful way of proceeding because what happens in an open economy is essentially the same as what happens in a closed economy but with one or two additional considerations. Thus, the closed-economy discussion is a helpful steppingstone to understanding what happens in an open economy like Canada.

One important variable that shifts the aggregate-demand curve is monetary policy. To see how monetary policy affects the economy in the short run, suppose that the Bank of Canada increases the money supply by buying government bonds in open-market operations. (Why the Bank of Canada might do this will become clear later after we understand the effects of such a move.) Let's consider how this monetary injection influences the equilibrium interest rate for a given price level. This will tell us what the injection does to the position of the aggregate-demand curve.

As panel (a) of Figure 16.6 shows, an increase in the money supply shifts the money-supply curve to the right from MS_1 to MS_2. Because the money-demand curve has not changed, the interest rate falls from r_1 to r_2 to balance money supply and money demand. That is, the interest rate must fall to induce people to hold the additional money the Bank of Canada has created.

Once again, the interest rate influences the quantity of goods and services demanded, as shown in panel (b) of Figure 16.6. The lower interest rate reduces the cost of borrowing and the return to saving. Households buy more and larger houses, stimulating the demand for residential investment. Firms spend more on new factories and new equipment, stimulating business investment. For all of these reasons, the quantity of goods and services demanded at the given price level, $\overline{P}$, rises. The increase in demand for goods and services increases the demand for money from MD_1 to MD_2, causing the interest rate to rise slightly from r_2 to r_3. This partial reversal in the fall in the interest rate reduces somewhat the stimulative effect on residential and firm investment. As a result, the shift in aggregate demand is smaller than it would otherwise have been. The net effect is an increase in the quantity of goods and services demanded at the given price level, $\overline{P}$, from Y_1 to Y_2, and thus a shift to the right of the aggregate-demand curve from AD_1 to AD_2. Of course, there is nothing special about $\overline{P}$: The monetary injection raises the quantity of goods and services demanded at every price level. Thus, the entire aggregate-demand curve shifts to the right.

To sum up: *When the Bank of Canada increases the money supply, it lowers the interest rate and increases the quantity of goods and services demanded for any given price level, shifting the aggregate-demand curve to the right. Conversely, when the Bank of Canada contracts the money supply, it raises the interest rate and reduces the quantity of*

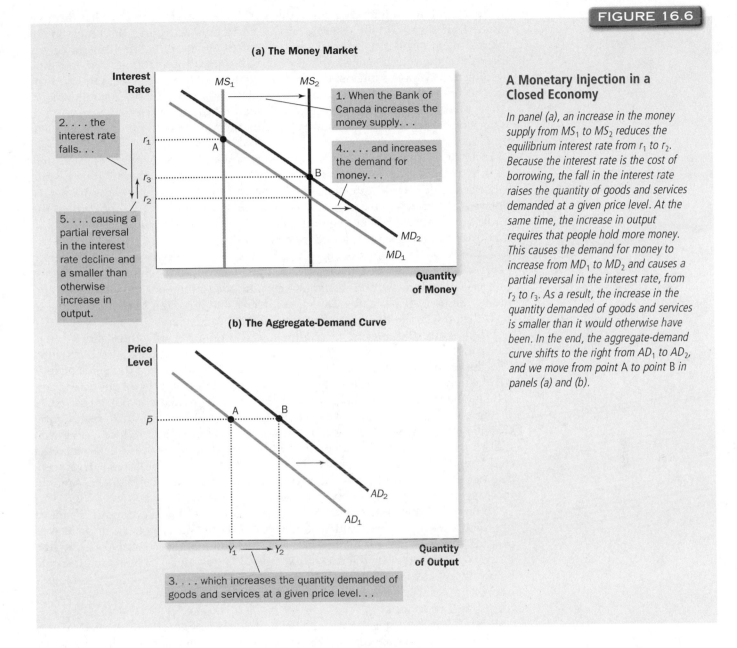

FIGURE 16.6

(a) The Money Market

1. When the Bank of Canada increases the money supply. . .

2. . . . the interest rate falls. . .

4. . . . . and increases the demand for money. . .

5. . . . causing a partial reversal in the interest rate decline and a smaller than otherwise increase in output.

(b) The Aggregate-Demand Curve

3. . . . . which increases the quantity demanded of goods and services at a given price level. . .

A Monetary Injection in a Closed Economy

In panel (a), an increase in the money supply from MS_1 to MS_2 reduces the equilibrium interest rate from r_1 to r_2. Because the interest rate is the cost of borrowing, the fall in the interest rate raises the quantity of goods and services demanded at a given price level. At the same time, the increase in output requires that people hold more money. This causes the demand for money to increase from MD_1 to MD_2 and causes a partial reversal in the interest rate, from r_2 to r_3. As a result, the increase in the quantity demanded of goods and services is smaller than it would otherwise have been. In the end, the aggregate-demand curve shifts to the right from AD_1 to AD_2, and we move from point A to point B in panels (a) and (b).

goods and services demanded for any given price level, shifting the aggregate-demand curve to the left.

Open-Economy Considerations

Our discussion of how monetary policy affects aggregate demand so far has ignored open-economy considerations. Earlier, we discussed how Canada is described by macroeconomists as a small open economy with perfect capital mobility. We saw that one implication of this is that Canada's interest rate must move up and down with changes in the world interest rate. Canada's interest rate differs from the world interest rate only by an amount reflecting differences in the tax treatment of financial capital and differences in default risk in Canada versus the rest of the world. For simplicity, we will ignore these differences and thus assume that Canada's interest rate adjusts to equal the world interest rate. We turn now to the question of how a monetary injection affects the aggregate-demand curve in a small open economy. We will see that the story we have told so far, while correct for a closed economy, is incomplete for a small open economy like Canada.

Panel (a) of Figure 16.7 shows money-demand and money-supply curves intersecting at the world interest rate, r^w. Because eventually Canada's interest rate must equal the world interest rate, we begin our discussion of how monetary policy affects aggregate demand from this point. To obtain a true measure of the impact of monetary policy, we must show all of the adjustments in the economy that return Canada's interest rate to the world interest rate.

An increase in the money supply shifts the money-supply curve to the right, from MS_1 to MS_2. Because the money-demand curve has not changed, the interest rate falls below the world interest rate to r_2 in order to balance money supply and money demand. That is, the Canadian interest rate must fall to induce people to hold the additional money the Bank of Canada has created.

Once again, the interest rate influences the quantity of goods and services demanded, as shown in panel (b) of Figure 16.7. By lowering the cost of borrowing and the return to saving, the lower interest rate stimulates the demand for residential and business investment. For these reasons, the quantity of goods and services demanded at the given price level, $\bar{P}$, rises. The increase in output increases the demand for money from MD_1 to MD_2, causing the interest rate to rise slightly from r_2 to r_3. This partial reversal in the fall in the interest rate reduces somewhat the stimulative effect on residential and firm investment. As a result, the increase in demand for goods and services is smaller than it would otherwise have been. The net effect is a shift in the aggregate-demand curve from AD_1 to AD_2 and an increase in the quantity of goods and services demanded from Y_1 to Y_2.

So far, all of this is exactly as it was previously. In a closed economy, the effect of a monetary injection would be summarized by the movement from point A to point B in panels (a) and (b) of Figure 16.7. In a small open economy like Canada, however, this cannot be the end of the story. We have left Canada's interest rate below the world interest rate. But, because of perfect capital mobility, Canada's interest rate must eventually adjust to equal the world interest rate. Something further must happen.

When Canada's interest rate falls below the world interest rate, Canadian and foreign savers find Canadian assets, which now pay interest rate r_3, less attractive than foreign assets that pay the world interest rate. As a result, Canadians and foreigners sell Canadian assets and buy foreign assets. Recall from our discussion in Chapter 14 that while people want to trade goods, services, and financial assets with people in other countries, they want to be paid for these things in their own currency. Thus the switch from Canadian assets to foreign assets requires a corresponding sale of Canadian dollars and purchase of foreign currencies. In the market for foreign-currency exchange, the supply of Canadian dollars therefore increases, causing the dollar to depreciate in value and the real exchange rate to fall. The fall in the real exchange rate makes Canadian-produced goods and services less expensive relative to foreign-produced goods and services.

FIGURE 16.7

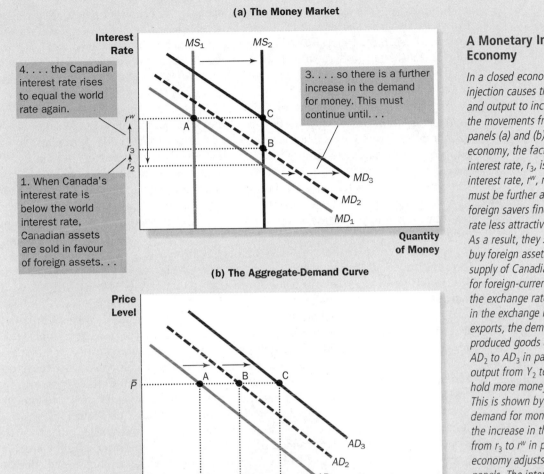

(a) The Money Market

4. . . . the Canadian interest rate rises to equal the world rate again.

3. . . . so there is a further increase in the demand for money. This must continue until. . .

1. When Canada's interest rate is below the world interest rate, Canadian assets are sold in favour of foreign assets. . .

(b) The Aggregate-Demand Curve

2. . . . which causes the exchange rate to fall, net exports to increase, and the demand for Canadian-produced goods and services to increase still further. . .

A Monetary Injection in an Open Economy

In a closed economy, a monetary injection causes the interest rate to fall and output to increase. This is shown by the movements from point A to point B in panels (a) and (b). In a small open economy, the fact that the domestic interest rate, r_3, is less than the world interest rate, r^w, means that the rate must be further adjusted. Canadian and foreign savers find the Canadian interest rate less attractive than the world rate. As a result, they sell Canadian assets to buy foreign assets. This increases the supply of Canadian dollars in the market for foreign-currency exchange and causes the exchange rate to fall. Because the fall in the exchange rate increases net exports, the demand for Canadian-produced goods and services rises from AD_2 to AD_3 in panel (b). The expansion of output from Y_2 to Y_3 requires that people hold more money to make transactions. This is shown by the increase in the demand for money from MD_2 to MD_3 and the increase in the Canadian interest rate from r_3 to r^w in panel (a). In the end, the economy adjusts to point C in both panels. The interest rate returns to the world interest rate, and output increases by more than it would in a closed economy.

Consequently, Canada's net exports increase, which causes the quantity of Canadian-produced goods and services demanded at the given price level, $\bar{P}$, to increase still further. This is shown in panel (b) of Figure 16.7 by the shift of the aggregate-demand curve from AD_2 to AD_3. This additional increase in output increases the demand for money, which causes the interest rate to rise still further. This is shown in panel (a) of Figure 16.7 by the shift of the money-demand curve from MD_2 to MD_3. This shift must be such that Canada's interest rate is once again equal to the world interest rate. The end result of all of these adjustments is an increase in the demand for money to MD_3, a return of Canada's interest rate to the world interest rate, an increase in the quantity of goods and services demanded to Y_3, and a shift in the aggregate-demand curve to AD_3.

To sum up: *In a small open economy, a monetary injection by the Bank of Canada causes the dollar to depreciate in value. Because this depreciation of the dollar causes net exports to rise, there is an additional increase in demand for Canadian-produced goods and services that is not realized in a closed economy. In the end, a monetary injection in an open economy shifts the aggregate-demand curve farther to the right than it does in a closed economy.*

An important part of our explanation of how a monetary injection affects aggregate demand is our assumption that the Bank of Canada allows the exchange rate to change. That is, we have assumed that the Bank of Canada has chosen to allow the exchange rate to be flexible. As we explained in Chapter 11, the Bank of Canada can, if it wishes, buy and sell foreign currencies in what are known as foreign exchange market operations. Foreign exchange market operations are very similar to open-market operations in that they both involve the central bank buying or selling something. When the central bank buys something, whether it is a government bond or foreign currency, it causes the money supply to increase. When the Bank sells something, whether it is a government bond or foreign currency, it causes the money supply to decrease. Now consider what would happen if the Bank of Canada wanted to expand the money supply while maintaining a constant value of the Canadian dollar.

By lowering the Canadian interest rate, a monetary injection causes Canadians and foreigners to sell Canadian assets in preference for foreign assets. This switch out of Canadian assets and into foreign assets increases the supply of Canadian dollars in the market for foreign-currency exchange, which causes the exchange rate to fall. If the Bank of Canada wanted to prevent this fall in the exchange rate, it would enter the market for foreign-currency exchange to sell foreign currency it holds and purchase Canadian dollars. This purchase of dollars would increase the demand for dollars in the market for foreign-currency exchange and offset the increased supply of dollars caused by Canadians and foreigners selling Canadian assets. In this way, the value of the Canadian dollar remains unchanged. But the sale of foreign currency by the Bank of Canada would also decrease the money supply. To prevent a fall in the value of the Canadian dollar, then, the Bank of Canada would need to contract the Canadian money supply. Because the purpose of the monetary injection was to expand the money supply, it would be counterproductive indeed for the Bank of Canada to try to prevent the value of the dollar from changing.

This explanation of why the Bank of Canada must allow the exchange rate to vary freely if it wants to change the money supply teaches an important lesson: *The Bank of Canada cannot simultaneously choose the size of the money supply and the value of the Canadian dollar.* By choosing to change the money supply, the Bank of Canada must allow the exchange rate to vary.

QuickQuiz Explain how a decrease in the money supply affects the money market and the position of the aggregate-demand curve. What is the effect for a closed economy and for a small open economy?

TABLE 16.1

The Effects of a
Monetary Injection:
Summary

How Does a Monetary Injection Shift the Aggregate-Demand Curve in a Closed Economy?

1. An increase in money supply causes the interest rate to fall.
2. The fall in the interest rate stimulates investment and consumption of durable goods. The increase in spending increases the demand for money, causing a partial reversal of the fall in the interest rate.
3. The increase in spending shifts the aggregate-demand curve to the right.

How Does a Monetary Injection Shift the Aggregate-Demand Curve in an Open Economy?

1. Due to perfect capital mobility, and ignoring differences in default risk and taxes, Canada's interest rate must equal the world interest rate. We begin with $r = r^w$.
2. An increase in the money supply causes Canada's interest rate to fall below r^w.
3. The fall in the interest rate stimulates investment and consumption of durable goods. The increase in spending increases the demand for money causing a partial reversal of the fall in the interest rate. Canada's interest rate remains below r^w.
4. With $r < r^w$, Canadian assets are sold in favour of buying foreign assets. The switch from Canadian to foreign assets requires that dollars be sold in the market for foreign-currency exchange. The real exchange rate falls.
5. The fall in the real exchange rate increases net exports, causing the aggregate-demand curve to shift even farther to the right.
6. This additional stimulus to spending increases the demand for money until $r = r^w$.
7. It makes sense for the Bank of Canada to cause a monetary injection only if it allows the exchange rate to be flexible.

Case Study

WHY CENTRAL BANKS WATCH THE STOCK MARKET (AND VICE VERSA)

"Irrational exuberance." That was how U.S. Federal Reserve Chairman Alan Greenspan once described the booming stock market of the late 1990s. He was right about the market being exuberant: Average stock prices in the United States increased about fourfold during the 1990s. While somewhat less exuberant, the average stock price in Canada nonetheless increased 2.5 times over this period. And perhaps stock markets were even irrational: In 2001 and 2002, stock markets took back some of these large gains, as stock prices experienced a pronounced decline.

Regardless of how they view booming (or crashing) stock markets, how should central banks respond to stock market fluctuations? Central banks have no reason to care about stock prices in themselves, but they do have the job of monitoring and responding to developments in the overall economy, and the stock market is a piece of the puzzle. When the stock market booms, households become wealthier, and this increased wealth stimulates consumer spending. In addition, a rise in stock prices makes it more attractive for firms to sell new shares of stock, and this stimulates investment spending. For both reasons, a booming stock market expands the aggregate demand for goods and services.

As we discuss more fully later in the chapter, one of a central bank's goals is to stabilize aggregate demand, because greater stability in aggregate demand means greater stability in output and the price level. To do this, a central bank might respond to a stock market boom by keeping the money supply lower and interest rates higher than it otherwise would. The contractionary effects of higher interest rates would offset the expansionary effects of higher stock prices.

The opposite occurs when the stock market falls. Spending on consumption and investment declines, depressing aggregate demand and pushing the economy toward recession. To stabilize aggregate demand, a central bank needs to increase the money supply and lower interest rates.

While central banks keep an eye on the stock market, stock market participants also keep an eye on the central banks. Because central banks can influence interest rates and economic activity, they can alter the value of stocks. For example, when a central bank raises interest rates by reducing the money supply, it makes owning stocks less attractive for two reasons. First, a higher interest rate means that bonds, the alternative to stocks, are earning a higher return. Second, the central bank's tightening of monetary policy risks pushing the economy into a recession, which reduces profits. As a result, stock prices often fall when central banks raise interest rates. ●

QuickQuiz Use the theory of liquidity preference to explain how a decrease in the money supply affects the equilibrium interest rate. How does this change in monetary policy affect the aggregate-demand curve?

HOW FISCAL POLICY INFLUENCES AGGREGATE DEMAND

The government can influence the behaviour of the economy not only with monetary policy but also with fiscal policy. Fiscal policy refers to the government's choices regarding the overall level of government purchases or taxes. Earlier in the book we examined how fiscal policy influences saving, investment, and growth in the long run. In the short run, however, the primary effect of fiscal policy is on the aggregate demand for goods and services.

Changes in Government Purchases

When policymakers change the money supply or the level of taxes, they shift the aggregate-demand curve by influencing the spending decisions of firms or households. By contrast, when the government alters its own purchases of goods and services, it shifts the aggregate-demand curve directly.

Suppose, for example, that the federal government chooses to introduce a $5 billion job-creation program. The program will finance expenditures on new roads, sewers, and bridges. The program raises the demand for construction work and induces construction firms to hire more workers. The increase in demand for construction work is reflected in an increase in the aggregate demand for goods and services. As a result, the aggregate-demand curve shifts to the right.

By how much does this $5 billion government expenditure shift the aggregate-demand curve? At first, one might guess that the aggregate-demand curve shifts to the right by exactly $5 billion. It turns out, however, that this is not correct. There are two macroeconomic effects that make the size of the shift in aggregate demand differ from the change in government purchases. The first—the multiplier effect—suggests that the shift in aggregate demand could be *larger* than $5 billion. The second—the crowding-out effect—suggests that the shift in aggregate demand could be *smaller* than $5 billion. We now discuss each of these effects in turn.

The Multiplier Effect

When the government spends $5 billion on construction work, that expenditure has repercussions. The immediate impact of the higher demand from the government is to raise employment and profits for the construction firms involved. Then, as the workers see higher earnings and the firm owners see higher profits, they respond to this increase in income by raising their own spending on consumer goods. As a result, the government expenditure of $5 billion raises the demand for the products of many other firms in the economy. Because each dollar spent by the government can raise the aggregate demand for goods and services by more than a dollar, government purchases are said to have a **multiplier effect** on aggregate demand.

multiplier effect
the additional shifts in aggregate demand that result when expansionary fiscal policy increases income and thereby increases consumer spending

This multiplier effect continues even after this first round. When consumer spending rises, the firms that produce these consumer goods hire more people and experience higher profits. Higher earnings and profits stimulate consumer spending once again, and so on. Thus, there is positive feedback as higher demand leads to higher income, which in turn leads to even higher demand. Once all these effects are added together, the total impact on the quantity of goods and services demanded can be much larger than the initial impulse from higher government spending.

Figure 16.8 illustrates the multiplier effect. The increase in government purchases of $5 billion initially shifts the aggregate-demand curve to the right from AD_1 to AD_2 by exactly $5 billion. But when consumers respond by increasing their spending, the aggregate-demand curve shifts still further to AD_3.

This multiplier effect arising from the response of consumer spending can be strengthened by the response of investment to higher levels of demand. For instance, the construction firms might respond to the higher demand for roads and bridges by deciding to buy more paving equipment or build another cement plant. In this case, higher government demand spurs higher demand for investment goods. This positive feedback from demand to investment is sometimes called the *investment accelerator*.

A Formula for the Spending Multiplier

A little high-school algebra permits us to derive a formula for the size of the multiplier effect that arises from consumer spending. An important number in this formula is the *marginal propensity to consume (MPC)*—the fraction of extra income that a household consumes rather than saves. For example, suppose that the marginal propensity to consume is 3/4. This means that for every extra dollar that a

FIGURE 16.8

The Multiplier Effect

An increase in government purchases of $5 billion can shift the aggregate-demand curve to the right by more than $5 billion. This multiplier effect arises because increases in aggregate income stimulate additional spending by consumers.

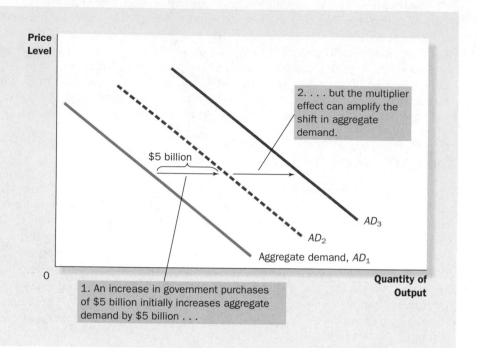

2. . . . but the multiplier effect can amplify the shift in aggregate demand.

$5 billion

AD_3

AD_2

Aggregate demand, AD_1

Quantity of Output

1. An increase in government purchases of $5 billion initially increases aggregate demand by $5 billion . . .

household earns, the household spends $0.75 (3/4 of the dollar) and saves $0.25. With an *MPC* of 3/4, when the workers and owners of the construction firms earn $5 billion from the government contract, they increase their consumer spending by 3/4 × $5 billion, or $3.75 billion.

To gauge the impact on aggregate demand of a change in government purchases, we follow the effects step by step. The process begins when the government spends $5 billion, which implies that national income (earnings and profits) also rises by this amount. This increase in income in turn raises consumer spending by *MPC* × $5 billion, which in turn raises the income for the workers and owners of the firms that produce the consumption goods. This second increase in income again raises consumer spending, this time by *MPC* × (*MPC* × $5 billion). These feedback effects go on and on.

To find the total impact on the demand for goods and services, we add up all these effects:

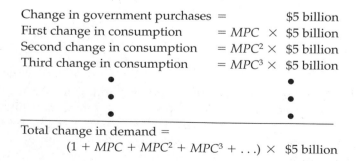

Change in government purchases = $5 billion
First change in consumption   = *MPC* × $5 billion
Second change in consumption   = MPC^2 × $5 billion
Third change in consumption   = MPC^3 × $5 billion
       •   •
       •   •
       •   •

Total change in demand =
$(1 + MPC + MPC^2 + MPC^3 + \ldots)$ × $5 billion

Here, "..." represents an infinite number of similar terms. Thus, we can write the multiplier as follows:

$$\text{Multiplier} = 1 + MPC + MPC^2 + MPC^3 + \ldots$$

This multiplier tells us the demand for goods and services that each dollar of government purchases generates.

To simplify this equation for the multiplier, recall from math class that this expression is an infinite geometric series. For x between -1 and $+1$,

$$1 + x + x^2 + x^3 + \ldots = 1/(1 - x)$$

In our case, $x = MPC$. Thus,

$$\text{Multiplier} = 1/(1 - MPC)$$

For example, if MPC is 3/4, the multiplier is $1/(1 - 3/4)$, which is 4. In this case, the $5 billion of government spending generates $20 billion of demand for goods and services.

In an open economy, the formula for the multiplier looks a bit different, because many of the goods and services that people purchase are imported. Recognition of this requires that we be a little more specific about how we define the multiplier. The government-spending multiplier tells us the demand for *Canadian-produced* goods and services generated by each additional dollar of government expenditure. Suppose that the fraction of extra income that a Canadian household spends on imported goods—what we call the *marginal propensity to import (MPI)*—is 1/4. Now for every extra dollar that a household earns, the household saves $0.25 and spends $0.75, as before, but only $0.50 of that spending is on Canadian-produced goods and $0.25 is spent on imported goods. When the construction workers and firms earn $5 billion from the government contract, they increase their spending on all goods by 3/4 × $5 billion, or $3.75 billion, but increase their spending on Canadian-produced goods by just 1/2 × $5 billion, or $2.5 billion. Only this second, smaller, amount adds to the incomes of other Canadians. Because Canadians spend some of their additional income on imported goods and services, therefore, the feedback effects are smaller than in a closed economy.

The relevant formula for the government-purchases multiplier in an open economy is

$$\text{Multiplier} = 1/(1 - MPC + MPI)$$

Now, because $MPC = 3/4$ and $MPI = 1/4$, the multiplier is $1/(1 - 3/4 + 1/4)$, which is 2. In this case, the $5 billion of government spending generates $10 billion of demand for Canadian-produced goods and services. This compares with the $20 billion of demand for goods and services generated by the $5 billion of government spending in a closed economy. The government-purchases multiplier is clearly much smaller in an open economy than in a closed economy.

These formulas for the multiplier show an important conclusion. The size of the multiplier depends on the marginal propensity to consume and, in an open economy, the marginal propensity to import. A larger MPC means a larger multiplier. To see why this is true, remember that the multiplier arises because higher income induces greater spending on consumption. The larger the *MPC*, the greater this induced effect on consumption and the larger the multiplier. In an open economy we also need to consider the marginal propensity to import. A larger *MPI* means a *smaller* multiplier. To see why this is true, remember that the *MPI* measures the amount of higher income that is spent on foreign-produced goods and services. The greater this amount, the smaller the amount by which spending on *Canadian-produced* goods and services increases for any increase in income. A larger *MPI*, then, means that every increase in income induces a smaller increase in spending on Canadian-produced goods and services.

An interesting implication of the role played by the marginal propensity to import in determining the size of the multiplier in Canada is the likelihood that the *MPI* has recently grown larger. We saw earlier how the implementation of free trade agreements in 1989 and 1994 has resulted in a dramatic increase in the amount of trade Canada does with the rest of the world, and the United States in particular. As a result of this growth in trade, it seems likely that any change in income now results in a larger change in spending on imported goods than would have been the case only ten years ago. The *MPI*, then, has likely grown larger. If so, the multiplier in Canada has grown smaller over the past ten years.

Other Applications of the Multiplier Effect

Because of the multiplier effect, a dollar of government purchases can generate more than a dollar of aggregate demand. The logic of the multiplier effect, however, is not restricted to changes in government purchases. Instead, it applies to any event that alters spending on any component of GDP—consumption, investment, government purchases, or net exports.

For example, suppose that a recession in the United States reduces the demand for Canada's net exports by $10 billion. This reduced spending on Canadian-produced goods and services depresses Canada's national income, which reduces spending by Canadian consumers. If the marginal propensity to consume is 3/4, the marginal propensity to import is 1/4, and the multiplier is 2, then the $10 billion fall in net exports means a $20 billion contraction in aggregate demand.

As another example, suppose that a stock market boom increases households' wealth and stimulates their spending on goods and services by $20 billion. This extra consumer spending increases national income, which in turn generates even more consumer spending. If the marginal propensity to consume is 3/4, the marginal propensity to import is 1/4, and the multiplier is 2, then the initial impulse of $20 billion in consumer spending translates into a $40 billion increase in aggregate demand.

The multiplier is an important concept in macroeconomics because it shows how the economy can amplify the impact of changes in spending. A small initial change in consumption, investment, government purchases, or net exports can end up having a large effect on aggregate demand and, therefore, the economy's production of goods and services. It is because of this amplified impact of initial changes in consumption, investment, government purchases, or net exports that policymakers must pay close attention to events such as the possibility of recession among our trading partners and the possibility of stock market booms or crashes.

The Crowding-Out Effect on Investment

The multiplier effect seems to suggest that when the government spends $5 billion on construction work, the resulting expansion in aggregate demand is necessarily larger than $5 billion. Yet another effect is working in the opposite direction. While an increase in government purchases stimulates the aggregate demand for goods and services, it also causes the interest rate to rise, and a higher interest rate reduces investment spending and chokes off aggregate demand. The reduction in aggregate demand that results when a fiscal expansion raises the interest rate is called the **crowding-out effect on investment.**

To see why crowding out occurs, let's consider what happens in the money market when the government spends $5 billion on construction work. As we have discussed, this increase in demand raises the incomes of the workers and owners of the construction firms (and, because of the multiplier effect, of other firms as well). As incomes rise, households plan to buy more goods and services and, as a result, choose to hold more of their wealth in liquid form. That is, the increase in income caused by the fiscal expansion raises the demand for money.

The effect of the increase in money demand is shown in panel (a) of Figure 16.9. Because the Bank of Canada has not changed the money supply, the vertical supply curve remains the same. When the higher level of income shifts the money-demand curve to the right from MD_1 to MD_2, the interest rate must rise from r_1 to r_2 to keep supply and demand in balance.

The increase in the interest rate, in turn, reduces the quantity of goods and services demanded. In particular, because borrowing is more expensive, the demand for residential and business investment goods declines. That is, as the increase in government purchases increases the demand for goods and services, it may also crowd out investment. This crowding-out effect partially offsets the impact of government purchases on aggregate demand, as illustrated in panel (b) of Figure 16.9. The initial impact of the increase in government purchases is to shift the aggregate-demand curve from AD_1 to AD_2, but once crowding out takes place, the aggregate-demand curve drops back to AD_3.

To sum up: *When the government increases its purchases by $5 billion, the aggregate demand for goods and services could rise by more or less than $5 billion, depending on whether the multiplier effect or the crowding-out effect on investment is larger.*

> **crowding-out effect on investment**
> the offset in aggregate demand that results when expansionary fiscal policy raises the interest rate and thereby reduces investment spending

Open-Economy Considerations

Our discussion of how fiscal policy affects aggregate demand has so far ignored open-economy considerations. Just as we found when we considered the open-economy implications for monetary policy, we will see that the story we have told so far, while correct for a closed economy, is incomplete for a small open economy like Canada.

Panel (a) of Figure 16.10 shows money-demand and money-supply curves intersecting at the world interest rate, r^w. Just as we did before, we begin our discussion of how fiscal policy affects aggregate demand from this point, because eventually Canada's interest rate must equal the world interest rate. To obtain a true measure of the impact of fiscal policy, we must show all of the adjustments in the economy that return Canada's interest rate to the world interest rate.

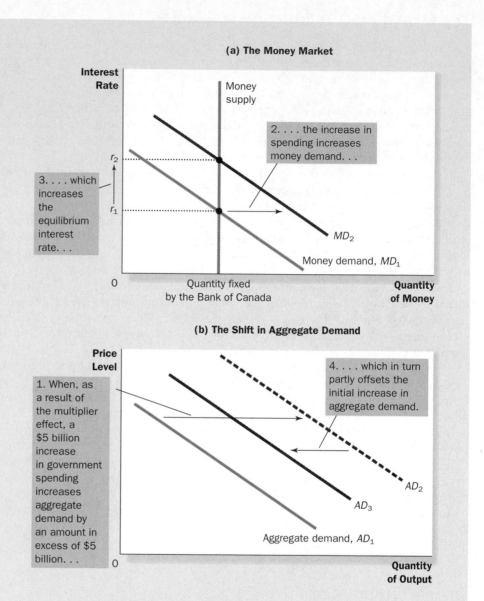

FIGURE 16.9

The Crowding-Out Effect on Investment

Panel (a) shows the money market. When the government increases its purchases of goods and services, the resulting increase in income raises the demand for money from MD_1 to MD_2, and this causes the equilibrium interest rate to rise from r_1 to r_2. Panel (b) shows the effects on aggregate demand. The multiplier effect of the increase in government purchases shifts the aggregate-demand curve from AD_1 to AD_2. Yet, because the interest rate is the cost of borrowing, the increase in the interest rate tends to reduce the quantity of goods and services demanded, particularly for investment goods. This crowding out of investment partially offsets the impact of the fiscal expansion on aggregate demand. In the end, the aggregate-demand curve shifts only to AD_3.

(a) The Money Market

Interest Rate

Money supply

2. . . . the increase in spending increases money demand. . .

r_2

3. . . . which increases the equilibrium interest rate. . .

r_1

MD_2

Money demand, MD_1

0   Quantity fixed by the Bank of Canada   **Quantity of Money**

(b) The Shift in Aggregate Demand

Price Level

1. When, as a result of the multiplier effect, a $5 billion increase in government spending increases aggregate demand by an amount in excess of $5 billion. . .

4. . . . which in turn partly offsets the initial increase in aggregate demand.

AD_2

AD_3

Aggregate demand, AD_1

0   **Quantity of Output**

The $5 billion job-creation program raises the incomes of those directly employed and increases the incomes of workers and owners of other firms. This is the multiplier effect, and it is represented by the shift of the aggregate-demand curve to the right from AD_1 to AD_2, as shown in panel (b) of Figure 16.10. The increase in demand for goods and services also increases the demand for money. In panel (a), this is shown by the shift of the demand for money curve from MD_1 to MD_2. Because the Bank of Canada has not changed the money-supply curve, the vertical money-supply curve remains the same. As a result, the interest rate must rise above the world interest rate, to r_2, in order to balance money supply and money demand.

FIGURE 16.10

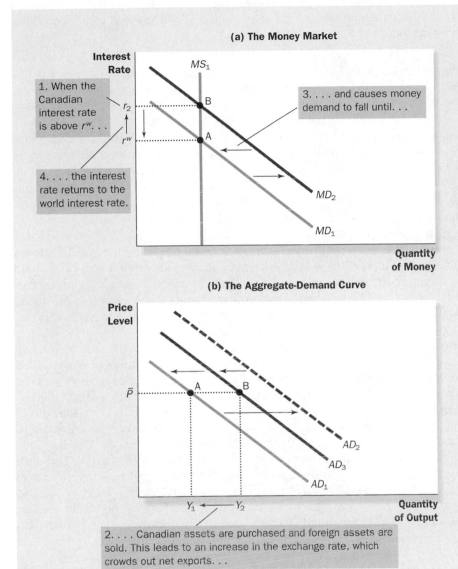

(a) The Money Market

1. When the Canadian interest rate is above r^w. . .

3. . . . and causes money demand to fall until. . .

4. . . . the interest rate returns to the world interest rate.

MS_1

B

r_2

r^w

A

MD_2

MD_1

Quantity of Money

(b) The Aggregate-Demand Curve

$\bar{P}$

A   B

AD_2

AD_3

AD_1

Y_1 Y_2

Quantity of Output

2. . . . Canadian assets are purchased and foreign assets are sold. This leads to an increase in the exchange rate, which crowds out net exports. . .

A Fiscal Expansion in an Open Economy with a Flexible Exchange Rate

In a closed economy, an increase in government purchases causes the interest rate to rise and output to increase. This is shown by the movement from point A to point B in panels (a) and (b). In a small open economy, the fact that the domestic interest rate, r_2, is greater than the world interest rate, r^w, means there must be further adjustment. Canadian and foreign savers find the Canadian interest rate more attractive than the world rate. As a result, they buy Canadian assets and sell foreign assets. This decreases the supply of Canadian dollars in the market for foreign-currency exchange and causes the exchange rate to rise. Because this increase in the interest rate decreases net exports, the demand for Canadian-produced goods and services falls from AD_2 to AD_1 in panel (b). The contraction of output from Y_2 to Y_1 requires that people hold less money to make transactions. This is shown by the decrease in the demand for money from MD_2 to MD_1 and the decrease in the Canadian interest rate from r_2 to r^w in panel (a). In the end, the economy adjusts back to point A in both panels, the interest rate returns to the world interest rate, and there is no lasting effect on aggregate demand.

Once again, the interest rate influences the quantity of goods and services demanded, as shown in panel (b). In particular, by increasing the cost of borrowing, the higher interest rate reduces the demand for residential and business investment. As a result, the quantity of goods and services demanded at the given price level, $\bar{P}$, falls. This is the crowding-out effect on investment, which is shown in panel (b) by the shift of the aggregate-demand curve from AD_2 to AD_3.

So far, all of this is exactly as it was previously. In a closed economy, the effect of a fiscal expansion would be summarized by the movement from point A to point B in panels (a) and (b) of figure 16.10. In a small open economy like Canada, however, this cannot be the end of the story. We have left Canada's interest rate above the world interest rate. But, because of perfect capital mobility, Canada's interest rate must eventually adjust to equal the world interest rate. Something else must happen.

Flexible Exchange Rate We begin by assuming that the Bank of Canada has chosen to allow the exchange rate to be flexible. As we saw in our examination of the effects of a monetary injection, the assumption about whether or not the exchange rate is flexible will prove to be an important one.

When Canada's interest rate rises above the world interest rate, Canadian and foreign savers find Canadian assets, which now pay interest rate r_2, to be more attractive than foreign assets that pay the world interest rate, r^w. As a result, Canadians and foreigners sell foreign assets and buy Canadian assets. Recall, again, our discussion in Chapter 14 that while people want to trade goods, services, and financial assets with people in other countries, they want to be paid for these things in their own currency. Thus, the switch from foreign assets to Canadian assets requires a corresponding purchase of Canadian dollars and sale of foreign currencies. In the market for foreign-currency exchange, the demand for Canadian dollars therefore increases, causing the dollar to appreciate in value and the real exchange rate to rise. The rise in the real exchange rate makes Canadian-produced goods and services more expensive relative to foreign-produced goods and services. Consequently, Canada's net exports decrease.

The reduction in net exports that results when a fiscal expansion in a small open economy with a flexible exchange rate raises the real exchange rate is called the **crowding-out effect on net exports.** The decrease in net exports causes the quantity of Canadian-produced goods and services demanded at the given price level, $\overline{P}$, to decrease. This is shown in panel (b) of Figure 16.10 by the shift of the aggregate-demand curve from AD_3 to AD_1. This fall in demand for Canadian-produced goods and services also decreases the demand for money. This is shown in panel (a) by the shift of the money-demand curve from MD_2 to MD_1. This shift must be large enough to cause Canada's interest rate to fall back to the world interest rate. The end result of all of these adjustments is a decrease in the demand for money back to MD_1, a return of Canada's interest rate to the world interest rate, and a decrease in the quantity demanded of Canadian-produced goods and services, represented by a shift in the aggregate-demand curve back to AD_1.

To sum up: *In a small open economy, an expansionary fiscal policy causes the dollar to appreciate. Because this appreciation of the dollar causes net exports to fall, there is an additional crowding-out effect that reduces the demand for Canadian-produced goods and services. In the end, fiscal policy has no lasting effect on aggregate demand.*

Fixed Exchange Rate Now consider the effect on aggregate demand of a fiscal policy in an open economy when the Bank of Canada chooses to prevent changes in the value of the exchange rate. Recall that the Bank of Canada can influence the value of the exchange rate by buying and selling foreign currencies in what are known as foreign exchange market operations. When firms and households are selling Canadian dollars in the market for foreign-currency exchange (thereby increasing the supply of dollars in that market), the Bank of Canada can prevent the value of the exchange rate from falling by increasing the demand for Canadian dollars in that market. It does this by selling foreign currencies and purchasing Canadian dollars. Similarly, when firms and households

---

crowding-out effect on net exports

the offset in aggregate demand that results when expansionary fiscal policy in a small open economy with a flexible exchange rate raises the real exchange rate and thereby reduces net exports are buying Canadian dollars in the market for foreign-currency exchange (thereby increasing the demand for dollars in that market), the Bank of Canada can prevent the value of the exchange rate from rising by increasing the supply of Canadian dollars in that market. It does this by buying foreign currencies and selling Canadian dollars.

Figure 16.11 shows how expansionary fiscal policy affects aggregate demand in this case. As always, we start with the Canadian interest rate equal to the world interest rate, r^w. In panel (a), the demand for money, MD_1, is equal to the supply of money, MS_1, at r^w. An increase in government expenditures increases the quantity of goods and services demanded for given price level $\bar{P}$. As a result of the multiplier effect, the quantity of goods and services demanded increases by more than

FIGURE 16.11

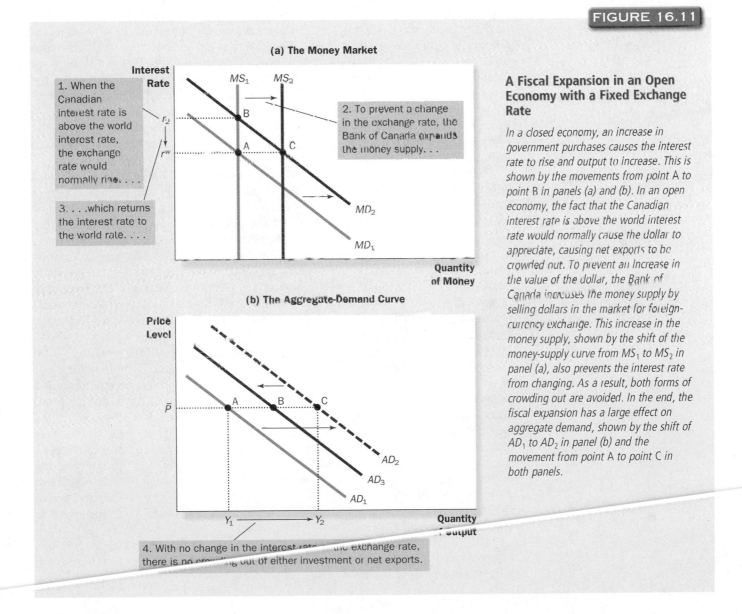

(a) The Money Market

1. When the Canadian interest rate is above the world interest rate, the exchange rate would normally rise. . . .

2. To prevent a change in the exchange rate, the Bank of Canada expands the money supply. . .

3. . . .which returns the interest rate to the world rate. . . .

(b) The Aggregate-Demand Curve

4. With no change in the interest rate or the exchange rate, there is no crowding out of either investment or net exports.

A Fiscal Expansion in an Open Economy with a Fixed Exchange Rate

In a closed economy, an increase in government purchases causes the interest rate to rise and output to increase. This is shown by the movements from point A to point B in panels (a) and (b). In an open economy, the fact that the Canadian interest rate is above the world interest rate would normally cause the dollar to appreciate, causing net exports to be crowded out. To prevent an increase in the value of the dollar, the Bank of Canada increases the money supply by selling dollars in the market for foreign-currency exchange. This increase in the money supply, shown by the shift of the money-supply curve from MS_1 to MS_2 in panel (a), also prevents the interest rate from changing. As a result, both forms of crowding out are avoided. In the end, the fiscal expansion has a large effect on aggregate demand, shown by the shift of AD_1 to AD_2 in panel (b) and the movement from point A to point C in both panels.

the increase in government expenditures. This is shown in panel (b) by the shift in the aggregate-demand curve from AD_1 to AD_2. As before, the increase in demand for goods and services requires that people hold more of their wealth as money. This is represented in panel (a) by the shift of the money-demand curve from MD_1 to MD_2. The increase in the demand for money increases the Canadian interest rate to r_2. As we have seen, this increase in the interest rate crowds out business and residential investment and reduces the demand for goods and services. In panel (b), this crowding-out effect on investment is shown by the shift of the aggregate-demand curve from AD_2 to AD_3.

So far, we have described the adjustment from point A to point B in panels (a) and (b). This is how a closed economy would respond to a fiscal expansion. In an open economy, because Canada's interest rate is above the world interest rate, there is a tendency for the exchange rate to change. In particular, because Canada's interest rate is above the world interest rate, Canadian assets are preferred to foreign assets. The switch from foreign to Canadian assets requires a corresponding purchase of dollars in the market for foreign-currency exchange, and this causes the dollar to appreciate in value. We have seen that if the Bank of Canada allows the exchange rate to appreciate, net exports will fall and the economy will adjust back to point A in panels (a) and (b), so that the fiscal expansion has no lasting impact on aggregate demand. If the Bank of Canada chooses to fix the value of the exchange rate, it must increase the supply of dollars in the market for foreign-currency exchange. To do this, the Bank of Canada purchases foreign currency in exchange for dollars.

The actions taken by the Bank of Canada to fix the exchange rate also has an effect on the money supply. As we explained in Chapter 11 and reviewed earlier in this chapter, when the Bank of Canada buys something, it causes the money supply to increase. When the Bank of Canada sells something, it causes the money supply to decrease. Thus, when the Bank of Canada buys foreign currency in order to prevent the value of the dollar from changing, it expands the money supply. This is shown in panel (a) of Figure 16.11 by the shift of the money-supply curve from MS_1 to MS_2. The shift of the money-supply curve must be sufficient to lower Canada's interest rate back to the world interest rate. Only when Canada's interest rate is equal to the world interest rate is there no reason for the exchange rate to change.

The expansion of the money supply has two effects. First, it lowers the Canadian interest rate back to the world interest rate. This eliminates the crowding-out effect of government expenditures on business and residential investment. This crowding-out effect is what shifted AD_2 back to AD_3. The second effect of the monetary expansion is that, by lowering the Canadian interest rate to the level of the world interest rate, it removes the reason for the appreciation of the dollar. This eliminates the crowding-out effect of government expenditures on net exports. This crowding-out effect is what shifted AD_3 back to AD_1. By preventing the exchange rate from changing, the Bank of Canada therefore removes both crowding-out effects. The end result, then, is that the aggregate-demand curve shifts from AD_1 to AD_2 and the quantity demanded of Canadian-produced goods and services expands from Y_1 to Y_2.

To sum up: *If the Bank of Canada chooses to prevent any change in the exchange rate, expansionary fiscal policy will have no crowding-out effects and will therefore cause a very large increase in the demand for goods and services.*

The Coordination of Monetary and Fiscal Policy   The dramatically different effects of a fiscal expansion on aggregate demand under a fixed exchange rate and under a flexible exchange rate teaches us an important lesson: *For fiscal policy to have a lasting effect on the position of the aggregate-demand curve, the Bank of Canada must choose the appropriate exchange rate policy.* Interestingly, fiscal policy decisions are made by Parliament and by provincial legislatures, while monetary policy is determined by the Bank of Canada. Therefore, for fiscal policies to have a lasting influence on aggregate demand, these two sets of policymakers, elected politicians on the one hand and the Bank of Canada on the other, must coordinate their choices.

TABLE 16.2

The Effects of Fiscal Policy: Summary

How Does Fiscal Policy Shift the Aggregate-Demand Curve in a Closed Economy?

1. An increase in government spending shifts the aggregate-demand curve to the right.
2. Increased spending increases money demand, and this increases the interest rate.
3. The rise in the interest rate crowds out investment and reduces somewhat the size of the shift in the aggregate-demand curve.

How Does Fiscal Policy Shift the Aggregate-Demand Curve in an Open Economy with a Flexible Exchange Rate?

1. Due to perfect capital mobility, and ignoring differences in default risk and taxes, Canada's interest rate must equal the world interest rate. We begin with $r = r^w$.
2. An increase in government spending shifts the aggregate-demand curve to the right.
3. Increased spending increases money demand, and this increases the interest rate.
4. The rise in the interest rate crowds out investment and reduces somewhat the size of the shift in the aggregate-demand curve. Now $r > r^w$.
5. Canadian assets now pay a higher interest rate than foreign assets. Increased demand for Canadian assets means an increased demand for dollars in the market for foreign-currency exhange. The dollar appreciates.
6. The appreciation of the dollar reduces net exports.
7. The fall in net exports means a fall in spending, a fall in money demand, and a fall in interest rates until $r = r^w$.
8. The increase in government spending has no lasting influence on the position of the aggregate-demand curve.

How Does Fiscal Policy Shift the Aggregate-Demand Curve in an Open Economy with a Fixed Exchange Rate?

1. Due to perfect capital mobility, and ignoring differences in default risk and taxes, Canada's interest rate must equal the world interest rate. We begin with $r = r^w$.
2. An increase in government spending shifts the aggregate-demand curve to the right.
3. Increased spending increases money demand, and this increases the interest rate.
4. The rise in the interest rate crowds out investment and reduces somewhat the size of the shift in the aggregate-demand curve. Now $r > r^w$.
5. Canadian assets now pay a higher interest rate than foreign assets. Increased demand for Canadian assets means an increased demand for dollars in the market for foreign-currency exchange. To fix the exchange rate, the Bank of Canada increases the supply of dollars traded in the market for foreign-currency exchange by purchasing foreign currency.
6. The purchase of foreign currency by the Bank of Canada causes the money supply to increase, and this causes the interest rate to fall until $r = r^w$.
7. The increase in the money supply shifts the aggregate-demand curve even farther to the right.

Such coordination has not always been observed. The most famous example of a lack of coordination was the Coyne Affair in 1961. In an attempt to stimulate an economy mired in an economic slowdown, the federal government of the day introduced tax cuts and expenditure increases in the hope of shifting the aggregate-demand curve to the right. Unfortunately, the governor of the Bank of Canada, James Coyne, was determined to allow the exchange rate to be flexible. The result—predictable on the basis of our analysis—was a serious conflict between the federal government and the Bank of Canada. By maintaining a flexible exchange rate, Coyne was causing the federal government's expansionary fiscal policy to have no lasting influence on the position of the aggregate-demand curve. In the end, Coyne was forced to resign, and the Bank of Canada adopted a fixed exchange rate in order to enable the government's expansionary fiscal policy to shift the aggregate-demand curve. As Donald Fleming, the federal minister of finance in 1961, concluded, "This budget and Mr. Coyne were simply not compatible."

Currently, the Bank of Canada allows the exchange rate to vary. Indeed, the Canada–U.S. exchange rate garners considerable attention, and changes in its value often lead off news programs. On occasion, however, the Bank of Canada influences the value of the exchange rate by buying and selling dollars in the market for foreign-currency exchange. It does this to try to slow the rate of change in the exchange rate and thereby ensure that changes are not too abrupt. When considering what you think will be the outcome of fiscal policy choices of Canadian governments, therefore, you need to have a sense of how much the Bank of Canada will choose to try to influence the exchange rate. If the Bank of Canada is likely to allow the exchange rate to vary freely, then fiscal policy changes will have no lasting effect on the position of the aggregate-demand curve. If, however, you judge that the Bank of Canada will try to minimize changes in the exchange rate, fiscal policy changes will have a lasting influence on the position of the aggregate-demand curve.

Changes in Taxes

The other important instrument of fiscal policy, besides the level of government purchases, is the level of taxation. When the government cuts personal income taxes, for instance, it increases households' take-home pay. Households will save some of this additional income, but they will also spend some of it on consumer goods. Because it increases consumer spending, the tax cut shifts the aggregate-demand curve to the right. Similarly, a tax increase depresses consumer spending and shifts the aggregate-demand curve to the left.

The size of the shift in aggregate demand resulting from a tax change is also affected by the multiplier and crowding-out effects. When the government cuts taxes and stimulates consumer spending, earnings and profits rise, which further stimulates consumer spending. This is the multiplier effect. At the same time, higher income leads to higher money demand, which tends to raise interest rates. Higher interest rates make borrowing more costly, which reduces investment spending. This is the crowding-out effect on investment. Depending on the size of the multiplier and crowding-out effects, the shift in aggregate demand could be larger or smaller than the tax change that causes it.

In a small open economy like Canada, whether the change in the position of the aggregate-demand curve that results from a change in taxes is a lasting one depends on the central bank's decision whether to allow the exchange rate to change. If the Bank of Canada chooses to allow the exchange rate to vary freely, tax changes will not have a lasting effect on the position of the aggregate-demand curve. For example, a tax cut, by pushing Canada's interest rate above the world interest rate, will cause the exchange rate to rise. Thus, the tax cut crowds out net exports just as an increase in government expenditures does. If, however, the Bank of Canada chooses to fix the value of the exchange rate, a tax cut has a large and lasting effect on the position of the aggregate-demand curve. This is so because the Bank of Canada, in order to fix the value of the exchange rate, must purchase dollars in the market for foreign-currency exchange, causing the money supply to increase. The increase in the money supply removes the crowding-out effects on investment and net exports that prevent fiscal policy from having a lasting influence on aggregate demand.

Deficit Reduction

In recent years, Canadian governments at both the federal and the provincial levels have taken steps to reduce or eliminate their budget deficits. Some governments have relied primarily on reductions in expenditures, others have relied

HOW FISCAL POLICY MIGHT AFFECT AGGREGATE SUPPLY

So far our discussion of fiscal policy has stressed how changes in government purchases and changes in taxes influence the quantity of goods and services demanded. Most economists believe that the short-run macroeconomic effects of fiscal policy work primarily through aggregate demand. Yet fiscal policy can potentially also influence the quantity of goods and services supplied.

For instance, consider the effects of tax changes on aggregate supply. One of the ten principles of economics in Chapter 1 is that people respond to incentives. When government policymakers cut tax rates, workers get to keep more of each dollar they earn, so they have a greater incentive to work and produce goods and services. If they respond to this incentive, the quantity of goods and services supplied will be greater at each price level, and the aggregate-supply curve will shift to the right. Some economists, called *supply-siders*, have argued that the influence of tax cuts on aggregate supply is very large. Indeed, some supply-siders claim the influence is so large that a cut in tax rates will actually increase tax revenue by increasing worker effort. Most economists, however, doubt that the supply-side effects of cuts to tax rates are as large as this.

The fact that tax cuts cause the aggregate-supply curve to shift to the right is important because it suggests that tax cuts have a permanent effect on output. As we saw in Chapter 15, any shift in the aggregate-demand curve has only a temporary effect on output. Over time, as perceptions, wages, and prices adjust, the short-run aggregate-supply curve shifts to where the aggregate-demand curve intersects the long-run aggregate-supply curve. Unless the long-run aggregate-supply curve shifts, the shift in the aggregate-demand curve will have only a temporary effect on output. If tax cuts cause a shift to the right in the long-run aggregate-supply curve, then this represents a permanent increase in the natural level of output.

While this sounds like an exciting policy prescription—keep cutting tax rates and cause more and more permanent increases in output—we must remember that we need taxes to finance useful government programs. There would be no national defence, no social programs, and no universal health care without taxes. A more sensible, though perhaps less exciting, policy prescription is to keep tax rates as low as possible given the need to finance desired government spending programs.

primarily on tax increases, and others have relied on a combination of both approaches. Some analysts have suggested that efforts to reduce government deficits are hazardous to the health of the Canadian economy because they cause a reduction in aggregate demand. Our discussion of the effects of changes in government expenditures and taxes under fixed and flexible exchange rates sheds light on this claim. As long as the Bank of Canada chooses to allow the exchange rate to vary freely, there is no reason to expect that efforts at deficit reduction will have any lasting influence on the position of the aggregate-demand curve. Once again, we see the importance of a coordinated effort between Canadian governments and the Bank of Canada. Deficit reduction can have a minimal impact on the level of aggregate demand if the central bank adopts the appropriate exchange-rate policy.

QuickQuiz Explain how a decrease in government expenditures affects the money market and the position of the aggregate-demand curve. What is the effect for (a) a closed economy and (b) an open economy when the Bank of Canada allows the exchange rate to vary, and for (c) an open economy when the Bank of Canada chooses to maintain a fixed value for the exchange rate?

USING POLICY TO STABILIZE THE ECONOMY

We have seen how monetary and fiscal policy can affect the economy's aggregate demand for goods and services. These theoretical insights raise some important policy questions: Should policymakers use these instruments to control aggregate demand and stabilize the economy? If so, when? If not, why not?

The Case for Active Stabilization Policy

The Canadian economy is often subject to the effects of unexpected events. Conflicts in the Middle East, fluctuations in energy prices, exchange-rate fluctuations, and stock market booms and busts can all have serious impacts on the Canadian economy. Events such as these have often been responsible for large changes in output, employment, and income. We have seen that fiscal and monetary policy can be used to influence the position of the aggregate-demand curve and thereby cause changes in output, employment, and income. If we put these ideas together, we seem to have a strong case in favour of using policy instruments to offset the negative consequences of unexpected events. Simply put, unexpected expansions and contractions in the economy impose costs on people and firms in the form of unemployment, inflation, and uncertainty. If monetary and fiscal policy can be used to stabilize the economy, then surely these tools should be used to offset the harmful effects of economic fluctuations. This is the case in favour of using monetary and fiscal policy to stabilize the economy.

As we discussed in the preceding chapter, John Maynard Keynes's *The General Theory of Employment, Interest, and Money* has been one of the most influential books ever written about economics. In it, Keynes emphasized the key role of aggregate demand in explaining short-run economic fluctuations. Keynes claimed that the government should actively stimulate aggregate demand when aggregate demand appeared insufficient to maintain production at its full-employment level. At the time Keynes wrote his book, the world's major economies were in the midst of the Great Depression. It is little wonder, then, that the Keynesian proposal to use policy instruments to lessen the severity of economic downturns proved popular. Keynes and his many followers were strong advocates of using policy instruments to stabilize the economy.

The Case against Active Stabilization Policy

Some economists argue that the government should avoid active use of monetary and fiscal policy to try to stabilize the economy. They claim that these policy instruments should be set to achieve long-run goals, such as rapid economic growth and low inflation, and that the economy should be left to deal with short-run fluctuations on its own. Although these economists may admit that monetary and fiscal policy can stabilize the economy in theory, they doubt whether it can do so in practice.

The primary argument against active monetary and fiscal policy is that these policies affect the economy with a long lag. As we have seen, monetary policy works by changing interest rates, which in turn influence investment spending. But many firms make investment plans far in advance. Thus, most economists believe that it takes at least six months for changes in monetary policy to have much effect on output and employment. Moreover, once these effects occur, they can last for several years. Critics of stabilization policy argue that because of this lag, the Bank of Canada should not try to fine-tune the economy. They claim that the Bank of Canada often reacts too late to changing economic conditions and, as a result, ends up being a cause of rather than a cure for economic fluctuations. These critics advocate a passive monetary policy, such as slow and steady growth in the money supply.

Fiscal policy also works with a lag, but unlike the lag in monetary policy, the lag in fiscal policy is largely attributable to the political process. In Canada, most changes in federal government spending and taxes must go through parliamentary committees in both the House of Commons and the Senate, and be passed by both legislative bodies. Completing this process can take months and, in some cases, years. By the time the change in fiscal policy is passed and ready to implement, the condition of the economy may well have changed.

These lags in monetary and fiscal policy are a problem in part because economic forecasting is so imprecise. If forecasters could accurately predict the condition of the economy a year in advance, then monetary and fiscal policymakers could look ahead when making policy decisions. In this case, policymakers could stabilize the economy, despite the lags they face. In practice, however, major recessions and depressions arrive without much advance warning. The best policymakers can do at any time is to respond to economic changes as they occur.

Automatic Stabilizers

All economists—both advocates and critics of stabilization policy—agree that the lags in implementation render policy less useful as a tool for short-run stabilization. The economy would be more stable, therefore, if policymakers could find a way to avoid some of these lags. In fact, they have. **Automatic stabilizers** are

automatic stabilizers
changes in fiscal policy that stimulate aggregate demand when the economy goes into a recession, without policymakers having to take any deliberate action

changes in fiscal policy that stimulate aggregate demand when the economy goes into a recession without policymakers having to take any deliberate action.

The most important automatic stabilizer is the tax system. When the economy goes into a recession, the amount of taxes collected by the government falls automatically because almost all taxes are closely tied to economic activity. The personal income tax depends on households' incomes, sales taxes depend on levels of consumption, and the corporate income tax depends on firms' profits. Because incomes, consumption spending, and profits all fall in a recession, the government's tax revenue falls as well. This automatic tax cut stimulates aggregate demand and, thereby, reduces the magnitude of economic fluctuations.

Government spending also acts as an automatic stabilizer. In particular, when the economy goes into a recession and workers are laid off, more people apply for Employment Insurance benefits, welfare benefits, and other forms of income support. This automatic increase in government spending stimulates aggregate demand at exactly the time when aggregate demand is insufficient to maintain full employment. Indeed, when the unemployment insurance system was first enacted in the 1930s, economists who advocated this policy did so in part because of its power as an automatic stabilizer.

The automatic stabilizers in the Canadian economy are not sufficiently strong to prevent recessions completely. Nonetheless, without these automatic stabilizers, output and employment would probably be more volatile than they are. For this reason, many economists oppose legislation that would require the federal government always to run a balanced budget, as some politicians have proposed. When the economy goes into a recession, taxes fall, government spending rises, and the government's budget moves toward deficit. If the government faced a strict balanced-budget rule, it would be forced to look for ways to raise taxes or cut spending in a recession. In other words, a strict balanced-budget rule would eliminate the automatic stabilizers inherent in our current system of taxes and government spending.

A Flexible Exchange Rate as an Automatic Stabilizer

In an open economy, policymakers can choose to make use of another type of automatic stabilizer: a flexible exchange rate. Suppose Canada's largest trading partner, the United States, slips into recession. As the incomes of American households and firms fall, they spend less and we can expect that they buy fewer Canadian-produced goods. Canada's net exports fall and the aggregate-demand curve shifts to the left.

If the Bank of Canada has chosen to allow the exchange rate to be flexible, we would expect the following to occur: The fall in net exports causes the incomes of Canadians to fall, and this reduces the demand for money. This causes Canada's interest rate to fall below the world interest rate. Both Canadians and foreigners sell Canadian assets in favour of foreign assets that pay the higher world interest rate. The switch from Canadian to foreign assets requires a corresponding sale of dollars in the market for foreign-currency exchange. The increased supply of dollars in the market for foreign-currency exchange causes the exchange rate to depreciate, and this causes net exports to increase. Canada's aggregate-demand curve now shifts back to the right, increasing the incomes of Canadians and increasing the demand for money until Canada's interest rate is again equal to the world interest rate. The recession in the United States has no lasting effects on the position of Canada's aggregate-demand curve.

This scenario demonstrates how allowing the exchange rate to be flexible enables policymakers to insulate the Canadian economy from the effects of foreign recessions. Given Canada's dependence on foreign trade, and hence Canada's exposure to the effects of foreign recessions, this would seem to be an attractive policy choice. Indeed, most economists favour flexible exchange rates, partly for this reason. Unfortunately, as economists are fond of saying, there is no such thing as a free lunch. That is, the benefits of a flexible exchange rate do not come without costs.

An important cost is the uncertainty that a flexible exchange rate introduces into the pricing decisions of exporting and importing firms. Unexpected changes in the exchange rate mean unexpected changes in the Canadian dollar prices of imported and exported goods. A firm hoping to produce goods for export might be discouraged from doing so if it cannot be sure of how many Canadian dollars it will end up receiving for goods it sells abroad.

These types of costs have led to proposals by Canadian economists Richard Harris and Thomas Courchene that Canada form a monetary union with the United States. Essentially they argue that Canada should adopt the U.S. dollar as its currency and thereby avoid all uncertainty about the price importers will have to pay for U.S.-produced goods and the price exporters will receive for Canadian-produced goods sold in the United States. By eliminating this uncertainty, an important impediment to trade will be eliminated and the benefits of free trade will be maximized. At this point, the majority of economists judge that the benefit of using a flexible exchange rate as an automatic stabilizer exceeds the costs of the price uncertainty that a flexible exchange rate introduces. However, the debate continues.

QuickQuiz How does a reduction in government spending affect the aggregate-demand curve? How does your answer differ if we consider a closed economy versus an open economy?

A QUICK SUMMARY

We have accomplished quite a lot in this chapter. We have shown how fiscal and monetary policy can influence the position of the aggregate-demand curve in a closed economy and in a small open economy under both a fixed and a flexible exchange rate. Throughout this chapter we have made the assumption that the price level is relatively unresponsive to changing economic conditions. To emphasize the role of such price stickiness, we have assumed that the price level is fixed. This assumption characterizes the short run, the focus of this chapter. Figure 16.12 (page 401) summarizes what we have discovered about how fiscal and monetary policy can be used to influence the position of the aggregate-demand curve in the short run.

Panel (a) in Figure 16.12 shows how the aggregate-demand curve shifts in response to expansionary fiscal and monetary policies in a closed economy. Our starting position is at point A on aggregate-demand curve AD_1. The price level is fixed at value $\overline{P}$. An expansionary fiscal policy (either an increase in government

INTEREST RATES IN THE LONG RUN AND THE SHORT RUN

At this point, we should pause and reflect on a seemingly awkward embarrassment of riches. We appear to have many explanations of how the interest rate is determined. This embarrassment of riches is due to the fact that we have sought to explain the determination of the interest rate under a number of circumstances: in the short run and the long run, and in a closed economy and a small open economy. All of these explanations are correct, and each is useful for understanding the rest. It might be a good idea at this point to summarize their relationship to one another.

It is important to remind ourselves of the differences between the long-run and short-run behaviour of the economy. Three macroeconomic variables are of central importance: the economy's output of goods and services, the interest rate, and the price level. According to the classical macroeconomic theory we developed in Chapters 7, 8, and 12, these variables are determined as follows:

1. *Output* is determined by the supplies of capital and labour and the available production technology for turning capital and labour into output. (We call this the natural level of output.) Changes in the price level have no influence on output.
2. In a closed economy, for any given level of output, the *interest rate* adjusts to balance the supply and demand for loanable funds. In a small open economy, the domestic interest rate is equal to the world interest rate. Net capital outflow (*NCO*) balances the supply and demand for loanable funds.
3. The *price level* adjusts to balance the supply and demand for money. Changes in the supply of money lead to proportionate changes in the price level.

These are three of the essential propositions of classical economic

theory. Most economists believe that these propositions do a good job of describing how the economy works *in the long run*.

Yet these propositions do not hold in the short run. As we discussed in the preceding chapter, many prices are slow to adjust to changes in the money supply; this is reflected in a short-run aggregate-supply curve that is upward sloping rather than vertical. For issues concerning the short run, then, it is best to think about the economy as follows:

1. The *price level* is stuck at some level (based on previously formed expectations) and, in the short run, is relatively unresponsive to changing economic conditions.
2. In a closed economy, for any given price level, the *interest rate* adjusts to balance the supply and demand for money. The price level cannot adjust to balance the supply and demand for money as it does in the long run because of price stickiness. In a small open economy, the interest rate must adjust to equal the world interest rate. With a flexible exchange rate, this adjustment requires a change in the exchange rate. By affecting net exports, a change in the exchange rate affects output and thus the demand for money. In this case, then, the demand for money adjusts to balance the supply and demand for money at the world interest rate. With a fixed exchange rate, the adjustment of the domestic interest rate to the world interest rate requires the Bank of Canada to buy and sell foreign currencies, and this causes changes in the supply of money. In this case, then, the supply of money adjusts to balance the supply and demand for money at the world interest rate.
3. The level of *output* responds to net changes in the aggregate demand for goods and services that remain after the crowding-out effects induced by interest rate and exchange-rate changes are taken into account.

Thus, the different theories of the interest rate are useful for different purposes. When thinking about the long-run determinants of interest rates, it is best to keep in mind the loanable-funds theory. By contrast, when thinking about the short-run determinants of interest rates, it is best to keep in mind the liquidity-preference theory and, in a small open economy, the fact that the Canadian interest rate must equal the world interest rate.

spending or a cut in taxes) and an expansionary monetary policy (an increase in the supply of money) both shift the aggregate-demand curve to the right (to position AD_2). In a closed economy, then, fiscal and monetary policies have the same effect on the position of the aggregate-demand curve. As we discussed in this chapter, they differ with respect to how they affect the interest rate: An expan-

FIGURE 16.12

The Effects of Expansionary Monetary and Fiscal Policies on the Aggregate-Demand Curve

How fiscal and monetary policy affect the position of the aggregate-demand curve depends on whether the economy is closed or open. If the economy is open, the effect of fiscal and monetary policy depends on whether the Bank of Canada chooses to fix the value of the exchange rate or allow it to be flexible.

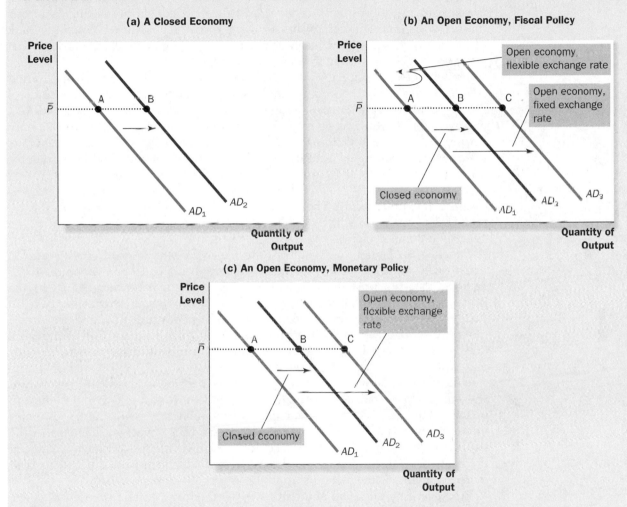

sionary fiscal policy causes the interest rate to increase because it causes the demand for money to increase; an expansionary monetary policy causes the interest rate to decrease because it involves an increase in the supply of money.

Panel (b) in Figure 16.12 shows how the aggregate-demand curve shifts in response to an expansionary fiscal policy in a small open economy. Once again, our starting position is at point A on aggregate demand curve AD_1, with the price level fixed at value $\bar{P}$. If this was a closed economy, an expansionary fiscal policy would shift the aggregate-demand curve to position AD_2, and we would move from point A to point B at the fixed price level $\bar{P}$. In an open economy, the influence of an expansionary fiscal policy on the position of the aggregate-demand curve depends on whether the exchange rate is fixed or flexible.

Under a fixed exchange rate, the same expansionary fiscal policy that shifted AD_1 to AD_2 would shift AD_1 to AD_3, and we move from point A to point C. This occurs because the expansionary fiscal policy forces Canada's interest rate above the world interest rate and thus causes an increase in the demand for dollars traded in the market for foreign-currency exchange. To prevent the exchange rate from changing, the Bank of Canada must increase the supply of dollars in this market, something it accomplishes by buying foreign currencies. When the Bank of Canada buys something, it causes the money supply to increase, which is what gives us the second shift in the aggregate-demand curve.

Under a flexible exchange rate, the same expansionary fiscal policy that shifted AD_1 to AD_2 in a closed economy would have no lasting impact on the position of the aggregate-demand curve. The aggregate-demand curve would return to AD_1, and we would return to point A. This occurs because, while the expansionary fiscal policy once again forces Canada's interest rate above the world interest rate, this time the resulting increase in the demand for dollars traded in the market for foreign-currency exchange is not offset by the actions of the Bank of Canada. Instead, the Bank of Canada allows the exchange rate to appreciate, and this causes net exports to fall. The fall in net exports offsets the expansionary fiscal policy, with the net result that there is no lasting impact on the position of the aggregate-demand curve.

Panel (c) in Figure 16.12 shows how the aggregate-demand curve shifts in response to an expansionary monetary policy in a small open economy. Once again, our starting position is at point A on aggregate-demand curve AD_1, with the price level fixed at value $\bar{P}$. If this was a closed economy, an expansionary fiscal policy would shift the aggregate-demand curve to position AD_2, and we would move from point A to point B at the fixed price level $\bar{P}$. In an open economy, it makes sense for the Bank of Canada to pursue an expansionary monetary policy only if it allows the exchange rate to be flexible.

Under a flexible exchange rate, the same expansionary monetary policy that shifted AD_1 to AD_2 would shift AD_1 to AD_3, and we would move from point A to point C. This occurs because the expansionary monetary policy forces Canada's interest rate below the world interest rate and thus causes an increase in the supply of dollars traded in the market for foreign-currency exchange. By causing the exchange rate to depreciate, the monetary expansion causes net exports to increase, giving us the second shift in the aggregate-demand curve.

Before leaving this quick summary, it is worthwhile to reiterate a point we have raised before: The predictions listed in this quick summary are based on an economic model characterized by a number of simplifications and assumptions. In macroeconomic courses you take in the future, some of these assumptions and simplifications will be relaxed. The result will be that some of the conclusions drawn from these models will need to be modified and restated. As we discussed in Chapter 2, constructing models based on simplifying assumptions and then observing how predictions generated by the model change with these assumptions is a part of the scientific method. Having said that, it is nonetheless true that the basic models presented in this chapter provide a very useful way of thinking about the effects of fiscal and monetary policies on aggregate demand in open and closed economies.

CONCLUSION

Before policymakers make any change in policy, they need to consider all the effects of their decisions. Earlier in the book we examined classical models of the economy that describe the long-run effects of monetary and fiscal policy. There we saw how fiscal policy influences saving, investment, and long-run growth, and how monetary policy influences the price level and the inflation rate.

In this chapter we examined the short-run effects of monetary and fiscal policy. We saw how these policy instruments can change the aggregate demand for goods and services and, thereby, alter the economy's production and employment in the short run. When Parliament reduces government spending in order to balance the budget, it needs to consider both the long-run effects on saving and growth and the short-run effects on aggregate demand and employment. When the Bank of Canada reduces the growth rate of the money supply, it must take into account the long-run effect on inflation as well as the short-run effect on production. In the next chapter we discuss the transition between the short run and the long run more fully, and we see that policymakers often face a tradeoff between long-run and short-run goals.

SUMMARY

- In developing a theory of short-run economic fluctuations, Keynes proposed the theory of liquidity preference to explain the determinants of the interest rate. According to this theory, the interest rate adjusts to balance the supply and demand for money.

- An increase in the price level raises money demand and increases the interest rate that brings the money market into equilibrium. Because the interest rate represents the cost of borrowing, a higher interest rate reduces investment and, thereby, the quantity of goods and services demanded. In a small open economy, an increase in the price level also increases the real exchange rate. An increase in the real exchange rate makes Canadian-produced goods and services more expensive relative to foreign-produced goods and services. As a result, Canada's net exports fall, reducing the quantity demanded of Canadian goods and services. The downward-sloping aggregate-demand curve expresses these negative relationships between the price level and the quantity demanded.

- Policymakers can influence aggregate demand with monetary policy. An increase in the money supply reduces the equilibrium interest rate for any given price level. Because a lower interest rate stimulates investment spending, the aggregate-demand curve shifts to the right. In a small open economy, the lower interest rate also means a fall in the exchange rate. Because a lower exchange rate increases the quantity demanded of Canadian-produced goods and services, a monetary injection in a small open economy shifts the aggregate-demand curve farther to the right than it does in a closed economy. Conversely, a decrease in the money supply raises the equilibrium interest rate for any given price level and shifts the aggregate-demand curve to the left. In a small open economy, the higher interest rate also means a rise in the exchange rate and, consequently, a fall in net exports. In a small open economy, then, a monetary contraction shifts the aggregate-demand curve farther to the left than it does in a closed economy.

- Policymakers can also influence aggregate demand with fiscal policy. An increase in government purchases or a cut in taxes shifts the aggregate-demand curve to the right. A decrease in government purchases or an increase in taxes shifts the aggregate-demand curve to the left.

- When the government alters spending or taxes, the resulting shift in aggregate demand can be larger or smaller than the fiscal change. The multiplier effect tends to amplify the effects of fiscal policy on aggregate demand. The crowding-out effect on investment tends to dampen the effects of fiscal policy on aggregate demand. The multiplier effect is much smaller in an open economy than in a closed economy.

- In a small open economy with perfect capital mobility, fiscal policy may or may not cause a lasting shift in the aggregate-demand curve. This depends on whether the Bank of Canada allows the exchange rate to vary freely. If the Bank of Canada allows the exchange rate to be flexible, fiscal policy has no lasting effect on the position of the aggregate-demand curve. This is so because the change in the exchange rate exerts an effect on net exports that is opposite to the fiscal policy in its influence on aggregate demand. If the Bank of Canada chooses to fix the value of the exchange rate, there is no such counteracting influence from net exports. In fact, by acting to fix the value of the exchange rate, the Bank of Canada causes the aggregate-demand curve to shift farther than it would in a closed economy. As a result, fiscal policy has a lasting effect on the position of the aggregate-demand curve.

- Because monetary and fiscal policy can influence aggregate demand, the government sometimes uses these policy instruments in an attempt to stabilize the economy. Economists disagree about how active the government should be in this effort. According to advocates of active stabilization policy, unexpected changes in economic conditions shift aggregate demand; if the government does not respond, the result is undesirable and unnecessary fluctuations in output and employment. According to critics of active stabilization policy, monetary and fiscal policy work with such long lags that attempts at stabilizing the economy often end up being destabilizing.

KEY CONCEPTS

theory of liquidity
    preference, p. 369
multiplier effect, p. 383

crowding-out effect on
    investment, p. 387

crowding-out effect on net
    exports, p. 390
automatic stabilizers, p. 397

QUESTIONS FOR REVIEW

1. What is the theory of liquidity preference? How does it help explain the downward slope of the aggregate-demand curve?

2. Use the theory of liquidity preference to explain how a decrease in the money supply affects the aggregate-demand curve. Consider the effects in both a closed economy and a small open economy.

3. The government spends $3 billion to buy police cars. Explain why aggregate demand might increase by more than $3 billion. Explain why aggregate demand might increase by less than $3 billion. Under what conditions might aggregate demand not change at all?

4. Suppose that survey measures of business confidence indicate a wave of pessimism about Canada's economic prospects is sweeping the country. As a consequence, firms announce their intention to delay new spending on plants and equipment. If policymakers do nothing, what will happen to aggregate demand? What should the Bank of Canada do if it wants to stabilize aggregate demand? If the Bank of Canada does nothing, what might Parliament do to stabilize aggregate demand?

5. Give an example of a government policy that acts as an automatic stabilizer. Explain why this policy has this effect.

PROBLEMS AND APPLICATIONS

1. Explain how each of the following developments would affect the supply of money, the demand for money, and the interest rate. For each case, show what happens in a closed economy and in a small open economy. Illustrate your answers with diagrams.
   a. The Bank of Canada's bond traders buy bonds in open-market operations.
   b. An increase in credit card availability reduces the cash people hold.
   c. Households decide to hold more money to use for holiday shopping.
   d. A wave of optimism boosts business investment and expands aggregate demand.
   e. An increase in oil prices shifts the short-run aggregate-supply curve to the left.

2. Suppose banks install automatic teller machines on every block and, by making cash readily available, reduce the amount of money people want to hold.
   a. Assume the Bank of Canada does not change the money supply. According to the theory of liquidity preference, what happens to the interest rate? What happens to aggregate demand? Assume a closed economy.
   b. If the Bank of Canada wants to stabilize aggregate demand, how should it respond?

3. This chapter explains that expansionary monetary policy reduces the interest rate and thus stimulates demand for investment goods. Explain how such a policy also stimulates the demand for net exports.

4. Suppose economists observe that in a closed economy an increase in government spending of $10 billion raises the total demand for goods and services by $30 billion.
   a. If these economists ignore the possibility of crowding out of investment, what would they estimate the marginal propensity to consume (MPC) to be?
   b. Now suppose the economists allow for crowding out. Would their new estimate of the MPC be larger or smaller than their initial one?

5. Suppose the government of a closed economy reduces taxes by $20 billion, that there is no crowding out of investment, and that the marginal propensity to consume is 3/4.
   a. What is the initial effect of the tax reduction on aggregate demand?
   b. What additional effects follow this initial effect? What is the total effect of the tax cut on aggregate demand?
   c. How does the total effect of this $20 billion tax cut compare with the total effect of a $20 billion increase in government purchases? Why?

6. Suppose government spending increases in a closed economy. Would the effect on aggregate demand be larger (a) if the Bank of Canada took no action in response or (b) if the Bank were committed to maintaining a fixed interest rate? Explain.

7. In which of the following circumstances is expansionary fiscal policy more likely to lead to a short-run increase in investment? Explain.
   a. when the investment accelerator is large, or when it is small
   b. when the interest sensitivity of investment is large, or when it is small
   c. when the marginal propensity to import is small, or when it is large

8. Suppose the Bank of Canada contracts the money supply in an effort to reduce aggregate demand by a particular amount, say $10 billion. If Canada was a closed economy, would the amount by which the Bank of Canada would need to reduce the supply of money to accomplish this goal be greater or smaller than the amount it would need to reduce the supply of money if Canada was an open economy with a flexible exchange rate?

9. Suppose that the world interest rate rises. What happens to the position of the aggregate-demand curve in Canada? Assume that the Bank of Canada allows the exchange rate to be flexible. How does your answer change if you assume that the Bank of Canada maintains a fixed exchange rate? Illustrate your answer with diagrams.

10. Suppose that U.S. income rises. As a result, Canada's exports to the United States increase. What happens to the position of the aggregate-demand curve in Canada? Assume that the Bank of Canada allows the exchange rate to be flexible. How does your answer change if you assume that the Bank of Canada maintains a fixed exchange rate? Illustrate your answer with diagrams.

11. Suppose that the Bank of Canada decides to expand the money supply.
    a. Why would it be counterproductive for the Bank of Canada to fix the value of the exchange rate?
    b. What is the effect of this policy on the interest rate in the long run? How do you know?

12. For various reasons, fiscal policy changes automatically when output and employment fluctuate.
    a. Explain why tax revenue changes when the economy goes into a recession.
    b. Explain why government spending changes when the economy goes into a recession.
    c. If the government were to operate under a strict balanced-budget rule, what would it have to do in a recession? Would that make the recession more or less severe?

INTERNET RESOURCES

- To learn more about the Bank of Canada and how it conducts monetary policy, visit its website at http://www.bankofcanada.ca. In the main menu, click on "Monetary Policy" to access a variety of links, including one to the bank's "Monetary Policy Report and Update," which summarizes current economic conditions and indicates how monetary policy will be used to address any problems that have been identified. Read about how and why the Bank of Canada intervenes in foreign exchange markets to influence the value of the exchange rate by selecting the "Backgrounders" link, where you can also access a number of other short articles explaining various topics related to the Bank of Canada's main functions.

- Finance Canada is the federal department in charge of Canada's fiscal policy. To learn more about this department and the conduct of fiscal policy in Canada, visit its website at http://www.fin.gc.ca.

- Provincial governments also collect and spend tax revenue and so influence the economy via their fiscal policy choices. To learn more about the fiscal policy choices made by the province in which you live, on the Finance Canada home page (http://www.fin.gc.ca), click on "Hot Links" in the main menu at the top of the page and then, under "Resources by Subject," click on "Public Finance." Links to departments of finance in other countries are also provided, so you can learn about how fiscal policy is conducted internationally.

http://   For more study tools, please visit http://www.mankiw3e.nelson.com.

17

Learning Objectives

In this chapter, you will …

- Learn why policymakers face a short-run tradeoff between inflation and unemployment
- Consider why the inflation–unemployment tradeoff disappears in the long run
- See how supply shocks can shift the inflation–unemployment tradeoff
- Consider the short-run cost of reducing the rate of inflation
- See how policymakers' credibility might affect the cost of reducing inflation

THE SHORT-RUN TRADEOFF BETWEEN INFLATION AND UNEMPLOYMENT

Two closely watched indicators of economic performance are inflation and unemployment. When Statistics Canada releases data on these variables each month, policymakers are eager to hear the news. Some commentators have added together the inflation rate and the unemployment rate to produce a *misery index,* which purports to measure the health of the economy.

How are these two measures of economic performance related to each other? Earlier in the book we discussed the long-run determinants of unemployment and the long-run determinants of inflation. We saw that the natural rate of unemployment depends on various features of the labour market, such as minimum-wage laws, the generosity of Employment Insurance, the market power of unions, the role of efficiency wages, and the effectiveness of job search. By contrast, the inflation rate depends primarily on growth in the money supply, which a nation's central bank controls. In the long run, therefore, inflation and unemployment are largely unrelated problems.

In the short run, just the opposite is true. One of the ten principles of economics discussed in Chapter 1 is that society faces a short-run tradeoff between inflation and unemployment. If monetary and fiscal policymakers expand aggregate demand and move the economy up along the short-run aggregate-supply curve, they can lower unemployment for a while, but only at the cost of higher inflation. If policymakers contract aggregate demand and move the economy down the short-run aggregate-supply curve, they can lower inflation, but only at the cost of temporarily higher unemployment.

In this chapter we examine this tradeoff more closely. The relationship between inflation and unemployment is a topic that has attracted the attention of some of the most important economists of the last half century. The best way to understand this relationship is to see how thinking about it has evolved over time. As we will see, the history of thought regarding inflation and unemployment since the 1950s is inextricably connected to the history of the economies of North America and Western Europe. These two histories will show why the tradeoff between inflation and unemployment holds in the short run, why it does not hold in the long run, and what issues it raises for economic policymakers.

THE PHILLIPS CURVE

Phillips curve
a curve that shows the short-run tradeoff between inflation and unemployment

"Probably the single most important macroeconomic relationship is the Phillips curve." These are the words of economist George Akerlof from the lecture he gave when he received the Nobel Prize in Economic Sciences in 2001. The **Phillips curve** shows the short-run tradeoff between inflation and unemployment. We begin our story with the discovery of the Phillips curve and its migration to North America.

Origins of the Phillips Curve

The origins and early development of the Phillips curve had an international flavour. In 1958, New Zealand economist A. W. Phillips published an article in the British journal *Economica* that would make him famous. The article was entitled "The Relationship between Unemployment and the Rate of Change of Money Wages in the United Kingdom, 1861–1957." In it, Phillips showed a negative correlation between the rate of unemployment and the rate of inflation. That is, Phillips showed that years with low unemployment tend to have high inflation, and years with high unemployment tend to have low inflation. (Phillips examined inflation in nominal wages rather than inflation in prices, but for our purposes that distinction is not important. These two measures of inflation usually move together.) Phillips concluded that two important macroeconomic variables—inflation and unemployment—were linked in a way that economists had not previously appreciated.

Two years later, Canadian economist Richard Lipsey confirmed and extended Phillips's observations. Lipsey used quantitative methods to derive a more accurate estimate of the change in inflation associated with particular rates of unemployment. In doing so, he introduced a methodology that economists would follow for many years to come.

Although the work of Phillips and Lipsey was based on data for the United Kingdom, researchers quickly confirmed their findings using data from many other countries. In the same year that Lipsey's article appeared, two American economists, Paul Samuelson and Robert Solow, entered the fray by testing the

Phillips–Lipsey hypothesis using U.S. data. In their contribution, Samuelson and Solow reasoned that the negative correlation between inflation and unemployment that they found in U.S. data, and that others were finding in data from other countries, arose because low unemployment was associated with high aggregate demand and because high demand puts upward pressure on wages and prices throughout the economy. Samuelson and Solow dubbed the negative association between inflation and unemployment the *Phillips curve*. Figure 17.1 shows an example of a Phillips curve that reflects the hypothesis put forward by Samuelson and Solow.

Samuelson and Solow were interested in the Phillips curve because they believed that it held important lessons for policymakers. In particular, they suggested that the Phillips curve offers policymakers a menu of possible economic outcomes. By altering monetary and fiscal policy to influence aggregate demand, policymakers could choose any point on this curve. Point A offers high unemployment and low inflation. Point B offers low unemployment and high inflation. Policymakers might prefer both low inflation and low unemployment, but the historical data as summarized by the Phillips curve indicate that this combination is impossible. According to Samuelson and Solow, policymakers face a tradeoff between inflation and unemployment, and the Phillips curve illustrates that tradeoff. Thus, at this very early stage in the development of the Phillips curve, it seemed to economists that policymakers faced a permanent tradeoff between inflation and unemployment.

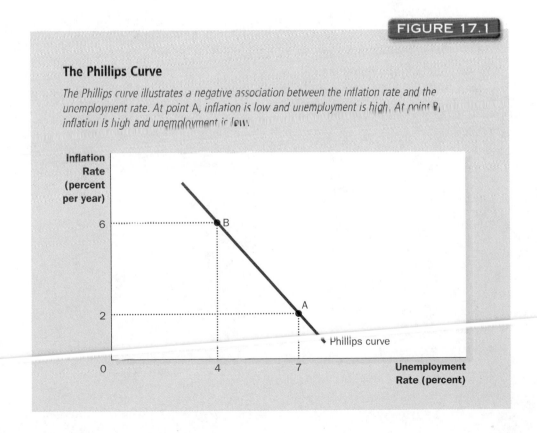

FIGURE 17.1

The Phillips Curve

The Phillips curve illustrates a negative association between the inflation rate and the unemployment rate. At point A, inflation is low and unemployment is high. At point B, inflation is high and unemployment is low.

Aggregate Demand, Aggregate Supply, and the Phillips Curve

The model of aggregate demand and aggregate supply provides an easy explanation for the menu of possible outcomes described by the Phillips curve. *The Phillips curve simply shows the combinations of inflation and unemployment that arise in the short run as shifts in the aggregate-demand curve move the economy along the short-run aggregate-supply curve.* As we saw in Chapter 15, an increase in the aggregate demand for goods and services leads, in the short run, to a larger output of goods and services and a higher price level. Larger output means greater employment and, thus, a lower rate of unemployment. In addition, whatever the previous year's price level happens to be, the higher the price level in the current year, the higher the rate of inflation. Thus, shifts in aggregate demand push inflation and unemployment in opposite directions in the short run—a relationship illustrated by the Phillips curve.

To see more fully how this works, let's consider an example. To keep the numbers simple, imagine that the price level (as measured, for instance, by the consumer price index) equals 100 in the year 2000. Figure 17.2 shows two possible outcomes that might occur in year 2001. Panel (a) shows the two outcomes using the model of aggregate demand and aggregate supply. Panel (b) illustrates the same two outcomes using the Phillips curve.

FIGURE 17.2

How the Phillips Curve Is Related to the Model of Aggregate Demand and Aggregate Supply

This figure assumes a price level of 100 for the year 2000 and charts possible outcomes for the year 2001. Panel (a) shows the model of aggregate demand and aggregate supply. If aggregate demand is low, the economy is at point A; output is low (7500), and the price level is low (102). If aggregate demand is high, the economy is at point B; output is high (8000), and the price level is high (106). Panel (b) shows the implications for the Phillips curve. Point A, which arises when aggregate demand is low, has high unemployment (7 percent) and low inflation (2 percent). Point B, which arises when aggregate demand is high, has low unemployment (4 percent) and high inflation (6 percent).

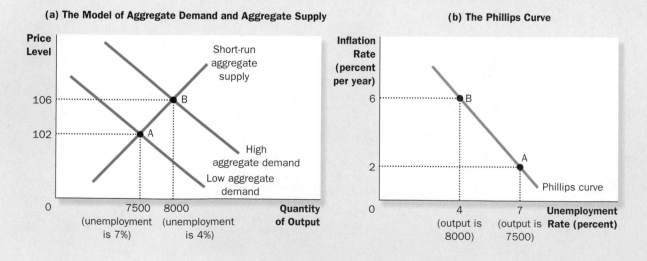

In panel (a) of the figure, we can see the implications for output and the price level in the year 2001. If the aggregate demand for goods and services is relatively low, the economy experiences outcome A. The economy produces output of 7500, and the price level is 102. By contrast, if aggregate demand is relatively high, the economy experiences outcome B. Output is 8000, and the price level is 106. Thus, higher aggregate demand moves the economy to an equilibrium with higher output and a higher price level.

In panel (b) of the figure, we can see what these two possible outcomes mean for unemployment and inflation. Because firms need more workers when they produce a greater output of goods and services, unemployment is lower in outcome B than in outcome A. In this example, when output rises from 7500 to 8000, unemployment falls from 7 percent to 4 percent. Moreover, because the price level is higher at outcome B than at outcome A, the inflation rate (the percentage change in the price level from the previous year) is also higher. In particular, since the price level was 100 in year 2000, outcome A has an inflation rate of 2 percent, and outcome B has an inflation rate of 6 percent. Thus, we can compare the two possible outcomes for the economy either in terms of output and the price level (using the model of aggregate demand and aggregate supply) or in terms of unemployment and inflation (using the Phillips curve).

As we saw in the preceding chapter, monetary and fiscal policy can shift the aggregate-demand curve. Therefore, monetary and fiscal policy can move the economy along the Phillips curve. Increases in the money supply, increases in government spending, or cuts in taxes expand aggregate demand and move the economy to a point on the Phillips curve with lower unemployment and higher inflation. Decreases in the money supply, cuts in government spending, or increases in taxes contract aggregate demand and move the economy to a point on the Phillips curve with lower inflation and higher unemployment. In this sense, the Phillips curve offers policymakers a menu of combinations of inflation and unemployment.

QuickQuiz   Draw the Phillips curve. Use the model of aggregate demand and aggregate supply to show how policy can move the economy from a point on this curve with high inflation to a point with low inflation.

SHIFTS IN THE PHILLIPS CURVE: THE ROLE OF EXPECTATIONS

The Phillips curve seems to offer policymakers a menu of possible inflation–unemployment outcomes. But does this menu remain stable over time? Is the Phillips curve a relationship on which policymakers can rely? These are the questions that economists took up in the late 1960s.

The Long-Run Phillips Curve

In 1968 economist Milton Friedman published a paper in the *American Economic Review,* based on an address he had recently given as president of the American Economic Association. The paper, entitled "The Role of Monetary Policy," contained sections on "What Monetary Policy Can Do" and "What Monetary Policy Cannot Do." Friedman argued that one thing monetary policy cannot do, other than for only a short time, is pick a combination of inflation and unemployment on the Phillips curve. At about the same time, another economist, Edmund Phelps, also published a paper denying the existence of a long-run tradeoff between inflation and unemployment.

Friedman and Phelps based their conclusions on classical principles of macroeconomics, which we discussed in Chapters 7 through 14. Recall that classical theory points to growth in the money supply as the primary determinant of inflation. But classical theory also states that monetary growth does not have real effects—it merely alters all prices and nominal incomes proportionately. In particular, monetary growth does not influence those factors that determine the economy's unemployment rate, such as the market power of unions, the role of efficiency wages, or the process of job search. Friedman and Phelps concluded that there is no reason to think the rate of inflation would, *in the long run*, be related to the rate of unemployment.

Here, in his own words, is Friedman's view about what central banks can hope to accomplish in the long run:

> The monetary authority controls nominal quantities—directly, the quantity of its own liabilities [currency plus bank reserves]. In principle, it can use this control to peg a nominal quantity—an exchange rate, the price level, the nominal level of national income, the quantity of money by one definition or another— or to peg the change in a nominal quantity—the rate of inflation or deflation, the rate of growth or decline in nominal national income, the rate of growth of the quantity of money. It cannot use its control over nominal quantities to peg a real quantity—the real rate of interest, the rate of unemployment, the level of real national income, the real quantity of money, the rate of growth of real national income, or the rate of growth of the real quantity of money.

These views have important implications for the Phillips curve. In particular, they imply that monetary policymakers face a long-run Phillips curve that is vertical, as in Figure 17.3. If the Bank of Canada increases the money supply slowly, the inflation rate is low, and the economy finds itself at point A. If the Bank of Canada increases the money supply quickly, the inflation rate is high, and the economy finds itself at point B. In either case, the unemployment rate tends toward its normal level, called the *natural rate of unemployment*. The vertical long-run Phillips curve illustrates the conclusion that unemployment does not depend on money growth and inflation in the long run.

The vertical long-run Phillips curve is, in essence, one expression of the classical idea of monetary neutrality. As you may recall, we expressed this idea in Chapter 15 with a vertical long-run aggregate-supply curve. Indeed, as Figure 17.4 illustrates, the vertical long-run Phillips curve and the vertical long-run aggregate-supply curve are two sides of the same coin. In panel (a) of this figure, an increase in the money supply shifts the aggregate-demand curve to the right from AD_1 to AD_2. As a result of this shift, the long-run equilibrium moves from point A to point B. The price level rises from P_1 to P_2, but because the aggregate-supply curve is vertical, output remains the same. In panel (b), more rapid growth in the money supply raises the inflation rate by moving the economy from point A to point B. But because the Phillips curve is vertical, the rate of unemployment is the same at

FIGURE 17.3

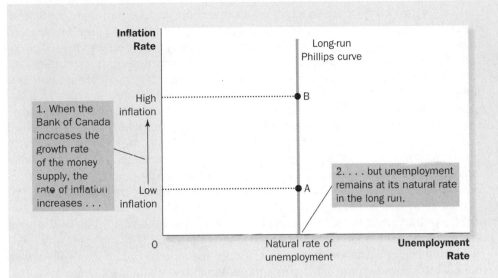

The Long-Run Phillips Curve

According to Friedman and Phelps, there is no tradeoff between inflation and unemployment in the long run. Growth in the money supply determines the inflation rate. Regardless of the inflation rate, the unemployment rate gravitates toward its natural rate. As a result, the long-run Phillips curve is vertical.

FIGURE 17.4

How the Long-Run Phillips Curve Is Related to the Model of Aggregate Demand and Aggregate Supply

Panel (a) shows the model of aggregate demand and aggregate supply with a vertical aggregate-supply curve. When expansionary monetary policy shifts the aggregate-demand curve to the right from AD_1 to AD_2, the equilibrium moves from point A to point B. The price level rises from P_1 to P_2, while output remains the same. Panel (b) shows the long-run Phillips curve, which is vertical at the natural rate of unemployment. Expansionary monetary policy moves the economy from lower inflation (point A) to higher inflation (point B) without changing the rate of unemployment.

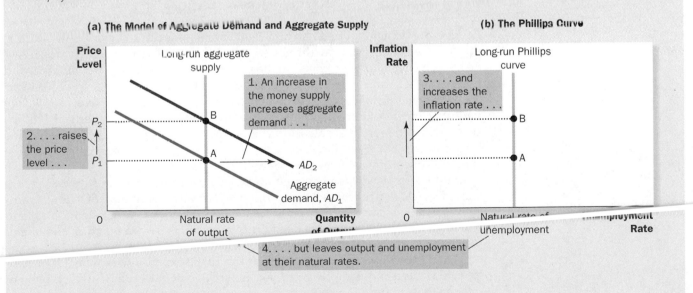

these two points. Thus, the vertical long-run aggregate-supply curve and the vertical long-run Phillips curve both imply that monetary policy influences nominal variables (the price level and the inflation rate) but not real variables (output and unemployment). Regardless of the monetary policy pursued by the Bank of Canada, output and unemployment are, in the long run, at their natural rates.

What is so "natural" about the natural rate of unemployment? Friedman and Phelps used this adjective to describe the unemployment rate toward which the economy tends to gravitate in the long run. Yet the natural rate of unemployment is not necessarily the socially desirable rate of unemployment. Nor is the natural rate of unemployment constant over time. For example, suppose that a newly formed union uses its market power to raise the real wages of some workers above the equilibrium level. The result is an excess supply of workers and, therefore, a higher natural rate of unemployment. This unemployment is "natural" not because it is good but because it is beyond the influence of monetary policy. More rapid money growth would not reduce the market power of the union or the level of unemployment; it would lead only to more inflation.

Although monetary policy cannot influence the natural rate of unemployment, other types of policy can. To reduce the natural rate of unemployment, policy-makers should look to policies that improve the functioning of the labour market. Earlier in the book we discussed how various labour-market policies, such as minimum-wage laws, collective-bargaining laws, Employment Insurance, and job-training programs, affect the natural rate of unemployment. A policy change that reduced the natural rate of unemployment would shift the long-run Phillips curve to the left. In addition, because lower unemployment means more workers are producing goods and services, the quantity of goods and services supplied would be larger at any given price level, and the long-run aggregate-supply curve would shift to the right. The economy could then enjoy lower unemployment and higher output for any given rate of money growth and inflation.

Expectations and the Short-Run Phillips Curve

At first, the denial by Friedman and Phelps of a long-run tradeoff between inflation and unemployment might not seem persuasive. Their argument was based on an appeal to *theory*. By contrast, the negative correlation between inflation and unemployment uncovered by Phillips and Lipsey using U.K. data, and confirmed by economists using data from many countries, was based on *observation*, not theory. Why should anyone believe that policymakers faced a vertical Phillips curve when the world seemed to offer a downward-sloping one? Shouldn't the large number of observations of downward-sloping curves lead us to reject the classical conclusion of monetary neutrality?

Friedman and Phelps were well aware of these questions, and they offered a way to reconcile classical macroeconomic theory with the finding of a downward-sloping Phillips curve in data from the United Kingdom, the United States, and elsewhere. They claimed that a negative relationship between inflation and unemployment holds in the short run but that it cannot be used by policymakers in the long run. In other words, policymakers can pursue expansionary monetary policy to achieve lower unemployment for a while, but eventually unemployment returns to its natural rate, and more expansionary monetary policy leads only to higher inflation.

Friedman and Phelps reasoned as we did in Chapter 15 when we explained the difference between the short-run and long-run aggregate-supply curves. (In fact, the discussion in that chapter drew heavily on the legacy of Friedman and Phelps.) As you may recall, the short-run aggregate-supply curve is upward sloping, indicating that an increase in the price level raises the quantity of goods and services that firms supply. By contrast, the long-run aggregate-supply curve is vertical, indicating that the price level does not influence quantity supplied in the long run. Chapter 15 presented three theories to explain the upward slope of the short-run aggregate-supply curve: sticky wages, sticky prices, and misperceptions about relative prices. Because wages, prices, and perceptions adjust to changing economic conditions over time, the positive relationship between the price level and quantity supplied applies in the short run but not in the long run. Friedman and Phelps applied this same logic to the Phillips curve. Just as the aggregate-supply curve slopes upward only in the short run, the tradeoff between inflation and unemployment holds only in the short run. And just as the long-run aggregate-supply curve is vertical, the long-run Phillips curve is also vertical.

To help explain the short-run and long-run relationship between inflation and unemployment, Friedman and Phelps introduced a new variable into the analysis: *expected inflation*. Expected inflation measures how much people expect the overall price level to change. As we discussed in Chapter 15, the expected price level affects the wages and prices that people set and the perceptions of relative prices that they form. As a result, expected inflation is one factor that determines the position of the short-run aggregate-supply curve. In the short run, the Bank of Canada can take expected inflation (and thus the short-run aggregate-supply curve) as already determined. When the money supply changes, the aggregate-demand curve shifts, and the economy moves along a given short-run aggregate-supply curve. In the short run, therefore, monetary changes lead to unexpected fluctuations in output, prices, unemployment, and inflation. In this way, Friedman and Phelps explained the downward-sloping Phillips curve that had been observed in the data from so many countries.

Yet the Bank of Canada's ability to create unexpected inflation by increasing the money supply exists only in the short run. In the long run, people come to expect whatever inflation rate the Bank of Canada chooses to produce. Because wages, prices, and perceptions will eventually adjust to the inflation rate, the long-run aggregate-supply curve is vertical. In this case, changes in aggregate demand, such as those due to changes in the money supply, do not affect the economy's output of goods and services. Thus, Friedman and Phelps concluded that unemployment returns to its natural rate in the long run.

The analysis of Friedman and Phelps can be summarized in the following equation (which is, in essence, another expression of the aggregate-supply equation we saw in Chapter 15):

$$\text{Unemployment rate} = \text{Natural rate of unemployment} - a\left(\text{Actual inflation} - \text{Expected inflation}\right)$$

This equation relates the unemployment rate to the natural rate of unemployment, actual inflation, and expected inflation. In the short run, expected inflation is given. As a result, higher actual inflation is associated with lower unemployment. (How much unemployment responds to unexpected inflation is determined by the size of *a*, a number that in turn depends on the slope of the short-run aggregate-supply curve.) In the long run, however, people come to expect whatever inflation the Bank of Canada produces. Thus, actual inflation equals expected inflation, and unemployment is at its natural rate.

This equation implies there is no stable short-run Phillips curve. Each short-run Phillips curve reflects a particular expected rate of inflation. (To be precise, if you graph the equation, you'll find that the short-run Phillips curve intersects the long-run Phillips curve at the expected rate of inflation.) Whenever expected inflation changes, the short-run Phillips curve shifts.

According to Friedman and Phelps, it is dangerous to view the Phillips curve as a menu of options available to policymakers. To see why, imagine an economy at its natural rate of unemployment with low inflation and low expected inflation, shown in Figure 17.5 as point A. Now suppose that policymakers try to take advantage of the tradeoff between inflation and unemployment by using monetary or fiscal policy to expand aggregate demand. In the short run when expected inflation is given, the economy goes from point A to point B. Unemployment falls below its natural rate, and inflation rises above expected inflation. Over time, people get used to this higher inflation rate, and they raise their expectations of

FIGURE 17.5

How Expected Inflation Shifts the Short-Run Phillips Curve

The higher the expected rate of inflation, the higher the short-run tradeoff between inflation and unemployment. At point A, expected inflation and actual inflation are both low, and unemployment is at its natural rate. If the Bank of Canada pursues an expansionary monetary policy, the economy moves from point A to point B in the short run. At point B, expected inflation is still low, but actual inflation is high. Unemployment is below its natural rate. In the long run, expected inflation rises, and the economy moves to point C. At point C, expected inflation and actual inflation are both high, and unemployment is back to its natural rate.

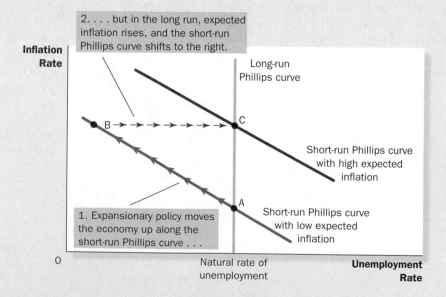

inflation. When expected inflation rises, firms and workers start taking higher inflation into account when setting wages and prices. The short-run Phillips curve then shifts to the right, as shown in the figure. The economy ends up at point C, with higher inflation than at point A but with the same level of unemployment.

Thus, Friedman and Phelps concluded that policymakers do face a tradeoff between inflation and unemployment, but only a temporary one. If policymakers use this tradeoff, they lose it.

The Natural Experiment for the Natural-Rate Hypothesis

Friedman and Phelps had made a bold prediction in 1968: If policymakers try to take advantage of the Phillips curve by choosing higher inflation in order to reduce unemployment, they will succeed at reducing unemployment only temporarily. This view—that unemployment eventually returns to its natural rate, regardless of the rate of inflation—is called the **natural-rate hypothesis.** A few years after Friedman and Phelps proposed this hypothesis, monetary and fiscal policymakers in Canada and the United States inadvertently created a natural experiment to test it. Their laboratory consisted of the Canadian and U.S. economics.

Before we see the outcome of this test, however, let's look at the data that Friedman and Phelps had when they made their prediction in 1968. Figure 17.6 shows the unemployment rate and the inflation rate in Canada for the period from 1956 to 1968. These data trace out a Phillips curve. As inflation rose over these 13 years, unemployment fell. The economic data from this era seemed to confirm the tradeoff between inflation and unemployment.

natural-rate hypothesis
the claim that unemployment eventually returns to its normal, or natural, rate, regardless of the rate of inflation

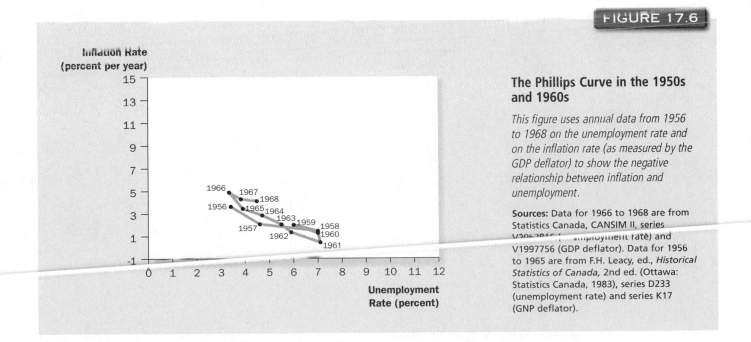

FIGURE 17.6

The Phillips Curve in the 1950s and 1960s

This figure uses annual data from 1956 to 1968 on the unemployment rate and on the inflation rate (as measured by the GDP deflator) to show the negative relationship between inflation and unemployment.

Sources: Data for 1966 to 1968 are from Statistics Canada, CANSIM II, series V206____ (unemployment rate) and V1997756 (GDP deflator). Data for 1956 to 1965 are from F.H. Leacy, ed., *Historical Statistics of Canada*, 2nd ed. (Ottawa: Statistics Canada, 1983), series D233 (unemployment rate) and series K17 (GNP deflator).

The apparent success of the Phillips curve in the 1950s and 1960s made the prediction of Friedman and Phelps all the more bold. In 1958 Phillips had suggested a negative association between inflation and unemployment. Another decade of data had confirmed the relationship for Canada, the United States, and many other countries. To some economists at the time, it seemed ridiculous to claim that the Phillips curve would break down once policymakers tried to use it.

But, in fact, that is exactly what happened. Beginning in the late 1960s, policies were enacted that expanded the aggregate demand for goods and services. In part, this expansion was due to fiscal policy: Federal and provincial government spending was increasing much faster than the economy. In part, it was due to monetary policy: Because the Bank of Canada was trying to hold down interest rates in the face of expansionary fiscal policy, during the period from 1969 to 1973 the quantity of money (as measured by M1) was allowed to increase at twice the annual rate it did during the period from 1956 to 1968. As a result, inflation stayed high (averaging 5.7 percent from 1969 to 1973, compared with 2.6 percent from 1956 to 1968). But, as Friedman and Phelps had predicted, unemployment did not stay low.

Figure 17.7 displays the history of inflation and unemployment from 1968 to 1973. It shows that the simple negative relationship between these two variables started to break down around 1970. In particular, as inflation remained high in the early 1970s, people's expectations of inflation caught up with reality, and the unemployment rate reverted to the 5 percent to 6 percent range that had prevailed in the early 1960s. Notice that the history illustrated in Figure 17.7 closely resembles the theory of a shifting short-run Phillips curve shown in Figure 17.5. By 1973, policymakers had learned that Friedman and Phelps were right: There is no tradeoff between inflation and unemployment in the long run.

FIGURE 17.7

The Breakdown of the Phillips Curve

This figure highlights annual data from 1968 to 1973 on the unemployment rate and on the inflation rate (as measured by the GDP deflator). Notice that the Phillips curve of the 1960s breaks down in the early 1970s.

Sources: Data for 1966 to 1973 are from Statistics Canada, CANSIM II, series V2062816 (unemployment rate) and V1997756 (GDP deflator). Data for 1956 to 1965 are from F.H. Leacy, ed., *Historical Statistics of Canada*, 2nd ed. (Ottawa: Statistics Canada, 1983), series D233 (unemployment rate) and series K17 (GNP deflator).

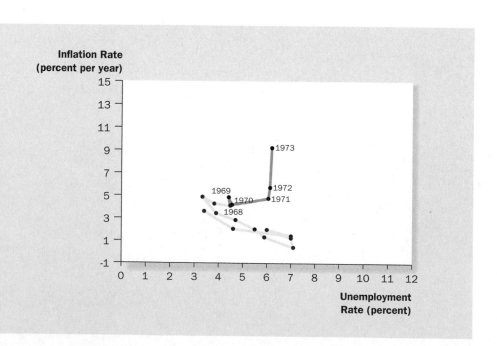

QuickQuiz   Draw the short-run Phillips curve and the long-run Phillips curve. Explain why they are different.

SHIFTS IN THE PHILLIPS CURVE: THE ROLE OF SUPPLY SHOCKS

Friedman and Phelps had suggested in 1968 that changes in expected inflation shift the short-run Phillips curve, and the experience of the early 1970s convinced most economists that Friedman and Phelps were right. Within a few years, however, the economics profession would turn its attention to a different source of shifts in the short-run Phillips curve: shocks to aggregate supply.

This time, the shift in focus came not from two American economics professors but from events in the Middle East. The Organization of Petroleum Exporting Countries (OPEC) was founded in 1960, but it was ineffectual at influencing oil prices until the early 1970s. Following a military takeover of the Libyan government in 1969, and following the success that country had in imposing new agreements on oil companies concerning pricing following the takeover, OPEC members began to act together to push up oil prices. At first, these efforts met with limited success. However, in the midst of the 1973 Middle East war, a war that had already caused oil prices to rise, OPEC met again and began to effectively exert its market power as a cartel in the world oil market. The countries of OPEC, such as Saudi Arabia, Kuwait, and Iraq, restricted the amount of crude oil they pumped and sold on world markets. Within a few years, this reduction in supply caused the price of oil to almost double.

A large increase in the world price of oil is an example of a supply shock. A **supply shock** is an event that directly affects firms' costs of production and thus the prices they charge; it shifts the economy's aggregate-supply curve and, as a result, the Phillips curve. For example, when an oil price increase raises the cost of producing gasoline, heating oil, tires, and many other products, it reduces the quantity of goods and services supplied at any given price level. As panel (a) of Figure 17.8 shows, this reduction in supply is represented by the leftward shift in the aggregate supply curve from AS_1 to AS_2. The price level rises from P_1 to P_2, and output falls from Y_1 to Y_2. The combination of rising prices and falling output is sometimes called *slugflation*.

This shift in aggregate supply is associated with a similar shift in the short-run Phillips curve, shown in panel (b). Because firms need fewer workers to produce the smaller output, employment falls and unemployment rises. Because the price level is higher, the inflation rate—the percentage change in the price level from the previous year—is also higher. Thus, the shift in aggregate supply leads to higher unemployment and higher inflation. The short-run tradeoff between inflation and unemployment shifts to the right from PC_1 to PC_2.

Confronted with an adverse shift in aggregate supply, policymakers face a difficult choice between fighting inflation and fighting unemployment. If they contract aggregate demand to fight inflation, they will raise unemployment further. If they expand aggregate demand to fight unemployment, they will raise inflation further. In other words, policymakers face a less favourable tradeoff between inflation and unemployment than they did before the shift in aggregate supply: They have to live with a higher rate of inflation for a given rate of unemployment,

supply shock
an event that directly alters firms' costs and prices, shifting the economy's aggregate-supply curve and thus the Phillips curve

FIGURE 17.8

An Adverse Shock to Aggregate Supply

Panel (a) shows the model of aggregate demand and aggregate supply. When the aggregate-supply curve shifts to the left from AS_1 to AS_2, the equilibrium moves from point A to point B. Output falls from Y_1 to Y_2, and the price level rises from P_1 to P_2. Panel (b) shows the short-run tradeoff between inflation and unemployment. The adverse shift in aggregate supply moves the economy from a point with lower unemployment and lower inflation (point A) to a point with higher unemployment and higher inflation (point B). The short-run Phillips curve shifts to the right from PC_1 to PC_2. Policymakers now face a worse tradeoff between inflation and unemployment.

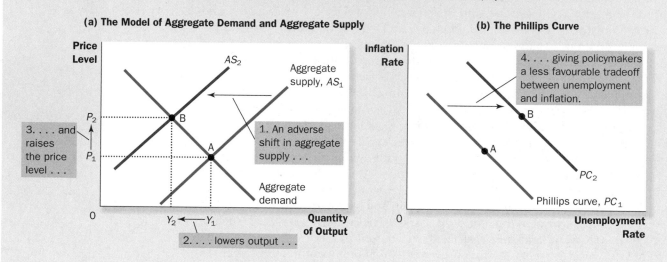

(a) The Model of Aggregate Demand and Aggregate Supply

(b) The Phillips Curve

a higher rate of unemployment for a given rate of inflation, or some combination of higher unemployment and higher inflation.

An important question is whether this adverse shift in the Phillips curve is temporary or permanent. The answer depends on how people adjust their expectations of inflation. If people view the rise in inflation due to the supply shock as a temporary aberration, expected inflation does not change, and the Phillips curve will soon revert to its former position. But if people believe the shock will lead to a new era of higher inflation, then expected inflation rises, and the Phillips curve remains at its new, less desirable position.

Figure 17.9 shows inflation and unemployment in the Canadian economy during the 1970s. It shows that in the mid-1970s inflation increased dramatically as a result of the OPEC oil price shock. The increase in the price of oil meant that Canadian firms using oil as an input in their production processes would soon suffer dramatically higher costs. If nothing was done, the result would be both higher inflation and a higher unemployment rate: stagflation. Canadian policymakers were therefore faced with a difficult choice brought about by the threat of stagflation: Should they respond to the threat of stagflation by contracting aggregate demand to fight inflation but contribute to an increase in unemployment, or should they expand aggregate demand to fight unemployment but at the cost of increasing inflation and inflationary expectations even further?

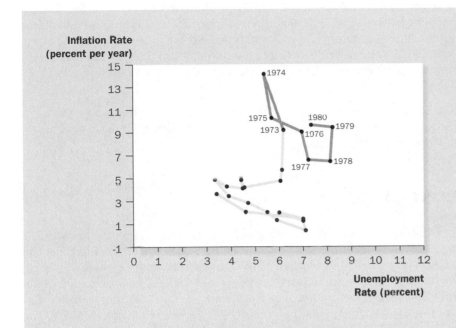

The Supply Shocks of the 1970s

This figure highlights annual data from 1973 to 1980 on the unemployment rate and on the inflation rate (as measured by the GDP deflator). Increases in the world price of oil in the early 1970s and again in 1979 caused large jumps in the rate of inflation and caused the short-run Phillips curve to shift to the right. In between these two oil price shocks, tight monetary policy and wage and price controls caused Canada to slide down a temporarily stable short-run curve.

Sources: Data for 1966 to 1980 are from Statistics Canada, CANSIM II, series V2062816 (unemployment rate) and V1997756 (GDP deflator). Data for 1956 to 1965 are from F.H. Leacy, ed., *Historical Statistics of Canada*, 2nd ed. (Ottawa: Statistics Canada, 1983), series D233 (unemployment rate) and series K17 (GNP deflator).

Policymakers chose to attack the problem of stagflation in two ways. First, the Bank of Canada instituted a tight monetary policy. From 1974 to 1978, the money supply increased by less than 1 percent per year. Thus, during this period, the Bank of Canada was reducing aggregate demand, which would reduce prices but also contribute to a further reduction in output. The second way policymakers chose to attack inflation was to impose wage and price controls. From 1976 to 1978, federal government legislation limited increases in wages and prices to below the rate of inflation. These controls were designed to be a direct attack on both inflation and inflation expectations. The hope was that controls would signal to workers and firms that, because everyone was being made to do so, they could moderate their own demands for higher wages and prices without losing ground to other workers and firms. The result of this two-pronged attack was a dramatic reduction in the rate of inflation but also an increase in the rate of unemployment. During the 1974 to 1978 period, the Canadian economy was sliding back down the short-run Phillips curve. Unfortunately, however, the effects of the OPEC price shock had shifted the curve to the right. As a result, by the time the rate of inflation returned to 1972 levels, unemployment was 2 percentage points higher. Moreover, just as inflation had moderated and price controls had been removed, OPEC once again started to exert its market power. As a result, the price of oil more than doubled in 1979.

In the wake of the second OPEC oil price shock, the Canadian economy was faced again with a much higher rate of inflation and the threat that expectations of inflation would remain high. In 1980, after two OPEC supply shocks, Canada had an inflation rate of 10 percent and an unemployment rate of 7.4 percent. This combination of inflation and unemployment was not at all near the tradeoff that seemed possible in the 1960s. (In the 1960s, the Phillips curve suggested that an unemployment rate of 7.5 percent would be associated with an inflation rate of less than 1.0 percent. Inflation of more than 10.0 percent was unthinkable.) With the misery index in 1980 near a historic high, the public was widely dissatisfied with macroeconomic performance. Something had to be done, and soon it would be.

QuickQuiz Give an example of a favourable shock to aggregate supply. Use the model of aggregate demand and aggregate supply to explain the effects of such a shock. How does it affect the Phillips curve?

THE COST OF REDUCING INFLATION

In October 1979, as OPEC was imposing adverse supply shocks on the world's economies for the second time in a decade, the Bank of Canada decided that the time for action had come. As guardian of the nation's monetary system, the Bank of Canada had little choice but to pursue a policy of *disinflation*—a reduction in the rate of inflation. There was no doubt that the Bank of Canada could reduce inflation through its ability to control the quantity of money. But what would be the short-run cost of disinflation? The answer to this question was much less certain.

The Sacrifice Ratio

To reduce the inflation rate, the Bank of Canada has to pursue contractionary monetary policy. Figure 17.10 shows some of the effects of such a decision. When the Bank of Canada slows the rate at which the money supply is growing, it contracts aggregate demand. The fall in aggregate demand, in turn, reduces the quantity of goods and services that firms produce, and this fall in production leads to a fall in employment. The economy begins at point A in the figure and moves along the short-run Phillips curve to point B, which has lower inflation and higher unemployment. Over time, as people come to understand that prices are rising more slowly, expected inflation falls, and the short-run Phillips curve shifts downward. The economy moves from point B to point C. Inflation is lower, and unemployment is back at its natural rate.

Thus, if a nation wants to reduce inflation, it must endure a period of high unemployment and low output. In Figure 17.10, this cost is represented by the movement of the economy through point B as it travels from point A to point C. The size of this cost depends on the slope of the Phillips curve and how quickly expectations of inflation adjust to the new monetary policy.

Many studies have examined the data on inflation and unemployment in order to estimate the cost of reducing inflation. The findings of these studies are often summarized in a statistic called the **sacrifice ratio**. The sacrifice ratio is the number of percentage points of one year's output lost in the process of reducing inflation by 1 percentage point. Macroeconomists have found it difficult to obtain a precise estimate of the sacrifice ratio. Typical estimates of the sacrifice ratio for Canada fall over quite a wide range of between 2 and 5. That is, for each percentage point that inflation is reduced, between 2 and 5 percent of one year's output must be sacrificed in the transition.

sacrifice ratio
the number of percentage points of one year's output lost in the process of reducing inflation by 1 percentage point

FIGURE 17.10

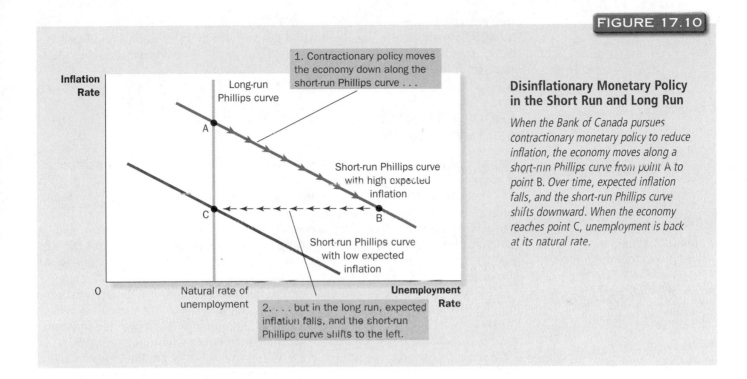

Disinflationary Monetary Policy in the Short Run and Long Run

When the Bank of Canada pursues contractionary monetary policy to reduce inflation, the economy moves along a short-run Phillips curve from point A to point B. Over time, expected inflation falls, and the short-run Phillips curve shifts downward. When the economy reaches point C, unemployment is back at its natural rate.

We can also express the sacrifice ratio in terms of unemployment. For this purpose we need an estimate of how much a 1 percentage-point fall in output translates into an increase in unemployment. **Okun's law** provides such an estimate. Okun's law suggests that a change of 1 percentage point in GDP translates into a change of 0.5 percentage points of unemployment. Therefore, the range of estimates for the sacrifice ratio suggest that reducing inflation by 1 percentage point requires a sacrifice of between 1 and 2.5 percentage points of unemployment.

Such estimates surely must have made the Bank of Canada apprehensive as it confronted the task of reducing inflation. In 1980, inflation was running at almost 10 percent per year and the unemployment rate was 7.4 percent. To reach moderate inflation of, say, 4 percent per year would mean reducing inflation by 6 percentage points. If the true size of the sacrifice ratio were at the top end of the range of estimates, so that each percentage point cost 5 percent of one year's output, then reducing inflation by 6 percentage points would require sacrificing 30 percent of one year's output. By the same token, it would cost 15 percentage points of unemployment.

According to studies of the Phillips curve and the cost of disinflation, this sacrifice could be paid in various ways. An immediate reduction in inflation would depress output by 30 percent and increase the unemployment rate by 15 percentage points in a single year. That outcome was surely too harsh even for inflation hawks. It would be better, many argued, to spread out the cost over several years. If the reduction in inflation took place over five years, for instance, then output would have to average only 6 percent below trend during that period to add up to a sacrifice of 30 percent. Similarly, reducing inflation by 6 percentage points over a five-year period would mean that the unemployment rate would need to rise by only 3 percentage points and remain at 10.4 percent for the

Okun's law
the number of percentage points the unemployment rate increases when GDP falls by 1 percentage point

five-year transition period. An even more gradual approach would be to reduce inflation slowly over a decade, so that output would have to be only 3 percent below trend. Whatever path was chosen, however, it seemed that reducing inflation would not be easy.

Rational Expectations and the Possibility of Costless Disinflation

Just as policymakers were pondering how costly reducing inflation might be, a group of economics professors was leading an intellectual revolution that would challenge the conventional wisdom on the sacrifice ratio. This group included such prominent economists as Robert Lucas, Thomas Sargent, and Robert Barro. Their revolution was based on a new approach to economic theory and policy called **rational expectations.** According to the theory of rational expectations, people optimally use all the information they have, including information about government policies, when forecasting the future.

This new approach has had profound implications for many areas of macroeconomics, but none is more important than its application to the tradeoff between inflation and unemployment. As Friedman and Phelps had first emphasized, expected inflation is an important variable that explains why there is a tradeoff between inflation and unemployment in the short run but not in the long run. How quickly the short-run tradeoff disappears depends on how quickly expectations adjust. Proponents of rational expectations built on the Friedman–Phelps analysis to argue that when economic policies change, people adjust their expectations of inflation accordingly. Studies of inflation and unemployment that tried to estimate the sacrifice ratio had failed to take account of the direct effect of the policy regime on expectations. As a result, estimates of the sacrifice ratio were, according to the rational-expectations theorists, unreliable guides for policy.

In a 1981 paper entitled "The End of Four Big Inflations," Thomas Sargent described this new view as follows:

> An alternative "rational expectations" view denies that there is any inherent momentum to the present process of inflation. This view maintains that firms and workers have now come to expect high rates of inflation in the future and that they strike inflationary bargains in light of these expectations. However, it is held that people expect high rates of inflation in the future precisely because the government's current and prospective monetary and fiscal policies warrant those expectations. . . . An implication of this view is that inflation can be stopped much more quickly than advocates of the "momentum" view have indicated and that their estimates of the length of time and the costs of stopping inflation in terms of forgone output are erroneous. . . . This is not to say that it would be easy to eradicate inflation. On the contrary, it would require more than a few temporary restrictive fiscal and monetary actions. It would require a change in the policy regime. . . . How costly such a move would be in terms of forgone output and how long it would be in taking effect would depend partly on how resolute and evident the government's commitment was.

According to Sargent, the sacrifice ratio could be much smaller than suggested by previous estimates. Indeed, in the most extreme case, it could be zero. If the

rational expectations
the theory according to which people optimally use all the information they have, including information about government policies, when forecasting the future

government made a credible commitment to a policy of low inflation, people would be rational enough to lower their expectations of inflation immediately. The short-run Phillips curve would shift downward, and the economy would reach low inflation quickly without the cost of temporarily high unemployment and low output.

Disinflation in the 1980s

As we have seen, when the Bank of Canada at the beginning of the 1980s faced the prospect of reducing inflation, the economics profession offered two conflicting predictions. One group of economists offered estimates of the sacrifice ratio and concluded that reducing inflation would have great cost in terms of lost output and high unemployment. Another group offered the theory of rational expectations and concluded that reducing inflation could be much less costly and, perhaps, could even have no cost at all. Who was right?

Figure 17.11 highlights data on inflation and unemployment from 1980 to 1989. As you can see, the Bank of Canada did succeed at reducing inflation. Inflation came down from 10 percent in 1980 and 1981 to about 3 percent in 1985 and 1986. Credit for this reduction in inflation goes completely to monetary policy. Fiscal policy at this time was acting in the opposite direction: Increases in the budget deficits of the provinces and the federal government were expanding aggregate demand, which tends to raise inflation. The dramatic fall in inflation from 1981 to 1985 is attributable to the equally dramatic anti-inflation policies of the Bank of Canada. From 1979 to 1982, the money supply, as measured by M1, shrank by an average of almost 6 percent per year. Economists David Laidler and William Robson suggested that monetary policy during this period was "excruciatingly" contractionary. The description certainly seems appropriate.

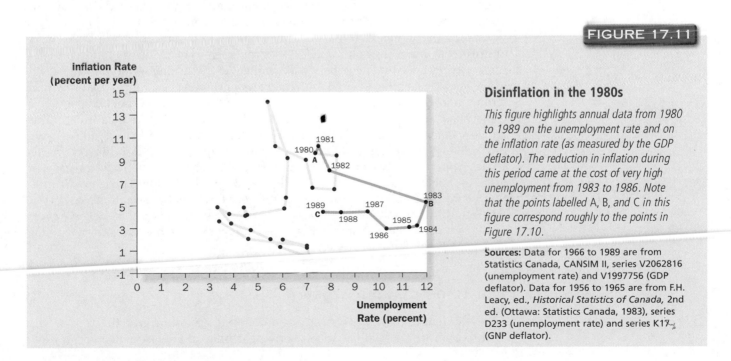

FIGURE 17.11

Disinflation in the 1980s

This figure highlights annual data from 1980 to 1989 on the unemployment rate and on the inflation rate (as measured by the GDP deflator). The reduction in inflation during this period came at the cost of very high unemployment from 1983 to 1986. Note that the points labelled A, B, and C in this figure correspond roughly to the points in Figure 17.10.

Sources: Data for 1966 to 1989 are from Statistics Canada, CANSIM II, series V2062816 (unemployment rate) and V1997756 (GDP deflator). Data for 1956 to 1965 are from F.H. Leacy, ed., *Historical Statistics of Canada*, 2nd ed. (Ottawa: Statistics Canada, 1983), series D233 (unemployment rate) and series K17 (GNP deflator).

Figure 17.11 shows that disinflation did come at the cost of high unemployment. In 1983, 1984, and 1985, the unemployment rate was more than 11 percent. At the same time, the production of goods and services as measured by real GDP was well below its trend level. (See Figure 15.1 in Chapter 15.) The disinflation of the early 1980s produced the deepest recession in Canada since the Great Depression of the 1930s.

Does this experience refute the possibility of costless disinflation as suggested by the rational-expectations theorists? Some economists have argued that the answer to this question is a resounding yes. Indeed, the pattern of disinflation shown in Figure 17.11 is very similar to the pattern predicted in Figure 17.10. To make the transition from high inflation (point A in both figures) to low inflation (point C), the economy had to experience a painful period of high unemployment (point B). At the beginning of this transition period (point A), the unemployment rate was 7.4 percent, approximately equal to the natural unemployment rate. By 1989, which marked the end of the transition period (point C), unemployment was again close to the natural unemployment rate. (As we showed in Figure 10.4 in Chapter 10, the natural unemployment rate is generally viewed as having increased during the 1980s; by 1988 it was roughly 8 percent. We use the estimates of the natural unemployment rate presented in Figure 10.4 in Chapter 10 in our calculations below.) If we add up the number of percentage points the unemployment rate remained above the natural rate and divide that amount by the number of percentage points inflation was reduced over this period, we arrive at an estimate of the sacrifice ratio defined in terms of sacrificed employment. The estimate we arrive at is 2.1. This indicates that during the period from 1981 to 1989, each reduction of 1.0 percentage point in inflation during this period required a sacrifice of about 2.1 percentage points of unemployment. This is at the upper end of estimates of the sacrifice ratio suggested by those economists who argued that reducing inflation could come only at great cost in terms of lost output and high unemployment. For those economists, then, the claims of rational-expectations theorists that less costly disinflation was possible seemed to carry little weight.

Despite the evidence supporting the view that inflation could be reduced only at great cost, many economists felt it was too soon to reject the notion that lower rates of inflation could be obtained at smaller cost. The main reason for this optimism was the fact that even though the Bank of Canada announced that it would aim monetary policy to lower inflation, much of the public did not believe it.

Because few people thought the Bank of Canada would reduce inflation as quickly as it did, expected inflation did not fall, and the short-run Phillips curve did not shift down as quickly as it might have. Some evidence for this hypothesis comes from the forecasts made by commercial forecasting firms: Their forecasts of inflation fell more slowly in the 1980s than did actual inflation. Thus, the disinflation of the 1980s does not necessarily refute the rational-expectations view that credible disinflation can be costless. It does show, however, that policymakers cannot count on people immediately believing them when they announce a policy of disinflation.

The Zero-Inflation Target

The latter half of the 1980s was a period of strong economic growth. By 1989, the unemployment rate had fallen by over 4 percentage points from its high in 1983.

Toward the end of the decade, however, this strong economic growth led to an increase in the rate of inflation. In 1988 the governor of the Bank of Canada, John Crow, made a speech known as the Hanson lecture. In that speech, Crow offered a clear statement defining the future direction of monetary policy in Canada. He asserted that the sole goal of the Bank of Canada would thereafter be to achieve and maintain a stable price level and zero inflation (for technical reasons that have to do with how inflation is measured, 1 percent inflation is generally accepted as being "zero").

The purpose of the Hanson lecture was to define a clear target for monetary policy and to announce this policy widely. Many macroeconomists believed that, because the new monetary policy target was so clearly and firmly stated by such a well-known inflation hawk as John Crow, the public ought to believe what he was saying and quickly adjust inflation expectations downward. In this way, inflation might be reduced to the targeted level with a smaller sacrifice in terms of unemployment and lost output than had been experienced previously. The Bank of Canada began contracting the money supply in 1989 and continued to do so in 1990 and 1991. Figure 17.12 shows that the unemployment rate increased from 7.7 percent in 1989 to 11.4 percent in 1994, while inflation fell from 4.5 percent to 1.1 percent. The inflation target was thus reached very quickly (the Bank of Canada's target for inflation is based on the "core" rate of CPI inflation, a rate slightly lower than that calculated here using the GDP deflator). From 1994 to 2002, the inflation rate averaged just 1.5 percent, so that the target was successfully maintained. By the end of 2002, the unemployment rate had returned to what it was in 1989, a level generally regarded as roughly equal to the natural rate.

FIGURE 17.12

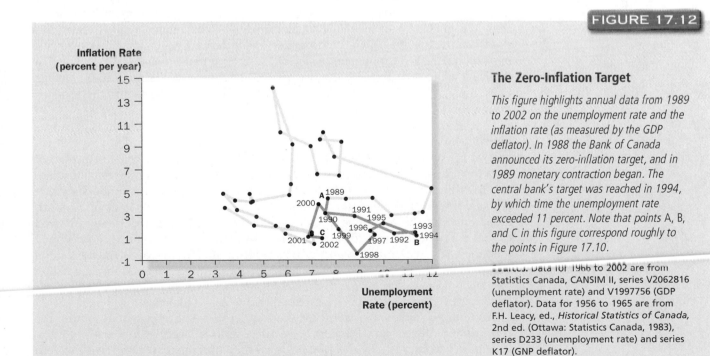

The Zero-Inflation Target

This figure highlights annual data from 1989 to 2002 on the unemployment rate and the inflation rate (as measured by the GDP deflator). In 1988 the Bank of Canada announced its zero-inflation target, and in 1989 monetary contraction began. The central bank's target was reached in 1994, by which time the unemployment rate exceeded 11 percent. Note that points A, B, and C in this figure correspond roughly to the points in Figure 17.10.

Sources: Data for 1966 to 2002 are from Statistics Canada, CANSIM II, series V2062816 (unemployment rate) and V1997756 (GDP deflator). Data for 1956 to 1965 are from F.H. Leacy, ed., *Historical Statistics of Canada*, 2nd ed. (Ottawa: Statistics Canada, 1983), series D233 (unemployment rate) and series K17 (GNP deflator).

Just as it did in response to the Bank of Canada's effort at disinflation in the early 1980s, the economy adjusted toward a lower rate of inflation from 1989 to 2002 in a way that closely corresponds to the pattern shown in Figure 17.10. If we label 1989 as point A, 1994 as point B, and 2002 as point C, the data in Figure 17.12 appear to show that inflation expectations were slow to adjust downward. As a result, it appears that the economy adjusted along a given short-run Phillips curve (from point A to point B) before inflation expectations adjusted, shifting the short-run curve to the left (to give us point C). If we add up the number of percentage points the unemployment rate remained above the natural rate and divide that amount by the number of percentage points inflation was reduced over the 1989–2002 period, we arrive at an estimate of the sacrifice ratio equal to 4.8, an estimate more than twice as large as our estimate (2.1) for the 1981–89 period. The experience of this most recent attempt to reduce inflation has confirmed the opinion of those macroeconomists who believe that inflation can be reduced only at great cost. The Bank of Canada clearly defined and announced its intention to contract the money supply so as to reduce inflation to zero, and yet the cost of reducing inflation seemed to be larger than ever before.

Despite this evidence, many macroeconomists are still not ready to reject the notion that lower rates of inflation can be obtained at smaller cost if the central bank makes a credible statement of its intention to deflate. They maintain their optimism by pointing to a number of factors in the transition to zero inflation that may have prevented inflation expectations from falling as quickly as they otherwise might have. One such factor was that the deficits of the provinces and the federal government remained very high throughout much of this period of transition. Concern over these deficits culminated in 1995, when credit agencies lowered the rating on federal government debt. High deficits and credit downgrades may have caused people to doubt whether the Bank of Canada could reach its target of zero inflation, and thereby caused people's expectations of inflation to remain high. Critics of the Bank of Canada argue that it should have foreseen this problem, because the main reason government deficits were increasing over this period was the tight monetary policy of the central bank. These critics argue that the Bank of Canada's credibility was in doubt because of its decision to launch a tight monetary policy before the federal and provincial governments reduced their deficits.

A second reason inflation expectations may not have fallen as quickly as was hoped when the Bank of Canada announced its zero-inflation target was that the federal government, in preparing its budgets, was using a forecast of 3 percent inflation. Thus, at the same time that the Bank of Canada was announcing its intention to achieve zero inflation, the federal government was in effect announcing that it was doubtful that the target could be reached. Once again, the lack of a coordinated effort by the central bank and the federal government may have conspired to cause individuals and firms to adjust their inflation expectations more slowly than they otherwise might have. Perhaps in recognition of this problem, the federal government issued a news release in conjunction with its 1998 budget reaffirming its commitment to supporting the Bank of Canada's inflation target. A similar statement has been released with each federal budget since that time.

Another possible explanation for the high costs associated with attaining the zero-inflation target may be that the sacrifice ratio is larger at low rates of inflation. Macroeconomists who hold this view argue that the reason the move to zero inflation proved so costly had less to do with the failure of inflation expectations to adjust and more to do with the short-run Phillips curve becoming much flatter at low rates of inflation. As a result, the cost of lowering inflation from 3 percent to 1 percent may be substantially greater than the cost of reducing inflation from 5 percent to 3 percent. Our calculations of the sacrifice ratio involved in reducing inflation from 10.3 percent in 1981 to 4.5 percent in 1989 (a sacrifice ratio of 2.1) versus the sacrifice ratio involved in reducing inflation from 4.5 percent in 1989 to 1.0 percent in 2002 (a sacrifice ratio of 4.8) seem to offer evidence in favour of this view. These macroeconomists also point to the recent experience of the United States to support this view. From 1984 to 2002, the inflation rate in the United States fluctuated between 3 and 5 percent, with relatively small changes in the unemployment rate. In Canada, the reduction in the inflation rate below 3 percent seemed to incur the greatest cost. The relative success of U.S. monetary policy in the 1990s may therefore be due to the Federal Reserve being satisfied with a higher rate of inflation than the Bank of Canada.

What does the future hold? Macroeconomists are notoriously bad at forecasting, but several lessons of the past seem clear. First, our interpretation of the evidence concerning the rates of unemployment and inflation since 1956 suggests that the existence of a short-run tradeoff between inflation and unemployment is well established. While policymakers may be able to influence output and unemployment, they can do so only temporarily. Second, those who claim that inflation can be reduced without increases in the unemployment rate face a good deal of contrary evidence against which they must present their case. Third, the possibility always exists for the economy to experience adverse shocks to aggregate supply, as it did in the 1970s. If that unfortunate development occurs, policymakers will have little choice but to confront a less desirable tradeoff between inflation and unemployment. Fortunately, while oil prices increased quite dramatically in 2000 and remain high as this edition goes to press (fall 2004), because the Canadian economy is far less dependent on oil than it was in the 1970s, the tradeoff does not seem to have worsened as it did earlier.

Fourth, as long as the Bank of Canada remains vigilant in its control over the money supply and, thereby, aggregate demand, there is no reason to allow inflation to heat up needlessly. Fifth, many macroeconomists remain convinced that the costs of disinflation can be minimized if the Bank of Canada clearly announces its intentions, so that people and firms have the opportunity to adjust their inflation expectations before a monetary contraction. Certainly the Bank of Canada remains convinced of this, and for this reason it continues to make clear statements of its intentions. Finally, the debate continues over the question of whether the costs of disinflation increase at lower rates of inflation.

Figure 17.12 stops with measures of unemployment and inflation for the year 2002: 7.4 percent and 1.0 percent, respectively. It is discouraging that achieving the low inflation target was realized only by suffering a long period of high unemployment. On the other hand, it is encouraging that unemployment and inflation in the first two years of the new millenium were at levels not seen since the early 1960s. It suggests the possibility that policymakers might face a more attractive short-run tradeoff between inflation and unemployment than they have for quite some time. Many economists are hopeful that the natural unemployment rate is falling in value so that data on unemployment and inflation for future years will lie to the left of point C in Figure 17.12. That is, these economists are hopeful that low inflation can be maintained even while realizing a reduction in the unemployment rate. The reason for their hope is the subject of the following case study.

Case Study

IS THE PHILLIPS CURVE NOW SHIFTING TO THE LEFT?

Figure 17.12 shows that since 1956, Canada's short-run Phillips curve has shifted to the right. In this chapter we highlighted the role oil price shocks played in causing these shifts. In the early 1970s and again in the late 1970s, rapid increases in oil prices shifted the Phillips curve to the right and thereby worsened the short-run trade-off. We referred to these oil price shocks as adverse supply shocks. (Recall that a supply shock is an event that directly alters firms' costs and prices.

IN THE NEWS

THE MOVING SHORT-RUN TRADEOFF BETWEEN INFLATION AND UNEMPLOYMENT

When has the unemployment rate fallen too low? The answer depends on how far one believes the economy is from the natural unemployment rate. In the following article, former Bank of Canada Governor Gordon Thiessen (who has since been replaced by David Dodge) expresses concern that strong growth and a falling unemployment rate might be signalling that the rate of inflation is about to increase. Economist Tim O'Neill discusses how the Bank of Canada is uncertain about when inflationary pressures might arise because it is uncertain about the effects productivity gains have had on the economy's ability to grow without inflation. In other words, the Phillips curve may be shifting to the left, allowing unemployment to fall further without inflation. If so, the Bank of Canada may be able to delay raising interest rates in an effort to prevent inflation. (Note: The reference in the article to the noninflationary rate of unemployment *is to what we know as the* natural rate of unemployment.*)*

Rate Rise Warning Flag Raised by Thiessen

By Jill Vardy

Ottawa—Gordon Thiessen, the Bank of Canada's governor, raised a warning flag yesterday that the economy may need a cooling dose of interest rate hikes to take some of the heat out of inflation.

But the point at which the economy overheats may be higher than it once was, and so the bank can afford to be less aggressive in its efforts to cool things down, Mr. Thiessen suggested.

Speaking to the Canadian Society in New York, he said Canada's economy is expanding faster than expected. That could spark higher inflation, something the Bank won't tolerate. "We continue to see strong momentum in our economy so far this year," he said. "By some calculations, we could be operating at full capacity.

"The Bank is now monitoring a wide range of indicators for early-warning signs of pressure on capacity and prices. Up to now, our inflation performance bodes well for the continued expansion of the Canadian economy."

He said even the unemployment rate appears to have room to drop further before higher wage demand starts to push up inflation.

An adverse supply shock shifts the short-run aggregate-supply curve to the left, lowering output and raising prices. It therefore increases both unemployment and inflation and shifts the short-run Phillips curve to the right.)

Many economists stress another reason why Canada's Phillips curve shifted to the right: adverse supply shocks in the form of higher taxes and higher government debt. Increases in tax burdens increase the costs to firms both directly, if corporate taxes are increasing, and indirectly, if personal taxes are increasing and firms must consequently offer higher wages to attract workers. To the extent that increased government debt causes interest rates to be higher, firms similarly face higher costs to finance capacity expansions. In both of these ways, then, the rising

The Bank of Canada has been grappling to define the noninflationary rate of unemployment for Canada. Productivity gains make it difficult to gauge how much further the jobless rate can fall, Mr. Thiessen said.

The Bank of Canada is expected to follow an anticipated 25-basis-point interest rate hike in the United States after that country's Federal Reserve meets on March 21. That will be the fifth jump in U.S. interest rates in eight months.

"I think the bank has been signalling they're ready to move and they will likely move if the Fed moves on the 21st of this month," said Tim O'Neill, chief economist at the Bank of Montreal. "On the other hand, other comments in Mr. Thiessen's speech suggest there is not a sense of urgency or panic here, that the moves will be gradual rather than very aggressive."

The Bank of Canada has increased its trendsetting bank rate twice, in November and February, following similar hikes in the United States.

Certainly Canada's economy is growing by more than expected. Real gross domestic product rose at a 4.6 percent annualized rate in the fourth quarter of 1999. Strong growth has

pulled the unemployment rate down to just 6.8 percent, its lowest level in almost 25 years.

Despite that, Canada's inflation performance to January has been better than expected, Mr. Thiessen said, with Canada's core inflation rate remaining around 1.3 percent, at the bottom half of the 1 percent to 3 percent target the central bank has set.

"The job of the Bank of Canada is to keep inflation in Canada low and stable," Mr. Thiessen said. "Without that, we will be risking both the economic expansion and the potential productivity gains."

The risk of inflation grows as the economy nears its peak capacity, because that's when workers start demanding higher wages and producers can pass on higher prices to consumers. But no one is sure now just what is Canada's potential capacity, Mr. O'Neill said.

The U.S. economy has shown remarkable improvements in its productivity, and in its capacity for noninflationary growth, thanks largely to investments in machinery, equipment, and technology. That appears to be happening in Canada, too—but no one knows to what extent.

"We're prepared to be less aggressive than we might have been previously, because we're not as confident about what precisely are the capacity limits on the economy. So we don't want to be overly aggressive here. The U.S. has done remarkably well by not overreacting to strong growth. The limits may be higher than they thought," Mr. O'Neill said.

Canada's capacity utilization rate—which measures actual production against the amount of production of which the economy is capable—rose to 86.8 percent in the fourth quarter, from 85.5 percent in the previous quarter.

"That suggests there may be more room for error here without dire consequences and I think it's that more balanced interpretation that I would give to the speech today," Mr. O'Neill said. "The situation is different and so the way in which the bank conducts monetary policy must be different."

Source: National Post, March 10, 2000, National Edition, p. C1/Front. Material reprinted with the express permission of The National Post Company, a CanWest partnership.

tax burden and rising levels of government debt Canadians faced during the 1980s contributed to the rightward shift of the Phillips curve.

Although it is still too early to be sure, the last few observations in Figure 17.12 suggest that the Phillips curve may be shifting back toward the left. Some economists suggest this may be happening because of a number of *favourable* supply shocks. By reducing a firm's costs and prices, a favourable supply shock shifts the short-run aggregate-supply curve to the right, raising output and reducing prices. The shock therefore reduces both unemployment and inflation and shifts the short-run Phillips curve to the left. In particular, these economists identify the following as causing favourable supply shocks:

- *Debt reduction*: Since the mid-1990s, Canadian federal and provincial governments have made great strides in eliminating their deficits and most are now regularly reporting budget surpluses. The result has been a reduction in the level of government debt and falling interest rates. Reduced interest rates lower the financing costs firms face for expanding capacity and thus represent a favourable supply shock.
- *Tax cuts:* In 2000, the federal government announced a set of major tax cuts. Most provincial governments are also making efforts to reduce taxes, and many are emphasizing cuts to corporate taxes. Tax cuts reduce producers' costs and in this way act as a favourable supply shock for the economy.
- *Technological advances:* Some economists believe that the Canadian economy has entered a period of more rapid technological progress. Advances in information technology, such as the Internet, have been profound and have influenced many parts of the economy. Such technological advances increase productivity and, therefore, are a type of favourable supply shock.
- *Free trade:* Exposing Canadian firms to greater foreign competition provides them with an incentive to minimize costs and adopt the latest technologies. For both of these reasons, many economists consider free trade agreements to be a type of favourable supply shock.

Economists debate whether the Phillips curve is in fact shifting back to the left and they debate which, if any, of the explanations listed above is responsible for this shift. In the end, the complete story may contain elements of each.

Keep in mind that none of these hypotheses denies the fundamental lesson of the Phillips curve—that policymakers who control aggregate demand always face a short-run tradeoff between inflation and unemployment. Canada's experience with this tradeoff suggests, however, that it changes over time and can worsen or improve. ●

QuickQuiz What is the sacrifice ratio? How might the credibility of the Bank of Canada's commitment to reduce inflation affect the sacrifice ratio?

CONCLUSION

This chapter has examined how economists' thinking about inflation and unemployment has evolved over time. We have discussed the ideas of many of the best economists of the twentieth century: from the Phillips curve of Phillips, Lipsey, Samuelson, and Solow, to the natural-rate hypothesis of Friedman and Phelps, to the rational-expectations theory of Lucas, Sargent, and Barro. Four of this group have already won Nobel prizes for their work in economics, and more are likely to be so honoured in the years to come.

Although the tradeoff between inflation and unemployment has generated much intellectual turmoil over the past 40 years, certain principles have developed that today command consensus. Here is how Milton Friedman expressed the relationship between inflation and unemployment in 1968:

> There is always a temporary tradeoff between inflation and unemployment; there is no permanent tradeoff. The temporary tradeoff comes not from inflation per se, but from unanticipated inflation, which generally means, from a rising rate of inflation. The widespread belief that there is a permanent tradeoff is a sophisticated version of the confusion between "high" and "rising" that we all recognize in simpler forms. A rising rate of inflation may reduce unemployment, a high rate will not.
>
> But how long, you will say, is "temporary"? . . . I can at most venture a personal judgment, based on some examination of the historical evidence, that the initial effects of a higher and unanticipated rate of inflation last for something like two to five years.

Today, more than 35 years later, this statement still summarizes the view of most macroeconomists.

SUMMARY

- The Phillips curve describes a negative relationship between inflation and unemployment. By expanding aggregate demand, policymakers can choose a point on the Phillips curve with higher inflation and lower unemployment. By contracting aggregate demand, policymakers can choose a point on the Phillips curve with lower inflation and higher unemployment.

- The tradeoff between inflation and unemployment described by the Phillips curve holds only in the short run. In the long run, expected inflation adjusts to changes in actual inflation, and the short-run Phillips curve shifts. As a result, the long-run Phillips curve is vertical at the natural rate of unemployment.

- The short-run Phillips curve also shifts because of shocks to aggregate supply. An adverse supply shock, such as the increase in world oil prices during the 1970s, gives policymakers a less favourable tradeoff between inflation and unemployment. That is, after an adverse supply shock, policymakers have to accept a higher rate of inflation for any given rate of unemployment, or a higher rate of unemployment for any given rate of inflation.

- When the Bank of Canada contracts growth in the money supply to reduce inflation, it moves the economy along the short-run Phillips curve, which results in temporarily high unemployment. The cost of disinflation depends on how quickly expectations of inflation fall. Some economists argue that a credible commitment to low inflation can reduce the cost of disinflation by inducing a quick adjustment of expectations. To this point, there has been little empirical evidence to support the theoretical possibility of costless disinflation.

KEY CONCEPTS

Phillips curve, p. 408
natural-rate hypothesis, p. 417

supply shock, p. 419
sacrifice ratio, p. 422

Okun's law, p. 423
rational expectations, p. 424

QUESTIONS FOR REVIEW

1. Draw the short-run tradeoff between inflation and unemployment. How might the Bank of Canada move the economy from one point on this curve to another?

2. Draw the long-run tradeoff between inflation and unemployment. Explain how the short-run and long-run tradeoffs are related.

3. What's so natural about the natural rate of unemployment? Why might the natural rate of unemployment differ across countries?

4. Suppose a drought destroys farm crops and drives up the price of food. What is the effect on the short-run tradeoff between inflation and unemployment?

5. Suppose the Bank of Canada decides to reduce inflation. Use the Phillips curve to show the short-run and long-run effects of this policy. How might the short-run costs be reduced?

PROBLEMS AND APPLICATIONS

1. Suppose the natural rate of unemployment is 6 percent. On one graph, draw two Phillips curves that can be used to describe the four situations listed here. Label the point that shows the position of the economy in each case.
   a. Actual inflation is 5 percent and expected inflation is 3 percent.
   b. Actual inflation is 3 percent and expected inflation is 5 percent.
   c. Actual inflation is 5 percent and expected inflation is 5 percent.
   d. Actual inflation is 3 percent and expected inflation is 3 percent.

2. Illustrate the effects of the following developments on both the short-run and long-run Phillips curves. Give the economic reasoning underlying your answers.
   a. a rise in the natural rate of unemployment
   b. a decline in the price of imported oil

   c. a rise in government spending
   d. a decline in expected inflation

3. Suppose that a fall in consumer spending causes a recession.
   a. Illustrate the changes in the economy using both an aggregate-supply/aggregate-demand diagram and a Phillips-curve diagram. What happens to inflation and unemployment in the short run?
   b. Now suppose that over time expected inflation changes in the same direction that actual inflation changes. What happens to the position of the short-run Phillips curve? After the recession is over, does the economy face a better or worse set of inflation–unemployment combinations?

4. Suppose the economy is in a long-run equilibrium.
   a. Draw the economy's short-run and long-run Phillips curves.

b. Suppose a wave of business pessimism reduces aggregate demand. Show the effect of this shock on your diagram from part (a). If the Bank of Canada undertakes expansionary monetary policy, can it return the economy to its original inflation rate and original unemployment rate?

c. Now suppose the economy is back in long-run equilibrium, and then the price of imported oil rises. Show the effect of this shock with a new diagram like that in part (a). If the Bank of Canada undertakes expansionary monetary policy, can it return the economy to its original inflation rate and original unemployment rate? If the Bank of Canada undertakes contractionary monetary policy, can it return the economy to its original inflation rate and original unemployment rate? Explain why this situation differs from that in part (b).

5. Suppose the Bank of Canada believed that the natural rate of unemployment was 6 percent when the actual natural rate was 5.5 percent. If the Bank of Canada based its policy decisions on its belief, what would happen to the economy?

6. The price of oil fell sharply in 1986 and again in 1998.
a. Show the impact of such a change in both the aggregate-demand/aggregate-supply diagram and in the Phillips-curve diagram. What happens to inflation and unemployment in the short run?
b. Do the effects of this event mean there is no short-run tradeoff between inflation and unemployment? Why or why not?

7. Suppose the Bank of Canada announced that it would pursue contractionary monetary policy in order to reduce the inflation rate. Would the following conditions make the ensuing recession more or less severe? Explain.
a. Wage contracts have short durations.
b. There is little confidence in the Bank of Canada's determination to reduce inflation.
c. Expectations of inflation adjust quickly to actual inflation.

8. Some economists believe that the short-run Phillips curve is relatively steep and shifts quickly in response to changes in the economy. Would these economists be more or less likely to favour contractionary policy in order to reduce inflation than economists who had the opposite views?

9. Imagine an economy in which all wages are set in three-year contracts. In this world, the Bank of Canada announces a disinflationary change in monetary policy to begin immediately. Everyone in the economy believes the Bank of Canada's announcement. Would this disinflation be costless? Why or why not? What might the Bank of Canada do to reduce the cost of disinflation?

10. Given the unpopularity of inflation, why don't elected leaders always support efforts to reduce inflation? Economists believe that countries can reduce the cost of disinflation by letting their central banks make decisions about monetary policy without interference from politicians. Why might this be so?

11. Suppose the governor of the Bank of Canada accepts the theory of the short-run Phillips curve and the natural-rate hypothesis and wants to keep unemployment close to its natural rate. Unfortunately, because the natural rate of unemployment can change over time, the governor is unsure about the value of the natural rate. What macroeconomic variables do you think the governor should look at when conducting monetary policy?

12. Figure 17.13 plots data on the unemployment rate and the inflation rate for two periods: 1956 to 1968 and 1989 to 1997. Observe that these two sets of observations span the same rates of inflation, from less than 1 percent to 5 percent. The two sets of observations also span a similar range of unemployment rates, from a low of 3.3 percent to a high of 7.1 percent (a range of 3.8 percentage points) for the early period, and from a low of 7.6 percent to a high of 11.4 percent (a range of 3.8 percentage points) for the later period. These two sets of data therefore define two very similar short-run Phillips curves. Explain why the 1989–97 curve lies to the right of the 1956–68 curve. If the government has the goal of permanently lowering the rate of unemployment, how might it do so?

FIGURE 17.13

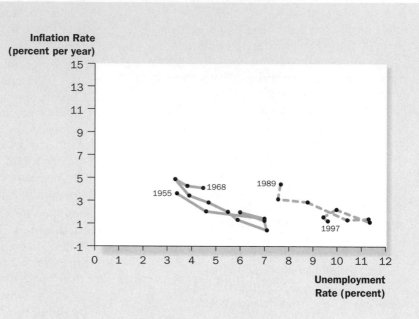

The Phillips Curve, 1956–68 and 1989–97

Sources: Data for 1966–1968 and 1989–1997 are from Statistics Canada, CANSIM II, series V2062816 (unemployment rate) and V1997756 (GDP deflator). Data for 1956 to 1965 are from F.H. Leacy, ed., *Historical Statistics of Canada*, 2nd ed. (Ottawa: Statistics Canada, 1983), series D233 (unemployment rate) and series K17 (GNP deflator).

INTERNET RESOURCES

- The Bank of Canada is charged with maintaining a low and stable rate of inflation. Go to the Bank of Canada's website at http://www.bankofcanada.ca and click on "Inflation" and then on "Backgrounders" to read about the central bank's inflation target and why the Bank judges this to be a key macroeconomic goal.

- In this chapter we have discussed the development of the Phillips curve using Canadian data on unemployment and inflation. However, we have also noted that the Phillips curve has also been measured and analyzed in other countries. J. Bradford DeLong, an economist at the University of California at Berkeley, maintains a website at http://econ161.berkeley.edu/multimedia/ Inflation.html, where he offers a multimedia presentation showing the history of the Phillips curve using U.S. data. You will find his discussion to be quite similar to that presented in this chapter.

  Nick Fawcett, an economist at Cambridge University, presents estimates of the Phillips curve using unemployment and inflation data from the United Kingdom at http://www.tutor2u.net/economics/content/topics/inflation/ philips_curve.htm. His presentation suggests the short-run Phillips curve in the United Kingdom shifted to the right during the 1970s and 1980s before shifting back to the left in the 1990s.

  What these presentations show is that the history of the Phillips curve we have offered using Canadian data is a story that is applicable to other countries as well.

For more study tools, please visit http://www.mankiw3e.nelson.com.

8

FINAL THOUGHTS

18

FIVE DEBATES OVER MACROECONOMIC POLICY

It is hard to open up the newspaper without finding some politician or editorial writer advocating a change in economic policy. The federal government should use the budget surplus to reduce government debt, or it should use it to finance increases in health care spending. The Bank of Canada should cut interest rates to stimulate a flagging economy, or it should avoid such a move in order not to risk higher inflation. Parliament should reform the tax system to promote faster economic growth, or it should reform the tax system to achieve a more equal distribution of income. Economic issues are central to the continuing political debate in Canada and other countries around the world.

Previous chapters have developed the tools that economists use when analyzing the behaviour of the economy as a whole and the impact of policies on the economy. This final chapter presents both sides in five leading debates over macroeconomic policy. The knowledge you have accumulated in this course provides the background with which we can discuss these important, unsettled issues. It should help you choose a side in these debates or, at least, help you see why choosing a side is so difficult.

Learning Objectives

In this chapter, you will consider the questions ...

- Should policymakers try to stabilize the economy?
- Should monetary policy be made by rule rather than by discretion?
- Should the central bank aim for zero inflation?
- Should fiscal policymakers reduce the government debt?
- Should the tax laws be reformed to encourage saving?

SHOULD MONETARY AND FISCAL POLICYMAKERS TRY TO STABILIZE THE ECONOMY?

In the preceding three chapters, we saw how changes in aggregate demand and aggregate supply can lead to short-run fluctuations in production and employment. We also saw how monetary and fiscal policy can shift aggregate demand and, thereby, influence these fluctuations. But even if policymakers *can* influence short-run economic fluctuations, does that mean they *should*? Our first debate concerns whether monetary and fiscal policymakers should use the tools at their disposal in an attempt to smooth the ups and downs of the business cycle.

Pro: Policymakers Should Try to Stabilize the Economy

Left on their own, economies tend to fluctuate. When households and firms become pessimistic, for instance, they cut back on spending, and this reduces the aggregate demand for goods and services. The fall in aggregate demand, in turn, reduces the production of goods and services. Firms lay off workers, and the unemployment rate rises. Real GDP and other measures of income fall. Rising unemployment and falling income help confirm the pessimism that initially generated the economic downturn.

Such a recession has no benefit for society—it represents a sheer waste of resources. Workers who become unemployed because of inadequate aggregate demand would rather be working. Business owners whose factories are left idle during a recession would rather be producing valuable goods and services and selling them at a profit.

There is no reason for society to suffer through the booms and busts of the business cycle. The development of macroeconomic theory has shown policymakers how to reduce the severity of economic fluctuations. By "leaning against the wind" of economic change, monetary and fiscal policy can stabilize aggregate demand and, thereby, production and employment. When aggregate demand is inadequate to ensure full employment, policymakers should boost government spending, cut taxes, and expand the money supply. When aggregate demand is excessive, risking higher inflation, policymakers should cut government spending, raise taxes, and reduce the money supply. Such policy actions put macroeconomic theory to its best use by leading to a more stable economy, which benefits everyone.

Con: Policymakers Should Not Try to Stabilize the Economy

Although monetary and fiscal policy can be used to stabilize the economy in theory, there are substantial obstacles to the use of such policies in practice.

One problem is that monetary and fiscal policy do not affect the economy immediately but instead work with a long lag. Monetary policy affects aggregate demand by changing interest rates, which in turn affect spending, especially residential and business investment. But many households and firms set their spending plans in advance. As a result, it takes time for changes in interest rates to alter the aggregate demand for goods and services. Many studies indicate that changes in monetary policy have little effect on aggregate demand until about six months after the change is made.

Fiscal policy works with a lag because of the long political process that governs changes in spending and taxes. To make any change in fiscal policy, a bill must go through Cabinet committees and then parliamentary committees, and then pass both the House of Commons and the Senate. It can take years to propose, pass, and implement a major change in fiscal policy.

Because of these long lags, policymakers who want to stabilize the economy need to look ahead to economic conditions that are likely to prevail when their actions will take effect. Unfortunately, economic forecasting is highly imprecise, in part because macroeconomics is such a primitive science and in part because the shocks that cause economic fluctuations are intrinsically unpredictable. Thus, when policymakers change monetary or fiscal policy, they must rely on educated guesses about future economic conditions.

All too often, policymakers trying to stabilize the economy do just the opposite. Economic conditions can easily change between the time when a policy action begins and when it takes effect. Because of this, policymakers can inadvertently exacerbate rather than mitigate the magnitude of economic fluctuations. Some economists have claimed that many of the major economic fluctuations in history, including the Great Depression of the 1930s, can be traced to destabilizing policy actions.

One of the first rules taught to physicians is "do no harm." The human body has natural restorative powers. Confronted with a sick patient and an uncertain diagnosis, often a doctor should do nothing but leave the patient's body to its own devices. Intervening in the absence of reliable knowledge merely risks making matters worse.

The same can be said about treating an ailing economy. It might be desirable if policymakers could eliminate all economic fluctuations, but that is not a realistic goal given the limits of macroeconomic knowledge and the inherent unpredictability of world events. Economic policymakers should refrain from intervening often with monetary and fiscal policy and be content if they do no harm.

QuickQuiz Explain why monetary and fiscal policy work with a lag. Why do these lags matter in the choice between active and passive policy?

SHOULD MONETARY POLICY BE MADE BY AN INDEPENDENT CENTRAL BANK?

As we first discussed in Chapter 11, the Bank of Canada determines the rate of monetary growth in Canada. On the basis of an evaluation of current economic conditions and forecasts of future conditions, the Bank of Canada chooses whether to raise, lower, or leave unchanged the supply of money in Canada. The rate of monetary growth is set so as to meet a monetary policy goal. Since 1988, the Bank of Canada has asserted that its goal would be to achieve and maintain a stable price level. In 1991 the Bank made this goal more specific by announcing its intention to conduct monetary policy in such a way as to hold inflation between 1 and 3 percent. In May 2001, the Bank announced its intention to extend this target band for inflation to the end of 2006. At that time the federal government and the Bank will determine whether this will remain the long-run target for monetary policy or whether a new target needs to be announced.

The relationship between the Bank of Canada and the federal government has evolved in such a way that the Bank has almost complete discretion over the conduct of monetary policy. The laws that created the Bank gave the institution vague recommendations about what goals it should pursue. However, these laws did not tell the Bank how to pursue these goals, nor did they indicate whether some of these goals might be more important than others. These choices have largely been left in the hands of the governor of the Bank. The Bank has used this independence to adopt a monetary policy rule: The rate of growth in the money supply will be sufficient to maintain a rate of inflation between 1 and 3 percent. This target rate of inflation was achieved in 1994 following a number of years of monetary contraction that caused considerable economic pain in the form of high unemployment.

Some economists are critical of the Bank of Canada's independence. Our second debate over macroeconomic policy, therefore, focuses on whether the Bank should be allowed to conduct monetary policy without being directly answerable to the electorate or to elected officials.

Pro: Monetary Policy Should Be Made by an Independent Central Bank

Allowing elected officials influence in conducting monetary policy has two problems. First, when given this power, politicians are sometimes tempted to use monetary policy to affect the outcome of elections. Suppose that the vote in an upcoming federal election is based on economic conditions at the time of the election. Politicians who are able to influence monetary policy might be tempted to pursue expansionary monetary policies just before the election in order to stimulate production and employment, knowing that the resulting inflation will not show up until after the election. In a small open economy with a flexible exchange rate, like Canada, monetary policy has very large effects on aggregate demand. As a result, the temptation to use monetary policy for political ends is even stronger. Thus, to the extent that politicians influence monetary policy, economic fluctuations may come to reflect the electoral calendar. Economists call such fluctuations the *political business cycle*.

The second, more subtle, problem with allowing elected officials a say in conducting monetary policy is that such influence might lead to more inflation than is desirable. Suppose that policymakers, knowing there is no long-run tradeoff between inflation and unemployment, announce that their goal is zero inflation. Economists believe that zero inflation is more likely to be achieved if the central bank is independent of political influence. Why? Economists believe that, once the public forms expectations of inflation, policymakers face a short-run tradeoff between inflation and unemployment. They are tempted to renege on their announcement of price stability in order to achieve lower unemployment.

This discrepancy between announcements (what policymakers say they are going to do) and actions (what they subsequently do) is called the *time inconsistency of policy*. When policymakers act in a time-inconsistent manner, people become skeptical about policy announcements. As a result, people always expect more inflation than policymakers claim they are trying to achieve. Higher expectations of inflation, in turn, shift the short-run Phillips curve upward. This not only causes the rate of inflation realized in the long run to be higher than it would otherwise be, but also causes a less favourable short-run tradeoff between inflation and unemployment. Since elected officials face a greater incentive to try to exploit the short-run tradeoff in order to curry favour with voters, the rate of inflation realized in the long run and the sacrifice ratio measuring the short-run costs of disinflation will always be higher than they would be if monetary policy were conducted by an independent central bank.

One way to avoid these difficulties is to conduct monetary policy independent of political influence. Because the governor of the Bank of Canada is not elected, the governor faces little incentive to try to exploit the short-run tradeoff between inflation and unemployment for political gain. In addition, because people know that the governor faces little incentive to exploit the short-run tradeoff, they are more likely to believe the Bank of Canada's announcements of low- or zero-inflation targets. In the long run, therefore, the rate of inflation will be lower. Empirical evidence seems to support this conjecture: When economists have compared average rates of inflation across countries, those countries with the most independent central banks tend to have the lowest rates of inflation.

Con: Monetary Policy Should Not Be Made by an Independent Central Bank

Although there are pitfalls in allowing elected policymakers a say in conducting monetary policy, there is also an important advantage: accountability. Giving central banks complete independence in conducting monetary policy is a problem because it does not limit incompetence and abuse of power. When the government sends police into a community to maintain civic order, it gives them strict guidelines about how to carry out their job. Because police have great power, allowing them to exercise that power in whatever way they want would be dangerous. When the government gives central bankers the sole authority to maintain economic order, it gives them no guidelines. Instead, it gives monetary policymakers undisciplined discretion and does not make them answerable for mistakes. In a small open economy with a flexible exchange rate, monetary policy has a large and lasting influence on aggregate demand. Since changes in aggregate demand translate into changes in employment and income, it is important that someone be accountable for monetary policy choices.

Moreover, the practical importance of time inconsistency is far from clear. Despite clear and forceful statements by the Bank of Canada, it is not obvious that enhancing the credibility of inflation targets has reduced the short-run cost of achieving lower inflation. The sacrifice ratio associated with the Bank of Canada's effort at disinflation in the early 1990s was not made obviously smaller by repeated announcements of a zero-inflation target. In fact, evidence suggests that the sacrifice ratio involved with this effort at disinflation was *larger* than that associated with earlier efforts. The supposedly enhanced credibility of monetary policy announcements that comes from central bank independence therefore seems to yield few dividends.

Finally, the idea that elected policymakers might use monetary policy to generate political business cycles seems at odds with the concept of rational expectations and the incentive people have to understand the implications of policy announcements. If people understand that reductions in unemployment before an election are temporary and will be followed by increases in unemployment following the election, it seems difficult to understand how elected policymakers can benefit from manipulating monetary policy.

What's more, monetary policy influences inflation and nominal interest rates. It is difficult to direct the benefits of changes in inflation and interest rates to any but very broad interest groups (for example, unexpectedly higher inflation benefits borrowers at the expense of savers). Thus, elected policymakers would not find monetary policy to be a very useful way of trying to influence voters. Fiscal policy seems much better suited for this purpose. Changes in government spending and tax laws can be more easily targeted to very specific interest groups with whom a policymaker might want to curry favour. Despite this, the fact that fiscal policy decisions are determined by elected policymakers has not been deemed a serious problem. On the contrary, political accountability with respect to fiscal policy decisions ("no taxation without representation") is a cornerstone of democracy. Why should this not also be true of monetary policy? Economists Lars Osberg and Pierre Fortin, editors of the book *Hard Money, Hard Times,* argue forcefully that

> it is inappropriate that major economic decisions, with implications for many aspects of Canadian life, are outside the influence of the democratic political process. As the legal mandate of the Bank of Canada recognizes, a complex market economy has a real need for macroeconomic stability. The Bank of Canada is rightly assigned the duty to "mitigate by its influence fluctuations in the general level of production, trade, prices and unemployment, so far as may be possible in the scope of monetary action, and generally to promote the economic and financial welfare of Canada." The citizens of a democracy also have a right to expect that their views will matter in major issues of public policy, such as the balance which is struck among these objectives. (page xv)

QuickQuiz Should the governor of the Bank of Canada be elected? Explain.

SHOULD THE CENTRAL BANK AIM FOR ZERO INFLATION?

One of the ten principles of economics discussed in Chapter 1, and developed more fully in Chapter 12, is that prices rise when the government prints too much money. Another of the ten principles of economics discussed in Chapter 1, and developed more fully in Chapter 17, is that society faces a short-run tradeoff between inflation and unemployment. Put together, these two principles raise a question for policymakers: How much inflation should the central bank be willing to tolerate? Our third debate is whether zero is the right target for the inflation rate.

Pro: The Central Bank Should Aim for Zero Inflation

Inflation confers no benefit on society, but it imposes several real costs. As we discussed in Chapter 12, economists have identified six costs of inflation:

1. Shoeleather costs associated with reduced money holdings
2. Menu costs associated with more frequent adjustment of prices
3. Increased variability of relative prices
4. Unintended changes in tax liabilities due to nonindexation of the tax code
5. Confusion and inconvenience resulting from a changing unit of account
6. Arbitrary redistributions of wealth associated with dollar-denominated debts

Some economists argue that these costs are small, at least for moderate rates of inflation, such as the 1.5 percent inflation experienced in Canada during the 1990s. But other economists claim these costs can be substantial, even for moderate inflation. Moreover, there is no doubt that the public dislikes inflation. When inflation heats up, opinion polls identify inflation as one of the nation's leading problems.

Of course, the benefits of zero inflation have to be weighed against the costs of achieving it. Reducing inflation usually requires a period of high unemployment and low output, as illustrated by the short-run Phillips curve. But this disinflationary recession is only temporary. Once people come to understand that policymakers are aiming for zero inflation, expectations of inflation will fall, and the short-run tradeoff will improve. Because expectations adjust, there is no tradeoff between inflation and unemployment in the long run.

Reducing inflation is, therefore, a policy with temporary costs and permanent benefits. That is, once the disinflationary recession is over, the benefits of zero inflation would persist into the future. If policymakers are farsighted, they should be willing to incur the temporary costs for the permanent benefits. This is precisely the calculation made by the Bank of Canada in the early 1980s and again in the early 1990s when it introduced monetary contractions designed to reduce the rate of inflation.

Moreover, the costs of reducing inflation need not be as large as some economists claim. If the Bank of Canada announces a credible commitment to zero inflation, it can directly influence expectations of inflation. Such a change in expectations can improve the short-run tradeoff between inflation and unemployment, allowing the economy to reach lower inflation at a reduced cost. The key to this strategy is credibility; People must believe that the Bank of Canada is actually going to carry through on its announced policy. Parliament could help in this regard by passing legislation that made price stability the Bank of Canada's primary goal. Such a law would make it less costly to achieve zero inflation without reducing any of the resulting benefits.

One advantage of a zero-inflation target is that zero provides a more natural focal point for policymakers than any other number. Suppose, for instance, that the Bank of Canada were to announce that it would keep inflation at 1.5 percent—the rate experienced during the 1990s. Would the Bank of Canada really stick to that 1.5 percent target? If events inadvertently pushed inflation up to 4 or 5 percent, why wouldn't they just raise the target? There is, after all, nothing special about the number 1.5. By contrast, zero is the only number for the inflation rate at which the Bank of Canada can claim that it achieved price stability and fully eliminated the costs of inflation.

Con: The Central Bank Should Not Aim for Zero Inflation

Although price stability may be desirable, the benefits of zero inflation compared to moderate inflation are small, whereas the costs of reaching zero inflation are large. Estimates of the sacrifice ratio suggest that reducing inflation by 1 percentage point requires giving up between 2 and 5 percent of one year's output. Using the midpoint of this range of estimates, to reduce inflation from, say, 4 percent to zero requires a loss of 14 percent of a year's output. At the 2002 level of gross domestic product, about $1200 billion, this cost translates into $168 billion of lost output, which is about $5300 per person. Although people might dislike inflation of 4 percent, it is not at all clear that they would (or should) be willing to pay this much to get rid of it.

The social costs of disinflation are even larger than this $5300 figure suggests, because the lost income is not spread equitably over the population. When the economy goes into recession, all incomes do not fall proportionately. Instead, the fall in aggregate income is concentrated on those workers who lose their jobs. The vulnerable workers are often those with the least skills and experience. Hence, much of the cost of reducing inflation is borne by those who can least afford to pay it.

Although economists can list several costs of inflation, there is no professional consensus that these costs are substantial. The shoeleather costs, menu costs, and others that economists have identified do not seem great, at least for moderate rates of inflation. It is true that the public dislikes inflation, but the public may be misled into believing the inflation fallacy—the view that inflation erodes living standards. Economists understand that living standards depend on productivity, not monetary policy. Because inflation in nominal incomes goes hand in hand with inflation in prices, reducing inflation would not cause real incomes to rise more rapidly.

Moreover, policymakers have recently taken steps to reduce many of the costs of inflation. In the fall of 2000, the federal government indexed income tax brackets to prevent inflation from pushing taxpayers into higher tax brackets. They can also reduce the arbitrary redistributions of wealth between creditors and debtors caused by unexpected inflation by issuing indexed government bonds, as in fact the Bank of Canada did in 1991. Such an act insulates holders of government debt from inflation. In addition, by setting an example, it might encourage private borrowers and lenders to write debt contracts indexed for inflation.

Reducing inflation might be desirable if it could be done at no cost, as some economists argue is possible. Yet this trick seems hard to carry out in practice. When economies reduce their rate of inflation, they almost always experience a period of high unemployment and low output. It is risky to believe that the central bank could achieve credibility so quickly as to make disinflation painless.

Indeed, a disinflationary recession can potentially leave permanent scars on the economy. Firms in all industries reduce their spending on new plants and equipment substantially during recessions, making investment the most volatile component of GDP. Even after the recession is over, the smaller stock of capital reduces productivity, incomes, and living standards below the levels they otherwise would have achieved. In addition, when workers become unemployed in recessions, they lose valuable job skills, permanently reducing their value as workers. Some economists have argued that the slow speed at which Canada's unemployment rate falls following recessions is the result of workers losing job skills while they are unemployed and thus finding re-employment difficult.

Why should policymakers put the economy through a costly, inequitable disinflationary recession to achieve zero inflation, which may have only modest benefits? Economist Alan Blinder, a former vice-chairman of the U.S. Federal Reserve, argued forcefully in his book *Hard Heads, Soft Hearts* that policymakers in countries like Canada and the United States—countries that typically experience moderate rates of inflation—should not make this choice:

> The costs that attend the low and moderate inflation rates experienced in the United States and in other industrial countries appear to be quite modest— more like a bad cold than a cancer on society. . . . As rational individuals, we do not volunteer for a lobotomy to cure a head cold. Yet, as a collectivity, we routinely prescribe the economic equivalent of lobotomy (high unemployment) as a cure for the inflationary cold.

Blinder concludes that it is better to learn to live with moderate inflation.

QuickQuiz Explain the costs and benefits of reducing inflation to zero. Which are temporary and which are permanent?

SHOULD FISCAL POLICYMAKERS REDUCE THE GOVERNMENT DEBT?

Perhaps the most persistent macroeconomic debate in recent years has been over government finances. Throughout most of the 1970s, 1980s, and 1990s, Canadian federal and provincial governments spent more than they collected in tax revenue and financed the resulting budget deficits by issuing government debt. As we discussed in Chapter 8, the result was an accumulation of a startling amount of government debt. In that chapter we saw how budget deficits affect saving, investment, and interest rates. Recently, however, most governments in Canada have taken measures to reduce and even eliminate their deficits. In February 1998, the federal government announced its first balanced budget since 1970. In November 2003, it predicted budget surpluses—an excess of tax revenue over government spending—were possible to at least 2009. Similarly, almost all provinces now regularly forecast budget surpluses and have announced plans on how they plan to use these projected surpluses to reduce taxes, increase spending, and repay debt.

Our fourth debate concerns what fiscal policymakers should do with projected surpluses: Should they use projected surpluses to reduce the debt they steadily accumulated over the past quarter-century, or should they eliminate the projected budget surpluses by cutting tax rates and increasing spending on social programs?

Pro: Policymakers Should Reduce the Government Debt

From the mid-1970s to the mid-1990s, governments in Canada spent substantially more than they received in tax revenue. At the federal level, the resulting budget deficits caused the federal debt to rise from $28 billion in 1975 to a peak of $612 billion in 1997. While some debt has been repaid since 1997, by 2003 it remained very high at $564 billion. If we divide that debt by the size of the population, we learn that each person's share of this debt is just under $18 000. If we include the

© PHOTODISC

"My share of the government debt is $26 000."

debts of provincial and territorial governments, the level of government debt in 2003 increases to about $806 billion, or about $26 000 per person.

The most direct effect of the government debt is to place a burden on future generations of taxpayers. When these debts and accumulated interest come due, future taxpayers will face a difficult choice. They can pay higher taxes, enjoy less government spending, or both, in order to make resources available to pay off the debt and accumulated interest. Or they can delay the day of reckoning and put the government into even deeper debt by borrowing once again to pay off the old debt and interest. In essence, when the government runs a budget deficit and issues government debt, it allows current taxpayers to pass the bill for some of their government spending on to future taxpayers. Inheriting such a large debt cannot help but lower the living standard of future generations.

In addition to this direct effect, budget deficits also have various macroeconomic effects. Because budget deficits represent *negative* public saving, they lower national saving (the sum of private and public saving). Reduced national saving causes the real exchange rate to rise and net exports to fall. Large and persistent budget deficits, and the accumulation of debt, also increase the default risk that lenders perceive when they consider buying Canadian debt. This causes the real interest rate in Canada to remain above the real interest rate in the rest of the world. Because higher real interest rates cause investment to fall, the capital stock grows smaller over time. A lower capital stock reduces labour productivity, real wages, and the economy's production of goods and services. Thus, when the government increases its debt, future generations are born into an economy with lower incomes as well as higher taxes.

There are, nevertheless, situations in which running a budget deficit is justifiable. Throughout history, the most common cause of increased government debt is war. When a military conflict raises government spending temporarily, it is reasonable to finance this extra spending by borrowing. Otherwise, taxes during wartime would have to rise precipitously. Such high tax rates would greatly distort the incentives faced by those who are taxed, leading to large deadweight losses. In addition, such high tax rates would be unfair to current generations of taxpayers, who already have to make the sacrifice of fighting the war.

Similarly, it is reasonable to allow a budget deficit during a temporary downturn in economic activity. When the economy goes into a recession, incomes and consumption expenditures fall and this causes income tax and sales tax revenues to fall. A recession also results in more unemployment and hence larger expenditures on Employment Insurance. If the government tried to balance its budget during a recession, it would need to offset the budgetary implications of these automatic tax and spending changes by increasing tax rates and chopping spending programs. Such a policy would tend to depress aggregate demand at precisely the time it needed to be stimulated and, therefore, would tend to increase the magnitude of economic fluctuations.

The budget deficits incurred by the federal and provincial governments since the mid-1970s are difficult to justify. The major culprit seems to be the failure of fiscal policymakers to take advantage of periods of strong economic growth to pay down the debt incurred during recessions. For example, the federal government's debt increased quite substantially as a result of the 1980–81 recession. This recession, the worst experienced in Canada since the Great Depression, caused a large fall in tax revenue and necessitated a large increase in spending on programs such as Employment Insurance.

Not surprisingly, the federal government's deficit was large during this period and its debt grew. From 1983 to 1988, however, real output grew by an average of 4.5 percent per year. During this period, the rapid growth in incomes caused tax revenue to grow quickly and expenditures on programs such as Employment Insurance to fall. This was the federal government's opportunity to run budget surpluses and pay down the debt incurred as a result of the recession. Instead, the federal government continued to run large deficits and to add to its debt. Indeed, in 1985, despite real output growth of 5.3 percent, the federal government announced a deficit in excess of $38 billion (equivalent to $56 billion in 2003 dollars).

It is hard to see any rationale for this policy. Although governments need not commit themselves to a balanced budget as an inflexible rule, the budget should be balanced over the course of a business cycle. This requires budget surpluses during good times to offset the budget deficits that naturally arise during bad times. If the federal government had been operating with such a plan in place since 1975, today's university and college graduates would be entering an economy that promised them greater economic prosperity.

It is time to reverse the effects of this policy mistake. A combination of fiscal prudence and good luck has left the federal government and most of the provinces with budget surpluses now and into the near future. We should use these surpluses to repay some of the debt that our governments have accumulated.

Compared to the alternative of ongoing budget deficits, a balanced budget means greater national saving, investment, and economic growth. It means that future college graduates will enter a more prosperous economy.

Con: Policymakers Should Not Reduce the Government Debt

The problem of government debt is often exaggerated. Although the government debt does represent a tax burden on younger generations, it is not large compared to the average person's lifetime income. The debt of the Canadian federal government is about $26 000 per person. A person who works 40 years for $25 000 a year will earn $1 million over his lifetime. His share of the government debt represents less than 3 percent of his lifetime resources.

Moreover, it is misleading to view the effects of budget deficits in isolation. The budget deficit is just one piece of a large picture of how the government chooses to raise and spend money. In making these decisions over fiscal policy, policymakers affect different generations of taxpayers in many ways. The government's budget deficit or surplus should be considered together with these other policies.

For example, suppose governments use their budget surpluses to pay off government debt instead of using it to pay for increased spending on education. Does this policy make young generations better off? The government debt will be smaller when they enter the labour force, which means a smaller tax burden. Yet if they are less well educated than they could be, their productivity and incomes will be lower. Many estimates of the return to schooling (the increase in a worker's wage that results from an additional year in school) find that it is quite large. Reducing the budget deficit rather than funding more education spending could, all things considered, make future generations worse off.

Single-minded concern about the budget deficit is also dangerous because it draws attention away from various other policies that redistribute income across generations. For example, the federal government recently increased the payroll tax used to finance Canada Pension Plan (CPP) payments to elderly people. This policy will redistribute income away from younger generations (who are paying the payroll tax) toward older generations (who are receiving the CPP payments), even though it does not affect the federal debt. Thus, government debt is only a small piece of the larger issue of how government policy affects the welfare of different generations.

To some extent, the adverse effects of government debt can be reversed by forward-looking parents. Suppose parents are enjoying the benefits of low taxes and high government spending on social programs but are worried about the impact of the resulting government debt on their children. Parents can offset the impact by using the income they are saving as a result of low taxes to leave their children a larger bequest. The bequest would enhance the children's ability to bear the burden of future taxes. Some economists claim that people do in fact behave this way. If this were true, higher private saving by parents would offset the public dissaving of budget deficits, and deficits would not affect the economy. Most economists doubt that parents are so farsighted, but some people probably do act this way, and anyone could. Deficits give people the opportunity to consume at the expense of their children, but deficits do not require them to do so. If the government debt were actually a great problem facing future generations, some parents would help to solve it.

Critics of budget deficits sometimes assert that the government debt cannot continue to rise forever, but in fact it can. Just as a bank evaluating a loan application would compare a person's debts to his income, we should judge the burden of the government debt relative to the size of the nation's income. Population growth and technological progress cause the total income of the Canadian economy to grow over time. As a result, the nation's ability to pay the interest on the government debt grows over time as well. As long as the government debt grows more slowly than the nation's income, there is nothing to prevent the government debt from growing forever.

Some numbers can put this into perspective. The real output of the Canadian economy grows on average about 3 percent per year. If the inflation rate is 2 percent per year, then nominal income grows at a rate of 5 percent per year. The government debt, therefore, can rise by 5 percent per year without increasing the ratio of debt to income. In 2003 the federal government debt was $564 billion; 5 percent of this figure is $28.5 billion. As long as the federal budget deficit is smaller than $28.5 billion, the policy is sustainable. There will never be any day of reckoning that forces the budget deficits to end or the economy to collapse.

If moderate budget deficits are sustainable, there is no need for the government to maintain the budget surpluses it is currently realizing. Let's put this excess of revenue over spending to better use. The government could use these funds to pay for valuable government programs, such as increased funding for education, or it could use them to finance a tax cut. In the late 1990s taxes reached a historic high as a percentage of GDP, so there is every reason to suppose that the deadweight losses of taxation reached a historic high as well. If all of these taxes aren't needed for current spending, the government should return the money to the people who earned it.

QuickQuiz Explain how reducing the government debt makes future generations better off. What fiscal policy might improve the lives of future generations more than reducing the government debt?

SHOULD THE TAX LAWS BE REFORMED TO ENCOURAGE SAVING?

A nation's standard of living depends on its ability to produce goods and services. This was one of the ten principles of economics in Chapter 1. As we saw in Chapter 1, a nation's productive capability, in turn, is determined largely by how much it saves and invests for the future. Our fifth debate is whether policymakers should reform the tax laws to encourage greater saving and investment.

Pro: The Tax Laws Should Be Reformed to Encourage Saving

A nation's saving rate is a key determinant of its long-run economic prosperity. When the saving rate is higher, more resources are available for investment in new plant and equipment. A larger stock of plant and equipment, in turn, raises labour productivity, wages, and incomes. It is, therefore, no surprise that international data show a strong correlation between national saving rates and measures of economic well-being.

Another of the ten principles of economics presented in Chapter 1 is that people respond to incentives. This lesson should apply to people's decisions about how much to save. If a nation's laws make saving attractive, people will save a higher fraction of their incomes, and this higher saving will lead to a more prosperous future.

Unfortunately, the Canadian tax system discourages saving by taxing the return to saving quite heavily. For example, consider a 25-year-old worker who saves $1000 of her income to have a more comfortable retirement at the age of 70. If she buys a bond that pays an interest rate of 10 percent, the $1000 will accumulate at the end of 45 years to $72 900 in the absence of taxes on interest. But suppose she faces a marginal tax rate on interest income of 40 percent, which is typical of many workers once federal and provincial income taxes are added together. In this case, her after-tax interest rate is only 6 percent, and the $1000 will accumulate at the end of 45 years to only $13 800. That is, accumulated over this long span of time, the tax rate on interest income reduces the benefit of saving $1000 from $72 900 to $13 800—or by about 80 percent.

The tax code further discourages saving by taxing some forms of capital income twice. Suppose a person uses some of his saving to buy shares in a corporation. When the corporation earns a profit from its capital investments, it first pays tax on this profit in the form of the corporate income tax. If the corporation pays out the rest of the profit to the shareholder in the form of dividends, the shareholder pays tax on this income a second time in the form of the individual income tax. This double taxation substantially reduces the return to the shareholder, thereby reducing the incentive to save.

In addition to the tax code, many other policies and institutions in our society reduce the incentive for households to save. Some government benefits, such as Old Age Security pension payments, are means-tested; that is, the benefits are reduced for those who in the past have been prudent enough to save some of their income. Colleges and universities grant financial aid as a function of the wealth of the students and their parents. Such a policy is like a tax on wealth and, as such, discourages students and parents from saving.

There are various ways in which the tax code could provide an incentive to save, or at least reduce the disincentive that households now face. Already the tax laws give preferential treatment to some types of retirement saving. When a taxpayer puts income into a registered retirement savings plan (RRSP), for instance, that income and the interest it earns are not taxed until the funds are withdrawn at retirement. There are, however, limits on the amount that can be put into an RRSP each year. After many years in which the limit was unchanged, in 2003 the limit was increased by $1000 to $14 500 and then by another $1000 in 2004. The RRSP contribution limit is scheduled to increase to $16 500 in 2005 and finally to $18 000 in 2006. While it is encouraging that the contribution limit is being increased, Canadian savers remain at a substantial disadvantage relative to savers in other countries. In the United States, for example, an individual taxpayer is currently able to contribute four times the Canadian maximum to a similar type of savings plan.

An important step the federal government took to encourage greater saving was to introduce the Goods and Services Tax (GST) in 1991. The great majority of federal tax revenue is collected through the personal income tax. Under an income tax, a dollar earned is taxed the same whether it is spent or saved. The GST is a consumption tax, meaning that a household pays tax only on the basis of what it spends. Income that is saved is exempt from consumption taxation until the saving is later withdrawn and spent on consumption goods. For this reason, a consumption tax increases the incentive to save. Because of this, economists were generally in favour of adding the GST to the federal government's tax mix, and many would favour an increased emphasis on consumption taxation, as opposed to income taxation. A switch from income to consumption taxation would increase the incentive to save.

Con: The Tax Laws Should Not Be Reformed to Encourage Saving

Increasing saving may be desirable, but it is not the only goal of tax policy. Policymakers also must be sure to distribute the tax burden fairly. The problem with proposals to increase the incentive to save is that they increase the tax burden on those who can least afford it.

It is an undeniable fact that high-income households save a greater fraction of their income than low-income households. As a result, any tax change that favours people who save will also tend to favour people with high income. Policies such as RRSPs may seem appealing, but they lead to a less egalitarian society. By reducing the tax burden on the wealthy who can take advantage of these plans, they force the government to raise the tax burden on the poor.

Moreover, tax policies designed to encourage saving may not be effective at achieving that goal. Many studies have found that saving is relatively inelastic—

that is, the amount of saving is not very sensitive to the rate of return on saving. If this is indeed the case, then tax provisions that raise the effective return by reducing the taxation of capital income will further enrich the wealthy without inducing them to save more than they otherwise would.

Economic theory does not give a clear prediction about whether a higher rate of return would increase saving. The outcome depends on the relative size of two conflicting effects, called the *substitution effect* and the *income effect*. On the one hand, a higher rate of return raises the benefit of saving: Each dollar saved today produces more consumption in the future. This substitution effect tends to raise saving. On the other hand, a higher rate of return lowers the need for saving: A household has to save less to achieve any target level of consumption in the future. This income effect tends to reduce saving. If the substitution and income effects approximately cancel each other, as some studies suggest, then saving will not change when lower taxation of capital income raises the rate of return.

There are other ways to raise national saving than by giving tax breaks to the rich. National saving is the sum of private and public saving. Instead of trying to alter the tax code to encourage greater private saving, policymakers can simply raise public saving by increasing the budget surplus, perhaps by raising taxes on the wealthy or by restraining government spending. This offers a direct way of raising national saving and increasing prosperity for future generations.

Indeed, once public saving is taken into account, tax provisions to encourage saving might backfire. Tax changes that reduce the taxation of capital income reduce government revenue and, thereby, lead to a budget deficit. To increase national saving, such a change in the tax code must stimulate private saving by more than the decline in public saving. If this is not the case, so-called saving incentives can potentially make matters worse.

QuickQuiz   Give three examples of how our society discourages saving. What are the drawbacks of eliminating these disincentives?

CONCLUSION

This chapter has considered five debates over macroeconomic policy. For each, it began with a controversial proposition and then offered the arguments pro and con. If you find it hard to choose a side in these debates, you may find some comfort in the fact that you are not alone. The study of economics does not always make it easy to choose among alternative policies. Indeed, by clarifying the inevitable tradeoffs that policymakers face, it can make the choice more difficult.

Difficult choices, however, have no right to seem easy. When you hear politicians or commentators proposing something that sounds too good to be true, it probably is. If they sound like they are offering you a free lunch, you should look for the hidden price tag. Few if any policies come with benefits but no costs. By helping you see through the fog of rhetoric so common in political discourse, the study of economics should make you a better participant in our national debates.

SUMMARY

- Advocates of active monetary and fiscal policy view the economy as inherently unstable and believe that policy can manage aggregate demand to offset the inherent instability. Critics of active monetary and fiscal policy emphasize that policy affects the economy with a lag and that our ability to forecast future economic conditions is poor. As a result, attempts to stabilize the economy can end up being destabilizing.

- Advocates of an independent central bank argue that such independence guards against politicians using monetary policy in an attempt to influence voters. They also assert that a lower rate of inflation and a more favourable short-run tradeoff between inflation and unemployment is possible when the central bank is independent of political influence. Critics of central bank independence argue that because monetary policy has large and lasting influences on aggregate demand, and hence on output and employment, citizens should have a say on the conduct of monetary policy, just as they do on the conduct of fiscal policy.

- Advocates of a zero-inflation target emphasize that inflation has many costs and few if any benefits. Moreover, the cost of eliminating inflation—depressed output and employment—is only temporary. Even this cost can be reduced if the central bank announces a credible plan to reduce inflation, thereby directly lowering expectations of inflation. Critics of a zero-inflation target claim that moderate inflation imposes only small costs on society, whereas the recession necessary to reduce inflation is quite costly.

- Advocates of reducing government debt argue that debt imposes a burden on future generations by raising their taxes and lowering their incomes. Critics of reducing the government debt argue that the debt is only one small piece of fiscal policy. Single-minded concern about the debt can obscure the many ways in which the government's tax and spending decisions affect different generations.

- Advocates of tax incentives for saving point out that our society discourages saving in many ways, such as by heavily taxing the income from capital and by reducing benefits for those who have accumulated wealth. They endorse reforming the tax laws to encourage saving, perhaps by switching from an income tax to a consumption tax. Critics of tax incentives for saving argue that many proposed changes to stimulate saving would primarily benefit the wealthy, who do not need a tax break. They also argue that such changes might have only a small effect on private saving. Raising public saving by increasing the government's budget surplus would provide a more direct and equitable way to increase national saving.

QUESTIONS FOR REVIEW

1. What causes the lags in the effect of monetary and fiscal policy on aggregate demand? What are the implications of these lags for the debate over active versus passive policy?

2. What might motivate a central banker to cause a political business cycle? What does the possibility of a political business cycle imply for the debate over whether monetary policy should be conducted by an independent central bank?

3. Explain how credibility might affect the cost of reducing inflation.

4. Why are some economists against a target of zero inflation?

5. Explain two ways in which a government budget deficit hurts a future worker.

6. What are two situations in which most economists view a budget deficit as justifiable?

7. Give an example of how the government might hurt young generations, even while reducing the government debt they inherit.

8. Some economists say that the government can continue running a budget deficit forever. How is that possible?

9. Some income from capital is taxed twice. Explain.

10. Give an example, other than tax policy, of how our society discourages saving.

11. What adverse effect might be caused by tax incentives to raise saving?

PROBLEMS AND APPLICATIONS

1. The chapter suggests that the economy, like the human body, has "natural restorative powers."
   a. Illustrate the short-run effect of a fall in aggregate demand using an aggregate-demand/aggregate-supply diagram. What happens to total output, income, and employment?
   b. If the government does not use stabilization policy, what happens to the economy over time? Illustrate on your diagram. Does this adjustment generally occur in a matter of months or a matter of years?
   c. Do you think the "natural restorative powers" of the economy mean that policymakers should be passive in response to the business cycle?

2. In Chapter 16 we learned that the multiplier effect associated with a change in government purchases could be expressed as $1/(1 - MPC + MPI)$, where MPC is the marginal propensity to consume and MPI is the marginal propensity to import. If $MPC = 0.60$ and $MPI = 0.20$, then we can use this formula to calculate that the multiplier effect associated with a change in government purchases is equal to 5. A problem with which fiscal policymakers must deal is the fact they are not absolutely certain what the true magnitudes of the MPC and MPI are. Suppose these values were actually 0.65 and 0.25, respectively. How would this affect the size of the multiplier effect? How does uncertainty about the size of the values of MPC and MPI affect your position on the debate over whether policymakers should try to stabilize the economy?

3. Suppose that people suddenly wanted to hold more money balances. For simplicity, assume Canada is a closed economy.
   a. What would be the effect of this change on the economy if the Bank of Canada followed a rule of increasing the money supply by 3 percent per year? Illustrate your answer with a money-market diagram and an aggregate-demand/aggregate-supply diagram.
   b. What would be the effect of this change on the economy if the Bank of Canada followed a rule of increasing the money supply by 3 percent per year *plus* 1 percentage point for every percentage point that unemployment rises above its normal level? Illustrate your answer.
   c. Which of the forgoing rules better stabilizes the economy? Would it help to allow the Bank of Canada to respond to predicted unemployment instead of current unemployment? Explain.

4. In earlier chapters, we learned about automatic stabilizers in the tax system and government spending programs.
   a. Provide an example of an automatic stabilizer that works via the tax system in Canada and another of an automatic stabilizer that works via a government spending program.
   b. How does the existence of automatic stabilizers affect your position on the debate over whether policymakers should try to stabilize the economy?

5. The problem of time inconsistency applies to fiscal policy as well as to monetary policy. Suppose the government announced a

reduction in taxes on income from capital investments, like new factories.

a. If investors believed that capital taxes would remain low, how would the government's action affect the level of investment?

b. After investors have responded to the announced tax reduction, does the government have an incentive to renege on its policy? Explain.

c. Given your answer to part (b), would investors believe the government's announcement? What can the government do to increase the credibility of announced policy changes?

d. Explain why this situation is similar to the time-inconsistency problem faced by monetary policymakers.

6. Chapter 2 explains the difference between positive analysis and normative analysis. In the debate about whether the central bank should aim for zero inflation, which areas of disagreement involve positive statements and which involve normative judgments?

7. Why are the benefits of reducing inflation permanent and the costs temporary? Why are the costs of increasing inflation permanent and the benefits temporary? Use Phillips-curve diagrams in your answer.

8. Suppose the federal government cuts taxes and increases spending, raising the budget deficit to 12 percent of GDP. If nominal GDP is rising 7 percent per year, are such budget deficits sustainable forever? Explain. If budget deficits of this size are maintained for 20 years, what is likely to happen to your taxes and your children's taxes in the future? Can you do something today to offset this future effect?

9. Explain how each of the following policies redistributes income across generations. Is the redistribution from young to old, or from old to young?

a. an increase in the budget deficit
b. more generous subsidies for education loans
c. greater investments in highways and bridges
d. indexation of Old Age Security benefits to inflation

10. Surveys suggest that most people are opposed to budget deficits, but these same people

elected representatives who in the 1970s and 1980s passed budgets with significant deficits. Why might the opposition to budget deficits be stronger in principle than in practice?

11. In 1991, the federal government simultaneously reduced the income tax rate and introduced the Goods and Services Tax (GST). Explain why economists applauded this switch from taxing incomes to taxing spending.

12. The following table presents data taken from Finance Canada's *Economic and Fiscal Update, November 2003*. It shows borrowing in the market for loanable funds by Canadian governments and Canadian businesses in fiscal years 1992–93 and 2001–02.

	1992–93	2001–02	Change
		(billions of dollars)	
Government	+$45.1	–$10.3	–$55.4
Business	+$22.0	+$59.1	+$37.1

In the earlier period, Canadian governments were running large deficits. As a result, they borrowed $45.1 billion in capital markets. In the later period, Canadian governments were realizing budget surpluses and as a result provided $10.3 billion in funds to capital markets. The table shows how the change in government borrowing has enabled the private sector greater access to loanable funds. How do you think this change in government policy has affected interest rates? How do you think this change has affected the ability of Canadian businesses to expand and create new employment?

13. The following table presents data taken from Finance Canada's *Economic and Fiscal Update, November 2003*. It shows federal government spending, after removing spending on interest payments on the debt, in fiscal years 1992–93 and 2001–02. The spending measured here is on health care, defence, pensions, Employment Insurance, and other goods and services.

	1992–93	2001–02	Change
		(percentage of GDP)	
Federal government program spending	16.8%	11.3%	–5.5%

In the earlier period, the federal government spent an amount equal to 16.8 percent of GDP on such programs. In the later period, federal spending on these programs amounted to only 11.3 percent of GDP. How do you think this change in government spending policy has affected Canadians receiving health care, pensions, and Employment Insurance?

INTERNET RESOURCES

- The following Canadian "think tanks" maintain websites that provide access to research on issues of economic and social policy:
    Institute for Research on Public Policy (Montreal): http://www.irpp.org
    C.D. Howe Institute (Toronto): http://www.cdhowe.org
    The Fraser Institute (Vancouver): http://www.fraserinstitute.ca
    Canadian Centre for Policy Alternatives (Ottawa):
        http://www.policyalternatives.ca

- An interesting website that provides access to current debates on economic and social policy in Canada and in other countries is the Policy Library at http://www.policylibrary.com/canada. From this site you can follow links that will provide you with access to current debates on economic issues in Canada, Australia and New Zealand, the United Kingdom, the United States, and Germany.

- The International Monetary Fund (IMF) publishes its *Finance and Development* magazine online at http://www.imf.org; just click on "Publications" at the top of the screen for a link to this and other IMF publications. *Finance and Development* presents information on interesting and current debates on a variety of issues of concern to those with an interest in international economic and social issues.

For more study tools, please visit http://www.mankiw3e.nelson.com.

GLOSSARY

absolute advantage   the comparison among producers of a good according to their productivity

aggregate-demand curve   a curve that shows the quantity of goods and services that households, firms, and the government want to buy at each price level

aggregate risk   risk that affects all economic actors at once

aggregate-supply curve   a curve that shows the quantity of goods and services that firms choose to produce and sell at each price level

appreciation   an increase in the value of a currency as measured by the amount of foreign currency it can buy

automatic stabilizers   changes in fiscal policy that stimulate aggregate demand when the economy goes into a recession, without policymakers having to take any deliberate action

balanced trade   a situation in which exports equal imports

Bank of Canada   the central bank of Canada

bank rate   the interest rate charged by the Bank of Canada on loans to the commercial banks

bond   a certificate of indebtedness

budget deficit   a shortfall of tax revenue from government spending

budget surplus   an excess of tax revenue over government spending

business cycle   fluctuations in economic activity, such as employment and production

capital flight   a large and sudden reduction in the demand for assets located in a country

catch-up effect   the property whereby countries that start off poor tend to grow more rapidly than countries that start off rich

central bank   an institution designed to regulate the quantity of money in the economy

circular-flow diagram   a visual model of the economy that shows how dollars flow through markets among households and firms

classical dichotomy   the theoretical separation of nominal and real variables

closed economy   an economy that does not interact with other economies in the world

collective bargaining   the process by which unions and firms agree on the terms of employment

commodity money   money that takes the form of a commodity with intrinsic value

comparative advantage   the comparison among producers of a good according to their opportunity cost

competitive market   a market in which there are many buyers and many sellers so that each has a negligible impact on the market price

complements   two goods for which an increase in the price of one leads to a decrease in the demand for the other

compounding   the accumulation of a sum of money in, say, a bank account, where the interest earned remains in the account to earn additional interest in the future

consumer price index (CPI)   a measure of the overall cost of the goods and services bought by a typical consumer

consumption   spending by households on goods and services, with the exception of purchases of new housing

core inflation   the measure of the underlying trend of inflation

cost   the value of everything a seller must give up to produce a good

crowding out   a decrease in investment that results from government borrowing

crowding-out effect on investment   the offset in aggregate demand that results when expansionary fiscal policy raises the interest rate and thereby reduces investment spending

crowding-out effect on net exports   the offset in aggregate demand that results when expansionary fiscal policy in a small open economy with a flexible exchange rate raises the real exchange rate and thereby reduces net exports

currency   the paper bills and coins in the hands of the public

cyclical unemployment   the deviation of unemployment from its natural rate

deadweight loss   the fall in total surplus that results from a market distortion, such as a tax

demand curve   a graph of the relationship between the price of a good and the quantity demanded

demand deposits   balances in bank accounts that depositors can access on demand by writing a cheque or using a debit card

demand schedule   a table that shows the relationship between the price of a good and the quantity demanded

depreciation   a decrease in the value of a currency as measured by the amount of foreign currency it can buy

depression   a severe recession

diminishing returns   the property whereby the benefit from an extra unit of an input declines as the quantity of the input increases

discouraged searchers   individuals who would like to work but have given up looking for a job

diversification   the reduction of risk achieved by replacing a single risk with a large number of smaller unrelated risks

economics   the study of how society manages its scarce resources

efficiency   the property of society getting the most it can from its scarce resources

efficiency wages   above-equilibrium wages paid by firms in order to increase worker productivity

efficient markets hypothesis   the theory that asset prices reflect all publicly available information about the value of an asset

Employment Insurance   a government program that partially protects workers' incomes when they become unemployed

equilibrium   a situation in which the price has reached the level where quantity supplied equals quantity demanded

equilibrium price   the price that balances quantity supplied and quantity demanded

equilibrium quantity   the quantity supplied and the quantity demanded at the equilibrium price

equity   the property of distributing economic prosperity fairly among the members of society

exports   goods and services that are produced domestically and sold abroad

externality   the impact of one person's actions on the well-being of a bystander

fiat money money without intrinsic value that is used as money because of government decree

finance the field that studies how people make decisions regarding the allocation of resources over time and the handling of risk

financial intermediaries financial institutions through which savers can indirectly provide funds to borrowers

financial markets financial institutions through which savers can directly provide funds to borrowers

financial system the group of institutions in the economy that help to match one person's saving with another person's investment

Fisher effect the one-for-one adjustment of the nominal interest rate to the inflation rate

foreign exchange market operations the purchase or sale of foreign money by the Bank of Canada

fractional-reserve banking a banking system in which banks hold only a fraction of deposits as reserves

frictional unemployment unemployment that results because it takes time for workers to search for the jobs that best suit their tastes and skills

fundamental analysis the study of a company's accounting statements and future prospects to determine its value

future value the amount of money in the future that an amount of money today will yield, given prevailing interest rates

GDP deflator a measure of the price level calculated as the ratio of nominal GDP to real GDP times 100

government purchases spending on goods and services by local, provincial, and federal governments

gross domestic product (GDP) the market value of all final goods and services produced within a country in a given period of time

human capital the knowledge and skills that workers acquire through education, training, and experience

idiosyncratic risk risk that affects only a single economic actor

import quota a limit on the quantity of a good that is produced abroad and sold domestically

imports goods and services that are produced abroad and sold domestically

indexation the automatic correction of a dollar amount for the effects of inflation by law or contract

inferior good a good for which, other things equal, an increase in income leads to a decrease in demand

inflation an increase in the overall level of prices in the economy

inflation rate the percentage change in the price index from the preceding period

inflation tax the revenue the government raises by creating money

informationally efficient reflecting all available information in a rational way

interest rate parity a theory of interest rate determination whereby the real interest rate on comparable financial assets should be the same in all economies with full access to world financial markets

investment spending on capital equipment, inventories, and structures, including household purchases of new housing

job search the process by which workers find appropriate jobs given their tastes and skills

labour force the total number of workers, including both the employed and the unemployed

labour-force participation rate the percentage of the adult population that is in the labour force

law of demand the claim that, other things equal, the quantity demanded of a good falls when the price of the good rises

law of supply the claim that, other things equal, the quantity supplied of a good rises when the price of the good rises

law of supply and demand the claim that the price of any good adjusts to bring the quantity supplied and the quantity demanded for that good into balance

liquidity the ease with which an asset can be converted into the economy's medium of exchange

macroeconomics the study of economy-wide phenomena, including inflation, unemployment, and economic growth

marginal changes small incremental adjustments to a plan of action

market a group of buyers and sellers of a particular good or service

market economy an economy that allocates resources through the decentralized decisions of many firms and households as they interact in markets for goods and services

market failure a situation in which a market left on its own fails to allocate resources efficiently

market for loanable funds the market in which those who want to save supply funds and those who want to borrow to invest demand funds

market power the ability of a single economic actor (or small group of actors) to have a substantial influence on market prices

medium of exchange an item that buyers give to sellers when they want to purchase goods or services

menu costs the costs of changing prices

microeconomics the study of how households and firms make decisions and how they interact in markets

model of aggregate demand and aggregate supply the model that most economists use to explain short-run fluctuations in economic activity around its long-run trend

monetary neutrality the proposition that changes in the money supply do not affect real variables

monetary policy the setting of the money supply by policymakers in the central bank

money the set of assets in an economy that people regularly use to buy goods and services from other people

money multiplier the amount of money the banking system generates with each dollar of reserves

money supply the quantity of money available in the economy

multiplier effect the additional shifts in aggregate demand that result when expansionary fiscal policy increases income and thereby increases consumer spending

mutual fund an institution that sells shares to the public and uses the proceeds to buy a portfolio of stocks and bonds

national saving (saving) the total income in the economy that remains after paying for consumption and government purchases

natural-rate hypothesis the claim that unemployment eventually returns to its normal, or natural, rate, regardless of the rate of inflation

natural rate of unemployment the rate of unemployment to which the economy tends to return in the long run

natural resources the inputs into the production of goods and services that are provided by nature, such as land, rivers, and mineral deposits

net capital outflow the purchase of foreign assets by domestic residents minus the purchase of domestic assets by foreigners

net exports the value of a nation's exports minus the value of its imports; also called the trade balance

nominal exchange rate the rate at which a person can trade the currency of one country for the currency of another

nominal GDP the production of goods and services valued at current prices

nominal interest rate the interest rate as usually reported without a correction for the effects of inflation

nominal variables variables measured in monetary units

normal good a good for which, other things equal, an increase in income leads to an increase in demand

normative statements claims that attempt to prescribe how the world should be

Okun's law the number of percentage points the unemployment rate increases when GDP falls by 1 percentage point

open economy an economy that interacts freely with other economies around the world

open-market operations the purchase or sale of Canadian government bonds by the Bank of Canada

opportunity cost whatever must be given up to obtain some item

overnight rate the interest rate on very short-term loans between commercial banks

perfect capital mobility full access to world financial markets

Phillips curve a curve that shows the short-run tradeoff between inflation and unemployment

physical capital the stock of equipment and structures that are used to produce goods and services

positive statements claims that attempt to describe the world as it is

present value the amount of money today that would be needed to produce, using prevailing interest rates, a given future amount of money

private saving the income that households have left after paying for taxes and consumption

production possibilities frontier a graph that shows the combinations of output that the economy can possibly produce given the available factors of production and the available production technology

productivity the amount of goods and services produced from each hour of a worker's time

public saving the tax revenue that the government has left after paying for its spending

purchasing-power parity a theory of exchange rates whereby a unit of any given currency should be able to buy the same quantity of goods in all countries

quantity demanded the amount of a good that buyers are willing and able to purchase

quantity equation the equation $M \times V = P \times Y$, which relates the quantity of money, the velocity of money, and the dollar value of the economy's output of goods and services

quantity supplied the amount of a good that sellers are willing and able to sell

quantity theory of money a theory asserting that the quantity of money available determines the price level and that the growth rate in the quantity of money available determines the inflation rate

random walk the path of a variable whose changes are impossible to predict

rational expectations the theory according to which people optimally use all the information they have, including information about government policies, when forecasting the future

real exchange rate the rate at which a person can trade the goods and services of one country for the goods and services of another

real GDP the production of goods and services valued at constant prices

real interest rate the interest rate corrected for the effects of inflation

real variables variables measured in physical units

recession a period of declining real incomes and rising unemployment

reserve ratio the fraction of deposits that banks hold as reserves

reserve requirements regulations on the minimum amount of reserves that banks must hold against deposits

reserves deposits that banks have received but have not loaned out

risk averse exhibiting a dislike of uncertainty

sacrifice ratio the number of percentage points of one year's output lost in the process of reducing inflation by 1 percentage point

scarcity the limited nature of society's resources

shoeleather costs the resources wasted when inflation encourages people to reduce their money holdings

shortage a situation in which quantity demanded is greater than quantity supplied

small open economy an economy that trades goods and services with other economies and, by itself, has a negligible effect on world prices and interest rates

stagflation a period of falling output and rising prices

sterilization the process of offsetting foreign exchange market operations with open-market operations, so that the effect on the money supply is cancelled out

stock a claim to partial ownership in a firm

store of value an item that people can use to transfer purchasing power from the present to the future

strike the organized withdrawal of labour from a firm by a union

structural unemployment unemployment that results because the number of jobs available in some labour markets is insufficient to provide a job for everyone who wants one

substitutes two goods for which an increase in the price of one leads to an increase in the demand for the other

supply curve a graph of the relationship between the price of a good and the quantity supplied

supply schedule a table that shows the relationship between the price of a good and the quantity supplied

supply shock an event that directly alters firms' costs and prices, shifting the economy's aggregate-supply curve and thus the Phillips curve

surplus a situation in which quantity supplied is greater than quantity demanded

tariff a tax on goods produced abroad and sold domestically

technological knowledge society's understanding of the best ways to produce goods and services

theory of liquidity preference Keynes's theory that the interest rate adjusts to bring money supply and money demand into balance

trade balance the value of a nation's exports minus the value of its imports; also called net exports

trade deficit an excess of imports over exports

trade policy a government policy that directly influences the quantity of goods and services that a country imports or exports

trade surplus an excess of exports over imports

unemployment rate the percentage of the labour force that is unemployed

union a worker association that bargains with employers over wages and working conditions

unit of account the yardstick people use to post prices and record debts

velocity of money the rate at which money changes hands

vicious circle cycle that results when deficits reduce the supply of loanable funds, increase interest rates, discourage investment, and result in slower economic growth; slower growth leads to lower tax revenue and higher spending on income-support programs, and the result can be even higher budget deficits

virtuous circle cycle that results when surpluses increase the supply of loanable funds, reduce interest rates, stimulate investment, and result in faster economic growth; faster growth leads to higher tax revenue and lower spending on income-support programs, and the result can be even higher budget surpluses

welfare economics the study of how the allocation of resources affects economic well-being

world price the price of a good that prevails in the world market for that good

INDEX